Madagascar

THE BRADT TRAVEL GUIDE

'France, Spain, Italy and the Indie... must be ransackt to make sauce for our meat; while we impoverish the land, air and water to enrich our private table... Besides, these happy people have no need of any foreign commodity, nature having sufficiently supplied their necessities wherewith they remain contented. But it is we that are in want, and are compelled like famished wolves to range the world about for our living, to the hazards of both our souls and bodies, the one by the corruption of the air, the other by the corruption of religion.'

Walter Hamond, *A Paradox Prooving that the Inhabitants of ... Madagascar ... are the Happiest People in the World*, 1640

Madagascar

THE BRADT TRAVEL GUIDE

Seventh Edition

Hilary Bradt

Bradt Travel Guides Ltd, UK
The Globe Pequot Press Inc, USA

This seventh edition published in 2002 by Bradt Travel Guides Ltd
19 High Street, Chalfont St Peter, Bucks SL9 9QE, England
web: bradt-travelguides.com
Published in the USA by The Globe Pequot Press Inc, 246 Goose Lane,
PO Box 480, Guilford, Connecticut 06475-0480

First published in 1988 by Bradt Publications

ISBN 1 84162 051 3

British Library Cataloguing in Publication Data
A catalogue record for this book is available from the British Library

Library of Congress Cataloging-in-Publication Data applied for

Photographs
Cover Parson's chameleon (Nick Garbutt)
Text Hilary Bradt (HB), Nick Garbutt (NG), Colin Palmer (CP), Brian Slobe (BS)

Illustrations Cherry-Anne Lavrih (orchids), Carole Vincer (baobabs),
Nick Garbutt (others)
Maps Alan Whitaker

Typeset from the author's disc by Wakewing
Printed and bound in Italy by Legoprint SpA, Trento

Author/Contributors

Hilary Bradt has visited Madagascar some 22 times since her first trip in 1976. Since then she has led numerous tours there and lectures, broadcasts and writes on the joys and perils of travelling in Madagascar and other countries. She is also the founder of Bradt Travel Guides.

SPECIALIST CONTRIBUTORS

Ian Anderson (*The music of Madagascar*) is the editor of the magazine *Folk Roots* and a regular broadcaster on the subject of folk music.

Oliver and Camilla Backhouse (*Blindness in Madagascar, Malagasy hats*) spent a year in Madagascar in 1993 and set up the charity MOSS (see page 146). Oliver is an ophthalmologist and Camilla is a milliner.

Jim Bond (*Baobabs*) is a medical doctor and an ethnobotanist. He worked for three years with the Mikea of the southwest researching their traditional use of plants.

Samantha Cameron (*Childbirth* and *Traditional healing...*) is a volunteer for Feedback Madagascar, co-ordinating their health programme.

Nick Garbutt (photos and *A layman's guide to lemurs*) is a zoologist, photographer, tour leader and the author of the definitive guide to Madagascar's mammals.

Clare and Johan Hermans (*Orchids* and travel information) have visited Madagascar nine times. They are co-authors of *The Orchids of Madagascar*.

Jonathan Hughes (*Natural history*) is an author and lecturer in ecology in London.

Julia Jones (*Crayfish* and Ranomafana information) is a PhD student from the University of Cambridge, studying the ecology of Malagasy crayfish.

Tim Ireland (*Geology* and *gemstones*) is a geologist and amateur gemologist currently doing postgraduate research at the University of Tasmania. He went to Madagascar to experience first-hand a modern mining 'rush', and maybe buy a gemstone or two.

Angus McCrae (*Ant-lions* and *Wild silk*) has been fascinated by insects since childhood and worked as a medical entomologist in Africa for some 25 years.

Colin Palmer (*Pangalanes* and *Cargo boats*) is a consultant who specialises in the role of water transport in developing countries.

Derek Schuurman (*Birding* and *Freshwater Fish*) works for a London-based tour operator. He is the author of two books and countless articles on Madagascar.

Seraphine Tierney (*Famadihana diary*) is the attaché at the Madagascar Consulate in London and runs the travel consultancy, Discover Madagascar.

Jane Wilson-Howarth (*Health*) is a medical doctor with a degree in biology. She has researched and practised medicine in several tropical countries, writes about travellers' health for *Wanderlust* magazine, and is the author of two travellers' health guides.

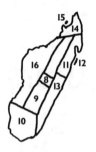

Contents

Introduction

Twenty-seven years ago I attended a slide show in Cape Town given by a zoo collector who had just returned from a country called Madagascar. By the end of the evening I knew I had to go there. It wasn't just the lemurs, it was the utter otherness of this little-known island that entranced me. So I went, and I fell in love, and I've been returning ever since.

Last June I was back for the total eclipse. Everything was running smoothly. Despite my anxieties the planes were not overbooked, the hotels had been built in time (just) and there were responsible government warnings about risking damage to eyesight. I felt that Madagascar had made its way into the 21st century. Then came eclipse day. Two zebu were sacrificed in Morombe in honour of the occasion, and the rural population of Madagascar went inside their huts, blocked the windows, covered their children's eyes, and waited, trembling, for it to be over. The next day one of the national papers declared, ominously, that three babies, delivered during the eclipse, were stillborn. That's Madagascar. Tradition and superstition are far more powerful than information media.

In the quarter century since my first visit nothing has changed and everything has changed. This is what's so magical about Madagascar... in so large an island you can still find yourself among people who have rarely seen a white person, or you can join other tourists in a fail-safe wildlife experience in Périnet or Berenty, where the accommodation is excellent, the guides superb, and the animals so accustomed to humans that you know you will get a close view. Or you can retreat to one of the new luxury resorts for the holiday of a lifetime.

The choice is yours – lucky you!

Some day, when I am old and worn and there is nothing new to see, I shall go back to the palm-fringed lagoons, the sun-drenched, rolling moors, the pink villages, and the purple peaks of Madagascar.

E A Powell, *Beyond the Utmost Purple Rim*, 1925

Acknowledgements

This guide has evolved from readers' letters, in addition to my own travels, and I owe them a debt of gratitude that can never be repaid. So many people have spent time and effort compiling new information, writing about their experiences, and keeping me up to date with changes in remote parts of Madagascar. There are evocative and amusing descriptions from earlier editions which I couldn't bear to delete, as well as wonderful new bits and pieces from numerous correspondents. I receive some astonishing letters, all of which add to my knowledge and understanding of the country.

For each edition there is a special correspondent who touches me with his or her enthusiasm or fortitude. This time it's Sarah Blachford who has done two extensive trips on her own, staying at C-rated hotels and travelling by taxi-brousse. Comments such as 'I was determined not to let illness get in the way of having a good time... Consequently fainted in the restaurant (thought I would nuke malaria with chilli & prawn soup)...' leave me wondering whether to smile or cry, but full of admiration!

A special thank you goes to Ony Rakototoarivelo of Akano Avoka, who tirelessly telephoned hotels all over the country to get their latest prices. Nivo Ravelojaona of Za Tours answered my endless queries, backed up by Judith de Witt and Derek Schuurman of Rainbow Tours. Rita Bachman of Unusual Destinations chipped in when needed.

The following residents in Madagascar contributed substantially to this edition: Charlie Welch and Andrea Katz (Toamasina), Brett Massoud and Christine Orengo (Taolagnaro), Julia Jones (Ranomafana), and Irene Boswell (Nosy Be). Andrew Cooke and Alisdair Harris helped with marine conservation and diving information. Frequent Mad visitors Quentin Bloxam, Jim Bond, Janice Booth, Angus Carpenter, Lorna Gillespie, Stuart Edgill, Clare and Johan Hermans, Philip Jones, Lyn Mair, and John and Valerie Middleton provided comparative views as well as new information. And a gaggle of wonderful first-timers visited, between them, almost every corner of the country and took the time to write to me with their findings. They are: Robert Bowker, Ann Callow, Rob Conway, Volker Dornheim, Frances Donovan, J Dudley, Debbie Fellner, Claire Graham, Jolijn Greel, Lawrence Harvey, Karl Lehmann, Taco Melissen, Bobbi Jo McCain, Marko Petrovic, Helen Ranger, Jenny Roberts, John Robertson, Angela Slater, Richard Smith, Bart Snyers, Ben Tapley, Wim van Alphen, Philippe Van den Eynde, Marja van Ipenburg, and Andrew Willis. Apologies if I have missed anyone out.

To everyone: *Misaotra!*

Perspectives on Madagascar

'[Madagascar is] the chiefest paradise this day upon earth.'

Richard Boothby, 1630

'I could not but endeavour to dissuade others from undergoing the
miseries that will follow the persons of such as adventure themselves for
Madagascar ... from which place, God divert the residence and adventures
of all good men.'

Powle Waldegrave, 1649

As it was in the 17th century, so it is today – although very few people these days
are disappointed. My love affair with Madagascar has lasted 26 years and, like any
lover, I tend to be blind to its imperfections and too ready to leap to its defence. I
am therefore fortunate to receive so much feedback from travellers both new and
experienced, wide-eyed or blasé, to help me see Madagascar with fresh eyes. It is,
I suppose, not a holiday island in the conventional sense, and as an exotic
destination it lacks tangible tourist sights and events. As one disappointed traveller
put it: 'I need to be hit in the face with garish temples, outrageous costumes,
bizarre practices. I agree toying with Grandad's bones is pretty bizarre but what
chance has a tourist like me of seeing a *famadihana*?'

Madagascar faces the dilemma of many developing countries: its government is
anxious to encourage tourism and there are a large number of potential visitors
who have seen television programmes about the island's natural history or are
looking for a new holiday destination. And yet this is one of the poorest countries
in the world and it is, perhaps, one of the most corrupt. Change will continue to
be slow, not helped by the fact that Malagasy culture is based on respect for the past
rather than anticipation of the future.

Nevertheless, I still rejoice that so much is special: the wildlife (of course), the
people – their beauty and gentle friendliness – the scenery, the food, and above all
the serendipity. Wander away from the main tourist places in any town and you are
likely to stumble across a market, a street fair, a group of musicians, or a gathering
that brings home what we seem to have lost in our culture: the ability to be joyful
despite poverty.

Here are some comments from letters I've received over the years:

'The beauty of the land I had expected, but the gentle openheartedness
and hospitality of the people took me by storm. I have lived and travelled
extensively in South America, Europe and Eastern Africa but I have never
encountered such lovely people as the Malagasy!'

'I got back from a two-month solo trip around Madagascar a few months ago and haven't yet managed to get it out of my system... I can't read enough about all things Malagasy and need a daily fix of Malagasy music.'

'We spent five days in Madagascar. We had intended to stay longer but found the poverty much too depressing...The country is a disaster.'

'My advice is to see Madagascar before the Malagasy finish with it.'

'It is such an extraordinary country – fascinating, exhilarating and depressing in one go. We couldn't get over how friendly everyone was, even in the most deprived areas, how incredible the wildlife is, and how precarious the whole balance of the island is.'

YOUR PERSPECTIVES WANTED!

One of the joys of publishing new editions of this guide is the chance to add readers' views on Madagascar as well as the all-important hard information on favourite hotels, restaurants, and travel off the beaten track. With the inevitable changes following the presidential struggle for power in 2002, this feedback is even more needed.

Whatever your experiences in Madagascar, irrespective of whether you travelled there independently or as part of an organised group, do write to tell me about it. Particularly welcome is hard information with accurately noted addresses and prices, and readers who include a map to show the location of their new find have me almost weeping with joy.

Whether you have loved Madagascar or hated it, I'd like to hear from you in time for the next edition which is scheduled for 2004.

Happy travelling

Hilary Bradt

19 High Street, Chalfont St Peter, Bucks SL9 9QE, England
Tel: 01753 893444 Fax: 01753 892333
Email: info@bradt-travelguides.com
Web: www.bradt-travelguides.com

Part One

General Information

Fanaloka

The Country

FACTS AND FIGURES
Location
Madagascar, also known as the Malagasy Republic ('Malagasy' is the correct adjective, not 'Madagascan'), lies some 250 miles (400km) off the east coast of Africa, south of the equator. It is separated from Africa by the Mozambique Channel and is crossed by the Tropic of Capricorn near the southern town of Toliara (Tuléar).

Size
The world's fourth largest island (after Greenland, New Guinea and Borneo), Madagascar is about 1,000 miles (1,580km) long by 350 miles (570km) at its widest point. Madagascar has an area of 227,760 square miles (590,000km²), 2½ times the size of Great Britain and a little smaller than Texas.

Topography
A chain of mountains runs like a spine down the east-centre of the island descending sharply to the Indian Ocean, leaving only a narrow coastal plain. These eastern mountain slopes bear the remains of the dense rainforest which once covered all of the eastern section of the island. The western plain is wider and the climate drier, supporting forests of deciduous trees and acres of savannah grassland. Madagascar's highest mountain is Maromokotro (9,450ft/2,876m), part of the Massif of Tsaratanana, in the north of the island. In the south is the 'spiny forest' also known as the 'spiny desert'.

Climate
A tropical climate with rain falling in the hottest season – coinciding with the northern hemisphere winter. The amount of rainfall varies greatly by region: the wettest area in the east averages 140ins (355cm) annually; in the dry zone (south-west) the annual average is 12ins (30cm). It is hot and humid in low-lying areas. Temperatures can drop to freezing in Antananarivo (4,100ft/1,250m) and close to freezing in the extreme south during the coldest month of June. In the last 30 years Madagascar has suffered 24 major cyclones.

Flora and fauna
A naturalist's paradise, most of the island's plants and animals are unique to Madagascar and new species and even new genera are being found by each scientific team that goes out there. Of the native plants 80% are endemic. All of the mammals are endemic, excluding those introduced by man; and half of the birds and well over 90% of the reptiles are found nowhere else. The incredible number of unique species is due to the island's early separation from the mainland some 165 million years ago, and to the relatively recent arrival of man (around 2,000 years ago).

History

Madagascar was first sighted by Europeans in 1500, but there were Arab settlements from about the 9th century. Marco Polo named it (perhaps confusing it with Mogadishu in Somalia). It was mostly united under one monarch from the early 19th century, a time of British influence through the London Missionary Society. It became a French colony in 1896 and regained independence in 1960.

Ethnic groups

The people of Madagascar, the Malagasy, are of Afro-Indonesian origin, officially divided into 18 main 'tribes' or clans. Other races include Indian/Pakistani, Chinese and European.

Government

A period of 'Christian Marxism' from 1975 to 1991 under president Didier Ratsiraka was followed by an attempt at parliamentary democracy which collapsed mainly because of the unconstitutional behaviour of the next president, Albert Zafy. In 1997 Ratsiraka was re-elected president and restored most of his dictatorial powers. Disputed presidential elections in December 2001 led to seven months of turmoil when Ratsiraka refused to relinquish power to the candidate who won the most votes, Marc Ravalomanana. Ratsiraka finally accepted the inevitable on July 5 when he fled the country (see pages 10 and 137).

Population

The estimated population is just under 15 million, nearly half of whom are under the age of 15. Three-quarters of the population live in rural areas. Since independence the population of Antananarivo has grown by 4% per annum and per capita consumption has dropped by 45%. A third of this decline has taken place since 1993. Some 75% of Madagascar's population live below the poverty line and 85% of the children in Tana are undernourished. 15% of all children die before their first birthday. The average mother has 6.6 children. The 'doubling time' of the population is approximately 22 years.

Some statistics

The average annual income in 2000 was US$102 per person or US$515 per household. In the poorest province, Toliara (Tuléar) the average annual household

RACIAL DISHARMONY

There has always been some tension between the Merina people of the highlands, historically the rulers of Madagascar, and the other clans. The political turmoil of 2002 brought this racial hatred out into the open, with Ratsiraka, a Betsimisaraka from the Toamasina region, at war with Ravalomanana, a Merina from Antananarivo. Clashes between their supporters resulted in about 70 deaths, many of which are likely to have been racially motivated. The traditional victims of racism, the Indians and Pakistanis who own many Malagasy businesses, tended to side with Ratsiraka (or the status quo). In Mahajanga, many lost the contents of their shops during the riots and looting that preceded Ravalomanana's conquest of Ratsiraka's former strongholds.

It may take several years for Madagascar to return to a semblance of racial harmony. Even in exile, Ratsiraka will attempt to destabilise the new government, and ethnic division is a powerful tool.

income is only US$81. Only 10% of all houses have electricity, 10% have running water and only 2% have WCs. 35% have a radio, 6% a telephone but only 1% has a refrigerator.

Religion

Christianity is the dominant organised religion, with the Catholic church slightly stronger than other denominations. Islam and Hinduism are also practised, mainly by the Asian community, but to the majority of Malagasy their own unique form of ancestor worship is the most important influence in their lives.

Economy

The economy suffered badly under Christian Marxism in the 1980s and declined further during the political upheavals from 1991 to 1997. Between 1970 and 1995 average annual GNP growth was 0% while the population doubled. There has been some improvement following economic reforms supported by international donors: inflation has fallen from 60% to 11% in 2000 and in recent years GNP growth has been around 3 to 4%. But Madagascar is still ranked as the eleventh poorest country in the world, with 75% of the population below the poverty line and over 60% classified as extremely poor. Hopes of recovery, based partly on expanding tourism, exports of shellfish and a more dynamic industrial sector, are threatened from time to time by destructive cyclones.

In October 2000 the IMF agreed to debt relief for Madagascar. In consequence its debt burden has been eased by 35%, with the rescheduled debt payable over 20 years. This will save US$62 million a year which will be diverted to health, education, rural infrastructure and other poverty-relieving measures.

Tourism statistics

The target for tourism in 2000 was 200,000 visitors but numbers dropped from 155,000 in 1999 to 138,000 because of bad publicity about cyclones and cholera. By comparison Mauritius receives 500,000 visitors a year. The majority of visitors to Madagascar are French (55%), then Italians (12.1%), Americans (4.2%) and Swiss, German and British at 2% each.

Education

The reduction of public funding and shortage of teachers in rural areas have resulted in a fall in educational standards. Of the school-age population only 66% reach the second primary year and only 28% finish primary school. In rural areas class sizes average 64 pupils. Private schools meanwhile are flourishing, with one quarter of Madagascar's children being educated privately. Over one third of its children receive no education at all. The literacy rate is approximately 45%.

Language

The first language is Malagasy, which belongs to the Malayo-Polynesian family of languages. French is widely spoken in towns, and is the language of business. English is only spoken in the capital and in major tourist areas.

Place names

Since independence the colonial names of some towns have been changed. Many foreigners – and people who deal with foreigners – still use the easier-to-pronounce old names. However, I use the Malagasy names (apart from one or two cases where there is exceptional resistance to the change) but with the other name in parenthesis so as to avoid confusion: Taolagnaro (Fort Dauphin), Toliara

(Tuléar), Toamasina (Tamatave), Andasibe (Périnet), Nosy Boraha (Ile Sainte Marie), Antsiranana (Diego Suarez), and Mahajanga (Majunga). Antananarivo (Tananarive) is often shortened to Tana.

Time
Greenwich Mean Time plus three hours.

Voltage
220.

Currency
The Malagasy franc (Franc malgache, Fmg) floats against hard currencies so these rates are approximate only: £1 = 9.095Fmg, US$1 = 6,375Fmg, 1€ = 5,790Fmg.

HISTORY
The first Europeans
The first Europeans to sight Madagascar were the Portuguese in 1500, although there is evidence of earlier Arab settlements on the coast. There were unsuccessful attempts to establish French and British settlements during the next couple of centuries; these failed due to disease and hostile local people. Hence a remarkably homogeneous and united country was able to develop under its own rulers.

By the early 1700s, the island had become a haven for pirates and slave-traders, who both traded with and fought the local kings who ruled the clans of the east and west coast.

The rise of the Merina Kingdom
The powerful Merina Kingdom was forged by Andrianampoinimerina (be thankful that this was a shortened version of his full name: Andrianampoinimerin-andriantsimitoviaminandriampanjaka!).

Succeeding to the tiny kingdom of Ambohimanga in 1787, by 1808 he had united the various Merina kingdoms and conquered the other highland tribes. In many ways the Merina Kingdom at this time paralleled that of the Inca empire in Peru: Andrianampoinimerina was considered to have almost divine powers and his obedient subjects were well provided for; each was given enough land for his family's rice needs, with some left over to pay a rice tribute to the king, and community projects such as the building of irrigation canals were imposed through forced labour (though with bonuses for the most productive worker). The burning of forests was forbidden.

Conquest was always foremost in the monarch's mind, however, and it was his son, King Radama I, who fulfilled his father's command to 'Take the sea as frontier to your kingdom'. This king had a friendly relationship with Britain, which in 1817 and 1820 signed treaties under which Madagascar was recognised as an independent state. Britain supplied arms and advisers to help Radama conquer most of the rest of the island.

The London Missionary Society
To further strengthen ties between the two countries, the British Governor of Mauritius, which had recently been seized from the French, encouraged King Radama I to invite the London Missionary Society to send teachers. In 1818 a small group of Welsh missionaries arrived in Tamatave (now Toamasina). David Jones and Thomas Bevan brought their wives and children, but within a few weeks only

ROBERT DRURY

The most intriguing insight into 18th-century Madagascar was provided by Robert Drury, who was shipwrecked off the island in 1701 and spent over 16 years there, much of the time as a slave to the Antandroy or Sakalava chiefs.

Drury was only 15 when his boat foundered off the southern tip of Madagascar (he had been permitted by his father to go to India with trade goods). The shipwreck survivors were treated well by the local king but kept prisoners for reasons of status. After a few days they made a bid for freedom by seizing the king and some of his courtiers as a hostage and marching east. They were followed by hundreds of warriors who watched for any relaxation in the guard; they were without water for three days as they crossed the burning hot desert, and just as they came in sight of the river Mandrare (having released the hostages) they were attacked and many were speared to death.

For ten years Drury was a slave of the Antandroy royal family. He worked with cattle and eventually was appointed royal butcher, the task of slaughtering a cow for ritual purposes being supposedly that of someone of royal blood – and lighter skin. Drury was a useful substitute. He also acquired a wife.

Wars with the neighbouring Mahafaly gave him the opportunity to escape north across the desert to St Augustine's Bay, some 250 miles away. Here he hoped to find a ship to England, but his luck turned and he again became a slave, this time to the Sakalava. When a ship did come in, his master refused to consider selling him to the captain, and Drury's desperate effort to get word to the ship through a message written on a leaf came to nothing when the messenger lost the leaf and substituted another less meaningful one. Two more years of relative freedom followed, and he finally got away in 1717, nearly 17 years after his shipwreck.

Ever quick to put his experience to good use, he later returned to Madagascar as a slave trader!

Jones remained alive; the others had all died of fever. Jones retreated to Mauritius, but returned to Madagascar in 1820 to devote the rest of his life to its people, along with equally dedicated missionary teachers and artisans. The British influence was established and a written language introduced for the first time (apart from some ancient Arabic texts) using the Roman alphabet.

'The wicked queen' and her successors

Radama's widow and successor, Queen Ranavalona I, was determined to rid the land of Christianity and European influence, and reigned long enough (33 years) largely to achieve her aim. These were repressive times for Malagasy as well as foreigners. One way of dealing with people suspected of witchcraft or other evil practices was the 'Ordeal by Tangena' (see box on page 9).

It was during Queen Ranavalona's reign that an extraordinary Frenchman arrived in Madagascar: Jean Laborde, who, building on the work of the British missionaries, introduced the island to many aspects of Western technology. He remained in the queen's favour until 1857 – much longer than the other Europeans (see box on pages 178/9).

The queen drove the missionaries out of Madagascar and many Malagasy Christians were martyred. However, the missionaries and European influence returned in greater strength after the Queen's death and in 1869 Christianity became the official religion of the Merina Kingdom.

After Queen Ranavalona I came King Radama II, a peace-loving and pro-European monarch, who was assassinated after a two-year reign in 1863. There is a widely held belief, however, that he survived strangulation with a silk cord (it was taboo to shed royal blood) and lived in hiding in the northwest for many years (see box on page 366). There is also a belief (less widely held) that he was assassinated because he was the illegitimate son of Queen Ranavalona I and Jean Laborde.

After the death of Radama II, Queen Rasoherina came to the throne, but the monarchy was now in decline and power shifted to the prime minister who shrewdly married the queen. He was overthrown by a brother, Rainilaiarivony, who continued the tradition by marrying three successive queens and exercising all the power. During this period, 1863-96, the monarchs (in title only) were Queen Rasoherina, Queen Ranavalona II and lastly Queen Ranavalona III.

The French conquest

Even during the period of British influence the French maintained a long-standing claim to Madagascar and in 1883 they attacked and occupied the main ports. The Franco-Malagasy War lasted thirty months, and was concluded by a harsh treaty making Madagascar a form of French protectorate. Prime Minister Rainilaiarivony, hoping for British support, managed to evade full acceptance of this status but the British government signed away its interest in the Convention of Zanzibar in 1890. The French finally imposed their rule by invasion in 1895. For a year the country was a full protectorate and in 1896 Madagascar became a French colony. A year later Queen Ranavalona III was exiled to Algeria and the monarchy abolished.

The first French Governor-General of Madagascar, Joseph Simon Gallieni, was an able and relatively benign administrator. He set out to break the power of the Merina aristocracy and remove the British influence by banning the teaching of English. French became the official language.

British military training and the two World Wars

Britain has played an important part in the military history of Madagascar. During the wars which preceded colonisation British mercenaries trained the Malagasy army to fight the French. During World War I 46,000 Malagasy were recruited for the allies and over 2,000 killed. In 1942, when Madagascar was under the control of the Vichy French, the British invaded Madagascar to forestall the possibility of the Japanese Navy making use of the great harbour of Diego Suarez (see box on page 326).

In 1943 Madagascar was handed back to France under a Free French Government. An uprising by the Malagasy against the French in 1947 was bloodily repressed (some 80,000 are said to have died) but the spirit of nationalism lived on and in 1960 the country achieved full independence.

The first 30 years of independence

The first president, Philibert Tsiranana, was 'pro-France' but in 1972 he stepped down in the face of increasing unrest and student demonstrations against French neo-colonialism. An interim government headed by General Ramanantsoa ended France's special position and introduced a more nationalistic foreign and economic policy.

In 1975, after a period of turmoil, a military directorate handed power to a naval officer, Didier Ratsiraka, who had served as Foreign Minister under Ramanantsoa.

TANGENA

When James Hastie, royal tutor, arrived in Madagascar in 1817 he witnessed and described one of the more barbaric tortures that King Radama I was using on his subjects: the Ordeal of Tangena. Tangena is a Malagasy shrub with a poisonous kernel in its fruit. This poison was used to determine the guilt or innocence of a suspected criminal. A 'meal' consisting of three pieces of chicken skin, rice and the crushed tangena kernel was prepared. The suspect was then forced to drink large quantities of water to make him – or her – vomit. If all three pieces of chicken skin reappeared the person was innocent (but often died anyway as a result of the poison). If the skin remained in the stomach the unfortunate suspect was killed, usually after limbs, or bits of limbs and other extremities, had been lopped off first.

One of the successes of Hastie's influence on the king was that the monarch agreed that, although the Ordeal by Tangena should continue, dogs could stand in for the accused. This decision was ignored by Queen Ranavalona who used it freely on the Christian martyrs she persecuted with such enthusiasm. Sir Mervyn Brown (from whose book, *A History of Madagascar*, this information is extracted) estimates that several thousand Malagasy met their deaths through the tangena shrub during Queen Ranavalona's long reign. Even during this period of xenophobia the queen was reluctant to subject the Europeans under arrest to the ordeal because of the inevitable political repercussions. Prudently, the poison was administered to chickens; all but one promptly died (the 'innocent' chicken/European was a bit too useful to condemn).

The Ordeal by Tangena was finally abolished by Queen Ranavalona's son, King Radama II, in 1861.

Ratsiraka established the Second Republic, changing the country's name from The Malagasy Republic to The Democratic Republic of Madagascar. He introduced his own brand of 'Christian-Marxism' and his manifesto, set out in a 'little red book', was approved by referendum. Socialist policies such as the nationalisation of banks followed. Within a few years the economy had collapsed and has remained in severe difficulties ever since. Ratsiraka was nevertheless twice re-elected, though there were claims of ballot rigging and intimidation.

Into the 21st century

In 1991 a pro-democracy coalition called the Forces Vives, in which the churches played an important part, organised a remarkable series of strikes and daily demonstrations calling for Ratsiraka's resignation. In August an estimated 500,000 demonstrators marched on the president's palace. Though unarmed and orderly, they were fired on by the presidential guards and an estimated 100 demonstrators died. This episode further weakened Ratsiraka and at the end of the year he was compelled to relinquish executive power and agree to a referendum which approved a new constitution and fresh elections.

A transitional administration was formed with Professor Albert Zafy, who had led the Forces Vives opposition to Ratsiraka, at its head and a coalition government with Ratsiraka's nominee Guy Razanamasy as prime minister. Presidential elections took place in 1992/93 and were won by Albert Zafy. The Third Republic, born in 1993, soon ran into trouble. The new parliamentary constitution provided for a constitutional president with a prime minister elected by the National Assembly. But Albert Zafy refused to accept the limitations on his presidential role and in 1995 won a referendum which gave him, rather than the Assembly, the right to appoint the prime minister.

Zafy's continuing breaches of the constitution led to his impeachment by the National Assembly. In the ensuing presidential election former president Ratsiraka emerged the winner, with Zafy a close second. Ratsiraka then piloted through major amendments to the constitution which restored most of the dictatorial powers that he had formerly enjoyed. In National Assembly elections in 1998 his party AREMA emerged as the largest, but had to rely on coalitition partners for a majority. Ratsiraka's position was further strengthened by a series of communal, provincial and senatorial elections in 2000 and 2001, which gave AREMA a dominant position at all levels, especially in the Senate.

The first round of presidential elections were held in December 2001. The mayor of Antananarivo, Marc Ravalomanana, appeared to have emerged the clear leader with a majority of 52% of the vote. Ratsiraka did not accept this verdict, however, and when Ravalomanana refused a second round of elections and declared himself president, the former president retreated to his home town of Toamasina and set up a rival government. See box on page 137 for the full story.

CLIMATE

Madagascar has a tropical climate: November to March – summer (wet season), hot with variable rainfall; April to October – winter (dry season), mainly dry and mild.

Southwest trade winds drop their moisture on the eastern mountain slopes and blow hot and dry in the west. North and northwest 'monsoon' air currents bring heavy rain in summer, decreasing southward so that the rainfall in Taolagnaro is half that of Toamasina. There are also considerable variations of temperature dictated by altitude and latitude. On the summer solstice of December 22 the sun is directly over the Tropic of Capricorn, and the weather is very warm. Conversely, June is the coolest month.

Average midday temperatures in the dry season are 77°F (25°C) in the highlands and 86°F (30°C) on the coast. These statistics are misleading, however, since in June the night-time temperature can drop to near freezing in the highlands and it is cool in the south. The winter daytime temperatures are very pleasant, and the hot summer season is usually tempered by cool breezes on the coast.

The east of Madagascar frequently suffers from cyclones during February and March and these may brush other areas in the north or west.

RAINFALL CHART

Region	Jan	Feb	Mar	Apr	May	Jun	Jul	Aug	Sep	Oct	Nov	Dec
West	●	●	●	●	✳	✳	✳	✳	✳	✳	●	●
Highlands	●	●	●	●	✳	○	○	○	✳	●	✳	●
East	●	●	●	●	●	●	●	●	✳	✳	✳	●
Southwest	✳	✳	✳	✳	✳	○	○	○	✳	✳	●	●
North	●	●	●	●	✳	✳	✳	✳	✳	✳	✳	●
Northwest (Sambirano)	●	●	●	●	✳	✳	✳	✳	✳	✳	●	●

● = rain   ✳ = driest months   ○ = fine but cool

The map on the right and chart below give easy reference to the driest and wettest months and regions but remember – nothing is as unpredictable as weather, and even in the rainiest months there will be sunny intervals, and in the driest there may be heavy showers. For advice on the best months to visit Madagascar see *When to Go*, *Chapter 4*.

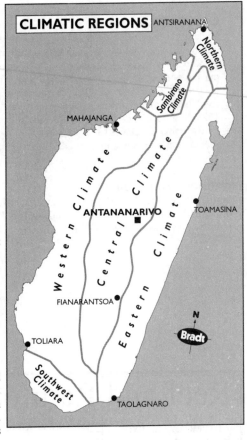

Climatic regions
West
Rainfall decreases from north to south. Variation in day/night winter temperatures increases from north to south. Average number of dry months: 7 or 8. Highest average annual rainfall within zone (major town): Majunga, 152cm. Lowest: Toliara, 36cm.

Central
Both temperature and rainfall are influenced by altitude. Day/night temperatures in Antananarivo vary by 14°C. The major rainy season starts end of November. Highest average annual rainfall within zone (major town): Antsirabe, 140cm.

East
In the northeast and central areas there are no months (or weeks) entirely without rain; but drier, more settled weather prevails in the southeast. Reasonably dry months: May, September, October, November. Possible months for travel: April, December, January (but cyclone danger in January). Difficult months for travel (torrential rain and cyclones) are February, March. Highest annual rainfall in zone: Maroantsetra, 410cm. Lowest: Taolagnaro (Fort Dauphin), 152cm.

Southwest
The driest part of Madagascar. The extreme west may receive only 5cm of rain a year, increasing to around 34cm in the east.

North
This is similar to the east zone except for the dry climate of the Antsiranana (Diego Suarez) region, which gets only 92cm of rain per year, with a long and fairly reliable dry season.

CYCLONES

Madagascar has always suffered from cyclones but media attention in 2000 raised awareness of this perennial destruction. Between 1968 and 1999 the country suffered 21 severe cyclones which affected 5.2 million people, making 445,000 homeless and killing 1,291. The cost has been estimated at US$1 billion. The year 2000 added to this toll with cyclones Eline, Gloria and Hudah affecting over a million people and killing 1,292. Agriculture lost 152,000 tons of rice paddy, 4,000 tons of maize, 2,500 tons of coffee, 3,400 tons of cloves and 870 tons of vanilla. The total cost of reconstruction has been put at US$128 million.

Northwest (Sambirano)

Dominated by the Massif of Tsaratanana, with Maromokotro the highest mountain, this region includes the island of Nosy Be and has a micro-climate with frequent heavy rain alternating with sunshine.

The People

ORIGINS

Archaeologists believe that the first people arrived in Madagascar from Indonesia/Malaya about 2,000 years ago. A journey in a reconstructed boat of those times has proved that the direct crossing of the Indian Ocean – 6,400km – was possible, but most experts agree that it is much more likely that the immigrants came in their outrigger canoes via Southern India and East Africa, where they established small Indonesian colonies. The strong African element in the coastal populations probably derived from later migrations from these colonies since their language is also essentially Malayo-Polynesian with only slightly more Bantu-Swahili words than elsewhere in the island. The Merina people of the highlands retain remarkably Indonesian characteristics and may have arrived as recently as 500–600 years ago.

Later arrivals, mainly on the east coast, from Arabia and elsewhere in the Indian Ocean were also absorbed into the Malagasy-speaking population while leaving their mark in certain local customs clearly derived from Islam. The two-continent origin of the Malagasy is easily observed, from the highland tribes who most resemble Indonesians, to the African type characterised by the Bara or Makoa in the south. In between are the elements of both races which make the Malagasy so varied and attractive in appearance. Thus there is racial diversity but cultural uniformity.

BELIEFS AND CUSTOMS

The Afro-Asian origin of the Malagasy has produced a people with complicated and fascinating beliefs and customs. Despite the various tribes or clans, the country shares not only a common language but a belief in the power of dead ancestors (*razana*). This cult of the dead, far from being a morbid preoccupation, is a celebration of life since the dead ancestors are considered to be potent forces that continue to share in family life. If the *razana* are remembered by the living, the Malagasy believe, they thrive in the spirit world and can be relied on to look after their descendants in a host of different ways. These ancestors wield considerable power, their 'wishes' dictating the behaviour of the family or community. Their property is respected, so great-grandfather's field may not be sold or changed to a different crop. Calamities are usually blamed on the anger of *razana*, and a zebu bull may be sacrificed in appeasement. Large herds of zebu cattle are kept as a 'bank' of potential sacrificial offerings.

Belief in tradition, in the accumulated wisdom of the ancestors, has shaped the Malagasy culture. Respect for their elders and courtesy to all fellow humans is part of the tradition. But so is resistance to change.

Spiritual beliefs

At the beginning of time the Creator was Zanahary or Andriananahary. Now the Malagasy worship one god, Andriamanitra, who is neither male nor female. (Andriamanitra is also a word for silk, the fabric of burial shrouds).

DID YOU KNOW?
- Earthquakes mean that whales are bathing their children.
- If a woman maintains a bending posture when arranging eggs in a nest, the chickens will have crooked necks.
- If the walls of a house incline towards the south, the wife will be the stronger one; if they incline towards the north it will be the husband.
- Burning a knot on a piece of string causes the knees to grow big.

Many rural people believe in 'secondary gods' or nature spirits, which may be male or female, and which inhabit certain trees or rocks (which are known as *ody*) or rivers. People seeking help from the spirit world may visit one of these sites for prayer. Spirits are also thought to possess humans who fall into a trance-like state, called *tromba* by the Sakalava and *bilo* by the Antandroy. Some clans or communities believe that spirits can also possess animals, particularly crocodiles.

The Malagasy equivalent of the soul is *ambiroa*. When a person is in a dream state it can temporarily separate from the body, and at death it becomes an immortal *razana*. Death, therefore, is merely a change and not an end. A special ceremony usually marks this rite of passage, with feasting and the sacrifice of zebu. The mood of the participants alternates between sorrow and joy.

Fady

The dictates of the *razana* are obeyed in a complicated network of *fady*. Although *fady* (the plural is also *fady*) is usually translated as 'taboo' this does not truly convey the meaning: these are beliefs related to actions, food, or days of the week when it is 'dangerous to…'. *Fady* vary from family to family and community to community, and even from person to person.

The following are some examples related to actions and food among the Merina: it may be *fady* to sing while you are eating (violators will develop elongated teeth); it is also *fady* to hand an egg directly to another person – it must first be put on the ground; for the people of Andranoro it is *fady* to ask for salt directly, so one has to request 'that which flavours the food'. A *fady* connected with objects is that the spade used to dig a grave should have a loose handle since it is dangerous to have too firm a connection between the living and the dead.

Social *fady*, like *vintana* (see below), often involve the days of the week. For example, among the Merina it is *fady* to hold a funeral on a Tuesday, or there will be another death. Among the Tsimihety, and some other groups, it is *fady* to work the land on Tuesdays; Thursday is also a *fady* day for some people, both for funerals and for farming.

A *fady* is not intended to restrict the freedom of the Malagasy but to ensure happiness and an improved quality of life. That said, however, there are some cruel *fady* which Christian missionaries have been trying, over the centuries, to eliminate. One is the taboo against twins among the Antaisaka people of Mananjary. Historically twins were killed or abandoned in the forest after birth. Today this is against the law but still persists and twins may not be buried in a tomb. Catholic missionaries have established an orphanage in the area for the twins born to mothers torn between social tradition and maternal love. Many mothers who would otherwise have to suffer the murder or abandonment of their babies can give them to the care of the church.

FADY AND THEIR ORIGINS
The intruders and the geese
During the rule of King Andrianampoinimerina, thieves once attempted a raid on the village of Ambohimanga. The residents, however, kept geese which caused a commotion when the intruders entered the compound, thus alerting the people who could take action. Geese are therefore not eaten in this part of Madagascar.

The baby and the drongo
Centuries ago the communities of the east coast were persecuted by pirates who made incursions to the hills to pillage and take captives. At the warning that a pirate band was on its way the villagers would flee into the jungle. When pirates approached the village of Ambinanetelo the women with young children could not keep up with the others so hid in a thicket. Just as the pirates were passing them a baby wailed. The men turned to seek the source of the cry. It came again, but this time from the top of a tree: it was a drongo. Believing themselves duped by a bird the pirates gave up and returned to their boats. Ever since then it has been *fady* to kill a drongo in Ambinanetelo.

The tortoise and the pot
A Tandroy man put a tortoise in a clay pot of boiling water to cook it, but the tortoise kicked so hard that the pot shattered to smithereens. The man declared that his descendants would never again eat tortoise because it broke his pot.

Many *fady* benefit conservation. For instance the killing of certain animals is often prohibited, and the area around a tomb must be left undisturbed. Within these pockets of sacred forest, *ala masina*, it is strictly forbidden to cut trees or even to burn deadwood or leaf litter. In southeast Madagascar there are *alam-bevehivavy* (sacred women's forests) along a stretch of river where only women may bathe. Again, no vegetation may be cleared or damaged in such localities.

For an in-depth study of the subject try to get hold of a copy of *Taboo* (see *Books* in the *Appendix*).

Vintana
Along with *fady* goes a complex sense of destiny called *vintana*. Broadly speaking, *vintana* is to do with time – hours of the day, days of the week, etc – and *fady* usually involves actions or behaviour. Each day has its own *vintana* which tends to make it good or bad for certain festivals or activities. Sunday is God's day; work undertaken will succeed. Monday is a hard day, not a good day for work although projects undertaken (such as building a house) will last; Tuesday is an easy day – too easy for death so no burials take place – but all right for *famadihana* (exhumation) and light work; Wednesday is usually the day for funerals or *famadihana*; Thursday is suitable for weddings and is generally a 'good' day; Friday, *Zoma*, is a 'fat' day, set aside for enjoyment, but is also the best day for funerals; Saturday, a 'noble' day, is suitable for weddings but also for purification.

As an added complication, each day has its own colour. For example Monday is a black day. A black chicken may need to be sacrificed to avoid calamity, dark-coloured food should not be eaten, and people may avoid black objects. Other day-colours are: Tuesday multicoloured, Wednesday brown, Thursday black, Friday red, Saturday blue.

Tody and Tsiny

A third force shapes Malagasy morality. In addition to *fady* and *vintana*, there is *tody* and its partner *tsiny*. *Tody* is somewhat similar to the Hindu/Buddhist kharma. The word means 'return' or 'retribution' and indicates that for any action there is a reaction. *Tsiny* means 'fault', usually a breach of the rules laid down by the ancestors.

After death

Burial, exhumation and second burial are the focus of Malagasy beliefs and culture. To the Malagasy, death is the most important part of life, when a person abandons his mortal form to become a much more powerful and significant ancestor. Since a tomb is for ever whilst a house is only a temporary dwelling, it follows that tombs should be more solidly constructed than houses.

Burial practices differ among the various tribes but all over Madagascar a ritual known as *sasa* is practised immediately after a death. The family of the deceased go to a fast-flowing river and wash all their clothes to remove the contamination of death.

Funeral practices vary from clan to clan. The Antankarana (in the north) and Antandroy (south) have 'happy' funerals during which they may run, with the coffin, into the sea. An unusual ritual, *tranondonaky*, is practised by the Antaisaka of the southeast. Here the corpse is first taken to a special house where, after a signal, the women all start crying. Abruptly, after a second signal, they dance. While this is happening the men are gathered in the hut of the local chief from where, one by one, they go to the house where the corpse is lying and attach money to it with a special oil. The children dance through the night, to the beat of drums, and in the morning the adults wrap the corpse in a shroud and take it to the *kibory*. These tombs are concealed in a patch of forest known as *ala fady* which only men may enter, and where they deliver their last messages to the deceased. These messages can be surprisingly fierce: 'You are now at your place so don't disturb us any more' or 'You are now with the children of the dead, but we are the children of the living'.

More disturbing, however, is the procedure following the death of a noble of the Menabe Sakalava people. The body may be placed on a wooden bench in the hot sun until it begins to decompose. The bodily fluids which drip out are collected in receptacles and drunk by the relatives in the belief that they will then take on the qualities of the deceased.

It is after the first burial, however, that the Malagasy generally honour and communicate with their dead, not only to show respect but to avoid the anger of the *razana* who dwell in the tombs. The best-known ceremony in Madagascar is the 'turning of the bones' by the Merina and Betsileo people: *famadihana* (pronounced 'famadeean'). This is a joyful occasion which occurs from four to seven years after the first burial, and provides the opportunity to communicate with and remember a loved one. The remains of the selected relative are taken from the tomb, rewrapped in a new burial shroud (*lamba mena*), and carried around the tomb a few times before being replaced. Meantime the corpse is spoken to and informed of all the latest events in the family and village. The celebrants are not supposed to show any grief. Generous quantities of alcohol are consumed amid a festive atmosphere with much dancing and music. Women who are trying to conceive take small pieces of the old burial shroud and keep these under their mattresses to induce fertility.

By law a *famadihana* may only take place in the dry season, between June and September. It can last up to a week and involves the family in considerable expense,

TOMB ARCHITECTURE AND FUNERARY ART

In Madagascar the style and structure of tombs define the different clans or tribes better than any other visible feature, and also indicate the wealth and status of the family concerned. Below is a description of the tombs.

Merina In early times burial sites were near valleys or in marshes. The body would be placed in a hollowed-out tree trunk and sunk into the mud at the bottom of a marsh. These *fasam-bazimba* marshes were sacred. Later the Merina began constructing rectangular wooden tombs, mostly under the ground but with a visible structure above. In the 19th century the arrival of the Frenchman Jean Laborde had a profound effect on tomb architecture. Tombs were built with bricks and stone, no longer just from wood. It was Laborde's influence which led to the elaborate structure of modern tombs, which are often painted with geometric designs. Sometimes the interior is lavishly decorated.

Sakalava During the Vazimba period, the Sakalava tombs were simple piles of stones. As with the Merina the change occurred with the introduction of cement and a step design was added. At a later stage, wooden stelae, *aloalo*, were placed on the tombs, positioned to face east. These were topped with carvings of a most erotic nature. Since Sakalava tombs are for individuals and not families, there is no attempt at maintaining the stelae as it is believed that only when the wood decays will the soul of the buried person be released. Not all the carvings, however, are erotic – they may just depict scenes from everyday life or geometric paintings.

Tomb construction commences only after the person's death and can take up to six weeks, the body meanwhile being kept in a house. While a tomb is under construction, many zebu are sacrificed to the ancestors. The Sakalava call their tombs *izarana*, 'the place where we are separated'.

Antandroy and Mahafaly The local name of these tombs is *fanesy* which means 'your eternal place'. Zebu horns are scattered on the tomb as a symbol of wealth (on Sakalava tombs, zebu horns are only a decoration, not an indication of status). The Antandroy and Mahafaly tombs have much the same architecture as those of the Sakalava, but are more artistically decorated. The Mahafaly *aloalo* bear figures depicting scenes from the person's life, and the entire length is often carved with intricate designs. These tombs are carefully maintained, and it is probably the Mahafaly tombs in the southern interior which are the most colourful and striking symbols of Malagasy culture. Antandroy tomb paintings tend to be merely decorative and do not represent scenes from the deceased person's life.

as befits the most important celebration for any family. In the Hauts Plateaux the practice of *famadihana* is embraced by rich and poor, urban and rural, and visitors fortunate enough to be invited to one will find it a strange but very moving occasion; it's an opportunity to examine our own beliefs and rituals associated with death. For an account of what *famadihana* means to a sophisticated London-based Merina woman, see page 18.

FAMADIHANA DIARY

Seraphine Tierney Ramanantsoa

I travelled across the seas to be here today. This day was long awaited, I would soon be in contact with my mother again. She had died seven years previously and I had not been able to be at her funeral. Tradition had always been so important to her so I knew she would be happy that I have come for her *famadihana*.

The meeting point is at 6am outside Cinema Soa in Antananarivo. My household woke up at about 4am to pack the food that had been prepared during the previous week. Drinks and cutlery are all piled into the car. A great number of people are expected as it is also the *famadihana* of the other members of my mother's family.

Fourteen cars and a big taxi-brousse carrying in all about 50 people, squashed one on top of the other, turn up. Everybody is excited. It is really great to see faces I haven't seen since my childhood. Everybody greets each other and exchanges news.

At 8am we all set off. We are heading towards Ifalimanjaka (meaning 'Joy Reigns Here'), in the *fivondronana* of Manjakandriana. Driving through villages with funny names like Ambohitrabiby (The Town of Animals) brings me back to the time when such names were familiar. We make one stop at Talatan'ny volon'ondry for a breakfast of rice cakes and sausages: another opportunity to re-acquaint myself with long lost cousins with whom I spent the long summer holidays as a child. We used to run around together playing games like catching grasshoppers and then finding carnivorous plants and dropping the insect in to see how long it took the plant to close its top to eat its prey.

10am. We arrive at the tombs. Faces are bright, full of expectancy. I ask what the day means to them. They all agree that it's a day for family togetherness, a day for joy, for remembrance.

We are in front of my mother's tomb. It is made out of stone and marble, very elegant. The family will have spent more money on keeping that tomb nice and well maintained than on their own house.

Everybody stands around in front of the tomb waiting for the main event to start: the opening of the tomb door. We have to wait for the president of the *fokon'tany* (local authority) to give permission to open the tomb. Although it had been arranged beforehand he cannot be found anywhere. This wait, after such anticipation, is taken patiently by all – just one of those things.

Mats are laid on the ground on one side of the tomb. The atmosphere of joy is so tangible! Music is blaring out. Permission is finally granted to enter the tomb. The *ray aman-dreny* (the elders) are the first to enter.

The inside of my mother's tomb looks very comfortable with bunk beds made out of stone. It is very clean. There are names on the side of the beds. The national flag is hoisted on top of the tomb as a sign of respect. The conversation goes on happily on the little veranda outside the tomb's door, people chatting about the event and what they have been doing in the last few days.

They start to take the bodies out. Voices could be heard above the happy

Variations of *famadihana* are practised by other tribes. The Menabe Sakalava, for example, hold a *fitampoha* every ten years. This is a royal *famadihana* in which the remains of deceased monarchs are taken from their tomb and washed in a river. A similar ritual, the *fanampoambe*, is performed by the Boina Sakalava further north.

murmur: 'Who is this one? This is your ma! This one your aunt! Here is your uncle! Just carry them around!' The closest relations carry the body but others could touch and say hello. When carrying them, they make sure that the feet go first and the head behind. Everybody carries their loved ones out of the tomb in a line, crying but happy.

When all the bodies are out, they are put on the ground on the front side of the tomb, the head facing east, with their immediate family seated around their loved one. This is a very important moment of the *famadihana*: the beginning of the wrapping of the body. The old shroud in which the body was buried is left on and the new silk shroud put on top of it, following the mummified shape and using baby safety pins to keep it in place. There are three new silk shrouds for my mother which have been donated in remembrance and gratitude. The belief is that she won't be cold and the top shroud befits her, being of top quality silk with beautiful, delicate embroidery. This is the time to touch her, give her something, talk to her. Her best friend is there, making sure that my mother is properly wrapped, as the ritual has to follow certain rules. Lots of touching as silent conversation goes on, giving her the latest news or family gossip, and asking for her blessing. Perfume is sprinkled on her and wishes made at the same time.

The music plays on, everyone happily sitting around the mummified bodies. Flowers are placed on the bodies. The feeling of togetherness and love is so strong. This occasion is not just for the immediate family, but for cousins, and cousins of cousins, uncles and aunts and everybody meeting, bonded by the same ties, belonging to one unique extended family.

Photographs of the dead person are now put on top of each body. There is a photograph of a couple on top of one body: they were husband and wife and are now together for ever in the same silk shroud.

Food is served in the forest area just next to the tombs. The huge feast and celebration begins.

Back to the bodies. We lift them, carrying them on our shoulders. We sing old rhymes and songs and dance in a line, circling the tomb seven times, moving the body on our shoulder and making it dance with us.

The last dance ends. The bodies have to be back inside the tombs by a precise time and the tomb is immediately closed after a last ritual cleaning. This moment of goodbye is very emotional. The next time the tomb will be opened will not be for happiness but grief because it will be for a burial. *Famadihana* only happens once every seven or ten years.

Everybody returns to the cars and drives to the next meeting place – my uncle's, where a huge party finishes the day. Everyone is happy at having done their duty, *Vita ny adidy!*

It has been a very special day for me. My mother was extremely traditional, spending endless energy and money during her lifetime to keep the traditions. It all makes sense now because this *famadihana* brought so much joy, a strong sense of belonging and identity, and giving a spiritual feeling that death is not an end but an extension into another life, linked somehow with this one.

Misaotra ry neny (thank you mum).

Healers, sorcerers and soothsayers

The 'Wise Men' in Malagasy society are the *ombiasy*; the name derives from *olona-be-hasina* meaning 'person of much virtue'. Traditionally they were from the Antaimoro clan and were the advisors of royalty: Antaimoro *ombiasy* came to

HAINTENY

References in this book to the Merina have hitherto been focused on their military abilities, but this tribe has a rich and complex spiritual life. Perhaps the shortest route to the soul of any society is through its poetry, and we are fortunate that there is a book of the traditional Malagasy poetry, *Hainteny*. Broadly speaking, *hainteny* are poems about love: love between parent and child, between man and woman, the love of nature, the appreciation of good versus evil, the acceptance of death. Through the sensitive translations of Leonard Fox, the spiritual and emotional life of the Merina is made available to the reader who cannot fail to be impressed by these remarkable people. As Leonard Fox says: 'On the most basic level, *hainteny* give us an incomparable insight into a society characterised by exceptional refinement and subtlety, deep appreciation of beauty, delight in sensual enjoyment, and profound respect for the spiritual realities of life.'

There are two examples of *hainteny* below, and others are scattered throughout this book.

What is the matter, Raivonjaza,
That you remain silent?
Have you been paid or hired and your mouth tied,
That you do not speak with us, who are your parents?
– I have not been paid or hired
and my mouth has not been tied,
but I am going home to my husband
and am leaving my parents,
my child, and my friends,
so I am distressed,
speaking little.
Here is my child, dear Mother and Father.
If he is stubborn, be strict, but do not beat him;
and if you hit him, do not use a stick.
And do not act as though you do not see him
when he is under your eyes, saying:
'Has this child eaten?'
Do not give him too much,
Do not give him the remains of a meal,
and do not give him what is half-cooked,
for I will be far and will long for him.

Do not love me, Andriamatoa, as one loves
the banana tree exposed to the wind,
overcome and in danger from cold.
Do not love me as one loves a door:
It is loved, but constantly pushed.
Love me as one loves a little crab:
even its claws are eaten.

Antananarivo to advise King Andrianampoinimerina and to teach him Arabic writing.

The astrologers, *mpanandro* ('those who make the day'), work on predictions of *vintana*. There is a Malagasy proverb, 'Man can do nothing to alter his destiny'; but the *mpanandro* will advise on the best day to build a house, or hold a wedding or *famadihana*. Though nowadays *mpanandro* do not have official recognition, they are present in all levels of society. A man (or woman) is considered to have the powers of a mpanandro when he has some grey hair – a sign that he is wise enough to interpret *vintana*. Antandroy soothsayers are known as *mpisoro*.

The Malagasy have a deep knowledge of herbal medicine and all markets display a variety of medicinal plants, amulets and talismans. The Malagasy names associated with these are *ody* and *fanafody*. Broadly speaking, *ody* refers to fetishes such as sacred objects in nature, and *fanafody* to herbal remedies – around 60% of the plants so far catalogued in Madagascar have healing properties. Travellers will sometimes come across conspicuous *ody* in the form of stones or trees which are sacred for a whole village, not just for an individual. Such trees are called *hazo manga*, 'good tree', and are presided over by the *mpisoro*, the senior man of the oldest family in the village. Another type of *ody* is the talisman, *aoly*, worn for protection if someone has transgressed a *fady* or broken a promise. *Aoly* are sometimes kept in the house or buried. *Ody fiti* are used to gain love (white magic) but sorcerers also sell other forms of *ody* for black magic and are paid by clients with either money, zebu or poultry (a red rooster being preferred).

Mpamonka are witch doctors with an intimate knowledge of poison and *mpisikidy* are sorcerers who use amulets, stones, and beads (known as *hasina*) for their cures. Sorcerers who use these in a destructive way are called *mpamosavy*.

On their death, sorcerers are not buried in tombs but are dumped to the west of their villages, barely covered with soil so that feral dogs and other creatures can eat their bodies. Their necks are twisted to face south.

Thanks to Nivo Ravelajaona who provided much of the above information.

The way it is...

Visitors from the West often find the beliefs and customs of the Malagasy merely bizarre. It takes time and effort to understand and respect the richness of tradition that underpins Malagasy society, but it is an effort well worth making.

Leonard Fox, author of *Hainteny*, sums it up perfectly:

> Whoever has witnessed the silent radiance of those who come to pray... at the house of Andrianampoinimerina in Ambohimanga and has experienced the nobility, modesty, unobsequious courtesy, and balanced wholeness of the poorest Merina who has remained faithful to his heritage can have no doubt as to the deep integrative value of the Malagasy spiritual tradition.

MALAGASY SOCIETY
Marriage and children

The Malagasy have a strong sense of community which influences their way of life. Just as the ancestors are laid in a communal tomb, so their descendants share a communal way of life, and even children are almost considered common property within their extended family. Children are seldom disciplined but learn by example.

Marriage is a fairly relaxed union and divorce is common. There is no formal dowry arrangement or bride price, but a present of zebu cattle will often be made. In rural communities the man should bring his new wife home to his village (not vice versa) or he will lose face. You often see young men walking to market wearing a comb in their hair. They are advertising their quest for a wife.

MALAGASY HATS
Camilla Backhouse

During my year working in Madagascar I was particularly struck by the wonderful array of different hats that were worn there. Market stalls were piled high with hats all shapes, colours and sizes. I had done some millinery before and was extremely interested in all the different weaves and so spent time learning about them.

Little had been noted about Malagasy headwear until the missionaries came in the early 19th century. At that time, apparently, few hats were worn as a person's hairstyle was regarded as more important and a sign of beauty. People from each region of Madagascar had different ways of plaiting their hair and they would often incorporate shells, coins or jewels. Oils and perfumes were massaged into the hair – the richer people used *Tseroka*, a type of castor oil mixed with the powdered leaf of *Ravintsara*, which produced a nutmeg scent while the poorest population were satisfied with the fat of an ox or cow.

The chiefs wore simple headdresses but it was not until the Europeans came that hats became more popular. Although plaiting and the art of weaving were already very well established, there was little or no evidence of woven hats. The cutting of hair was introduced in 1822 which may have changed the Malagasy attitudes to wearing hats – to cover an unplaited head certainly would not be any detriment to their beauty. Initially hats were worn by the more wealthy people. Chiefs could be seen wearing caps made of neatly woven rushes or coarse grass and the people of Tana began to wear hats of more costly and durable material (often imported from overseas). It was Jean Laborde in the 1850s who started the industry of hat-making and helped to increase the production of them.

Most Malagasy (and all Christians) have only one wife, but there are exceptions. There is, for example, a well-known man living in Antalaha, in the northeast, who has 11 wives and 120 children. This arrangement seems to work surprisingly well, with each wife working to support her own children, and a head wife to whom the others defer. The man is wealthy enough to provide housing for all his family.

The village community

Malagasy society is a structured hierarchy with two fundamental rules: respect for the other person and knowing one's place. Within a village, the community is based on the traditional *fokonolona*. This concept was introduced by King Andrianampoinimerina when these councils of village elders were given responsibility for, among other things, law and order and the collection of taxes. Day-to-day decisions are still made by the *fokonolona*.

Rural Malagasy houses are always aligned north/south and generally have only one room. Furniture is composed of mats, *tsihy*, often beautifully woven. These are used for sitting and sleeping, and sometimes food is served on them. There are often *fady* attached to *tsihy*. For example you should not step over a mat, particularly one on which meals are eaten.

Part of the Malagasy culture is the art of oratory, *kabary*. Originally *kabary* were the huge meetings where King Andrianampoinimerina proclaimed his plans, but the word has now evolved to mean the elaborate form of speech used to inspire and control the crowds at such gatherings. Even rural leaders can speak for hours, using

In each region the hats vary – they use different plant fibres (depending on what grows well near them), different weaves and occasionally dyes. The colours used are not the vegetable or plant dyes I had imagined but imported from China. The fibres are usually from palms (raffia, *badika*, *manarana*, *dara*), reeds (*penjy*, *harefo*) or straw. Some of the best regions that I came across for seeing weaving were near Lac Tritriva (straw), Maroantsetra (raffia), Mananjary (*penjy*, *dara*), Mahsoabe near Fianarantsoa (*badika*) and Vohipeno (*harefo*).

The ways of preparing the fibres differ, but in general they are dried, flattened and then, if necessary, using a sharp knife, are stripped into thin fibres. They are then ready for weaving. Some are woven into strips which are eventually machined together, while other regions use a continuous weave method to make the entire hat. The latter method can be extremely complicated and is an amazing art to watch. The weaver will place their foot on the central part of the woven circle and gradually intertwine hundreds of different fibres into position. One of my lasting memories was spending time in Maroantsetra where they make the most beautiful crochet style raffia hat. Women sit on palm mats outside their houses weaving, while children play, plait hair or busily prepare food for the next meal. Occasionally the hats are blocked (a method of shaping a crown or brim over a wooden block). There are places in Tana where they heat steel blocks on a fire and then press the woven hat into a trilby style for example. This was a fascinating sight to see as normally these blocks are electrically heated.

The variety of hats is astounding. It can take a day for a woman to weave a hat, and this can be a main source of family income. If you are interested in getting a Malagasy hat, it is worthwhile getting to know a weaver so they may be able to make one large enough for the *vahaza* head!

highly ornate language and many proverbs; a necessary skill in a society that reached a high degree of sophistication without a written language.

The market plays a central role in the life of rural people, who will often walk 15–20km to market with no intention of selling or buying, but simply to catch up on the gossip or continue the conversation broken off the previous week. You will see well-dressed groups of young people happily making their way to this social centre. Often there is a home-made tombola, and other outlets for gambling.

Festivals and ceremonies

Malagasy Christians celebrate the usual holy days, but most tribes or clans have their special festivals.

Ala volon-jaza

This is the occasion when a baby's hair is cut for the first time. With the Antambahoka people in the south the haircut is performed by the grandparents. The child is placed in a basin filled with water, and afterwards bathed. Among the Merina the ceremony is similar but only a man whose parents are still alive may cut a baby's hair. The family then have a meal of rice, zebu, milk and honey. Coins are placed in the bowl of rice and the older children compete to get as many as possible.

Circumcision

Boys are usually circumcised at the age of about two; a baby who dies before this operation has been performed may not be buried in the family tomb.

The operation itself is often done surgically, but in some rural areas it may still be performed with a sharpened piece of bamboo. The foreskin is not always simply discarded. In the region of the Antambahoka it may be eaten by the grandparents, and in Antandroy country it could be shot from the barrel of a gun!

Different clans have their own circumcision ceremonies. Among the Antandroy, uncles dance with their nephews on their shoulders. But the most famous ceremony is *Sambatra*, which takes place every seven years in Mananjary.

Tsangatsaine

This is a ceremony performed by the Antankarana. Two tall trees growing side by side near the house of a noble family are tied together to symbolise the unification of the tribe, as well as the tying together of the past and present, the living and the dead.

Fandroana

This was the royal bath ceremony which marked the Malagasy New Year. These celebrations used to take place in March, with much feasting. While the monarch was ritually bathed, the best zebu was slaughtered and the choicest rump steak presented to the village nobles. The day was the equivalent of the Malagasy National Day, but the French moved this to July 14, the date of the establishment of the French Protectorate. This caused major resentment among the Malagasy as effectively their traditional New Year was taken from them. After independence the date was changed to June 26 to coincide with Independence Day. These days, because of the cost of zebu meat and the value attached to the animals, the traditional meat has been replaced by chicken, choice portions again being given to the respected members of the community. In the absence of royalty there is, of course, no royal bath ceremony.

Music

Music infuses the lives of the Malagasy people, and like *Hainteny* it is the outward expression of their feelings towards nature and human relationships. Traditional musical instruments are often unadapted natural objects – dried reeds or gourds, rubbed together or shaken to the beat of the music – while the words reflect the spiritual essence of the culture. Pop music is encroaching on this tradition, of course, but the charity Valiha High (see page 146) is helping preserve the traditions.

ETHNIC GROUPS

This section was originally taken from A Glance at Madagascar by Ken Paginton in 1973 (and at that time the only authoritative source on Madagascar) and has subsequently been added to from a variety of sources.

The different clans of Madagascar are based more upon old kingdoms than upon ethnic grouping. Traditions are changing: the descriptions below reflect the tribes at the time of Independence, rather than in the more fluid society of today.

Antaifasy (People-of-the-sands)

Living in the southeast around Farafangana they cultivate rice, and fish in the lakes and rivers. Divided into three clans each with its own 'king' they generally have stricter moral codes than other tribes. They have large collective burial houses known as *kibory*, built of wood or stone and generally hidden in the forest.

Antaimoro (People-of-the-coast)

These are among the most recent arrivals and live in the southeast around Vohipeno and Manakara. They guard Islamic tradition and Arab influence and still

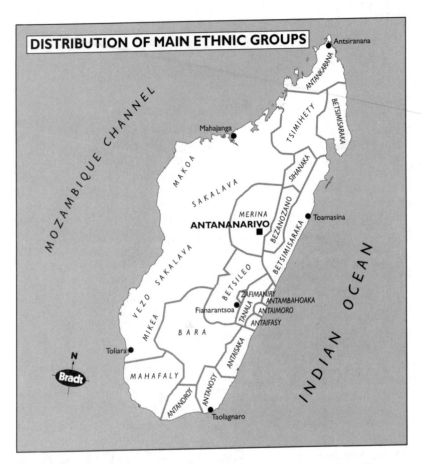

DISTRIBUTION OF MAIN ETHNIC GROUPS

use a form of Arab writing known as *sorabe*. They use verses of the Koran as amulets.

Antaisaka

Centred south of Farafangana on the southeast coast but now fairly widely spread throughout the island, they are an off-shoot of the Sakalava tribe. They cultivate coffee, bananas and rice – but only the women harvest the rice. There are strong marriage taboos amongst them. Often the houses may have a second door on the east side which is only used for taking out a corpse. They use the *kibory*, communal burial house, the corpse usually being dried out for two or three years before finally being put there.

Antankarana (Those-of-the-rocks)

Living in the north around Antsiranana (Diego Suarez) they are fishermen or cattle raisers whose rulers came from the Sakalava dynasty. Their houses are usually raised on stilts. Numerous *fady* exist amongst them governing relations between the sexes in the family; for example a girl may not wash her brother's clothes. The legs of a fowl are the father's portion, whereas amongst the Merina, for instance, they are given to the children.

Antambahoaka (Those-of-the-people)

The smallest tribe, of the same origin as the Antaimoro and living around Mananjary on the southeast coast. They have some Arab traits and amulets are used. They bury in a *kibory*. Group circumcision ceremonies are carried out every seven years.

Antandroy (People-of-the-thorns)

Traditionally nomadic, they live in the arid south around Ambovombe. A dark-skinned people, they wear little clothing and are said to be frank and open, easily roused to either joy or anger. Their women occupy an inferior position, and it is *fady* for a woman to milk a cow. The villages are often surrounded by a hedge of cactus plants. Until recently they ate little rice, their staples being maize, cassava and sweet potatoes. They believe in the *kokolampo*, a spirit of either good or bad influence. Their tombs are similar to those of the Mahafaly tribe. Sometimes it is *fady* among them for a child to say his father's name, or to refer by name to parts of his father's body. Thus he may say *ny fandiany* (the-what-he-moves-with) for his feet, and *ny amboniny* (the-top-of-him) for his head.

Antanosy (People-of-the-island)

The island is a small one in the Fanjahira river. They live in the southeast principally around Taolagnaro (Fort Dauphin). Their social structure is based on clans with a 'king' holding great authority over each one. There are strict *fady* governing relationships in the family. For example, a brother may not sit on or step over his sister's mat. As with many other tribes there are numerous *fady* regarding pregnancy: a pregnant woman should not sit in the doorway of the house; she should not eat brains; she should not converse with men; people who have no children should not stay in her house overnight. Other *fady* are that relatives should not eat meat at a funeral and the diggers opening a tomb should not wear clothes. When digging holes for the corner posts of a new house it may be *fady* to stand up so the job must be performed sitting down.

Bara

Originally in the southwest near Toliara, these nomadic cattle raisers now live in the south-central area around Ihosy and Betroka. Their name has no special meaning but it is reputed to derive from an African (Bantu) word. They may be polygamous and women occupy an inferior position in their society. They attach importance to the *fatidra* or 'blood pact'. Cattle stealing is regarded as proof of manhood and courage, without which a man cannot expect to get a wife. They are dancers and sculptors, a unique feature of their carved wooden figures being eyelashes of real hair set into the wood. They believe in the *helo*, a spirit that manifests itself at the foot of trees. In the past a whole village would move after somebody died owing to the fear of ghosts. They use caves in the mountains for burial. It is the custom to shave the head on the death of a near relative.

Betsileo (The-many-invincibles)

They are centred in the south of the Hauts Plateaux around Fianarantsoa but about 150,000 of them also live in the Betsiboka region. They are energetic and expert rice-producers, their irrigated, terraced rice-fields being a feature of the landscape. *Famadihana* was introduced to their culture by the Merina at the time of Queen Ranavalona I. It is *fady* for the husband of a pregnant woman to wear a *lamba* thrown over his shoulder. It may be *fady* for the family to eat until the father is present or for anyone to pick up his fork until the most honourable person present has started to eat.

Betsimisaraka (The-many-inseparables)

They are the second largest tribe and live on the east coast in the region between Toamasina and Antalaha. Their culture has been influenced by Europeans, particularly pirates. They cultivate rice and work on vanilla plantations. Their clothes are sometimes made from locally woven raffia. Originally their society included numerous local chiefs. The *tangalamena* is the local official for religious rites and customs. The Betsimisaraka have many superstitious beliefs: *angatra* (ghosts), *zazavavy an-drano* (mermaids), and *kalamoro*, little wild men of the woods, about 25 inches high with long flowing hair, who like to slip into houses and steal rice from the cooking pot. In the north coffins are generally placed under a shelter, in the south in tombs. It may be *fady* for a brother to shake hands with his sister, or for a young man to wear shoes while his father is still living.

Bezanozano (Many-small-plaits)

The name refers to the way in which they do their hair. They were probably one of the first tribes to become established in Madagascar, and live in an area between the Betsimisaraka lowlands and the Merina highlands. Like the Merina, they practise *famadihana*. As with most of the coastal tribes their funeral celebrations involve the consumption of considerable quantities of *toaka* (rum).

Mahafaly (Those-who-make-taboos or Those-who-make-happy)

The etymology of the word is sometimes disputed but the former meaning is generally regarded as being correct. They probably arrived around the 12th century, and live in the southwest desert area around Ampanihy and Ejeda. They are farmers, with maize, sorgho and sweet potatoes as their chief crops; cattle rearing occupies a secondary place. They kept their independence under their own local chiefs until the French occupation and still keep the bones of some of their old chiefs – this is the *jiny* cult. Their villages usually have a sacrificial post, the *hazo manga*, on the east side where sacrifices are made. Some of the blood is generally put on the foreheads of the people attending.

The tombs of the Mahafaly attract a great deal of interest. They are big rectangular constructions of uncut stone rising some three feet above the ground and decorated with *aloalo* and the horns of the cattle slain at the funeral feast. The tomb of the Mahafaly king Tsiampody has the horns of 700 zebu on it. The *aloalo* are sculpted wooden posts set upright on the tomb, often depicting scenes from the person's life. The burial customs include waiting for the decomposition of the body before it is placed in the tomb. It is the practice for a person to be given a new name after death – generally beginning with 'Andria'.

THE VAZIMBA

Vazimba is the name given to the earliest inhabitants of Madagascar, pastoralists of the central plateaux, who were displaced or absorbed by later immigrants. Once thought to be pre-Indonesian aboriginals from Africa, it is now generally accepted that they were survivors of the earliest Austronesian immigrants who were pushed to the west by later arrivals.

Vazimba come into both legends and history of the Malagasy. Vazimba tombs are now places of pilgrimage where sacrifices are made for favours and cures. It is *fady* to step over such a tomb. Vazimba are also thought to haunt certain springs and rocks, and offerings may be made here. They are the ancestral guardians of the soil.

SOME MALAGASY PROVERBS

Tantely tapa-bata ka ny foko no entiko mameno azy.
This is only half a pot of honey but my heart fills it up.

Mahavoa roa toy ny dakam-boriky.
Hit two things at once like the kick of a donkey.

Tsy midera vady tsy herintaona.
Don't praise your wife before a year.

Ny omby singorana amin' ny tandrony, ary ny olona kosa amin' ny vavany.
Oxen are trapped by their horns and men by their words.

Tondro tokana tsy mahazo hao.
You can't catch a louse with one finger.

Ny alina mitondra fisainana.
The night brings wisdom.

Aza manao herim-boantay.
If you are just a dung beetle don't try to move mountains.

Aza midera harena, fa niter-day.
Do not boast about your wealth if you are a father.

Ny teny toy ny fonosana, ka izay mamono no mamaha.
Words are like a parcel: if you tie lots of knots you will have to undo them.

The divorce rate is very high and it is not at all uncommon for a man to divorce and remarry six or seven times. It is very often *fady* for children to sleep in the same house as their parents. Their *rombo* (very similar to the *tromba* of the Sakalava) is the practice of contacting various spirits for healing purposes. Amongst the spirits believed in are the *raza* who are not real ancestors and in some cases are even supposed to include *vazaha* (white foreigners), and the *vorom-be* which is the spirit of a big bird.

Makoa

The Makoa are descended from slaves taken from the Makua people of Mozambique, and although often classified as Vezo, they maintain a separate identity. They inhabit forest areas, mainly in the southwest, and are considered to be the most 'primitive' (ie: traditional) group in Madagascar.

Merina (People-of-the-Highlands)

They live on the Hauts Plateaux, the most developed area of the country, the capital being 95% Merina. They are of Malayo-Polynesian origin and vary in colour from ivory to very dark, with straight hair. They used to be divided into three castes: the Andriana (nobles), the Hova (freemen) and the Andevo (serfs); but legally these divisions no longer exist. Most Merina houses are built of brick or mud; some are two-storey buildings with slender pillars, where the people live mainly upstairs. Most villages of any size have a church – probably two, Catholic and Protestant. There is much irrigated rice cultivation, and the Merina were the first tribe to have any skill in architecture and metallurgy. *Famadihana* is essentially a Merina custom.

Mikea

The Mikea are an off-shoot of the Sakalava. The name refers not so much to a tribe as to a lifestyle. They subsist by foraging in the dry forests of the west and southwest. Various groups of people up the west coast are called Mikea, although their main area is the Forêt des Mikea between Morombe and Toliara. The Mikea are Malagasy of various origins, having adopted their particular lifestyle (almost unique in Madagascar) for several reasons, including fleeing from oppression, taxation etc exerted on them by various powers: Sakalava, French, and the Government of the 2nd Republic. (Information from Dr J Bond.)

Sakalava (People-of-the-long-valleys)

They live in the west between Toliara and Mahajanga and are dark skinned with Polynesian features and short curly hair. They were at one time the largest and most powerful tribe, though disunited, and were ruled by their own kings and queens. Certain royal relics remain – sometimes being kept in the northeast corner of a house. The Sakalava are cattle raisers, and riches are reckoned by the number of cattle owned. There is a record of human sacrifice amongst them up to the year 1850 at special occasions such as the death of a king. The *tromba* (trance state) is quite common. It is *fady* for pregnant women to eat fish or to sit in a doorway. Women hold a more important place amongst them than in most other tribes.

Sihanaka (People-of-the-swamps)

Their home is the northeast of the old kingdom of Imerina around Lake Alaotra and they have much in common with the Merina. They are fishermen, rice growers and poultry raisers. Swamps have been drained to make vast rice-fields cultivated with modern machinery and methods. They have a special rotation of *fady* days.

St Marians

The population of Ile Sainte Marie (Nosy Boraha) is mixed. Although Indonesian in origin there has been influence from both Arabs and European pirates.

Tanala (People-of-the-forest)

These are traditionally forest-dwellers, living inland from Manakara, and are rice and coffee growers. Their houses are usually built on stilts. The Tanala are divided into two groups: the Ikongo in the south and the Menabe in the north. The Ikongo are an independent people and never submitted to Merina domination, in contrast to the Menabe. Burial customs include keeping the corpse for up to a month. Coffins are made from large trees to which sacrifices are sometimes made when they are cut down. The Ikongo usually bury their dead in the forest and may mark a tree to show the spot.

Some recent authorities dispute that the Tanala exist as a separate ethnic group.

Tsimihety (Those-who-do-not-cut-their-hair)

The refusal to cut their hair (to show mourning on the death of a Sakalava king) was to demonstrate their independence. They are an energetic and vigorous people in the north-central area and are spreading west. The oldest maternal uncle occupies an important position.

Vezo (Fishing people)

More usually referred to as Vezo-Sakalava, they are not generally recognised as a separate tribe but as a clan of the Sakalava. They live on the coast in the region of Morondava in the west to Faux Cap in the south. They use little canoes

MALAGASY WITHOUT (TOO MANY) TEARS
Janice Booth

Once you've thrown out the idea that you must speak a foreign language correctly or not at all, and that you must use complete sentences, you can have fun with only a few words of Malagasy. Basic French is understood almost everywhere, but the people – particularly in villages – warm instantly to any attempts to speak 'their own' language.

If you learn only three words, choose *misaotra* (thank you), pronounced misowtr; *veloma* (goodbye), pronounced veloom; and *manao ahoana* (pronounced roughly manna owner), which is an all-purpose word meaning hello, good morning or good day. If you can squeeze in another three, go for *tsara* (good); *aza fady* (please), pronounced azafad; and *be* (pronounced beh), which can be used – sometimes ungrammatically, but who cares! – to mean big, very or much. Thus *tsara be* means very good; and *misaotra be* means a big thank you. Finally, when talking to an older person, it's polite to add *tompoko* (pronounced toompk) after thank you or goodbye. This is equivalent to Madame or Monsieur in French. If your memory's poor, write the vocabulary on a postcard and carry it round with you.

In a forest one evening, at dusk, I was standing inside the trunk and intertwining roots of a huge banyan tree, looking up through the branches at the fading sky and a few early stars. It was very peaceful, very silent. Suddenly a small man appeared from the shadows, holding a rough wooden dish. Old and poorly dressed, probably a cattle herder, he stood uncertainly, not wanting to disturb me. I said 'Manao ahoana,' and he replied. I touched the bark of the tree gently and said 'tsara'. 'Tsara,' he agreed, smiling. Then he said a sentence in which I recognised *tantely* (honey). I pointed questioningly to a wild bees' nest high in the tree. 'Tantely,' he repeated quietly, pleased. I pointed to his dish – 'Tantely sakafo?' Yes, he was collecting wild honey for food. 'Tsara. Veloma, tompoko.' I moved off into the twilight. 'Veloma,' he called softly after me. So few words, so much said.

Another day, in Tana, a teenaged girl was pestering me for money. She didn't seem very deserving, but wouldn't give up. Then I asked her in Malagasy, 'What's your name?' She looked astonished, eyes suddenly meeting mine instead of sliding furtively. 'Noro.' So I asked, very politely, 'Please Noro, go away. Goodbye.' Nonplussed, she stared at me briefly before moving off, the cringing attitude quite gone. By using her name, I'd given her dignity. You can find that vocabulary – all seven words of it! – in the Language Appendix on page 401.

'What's your name?' is probably the phrase I most enjoy using. Say it to a child and its eyes grow wider, as a timid little voice answers you. Then you can say 'Manao ahoana', using the name, and you've forged a link. Now find out from the Appendix how to say 'My name is...' – and you're into real conversation!

When I'm in Madagascar I still carry a copy of the Language Appendix in my bag. It's dog-eared now, and scribbled on. But it's my passport to a special kind of contact with friendly, gentle and fascinating people.

hollowed out from tree trunks and fitted with one outrigger pole and a small rectangular sail. In these frail but stable craft they go far out to sea. The Vezo are also noted for their tombs, which are graves dug into the ground surrounded by wooden palisades, the main posts of which are crowned by erotic wooden carved figures.

Zafimaniry

A clan of some 15,000 people distributed in about 100 villages in the forests between the Betsileo and Tanala areas southeast of Ambositra. They are known for their wood carvings and sculpture, and are descended from people from the Hauts Plateaux who established themselves there early in the 19th century. The Zafimaniry are thus interesting to historians as they continue the forms of housing and decoration of past centuries. Their houses, which are made from vegetable fibres and wood with bamboo walls and roofs, have no nails and can be taken down and moved from one village to another.

In the last few years there have been several anthropological books published in English about the people of Madagascar. See *Books* in the *Appendix*.

The tribes may differ but a Malagasy proverb shows their feeling of unity: *Ny olombelona toy ny molo-bilany, ka iray mihodidina ihany*; 'Men are like the lip of the cooking pot which forms just one circle'.

LANGUAGE

The Indonesian origin of the Malagasy people shows strongly in their language which is spoken, with regional variations of dialect, throughout the island. (Words for domestic animals, however, are derived from Kiswahili, indicating that the early settlers, sensibly enough, did not bring animals with them in their outrigger canoes.) Malagasy is a remarkably rich language, full of images, metaphors and proverbs. Literal translations of Malagasy words and phrases are often very poetic. 'Dusk' is *Maizim-bava vilany*, 'Darken the mouth of the cooking pot'; 'two or three in the morning' is *Misafo helika ny kary*, 'When the wild cat washes itself'. The richness of the language means that there are few English words that can be translated into a single word in Malagasy, and vice versa. An example given by Leonard Fox in his book on the poetry of Madagascar, *Hainteny*, is *miala mandry*. *Miala* means 'go out/go away' and *mandry* means 'lie down/go to sleep'. Together, however, they mean 'to spend the night away from home, and yet be back in the early morning as if never having been away'!

Learning, or even using, the Malagasy language may seem a challenging prospect to the first-time visitor. Place names may be 15 characters long (because they usually have a literal meaning, such as Ranomafana: Hot water), with seemingly erratic syllable stress. However, as a courtesy to the Malagasy people you should learn a few Malagasy words. Get started with the helpful hints page 401, then memorise some of the Malagasy vocabulary on page 402. Dictionaries and phrase books can be bought in Antananarivo. A new one (published by Hippocrene Books, New York) combines dictionary and phrase book in one volume; website (UK): www.wermter.fsnet.co.uk.

▥▥▥▥▥

> The mercies of God [be bestowed on] this people, whose
> simplicity hath herein made them more happy than our too dear-
> bought knowledge hath advantaged us.
>
> Walter Hamond

32

Natural History

This section, with the exception of Geology *and as far as* Conservation, *is written by Jonathan Hughes with additional information by Nick Garbutt and others. Jonathan Hughes's involvement with Madagascar began while working at the Royal Botanic Gardens, Kew, mapping and classifying the conservation needs of the island's habitats.*

INTRODUCTION

Madagascar's natural history is its most striking single feature. There are over 200,000 species on the island, living in habitats ranging from rainforests to deserts and from mountain tops to mangrove swamps. The residents are as unique as they are diverse, so that a list of Malagasy species reads like a hurried appendix tagged on the end of a catalogue of the world's wildlife – 'The ones found nowhere else'. Six whole plant families exist only on Madagascar, as do 1,000 orchid species, many thousands of succulents, countless insects, over 300 species of frog, 270 kinds of reptile, five families of birds and more than 100 different mammals, including an entire group of primates, the order to which we belong. One thing is certain: whatever animal or plant you gaze upon during your visit, you are unlikely to see it anywhere else.

This magnificent menagerie is the product of a spectacular geological past. More than 165 million years ago, Madagascar was a land-locked plateau at the centre of the largest continent the Earth has ever seen, Gondwanaland or Gondwana. This was during the age of the reptiles at about the time when the flowering plants were beginning to blossom and primitive mammals and birds were finding a niche among their giant dinosaur cohabitants. With a combination of sea-level rises and plate movements Gondwanaland subsequently broke into the island continents of Australia, Antarctica, South America and Africa. As the Indian Ocean opened up between once neighbouring territories, Madagascar cast away from the African coast, setting itself adrift as one of the Earth's great experiments in evolution.

Some of the plants and animals present on the island today are the results of adaptation from the original, marooned Gondwanaland stock. Ancient groups such as the ferns, cycads, palms and pandans, and primitive reptiles such as the boas and iguanids, are descendants of this relic community. Yet, the magic of Madagascar is that a select band of species have enriched the community by arriving *since* the break-up. Flying, swimming, journeying as seeds or riding the floodwaters of the east African rivers in hollow trunks, wave after wave of more recent plants and animals came from over the horizon during a period of 100 million years, bringing with them the latest adaptations from the big world beyond. Colonisers, such as the lemurs and carnivores, may have had a helping hand from a partial land-bridge which is thought to have appeared from beneath the waves of the Mozambique Channel about 40 million years ago.

Yet, whatever their mode of transport, upon land-fall each species spread outwards in every direction, through the tremendous range of habitats on offer,

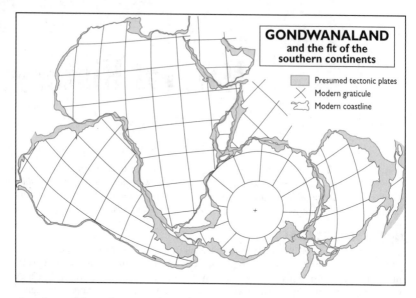

GONDWANALAND
and the fit of the
southern continents

☐ Presumed tectonic plates
✕ Modern graticule
〜 Modern coastline

changing subtly as they encountered new environments, sometimes to the extent that new species were formed. This evolutionary process is termed 'adaptive radiation' and it results in the creation of an array of new species found nowhere else.

The patterns in the island's diversity tell us something of the timing of these colonisations. A large number of unique succulent plants indicates an early arrival from Africa in the dry west, followed by a radiation eastwards ending in the rainforests. On the contrary, the two Malagasy pitcher plants found on the east coast probably arrived at about the same time as the Malagasy, and from the same direction. The remoteness of Madagascar's rainforests, positioned as they are, across a stretch of dry plateaux and over a spine of high mountains, may have made these humid lands tantalisingly out of reach for African rainforest species. Certainly many of the Malagasy species seem to have closer associations with Asian and South American groups with whom they share Gondwanaland ancestors. As a result of these various evolutionary processes and chance events, the island is blessed with animals and plants of many descriptions, most unique to the island, and about a fair proportion of which we have very little knowledge.

GEOLOGY
Tim Ireland
Note: Ma = millions of years ago, Ga = billions of years ago
The geology of Madagascar raises plenty of interesting questions, many of them unanswered, and attracts geologists and mining companies from around the world. Madagascar comprises three main geological terranes; a **crystalline core** comprising the central highlands, **a sedimentary shelf** that flanks this core on the west, and dispersed **volcanic edifices**.

The **crystalline core** dates to the Late Proterozoic (900-550 Ma); a period long before the evolution of complex life, and before the assembly of the continents as we know them. Yet these rocks contain tiny crystals of the resistant mineral zircon, which testify to a far greater antiquity (2.6 Ga). At that stage the atmosphere was rich in carbon dioxide, the now-geologically distinctive continents and oceans differed less than they do today ... little is known confidently about those times. Probably the zircon crystals record the formation of a continent that would later become part of Gondwana. Other continental masses also existed, several that would later become the northern continents, and one that would split and become South America and Africa.

Two of these (South America-Africa and Australia-Antarctica-India-Madagascar) had been drifting slowly closer together, and then at 690 Ma, almost at the same time as the first large multicellular marine creatures evolved, they collided, as India and Asia collided to form the Himalaya. During such collisions the edges of the continents crumple and snap, and kilometre-thick sheets are thrust over each other. Mountain ranges (orogenic belts) are thus created that suture together the original continental blocks. This ·so-called 'Mozambique Belt' of mountains (Pan-African Orogen) was immense, extending 7,000km from modern Kenya to Antarctica, and Madagascar was at the centre of it. The rocks buried during mountain building are recrystallised and partially melted under the subsequent pressure and heat. The Central Highlands of Madagascar are just a small part of the exhumed roots of this vast and ancient mountain belt, and consist of intensely recrystallised rocks such as gneisses and granulites (formed in the solid-state), and subordinate migmatites and granites (crystallised from molten rock). The ramparts of the 'Mozambique Belt' then stood sentinel, slowly eroding but largely unchanged, for several hundred million years, while soft-bodied life in the oceans experimented and toyed with the idea of greater progression.

The **sedimentary shelf** began to form early in the Palaeozoic (500 Ma), as three-dimensional macroscopic organisms with external skeletons evolved and explosively diversified. The old mountain belt had been eroded down near sea-level, and the waning of an ice age cause marine flooding of the land. Across the world, life evolved dramatically toward a climax of vegetation productivity in the Carboniferous (when much of the world's coal was deposited: 320 Ma) and then shivered through its most severe ice age and most catastrophic extinction only 30 million years later (96% of marine species vanished). That ice age scraped all evidence of the preceding sedimentation from proto-Madagascar, and the geological record there is reset, beginning with gravel and boulder deposits laid down as the glaciers retreated. In the middle Permian (270 Ma), the southern continents were still assembled as one (Gondwana) in which Madagascar was a central part without identity, bound on the west by Africa, the east by India and the south by Antarctica.

Gondwana began to split apart soon after, toward the modern continental distribution. As a continent divides, rifts form (like modern East Africa), then become nascent seas (like the Red Sea), and eventually widen into oceans. The rocks of the sedimentary shelf record 100 million years of deposition spanning that cycle, for the rift separating Madagascar from Africa. The earliest (basal) sediments are mixed glacial and river and lake (terrestrial) deposits that contain a fossil flora common to all the modern southern continents. Later, the land was inundated and marine carbonates were deposited in this new shallow sea, which preserve the remains of some primitive fish. During the Triassic (240-210 Ma) the landscape was uplifted (rejuvenated) and terrestrial gravels and sands were deposited, including those exposed in Isalo National Park. Major marine transgression followed, and from this time, until after the demise of the dinosaurs (63 Ma), fossiliferous marine limestone (carbonate) sedimentation dominated in the growing Mozambique Channel. These sediments today make up the Bemahara Plateau and the *tsingy* landscapes of western Madagascar. The shallow marine

THE EXTINCT MEGAFAUNA

Today, Madagascar's wildlife is as rich as anywhere on Earth. The tragedy is that it was once richer still. When, just 2,000 years ago, humans arrived they found a world covered with forests and populated by huge tortoises, dwarf hippos, lemurs the size of gorillas and the 'elephant bird' which, at three metres high, made an ostrich look like a goose. All are now extinct, possibly as a result of both direct hunting and indirect effects such as competition with humans for food, habitat or space. It is no accident that these animals represent what, at the time, would have been the 'biggest ones' on the island – the *megafauna*. Large animals are not only more worthwhile prey for humans, but they are also more impinged by human activities for they have higher demands on the environment.

The 16 or so species of lemur that became extinct were all larger than the present title-holders – the indri and diademed sifaka. Some species hung like a sloth from branches, while others browsed on the forest floor. The elephant bird, or *Aepyornis*, was not one species but several, one of which, *A. maximus*, weighing over 300kg, may have been the largest bird that has ever lived. Recent finds reveal that the birds only became extinct a few hundred years ago. Indeed tales of 'vorombe', or big bird, are still fresh in Malagasy folklore. Such tales may have filtered through to Marco Polo who wrote of the giant roc able to lift an elephant, on the island south of Zanzibar.

The roc as visualised by an artist in 1598

ecosystems at that stage were characterised by the super-abundance of squid-like animals with planar, segmented, spiral shells (*ammonites*), and the west-Madagascan sedimentary carbonate sequences are an incredible repository of these fossils. Tectonic landscape rejuvenation occurred again between 50 and 30 Ma as a major eastern rift developed between India and Madagascar, and ended sedimentation on the shelf.

The **volcanic edifices** of Madagascar are less obvious than related volcanoes responsible for the Comoros, Réunion and Mauritius islands. They are widespread in the north and along the east coast, and inland, make up the Ankaratra Massif, Itasy Highlands, and Montagne d'Ambre. Underwater volcanic activity began during the Cretaceous (120 Ma), related to the eventual departure of India, and has persisted off the north Malagasy coast up to the present day, due to anomalously high heat flow similar to the case in Hawaii. The lavas and intrusive rocks produced have rare and bizarre chemistry, consisting of a bimodal super-alkalic (Na-rich) suite dominated by basaltic andesites and Na-amphibole-bearing syenitic rocks. The most recent major volcanism occurred less than two million years ago, of note giving birth to Nosy Be, where modern hot springs testify to the relative youth of volcanic activity. There are suggestions that the volcanic focus is moving southeast, from the Comoros toward Madagascar; the volcanic record in the island is potentially far from over.

Significant **landscape evolution** has occurred over the last 40 Ma. At and after the time India began to head northeast, the rift between Africa and Madagascar stabilised and topographic relief was regenerated by activity on major NNE- and NNW-oriented faults. These orientations can be recognised across the country bounding smaller sedimentary basins and mountain ranges, and most noticeably, control the geometry of the east coast. The centre and east were uplifted more than the west, providing the basis for the modern geomorphology of the island. Completely emergent for the first time for several hundred million years, during this time land plants and animals evolved and proliferated toward the present unique flora and fauna for which Madagascar is famous. Local lake and river deposits developed in the lowlands, and erosion cut back the highlands. In the centre and east, the entire marine record was stripped away, revealing the crystalline core and resulting in undulating dome-like mountains (eg: Pic Boby). In the west, the sedimentary sequences were eroded flat, to near sea-level. Tectonic activity in the last million years has again uplifted the Malagasy terrain, and this ancient erosional surface (peneplain) now defines the Bemahara (and other) plateaux of the west, dissected by the modern west-flowing rivers.

The final chapter starts just two thousand years ago, when skilled Malay boatmen found their way to then uninhabited Madagascar (while their brethren discovered all but two of the Pacific Islands). Humans can affect geological processes; reduction in primary forest since the colonisation of Madagascar has indisputably influenced the shape of the land. Soils stabilised by deep root systems and high inputs of organic matter become susceptible to erosion, and the sediment load in the rivers has increased. In the 50 years to 1945, 40m of clay was deposited in the delta of the Betsiboka River at Mahajanga, immensely more than the underlying sedimentary record suggests was usual prior to deforestation. Ubiquitous hillside scars called *lavaka* are the inland testimony to this accelerated redistribution of material from highlands to coast, an inexorable environmental response to deforestation that is sending the Malagasy highlands toward eventual peneplanation at an incredible rate; if mean annual erosion of 1mm takes place continuously without volcanic or tectonic rejuvenation, Madagascar will be reduced to near sea level in a short three million years.

MADAGASCAR'S BIODIVERSITY

Madagascar is one of the 12 most important countries for biodiversity on the planet. It is home to so many species for two reasons: it is near to the equator and it contains an astonishing array of habitats. The tropical climate is a perfect host to the processes of life – far more living things survive within the tropics than in cooler regions, while the habitat variety provides more opportunity for animal and plant variation. It is in this evolutionary playground that every now and then a member of a mainland plant or animal group has found itself marooned. Little wonder then that Madagascar has such biodiversity – a feature that has served to fascinate centuries of travellers, but one that has also placed a tremendous responsibility upon a troubled nation.

FLORA

Madagascar has one of the richest floras in the world. The upper estimates of its diversity, at 12,000 species, make the island the world's number one floral hotspot for an area of its size. The key to this richness is its endemism – 80% of Madagascar's plant species are not found anywhere else. The fortuitous break from Africa and Asia at a time when the flowering plants were just beginning to diversify, allowed many groups to develop their own lineage, supplemented occasionally by the later colonisations of more advanced forms.

Ferns and cycads

Ferns were in their heyday before even Gondwanaland was formed. Their best efforts were the impressive tree-ferns, which had large spreading fronds sprouting from a tall, scaly stem. These structures created vast forests in all warm, humid areas during the Carboniferous Period, 350 million years ago; forests that were later to persist only as coal seams in the rocks. Although they eventually lost ground to seed-bearing plants in the age of the dinosaurs, it is a credit to the fern design that they are still abundant and successful. Indeed the soft, symmetrical foliage of ferns very much symbolises the lushness of wet, hot places. It's true that they have been relegated to a life in the shade of more recently evolved plants, but at this they excel, out-competing all others.

Although some species are present in dry habitats, the vast majority of Madagascar's ferns decorate the branches and trunks of the eastern rainforest. One noticeable species is the huge **bird's nest fern** (*Asplenium nidus*), which adorns most of the large trunks with luxuriant balconies of leaves. The ancient **tree-ferns** (*Cyathea* spp), that once supplied the forest canopy, are still present on its floor, contributing to the prehistoric atmosphere of the forest. Many other species inhabit the shady world among the tree roots or swell the foliage at riverbanks. In all, the diversity and delicacy of the ferns much enhance the rainforest experience.

Often mistaken for a tree-fern, the **cycad** (*Cycas* spp), is significantly different. It is one of the original seed-bearing plants which marked the end of the ferns' dominance on Earth. Its innovation, leading eventually to the evolution of the flowering plants which currently command all of the world's habitats. Ironically, cycads are much more unusual today than their fern predecessors. Resembling a tree-fern with palm-like leaves, the single Malagasy representative of the genus *Cycas* is found only in the eastern rainforest. If seen, it is worth a close look. The cone that it bears holds seeds which, 300 million years ago, became the most significant single plant adaptation in Earth's history.

Palms

Madagascar is home to one of the world's richest palm floras. There are around 170 species, three times more than in the rest of Africa put together, and of these 165 are found nowhere else. Experts claim that this diversity is evidence that south Gondwanaland was rich in palms at about the time the island was created. The dominance of species with Asian relatives betrays the fact that Madagascar severed with India millions of years ago it left Africa's shores.

The species present range from the famous to the recently discovered, from dwarf to giant, and almost all have intriguing characteristics. One palm has led to a Malagasy word entering our language – the **raffia palm** (*Raphia ruffia*). The fibres from its leaves are woven into the hats, baskets and mats that characterise the Malagasy. Of the 50 new palm species discovered in the last decade, one is worth particular attention – *Ravenea musicalis*, the world's only 'water palm'. It starts life

MADAGASCAR'S DINOSAURS

Visitors to the museum in Tsimbazaza, in Tana, will see a display of dinosaur bones, confirming that these ancestors to today's remarkable lizards lived on Madagascar before the break up of Gondwanaland. The oldest dinosaur fossils yet discovered were found in 2000 in southern Madagascar and date back 230 million years! Another find was of a bizarre blunt-snouted herbivorous crocodile, *Simosuchus clarki*, discovered in northwest Madagascar, which dates from the late Cretaceous era, between 97 million and 65 million years ago. Hitherto, crocodiles were assumed to have changed little for millions of years.

The news that really hit the headlines in 2001, however, was of *Masiakasaurus knopfieri*, possibly the first animal to be named after a pop star. The palaeontologists who discovered it called it after the lead guitarist of Dire Straits, because whenever they played his music they found dinosaur fossils. *M. knopfieri* was a ferocious little two-legged carnivore, whose larger cousin *Majungatholus atopus* was discovered by the same team from the State University of New York Stony Brook, led by David Krause.

actually underwater in only one of Madagascar's rivers. As it grows it surfaces, eventually bears fruit, and then seeds. Its discoverer named it *R. musicalis* after being charmed by the chimes of its seed pods as they hit the water below. There are other riverside palms in Madagascar adapted to tolerate the recurrent floods of the island's lowland rainforest, but none as perfectly as the musical water palm.

One other unusual group is named the '**litter-trapping palms**'. The crown of their leaves is arranged like an upturned shuttlecock, sprouting at first from the forest floor, and then gaining height as the stem grows from below. Its watertight crown catches leaves falling from the canopy, perhaps to obtain trace minerals, but no one really knows. A strange consequence of this growth is that the roots of other plants, which originally grew through the soil into the crown by mistake, later dangle down from its heights as alabaster-white zigzags.

Although the vast majority of palms live among the hardwoods of the lowland rainforest, there are species which brave the more arid environments, notably the **feather palms** (*Chrysalidocarpus* spp), which nestle in the canyons of Isalo National Park and stand alone amongst the secondary grasslands of the west. An extremely rare and unusual palm, *Ravenea xerophila*, is even to be found within the semidesert of the spiny forest.

A distinct lack of large herbivores in Madagascar has left its palms spineless and without poisons. Pollination is mostly by bees and flies, but some species have tiny flowers to entice unknown insect guests. For seed dispersal lemurs are often employed. The ring-tailed, black, red-ruffed and the browns all assist in scattering the seeds. The bright colours of some fruits serve to attract birds and forest pigs. While the few African palms, which normally use elephants as dispersers, presumably make do with zebu.

Looking like a messy cross between a palm and a pine tree, **pandan palms**, or screw pines (*Pandanus* spp), are different from those above, but equally fond of Madagascar. Their foliage consists of untidy grass-like mops which awkwardly adorn rough branches periodically emerging from their straight trunks. Common in both rain and dry forests, there are 75 species, only one of which is found elsewhere, placing the country alongside Borneo in the pandan diversity stakes.

Trees

Until the arrival of humans, Madagascar was almost entirely cloaked in forest. There remain examples of each of the original forests, but vast areas of Madagascar have become treeless as a result of *tavy* (slash and burn) agriculture and soil erosion. Most of the **evergreen trees** remaining form the superstructure of the rainforest. They are normally 30m high, with buttressed roots, solid hardwood trunks and vast canopies. There can be up to 250 species of trees per hectare in the lowland rainforest, but from the ground they all look very similar. To identify a species, botanists must often wait for flowering, an event that is not only extremely difficult to predict, but also one that takes place 30m above the ground. One obvious tree is the **strangler fig** (*Ficus* spp), which germinates up in the canopy on a branch of its victim, grows down to the floor to root, and then encircles and constricts its host leaving a hollow knotted trunk. The Malagasy prize the forest hardwoods; one canopy tree is called the 'kingswood' because its wood is so hard that, at one time, any specimens were automatically the property of the local king for use as a staff.

The only evergreen species to be found outside the rainforest are the **tapia tree** (*Uapaca bojei*), the nine species of **mangrove tree** and some of the **succulent trees** to be found in the extreme southwest where sea mists provide water year-round. In tolerating the conditions of west Madagascar, these evergreens have borne their own unusual communities.

The rest of Madagascar's trees are **deciduous**, that is they lose their leaves during the dry season. The largest dry forests of the west are dappled with the shadows of **leguminous trees** such as *Dalbergia* and *Cassia*, characterised by their long seed pods and symbiotic relationships with bacteria which provide fertilisers within their roots. Sprawling **banyan figs** (*Ficus* spp), and huge **tamarind trees** (*Tamarindus indica*), create gallery forest along the rivers of the west and south, yielding pungent fruit popular with lemurs. Where the soil is rich in lime, Madagascar's most celebrated trees, the **baobabs** (*Adansonia* spp), dominate. See below for an expert's account of Madagascar's baobabs.

One last species deserves a mention. The **traveller's tree** (*Ravenala madagascariensis*) is one of Madagascar's most spectacular plants. It earns its name from the relief it affords a thirsty traveller: water is stored in the base of its leaves and can be released with a swift blow. A relation of the banana, its elegant fronds are arranged in a dramatic vertical fan, which is decorative enough to have earned it a role as Air Madagascar's symbol. Its large, bulbous flowers sprout from the leaf axils and, during the 24 hours that they are receptive, are visited by unusual pollinators – ruffed lemurs. The lemurs locate flowers which have just opened, and literally pull them apart to get at the large nectary inside. Keeping a lemur fed is quite a demand on the tree, but it produces flowers day after day for several months, and during this time, the lemurs eat little else. The traveller's tree is perhaps the only native species to have benefited from *tavy* agriculture, for it dominates areas of secondary vegetation on the central plateau and east coast.

Baobabs
Jim Bond

The baobabs *(Adansonia* sp.) of Madagascar are one of its main attractions and a 'must see' on the list of many visitors on account of their extraordinary size and beauty. To the Malagasy who live alongside them, they are important economically, yielding highly nutritious fruits, oil from the seeds, strong fibre for rope and bark for roofing material, as well as often having a deeper spiritual significance by providing a home for the Ancestors. The Malagasy name for the

SCIENTIFIC CLASSIFICATION

Since many animals and plants in Madagascar have yet to be given English names, I have made use of the Latin or scientific name. For those not familiar with these and the associated terminology, here is a brief guide:

Having been separated into broad **classes** like mammals (*mammalia*), angiosperms (*angiospermae*) – flowering plants – etc, animals and plants are narrowed down into an **order**, such as Primates or Monocotyledons. The next division is **family**: Lemur (*Lemuridae*) and Orchid (*Orchidaceae*) continue the examples above. These are the general names that everyone knows, and you are quite safe to say 'in the lemur family' or 'a type of orchid'. There are also subfamilies, such as the 'true lemurs' and 'the indri subfamily' which includes sifakas. Then come **genera** (**genus** in the singular) followed by **species**, and the Latin names here will be less familiar-sounding. It is these two names that are combined in the scientific name precisely to identify the animal or plant. So *Lemur catta* and *Angraecum sesquipedale* will be recognisable whatever the nationality of the person you are talking to. We call them ring-tailed lemur and comet orchid; the French say *maki* and *orchidée comète*. With a scientific name up your sleeve there is no confusion.

largest species, the magnificent *Adansonia grandidieri,* is *renala* or *reniala,* literally: 'mother-of-the-forest' – which is particularly apt, considering the 'keystone' role these trees play in the dry forest ecosystems.

Diversity

There are eight baobab species in the world, of which six are endemic to Madagascar, with only one found in the whole of Africa and one in NW Australia. The diversity in Madagascar would suggest that this is where baobabs first evolved, a theory that has now been supported by molecular studies of the baobab 'family tree'. It also appears that this happened long after the separation of the continents, which means that the African and Australian species must have arisen from colonising fruits floating across the Indian Ocean, rather than any Gondwanaland explanation.

Within Madagascar, the other six species each evolved to fit their own niche within the dry forest zones. What kept them isolated from each other here, unlike in Africa, was partly a north-south divide (the Sambirano barrier) and partly having three different flowering seasons within both northern and southern groups. However, even within the same species, baobabs can assume quite widely different forms, or 'ecotypes', depending on local conditions. For example, some of the *renala* near Morondava are almost 30 metres tall, smooth, columnar giants, but in the spiny scrub by Andavadoaka, mature trees of the same species reach only three metres, are quite knobbly, almost spherical in shape, and wonderfully grotesque-looking! (See illustrations on the following page.) It is not always easy, even to the trained eye, to tell the species apart so below are some working guidelines that I use when in doubt.

Form and function

Baobabs are dryland plants, in the sense that they are 'drought survivors'. They are able to take up and store water from a sporadic downpour very efficiently within the soft, porous 'wood' of their big, fat trunks, which acts like a giant sponge. However, they do not like getting their roots too wet, which is why they are not found in the east, nor do they tolerate frost well, which limits their distribution inland. The thick bark is relatively (but not completely) fire-resistant and can be removed in moderation without causing the tree too much harm. All baobabs are deciduous in the dry season, although two Malagasy species also flower at this time, providing an important source of pollen for bees when few other plants are in flower.

Taxonomy

There are technically seven species in Madagascar, although one is a bit of a red herring, as it is the African species, *A. digitata,* which was introduced by Arab traders and planted as street trees in a few towns such as Diego and Mahajanga. These should be fairly obvious.

The six true Malagasy species fall into two sub-genera, based on flower characters: the Brevitubae ('short-tubed') and the Longitubae ('long-tubed'). This may all seem rather academic, but understanding the function behind these differences should help to explain the overall shape and position of the tree, and hence point to which one it might be...

Brevitubae

These comprise *A. grandidieri* in the south and *A. suarezensis* in the north. The distinctive feature of both is that they have flat-topped crowns of predominantly horizontal branches, which emerge just above the canopy height of the forest in which they grow. The *reason* these species invest so much extra energy is thought to be to make things easier for their favoured pollinator, a large and clumsy fruit bat, to fly in to at night. The idea is that the bats could land easily on the flat, bare branches and hop about between flowers. These in turn are short in length and sit presented nicely upwards like cups and saucers, their long stamens fanning out ready to brush the bats' chins when they feed on the nectar. The flowers only come out at dusk and are cream-coloured in order to catch the moonlight, although by the next morning they start to wilt, turning red before falling off about four days later. The flowers are also visited by sunbirds, bees and small lemurs.

Longitubae

The remaining Malagasy species, *A. za* and *A. rubrostipa* (or *A. fony*) in the south, and *A. perrieri* and *A. madagascariensis* in the north, have long floral parts, mostly yellow or red, which tend to dangle down. The nectaries are at the end of a long tube, so have almost certainly evolved to accommodate the tongues of large hawkmoths. The trees have no need to emerge from the canopy and they have round crowns, with branches forking upwards and outwards. Where they happen to live is more determined by soil type and manner of seed dispersal.

Identification

So, for the simplified guide to working out which baobab is which:

1 Is it really a baobab? – there are other big, fat grey trees in the dry zones, eg: *Pachypodium* sp. (which has spines towards the top) or *Moringa* (bean-shaped pods). If it has large, round or ovoid, hard fruits, with a velvety coat then you can be pretty sure it's a baobab.
2 Does it have a flat-topped, emergent crown or a round-topped crown at the level of the other trees? Are its branches trying to be horizontal or generally reaching up?
3 Can you see any flowers and what are they like? (Remember they all turn red on the ground.) Is there thick foliage at the same time?

4 Is it in the northern dry zone or in the south/west?
5 What is the soil like?
6 Other special characters (see below) – fruit, stalk, trunk constriction, leaf margin, staminal tube proportions...
7 What do the *local* people call it? In areas with two or three baobab species coexisting, especially in the south and west, they are usually right.

Individual species
'Southern three'
Adansonia grandidieri. Malagasy name: *renala* or *reniala*
Perhaps the most famous of the Malagasy baobabs and certainly the grandest of them all, it was actually named in honour of the pioneering French botanist and explorer, Alfred Grandidier. This is generally the largest of the three 'southern species', although

A. grandidieri
Andavadoaka

as mentioned earlier, this all depends on the natural height of the surrounding vegetation. Heights of over 30m have been

A. grandidieri
Morondava

recorded and a diameter of 7.5m. Some have even been hollowed out to house people. Usually found on richer alluvial soils, ie: flood-plains, or near watercourses where it grows tallest, but also adjacent to mangroves and salt marshes, which may be the cause of characteristic ring patterns on the bark in some areas. It has quite a restricted distribution, between the Manambolo lakes system in the north and the fringes of the Mikea Forest in the south. Best examples, in relatively undisturbed forest, are to be seen in the Mangoky valley. Flowering season: May–August

Adansonia za. Malagasy name: *za*
Intermediate in size of the southern species, this one has the widest distribution, from just west of Fort Dauphin up to Analalava. It tends to prefer calcareous soils and is the only species in the spiny forest on limestone of the Mahafaly Plateau in the deep south. Probably more frost tolerant than the others, it is found more inland, notably around Zombitsy. Typically it has a tall, straight trunk with grey bark and round crown, although there are stunted versions in the very dry south. Fruits are more ovoid than round and have a peculiarly swollen stalk. Flowering season: Nov–Jan.

Adansonia rubrostipa (synonym: *A. fony*). Malagasy name: *fony*
(Originally described and named in 1890 as *A. fony*, after the local name, by the French botanist, Baillon, this species was officially renamed in 1995 on a technicality relating to the original publication. Not surprisingly, this has caused much offence in Madagascar and there are now moves afoot to try and get the old name conserved. Out of respect to all concerned, I shall therefore only refer to it by the Malagasy name.)
Fony is generally the smallest of the southern group and it tends to grow on sandy soil. It may be found up the west

coast from Itampolo to Soalala. The classic form is the bottle-shaped tree in the spiny forest, although further north at Kirindy, a taller and more slender model appears, which is in fact the dominant tree in some parts of that forest. *Fony* do not seem to mind growing almost on top of one another and they can often be quite concentrated, presumably due to their thin-walled fruits not being naturally carried very far. Definitive characters include: a characteristic constriction in the trunk just below the branches (not necessarily in every tree) and a serrated leaf margin. *Fony* also tend to have more of a reddish tinge to the bark, but there is some overlap either way on this with other species. Flowering season: February–March

'Northern three'
In the north, the local names, *bojy* or *bozy*, are not specific, presumably because baobabs have less economic importance.

Adansonia suarezensis
This is the northern flat-top, and a much smaller version of its cousin the *renala*. It has an even more restricted distribution in various small patches of remaining woodland around Diego plus the forests of Mahory and Analamera to the south. The conservation status of *A. suarezensis* is listed as 'critical' due to ongoing clearance of the surrounding vegetation. However, some individual trees are regarded as sacred and are locally protected, together with one intact small wood on a basalt outcrop near the village of Ambilo, about 6km east of Mahavanona – do be generous in your encouragement of this if you visit! Flowering season: May–July.

RAINFOREST COMMUNITIES
If a plant could pick a place to live, it would choose one with constant high temperatures and an abundance of water. The hottest, wettest places on Earth occur near to the Equator and they are covered in the world's greatest conglomerations of plants – the tropical rainforests. The rainforests have thrived here for millennia, bathing in the planet's most powerful sunlight and heaviest, most dependable rainfall. In this evergreen habitat there is no autumn, though leaves are individually shed as they age and become inefficient. This constant shower of leaf litter builds up on the forest floor to become the fodder of fungi and soil bacteria, which work unceasingly to decompose the material. A quick turn around of nutrients is vital in a habitat that bears high rainfall, for with each torrent much of the soil surface is washed into the river systems. For the same reason rainforest soils are remarkably shallow, yet rainforest trees are remarkably tall, so throughout the world the trees employ buttress or stilt roots to give them some stability. Another common feature is the broad-leaf which comes to a point, known as a drip-tip, designed to shed the heavy rain as it lands.

The dominant trees block out the sun from below with a solid canopy many metres above the ground. Their broad branches inadvertently support tonnes of epiphytic plants such as orchids and ferns which, embedded in tiny patches of soil, sip water directly from the super-saturated air with bizarre 'air roots'. Trapped amongst their foliage are numerous pools of rainwater used by insects to raise larvae, which in turn serve as food for the tadpoles of tree frogs. On emerging, the vast numbers of insect species harvest the leaves, buds and shoots around them, each specialised to tolerate its host's defensive poisons. The insects themselves are food for birds, bats, tree frogs, lizards, spiders and

Adansonia perrieri
This is the largest baobab in the north and the rarest. It has the most restricted distribution of all, limited to only four known populations in and around the Montagne d'Ambre massif. Sometimes known as 'the rainforest species', this baobab appears to have found a very specialised niche on the sheltered banks of small streams running off the old volcano. One of the best sites to see it in its full glory is on the stream in the Park that runs down from the Grande Cascade, although you need to walk down an entirely separate path. Rising tall and majestic up to 25m from the steep valley floor, its crown merges neatly with those of other trees on the slopes. Note how few there are though! Key features are: somewhat thickened distal branches and a distinctive large, pale yellow flower, with relatively wide petals and stamens fused for most of their length, a bit like a hibiscus. Flowering season: November–December.

Adansonia madagascariensis
This is another extremely plastic species that is often mistaken for others! Growing beside *A. suarenzensis* in at least two places, *A. madagascariensis* looks much smaller and scruffier with its irregular tangle of branches. However, given more favourable soil and water conditions it can grow much taller, such as at the east entrance to Ankarana, where it starts to resemble the stature of *A. perrieri*. Up on the nearby karst itself, it looks quite wee and delicate with a pear-shaped trunk. Essentially, it is only found from the Ankara (sic) plateau, just south of Mahajanga, north. It can be distinguished most readily from *A. za* by having round or grapefruit-shaped fruits and a lack of swollen stalk, as well as having other minor floral differences. Flowering season: March–April.

other insects, and to complete the food chain, there are predatory snakes within the canopy, birds of prey above, and mammalian carnivores below.

Rainforest animals have other roles. They are employed by plants to courier pollen about the forest. The plants advertise their nectar with magnificent, pungent flowers, each species timing the flowering event for a particular period in the month, year or even decade, so that its dispersed members can swap genes effectively. Once fertilised, the fruits and seeds of the plants are unwittingly dispersed by a different set of animal carriers, such as fruit bats, nut-cracking birds and the lemurs.

Many of the rainforest's residents never leave these hanging gardens, but below the canopy there is another world. An under-storey of smaller plants, such as palms and shrubs, lap up what light is allowed through from above. The huge trunks of the canopy trees are encumbered with lianas, creepers and ferns, and at their bases the forest floor, cloaked in darkness and largely devoid of plant growth, is the realm of fungi, ants and termites. Despite appearances, the floor is more dormant than dead, for its soil is riddled with baby trees, stunted by the darkness, but waiting patiently for their one chance to join the others above – a tree fall. If this occurs, the light comes streaming down from above, and opportunistic saplings take their chance by throwing their growth into top gear. In the years it takes for the saplings to climb and close up the canopy once more, a flourish of 'chablis' plants and animals revel in this short-lived paradise, their entire lifecycles designed to support the precarious existence of jumping between tree fall events.

This, then, is the rainforest, the most complex, productive and dynamic community on Earth.

Conservation and respect

Baobabs are fairly long-lived, but do not grow as old as previously thought. Although they are generally left standing by people when forests are cleared, this is not always the case. Where there is regular burning of the undergrowth to stimulate new grazing, like in the *renala* forest south of Lac Ihotry, a few mature trees fall each year. Few young trees survive the flames and those that do are promptly eaten by zebu, so there is little regeneration. Left unchecked it will not take long before such healthy-looking forests resemble the sad scene around the famous 'avenue de baobabs' north of Morondava – just imagine how tall the surrounding forest there must have been there before it was all degraded!

There are many complex interactions in the dry forests, which are only now becoming appreciated. Baobabs are known to provide food, support and homes to all sorts of creatures, both directly and indirectly, including: ants, moths, bees, sunbirds, eagles, geckos, fruit bats, lemurs, humans, fungi and even other plants. Reflect a moment on all these potential dependants before you take your photos. Pay your respects to these true mothers of the forest and be seen to do so. And, if possible, ask permission first – that tree might be sacred *(faly)* to someone!

Estimating the age of a baobab

Estimating the age of baobabs is not easy, since counting rings is pointless because of the sponginess of the 'wood'. David Livingstone gave himself a major headache by trying, both physically and theologically! The girth of the trees appears to vary not only with the species, but also with the local soil, water table and the amount of rainfall in the previous few months.

I did a study on *A. grandidieri* a couple of years ago, from which we now have a rough guide, at least for this species... I noticed an unusual population of protected 'baby' *renala* in one village, that all turned out to have been planted during the famine years of 1934-6 from fruits gathered elsewhere. We can be pretty sure of this because: a) it lies outside the natural distribution limits for *renala* (which I have mapped), and b) we have documented three independent oral accounts of the 'great trek north' to find food at that time. One of these was an eye witness who actually took part, at the age of 12 or 13. We measured most of these known sexagenarian baobabs and averaged out the data to get a crude measure of annual growth.

Extrapolating from these data, even the biggest, fattest *renala* that we know of, in the Mangoky valley, are probably no more than 600 years old, and that's being generous! Most are far younger. From a conservation point of view, this is quite significant since older-living trees do not need such a high rate of regeneration in order to replicate their numbers and so maintain a sustainable population.

Pitcher plants

There are only two species of pitcher plant (*Nepenthes* spp) on Madagascar, but they are spectacular enough to deserve a mention. In wetlands in the south, they poke out of the marsh beds like triffids planning an ambush. One of their leaves wraps upon itself to create a fly trap, which then serves up trace elements, from the flies' remains, unobtainable from the mud below. The rest of the family live thousands of miles away in Southeast Asia, and it is thought that the arrival of these two species stemmed from a fortuitous migration along the same path that originally brought the Malagasy – perhaps they inadvertently shared the boats!

Succulents

In Madagascar, wherever rainfall is below about 400mm a year, succulents reign. The entire southwest of the island is dominated by their swollen forms. Further north they decorate the natural rock gardens of Isalo, Itremo and the countless outcrops on the central plateau. They also appear within the sparse dry forests of the west, among the stone chaos of the *tsingy*, and even venture on to the grasslands and into the rainforests. The **euphorbias** are the most widespread group. They have diversified into a thousand different forms, from bushes resembling strings of sausages, to trees sprouting smooth green branches, but few leaves, to spiny stalks emerging from an underground swollen tuber. Many species shed their leaves at the start of the dry season, but when present they are swollen with water, and shining with wax. To replace the leaves they often yield wonderful flowers and, in so doing, brighten up the landscape. Another succulent group, the **pachypodia**, is perhaps even more unusual. They are stem succulents with sometimes grotesquely swollen bodies, so that the tallest look like short, fat trees sprouting at their tips, whereas the smaller species resemble grey bottles sprouting either stubby leaves or flowers, depending on the season. **Aloes**, **kalanchoes** and **senecios** are leaf succulents, existing essentially as a collection of swollen leaves sprouting from the earth. The leaves are often ornamental, tinged with terracotta and bearing harsh spines, but also showy red flowers during the drought. Some species do have stems to raise their broad foliage above the ground. The largest aloes have stocky 3m stems covered in untidy dead scales which sport the huge succulent leaves and, in June and July, a large, red inflorescence. Other succulents in Madagascar include *Adenia*, which looks even more rock-like than the pachypodia, swollen, straggling milkweed and succulent relatives of the cucumber family with disc-shaped leaves.

Didierea

To botanists the ***Didiereaceae*** of the arid southwest are the most intriguing plants in Madagascar, for they are an entire family of bizarre plants found nowhere else on

XEROPHYTES AND SUCCULENTS – PLANTS IN DRY HABITATS

Unlike animals, plants cannot escape harsh environments. The plants of Madagascar's dry southwest have therefore adapted to tolerate strong sunlight, high temperatures and most restricting of all, desiccation. Here, as elsewhere in the world, these high demands have produced unusual-looking, but fascinating, plant species called xerophytes.

All xerophytes have deep root systems to acquire what little water there is available. Their leaves are usually small and covered in hairs, and much of the photosynthesis is done by the green stems. This design lowers the surface area of the plant and traps still air adjacent to the leaf, reducing water loss – the key aim. In addition to desiccation, overheating is as much a problem for plants as it is for animals. Many xerophytes are therefore orientated to minimise heating, usually having their narrowest edge facing the sun, and they often add grey pigments to their leaves to deflect the intense light of midday.

The most extreme adaptations for a dry life are to be seen in the succulents. This general term describes all xerophytes which store water in their waxy leaves, roots or stems. Such water is a valuable commodity in a dry habitat, and one that must be protected from thirsty grazers. Succulents usually employ toxins, or spines, and this need for defence has given rise to the most spectacular plants on the island – the didierea 'trees' of the spiny forest.

ORCHIDS IN MADAGASCAR
Clare and Johan Hermans

Like so many other living things on the island, the orchids of Madagascar are extremely varied and well over three-quarters are endemic. More than 950 different species have been recorded so far, and new ones are still being discovered. The orchids have adapted to every possible habitat, including the spiny forest and the cool highland mountain ranges but their highest density is in the wet forests of the east. Whilst orchid habitats are becoming scarcer, something can be seen in flower at most times of the year; the best season for flowers is the rainy season from January to March.

Some of the most memorable orchids are to be found in the **eastern coastal area**, which is the habitat of large Angraecums, Eulophiellas and Cymbidiellas. Many orchids here are epiphytes – they live on tree branches or stems with their roots anchoring the plants and although they scramble over their host, collecting moisture and nutrients, they are not parasites.

Angraecum eburneum can be seen in flower from September to May, its thick leathery leaves form a half-metre wide fan shape; the flower stems reach above the leaves carrying a number of large greenish white fragrant flowers. Like many Malagasy orchids the blooms are strongly night-scented and white in colour to attract pollinating moths.

The comet orchid, *Angraecum sesquipedale*, is one of the most striking. It flowers from June to November and the plants are similar to *eburneum* but slightly more compact. Individual flowers can be almost 26cm across and over 30cm long including the long nectary spur, characteristic for the Angraecoid orchids, at the back of the flower. The flower was described by Charles Darwin at the end of the 19th century when he predicted that there would be a moth with a very long tongue that could reach down to the nectar at the bottom of the spur. This idea was ridiculed by his contemporaries but in 1903 a moth with a proboscis of over 30cm was found in Madagascar!

Aeranthes plants look similar to Angraecums. Their spider-like greenish flowers are suspended from a long thin stem, gently nodding in the breeze.

Eulophiella roempleriana is now very rare. One of the few remaining, almost two-metre-high plants can be seen on Île aux Nattes, off Ile Sainte Marie. The large, deep pink flowers are well worth the *pirogue* trip to the island. A few more of these plants survive in the reserves around Andasibe. The plant is normally in flower from October onwards.

Earth. The common name of one species, the octopus tree, gives some indication of their eccentricities. They look similar to some forms of cacti and they are often quoted as examples of convergent evolution – where two separate groups of organisms have adapted similar features to cope with a similar environment. However they do differ from typical cacti in that they do not have green swollen stems, but instead bear small, deciduous leaves, protected by immense thorns, on grey, wooded branches. A number of these spiny branches sprout from near the base of each plant and soar unsteadily into the sky, so that the entire structure has an unkempt and uninviting appearance from afar. In various guises, these magnificent didierea join the succulent trees to create the unworldly landscape of the spiny forest in the southwest.

At first sight the mass of thorns and branches confuses the eye, let alone identification, but if you want to name a species try to recognise individual silhouettes, and look for the following features:

Cymbidiella orchids are also very striking; they generally flower from October to January. *Cymbidiella pardalina*, with its huge crimson lip, cohabits with a stag-horn fern, while *Cymbidiella falcigera*, with large black spotted yellow flowers, prefers the exclusive company of the raffia palm.

The highlands of Madagascar with their cooler and more seasonal climate are inhabited by numerous terrestrial orchids, growing in soil or leaf litter; underground tubers produce deciduous leaves and flower stems – not dissimilar to orchids seen in temperate regions.

Eulophia plantaginea is a relatively common roadside plant; large colonies can sometimes be found, especially in boggy areas.

Cynorkis can also be seen along the roads. Many are terrestrials, others grow on wet rock or in swamps. Epiphytes like *Angraecum* and *Aeranthes* can still be found in the few remaining pockets of forest in the highlands.

Aerangis plants are instantly recognisable by their shiny, dark green foliage. The flowers superficially resemble those of *Angraecum* but they are often much smaller, carried on elegant racemes, and their scent is exquisite. The plants are commonly seen in the wet shade of the rainforest reserves of Périnet and Ranomafana.

Jumellea are again similar but have a more narrow, folded back single flower on thin stems.

Bulbophyllum orchids are easily missed by the untrained eye; their rounded, plump pseudo-bulbs are often seen on moss-covered trees. They are always worthwhile investigating: small gem-like blooms may be nestled amongst the foliage.

Oeonia with its huge white lip and two red dots in its throat can be found rambling amongst the undergrowth.

The apparently bare higher peaks of the Hauts Plateaux, like Ibity near Antsirabe, also contain a very specialised community of orchids. The thick-leaved, sun-loving Angraecoids and Bulbophyllums share the rock faces with succulents; these rock dwellers are known as lithophytes.

One of the best and easiest places to see orchids, such as *Angraecum*, *Cymbidiella* and *Gastrorchis*, is in hotel and private gardens but one must be aware that these domesticated collections may contain the odd foreign interloper. Orchids from the Orient and South America are brought in as pot plants, the flowers being often bigger and brighter than the natives.

Import and export permits are required to take orchids out of Madagascar.

- *Didierea madagascariensis*, the octopus tree – most abundant between Morondava and Toliara (Tuléar), the erratic branches of this tree, which sprout from close to the base, are covered with very long thorns and, in the wet season, long thin leaves, giving it a fuzzy appearance.
- *Didierea trolli* – when adult they are similar to *D. madagascariensis*, but are distinguished when younger by having lateral branches at the base of the stem, which creep over the ground keeping browsing animals at a distance.
- *Decaryia madagascariensis*, the zigzag plant – found between Ampanihy and Ambovombe, it has a complex crown of thorny, zigzagging branches and produces small, white flowers.
- *Alluaudiopsis fiherenensis* – found north of Toliara (Tuléar), it is bushy but short (up to 2m) and sprouts yellow-white flowers.
- *Alluaudia procera* – this is the most abundant of the trees in much of the spiny

forest. When young it is little more than a mesh of wild, extremely thorny bush. However, when closer to its maximum height of 15m, it takes on a more regal appearance with a single trunk crowned by a series of substantial branches. Its leaves sprout in curious lines which spiral up the branches during the wet season to be shed at the start of the dry. Thorns patrol the leaves on each side and hence themselves form further spirals. Tiny flowers sometimes adorn tufts on the tips of the branches.

- *Alluaudia ascendens* – Up to 20m tall, this tree shares the skies with *A. procera*. A solitary woody trunk divides into a series of long slim, skyward branches, hence the Latin name. Even when juvenile the single stem is present with its spiralling thorns.
- *Alluaudia montagnacii* – only found near Itampalo, it has few leaning branches, covered in spirals of thorns and finishing in bouquets of leaves and flowers. The fact that they look like a cross between *A. procera* and *A. ascendens* has led some to suggest that they are nothing more than hybrids.
- *Alluaudia comosa* – common along the road from Toliara (Tuléar) to Andranavory, these trees resemble very thorny, squat acacia, their dark crowns often formed into an anvil shape.
- *Alluaudia dumosa* – grows between Ampanihy and Taolagnaro (Fort Dauphin). It has a woody trunk with few leaves and even fewer spines. The diverging greyish-brown branches above the main trunk carry out most of the photosynthesis. The flowers are white with red stigmas.

Foreigners

In common with many islands around the globe, Madagascar has suffered from accidental or intended introductions of 'alien' species. Referred to as 'weedy' species, these are the botanical equivalents of cats and rats – species that should not really be there, but that cause havoc when they arrive. Out-competing native species, sharp tropical grasses from South America permanently deface the burnt woodlands of the west and, avoided by cattle, their populations explode. Where thick forest is cleared, fast-growing *Eucalyptus* and *Psidium* trees step in. They either

WATCHING WILDLIFE IN THE FOREST

Although the forest is full of life, a stroll among its trunks can be disappointing. To see its characters you must be patient and quiet, and it doesn't hurt to maximise your chances of sightings by employing a local guide, or enhancing your vantage point. A good location is on the lip of a slope. This places the canopy below you at eye level, so that you are staring straight at the action among its branches. Another good position is on a riverbank, where light penetrates further and walls of palms, pandans and ferns exploit the illumination. Numerous rivers and streams dissect the forest and are the favourite spots of insects, particularly butterflies which 'puddle' on the damp earth of the riverbanks. If nothing else you may get to see some of the freshwater eels! An extremely good time to see wildlife is actually after dark when a totally different set of players appear to enact their lives. Caught in the torchlight you can often see the eyes of nocturnal species such as the mouse lemurs, carnivores and perhaps, if you are in the right place, the aye-aye. Set up a torch behind a mosquito net, and within a short time you will have species of moths and beetles unknown to science to inspect.

suffocate competitors with their dense growth, or poison the soil with their toxins. In drier areas, superbly adapted and profoundly damaging cacti spread from the nearby sisal plantations and flourish where there was once spiny forest. Needless to say, the native animal populations, unable to adapt to these invaders, also suffer, and this, perhaps more than the endangerment of plant species, has prompted action from conservation bodies.

The value of the flora

Many Malagasy plants crop up in garden centres throughout Europe. Familiar to horticulturalists are the dragon tree (*Dracaena marginata*), the crown of thorns (*Euphorbia millii*), the *Areca* palm, the flamboyant tree (*Delonix regia*) and the Madagascar jasmine (*Stephanotis floribunda*) of bridal bouquet fame. Other natives are valued for their uses rather than their aesthetic qualities. Recent interest has grown in Madagascar's various wild coffees, *Rubiaceae*. Many are naturally decaffeinated and hybrids with tastier coffees are currently being produced. More seriously, the rosy periwinkle (*Catharanthus roseus*) is a champion of those who campaign to conserve natural habitats. It contains two alkaloid chemicals proven to assist treatment of leukaemia and other cancers in children. There may well be other plants in a position to offer equally useful products, but the rate of forest destruction may be extinguishing these before we have a chance to appreciate them. Slowly we are learning that there is great value in diversity alone.

FAUNA

Compared with the breathtaking ecosystems of mainland Africa, Madagascar's fauna has far more subtle qualities. A combination of ancient Gondwanaland stock and the descendants of the last 165 million years' wayfarers, it is more intriguing than dynamic. Here are a seemingly random collection of animal groups that had the opportunity to prove themselves in the absence of big predators and herbivores. The resulting 180,000 species existing in habitats from rainforests to coral reefs bring human opportunity too, for dozens of truly unique safaris.

Invertebrates

There are well over 150,000 species of invertebrate on Madagascar, the majority in the eastern rainforests. To spot them turn over leaves and logs on the forest floor, peer very closely at the foliage or switch on a bright light after dark. Although creepy, let alone crawly, they do contribute substantially to the experience of wild areas on the island and, providing you can suppress the spine shivers, your mini-safaris will be well worthwhile.

It is a difficult task to pick out the most impressive invertebrates, but notable are the huge **golden orb-web spiders** (*Nephila madagascariensis*), which gather on telephone lines in all the towns. Their silk is so strong that it was once used as a textile – Queen Victoria even had a pair of Nephila silk stockings! Equally oversized are the **pill millipedes** (*Sphaerotherium* spp) which roll up when startled to resemble a striped, brown golf ball. Among the forest foliage are superbly camouflaged **praying mantis**, **net-throwing spiders**, which cast their silk nets at fliers-by, and **nymphs** and bugs of all shapes, colours and adornments. Among the leaf litter there are spectacular, striped **flatworms** and vast numbers of wonderful **weevils**.

The 300 species of **butterfly** are all descendants of African voyagers. The most visible are the heavily-patterned swallowtails, and the nymphalids with their dominant blue and orange liveries. Madagascar's **moths** are significantly older in origin and are probably descendants of the Gondwanaland insects marooned on

ANTS BEWARE!
Angus McCrae

Should you come across perfectly conical little craters up to 5cm across with little or no evidence of spoil around them in dry, sandy places you're looking at evidence of ant lions (Fam. *Myrmeleontidae*, of the minor order *Neuroptera*). Out of sight at the bottom of each pit may lurk the strange and ravenous ant lion larva, buried but for the tips of its needle-sharp mandibles. Should an unwary ant or other small prey stray over the brink and loosen some sand, a blur of action may suddenly erupt: showers of sand are hurled back by the ant lion's jerking head and the resultant landslide carries the intruder helplessly down into the waiting jaws. Only if you're British might they come as a big surprise – ant lions are found in most countries. In North America their common name is doodle-bug.

Seen close up, the larval ant lion looks like some kind of termite-like alien with a large, hard and somewhat flattened head attached apparently upside down to its softer, hunched body. It has eyes arranged in a group on each side of the head, and thin vibrissae sprout from around its sickle-like jaws. Its mouth is permanently sealed, and it feeds instead through a narrow groove between each mandible and its close-fitting maxilla, thus being incapable of chewing or taking in anything but liquid. With no solids to be excreted the stomach ends blindly, disconnected from the hind-gut. On pupation the larva digs deeper and makes a stout, round cocoon of silk secreted by its malpighian tubules (the insect equivalent of kidneys) and stored in its rectum. The silk simply oozes out from its otherwise unused anus which is unmodified with any kind of spinneret. Sand adheres to the outside as the cocoon is formed.

The adults are seldom noticed by non-speciaiasts as most are of unexciting grey to pale fawn colours and they usually fly only at dusk or at night. They superficially resemble dragonflies but fly more clumsily and have smaller eyes and short, stout and clubbed antennae. At rest they fold their wings lengthwise, hiding the abdomen. Unlike their larvae they have a fully functional mouth, chewing mouthparts and a complete gut, but very little is known of their food or how they catch it.

The genus *Palpares* includes several endemic Malagasy species of striking size and colour which sometimes take to flight by day under dull conditions or when disturbed, as well as at night. Of these, *P. voeltzkowi* is one of the largest and perhaps the most handsome of any ant lion in the world with its violet-black and white-blotched wings more than 16cm in span and its reddish-brown body exceeding 16cm.

About 20 ant lion species have been described from Madagascar but more can be expected as they have not been revised for half a century. Their greatest diversity is in the dry west and south, but so far no endemic Malagasy genera are known and their affinities appear strongly African.

the island. This explains the diversity in place – there are 4,000 species, and many groups are active in the daylight, filling niches that elsewhere are currently the realm of butterflies. Most dramatic is the huge, yellow comet moth (*Argema mittrei*), which has a wingspan of up to 25cm, and the elaborate urania moths (*Chrysiridia*), which look just like swallowtails decorated with emeralds. A very close relative is found in the Amazon rainforest.

Fish

The inhabitants of Madagascar's abundant lakes, marshes, estuaries, rivers and mountain brooks have been as much isolated by history as those of the land. The most interesting species are the **cichlids**, with their huge variety, colourful coats and endearing habits of childcare – they protect their young by offering their mouths as a retreat in times of danger. Other Malagasy species demonstrate the parental instinct, a feature rare in fish. Some of the island's **catfish** also mouth-brood and male **mudskippers** in the mangroves defend their nest burrows with the vigour of a proud father.

Another major group is the **killifish**, which resemble the gouramis to be found in pet shops. Specialised **eels** live high up in mountain brooks, and in the underground rivers of west Madagascar blind **cave fish** live, sometimes entirely on the rich pickings of bat guano. The one problem with the island's fish is that they are not big and tasty. Consequently many exotic species have been introduced into the rivers and are regularly on display in the nation's markets. These new species naturally put pressure on the native stock and, as is often the story, the less-vigorous Malagasy species seem to be on the retreat.

More robust are the marine species to be found swimming off the island's 4,000km of coastline. Madagascar is legendary for its **shark** populations and a quick dip off the east coast should be considered carefully, but on the west coast there are **coral reefs** bursting with life, outdoing even the Red Sea for fish diversity. The reefs are host to a typical Indo-Pacific community of clownfish, angelfish, butterflyfish, damselfish, tangs and surgeons, triggerfish, wrasse,

LEECHES

Hilary Bradt

Few classes of invertebrates elicit more disgust than leeches. Perhaps some facts about these extraordinarily well-adapted animals will give them more appeal.

Terrestrial leeches such as those found in Madagascar are small (1–2cm long) and find their warm-blooded prey by vibrations and odour. Suckers at each end enable the leech to move around in a series of loops and to attach itself to a leaf by its posterior while seeking its meal with the front end. It has sharp jaws and can quickly – and painlessly – bite through the skin and start feeding. When it has filled its digestive tract with blood the leech drops off and digests its meal. This process can take several months since leeches have pouches all along their gut to hold as much blood as possible – up to ten times their own weight. The salivary glands manufacture an anticoagulant which prevents the blood clotting during the meal or period of digestion. This is why leech wounds bleed so spectacularly. Leeches also inject an anaesthetic which is why you don't feel them biting.

Leeches are hermaphrodite but still have pretty exciting sex lives. To consummate their union they need to exchange packets of sperm. This is done either the conventional way via a leechy penis or by injection, allowing the sperm to make its way through the body tissues to find and fertilise the eggs.

Readers who are disappointed with the small size of Malagasy leeches will be interested to hear that an expedition to French Guiana in the 1970s discovered the world's largest leech: at full stretch 45cm long!

THE FRESHWATER FISH OF MADAGASCAR

Derek Schuurman

Most of Madagascar's freshwater ecosystems are in poor condition today. Across the island, lakes and marshes – except those too saline for riziculture – have been converted into paddy-fields. Many rivers have suffered massive siltation due to the erosion which follows large-scale deforestation. Add to this the widespread invasion of introduced fish, particularly various tilapia species, the spotted and striped snakeheads (both introduced as food fish) and mosquito-fish (tiny fish brought in to control mosquitoes, but which instead wreaked havoc on the endemic fish), plus over-fishing by a burgeoning rural population, and you have a recipe for disaster as far as endemic freshwater wildlife is concerned.

With Madagascar's freshwater fish fauna still being quite poorly understood, estimates vary from 32 to 49 for the number of endemic species. The status of several remains uncertain at this point, with some never having been photographed or studied, and others very likely being extinct in the wild. Perhaps best known in international aquaria are the popular rainbow fishes (especially *Bedotia geayi*) and one killifish (*Pachypanchax omalonotus*) while the three blind cave gobies, (*Glossogobius ankaranensis* in particular), receive frequent mention in literature on Malagasy cave systems like Ankarana.

The group which has been receiving much international attention during the last few years, are the cichlids. Some of these, like the lamena (*Lamena nourissati*, its name meaning 'red one') are very attractive, but until the 1980s only one species, the carnivorous marakely (*Paratilapia polleni*, 'the black one') had been seen alive outside Madagascar. During the late 1990s, expeditions to remote parts of the island came up with a number of new discoveries on the cichlid front, such as a new lamena species with blue lips.

The seven omnivorous and herbivorous *Paretroplus* cichlids or Damba have also been studied fairly intensively lately, their status varying from widespread and not threatened (a few of them) to probably extinct in the wild (pin-stripe Damba). One expedition member indicated the severity of the tilapia invasion, reporting that for every one cichlid they caught, they had to catch more than 100 tilapia! Fortunately, various captive breeding programmes have been started around the world to save the Malagasy cichlids.

groupers, batfish, blennies and gobies, boxfish, lionfish, moray eels, flutefish, porcupinefish, pufferfish, squirrelfish, sweetlips and the Moorish idol.

Frogs

The only amphibians on Madagascar are frogs. Newts, salamanders and toads are absent, but the frog abundance more than makes up for these omissions. On average a new species of Malagasy frog is discovered every eight weeks. There are currently 170 catalogued species, but the actual number may be closer to 300 and all but two of these are endemic.

Most of the species, restricted by their permeable skins, spend their lives in the humid forests of the east. With their bulbous finger tips, which help them to grip on to the waxy forest leaves, large brightly-coloured eyes and loud whistles, the **tree frogs** are appealing to most visitors. They either return to small streams to breed, hang their egg batches from overhanging branches (a habit which demands high-dive routines from the tadpoles), or abandon the waterways altogether to raise their young in the miniature pools among pandan leaves or between the epiphytes of the canopy. Closer to the forest floor there are other, more brightly-coloured frogs, such as the large, blushing **tomato frog** (*Dyscophus antongili*) and the magnificent miniature *Mantella* species, which resemble the famed poison arrow frogs from the Amazon in that they display their toxic inners with lurid coats of black, gold and blue.

Away from the mature forest, frogs congregate around fast-flowing mountain streams littered with mossy rocks, alongside the sticky marshes that house pitcher plants and even in the drier Hauts Plateaux and Isalo regions where they rumble through the floor litter defying dehydration.

Reptiles

The unique evolutionary history of Madagascar is particularly evidenced by the reptiles on the island. There are scattered species derived from ancient Gondwanaland stock, many of which are more closely related to South American or Asian reptiles than to African. There are also large groups of closely related species marking the radiations that stemmed from African immigrations in more recent times. The most dramatic example of the latter concerns chameleons. Madagascar is home to about half the world's chameleon species including the smallest and the largest. With impressive adaptive dexterity, they have dispersed throughout the habitats of the island to occupy every conceivable niche (see box, pages 56–7).

Similar in their success have been the **geckoes**. The 70-odd gecko species seem to be split between those that make every effort imaginable to camouflage themselves and those that are quite happy to stick out like a sore thumb. The spectacular **day gecko** (*Phelsuma madagascariensis*) and its relatives can be seen by passing motorists from some distance. Their dazzling emerald coats emblazoned with day-glo orange splashes are intended for the attentions of the opposite sex and competitors. Once in their sights they bob their heads and wave their tails as if an extra guarantee of visibility is needed. In contrast a magnificently-camouflaged **leaf-tailed gecko** (*Uroplatus* spp*)* could easily be next to your hand on a tree trunk without you noticing it. With its flattened body, splayed tail, speckled eyes, colour-change tactics and complete lack of shadow, you may remain ignorant until, nervous, it gapes a large, red tongue in your direction.

A quiet scuttle on the floor of a western forest may well be a **skink**, while louder ramblings could be due to one of the handsome **plated lizards**. However, the most significant disturbances, both in the forest and the academic world, are made by the **iguanids**. This group of large lizards is primarily found in the Americas, and never in Africa. Hence its presence on Madagascar is a sign that its ancestors were members of the original party that separated from Africa.

Madagascar's three **boas** are in the same boat. They only exist as fossils in Africa, supplanted by the more stealthy pythons, but they do have distant relatives in South America. Most often seen is the Madagascar tree boa (*Sanzinia madagascariensis*), which although decorated in the same marbled glaze, varies in colour from orange (when juvenile) to grey and black, brilliant green or brown and blue, depending on the location. Its larger relative the ground boa (*Acrantophis madagascariensis*) is also often spied at the edge of waterways in the humid east and north. Of the remaining species of snake, the one-metre long **hog-nosed snake** (*Leioheterodon madagascariensis*), in its dazzling checkerboard of black and yellow, is most frequently encountered, usually gliding across a carpet of leaves on the lookout for frogs.

CHAMELEONS

Hilary Bradt

Everybody thinks they know one thing about chameleons: that they change colour to match their background. Wrong! You have only to observe the striking *Calumma parsonii*, commonly seen at Périnet, staying stubbornly green while transferred from boy's hand to tree trunk to leafy branch, to see that in some species this is a myth. Most chameleons are cryptically coloured to match their preferred resting place (there are branch-coloured chameleons, for instance, and leaf-coloured ones) and some do respond to a change of background, but their abilities are mainly reserved for expressing emotion. An anxious chameleon will darken and grow stripes and an angry chameleon, faced with a territorial intruder, will change his colours dramatically. The most impressive displays, however, are reserved for sexual encounters. Chameleons say it with colours. Enthusiastic males explode into a riot of spots, stripes and contrasting colours, whilst the female usually responds by donning a black cloak of disapproval. Only on the rare occasions that she is feeling receptive will she present a brighter appearance.

Chameleons use body language more than colour to deter enemies. If you spot a chameleon on a branch you will note that his first reaction to being seen is to put the branch between you and him and flatten his body laterally so that he is barely visible. If you try to catch him, he will blow himself up, expand his throat, raise his helmet (if he has one) and hiss. His next action will be to either bite, jump, or try to run away. Fortunately they must be the slowest of all lizards, are easily caught, and pose for the camera with gloomy resignation (who can resist an animal that has a constantly down-turned mouth like a Victorian headmistress?). This slowness is another aspect of the chameleon's defence: when he walks, he moves like a leaf in the wind. This is fine when the danger is an animal predator, but less effective when it is a car. In a tree, his best protection is to keep completely still. He can do this by having feet shaped like pliers and a prehensile tail so he can effortlessly grasp a branch, and eyes shaped like gun-turrets which can swivel 180 degrees independently of each other, enabling him to view the world from front and back without moving his head. This is the chameleon's true camouflage.

The family Chamaeleonidae is represented by three genera, the 'true chameleons' *Calumma* and *Furcifer*, and the little stump-tailed chameleons,

Despite the fact that none of the island's snakes are a danger to humans, the Malagasy are particularly wary of some species. The blood-red tail of one harmless tree snake (*Ithycyphus perineti*), known to the Malagasy as the *fandrefiala*, is believed to have powers of possession. It apparently hypnotises cattle from up high, then drops down tail-first to impale its victim. Similar paranormal attributes are bestowed on other Malagasy reptiles. The chameleons, for example, are generally feared by the Malagasy, and when fascinated *vazaha* go to pick one up, there is often a bout of surprised gasps from the locals. Another reptile deeply embedded in the folklore is the **Nile crocodile** (*Crocodilus niloticus*) which, although threatened throughout the island, takes on spiritual roles in some areas (see Lac Antanavo).

A number of Madagascar's **tortoises** are severely threatened with extinction. Captive breeding programmes at Ampijoroa are currently successfully rearing the ploughshare (*Geochelone yniphora*) and flat-tailed tortoises (*Pyxis planicauda*) and further south, the Beza-Mahafaly reserve is protecting the handsome radiated

Brookesia. Unlike the true chameleons, the *Brookesia*'s short tail is not prehensile.

In chameleons there is often a striking colour difference between males and females. Many males have horns (occasionally used for fighting) or other nasal protuberances. Where the two sexes look the same you can recognise the male by the bulge of the scrotal sac beneath the tail, and a spur on the hind feet.

It is interesting to know how the chameleon achieves its colour change. It has a transparent epidermis, then three layers of cells – the top ones are yellow and red, the middle layer reflects blue light and white light, and the bottom layer consists of black pigment cells with tentacles or fingers that can protrude up through the other layers. The cells are under control of the autonomic nervous system, expanding and contracting according to a range of stimuli. Change of colour occurs when one layer is more stimulated than others, and patterning when one group of cells receives maximum stimulation.

In the early 17th century there was the firm conviction that chameleons subsisted without food. A German author, describing Madagascar in 1609, mentions the chameleon living 'entirely on air and dew' and Shakespeare refers several times to the chameleon's supposed diet: 'The chameleon ... can feed on air' (*Two Gentlemen of Verona*) and 'of the chameleon's dish: I eat the air promise-crammed' (*Hamlet*). Possibly at that time no-one had witnessed the tongue flash out through the bars of its cage to trap a passing insect. This tongue is as remarkable as any other feature of this remarkable reptile. It was formerly thought that the club-shaped tip was sticky, allowing the chameleon to catch flies, but researchers discovered that captive chameleons had been catching much larger prey – lizards, intended to coexist as cage-mates. These animals were far too heavy to be captured simply with a sticky tongue, so a high-speed video camera was brought into use. This showed that a chameleon is able to use a pair of muscles at the tip of its tongue to form a suction cup milliseconds before it hit its prey. The whole manoeuvre, from aim to mouthful, takes about half a second.

The name apparently comes from Greek: *chamai leon*, dwarf lion. I suppose a hissing, open-mouthed reptile could remind one of a lion, but to most visitors to Madagascar they are one of the most appealing and bizarre of the 'strange and marvellous forms' on show.

tortoise (*Geochelone radiata*). Four species of fresh-water **turtle** inhabit the western waterways; the only endemic being the big-headed or side-necked turtle (*Erymnochelys madagascariensis*), and beyond in the Mozambique Channel, there are **sea turtles** (Ridley, hawksbill and green) which periodically risk the pot as they visit their nesting beaches.

Birds

Madagascar's score sheet of resident birds is surprisingly short. There are only about 270 species of birds on the island. However, of these, 120 species are endemic, there are five endemic families, and 36 endemic genera – rendering Madagascar the hot-spot for bird endemism in Africa.

The key endemics include the three extremely rare **mesites** – the brown mesite (*Mesitornis unicolor*) in the rainforests, the white-breasted mesite (*Mesitornis variegata*) in the western dry forests and the subdesert mesite (*Monias benschi*) in the south's spiny forest. A similar allocation of habitats is more generously employed by the ten species of **couas** which brighten the forests throughout the island with their blue-masked faces. Six species are ground-dwellers, occupying the roles filled elsewhere by pheasants and roadrunners. Much harder to see are the **ground-rollers**, which patrol the rainforest floors in their pretty uniforms. One rebellious

BIRDING IN MADAGASCAR
Derek Schuurman

To see a fair spectrum of Madagascar's endemic birds, you'll need to visit at least one site in each of the island's three chief climatic/floristic zones: eastern rainforest, southern 'spiny forest', and western dry deciduous forests. Each holds its own compliment of regional endemics. In addition a select band of birds is dependent on the dwindling wetlands, so include those in your itinerary. The transition forest of Zombitse should also be included if possible. During a stay of two or three weeks and armed with two helpful new field guides (see *Further Information*, page 411) you should be able to tick off most of the sought-after 'lifers'.

Below is a review of the sites on the standard birding route.

Eastern rainforest
Rainforest birding is best in spring and early summer (late August to January).

Ranomafana National Park
Above all, Ranomafana is known for its ground-rollers (pitta-like, short-legged and rufous-headed especially). Other 'megaticks' often seen include brown mesite, the three oxylabes (white-throated and yellow-browed oxylabes, and Crossley's babbler), grey-crowned greenbul, forest rock-thrush and Pollen's vanga. Velvet and common sunbird asitys are plentiful. On ridges, look for yellow-bellied sunbird asity, brown emutail and cryptic warbler. In the Vohiparara Marsh, you might find Madagascar rail, grey emutail and Madagascar flufftail.

Andasibe-Mantadia National Park (Périnet) and surrounds
At Périnet (Analamazaotra), you'll easily find most of the generally distributed Malagasy endemics. 'Specials' include red-fronted coua, Rand's warbler, coral-billed nuthatch vanga and tylas. With luck, you'll locate Madagascar wood-rail, Madagascar flufftail and collared nightjar.

In Mantadia, the pittalike, scaly (rare), rufous-headed and shortlegged ground-rollers occur, as do the three oxylabes, velvet asity, common and yellow-bellied sunbird asitys, Ward's flycatcher and brown emutail. Two wetlands nearby, the Torotorofotsy Marsh, and more accessible Ampasipotsy Marsh, hold Madagascar rail, Madagascar snipe, Meller's duck, grey emutail, Madagascar swamp warbler and even the ultra-rare slender-billed flufftail.

Masoala National Park
Birding in this lowland rainforest is exceptional. Aside from nearly all the broadly distributed rainforest birds, the 'specials' here include brown mesite, red-breasted coua, scaly ground-roller and the helmet and Bernier's vangas. Two extremely rare species are protected here: the Madagascar serpent

member of the family, the long-tailed ground-roller (*Uratelornis chimaera*), has left the forest for the challenge of living among the didierea in the southwest. More restricted in range are the **sunbird asities** (*Neodrepanis* spp) which appear as flashes of blue and green in the canopies of montane rainforests, their down-turned beaks designed for the nectaries of canopy flowers.

eagle and Madagascar red owl. But seeing them is not guaranteed as both are elusive.

Tropical dry deciduous forests (western region)
Ampijoria Forest Station
This is an outstanding birding locality year round and is included in all birding itineraries because there you'll get most of the birds local to western Madagascar. They include white-breasted mesite, Coquerel's coua, Schlegel's asity and Van Dam's vanga. Several other vangas (sicklebill, rufous, Chabert's, white-headed, blue and rufous) are commonly seen. Raptors abound, including Madagascar fish eagle, Madagascar gymnogene, Madagascar buzzard, Madagascar sparrow-hawk and Frances's sparrow-hawk. Broadly distributed endemics easily ticked off include Madagascar crested ibis, white-throated rail and Madagascar pygmy kingfisher. At nearby wetlands, the chances of seeing Humblot's heron, Madagascar white ibis and Madagascar jacana are excellent.

Transition Forest
Zombitse National Park
A serious 'OOE' (Orgasmic Ornithological Experience) and long included in all birding itineraries for its 'megatick', the Appert's greenbul, this forest also holds an impressive variety of other endemics, like giant and crested couas as well as the recently described olive-capped coua.

Vangas include blue, sicklebill, hook-billed, rufous, white-headed and Chabert's. Look out for Madagascar partridge, Madagascar buttonquail, Madagascar sandgrouse, greater and lesser vasa parrots, grey-headed lovebird, Madagascar green pigeon, Madagascar hoopoe, Thamnornis warbler, common newtonia, common jery, longbilled green sunbird and Sakalava weaver. Great birding all year.

Southern sub-arid thorn thicket ('spiny bush' or 'spiny forest')
Excellent birding year-round; start just before daybreak.

Ifaty
Ifaty's bizarre Euphorbia-didieraceae bush holds some extremely localised 'megaticks': sub-desert mesite, long-tailed ground-roller, La Fresnaye's vanga and Archbold's newtonia. Look also for running coua and sub-desert brush-warbler. This is a good place for banded kestrel and white-browed owl too.

St Augustine's Bay and the Arboretum d'Antsokay
The bush in St Augustine's Bay is lower and more scrubby than in Ifaty. The following endemics are best sought here: Verreaux's coua, littoral rockthrush and the recently described red-shouldered vanga. At puddles along the road, look for the rare Madagascar plover.

The Arboretum provides excellent and easy birding.

Yet, beak variation is more the domain of Madagascar's most celebrated endemic family – the **vangas**. All 15 member species have perfected their own craft of insect capture, filling the niches of various absent African birds, so that, physically, they are very dissimilar. They often flock together, or with other Malagasy birds, presenting a formidable offensive for the local insects. The most prominent is the sickle-billed vanga (*Falculea pallinata*) which parallels the tree-probing habits of African woodhoopoes. The heavy carnivorous diet of the shrikes is adopted here by the hook-billed vanga (*Vanga curvirostris*), while the dramatic, blue-billed helmet vanga (*Euryceros prevostii*) resembles a small hornbill. Other species mimic nuthatches, treecreepers and tits. In short, if *The Beagle* had been caught by the West Wind Drift and Darwin had arrived in Madagascar instead of the Galapagos, the vangas would certainly have ensured that his train of thought went uninterrupted.

Malagasy representatives of families found elsewhere make up the bulk of the remaining birdlife. Herons, coots, grebes and ducks take up their usual positions in the wetlands alongside endemics such as the Madagascar teal (*Anas bernieri*) and the Madagascar malachite kingfisher (*Alcedo vintsioides*). In the forests and open scrub small game birds, the impressive crested ibis (*Lophotibis cristata*), doves and the drab but tuneful vasa parrots (*Coracopsis* spp) occupy the various strata of the vegetation. More colourful birds in the air include the grey-headed lovebird (*Agapornis cana*), the olive bee-eater (*Merops superciliosus*), the paradise flycatcher (*Terpsiphone mutata*) and the blushing pink hoopoe (*Upupa epops*) with bold black-and-white stripes and crest feathers. Unmistakable, and common, are the red fody (*Foudia madagascariensis*), which dance about the savannah landscape dressed in scarlet during the breeding season (November to April), and the crested drongo (*Dicrurus forticatus*), which has coal-black plumage and a strongly forked tail. The rock-thrushes (*Monticola* spp) of the drier south look just like European robins in morning suits. The real thing, the endemic Madagascar magpie robin (*Copsychus albospecularis*), sports black-and-white attire and has the habit of flirting fearlessly with humans.

The Madagascar kestrel (*Falco newtoni*) is joined by other **birds of prey** such as the banded kestrel (*Falco zoniventris*), the Madagascar harrier-hawk (*Polyboroides radiatus*), Frances's sparrow-hawk (*Accipiter francesii*), the Madagascar buzzard (*Buteo brachypterus*), the Madagascar cuckoo-falcon (*Aviceda madagascariensis*) and seven species of owl. The two eagles found on the island are both extremely rare. The Madagascar fish eagle (*Haliaeetus vociferoides*) is sparsely distributed on the west coast, fishing the freshwater lakes, mangroves and estuaries between Morondava and Antsiranana. The Madagascar serpent eagle (*Eutriorchis astur*) was recently rediscovered, after a period of 50 years, hunting on the Masoala peninsula.

Mammals

Madagascar's mammals are the prize exhibit in the island's incredible menagerie. They exist as an obscure assortment of primates, insectivores, carnivores, bats and rodents, representing the descendants of parties of individuals who, curled up in hollow trunks or skipping across temporary islands, accidentally completed the perilous journey from eastern Africa to the island beyond the horizon at different times over the last 100 million years. Once established, they gradually spread through the diverse habitats of their paradise island, all the time evolving and creating new species.

Biologists often refer to Madagascar as a 'museum', housing 'living fossils'. This is because almost all the mammals on the island today closely resemble groups that once shone on the mainland but have since been replaced by more advanced species. Although evolution has certainly occurred on the island, it seems to have had less momentum than it had back in Africa. Hence, while their cousins on the mainland were subjected to extreme competition with the species that were to develop subsequently, the Malagasy mammals were able to stick more rigidly to their original physiques and behaviours.

The word 'cousins' is especially poignant when applied to the lemurs, for back in Africa primate evolution was eventually to lead to the ascent of humankind. How opportune then for our understanding of our own natural history that one of our direct ancestors managed to end up on this island sanctuary and remain, sheltered from the pressures of life elsewhere, relatively true to its original form for us to appreciate 35 million years later.

The lemurs

Lemurs are to a biologist what the old masters are to an art critic: they may not be contemporary, but historically they are very important and they are still beautiful to look at. Lemurs belong to a group of primates called the *prosimians*, a word which means 'before monkeys'. Their basic body design evolved about 40 to 50 million years ago. With stereoscopic-colour vision, hands that could grasp branches, a brain capable of processing complex, learned information, extended parental care and an integrated social system incorporating a wide range of sound and scent signals, the lemurs were the latest model in evolution's comprehensive range of arboreal (tree-living) mammals. Their reign lasted until about 35 million years ago, when a new model, the monkey, evolved. Monkeys were superior in a number of ways: they were faster, could think more quickly, used their vision more effectively and were highly dextrous. Thus monkeys quickly replaced the lemurs which, destined for the fossil records, vanished from the forests of the world. That is, all but one forest, for on the island of Madagascar, a few stowaway lemurs had managed to take refuge. Today we see the results of 35 million years of their evolution. The single ancestral species has adapted into 51 recognised varieties (see *Appendix 3*), and instead of gazing down at inanimate rocks, we have the luxury of being able to watch, hear and smell the genuine article.

Smell is an extremely important aspect of lemur lives. Through scents, lemurs communicate a wide range of information, such as who's in charge, who is fertile, who is related to whom and who lives where. They supplement this language with an audible one. Chirps, barks and cries reinforce hierarchies in lemur societies, help to defend territories against other groups and warn of danger. Socially the lemurs show a great variety of organisations and the strategy used by each species is largely dependent on the nature of their diet. The small, quick-moving, insectivorous lemurs such as the mouse lemurs and dwarf lemurs are nocturnal and largely solitary except during the mating season when they pair with a member of the opposite sex. Literally surrounded by their insect food, they only require small territories, hence they never cover large distances and spend their entire lives in the trees. A different way of life is led by the larger leaf-eating species such as the indri. In a rainforest there is no shortage of leaves, however as a food source leaves are fairly poor in nutrients, hence each lemur needs to consume a large amount. Leaf-eaters therefore tend to collect in small groups, together defending their territory of foliage with scents and often loud calls, which, in the dense forests, are the best forms of communication.

Their sex lives vary, but most of these species have 'family' groups in which a single male dominates. The most social lemurs on the island are those with a more varied diet concentrating on fruit, but also including seeds, buds and some leaves. This group includes the ring-tailed lemur, the ruffed lemur and the 'true' lemurs

A LAYMAN'S GUIDE TO LEMURS
Nick Garbutt

Unless you are a keen natural historian, sorting out Madagascar's 50 varieties (taxa) of lemur is challenging. The information below, together with the scientific classification (see box on page 41), should help you put names to faces: and if you know in which region/reserve the most common species are found you'll be better able to decide what that leaping animal high in the trees is likely to be.

Diurnal lemurs (active during the day)
The largest and the easiest to identify, these are usually found in groups of between three and twelve individuals.

Ring-tailed lemurs (*Lemur catta*) Recognisable by their banded tails, and more terrestrial than other lemurs, these are seen in troops of around 20 animals in the south and southwest, notably in Berenty reserve.

Ruffed lemurs These are large lemurs (genus *Varecia*) and commonly found in zoos but seldom seen in the wild. There are two species: black-and-white ruffed lemur and red ruffed lemur. Both live in the eastern rainforest, the black-and-white in Mantadia or Nosy Mangabe, and the red in Masoala.

True lemurs This family has only fairly recently been grouped under a new generic name, *Eulemur*. They are all roughly cat-sized, have long noses, and live in trees. A confusing characteristic is that males and females of each species are coloured differently. The best-known *Eulemur* is the black lemur, *E. macaco* (called *maki* by the Malagasy), of northwest Madagascar, notably Nosy Komba and Lokobe. Only the males are black; females are chestnut brown. Visitors to Ranomafana usually see the red-bellied lemur; the male has white 'tear-drop' face markings. In the northern reserves you'll find the crowned lemur, *Eulemur coronatus*.

Brown lemurs (*Eulemur fulvus*) present the ultimate challenge. There are six subspecies and, since the males mostly look quite different from the females, you have 12 animals to sort out. Fortunately for you their ranges do not overlap. Two neighbouring brown lemurs have beautiful cream or white eartufts and side whiskers: Sanford's brown lemur (*E. f. sanfordii*) is found in the northern reserves; the white-fronted brown lemur, *E. f. albifrons* (the males

(see box). The diet of these species requires active foraging over large areas during the day, so in order to defend their expansive territory, and to protect themselves in daylight, these lemurs form distinctive troops. The societies are run by matriarchs, which organise the troop's movement, courtship and defence, but there are also whole groups of males, which often separate for week-long excursions away from the home base. Usually operating in more open country these lemurs use a wide range of visual signals to accompany their scents and sounds. This makes them particularly entertaining to watch.

Perhaps the most entertaining of all the lemurs is the ring-tailed lemur (*Lemur catta*). Among lemurs it forms the largest and liveliest troops. Each troop typically stirs at dawn, warms up with a period of sunning and then, guided by have bushy white heads and side whiskers of almost Santa Claus proportions), in the northeast. Moving south you'll find the common brown lemur (*E. f. fulvus*) in the east and also the west. The red-fronted brown lemur (*E. f. rufus*) lives in the southeast and southwest. Females all look pretty much the same – boring and brown.

Bamboo lemurs (genus *Hapalemur*) These are smaller than the 'true lemurs', with short muzzles and round faces. They occur in smaller groups (one to three animals), cling to vertical branches, and feed on bamboos. You may see these in the eastern reserves of Périnet and Ranomafana; the commonest species is the grey bamboo lemur (*Hapalemur griseus*), although in Ranomafana you could see the golden bamboo lemur, *H. aureus*.

Indri The largest of the lemurs, and the only one without a tail, this black-and-white 'teddy bear' lemur is unmistakable. It is seen in Périnet.

Sifakas (genus *Propithecus*) The sifakas (sometimes pronounced Shee-fahk) belong to the same family as the indri, sharing its characteristic of long back legs; sifakas are the 'dancing lemurs' that bound upright over the ground and leap spectacularly from tree to tree. The commonest sifakas are white or mainly white and so are unlike any other lemur. The white sifaka (*P. verreauxi verreauxi*) shares its southern habitat with the ring-tailed lemur, and its cousin the Coquerel's sifaka (*P. V. coquerel*), which has chestnut arms and legs, is seen in Ampijoroa, in the northwest. You may also see the dark-coloured Milne-Edwards sifaka (*P. diadem edwardsi*) in Ranomafana.

Nocturnal lemurs Two genera of nocturnal lemur helpfully sleep or doze in the open so are regularly seen by tourists: sportive lemurs (lepilemurs) and woolly lemurs or avahis (guides may use both popular and generic names). Most species of lepilemur spend the day in a tree-hole from which they peer drowsily, and the woolly lemur sleeps in the fork of a tree or shrub.
During guided night walks you may see the eyes of dwarf lemurs – most likely the greater dwarf lemur at Périnet . The tiny mouse lemurs are quite common, and easiest to see at Ranomafana or Berenty.
You're very unlikely to see an unplanned aye-aye, but check the description on page 64 if you think you did...

See *Appendix 3* for a checklist of lemurs and where to find them.

the matriarchs, heads off to forage, breaking at noon for a siesta. The troop moves along the ground, each individual using its distinctive tail to maintain visual contact with the others. If out of eyesight the troop members use the cat-like mews that prompted their scientific name. By dusk they return to the sleeping trees which they use for three or four days before the females move the group off to another part of the territory to harvest the food there. During the April breeding season, the males become less tolerant of each other and engage in 'stink-fights' where, after charging their tails with scent from glands on their wrists, they waft them antagonistically at opponents. Similar aggressive interactions occur when two ring-tailed troops meet, yet actual physical violence is rare.

THE AYE-AYE
Hilary Bradt

The strangest lemur is the aye-aye, *Daubentonia madagascariensis*. It took a while for scientists to decide that it was a lemur at all: for years it was thought to be a peculiar type of squirrel. Today it is classified in a family of its own, Daubentonidae. The aye-aye seems to have been assembled from the leftover parts of a variety of animals. It has the teeth of a rodent (they never stop growing), the ears of a bat, the tail of a fox, and the hands of no living creature since the middle finger is like that of a skeleton. It's this finger which so intrigues scientists as it shows the aye-aye's adaptation to its way of life. In Madagascar it seems to fill the ecological niche left empty by the absence of woodpeckers. The aye-aye evolved to use its skeletal finger to winkle grubs from under the bark of trees. It has added the skill (shown by the Chinese when using chopsticks to eat soup) of flicking coconut milk into its mouth; coconuts are now a favoured food. The aye-aye's fingers are unique among lemurs in another way – it has claws not fingernails (except on the big toe). When searching for grubs the aye-aye taps on the wood with its finger, its enormous ears pointing like radar dishes to detect a cavity. It can even tell whether this is occupied by a nice fat grub.

Another anatomical feature of the aye-aye that sets it apart from other primates is that it has inguinal mammary glands. In other words, its teats are between its back legs. This fascinating animal was long considered to be on the verge of extinction, but recently there have been encouraging signs that it is more widespread than previously supposed. Although destruction of habitat is the chief threat to its survival, it is also at risk because of its supposedly evil powers. Rural people believe the aye-aye to be the herald of death. If one is seen near a settlement it must be killed, and even then the only salvation may be to burn down the village. Nevertheless there are several places where you are likely to see wild aye-ayes: Mananara is the easiest, and Nosy Mangabe if you are fortunate. Being strictly nocturnal, aye-ayes can only be watched with the help of a torch (flashlight); so for a prolonged session with these amazing animals treat yourself to a visit to Jersey Zoo, Channel Islands, where the purpose-built 'night-into-day' aye-aye house allows you to watch their behaviour to your heart's content, or pay your fee for a night-time visit at Tana's zoo, Tsimbazaza (but there is no infra-red lighting).

Other mammals

Employing one of the most primitive mammalian body plans the **tenrecs** have been able to fill the vacancies created by an absence of shrews, moles and hedgehogs, and in doing so diversified into at least 24 different species. Five of the species are called the spiny tenrecs, most looking just like hedgehogs, some with yellow and black stripes. However, the largest of these, the tail-less common tenrec (*Tenrec ecaudatus*), has lost the majority of its spines. Not only is this species, at 1.5kg, the largest insectivore in the world, but it can also give birth to enormous litters, which the mother feeds with up to 24 nipples. The 19 species of furred tenrecs are mostly shrew-like in stature, although three species look and act more like moles, and one has become aquatic, capturing small fish and freshwater shrimps in the fast-flowing streams of the Hauts Plateaux.

Highly successful elsewhere, **rodents** have made little impression on Madagascar. There are 20 species, most of which are nocturnal. The easiest to see is the red forest rat (*Nesomys rufus*) which is active during the day. The most unusual are the rabbit-like giant jumping rat (*Hypogeomys antimena*) from the western forests and the two tree-dwelling *Brachytarsomys* species which have prehensile tails.

The island's eight **carnivores** belong to the civets and mongooses, *Viverridae*, which evolved 40 million years ago, at about the same time as the cats. The largest, known as the *fosa* (*Cryptoprocta ferox*), is very cat-like with an extremely long tail which assists balance during canopy-based lemur hunts. The size of a chubby cat, the striped civet (*Fossa fossana*) hunts in the eastern rainforests for rodents, and a third, very secretive animal, the *falanouc* (*Eupleres goudotii*) inhabits the northeastern rainforests where it lives almost entirely on earthworms. Each of Madagascar's forest types play host to mongooses. There are five species in all, the most obvious being the ring-tailed mongoose (*Galidia elegans*) which varies in colour, but is typically a handsome, rusty red.

Possessing, among mammals, the unique gift of flight, it is not surprising that most of Madagascar's **bats** are also found on mainland Africa or Asia. There are three species of fruit bat which are active during the day, very noisy, large (a wingspan of up to 1.5m) and unfortunately often on the Malagasy menu. If the fruit bats look like flying foxes (and they do), then the remaining 20 plus species are not unlike flying mice. These are nocturnal, prefer moths to figs and find them by echo-location, employing shell-like ears and distorted noses. It is known that some moths outdo the bats by chirping back at them in mid-flight, scrambling the echo and sending the aggressor off into the night.

The Bay of Antongil marks the northern extent of **humpback whale** migrations. The whales calve just beyond the coral reefs in July and August, and after this period migrate south as far as the Antarctic coast to feed. **Dugongs**, or sea cows, are extremely rare. The Vezo of the west coast share their fishing grounds with an abundance of **dolphins**, and regard them as kin. If a dolphin is discovered dead, they wrap it in shrouds and bury it with their ancestors.

MADAGASCAR'S WILDERNESS

For many of us it is the experience of wandering through the unique wilderness of Madagascar that draws us to the island. As evidenced by the previous section, Madagascar has some of the most unusual plants and animals on Earth, and alone each one is fascinating, but of course these species do not lead isolated lives. Each one contributes to the structure, function and diversity of an ecosystem. Ecologists have been aware for some time now that it is only when observing a species within its natural ecosystem that we can fully comprehend characteristics such as its behaviours, life cycle, physical structures and interactions with other species. An ecosystem is more than the sum of its parts. It is an abstract combination of all the species, the landforms, the soil types, the atmosphere and the waterways in an area. When walking into a rainforest or the spiny forest or the *tsingy* or swimming over a coral reef, it isn't an individual species that takes your breath away – it is the spectacle of the whole functioning ecosystem.

As mentioned earlier, Madagascar has an amazing array of habitats. The variety of habitats on the island is a result of the effects of ocean currents, prevailing winds and geology. Rain is heaviest in the east, and lightest in the west; but at the same time, heaviest in the north and lightest in the south. Since rainfall is the single most significant factor in creating habitat characteristics, a complex spectrum of the world's tropical and subtropical habitats is therefore accommodated in a relatively

ECOLOGICAL CLASSIFICATION

Ecology is the science that investigates the relationships organisms have with each other and with their environment. It is a fairly recent science, but it has already taught us much about the world.

To an ecologist some common-use words have quite precise meanings. A **population** is a group of members of one species, found in a particular location, and partly isolated from other members of the species. Hence we can talk of a population of lemurs in a nature reserve. A **community** is a group of populations, ie: all the lemurs, tenrecs, tamarind trees etc in a nature reserve. An **ecosystem** is a community together with its non-living environment. For example, the nature reserve ecosystem would not only include the lemurs, tenrecs and tamarinds, but also take into account the climate, soil type, nutrient content, hydrology and landform of the area. A **biome** is a large-scale ecosystem with a typical community and environment, eg: a lowland tropical rainforest or a mangrove. The species found in different mangroves around the world may vary but the basic ecosystem does not. A **habitat** is simply the environment in which an organism lives, while a **niche** is a more complex term which describes the role and place of an organism within its ecosystem, eg: the niche of an aye-aye is similar to that of a woodpecker in that it extracts insects from under bark, but it is also similar to that of a squirrel, in that it eats a variety of nuts and makes nests out of twigs. However, it is different from both squirrel and woodpecker in many other ways; hence ecologists regard the aye-aye as occupying a broad niche, which elsewhere in the world, where competition forces specialist lifestyles, would be divided among several organisms.

small area of land – the wettest of rainforests in the northeast to the driest of deserts in the southwest. In addition, Madagascar's geology brings further variety by creating undulating coastlines, broad riverbeds and estuaries, shallow ocean shelves for coral reefs, high mountainous slopes and plateaux, a wealth of soil types and even bizarre limestone 'forests' riddled with caves. These various habitats house a wealth of ecosystems, and in this section each of the dominant ecosystem types found on and around the island will be described.

Terrestrial ecosystems

Before the arrival of humans, Madagascar was almost entirely covered with forests, each suited to the rainfall and altitude of the local area. In the east, where rainfall was sufficient, there was evergreen rainforest, '*lowland*' near the coast and '*montane*' in the highlands. The peaks of the tallest mountains supported thicket communities isolated as if on an island in a 'low-altitude sea'. The Hauts Plateaux, or highlands, were covered with deciduous wet forests interrupted occasionally by rocky outcrops, themselves infested with succulents. The western slopes of the highlands bore tapia trees adapted to the rain shadow of the highlands, and on the western coast vast belts of dry deciduous forest composed of baobabs and leguminous trees were a paradise for troops of lemurs. The southern arid region did not relent to desert, but instead kept the forest theme with the remarkable succulent trees and didierea, and along the west coast there were smatterings of mangrove swamps maintaining the coast margin and bringing a violent green trim to the reddish-brown of the interior.

Much of this once vast canopy which sheltered the soils of the entire island is now gone. In its place are poorer *secondary communities* of grasslands, forest mosaics and scrub, relying on impoverished soils which are constantly being washed into the sea. The communities are annually burnt in the practice of *tavy* (slash-and-burn) agriculture, and in the process foreign, virile species take the place of native plants. However, the original *primary communities* do exist in patches. There are still expanses of rainforest, spiny forest and mangroves. The great dry forest of the west is much reduced, but in evidence near to the coast. The remaining communities are particularly fragmented, harbouring amongst geological oddities such as the massif of Isalo and the *tsingy*, or depending on altitude or awkward slopes for their isolation. The one complete loss is the forest of the Hauts Plateaux which has been replaced by grasslands, ricefields and zebu.

Of these remnant communities, none is truly virgin. We know that there were many more lemurs, birds and plants on Madagascar before human settlement. These presumably became extinct as a result of the changes that occurred on the island after the advent of human colonisation. In removing such species communities are inevitably altered, but it is true to say that there are still good examples of natural communities on the island – and it is these primary communities that are of most interest to wildlife watchers.

Rainforests

The spine of mountains which border the central plateau force the wet air arriving from over the Indian Ocean to drop its moisture on the east coast of the island. Madagascar's rainforests therefore exist in a distinct band adjacent to the east coast where the continuous rainfall is high enough to sustain the evergreen canopy trees. Known as the *Madagascar Sylva*, this band of forest extends inland only as far as the mountain range, hence it is thickest in the northeast, even crossing to the west coast around Nosy Be, and becomes thinner as the mountain range approaches the coast towards Taolognaro. The end of the mountain range, just northwest of Taolognaro, forms a unique but fragile divide between the evergreen rainforest to the east and the arid spiny forest beyond. This region is particularly unusual in that it is actually *subtropical*, below the Tropic of Capricorn, and there are few areas in the world able to boast subtropical rainforests.

The *Sylva* is not one standard forest, but more a collection of local forest types. Variations occur due to latitude, underlying rock type, angle of slope, frequency of flooding and, towards Nosy Be, seasonality; but the most profound variation is due to altitude. In the tropics, temperature drops by up to 0.7°C for every 100m gained in altitude. As the climate changes so do the flora and fauna, hence rainforests are typically classified by their height above sea level.

Coastal rainforest (sea level)

Very little of Madagascar's unique coastal rainforest remains. Rooted in sand, washed with salty air, battered by cyclones and bordering lagoons and marshes the coastal forest harbours a very unusual community. The architecture of the forest is similar to the more widespread lowland forest, but the plants here are different: they are salt-tolerant and highly efficient at extracting water and nutrients from the shallow, porous sand beneath them. However, the very material that these plants flourish on, the sand, has recently become their downfall – titanium-rich sand in the most fragile of the coastal forests, that near Taolognaro, has attracted mining developments, which are likely to permanently disfigure the community.

Good examples: south of Antalaha and north of Sambava on the coast near Amboasary.

THE BIODIVERSITY OF THE RAINFOREST

Scientists still don't really understand how the rainforests are so diverse. Their rates of photosynthesis are the highest on Earth, and this leads to an abundance of food unparalleled in other habitats, but it still doesn't account for the incredible diversity. We don't know how many species there are in the rainforest, but it is estimated that they hold 50% of the species on the planet, yet they take up only 7% of the land area. The vast majority of these species are insects. It seems that in any one rainforest the numbers of endemic insects are astronomical. One ecologist sprayed a single rainforest tree with poison and collected the insects that fell down from the tree in nets. Seventy-five per cent of them were new to science, and many of these would only ever be found on that one tree species. By working out what would happen if he sprayed all the tree species in the world's rainforests, he decided that there may be up to 15 million species in rainforests – far more than the 1.8 million recorded so far.

An important feature of the rainforest is its tree diversity. When walking through a temperate forest you are unlikely to see more than three or four species of trees, and one almost always dominates. In rainforests it is common to find 250 species of tree per hectare, none dominating. Naturally this will increase the number of insect species, which are normally exclusive to one plant, and in turn the number of insect-eaters such as birds, lizards, spiders and bats. But why isn't one type of tree dominant in the rainforest? One suggestion is that the numerous seed-eaters on the forest floor have a strong influence. They tend to devour all the seeds that fall in a bunch around a parent tree, but perhaps leave those that have been dispersed further afield. This would create a mosaic of tree species, each widely dispersed throughout the forest – in fact, exactly what happens.

Other theories target the great age of the rainforests. Perhaps time alone can account for the development of so many intricate niches; after all in many places rainforests have remained undisturbed for millennia. Not everyone is convinced. Some of the most diverse forests are still relatively young. Perhaps the constant climate is important, for it brings stability to the forest. Further away from the equator, where conditions change from hot summers to cold winters, species must put up with a range of discomforts, and thus may not have the luxury of specialising to the same extent. A lack of specialisation certainly reduces diversity.

Whatever the answer, the rainforests exist as a biodiversity phenomenon. It is a great misfortune that the forest's complexity, as well as being its major contribution, may also be its downfall. Constructed of such specialist niches, rainforests are fragile ecosystems, and the escalating extent of human disturbance is having far-reaching and catastrophic results.

Lowland rainforest (0–800m)

Most of the rainforest in Madagascar can be described as lowland rainforest, that is the forest rising from sea level to around 800m. This type of forest is hot and sticky, with a saturated humidity of 100% and annual rainfall of up to 5,000mm. The forest canopy resides 30m above the ground, and there are few emerging trees beyond this height. As well as hardwoods, palms (including the litter-trappers) and pandans contribute to the canopy and under-storey. Most of Madagascar's orchid and fern species live epiphytically on the tree branches, providing rainwater pools for beautiful tree frogs and insects. Vast numbers of insect species hide amongst the foliage. Those that flaunt their bodies with bright colours are either dangerous, distasteful or pretending to be dangerous/distasteful. The most obvious insects are the flitting butterflies, monstrous beetles and the myriad ants and termites which patrol the forest floor. Ant colonies are extremely well organised and assign the infestation of every part of the forest within their territory to predictable days in each month. Within the dark field layer of tree roots, tree-ferns and cycads, are leeches, spiders and occasionally chameleons. The abundance and diversity of chameleons is one of the characteristic features of Malagasy forests, and it is wise to spend some time looking for them.

The stars of the forest, the lemurs, nonchalantly skip among the forest branches and the liana climbers which serve as highways between the forest floor and the world above. Most common are the brown lemurs and wherever you find bamboo growing in clumps under the canopy, the grey bamboo lemur. The lemurs dominate the ecosystem, quite capable of eating virtually every plant food that it yields. Preying on the lemurs, fosa are at home among the canopy branches, and above the leaves, birds of prey and fruit bats patrol. An unusual sight from ground-level are what look like strange fungi blossoming from the bark of the canopy trees. These are in fact the trees' flowers and fruit sprouting directly from their trunks and branches. A habit known as *cauliflory*, it is intended to make life easier for their pollinators and seed-bearers. Below this vivid display, tenrecs and forest birds rummage through the litter on the floor, and the Madagascar striped civet and mongooses wait to pick off any unsuspecting prey.

Good examples: Lokobe (Nosy Be); Masoala (the most diverse area on the island); Nosy Mangabe and Marojejy.

Montane rainforest (800–1,300m)

As altitude increases and air temperature drops, the tree species of the lowland rainforest give way to those more able to tolerate the cooler conditions. These species have lower canopies, and are the foundation of a different type of rainforest known as *montane*. The change from lowland to montane forest is a gradual one, influenced by a number of factors. In southern Madagascar, due to the effects of higher latitudes, montane forest occurs further down the mountains, and in the north where it is warmer, lowland forest continues from sea level up to about 900m. To accommodate this variation an arbitrary altitude of 800m is often used to define the boundary between the two types of forest in Madagascar.

Once in true montane forest the landscape is very different from the lowland forest below. Not only is the canopy lower and the temperature very much cooler, but the under-storey is far more dense. Tree-ferns and bamboos litter the forest floor and the gallery above is festooned with epiphytes and mosses lazily hanging off its branches. There is a tight tangle of trunks, roots and woody lianas, all sporting furry lichens and lines of bright fungi. Some orchid species have abandoned the branches and have rooted on the forest floor, where they are joined by determined succulent species.

Montane reserves are excellent places to spot mammals and birds. At the three best sites there are many lemur species harbouring amongst the trunks and climbers, some only recently discovered. Bright forest birds, chameleons and boas are also at large.

Good examples: Ranomafana (with its newly discovered golden bamboo lemur and many other mammal species); Périnet (for indri and other lemurs); Montagne d'Ambre (with many easy trails and beautiful scenery).

Cloudforest (above 1,300m)

The forest beyond 1,300m has an even lower canopy and is characteristically thick with ferns and mosses. Its proper title is 'high-altitude montane', but because it is often cloaked in mists, the emotive label of 'cloudforest' is often applied. The low temperature of the cloudforest slows down decomposition, creating waterlogged peaty soils in valleys. Termites do not live this high up, so large earthworms and beetles take the role of detritivores. The canopy is as low as 10m above the ground and in places the under-storey gives way to a thicket of shrubs. Mosses, lichens and ferns inhabit every branch and stone, and cover the floor along with forest succulents and *Bulbophyllum* orchids. A variety of lemurs brave the low temperatures and thick vegetation.

Good examples: Marojejy; Andringitra.

Montane scrubland

On the peaks of Madagascar's tallest mountains there are extremely isolated and unusual communities, which have yet to be studied to satisfaction. In a climate that often provides snow, the canopy here is so low that it eventually reaches a habitat which is less like a forest and more like dense scrub. It is characterised by a single stratum of strange, evergreen heath-trees belonging to the daisy family and an unusual genus called *Philippia*. Among these, and on exposed rocks, are specialist euphorbia and orchids. With the nearest equivalent habitat thousands of kilometres away, these species have evolved isolated on 'high-altitude islands' as remote as any in the ocean. Even at these heights lemurs are found, such as bamboo lemurs and troops of ring-tails with specialised diets.

Good example: Andringitra (higher up).

Tapia woodland

Growing in fragmented clumps among the canyons of the rocky western slopes of the Hauts Plateaux are the wonderful tapia trees (*Uapaca bojeri*). Although deprived of rain by the highlands to their east and pounded by hot sunlight throughout the year, the tolerant tapias manage to maintain a canopy year round by feeding upon the little water that rolls down over the rocks into their canyon homes. Similar in appearance to the stunted cork oaks of the Mediterranean, they share the 10m high canopy with other evergreens, which, unable to withstand fires to the same degree, are becoming less of a feature. The canopy is not as closed as that of the rainforest, so an under-storey of shrubs is well developed, criss-crossed with lianas. Although pandans are common, in this drier habitat, tree ferns and most palms and epiphytes are absent. One exception is the beautiful feather palm (*Chrysalidocarpus isaloensis*), endemic to Isalo National Park.

The tapia forests are the sole home of Madagascar's endemic silkworm which lives off the leaves of the tapia trees. Mammals are uncommon, but troops of ring-tailed lemurs and Verreaux's sifaka are sometimes seen.

Good example: Isalo National Park.

Dry deciduous forest

The magnificent dry forests of the west once covered the vast lowland plain west of the Hauts Plateaux. Now, this kind of forest is only to be found in patches sharing the coast with the mangroves, bordering the largest rivers of the south and dotted about the plains near Isalo and inland from Mahajanga. The forest supports far fewer species than the eastern rainforests, but has higher rates of endemism, and so has attracted the attentions of conservationists. The trees of these dry forests are less densely arranged, and the canopy is lower, at 12–20m. It is too dry here for

SUCCESSION

Natural communities do not instantly appear, they are built up over long periods of time in a process known as succession. It is succession that, with time, transforms a derelict area of land, or a badly-kept lawn, into a patch of scrub or a full-blown forest. In general, as time goes on, it is natural for soils to become deeper, for taller plants to arrive and for animals to become more abundant. In mowing the lawn we prevent all this from happening.

When cutting down or setting fire to natural communities we are in effect knocking back succession, so that the process has to start again from an earlier point. With time the original community should return, but more often than not, its succession is interfered with by human activities. New plants are grown, new animals imported, the soil is exploited for nutrients and waterways are redirected or overused. The result is that the land cannot support the original primary community, and instead a new, poorer community tends to develop on the site, full of fast-growing, 'weedy' species. Often where there were forests, there are now grasslands, and where there were grasslands there are semideserts. Ecologists call these artificial wildernesses secondary communities, and they are sadly common in today's world.

any epiphytes except some tolerant orchids in wetter areas, but the adventurous lianas are still to be found.

There are several distinct types of dry deciduous forest varying with soil conditions. Growing on the clayey and sandy soils near to the west coast are forests dominated by leguminous trees such as *Dalbergia* and *Cassia*. Where these forests meet the broad rivers of the west and south, enormous tamarind trees, *Tamarindus indica*, and sprawling banyan figs, *Ficus* spp, are common. The banyans, with typical fig audacity, can cover a significant area with their numerous stilt trunks, so that each individual creates its own miniature forest. On the limestone plateaux near the west coast, the alkalinity of the soil allows the baobabs (*Adansonia* spp) to take over. There are seven species of baobab in Madagascar and they are symbols of this vegetation, often forming impressive avenues about the forest tracks.

The title 'deciduous' refers to the shedding of the canopy during the seven or eight months of the dry season. A carpet of leaves begins to accumulate on the forest floor shortly after the rains stop in May, and through decomposition, they help to create a thick humus layer in the soil. During 'the dry' much of the animal life goes to ground, quite literally. Amphibians and insects bury themselves in the soil and await October when the rains return. Upon the advent of the first rainstorm the forest floor bubbles with emerging animal life and the canopy branches sprout leaves once again.

Foraging within this landscape are many bird and mammal species, each adapted to extract one element of the forest's bounty. Sifakas, sportive lemurs, brown lemurs and the ubiquitous mouse lemurs are particularly in evidence, but more obscure species also inhabit specialised niches within the forest ecosystem. The tamarind forests are the classic backdrop in pictures of ring-tail troops patrolling the floor with their tails in the air. Vangas and other birds form multi-species flocks within the canopy, and the tuneful vasa parrots make territories in the under-storey. The deep litter layer is home to tenrecs, tortoises, boas and hog-nosed snakes. Fosas and mongooses regularly run along their patrol trails, and are prepared to pursue prey into the canopy if the need arrives.

Good examples: Kirindy (jumping rat, lemurs and birds); Ampijoroa; Berenty (ring-tailed lemurs).

Inselberg and tsingy communities

Where the island's underlying rocks break through the landscape in the west, localised communities develop, composed of specialised plants and animals. Rain simply rolls off the rock surfaces or passes through its porous body, so all the residents must be tolerant to desiccation. These communities, known in Africa as 'rupicolous shrubland', are particularly interesting in Madagascar, because they are the sole retreat for many of the island's more ornamental succulents. Magnificent euphorbias, aloes, kalanchoes and pachypodia tuck themselves into the tiny pockets of soil available among the crevices, bringing foliage and flowers to the smooth rock face. Insects, birds and lemurs rely on these structures for sustenance, only retreating, in the heat of the day, to the copses of trees in nearby canyons.

Such plants are also to be found harbouring among the knife-edge pinnacles of three spectacular limestone karst massifs known locally as the *tsingy*. A result of unimaginable periods of erosion, the jigsaw landscape of the *tsingy* enables a complex mosaic of communities to live side-by-side. For this reason, a trip to the *tsingy* can be an extremely rewarding wildlife event. The towering pinnacles which sport the succulents are in fact the ornate roofs of extensive cave systems below. The caves are inhabited by bats, rodents and tonnes of arthropods feeding on the bat guano. Blind cave fish swim in the broad, dark rivers, as do, it is rumoured, cave crocodiles. Where the cave roofs have collapsed sunny gullies are crowded with dense, dry forests, rich in baobabs.

This diversity of habitat naturally supports a diversity of birds and mammals, and the *tsingy* massifs are good places to see a wealth of lemur species. It has even been said that Ankarana has the highest density of primates on Earth. It is certainly famous for its 'blade-running' crowned lemurs, *Eulemur coronatus*, troops of Sanford's brown lemurs, *Eulemur fulvus sanfordi*, and even the aye-aye, *Daubentonia madagascariensis*, but for a dry habitat to boast that claim the Ankarana ecosystem must be very special indeed.

Good examples: Isalo National Park (for inselberg communities); the *tsingy* massifs of Ankarana, Bemaraha and Namoroka.

Spiny forest

Whenever photographers wish to startle people with the uniqueness of Madagascar, they head for the 'spiny forest'. Its mass of tangled, spiny branches and swollen succulent trunks creates a habitat variously described by naturalists as 'a nightmare' and 'the eighth wonder of the world'. Stretching in a band around the southwest coast from Morombe to Taolagnaro, the spiny forest is the only primary community able to resist the extreme arid environment of this region. All the plants here are beautifully adapted to sporadic rainfall, even surviving without water for more than a year. The unworldly landscape of this community is largely a result of the striking forms of didierea trees (see descriptions in *Flora* section), which also provide most of the spines in the forest. Side-by-side with the didierea, forming impenetrable thickets, are emergent baobabs, bloated 'bottle-tree' pachypodia and tree euphorbia. Of the latter group the most recognisable are the huge *E. enterophora*, with its umbrella-shaped crown of slender green branches atop a black trunk, the sausage tree, *E. oncoclada*, and the spiky grey-green *E. stenoclada* which is so designed to capture the condensing sea mist near the coast. Dramatic, tall aloes and broad-leaved grey kalanchoe 'trees' can be found amongst the spiny branches contributing to the peculiar visage, and endemic orchids and palms, extremely specialised to withstand the aridity, are additional oddities. Where bordering the coast, the community can benefit from condensing sea mists and is in places evergreen.

The most evident animal life, aside from reptiles and desert arthropods, are the groups of sifakas which somehow avoid the nasty spines of the didierea as they leap from one trunk to another. These leaps can be impressive, assisted by the frog-like back legs of this group of lemurs. However, if the forest is too sparse the sifaka is forced to skip along the hot sandy floor in a comic routine likened by John Cleese to a mad butler doing the tango.

Good examples: Berenty; Ifaty; along the Taolagnaro-Ambovombe road; Beza-Mahafaly.

Secondary communities

Plants are the foundation of any community. Wherever plants have been removed directly or indirectly by human activities the entire community collapses. It sometimes returns later but in a poorer form called a secondary community. Madagascar is particularly prone to this degrading process as a result of its frightening rate of soil erosion. The resulting communities are typically infested with competitive foreign plants and are poor in animal life. There are several widespread secondary communities on the island, but as with primary communities there are limitless gradations of these where two meet.

Savoka

This is the local name for the secondary rainforest that tends to grow back after *tavy*. It is sadly dominated by foreign tree species which will eventually infest all returning forest, changing Madagascar's rainforest communities for ever. Some native plants have managed to compete with these exotics. The traveller's tree (*Ravenala madagascariensis*), really comes into its own in *savoka*, dominating vast tracts. Malagasy bamboos and pandans also line the remaining primary forest, but there are few animals living in this vegetation. *Tavy* has reduced the rainforest to *savoka* along much of the east coast, particularly inland of the Pangalanes Canal where slash-and-burn has been particularly ruthless.

Hauts Plateaux grassland ('bosaka')

Over a thousand years of *tavy* has destroyed the wet forests that existed on the central highlands. At first the forest must have battled to return, but eventually it failed, smothered by vigorous grass species which provided grazing for the introduced zebu cattle. All that remains now is a barren, sterile grassland dominated by uninviting species such as the knife-sharp *Heteropogon*.

Once dependent upon zebu the Malagasy continued burning the high country in order to bring fresh 'green bite' grass shoots for their cattle. This has, over hundreds of years, left the landscape scarred with deep cuts in the topsoil, called *lavaka*. The soil from these unsightly scars is washed into Madagascar's rivers, turning them iron red in the process. Eventually the sediment flows out into the sea clogging up mangroves and coral reefs. The net loss of soil from the surface of Madagascar as a result of *tavy* is the country's most pressing problem.

Parts of the plateaux support plantations of imported *Eucalyptus* and pine trees. Quick-growing, they are used for firewood by the highlanders. The establishment of these trees is at least proof that in parts of the plateaux, the soils are still rich enough to support the forest that once covered the area.

TAVY

Jamie Spencer

Slash and burn farming, or in Malagasy *tavy*, is blamed for the permanent destruction of the rainforest. Those practising *tavy* agree with this. They also respect this forest and they can see that *tavy* greatly jeopardises the future for the next generations. So why destroy what you love and need?

One answer to a very complex question is the practical need. The poverty is extreme and there are few options. Life's priority is to feed your family and children. Rice, the food staple, is grown both on the flat ground in sustainable paddy fields, and on the steep slopes of slashed and burned forest. The last cyclone washed away much of the paddy rice crop and wiped out the earth dams and irrigation waterways built at great cost and effort. Some farmers had recently invested a lifetime's savings employing labour for their construction. So if floods strike, people rely on the hill rice. Fertility in these fields is not replenished as in paddies where nutrients are carried in the water. The soil quickly becomes unproductive so new slopes must be cut after a few years.

The cultural explanation for *tavy* is less obvious. The people of Sandrakely are Tanala, meaning 'people of the forest'. The forest is their world and to survive in this surprisingly harsh environment they clear the land with fire – the ancient agricultural technique brought by the original immigrants from Indonesia perhaps 2,000 years ago. In more recent history the Tanala were forced into the forest by warring neighbours and colonial occupants of more fertile areas.

As the traditional means of survival and provision *tavy* can be seen as central to society's make-up and culture. The calendar revolves around it, land ownership and hierarchies are determined by its practice, and politics are centred on it. It is the pivot and subject of rituals and ceremonies. The forest is the domain of the ancestors and site of tombs and religious standing stones. *Tavy* is an activity carried out between the living and the dead: the ancestors are consulted and permit its execution to provide for the living. The word *tavy* also means 'fatness', with all the associations of health, wealth and beauty.

If they have the choice, many people are happy to pursue the sustainable kind of agriculture so Feedback is ready to help them. But the practical and cultural context must always be respected. The new alternatives must be rock solid when people's lives are at stake and to be truly enduring they must be accommodated within the culture by the people themselves. It is they who understand the problems and know the solutions that are acceptable. They must not be forced.

Jamie Spencer runs the charity Feedback Madagascar; see page 146.

Palm savannah

Further west where dry forests have suffered the same fate as those of the highland, a dramatic 'palm savannah' exists. Again, the majority of the ground is covered by tall grasses, but there are also scattered palm and baobab trees which can withstand the annual burning. Unfortunately this is likely to be a temporary landscape. The saplings of the trees are less resistant to the flames, so no new trees will be replacing the few remaining ones.

Southern cactus scrub

The harsh environment of the south prevented serious agriculture in this region until recently, hence the spiny forest had remained relatively protected. New sisal plantations have, however, led to colonisation by Mexico's *Agave* cactus creating a secondary cactus scrub in some areas. Another import is the prickly pear cactus (*Raketa*) used for fencing and food for both humans and cattle. The cochineal beetle, introduced by the French in 1928/9 destroyed this important food source and, coupled with the drought of those years, contributed to wide-spread famine.

Aquatic ecosystems

Madagascar's aquatic ecosystems are under-rated as sites of ecological interest. On the coast there are excellent stands of mangrove swamp, numerous lagoons and estuaries and, fringing the shore and forming barriers out at sea, magnificent coral reefs. Inland, the island's high lakes and marshes provide isolated havens for unusual bird species and even rare lemurs. Aquatic ecosystems are less restricted by the terrestrial climate and tend to offer more stable habitats for a rich diversity of species.

Wetlands

Wetlands everywhere are regarded as important habitats. Where water accumulates there is an abundance of plants and insects. The plants are terrestrial species adapted to tolerate waterlogging and periodic dry spells, and the insects depend on the water for reproduction, for many species have underwater larval stages. Lakes, swamps and marshes all over the island are therefore popular with birds, attracted by the shelter and materials of the reeds and rushes, and the sustenance to be gained from the insect life. On open water and lagoons near the coast, flamingos group in large flocks, accompanied in their feeding by a variety of waders. The rare Madagascar fish eagle can be seen in some locations, and among the marshes that border the inland lakes are white-throated rails, cuckoo-rollers and the Madagascar pygmy kingfisher.

However, in Madagascar it is not only birds that make their homes among the reeds. In the reed beds of Lake Alaotra, a rare subspecies of the grey bamboo lemur, *Hapalemur griseus alaotrensis*, has given up bamboo for papyrus to become the world's only reed-dwelling primate. Currently under surveillance by primatologists, this subspecies is known to be critically endangered due to the draining of the lake for agriculture. In southern Madagascar another marsh character hides among the foliage, although this time it's a fellow plant. The insectivorous pitcher plant, *Nepenthes madagascariensis*, overcomes the low nutrient levels of the boggy soil beneath by enticing unwitting flies into its smelly pitcher. Once inside they are slowly digested to relinquish their valuable trace elements. An equivalent fate is sometimes faced by the Malagasy themselves in the lakes and waterways that play host to healthy and even sacred populations of crocodiles.

Good examples: The Antsalova lakes in the west; Lake Alaotra; Lake Ampitabe; Lake Ravelobe, Ampijoroa (fish eagle).

Mangroves

Where trees dominate the wetlands instead of grasses, there are swamps. By far the most important swamps on the island are the mangroves. Madagascar possesses the largest area of mangroves in the western Indian Ocean. About 330,000ha of the land/water margin are dominated by their characteristic salt tolerant trees, which straddle the water at low tide with weight-bearing roots, their tips sticking upwards, unable to gain oxygen in the thick estuarine mud. Some of the trees get a headstart in life by germinating their seeds whilst still on the parent tree. Sporting a shoot and leaves, the seed then drops at low tide into the mud below to attempt a planting.

Mangroves are important and rich ecosystems. They support a wealth of bird species, which arrive to feast on the swarms of swamp insects above the water and shoals of fish below. Many marine fish and crustacean populations treat the underwater architecture of the mangroves as a nursery, coming in from the sea to mate, breed and rear their young in relative safety. Consequently, as mangroves are being uprooted to make way for hotels elsewhere around the Indian Ocean, the local fishermen are finding their livelihood disappearing. So far, no such problems face the Malagasy; Malagasy mangroves are inaccessible enough to serve as their own protection.

Good examples: All the important mangrove sites are on the west coast, with some of the best areas a short trip from Mahajanga: Katsepy; Marovoay; also Morombe.

Coral reefs

Madagascar has 1,000km of coral reef, and some of the best dive sites in the western Indian Ocean. As with other coral reef areas about the world, most of the species are from a community of globetrotting fish, corals and invertebrates, which crop up wherever the environment is just right. However, Madagascar's reefs are less polluted than those of India and East Africa, and hence in comparison they are diverse and healthy.

CORAL REEF COMMUNITIES

Coral reefs earn their glamorous title, the 'rainforests of the sea', for they are easily as diverse as rainforests, and for similar reasons. The foundation species, the reef-building corals, are miniature relatives of the jellyfish, who have taken to living in vast colonies, surrounding themselves with a protective skeleton of calcium carbonate and grabbing plankton out of the water with their stinging tentacles. Together, these colonies can, over many years, create massive solid structures, full of nooks and crevices, in and on which a myriad of fish and invertebrates live.

There are two basic types of corals – the slow-growing massive corals, which add 1cm each year to their bulk; and the more delicate branching corals, which grow ten times faster, but fracture easily during storms. The resulting architecture of a reef is similar to that of a rainforest for one very good reason – corals, like trees, grow towards the light. They do this in order to sustain the most intimate of symbiotic relationships, for, living within the tentacles of each coral individual, or polyp, are millions of single-celled algae. The algae, bathed in the tropical light, provide the polyp with food, while the polyp returns the favour by protecting the algae from predators. This in-house harvesting system works most efficiently in clear, tropical waters, where nutrient levels are poor enough to deter smothering seaweeds and temperatures high enough to permit active reef-building. It is therefore a very fruitful relationship for it creates a prosperity of life in waters that are essentially the subaqua equivalent of a desert.

Competition between corals for a place in the sun is remarkably heated. If two colonies of the same species grow close to each other they tend to fuse, but if different species are neighbours warfare begins. The corals launch filaments which digest the skeleton of the enemy, and this explains the

There are 63 genera of reef-building corals working to manufacture the island's numerous fringing and barrier reefs. The 1,600km of latitude that Madagascar has to offer creates a gradual cooling of the waters towards the south of the island enabling different corals, and therefore different communities, to predominate. The continental shelf surrounding Madagascar also contributes to diversity. A speedy drop-off on the east coast into deep waters allows only limited fringing reef growth stretching in patches from Fenoarivo to the Masoala peninsula. Off the west coast, the vast and shallow shelf spreading out under the Mozambique Channel, warmed by the Agulhas current coming down from the equator, creates far more reef opportunities. Along this coast there are fringing and barrier reefs sporting remote cays and a wealth of fish and invertebrates. Loggerhead, green and hawksbill turtles cruise the underwater meadows between corals and nest on the beaches. International travellers such as boobies, terns and tropic birds feed on reef residents such as lobsters, oysters and the enormous prawns that Madagascar is now famed for in Western restaurants. In July–September, migrating humpback whales use the warm waters of eastern Madagascar for breeding, before heading to Antarctica for a plankton feast.

Good examples: Ile Sainte Marie; islands off Nosy Be; Ifaty, islands south of Toliara; Lokaro.

CONSERVATION
An age-old problem
When people first settled in Madagascar, the culture they brought with them depended on rice and zebu cattle. Rice was the staple diet and zebu the spiritual

significant gaps between colonies on a reef. Their sex life is equally dramatic. It was only relatively recently that divers swimming at night, just after the full moon, stumbled upon corals engaging in mass spawning events, where the water is filled with sperm and eggs, all desperately trying to locate an ideal partner. Fish time their migrations to coincide with this phenomenon, which may take place only once a year, and feed in a frenzy on the abundant platter.

More permanent residents light up the habitat with their colours and behaviours. Unlike their oceangoing relatives, reef fish have an interest in defending their favourite location – a protective crevice or a bountiful patch of sponge. They do this with a combination of poisons, startling territorial displays and plain aggression. For human voyeurs the effect is one of constant theatre, each fish and invertebrate playing its role with finesse. Parrotfish have strong enough 'beaks' to chip away at the coral and extract polyps. Clownfish harbour among stinging anemones, free from harm due to an oily secretion on their scales. Cleaner wrasse run 'cleaning stations', which fish periodically visit to have their parasites removed, while a mimic of the wrasse exploits this chance for deception, and instead of removing unwanted hangers-on, removes chunks of flesh. The goby and the bulldozer shrimp team up to build burrows. The shrimp does the digging and the more vigilant goby watches for danger. All are kept on edge by small sharks patrolling the reef edges and trapped lagoons for stray prey.

Such a wondrous play is enacted daily on the stage of the coral reef, and has been for millions of years. The only threat to its continued run is, in effect, its audience. Soil erosion, pollution, the direct removal of fish and shells, and insensitive tourist activities add to the natural disturbances of storms and pest plagues to take their toll on the health of reefs all over the world.

staple, the link with the ancestors. Rice and zebu cannot be raised in dense forest, so the trees were felled and the undergrowth burned.

Two hundred or so years ago King Andrianampoinimerina punished those of his subjects who wilfully deforested areas. The practice continued, however. In 1883, 100 years later, the missionary James Sibree commented: 'Again we noticed the destruction of the forest and the wanton waste of trees.' The first efforts at legal protection came as long ago as 1927 when ten reserves were set aside by the French colonial government, which also tried to put a stop to the burning. Successive governments have tried – and failed – to halt this devastation.

Since independence in 1960, Madagascar's population has more than doubled (to nearly 15 million) and the remaining forest has been reduced by half. Only about 10% of the original cover remains and an estimated 2,000km² is destroyed annually – not by timber companies (although there have been some culprits) but by impoverished peasants clearing the land by the traditional method of *tavy*, slash and burn, and cutting trees for fuel or to make charcoal. However, Madagascar is not overpopulated: the population density averages only 21 people per square kilometre, while in Great Britain it is 228. The pressure on the forests is because

THE DURRELL WILDLIFE CONSERVATION TRUST
Lee Durrell

The Durrell Wildlife Conservation Trust (formerly the Jersey Wildlife Preservation Trust) was founded by Gerald Durrell in 1963. Our headquarters is at Jersey Zoo on the English Channel Island of Jersey. We began working in Madagascar in the early 1980s. Our current efforts concern eight threatened species, all inhabiting western forests or wetlands – fragile and poorly studied ecosystems only now beginning to receive attention from conservationists.

Our most advanced programme is for the endangered ploughshare tortoise, or *angonoka*. This animal is found only in the remote bamboo scrub of the northwest and probably numbers no more than a thousand. Our work on the *angonoka* began in 1986 with the establishment of a breeding centre at the Ampijoroa Forestry Station. An adult herd of 20 tortoises has produced more than 300 young. These and future offspring are being used to bolster the remaining wild populations, which number less than a thousand and are restricted to fragmented sites threatened by bush fires, as needed. We have also undertaken field research, both on the wild tortoises and on the way of life of the people who live near them, and have offered training opportunities for young Malagasy conservationists. With the results to date we are optimistic that the *angonoka* will eventually recover its numbers and become viable as a species once again. This programme has become the model on which our work with other threatened species in Madagascar is based.

Lake Alaotra is the largest freshwater wetland in Madagascar. Loss of forest in the watershed, transformation of the marshes into ricefields, use of pesticides and introduction of non-native fish and plants have turned what was once a biologically rich and productive region of Madagascar into an ecological disaster. Pockets of intact marsh and clean water still exist, supporting fishing, reed-gathering and, potentially, recreation, but native wildlife has suffered. We maintain breeding groups of the endangered Alaotran grey bamboo lemur and Meller's duck at Jersey Zoo, and at Lake Alaotra we have catalysed a strong community initiative to protect the remaining marshes.

The Madagascar giant jumping rat, flat-tailed tortoise and narrow-striped so much of the country is sterile grassland. Unlike in neighbouring Africa, this savannah is lifeless because Malagasy animals evolved to live in forests; they are not adapted to this new environment.

Change in Madagascar's vegetation is by no means recent. Scientists have identified that the climate became much drier about 5,000 years ago. Humans have just speeded up the process.

The race against time

Madagascar has more endangered species of mammal than any other country in the world. The authorities are not unaware of this environmental crisis: as long ago as 1970 the Director of Scientific Research made this comment in a speech during an international symposium on conservation: 'The people in this room know that Malagasy nature is a world heritage. We are not sure that others realise that it is *our* heritage.' Resentment at having outsiders make decisions on the future of their heritage without proper consultation with the Malagasy was one of the reasons there was little effective conservation in the 1970s and early 1980s. This was a time when Madagascar was demonstrating its independence from Western influences.

mongoose are all confined to a small area of western deciduous woodlands. Their severely restricted distribution coupled with deforestation for slash-and-burn maize cultivation and non-sustainable logging which are degrading the remaining forests of this area renders these species extremely vulnerable. Jersey Zoo coordinates the breeding of the jumping rat in Europe, and the breeding centre at Ampijoroa has had good success with the little tortoise. Research on the three species in the wild is ongoing. Also severely endangered are the Madagascar teal and the Madagascar side-necked turtle in the west. The teal probably number less than a thousand. Our field team has been the first to study breeding of the teal in the wild, and first breeding of the teal in captivity occurred in Jersey in 1998. Similarly, our teams worked with villagers to observe wild nests and to establish a breeding nucleus of the turtle at Ampijoroa. Biological field research and community work related to these species and their habitat are intensifying.

In addition to the focus on species, our other efforts include technical and financial aid to two zoos and conservation education centres in Madagascar. Also, we offer off-site training in endangered species management for Malagasy students at the International Training Centre based at Jersey Zoo. Fifteen Malagasy had graduated from the Centre by the end of 2001.

The Durrell Wildlife Conservation Trust carries out recovery programmes for threatened species all over the world, in partnership with governments and non-governmental organisations, both international and local. Each programme is tailored to address the particular conservation opportunities and constraints as defined by human (and other) impacts on the species in question both on-site and off-site. The programmes are usually long-term, in recognition of the fact that there are no quick fixes to the problems most endangered species face today. The strategic use of partnerships and grassroots-led action make the Trust's programmes more effective at less cost than those of many larger conservation organisations. Donations are welcome at the following address: Durrell Wildlife Conservation Trust, Les Augrès Manor, Trinity, Jersey JE3 5BP, Channel Islands, British Isles; tel: +44 (0)1534 860000; fax: +44 (0)1534 860001; email: jerseyzoo@durrell.org.

MARINE CONSERVATION IN MADAGASCAR
Andrew Cooke

While rightly famous for its unique terrestrial flora and fauna, Madagascar also possesses a spectacular diversity of marine ecosystems and species. Straddling about 15 degrees of latitude from 10° south to 25° south, with east and west-facing coasts subject to the varying influences of ocean currents, tides, waves, winds and rivers, Madagascar may possess the largest variety of marine habitats of any Western Indian Ocean country. It also harbours many species of global conservation concern, including whales, dolphins, dugongs, sea turtles (five species), certain sharks, sawfish and the coelacanth.

Madagascar possesses an estimated 3,000km of coral reefs, including barrier reefs, fringing reefs, patch reefs and submerged reefs, of which about 90% are along the relatively sheltered west coast, with the principal concentrations in the southwest (Androka to Morombe). There are also reefs in the northwest (Analalava to Antsiranana) and the northeast (Tamatave to Masoala). These reefs provide habitat for at least 6,000 species including 350 sponges, 250 corals, 750 crabs, 1,500 mollusks, 325 echinoderms (starfish, urchins, sea cucumbers etc), about 1,000 fishes and many more. In 2002 at least 12 new fish and coral species were discovered in the northwest during a marine survey by Conservation International.

For visitors the most accessible reefs are those near Toliara, Nosy Be, Ile Sainte Marie, Antsiranana, Antalaha (for the Masoala reefs) and Vohémar.

Apart from coral reefs, Madagascar is very important for its mangroves, with a total area of about 300km², 98% of which are on the west coast. Mangroves are an important nursery ground for numerous commercially important species, notably the high-value paeneid shrimps or 'pink gold'; mangroves also provide suitable conditions for the growing shrimp farming industry. The main conservation problem is cutting wood for fuel (so far shrimp farming has done little harm to mangroves, in contrast with other countries).

Marine conservation is only just beginning to take off in Madagascar now that the network of terrestrial parks has become well established. Most of the conservation effort is being concentrated on coral reefs (because of their species richness, high amenity value and scientific interest) and on species of global conservation concern (especially sea turtles). ANGAP and the National

Things changed in 1985, when Madagascar hosted a major international conference on conservation for development. The Ministry of Animal Production, Waters and Forests, which administered the protected areas, went into partnership with the World Wide Fund for Nature (WWF). Their plan was to evaluate all protected areas in the country, then numbering 37 (2% of the country), and in their strategy for the future to provide people living near the reserves with economically viable alternatives. They have largely achieved their aims. All the protected areas have been evaluated and recommendations for their management made. They are now the responsibility of the National Association for Management of Protected Areas (Association Nationale pour la Gestion des Aires Protegées, ANGAP) which was established under the auspices of the Environmental Action Plan (EAP), sponsored by the World Bank. Among their successes has been the establishment of several new national parks and a three-year 'Debt for Nature' swap negotiated by the WWF with the Central Bank of Madagascar.

Environment Office (ONE) have established a special working group to oversee the establishment of a marine protected areas system.

National marine parks with coral reefs already exist at Mananara-Nord (the coral reefs around Nosy Atafana) and the Masoala Peninsula (three separate marine parks at Tampolo, Cap Masoala and Tanjona). In addition there are small but significant community-based conservation efforts, such as the island of Nosy Ve, Anakao (Toliara) which is protected by a traditional by-law (*dina*). Progress is also being made to conserve parts of the reefs around Ifaty (Toliara) and the island of Sakatia (Nosy Be) under *dina*. The reefs of Nosy Tanikely have been protected under a ministerial decree since 1968, backed up by a local decree in 1995.

There are plans for several more marine conservation areas: Nosy Hara (Antsiranana), Sahamalaza (including the Radama islands), Lokaro (Taolagnaro), Toliara (Ifaty, Grand Récif, Nosy Ve), Belo sur Mer, and Manambolomaty (an area of wetlands and mangroves near Bemaraha).

While small in scale, results of marine conservation so far have been very encouraging. Scientists recently confirmed that protection of Nosy Atafana from intensive fishing is associated with 40% higher fish diversity relative to unprotected areas, and fishermen using surrounding areas have reported improved catches. Similar observations have been made for Nosy Tanikely and Nosy Ve. However, local conservation initiatives cannot hope to deal with large scale problems such as generalised impacts of over-fishing, sedimentation (due to upland soil erosion) or coral bleaching (an effect of global warming) which require regional, national or even global action.

There is mounting evidence that awareness-raising at the village level of the impacts of turtle hunting has been quite effective, with a substantial reduction in turtle hunting being reported for the Toliara region and several examples of local *dina* banning turtle hunting around both Nosy Be and Toliara.

Visitors can make an important contribution to marine conservation by visiting marine conservation areas and respecting their rules, including payment of entry fees (especially for local conservation efforts where even modest revenues can make all the difference for conservation). And please report any significant observations or experiences to a concerned institution (there is a list in *Appendix 4*), such as the breach of park rules, sea turtle hunting or sightings of rare species, especially dugongs (sea cows).

The WWF funds a number of projects in Madagascar. Other outside agencies involved in conservation are the Durrell Wildlife Conservation Trust, Conservation International, Missouri Botanical Gardens, Duke University Primate Center, and the Peregrine Fund; also USAID (US Agency for International Development), UNDP (United Nations Development Programme) and UNESCO.

The stated aims of the WWF and other conservation agencies working in Madagascar are to: 'Ensure the conservation of Malagasy biodiversity and ecological processes by stopping, and eventually reversing, the accelerating environmental degradation, and by helping to build a future in which humans live in harmony with nature'.

How you can help
- Support the organisations listed in *Chapter 7*.
- Do not interrupt the work of scientists in the reserves.

BURNING ISSUES

The following three stories show the tragedy – and the hope – of people versus forests in Madagascar.

> Our only low point here was on our return from Antonibe when we passed through an area of freshly burnt forest (in fact it was still burning). More or less in the centre there was only one large tree left standing and at the top of this was a forlorn group of Coquerel's sifaka. We knew that we were really looking at dead lemurs as there was nothing for them to eat and they would have to traverse a kilometre of burnt forest in any direction to get out – highly unlikely. There was nothing we could do. As there are so few people and zebu in the area our guide suggested that often local people do this out of frustration with the government!(?)
>
> *John and Valerie Middleton*

> Several times that day [during a hike in a wildlife-rich but unprotected area near Andapa] I paused to take in the surroundings, and I kept thinking 'something is amiss here'. And then it dawned on me – the ubiquitous pillars of smoke one tends to see in Madagascar during the 'burning season' (this was October), were Not There. I asked Gaston why. He told us that the elders of various village communities in this district had met up, following educational efforts on the part of the WWF, and had elected to implement a local law to the effect that if any farmers were caught burning the forest, they would be fined something like £23 - a fair whack for a Malagasy farmer. Apparently, enforcing this law was not problematic and it didn't take more than a handful of instances where people were fined, to establish it.
>
> *Derek Schuurman*

- Do not buy products made from endangered species, including shells. (Crocodiles are farmed for their skins and butterflies bred for the trade in mounted specimens, so buying these does not endanger the species' survival).
- Do not encourage the illegal domestication of protected species by admiring or paying to photograph pet animals.
- Pay the full park/reserve fees with good grace. The money is used for conservation.
- Do not berate the Malagasy for destroying their forests, nor impose your own cultural values in respect to their treatment of animals. Try to learn about the people whose country you are visiting.

NATIONAL PARKS AND RESERVES
Categories

The six categories of protected area are becoming blurred, as more and more reserves become national parks and open to tourists. The first three categories below were established to protect natural ecosystems or threatened species:

1 Réserves Naturelles Intégrales (strict nature reserves)
2 Parcs Nationaux (national parks)
3 Réserves Spéciales (special reserves)
4 Réserves de Chasse (hunting reserves)
5 Forêts Classées (classified forests)
6 Périmètres de Reboisement et de Restauration (reafforestation zones).

I'd imagined tracking down one of the world's 25 most endangered primates would be tough. I imagined long treks through inhospitable forests with only a fleeting glimpse of the rarity as it disappeared through the canopy. But I should have known better – Madagascar never stops surprising me.

I travelled to Daraina to look for the golden-crowned sifaka. An hour and a half's walk from the town, near a village, I found the last fragments of forest. In the river beds gallery forest formed bright green corridors linking them together.

The village was tiny: perhaps 20 people. They eked out a living digging for gold, excavating tonnes of soil for a very meagre reward – a day's panning producing little more than a few grains of metal, equivalent to a cup or two of rice. Yet despite their austere lives, these people have built a remarkable relationship with the sifakas in the neighbouring forest. It's *fady* to hunt and eat them, so instead they feed them – brandishing nothing more than a banana, villagers call the sifaka down from the canopy to accept their fruit offerings. Several groups of animals have become accustomed to this and live very happily in the degraded forests adjacent to the village.

This encapsulated Madagascar's magic and environmental vulnerability in a nutshell – a beautiful animal, and one of the rarest of all lemurs, surviving side by side with people scratching to make ends meet – but one whose continued survival remains in constant jeopardy from pressures exerted upon it by humanity (and further recent discoveries of gold and semi-precious stones in the area are exacerbating the problems).

Nick Garbutt

1 Several of the former strict nature reserves that denied access to tourists have now been gazetted as national parks. The remaining ones in this category protect representative ecosystems, and are open only to authorised scientific research (although tourists can often get permission to visit).

2 As in other countries, national parks protect ecosystems and areas of natural beauty, and are open to the public (with permits). There are now nine national parks: Montagne d'Ambre, Marojejy, Masoala, Andringitra, Ranomafana, Zombitse and Vohibasia, Andohahela, Isalo, and Tsingy de Bemaraha.

3 There are 18 or so special reserves, of which Ankarana, Cap Sainte Marie, Beza-Mahafaly, Andranomena, Anjanaharibe-Sud and Nosy Mangabe are described in this book. These reserves are for the protection of ecosystems or threatened species. Not all are supervised. Access may be limited to authorised scientific research.

4 Four lakes (including Kinkony and Ihotry) are duck-hunting reserves.

5 and 6 The 158 classified forests and 77 reafforestation zones conserve forests and watersheds using accepted forestry principles. Ampijoroa and Manjakatompo classified forests are described in this book.

There are also some private reserves, the most famous of which is Berenty.

Ecotourism

Ecotourism, or 'discovery tourism' (as opposed to mass tourism), was part of the National Environmental Action Plan set up in 1990. The aim was that tourism should generate about a third of the funding for 'protected area' maintenance by the end of the century. Now we have reached the end of the century and, although the target has not been met, the statistics are encouraging. Tourism to Madagascar is rising (23% in one year) and encouragingly, there was an eightfold increase in visitors to protected areas between 1992 and 1997. In 1995 only 20% of visitors to Madagascar went to a national park or reserve; now it is 50%. At present only four national parks – Isalo, Montagne d'Ambre, Ranomafana and Andasibe-Mantadia – are easy to visit, and these generate 60% of the total revenue from entrance fees.

There are two main reasons that the protected areas are not yet self supporting. One is that half the revenue from entrance fees goes (thank goodness!) to local community development projects, and the other is that of the entire network of national parks and reserves, many are not open to tourists at all, and those that are may be difficult to reach or have no facilities (not that that stops my readers getting there and enjoying the solitude!).

Permits

Permits to visit the reserves and national parks cost foreigners 50,000Fmg per person per reserve. Half this entrance fee goes to ANGAP and half to local communities, so each visitor is playing his or her part. Permits are mostly available at the park/reserve entrance (be sure to get a receipt) but you may wish to visit the ANGAP office in Antananarivo for the latest information or a 'passport' which covers all the protected areas you want to visit.

Hiring guides

After years of confusion and consequent resentment, fees for guides are more or less standardised and posted by the entrance to the popular parks and reserves: currently 20,000Fmg (about £2/US$3) for a two-hour day walk or 40,000Fmg for a night walk. This is for a maximum of three people – larger groups pay more. However, guides now expect a hefty tip on top of this fee. This is fair enough if the guide has been exceptional, but if they have been sloppy or lazy be brave and omit the tip but explain why. Discourage guides (again, with a polite explanation) from disturbing or frightening animals to make them move into range of your camera. When tipping, bear in mind the enormous earnings of these people compared with, say, the 160,000Fmg (£16/US$25) per month earned by a labourer in the sisal plantations.

Always check, and confirm, the fee before setting out.

There are some birds the size of a large turkeycock which have the head made like a cat and the rest of the body like a griffin; these birds hide themselves in the thick woods, and when anyone passes under the tree where they are they let themselves fall so heavily on the head of the passengers that they stun them, and in the moment they pierce their heads with their talons, then they eat them.'

Sieur de Bois, 1669

Planning and Preparation

WHEN TO GO

Read the section on climate (page 10) before deciding when to travel. Broadly speaking, the dry months are in the winter between April and September, but rainfall varies enormously in different areas. The months you may want to avoid are August and during the Christmas holidays, when popular places are crowded, and February and March (the cyclone season) when it will probably rain. However, the off-peak season can be rewarding, with cheaper international airfares and accommodation and fewer other tourists. September is nice, but often windy in the south. April and May often have lovely weather, and the countryside is green after the rainy season.

Keen naturalists have their own requirements: botanists will want to go in February when many of the orchids are in flower, and herpetologists will also prefer the spring/summer because reptiles are more active – and brightly coloured – during those months. Bear in mind that giant jumping rats, dwarf lemurs, tenrecs and some reptiles are less active so harder to see during the cold dry months of June, July and August.

My favourite months to visit Madagascar are October and November, when the weather is usually fine but not too hot, the jacarandas are in flower, the lemurs have babies, and lychees are sold from roadside stalls in the east.

RED TAPE
Visas

A visa is required by everyone and is normally issued for a stay of 30 days. Visas, costing €41 or the equivalent in US dollars ($32), are issued at the airport in Antananarivo on arrival. This is an easier and often cheaper option than applying through your local embassy or consulate, but only US dollars cash and Euros will usually be accepted. The situation could change, however, and if you require more than 30 days or are travelling on business you should obtain your visa before leaving home. Long-term visas are usually available for stays of more than 90 days, but need authorisation from Antananarivo so can take about two months to process. Travellers who apply for a visa extension during their stay are usually successful.

Embassy and consulate addresses

Australia Consulate; 3rd level, 100 Clarence St, Sydney, NSW 2000; tel: 02 9299 2290; fax: 02 9299 2242; email: tonyknox@ozemail.com.au. Hours 09.00–13.00. Visas are issued within 24 hours and cost AUS$50.00. The consul-general, Anthony Knox, is very enthusiastic and helpful. He is also the agent for Air Madagascar.
Austria Consulate; Pötzleindorferstr 94, A-1184 Wien; tel: 47 91 273; fax: 47 91 2734.
Belgium Embassy; 276 Av de Tervueren, 1150 Bruxelles; tel: 770 1726 & 770 1774; fax: 722 3731; email: ambassade.madagascar@skynet.be.
Canada Embassy; 649 Blair Rd, Gloucester, Ontario K1J 7M4; tel: 613 744 7995; fax: 613 744 2530; email: ambmgnet@inexpres.net.

Honorary Consulate; 8530 Rue Saguenay, Brossard, Québec, J4X IM6; tel/fax: 450 672 0353.

Honorary Consulate; 8944 Bayridge Drive SW, Calgary, Alberta T2V 3M8; tel: 403 262 5576; fax: 403 262 3556.

France Embassy; 4 Av Raphael, 75016 Paris; tel: 1 45 04 62 11; fax: 1 45 03 31 75. Visas take up to three days and cost 26 Euros (single) or 31 Euros (multiple).

Consulate; 234 Bd Perrier, 13008 Marseille; tel: 4 91 15 16 91; fax: 4 91 53 79 58.

Germany Consulate; Rolandstrasse 48 (Postfach 1200251), 53179 Bonn; tel: 0228 95 35 90; fax: 0228 33 46 28; email: 320044351112-0001@t-online.de.

Italy Embassy; Via Riccardo Zandonai 84/A, Roma 400194; tel: 36 30 77 97; fax: 396 329 43 06.

Kenya Honorary Consulate; First floor, Hilton Hotel (PO Box 41723), Nairobi; tel: 225 286; fax: 252 347. Allow 24 hours.

Mauritius Embassy; Av Queen Mary, Port Louis; tel: 686 3956; fax: 686 7040.

Réunion Consulate; 73 Rue Juliette Dodu, 97461 Saint-Denis; tel: 21 05 21/21 65 58. Visas cost the same as in France.

South Africa Consulate; No 13 6th St, Houghton Estate, Johannesburg; tel: 442 3322; fax: 442 6660; email: consul@infodoor.co.za; website: madagascarconsulate.org.za; 30-day visa, single entry R120, multiple entry R140; 90-day visa, single entry R180, multiple entry R200.

Consulate; Hon Consul: David Fox; 201 Percy Osborne Rd, Morningside, Durban; tel/fax: 31 312 9704; email: mdconsul@icon.co.za. Visas issued for 90 days only, single entry R120, multiple entry R140.

Spain Honorary Consulate; Balmes 202–2a, 08006 Barcelona; tel: 415 1006; fax: 415 2953.

Switzerland Honorary Consulate; 2 Theaterplatz, 3011 Bern; tel: 311 3111; fax: 311 0871; email: Hocomad@Datacomm.ch.

UK Honorary Consulate; 16 Lanark Mansions, Pennard Rd, London W12 8DT; tel: 020 8746 0133; fax: 020 8746 0134. Hours 09.30–13.00. Visas supplied immediately or by post; very helpful. £40 (single entry) or £50 (multiple entry). Business visas cost £55. Note: a visa can be easily bought at the airport in Antananarivo for only £23, but for a short stay (max 30 days).

United States Embassy; 2374 Massachusetts Av NW, Washington DC 20008; tel: 202 265 5525. Permanent Mission of Madagascar at the UN; 801 Second Street, New York NY 10017; tel: 212 744 3816; fax: 212 986 6271; email: mission.madagascar@itu.ch. For some reason visas from here cost double the normal rate! Honorary Consulate; It's convenient that the Hon Consul in California is Monique Rodrigues, who runs the specialist tour operator, Cortez Travel; 124 Lomas Santa Fe Dr, No 208, Solana Beach, CA 92075; tel: 619 792 6999. Visas in the US usually cost US$33.45 for a single-entry visa.

Extending your visa

A visa extension is usually easy to obtain. As early in your trip as possible go to the Ministry of the Interior, five minutes from the Hilton Hotel in Antananarivo. For your *prolongation* you will need three photos, a photocopy of your currency declaration, a typewritten declaration (best done at home) of why you want to stay longer, a *Certificat d'Hébergement* from your hotel, your passport, your return ticket and 180,000Fmg (£18/US$26). Every provincial town has an immigration office, or at least a Commissariat de Police, so in theory you can extend your visa anywhere.

GETTING THERE
By air

If you are planning to take several domestic flights during your stay, Air Madagascar should be the international carrier since they offer a discount called 'Decomad' which gives a low-season 30% discount on flights between the most popular destinations in Madagascar, providing visitors also book their international flight on Air Madagascar. This is reduced to 20% in the high-season (July and August). This pass is only valid for visitors staying one to four weeks; those on an extended visit pay the full rate. Also South Africa counts as 'regional' not international (so no discount).

From Europe

As with any long-haul flight it is often cheaper to book through an agency such as Trailfinders (tel: 020 7938 3366), WEXAS (tel: 020 7581 8768), STA (tel: 020 7361 6262), or The Flight Centre (tel: 01892 530030) rather than phoning the airline direct. At the time of writing only Air Madagascar and Air France fly to Madagascar from the UK.

Air Madagascar The country's national airline is due to be privatised (but that has been the case for several years). Contact Air Madagascar, Oak House, County Oak Way, Crawley, West Sussex RH11 7ST; tel: 01293 596 665. There are, as yet, no Air Madagascar flights from London – it is necessary to fly to Paris and connect with the Air Mad flight from CDG Airport (section 2a). Air Madagascar has teamed up with British Midland to provide the best add-on fare from London or Manchester to CDG. 2002 airfares from London are quoted at £750 plus taxes, and £633 from Paris, but there are often special promotions with lower fares. Flight schedules are reviewed half-yearly. At the time of writing (October 2001) they leave Paris on Mondays, Wednesdays, and Fridays (direct), plus Sundays (via Rome and Nairobi). These flights are overnight, taking approximately 14 hours. Travellers from mainland Europe will want to contact the nearest Air Madagascar office: the address of the head office in Paris is 29, Rue des Boulets, Paris 75011; tel: 53 27 21 10 or 43 79 42 10; fax: 43 79 30 33. There are also Air Madagascar offices in Brussels (tel: 02 712 6420); Rotterdam (tel: 010 437 9911); Munich (tel: 089 2900 3940) Vienna (tel: 01 5853 63088); Geneva (tel: 022 732 42 30, fax: 022 731 16 90), Zürich (tel: 01 816 40 51). In Italy there are offices in Rome (tel: 47 47 368), Verona (tel: 04 5670 0802), Palermo (tel: 09 1611 3366/7), and Florence (tel: 05 5496 663).

Air France Flights depart from Heathrow via Paris on Mondays, Wednesdays, Fridays and Saturdays. These are day flights, in contrast to Air Madagascar which flies overnight. The fares are the same as Air Madagascar.

CORSAIR This is the cheapest option, but tickets can only be purchased in Paris through Nouvelles Frontières, 3 Boulevard Saint-Martin, 75003 Paris; tel: 01 4027 0208; fax: 01 4027 0019; web: www.nouvelles-frontieres.fr.

On most airlines serving Madagascar there are different rates according to the season (based on popularity). High season is usually July and August, and the Christmas holiday, and low-season from January to the end of June.

From other Indian Ocean islands
Réunion

The following airlines fly from Paris to Réunion: Air France, AOM French Airlines, Air Liberté, and British Airways. From Réunion there are almost daily Air

---

A STAY IN REUNION?

If you have time, it's sensible to consider a stay in Réunion before or after tackling Madagascar. This is a fabulous place for mountain hiking and beach relaxation, and you can brush up your French while knowing that the place is almost entirely hassle-free.

The people to contact for all arrangements are Anthurium@guetali.fr.

Madagascar flights to Antananarivo, and also to Toamasina and Mahajanga. Air Austral flies three times a week to Nosy Be. A return flight between Réunion and Nosy Be currently (2001) costs US$329.

Mauritius
Air Mauritius and Air Madagascar fly between Mauritius and Antananarivo.

Comoro Islands
Air Madagascar flies from Mayotte and Air Mauritius from Moroni.

Seychelles
There is one flight a week (Tuesday) from the Seychelles.

From Africa
Kenya
There are several flights per week (Air Madagascar, Air Mauritius and Air France) from Nairobi. With so many cheap flights from London to Nairobi, this may be a good option. Air Madagascar flies on Mondays, Wednesdays and Saturdays. Avoid the Monday one which is coming from Paris so is likely to be both late and overbooked (at 1.45am this matters!). The current fare for a 30-day excursion is US$428 (excluding tax).

South Africa
Flights go three times a week from South Africa. Air Madagascar (tel: 011 289 8222) flies from Johannesburg on Thursdays and Saturdays, and their partner InterAir (tel: 011 616 0636) goes on Mondays. They return the following day. All flights leave Johannesburg at 08.30, getting you to Tana in the early afternoon. The flight takes four hours and, at a discounted rate through a tour operator, costs about R3,660 (US$436) low season, R4,020 (US$480) high season.

InterAir can be contacted in London: tel: 0207 707 4581; fax: 0207 707 4165; email: gsa.1.gsa@britishairways.com.

From the USA
Madagascar is about as far from California as it is possible to be. Indeed, San Francisco and the southern town of Toliara *are* as far apart as it is possible to be. Understandably, therefore, fares from the USA are expensive, but are coming down. Currently the best deal from New York is US$1,300 (November and February) or US$2,200 (July and August); from California you can travel west via Singapore for about US$1,800. Phone Air Madagascar on 800 821 3388; fax: 619 792 5280.

A DAY IN JOHANNESBURG
I have arrived exhausted in Tana after an overnight flight so many times I now prefer to fly via Johannesburg and catch up on sleep (not to mention good food and shopping) in my favourite suburb: Melville. This feels like Islington or Greenwich Village: cosmopolitan, lively and safe, with numerous excellent restaurants. This is a book about Madagascar, not South Africa, so I'll limit the space I give it to recommending the Melville Turret Guest House (tel: 011 482 7197; email: turret@totem.co.za). It's comfortable, leafy, inexpensive, charming. Melville is a £25/US$38 taxi ride from the airport.

An agency providing cheap flights to Africa, including Madagascar, is Africa Air Center; tel: 800 727 7207.

From Australia

Air Madagascar has an office in the same building as the Sydney Consulate. Flights are usually routed via Singapore, from where there is an Air Madagascar flight to Antananarivo, via Réunion, on Wednesdays and Saturdays. Alternatively you can go from Melbourne or Perth to Mauritius (Air Mauritius) connecting with an Air Madagascar flight to Antananarivo, or flying from Perth via Johannesburg.

By sea
From South Africa

There is no longer a passenger-carrying cargo boat running from Durban, but many people sail their own yachts to Madagascar.

Yacht clubs

Royal Natal Yacht Club PO Box 2946, Durban 4000; tel: 031 301 5425; fax: 031 307 2590.
Point Yacht Club PO Box 2224, Durban 4000; tel: 031 301 4787; fax: 031 305 1234.
Zululand Yacht Club PO Box 10387, Meer'en'see 3901; tel: 035 788 0256; fax: 035 788 0254.
Royal Cape Yacht Club PO Box 777, Cape Town 8000; tel: 021 4211 354; fax: 0214216 028.

Many yachts sail from Natal to Madagascar and the Durban consulate was set up to cope with their visas. It takes six to seven days to sail to Anakao, the most popular port (south of Toliara). Most stop en route at Europa island, where a French garrison will advise on the next stage. Experienced sailors and divers will want to reach the atoll of Bassas da India which offers superb diving but has been responsible for the shipwreck of numerous vessels.

Because of the increasing number of yachts visiting the northwest of Madagascar, I give information for 'yachties' in the *Nosy Be* chapter.

WHAT TO TAKE
Luggage

A soft bag or backpack is more practical than a hard suitcase (and you may not be allowed to take a suitcase on a Twin Otter plane). Backpackers should consider buying a rucksack with a zipped compartment to enclose the straps when using them on airlines. Or – a cheaper option – roll up the straps and bind them out of the way with insulating tape. Bring a light folding nylon bag for taking purchases home, and the largest permissible bag to take as hand baggage on the plane. Pack this with everything you need for the first four days or so (security restrictions permitting). Lost or delayed luggage is then less of a catastrophe.

Clothes

Before deciding what clothes to pack, take a look at the *Climate* section on page 10. There is quite a difference between summer and winter temperatures, particularly in the highlands and the south where it is distinctly cold at night between May and September. A fibre-pile jacket or a body-warmer (down vest) is useful in addition to a light sweater. In June and July a scarf (muffler) can give much-needed extra warmth. At any time of the year it will be hot during the day in low-lying areas, and very hot between October and March. Layers of clothing – T-shirt, sweatshirt, light sweater – are warm and versatile, and take less room than a heavy sweater.

Don't bring jeans, they are too heavy and too hot. Lightweight cotton or cotton mix trousers such as Rohan Bags are much more suitable. The Bags have a useful inside zipped pocket for security. At any time of year you will need a light showerproof jacket, and during the wet season, or if spending time in the rainforest, appropriate raingear and perhaps a small umbrella. A light cotton jacket is always useful for breezy evenings by the coast. Don't forget a sunhat.

For footwear, trainers (running shoes) and sandals are usually all you need. 'Sports sandals' which strap securely to the feet are better than flip-flops. Hiking boots may be required in places like Ankarana, Andringitra and Isalo but are not necessary for the main tourist circuits.

Give some thought to beachwear if you enjoy snorkelling. You may need an old pair of sneakers (or similar) to protect your feet from coral and sea urchins, and a T-shirt and shorts to wear while in the water to prevent sunburn.

Toiletries

You can buy just about everything in Madagascar, but many essentials such as sunblock are quite expensive so it's best to bring all you need. It's still worth bringing your favourite brand of soft toilet paper – don't rely on the local WCs having any sort of paper.

A correspondent notes with satisfaction that condoms are very cheap and reliable. Certainly Madagascar is addressing the problem of AIDS with enthusiasm: in the drawer of my posh Tana hotel was a Gideon's Bible and a condom!

Bring baby-wipes or – better – moist toilet tissues for freshening up during a long trip. There is now an excellent hand-gel which cleans and disinfects your hands. When used regularly, I have found this a real help in preventing travellers' diarrhoea.

Some toilet articles have several uses: dental floss is excellent for repairs as well as for teeth, and a nail brush gets clothes clean too.

Don't take up valuable space with a bath towel – a hand towel is perfectly adequate.

Protection against mosquitoes
Repellents

With malaria on the increase, it is vital to be properly protected. For maximum protection use repellent containing at least 50% DEET. Other nicer-smelling and arguably as effective repellents may also be used. Buzz-Bands (made by Traveller International Products) which slip over the wrists and ankles are recommended as easy to use and effective.

For hotel rooms, pyrethrum coils which burn slowly through the night and repel insects with their smoke are available all over Madagascar. The brand name is Big-Tox. They really do work. Plug-in repellents which work in a similar way are also effective.

Mosquito nets

Most Category A and B hotels either have effective screening or provide mosquito nets, but if you are staying in C hotels or travelling by overnight taxi-brousses (which may stop or break down) you should bring a mosquito net. Because most hotels do not have anything to hang a net from, a free-standing net is more practical (though a lot more expensive). They have a built-in groundsheet giving protection from bed bugs and fleas as well as mosquitoes. This means, however, that you must use your own sleeping bag inside it. You should also treat these nets with Permethrin, which kills bugs on contact.

A range of mosquito nets and other anti-bug devices, plus advice, can be had from Nomad Travel Store in London: tel: 020 8889 7014; email: sales@nomadtravel.co.uk; website: www.nomadtravel.co.uk.

Rough travel equipment

Basic camping gear gives you the freedom to travel adventurously and can add a considerable degree of comfort to overland journeys. Nomad (see above) sells an excellent range of adventure travel gear.

The most important item is your backpack: this should have an internal frame and plenty of pockets. Protect it from oil, dirt and the effluent of young or furry/feathered passengers with a cover. You can buy a commercially-made one or make your own: the plastic woven rice sacks sold in Madagascar markets are ideal for this purpose (bring a large needle and dental floss to do the final custom-fitting in Tana). For security consider bringing a lockable mesh backpack cover, such as Pacsafe, which is available in the UK; tel: 0116 234 0800.

In winter (June to August) a lightweight sleeping bag will keep you warm in cheap hotels with inadequate bedding, and on night stops on – or off – 'buses'. A sheet sleeping bag plus a light blanket (buy it in Tana) or space blanket are ideal for the summer months (October to May) and when the hotel linen may be missing or dirty.

An air-mattress or pillow pads your bum on hard seats as well as your hips when sleeping out. One of those horseshoe-shaped travel pillows lets you sleep sitting up (which you'll need to do on taxi-brousses).

A lightweight tent allows you to strike out on your own and stay in national parks, on deserted beaches and so forth. It will need to have a separate rain-fly and be well-ventilated.

Most people forgo a stove in order to cut down on weight, but if you will be camping extensively bring a stove that burns petrol (gasoline) or paraffin (kerosene). Meths (*alcohol à bruler*) is usually available as well. There are always fresh vegetables for sale in the smallest village so bring some stock cubes to make vegetable stew.

Take your own mug and spoon (and carry them with you always). That way you can enjoy roadside coffee without the risk of a cup rinsed in filthy water, and market yoghurt without someone else's germs on the spoon. Milk powder tastes (to most people) better in tea or coffee than condensed milk. You can buy it locally, or bring it from home. Don't forget a water-bottle. The sort that has a belt attached – or that can be attached to a belt – is ideal.

Give some thought to ways of interacting with the locals. A Malagasy phrase-book (best bought in Tana) provides lots of amusement as you practise your skills on fellow-passengers, and playing cards are universally understood.

A good book allows you to retreat from interaction for a while (but you won't be able to read on a taxi-brousse). Bring enough reading matter with you – English-language books are not easy to find in Madagascar. If you want to read at night, buy a 100-watt bulb (bayonet type) to substitute for the 40-watt one supplied by Category C hotels.

Photographic equipment

Ordinary print film is available in Madagascar, but it is safer to bring plenty. It can be competently developed in Tana, Fianarantsoa and Nosy Be. Slide film is harder to find. Bring twice as much film as you think you'll need.

You will not need a telephoto lens for the lemurs of Berenty and Nosy Komba (wide-angle is more useful for these bold animals) but you'll want a long lens plus very fast film (400 ASA) and a flash for most forest creatures. For landscapes 64 or 100 ASA is ideal. A macro lens is wonderful for all the weird insects and reptiles. Don't overburden yourself with camera equipment – there's no substitute for the eye/brain combination!

Miscellaneous

Bring a roll of insulating tape or gaffer tape which can be used for all manner of things. Blu-Tack is equally versatile; bring enough to make a plug for your sink, to stop doors banging or to hold them open. A Swiss Army knife (or similar) is essential. A rubber wedge will secure your hotel door at night, and a combination lock is useful in a variety of ways (see the section on safety, page 116). Many readers report (and I agree) that a small tape recorder/Walkman is a great asset during lone evenings in dingy hotel rooms or on an all-night taxi-brousse. Earplugs are just about essential, to block out not only the sounds of the towns but those of enthusiastic nocturnal animals when camping in reserves! (Personally I think it's worth being kept awake by these, but it can pall after several nights.) A large handkerchief or bandana has many uses and protects your hair and lungs from dust, and the uses for a *lamba* (Malagasy sarong) are too numerous to list.

Checklist

Small torch (flashlight) with spare batteries and bulb, or headlamp (for nocturnal animal hunts), travel alarm clock (or alarm wristwatch), penknife, sewing kit, scissors, tweezers, safety pins, insulating tape or Sellotape (Scotchtape), string, felt-tipped pen, ballpoint pens, a small notebook, a large notebook for diary and letters home, envelopes, plastic bags (all sizes, sturdy; Zip-loc are particularly useful), universal plug for baths and sinks (though Blu-Tack does the job just as well), elastic clothes line or cord and pegs, concentrated detergent, ear plugs, insect repellent, sunscreen, lipsalve, spare glasses or contact lenses, sunglasses, medical and dental kit (see *Chapter 5*), dental floss, a water bottle, water purifying tablets or other sterilising agent, compact binoculars, camera and film, books, miniature playing cards, Scrabble/pocket chess set, French dictionary and Malagasy phrasebook.

Goods for presents, sale or trade

This is a difficult area. In the past tourists have handed out presents to children and created the tiresome little beggars you will encounter in the popular areas (if you don't now know the French for pen or sweets, you soon will). They have also handed T-shirts to adults with similar consequences. There are, however, plenty of occasions when a gift is appropriate, although as Will Pepper points out 'On a number of occasions people said this souvenir of Ireland is all well and good but I would prefer cash'. Giving money in return for services is entirely acceptable so in rural areas it's best to pay cash and refrain from introducing a new consumer awareness.

In urban areas or with the more sophisticated Malagasy people, presents are a very good way of showing your appreciation for kindness or extra good service. Music cassettes often go down well with taxi-brousse drivers, but only pop music. It's worth bringing some duty-free cigarettes, however much you disapprove of smoking. It is probably the present most gratefully received.

If you want to contribute something a little more intellectually satisfying, here is a suggestion from Dr Philip Jones, who travels in Madagascar on behalf of the charity Money for Madagascar. 'I was asked several times for an English Grammar, so any such books would be valued gifts. If visitors take a French–English dictionary, why not leave it in Madagascar?' Frances Kerridge suggests English-language tapes as an alternative to books: 'Almost everyone seems to want to learn English.'

MONEY

How much money to take, and how to get emergency funds, is covered in *Chapter 6*, but give some thought to how to take it.

It is far easier to change cash (any hard currency) than travellers' cheques, so this is the best option if you are on a prepaid group tour. Be wary of bringing many US$100 bills – these are not always accepted because of the large number of counterfeit ones doing the rounds.

Most of the large hotels now accept credit cards, but there are some notable exceptions, such as the Dauphin in Taolagnaro. However, credit cards may be used to draw cash, but with restrictions. The Banque Malgache de l'Océan Indien accepts Visa cards only; the French for Visa card is Carte Bleue. There are a growing number of ATM machines which provide the most straight-forward way of getting cash using your debit card.

WAYS AND MEANS

I used to think (and write) that Madagascar was not for everyone; this is the point in the book where I wrote 'Are you sure you want to go?'. Now I've come to believe that everyone *can* enjoy Madagascar but not everyone does because they do not take sufficient care in matching the trip to their personality. When planning a holiday most people only consider their interests and how much they are prepared to spend. I feel that a vital component has been missed out.

What sort of person are you?

The Catch 22 of tourism in Madagascar is that the type of person who can afford the trip is often the type least suited to cope with the Malagasy way of life. In our culture assertiveness, a strong sense of right and wrong, and organisational skills are the personality traits which lead to success in business, and thus the income to finance exotic travel. But these 'A' type personalities often find Madagascar unbearably 'inefficient' and frustrating. By having control over their itinerary through a tailor-made tour, or by renting a vehicle and driver, such people are more likely to get the most out of their trip. A group tour, where they must 'go with the flow', may be the least successful option.

Conversely, the happiest travellers are often either those who choose to travel on a low budget (providing they're not obsessed with being ripped off) or those who can adopt the attitude of one elderly woman on a group tour who said 'I'm going to give up thinking; it doesn't work in Madagascar'. It doesn't, and she had a great time!

These days there is a trip to suit everyone in this extraordinary country. It won't be a cheap holiday, but it will be one you never forget so choose wisely. In the UK, travel consultant Seraphine Tierney, at Discover Madagascar, can help your planning. This Malagasy woman (and contributor to this book) has the advantage that she straddles the two cultures, and so understands expectations from both sides. Tel: 020 8 995 3529 or email: info@discovermadagascar.co.uk.

Below are the main options, in descending order of price and comfort.

The luxury package

The owners of Tsarabanjina (Nosy Be) and Anjajavy (north of Mahajanga) have ensured that holiday makers (such as honeymooners) looking for a trip-of-a-lifetime are shielded from Madagascar's efforts to introduce some surprises. International flights are met by a private plane which whisks passengers off to first a magnificent island surrounded by coral, and then to a beach resort and forest reserve, where there are lemurs as well as every activity imaginable. This is a well-rounded package (you visit small villages as well as wildlife) and well worth the expense. See pages 359 and 373 for details.

Expedition cruising

With ships you know that you will sleep in a comfortable bed each night and eat familiar food. It is thus ideal for the adventurous at heart who are no longer able to take the rigours of land travel. It is also sometimes the only way of getting to remote offshore islands and for snorkelling over some of the best reefs in the world. Since I accepted (without too much delay) an offer to lecture on the ships chartered by Noble Caledonia (UK) and Special Expeditions (US) I have become a convert – indeed, I've had some of my best Madagascar experiences ever from the *Caledonian Star* and the *Professor Khromov*. Contact Noble Caledonia Ltd, 11 Charles St, London W1X 7HB (tel: 020 7409 0376; www.noble-caledonia.co.uk) or Quark Expeditions, 980 Post Rd, Darien, CT 06820, USA (tel: 800 356 5699) or Lindblad Special Expeditions (tel: 800 397 3348). In South Africa try Starlight Cruises (tel: 011 884 7680 (Alan Foggitt)), and in Australia Adventure Associates (tel: 02 9389 7466).

Tailor-made tours

This is the ideal option for a couple or small group who are not restricted financially. It is also the best choice for people with special interests or who like things to run as smoothly as possible. You will be the decision-maker and will choose where you want to go and your preferred level of comfort, but the logistics will be taken care of.

You can organise your tailor-made trip through a tour operator in your home country, or approach some Malagasy tour operators. In these days of electronic communication when most people have email facilities, this is becoming an increasingly attractive option. Let the tour operator know your interests, the level of comfort you expect, and whether you want to cram in as much as possible or concentrate on just a few centres. Then compare prices and itineraries.

Tour operators which specialise in tailor-made tours in Madagascar are listed later in this chapter.

Special interests

It is easy for groups with a shared interest to have a tour organised for them with an expert leader and local guide. Some sample tours to consider are: fishing, diving, trekking, climbing, river journeys, sailing, mineralogy, speleology, birdwatching, herpetology, botany (which can be further split into orchids and succulents) and entomology. Specialist tour operators are included in the list below.

Group travel

Group travel is usually a lot of fun, ideal for single people who do not wish to travel alone, and if you choose the tour company and itinerary carefully you will see a great deal of the country, gain an understanding of its complicated culture and unique wildlife, and generally have a great time without the need to make decisions (but you need to be able to relinquish the decision-making; not everyone can do this).

Many of the listed tour operators in the UK and the USA do set departures (ie: group tours rather than tailor-made trips) to Madagascar.

TEENAGE TRAVEL IN MADAGASCAR

I have had some very adventurous correspondents in their late teens, travelling in Madagascar as part of their gap year. Reading 19-year-old Marko Petrivic's accounts of his travels in the southeast leaves no doubt about the possibilities for genuine exploration in this huge island.

My youngest correspondent, 14-year-old Clare Graham and nine others from her school, took part in a World Challenge expedition to Madagascar. This involved some long treks, arduous taxi-brousse rides, and work on a community project. This is her account, from the perspective of a school girl.

We spent four amazing weeks in Madagascar, each day different and new and providing us with memories which will stay with us for a long, long time. I am lucky that I grabbed the opportunity when I am still young enough for my experiences in Madagascar to maybe change or shape my opinions on things. One example of this is when we stayed at Ambalavao for a week, when we were doing our project phase. We spent a week cutting a field full of mulberry trees for an organisation called CCD Namana. The organisation helps the local community by teaching women how to weave and sew silk, so that they can start bringing in some income for themselves and family. The mulberry trees were planted to feed the silkworms on the farm they had built there. During the week we hardly interacted or even saw any locals and by the end of the week were starting to get a bit disheartened as to whether we were doing anything useful. On the last day, however, we were treated to a nice guided tour by one of the employees of the organisation. He explained what we were doing to help, and the purposes of the organisation. After the talk, I finally realised that we were doing something helpful. Albeit very indirectly, we were helping to put something back into Madagascar. Whenever I now see an article in a newspaper or a magazine about someone who has done 'community work' in a foreign country, it doesn't seem far off, and I can relate to it. It brings back memories.

Another aspect of Madagascar that I will not forget is the transport and travel! It makes me feel extremely lucky that I can just pop into my mum and dad's car whenever I want. Fortunately, we only had one breakdown on our expedition, but the state of the roads there is also quite an experience! Until then I didn't really realise how true people's accounts of them were!

Working holidays

There is a growing interest in paying to be a volunteer in a scientific or community project in Madagascar. The pioneer here is **Earthwatch**. Among other things in Madagascar you can work with Dr Alison Jolly on lemur research. Addresses: Belsyne Court, 57 Woodstock Rd, Oxford OX2 6HU, England; tel: 01865 311600; and PO Box 9104, Watertown, MA 02272-9104, USA; tel (800) 776 0188; email: info@earthwatch.org. A similar organisation for students is **World Challenge Expeditions**, Black Arrow House, 2 Chandos Rd, London NW10 6NF; tel: 020 8961 1122; fax: 020 8961 1551; email: welcome@world-challenge.co.uk. **Frontier**, 50-52 Rivington St, London EC2A 3QP; tel: 020 7613 2422 takes paying volunteers for their marine research programmes. More from their website www.frontierprojects.ac.uk. **Pioneer Madagascar** is the new volunteering scheme of Azafady (see page 145); tel: 020 8960 6629; website: www.madagascar.co.uk. The ten week scheme is run four times a year, with volunteers working on conservation and community projects.

SOME DAYS IN THE LIFE OF A WILDLIFE RESEARCHER

Frances Kerridge (Frankie Be) worked for several years in the southeast of Madagascar, studying carnivores with the organisation MICET. Her letters from the field were a regular source of entertainment. Here are some extracts.

It took nearly two weeks to get from Tana to Vevembe. The vehicle broke down and we were stuck for two days in torrential rain. My fruit and veg started rotting, all the cardboard boxes full of food dissolved, rice and coffee went mouldy, and beans and peanuts started sprouting... Then the river we had to ford was too high for the (mended) car so I had to pay porters to carry everything – traps and other research equipment, tents, tarps, all the kitchen stuff, three months' supply of food etc – the rest of the way. Cost a bloody fortune but we're there. Rosette gets on with her mapping and the student and I get down to the radio-tracking. Then the student breaks his antenna, gets water in his receiver and tells me he really can't do the work, it's too hard and he will be ill. Back to Tana while I search for another student. Another highlight was my guide getting a leech on his eyeball. Mega shouting and screaming, and I thought the student was going to faint. Got it off by killing it (slowly) with a tobacco leaf.

[After setting my tent on fire] I stayed in the guide's tent overnight. This was indeed an experience and not one I wish to repeat ever. Iato lit the candle every 15 minutes to see what time it was (as he has to get up first to start cooking breakfast) but as he can't tell the time he had to wake Baby to read the watch. Zaman'dory got up every 15 minutes to go for a pee and Baby alternatively ground his teeth and talked in his sleep. I was very relieved when the night was over...

The next drama involved Baby, who was complaining of toothache – I got a shock when I looked inside his mouth – one tooth had a massive hole in it, another was just a splintered fragment and there were quite a few missing (remember he is only 22). I walked down to Vondrozo with him (25km) to see if the hospital would pull his tooth out, there being no dentist there. However they were not very helpful so I arranged for him to go to Farafangana with me. This was to be his first trip beyond Vondrozo and his first sight of the sea, which he found suitably impressive; in fact he lost the power of speech for quite a while.

Zely's wife gave birth to their sixth offspring – a messenger arrived to say she was in labour and I sent down a knitted baby jacket and some sardines and chocolate to sustain her through the ordeal. When Zely returned from paternity leave he said we should choose his new son's name. I tried to make something suitable from our initials but the best I could manage was Frisbe, so we all chose a name and put them in a hat. Zely chose mine which was 'Faly' which means happy in Malagasy. It could have been much worse – we had run out of glue and a guide was going to Vondrozo to do some shopping. I had written down 'Araldite' on a piece of paper and somehow that got into the hat!

Semi-independent travel

If you have a fax machine or email and are willing to persevere with Madagascar's erratic telecommunications (which are rapidly improving), you can save money by dealing directly with a tour operator in Madagascar. The best ones are listed later in this chapter. The level of satisfaction in arranging a tour this way is very high. Now tourism is established in Madagascar, local operators have a clear understanding of tourists' needs and are impressively efficient. Of course things go wrong (and if they do there is no point in suing) but the cause is usually poor infrastructure rather than incompetence.

Perhaps the ideal do-it-yourself trip is to hire a local driver/guide and vehicle when you arrive in Tana. This way you are wonderfully free to stop when you please and stay where you wish. If you want to get fixed up before leaving home, try Claude Rambeloson who is personable, fun and has his own 4WD vehicle. Claude speaks excellent English and German, is knowledgeable on a wide range of subjects, and an expert on orchids. He can be contacted on BP 1223, Antananarivo 101; tel/fax: (261 20) 22 54 166; cellphone: (261) 3204 13 630; email: madamonde@simicro.mg.

Independent travel

Truly independent travellers usually have a rough idea of where they want to go and how they will travel, but are open to changes of plan dictated by local conditions, whim and serendipity. Independent travellers are not necessarily budget travellers: those who can afford to fly to major towns, then rent a vehicle and driver, can eliminate a large amount of hassle and see everything they set out to see – providing they set a realistic programme for themselves. What they may miss out on is contact with the local people, and some of the smells, sounds and otherness of Madagascar.

The majority of independent travellers use public transport and stay in B or C Category hotels. They are exposed to all Madagascar's joys and frustrations and most seem to love it, even if they agree that they have never travelled in a country that is so difficult to get around in (though this is changing – the popular circuits are usually pretty trouble-free). The key here is not to try too much. *Chapter 6* tells you about the trials and tribulations of travelling by taxi-brousse: no problem providing you allow time for delays.

The seriously adventurous

Madagascar must be one of the very few countries left in the world where large areas are not yet detailed in a guidebook. A study of the standard 1:2,000,000 map of Madagascar reveals some mouth-watering possibilities, and a look at the more detailed 1:500,000 maps confirms the opportunities for people who are willing to walk or cycle. In my very thick Readers' Letters file I have some wonderful accounts from travellers who did just that. Not everyone is courageous enough to step or pedal into the unknown like this, but in fact it's one of the safest ways to travel: the Malagasy that you meet will, once they have got over the shock of seeing you, invariably be welcoming and hospitable (see box on page 384). The risk of crime is very low.

It's how I first saw Madagascar and why I fell in love with the place.

Travelling alone

The particular problems facing solo men or women travellers are covered on pages 119–20, but if you choose to travel alone, be prepared for the long evenings. Robert Bowker found nights at national parks particularly lonely: 'Dinner is early, and after that nothing to do but go to your bungalow. Take a powerful torch and lots to read. I got through a fair number of crossword puzzles. Also take music…'. For budding writers evenings alone are the perfect time to develop your diary skills. You can buy exercise books in Madagascar for this purpose.

Tour operators
UK

The internet is the ideal way of finding out the best tour operator for your purposes. ATTA (African Travel and Tourism Association) has a comprehensive listing for Madagascar, separated into different interests; www.ATTA.co.uk. Safarilink (www.safarilink.com) has a listing of Madagascar specialists. Responsibletravel.com promotes ethical tour operators.

Here are the ones I know about:

Aardvark Safaris Tel: 01980 849160; fax: 01980 849161; email: mail@aardvarksafaris.com; web: www.aardvarksafaris.com. Tailor-made tours for couples or private groups.

Abercrombie and Kent Travel Tel: 0845 0700611; email: info@abercrombiekent.co.uk; web: www.abercrombiekent.co.uk. Escorted wildlife tours.

ACE Study Tours Tel: 01223 835055; fax: 01223 837394; email: ace@study-tours.org. Occasional Madagascar trips.

Africa Exclusive Tel: 01604 628979; fax: 01604 639879; email: africa@africaexclusive.co.uk. Tailor-made trips.

Africa Travel Centre Tel: 0207 387 1211; fax: 0207 383 7512; email: info@africatravel.co.uk; web: www.africatravel.co.uk. Flights and tailor-made holidays.

Alpha Holidays Tel: 020 7793 1667; fax: 020 7793 1985; email: alphaholidays@clara.co.uk

Animal Watch Tel: 01732 811838; fax: 01732 455441; email: mail@animalwatch.co.uk. Regular wildlife trips to Madagascar.

Arc Journeys Tel: 020 7681 3175 (24hr phone and fax line); cellphone: 0370 986653; email: arc@travelarc.com. Tailor-made cultural and nature tours.

Cox & Kings Travel Tel: 020 7873 5000; fax: 020 7630 6038; email: Cox.Kings@coxandkings.co.uk. Dedicated group departures and tailor-made itineraries.

Crusader Travel Tel: 020 8744 0474; fax: 020 8744 0574; email: info@crusadertravel.com. Includes diving trips.

David Sayers Travel Tel: 01572 821330; fax: 01572 821072; email: ABROCK3650@aol.com. Regular trips to Madagascar with a botanical angle. All tours are escorted by David Sayers.

Discover the World Ltd Tel: 01737 218800; fax: 01737 362341; email: sales@arctic-discover.co.uk. Regular trips to Madagascar; no special focus.

Earthwatch Tel: 01865 311600; fax: 01865 311383; email: info@uk.earthwatch.org. Several trips focus on Madagascar (wildlife). See *Working holidays*, page 95.

Explore Worldwide Ltd Tel: 01252 319448; fax: 01252 319100; email: res@explore.co.uk. Regular Madagascar trips; no special focus.

Footloose Adventure Travel Tel: 01943 604030; fax: 01943 604070; email: footrv@globalnet.co.uk; web: www.footlooseadventure.co.uk.

Naturetrek Tel: 01962 733051; fax: 01962 736426; email: info@naturetrek.co.uk. Special focus: birds and mammals.

Ocean Marketing Tel: 023 9238 6401; fax: 023 9238 6402; email: info@oceanmarketing.co.uk. Agents for Tropic Tours and Travel in Madagascar.

Okavango Tours & Safaris Tel: 020 8343 3283; fax: 020 8343 3287; email: jane@okavango.com; web: www.okavango.com.

Papyrus Tours Tel: 01302 371321. Small group wildlife tours.

Partnership Travel Tel: 020 8343 3446; fax: 020 8349 3439; email: info@partnershiptravel.co.uk.

Rainbow Tours Tel: 020 7226 1004; fax: 020 7226 2621; email: info@rainbowtours.co.uk. Tailor-made and small group tours with an emphasis on wildlife, birds, and community tourism. They are the UK agents for **Madventures**, organised by Feedback Madagascar (see page 148), where local fishermen take tourists in outrigger canoes up the west coast.

Reef & Rainforest Tours Tel: 01803 866965; fax: 01803 865916; email: reefrain@btinternet.com. Specialists in Madagascar with a wide variety of tours.

Safari Consultants Tel: 01787 228494; fax: 01787 228096; email: bill@safariconsultantuk.com; web: www.safari-consultants.co.uk. Tailor-made tours.

Scott Dunn World Tel: 020 8682 5010; fax: 020 8767 2026; email: world@scottdunn.com; www.scottdunn.com.

Steppes Africa Tel: 01285 650011; fax: 01285 885888; email: info@steppesafrica.co.uk; web: www.steppesafrica.co.uk.

Sunbird Tel: 01767 682969; fax: 01767 692481; email: sunbird@sunbird.demon.co.uk. Regular Madagascar birding trips.

Tim Best Travel Tel: 020 7591 0300; fax: 020 7591 0301; email: info@timbesttravel.com; web: www.timbesttravel.com. Tailor-made tours (especially wildlife and birds).

Wildlife Worldwide Tel: 020 8667 9158; fax: 020 8667 1960; email: jo@wildlifeworldwide.com; web: www.wildlifeworldwide.com.

Worldwide Adventures Abroad Tel: 0114 247 3400; fax: 0114 251 3210; email: abroad@globalnet.co.uk; web: www.adventures-abroad.com.

Worldwide Journeys & Expeditions Tel: 020 7386 4646; fax: 020 7381 0836; email: enquiry@worldwidejourneys.co.uk. Tailor-made trips, and guided tours led by naturalist Nick Garbutt.

USA

Blue Chameleon PO Box 643, Alva, FL 33920, USA; tel: +1 941 728 2390; fax: +1 941 728 3276; email: Bill@bluechameleon.org; www.bluechameleon.org

Cortez Travel Services 124 Lomas Santa Fe Dr, Solano Beach, CA 92075; tel: 619 755 5136 or 800 854 1029; fax: 619 481 7474; email: cortez-usa@mcimail.com. Cortez is the specialist Madagascar operator in the US; Monique Rodriguez has been running trips there for nearly two decades and knows the practicalities better than anyone else in the travel business. She is agent for Air Madagascar and Honorary Consul.

Field Guides Incorporated 9433 Bee Cave Rd, bldg. 1, Ste. 150, Austin, Texas; tel: 512 263 7295 or 800 728 4953; email: fieldguides@fieldguides.com; web: www.fieldguides.com. Birding tours.

Mountain Travel-Sobek 6420 Fairmount Ave, El Cerrito, CA; tel: 888 687 6235; email: info@mtsobek.com.

Remote River Expeditions PO Box 299, Fort Collins, CO 80522; tel: 800 558 1083; fax: 303 239 6065; email: Gary@remoterivers.com; web: www.remoterivers.com.

Australia

Adventure Associates Pty Ltd 197 Oxford St Mall, Bondi Junction, Sydney, NSW 2022 (PO Box 612, Bondi Junction, NSW 1355); tel: 02 9389 7466; fax: 02 9369 1853; email: mail@adventureassociates.com; web: www.adventureassociates.com. They are the only tour operator in Australia with regular Madagascar departures.

South Africa

Falcon African Safaris (Pty) Ltd PO Box 3490, Randburg, 2125; tel: 011 886 1981; fax: 011 886 1778; email: nicci@falcon-africa.co.za; web: www.falcon-africa.co.za. 10 years experience of running trips into Madagascar.

Unusual Destinations PO Box 97508, Petervale 2151 Gauteng, SA; tel: 011 706 1991; fax 011 463 1469; email: info@unusualdestinations.com; web: www.unusualdestinations.com. The SA experts in Madagascar. Very helpful and knowledgeable. Regular group departures and specialist natural history trips.

CAVING

Madagascar has some fabulous caves, and several expeditions have been mounted to explore them. Caving is not a popular Malagasy pursuit, however, so cavers should take particular care to explain what they are doing and get the necessary permits for exploring protected areas. An experienced local tour operator will help with the red tape.

The best karst areas are in the north and west, as follows.

Ankarana Known for its *tsingy*, this is the best explored and mapped of all karst areas.

Narinda The longest cave, Anjohibe, is 5,330m.

Namoroka Access difficult and safety a problem in this area.

Bemaraha Excellent possibilities for exploration now this *tsingy* area is being opened up to tourism.

Toliara region Mickoboka Plateau to the north has pits to a depth of 165m, and the Mahafaly Plateau to the south contains numerous small caves.

Wildlife Adventures Tel: 021 461 2235; fax: 021 461 2068; email: wildlady@mweb.co.za; web: www.wladventures.com. Tours and tailor-made trips.

Madagascar

There are many tour operators in Madagascar. This is by no means a complete list, just a selection of those that I can recommend. For a complete list of accredited tour operators (member of TOP – Tours Opérateurs Professionnels) contact TOP: tel/fax: 22 665 82 or 22 788 59; email: topmad@dts.mg.

The full telephone code for Tana is (261 20) 22 followed by the number.

Boogie Pilgrim Villa Michelet, Lot A11, Faravohitra, Antananarivo; tel: 258 78; fax: 625 56; email: bopi@dts.mg. Organise tours of every sort, including some by light aircraft. Owners of Bush House (Pangalanes). Recommended.

Cortez Expeditions 25 Rue Ny Zafindraindiky, Antanimena, Antananarivo; tel: 219 74; fax: 247 87; email: cortez@dts.mg. Probably the most experienced tour operator in Madagascar and owner of the Relais du Masoala in Maroantsetra.

Mad Caméléon Lot II K6, Ankadivato, Antananarivo; BP 4336; tel: 630 86; fax: 344 20; email: madcam@dts.mg. Specialise in river trips and are the only operator to offer the Manambolo river.

Madagascar Airtours 33 Av de l'Indépendance, Antananarivo; BP 3874; tel: 241 92; fax: 641 90. Also at the Hilton Hotel. The most experienced agency, with offices in most major towns, they can organise a wide variety of specialist tours including natural history, ornithology, speleology, trekking, mineralogy, river trips, sailing, etc.

Madagascar Discovery BP 3597, Antananarivo; tel: 351 65; fax: 351 67; email: mda@dts.mg; web: www.madagascar-contacts.com/mda.

Malagasy Tours Lot VX29, Avaradrova, Antananarivo; tel/fax: 356 07. The owner, Olivier Toboul, runs specialised itineraries for ethnobotany (amongst other things) using local people who can explain the complexities of the Malagasy culture. Good for off-the-beaten-track exploration, too.

Rova Travel Tours 35 Rue Refotaka, Analakely; tel: 276 67; fax: 276 89; email: rtt@bow.dts.mg.

SETAM 56, Av du 26 Juin 1960, Analakely, Antananarivo; tel: 324 31 or 324 33; cellphone:

032 07 324 33 or 032 07 243 73; fax: 324 35 or 347 02; email: setam@dts.mg. Very helpful and efficient. Recommended.

Transcontinents 10 Av de l'Indépendance, Antananarivo; BP 551; tel: 223 98; fax: 283 65; email: transco@dts.mg. Efficiently run. Recommended.

Tropic Tours and Travel 30, Rue de Russie, Isoraka, Antananarivo; BP 8019; tel: 645 16; fax: 645 17; email: tropic@bow.dts.mg.

Tropika Touring 41 Rue Ratsimilaho; BP 465; tel: 222 30 or 276 80; fax: 349 01; email: tropica@dts.mg.

Za Tour Lot ID 33 Bis, Ambohitsorohitra, Antananarivo 101; tel: 656 48; fax: 656 47; email: za.tour@dts.mg. Highly recommended.

HIGHLIGHTS AND ITINERARIES

Having sorted out the 'hows' of travelling in Madagascar you must turn your attention to the all-important subject of 'where'. One of the hardest decisions facing the first-time visitor to a country as large and diverse as Madagascar is where to go. Even a month is not long enough to see everything, so itineraries must be planned according to interests and the degree of comfort wanted. First, the highlights, according to interests.

Highlights
Wildlife

The best reserves and national parks (starting from the north and going clockwise) are: Montagne d'Ambre, Ankarana, Masoala, Nosy Mangabe, Andasibe-Mantadia (Périnet), Ranomafana, Berenty, Kirindy, Ampijoroa. Others, for enthusiasts, are Marojejy, Andohahela and Tsingy de Bemaraha.

Scenery

The central highlands between Fianarantsoa and Ambalavao, Andringitra, Isalo and Andohahela National Parks, Avenue of the Baobabs (Morondava), Ankarana, Montagne d'Ambre.

Beaches and watersports

Madagascar's best beaches are on the west coast, but many people are disappointed because of the shallow water (it is often impossible to swim at low tide). The beautiful beaches of the east coast are for sunbathing only – sharks

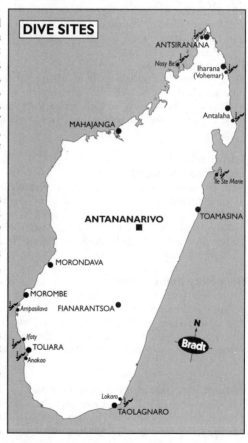

are a danger to swimmers. The very best beaches are in remote areas such as Anjajavy, islands around Nosy Be, Ile Sainte Marie and south of Toliara.

Diving and snorkelling have become much more organised in recent years, hence the extra coverage in this edition. The main centres are Nosy Be, Ile Sainte Marie, Toliara (Ifaty), and hotels specialising in diving down the west coast (see map on page 102). Taolagnaro (Fort Dauphin) is a new centre. Lists of diving centres are given in each relevant chapter: check the index.

Surfing is a growing sport in the Taolagnaro (Fort Dauphin) area and in some places in the southwest.

Sport fishing can be organised from Nosy Be.

Fun times
The people of southern Madagascar are the most outgoing on the island, with good discos in Taolagnaro and Toliara, but Nosy Be (and specifically Ambataloaka) is undoubtedly where the action is for tourists.

Museums
Madagascar has only a few good museums so it is worth listing them here. The best by far – really super! – is the Museum of the Antandroy in Berenty Reserve. Toliara has a good ethnological museum (and you can see a coelacanth at its marine museum). The Museum of Art and Archaeology in Antananarivo is nicely laid out and interesting, as is the Museum Akiba in Mahajanga. The only natural history museum that I am aware of is in Tsimbazaza in Tana.

People and tombs
Your tour operator may be able to organise a visit to a *famadihana* (only in the highlands and only between June and September). An unforgettable experience. Merina tombs can easily be seen between Antananarivo and Antsirabe, but the most intriguing and interesting tombs are those of the Mahafaly in the Toliara region.

Itineraries
Luxurious Madagascar
The opening of several top-class hotels in recent years means that it is now possible to see the highlights of Madagascar in style. The following hotels are in the very good to luxury class: Anjajavy and Tsarabanjina (secluded beach resorts), Relais de la Reine (Isalo National Park), Centerest (Ranomafana National Park), Vakôna Lodge (Andasibe-Mantadia/Périnet), Relais de Masoala (Maroantsetra) and Cocoterie Robert (Ile Sainte Marie).

Reliability and comfort
An itinerary which includes the following will provide a good overview of the country and its wildlife, with hotels of international standard: Antananarivo, Andasibe-Mantadia (Périnet), Antsirabe, Toliara, Taolagnaro (Fort Dauphin) and Berenty, and Nosy Be or Ile Sainte Marie. The stretches between Antananarivo and Antsirabe should be done by taxi or private car, and the rest by plane.

Nature reserves in moderate comfort
These are accessible by good road and have good-to-moderate accommodation: Ranomafana, Ampijoroa (as a day trip from Mahajanga), Montagne d'Ambre (as a day trip from Antsiranana), Mandena and Berenty.

Camping only reserves

Some of the following can be visited as a day trip, but you will miss the best animal viewing times of dawn and dusk: Kirindy, Tsingy de Bemaraha, Ampijoroa, Ankarana, Marojejy, Masoala, Nosy Mangabe, Andohahela and Beza Mahafaly.

Birding

See pages 58–9 for full details on the best birding places, but these cover all the different habitats: Ampijoroa (and along the road from Mahajanga), Ranomafana, Marojejy, Masoala, Andohahela or Ifaty (spiny forest), and Zombitse.

Here's a special place for birders: a hotel/restaurant in Tana, the Tonga Soa (see page 164), is planning to become a birding centre. Nick Garbutt reports: 'Brian Finch, the owner's brother, is a well-known birding tour leader (what else could he do with a name like his?) in Madagascar and both he and Patrick are keen to establish Tonga Soa as a place for the exchange of up-to-date information about wildlife. Their intention is to establish a small reference library relating to Malagasy natural history and have a visitor's book that anyone can contribute too as they pass through Tana and say what's been seen where and when. Others looking in may then be able to take advantage of such recent news.'

Landscape, people and tombs

For those whose interest lies more in the people and the countryside, a journey overland is recommended. RN7 from Antananarivo to Toliara gives a wonderful overview from rice-paddies in the highlands to the magnificent granite mountains of Andringitra, and the small villages between Ihosy and Toliara. It also gives you a chance to see Isalo National Park. The journey is best done in a private vehicle so you can stop and look; there are good hotels in the main towns.

A more adventurous alternative (but still on a good road) is by plane or bus to Toamasina then north by public transport to Soanierana-Ivongo and by boat to Ile Sainte Marie.

Mountain biking

Madagascar is becoming increasingly popular for travelling using your own muscle-power. The advantages are obvious: bad roads and broken down vehicles do not delay you, con-men will not overcharge you and – most important – by passing slowly through Madagascar's small villages and communities you will experience the Malagasy culture in an unforced way. These advantages far outweigh the inevitable security risks of being totally at the mercy of local people. You are far more likely to be overwhelmed by hospitality than robbed.

Mountain biking is covered in detail under *Transport,* pages 128–9.

DISTANCES FROM TANA IN KILOMETRES

Antananarivo–Ambositra	330km
Antananarivo–Antsirabe	170km
Antananarivo–Fianarantsoa	408km
Antananarivo–Mahajanga	572km
Antananarivo–Morondava	665km
Antananarivo–Perinet	142km
Antananarivo–Toamasina	365km
Antananarivo–Toliara	941km

Trekking

At long last there is organised trekking in the mountains of Madagascar! For decades I've looked longingly at the rugged landscape around Fianarantsoa and wanted to hike there. Now, with the opening of Andringitra National Park, the country's second highest mountain is open for climbers (non-technical, but strenuous) and a series of hiking trails range from gentle to tough. Andringitra seems to have inspired other areas to follow suit, and ANGAP is developing some two- or three-day treks at Ranomafana National Park. Then there's Isalo National Park which has some wonderful treks through the sandstone outcrops and canyons.

The leader in trekking organisation is the Tsara Guest House in Fianarantsoa. They will arrange a complete package for you in the region.

If you want to strike out on your own, the 'road' that runs down the east coast is just about perfect for a combination of walking and hitchhiking. In places it carries little or no traffic, yet is sufficiently populated that you will never be lost (for long) and can be sure of being able to buy food.

Climbing and paragliding

The granite rocks of the Andringitra area have always looked to me ideal for climbing and there is now a base for climbers and paragliders at Camp Catta, owned by Hotel Cotsoyannis in Fianarantsoa.

Working in Madagascar

Many tourists, having fallen in love with Madagascar, want to return to work. A few achieve it, but only after much perseverance. Madagascar does not have enough jobs for its own citizens, so only welcomes outsiders who have specialised skills. This also applies to volunteers. Adela Stockton, who worked in Madagascar as a midwife, gives this advice: 'White people are rarely seen outside the main cities. Many Malagasy are actively afraid of them and in some areas there are people who have never seen a white person. In the light of this the role of the Western volunteer worker is a sensitive one. If you are professionally skilled in your field of expertise and have a good working knowledge of French, your pair of hands may be useful in certain circumstances. I would suggest you approach specific organisations appropriate to the skills you offer, either in your own country or when in Madagascar. Be prepared to prove your qualifications and expertise and to adapt your skills to local practice rather than imagine that you know best. Remember, the Malagasy may prefer to place their trust in their own people.'

Many people fondly visualise a job working in conservation but this is very difficult to achieve unless you are already skilled in this area. It is probably best to start by being a paying volunteer through the organisations which sponsor such holidays.

Finally...

Remember that you are in Madagascar to enjoy yourself. Here's a comment from a traveller who did the unthinkable: spent eight days in Ranomafana without entering the national park.

> Now I will make my confession: I never actually went into the park itself!
> ... I'm not that keen on lemurs anyway – they look like half monkeys and
> half cat and I don't much like either animal. I absolutely love the thermal
> baths, though!

Good for Sarah for knowing what she wants and doesn't want to do!

Health and Safety

5

HEALTH
Dr Jane Wilson-Howarth
Before you go
Malaria prevention
Malaria (including cerebral malaria) is a risk in Madagascar and it is important to protect yourself by avoiding bites between dusk and dawn and also by taking tablets. There is some chloroquine resistance so Mefloquine (Lariam) taken weekly is probably the best prophylactic if it suits you. It is only available on prescription and would cost about £25 for a two-week trip. Perhaps around one quarter of people who try this tablet will experience unacceptable side effects, so take it for two and a half weeks (three doses) before departure and if it makes you feel weird or gives you nightmares stop it and take another regime. Malarone, a once a day preparation, is a new alternative although this is only presently licensed for use for up to 28 days and it is by far the most expensive prophylactic: it will cost you about £90 for a two-week trip. Another good alternative, although unsuitable in pregnancy, while breast-feeding or in children under 12, is Doxycycline capsules daily (at around £28 on prescription). Take advice from a travel clinic, your GP or the website www.fitfortravel.scot.nhs.uk.

All prophylactics are best taken after food (or milk or biscuits); nausea is more likely if they are taken on an empty stomach. If pregnant or planning a pregnancy take medical advice before travelling. Some travellers like to carry tablets for the emergency treatment of malaria; if you choose to do this make sure you understand when and how to take them. Pack a non-mercury thermometer.

Take plenty of insect repellent (DEET-based are best), long-sleeved shirts, long trousers, and consider carrying a mosquito net (see page 00). Nets are most effective if treated with Permethrin or a similar contact insecticide. Kits are sold at many travel clinics and the impregnation remains effective for six months.

Immunisations
Seek advice about immunisations a couple of months before travel; in the UK you can see your GP or visit a travel clinic such as those operated by MASTA (phone 01276 685040 for the nearest clinic); they offer constantly updated health briefs as well as immunisations. It's important that your immunisations for tetanus, polio and typhoid are up to date. Highly effective vaccines against hepatitis A are recommended for those travelling for several months. Two shots provide protection for ten years.

'Ordinary' intramuscular shots against rabies are now available and may be worth arranging if you are travelling in remote areas. The disease is a problem in Madagascar because of the half-wild dogs found in many parts of the island. Remember that 'live' vaccines cannot be given within a fortnight of each other, so plan well ahead. There is a list of vaccination centres at the end of this section.

LONG-HAUL FLIGHTS
Dr Felicity Nicholson

There is growing evidence, albeit circumstantial, that long-haul air travel increases the risk of developing deep vein thrombosis. This condition is potentially life threatening, but it should be stressed that the danger to the average traveller is slight.

Certain risk factors specific to air travel have been identified. These include immobility, compression of the veins at the back of the knee by the edge of the seat, the decreased air pressure and slightly reduced oxygen in the cabin, and dehydration. Consuming alcohol may exacerbate the situation by increasing fluid loss and encouraging immobility.

In theory everyone is at risk, but those at highest risk are shown below:

- Passengers on journeys of longer than eight hours duration
- People over 40
- People with heart disease
- People with cancer
- People with clotting disorders
- People who have had recent surgery, especially on the legs
- Women who are pregnant, or on the pill or other oestrogen therapy
- People who are very tall (over 6ft/1.8m) or short (under 5ft/1.5m)

A deep vein thrombosis (DVT) is a clot of blood that forms in the leg veins. Symptoms include swelling and pain in the calf or thigh. The skin may feel hot to touch and becomes discoloured (light blue-red). A DVT is not dangerous in

Teeth
Have a dental check-up before you go and if you have a lot of fillings and crowns carry a Dental Emergency Kit (from some pharmacies or ask your dentist).

Insurance
Make sure you have insurance covering the cost of an air ambulance and treatment in Réunion or Nairobi, which offer more sophisticated medical facilities than are available in Madagascar. Europ Assistance International, which has an office in Antananarivo, gives cover for scuba-diving.

Water sterilisation
Bringing water to the boil kills all the microbes that are likely to make you ill on your travels so tea, coffee or *ranovola* (the water rice is boiled in) bought in *hotelys* are probably the most convenient safe drinks. If travelling with small children you can take a thermos flask; almost-boiling water kept in this for 15 minutes will be thoroughly sterilised. Mineral water is not always available and can be quite expensive, and studies in other countries suggest it may be contaminated. Chemical sterilisation methods do not render water as safe as by boiling, but it is good enough for most purposes. The cheapest and most effective sterilising agent is iodine (preferable to chlorine and silver because it kills amoebic cysts), which is available in liquid or tablet form. To make treated water more palatable, add vitamin C after the sterilisation time is complete or bring packets of powdered drink. Silver-based sterilising tablets (sold in Britain under the trade name Micropur) are tasteless and have a long shelf life but are less effective than both iodine and chlorine products. An alternative is a water filter such as the Pur system,

itself, but if a clot breaks down then it may travel to the lungs (pulmonary embolus). Symptoms of a pulmonary embolus (PE) include chest pain, shortness of breath and coughing up small amounts of blood.

Symptoms of a DVT rarely occur during the flight, and typically occur within three days of arrival, although symptoms of a DVT or PE have been reported up to two weeks later.

Anyone who suspects that they have these symptoms should see a doctor immediately as anticoagulation (blood thinning) treatment can be given.

Prevention of DVT

General measures to reduce the risk of thrombosis are shown below. This advice also applies to long train or bus journeys.

- Whilst waiting to board the plane, try to walk around rather than sit.
- During the flight drink plenty of water (at least two small glasses every hour).
- Avoid excessive tea, coffee and alcohol.
- Perform leg-stretching exercises, such as pointing the toes up and down.
- Move around the cabin when practicable.

If you fit into the high-risk category (see above) ask your doctor if it is safe to travel. Additional protective measures such as graded compression stockings, aspirin or low molecular weight heparin can be given. No matter how tall you are, where possible request a seat with extra legroom.

or Aqua-pure Traveller, which provide safe water with no unpleasant flavour; they are expensive, however. Cheaper and more versatile, is a plug-in immersion heater, so that you can have a nice hot cuppa (if you bring teabags).

Note that most travellers acquire diarrhoea from inadequately cooked, or reheated, contaminated food – salads, ice, ice-cream etc – rather than from disobeying the 'don't drink the water' rule.

Some travellers' diseases
Malaria and insect-borne diseases

Tablets do not give complete protection from malaria, though they will make it less serious if it does break through; it's important to protect yourself from being bitten. The mosquitoes that give you malaria usually bite in the evening (from about 17.00) and throughout the night, so it's wise to dress in long trousers and long-sleeved shirts, and to cover exposed skin with insect repellent. *Anopheles* mosquitoes generally hunt at ankle level, and tend to bite the first piece of exposed flesh they encounter, so DEET-impregnated ankle bands are fairly effective in reducing bites. In most countries, malaria transmission is rare in urban environments, but it does occur around Antananarivo because ricefields are so close to the city. Most hotels have screened windows or provide mosquito nets. Bring your own net if staying in cheap hotels. Burning mosquito coils reduces but does not eliminate the risk of bites.

Be sure to take your malaria tablets meticulously for the requisite time after you get home. Even if you have been taking your malaria prophylaxis carefully, there is still a slight chance of contracting malaria. The symptoms are fevers, chills, joint pain, headache and sometimes diarrhoea – in other words the symptoms of many illnesses including flu. Bear in mind that malaria can take as little as seven days to

TRADITIONAL HEALING AND ETHNOBOTANY IN MADAGASCAR

Samantha Cameron

The author is a volunteer for the NGO Feedback Madagascar, and is co-ordinator of their health programme in the Fianarantsoa region. She recently led an RGS-supported expedition researching ethnobotanical knowledge in an area bordering the rainforest, and hopes that findings can be used to ease collaboration and understanding between traditional healers and the medical establishment, in the same way as is being done with traditional birth attendants.

Anyone interested in borrowing an extensive photo exhibition, complete with captions, about village life in Madagascar, should write to: samcam77@hotmail.com.

Faced with environmental degradation and increasing exposure to western medicine, there are many people who fear for the future of ethnobotanical knowledge. However, recent research in rural southeast Madagascar found that traditional healing practices continue to be widespread and that, although older people generally have more faith in them, the younger generation are also very knowledgeable about traditional remedies.

In this area of Madagascar, access to western medicine is almost irrelevant to the use of traditional remedies. Villagers living far from the hospital do not necessarily use less western medicine, or more traditional medicine, since most people go to the weekly market, near to the hospital, or are able to send someone in their place. Many people consult both healers and the hospital, depending on the disease they are suffering from and, to a lesser extent, the cost of treatment. Often healers are seen when people have an illness that they believe western medicine cannot cure. The two are also used in combination, or people resort to one having found the other ineffective. If symptoms of a disease are recognised, treatment is often self-administered. Some health problems of a sensitive nature, such as gynaecological problems and sexually transmitted diseases, are commonly treated by healers; women being afraid or too embarrassed to go to the hospital. Other conditions are often of a more psychological or supernatural nature, such as phobias and spirit possessions.

Healers commonly first receive their powers on the death of another healer, usually their parent or grandparent, and often through a dream. Many practise clairvoyance, using cards or mirrors, in order to communicate with their ancestors so as to diagnose illness and treatment. Sometimes, even if the disease is known, there is no fixed recipe but treatment varies according to what is identified as the cause of that disease. So two people with the same illness would not necessarily be administered the same treatment. These

develop. Consult a doctor (mentioning that you have been abroad) if you develop a flu-like illness within a year of leaving a malarious region. The life-threatening cerebral malaria will become apparent within three months and can kill within 24 hours of the first symptoms.

Mosquitoes pass on not only malaria but also elephantiasis, dengue fever and a variety of other serious viral fevers. By avoiding mosquito bites you also avoid illness, as well as those itching lumps which so easily become infected. Once you've been bitten, tiger balm, calamine lotion or calamine-based creams help stop the itching.

Travellers' diarrhoea

Diarrhoea is very common in visitors to Madagascar, and you are more likely to diagnostic powers of healers are all important, and are the reason why they could never be replaced. Some healers update treatments annually, on the advice of their ancestors, and many are blessed with healing hands; so the medicinal plants they use would not be as effective if self-administered. It is therefore difficult to know to what extent people are successfully cured by a plant's medicinal properties and how much is due to the healer's power or is just psychological.

Despite evident deforestation in the area, people living close to the forest do not suggest any consequent dramatic change in the abundance of medicinal plants, only stating that they have to go slightly further afield to find them. In fact, users of medicinal plants originating from secondary vegetation note that their abundance has actually increased as a direct result of environmental degradation. Other healers are unaware of availability since they are not responsible for plant collection. Some even claim to know nothing about medicinal plants or where they are found, being led to them whilst in a trance, their body possessed by ancestral spirits.

Although use of forest plants is generally higher in villages near the forest, some healers living near the forest use exclusively savannah-originating medicinal plants, and some living far from the forest use forest plants. Such patterns of medicinal plant use can result from the method of plant collection; some healers have plants come to them overnight by a supernatural force, some send people to harvest them, and some buy in the market or elsewhere. Many healers also conserve plants by drying them, thus making frequent collection unnecessary. Migration is another cause, some healers originating from forested areas later moving away but continuing to use the forest plants that tradition has passed on to them. Medicinal plant knowledge therefore changes more according to the speciality of the healer, and the healer's origin, as opposed to their proximity to the forest.

Although traditional healing does not appear to be dying out and western medicine does not seem to pose a real threat, perhaps its greatest threat is from religion. Common belief has it that traditional healing is the devil's work as it comes from the power of the ancestors rather than the power of God. The risk is that young people may resist the healing power they inherit. Recording traditional medicine practices enhances understanding of the context in which it is used in Madagascar, by distributing the results to local communities, authorities and scientists. It is also necessary to increase appreciation and valuation of these secondary forest products, with the aim of conservation and sustainable natural resource management.

suffer from this if you are new to tropical travel. Tourists tend to be obsessed with water sterilisation but, contrary to popular belief, travellers' diarrhoea usually comes from contaminated food not contaminated water. Ice-cream, sadly, is particularly risky: a survey in Antananarivo some years ago showed that 100% of homemade and 60% of factory-made ice-creams contained the faecal bacteria which cause diarrhoea. So if you want to stay healthy avoid ice-cream, and also ice, salads, fruit with lots of crevices such as strawberries, uncooked foods and cooked food that has been hanging around or has been inadequately reheated. Sizzling hot street food is likely to be far safer than the food offered in buffets in expensive hotels, however gourmet the latter may look. Yoghurt is usually safe, as are sorbets. Remember **peel it, boil it, cook it or forget it!**

The way to the quickest recovery from travellers' diarrhoea is to reduce your normal meals to a few light or high carbohydrate items, avoid milk and alcohol and drink lots of clear fluids. You need to replace the fluids lost down the toilet, and drinks containing salt and sugar are most easily absorbed. Add a little sugar to a salty drink, such as Marmite or Oxo, or salt to a sugary drink like Coca-Cola. Sachets of rehydration mixtures are available commercially, but you can make your own by mixing a rounded dessertspoon (or four teaspoons) of sugar with a quarter-teaspoon of salt and adding it to a glass of boiled and cooled water. Drink two glasses of this every time you open your bowels – more often if you are thirsty. Substituting glucose for sugar will make you feel even better. If you are in a rural area drink young coconut water or *ranovola* (water boiled in the pot that rice is cooked in).

Hot drinks and iced drinks cause a reflex emptying of the bowel and cause belly-ache, so take drinks tepid or at room-temperature while the diarrhoea is at its worst. Once the bowel has ejected the toxic material causing the diarrhoea, the symptoms will settle quite quickly and you should begin to feel better again after 24–36 hours. Should the diarrhoea be associated with passing blood or slime, it would be sensible to have a stool check at some stage, but provided you continue to drink clear fluids, no harm will come from waiting for a few days.

Holiday schedules often make it impossible to follow the 'sit it out' advice. When a long bus journey or flight is anticipated you may wish to take a blocker such as Imodium. Just remember that such drugs slow up the action of the bowel so you tend to feel ill for a longer period of time and they are dangerous if you have dysentery. Safer and far more effective is the antibiotic Ciprofloxacin taken as a three-day course (500mg twice daily). Discuss this with your doctor or travel clinic. Drink lots whatever treatment you are taking and if you are worried or feel very ill, seek local medical advice. As long as you keep well hydrated the symptoms will usually settle without further treatment. Even bacillary dysentery and cholera will usually resolve within a week without treatment, as long as you drink plenty of clear fluids.

Cholera

In the last few years cholera has been a problem in Madagascar. By the end of 2000, 39,400 cases had been reported and 2,245 Malagasy had died. Although it has a fearsome reputation, cholera doesn't usually make healthy people ill. It takes the debilitated, poor and half-starved of famine or conflict zones, or it is present along with other gastro-intestinal infections. Cholera is avoided in the same way as other 'filth-to-mouth' diseases and – if there are symptoms – it can be treated with the usual oral rehydration fluids that all wise travellers know about.

Other bowel beasties

There is a high prevalence of tapeworm in Malagasy cattle, so eat your steaks well done. If you do pass a worm, this is alarming but treatment can wait, and indeed travellers often carry only one and so need no treatment.

Bilharzia

This is a nasty, debilitating disease which is a problem in much of lowland Madagascar. The parasite is also carried by pond snails and is caught by people who swim or paddle in clean, still or slow-moving water (not fast-flowing rivers) where an infected person has defecated or urinated. The parasite causes 'swimmer's itch' when it penetrates the skin. Since it takes at least ten minutes for the tiny worm to work its way through your skin, a quick wade across a river, preferably followed by vigorous towelling off, should not put you at risk. Bilharzia is cured with a single

CLOSE ENCOUNTERS OF THE TURD KIND

The surf sparkled in the early morning sun and the sand was firm underfoot as the tourist strode along the beach, revelling in the freedom of miles and miles of eastern coastline. As he approached the picturesque fishing village of bamboo and reed huts he saw people on the beach: the villagers, wrapped in their *lambas*, were squatting near the water. He approached, curious to see every aspect of their daily lives, and the men greeted him politely. Then he saw what they were doing. Turning away in acute embarrassment and disgust, he headed quickly back to the hotel. His morning's walk was spoiled.

Even the most basic pit toilets are unknown to most rural Malagasy. This lack of concern over one of the West's most taboo bodily functions is rightly disturbing. No rationalisation can diminish the disgust we feel when confronted by a neat pile of human faeces in a rural beauty spot. And disgust turns to anxiety when we consider the role that flies play in spreading disease.

The tourist involved in the beach experience asked a Malagasy why they do not bury their faeces. He was told that this would be *fady* because the dead (ie: ancestors) are interred in the earth. Dr Jane Wilson-Howarth, who studied schistosomiasis and intestinal parasites in western Madagascar, made the following observations in *Journal of Tropical Medicine and Hygiene*: 'It is common to find human faeces within 10 metres of houses. It is *fady* for Sakalavas to use latrines, or to defaecate in the same place as siblings of the opposite sex. There are several well-defined areas for defaecation, and also places where it is *fady* – but usually out of respect for the ancestors rather than for reasons of public health.'

Much as I support the adherence to local customs and traditions, this is one that I hope disappears soon.

dose of Praziquantel. If you think you may have been exposed to the disease, ask your doctor to arrange a blood test when you get home. This should be done more than six weeks after but ideally within 12 weeks of the last exposure.

Sexually transmitted infections
These are common in Madagascar and AIDS is on the increase. If you enjoy nightlife, male or female condoms will make encounters less risky.

Rabies and animal bites
Bites from pet lemurs and habituated animals are on the increase in Madagascar and even the smallest danger of the animal being rabid has to be taken seriously. Do not try to stroke wild or captive animals. Should you be unfortunate enough to be bitten by any mammal, wild or domesticated, you are at risk from both rabies and tetanus. If you're not immunised against tetanus, you must seek medical help speedily. The risk of rabies should also be taken seriously, especially if you haven't been immunised, particularly if a dog has bitten you. Whether immunised or not, you should immediately scrub the wound under running water for five minutes, then flood it with alcohol or iodine. Once the rabies virus enters the body, it migrates slowly along the nerves until the virus reaches the brain and causes an agonising death. Once symptoms have appeared, rabies is untreatable and invariably fatal. Before the onset of symptoms, the disease can be prevented by a simple course of

injections into the arm (the painful ones in the abdomen have long been superseded). Although it's wise to seek medical help as soon as possible after you are bitten (and bites to the face must be attended to within days) it may not be too late to do so after you get home. The incubation period, and thus the amount of time you have while treatment is still possible, depends upon the severity of the bite and the distance from the brain. If the bite was trivial and on the leg you probably have weeks or even months, but seek help as soon as you can. Even if you have been immunised, you must seek medical attention and especially if the bite is severe, or if the wound is dirty or deep. Two rabies boosters are recommended after any suspect bite in immunised people. For unimmunised people five post-bite injections are necessary.

Infection and trivial breaks in the skin

The skin is very prone to infection in hot, moist climates, so anything that makes even the slightest break to its surface is likely to allow bacteria to enter and so cause problems. Mosquito bites – especially if you scratch them – are a common route of infection, so apply a cream to reduce the itching. Toothpaste helps if you are stuck for anything better. Cover any wounds, especially oozing ones, so that flies don't snack on them. Significant skin infections can arise through even a small nick or graze. Antiseptic creams are not advised, since they keep the wounds moist and this encourages further infection. A powerful antiseptic, which also dries out moist wounds, is potassium permanganate crystals dissolved in water. Another alternative is diluted tincture of iodine (which you may be carrying anyway as a water steriliser). Bathe the wound twice a day, more often if you can, by dabbing with cotton wool dipped in dilute potassium permanganate or iodine solution. Bathing in sulphur springs cures too.

Sunburn

Light-skinned people burn remarkably quickly near the equator, especially when snorkelling. Wearing a shirt, preferably one with a collar, protects the neck and back, and long shorts can also be worn. Use a sunscreen with a high protection factor (up to 25) on the back of the neck, calves and other exposed parts.

Prickly heat

A fine pimply rash on the trunk is likely to be heat rash; cool showers, dabbing (not rubbing) dry and talc will help relieve it. Treat the problem by slowing down to a relaxed schedule, wearing only loose, baggy 100% cotton clothes and sleeping naked under a fan; if it's bad you may need to check into an air-conditioned hotel room for a while.

Foot protection

Wear old trainers (running shoes) by or in the sea to avoid getting coral or urchin spines in the soles of your feet, and for some protection against venomous fish spines. If you tread on a venomous fish or stingray, or are charged by a lionfish soak the foot (or affected part) in hot (up to 45°C) water until some time after the pain subsides; this may mean 20–30 minutes' submersion in all. If the pain returns re-immerse. Once the venom has been heat-inactivated, get a doctor to check and remove any bits of fish spines in the wound.

The nasty side of nature
Animals

Malagasy **land-snakes** are back-fanged, and so are effectively non-venomous. **Sea-snakes**, although venomous, are easy to see and are rarely aggressive.

It's wise to be wary of **scorpions** and **centipedes**, particularly when in the dry forest. Neither is fatal, but their sting is very unpleasant. Scorpions often come out after rain. They are nocturnal, but they like hiding in small crevices during the day. If you are camping in the desert or the dry forest, it's not unusual to find they have crept into the pocket of a rucksack – even if you have taken the sensible precaution of suspending it from a tree. Scorpion stings are very painful for about 24 hours. After a sting on the finger, I had an excruciatingly painful hand and arm for several days. The pain was only eased with morphine. My finger had no feeling for a month, and over fifteen years later it still has an abnormal nerve supply.

Large **spiders** can be dangerous – the black widow is found in Madagascar, as well as an aggressive hairy spider with a nasty bite. Navy digger **wasps** have an unpleasant sting, but it's only the scorpions that commonly cause problems because they favour hiding places where one might plunge a hand without looking. If you sleep on the ground, isolate yourself from these creatures with a mat, a hammock or a tent with a sewn-in ground sheet.

Leeches can be a nuisance in the rainforest, but are only revolting, not dangerous (AIDS cannot be spread via leeches). They are best avoided by covering up, tucking trousers into socks and applying insect repellent (even on shoes – but beware, DEET dissolves plastics). Once leeches have become attached they should not be forcibly removed or their mouthparts may remain causing the bite to itch for a long time. Either wait until they have finished feeding (when they will fall off) or encourage them to let go by applying a lit cigarette, a bit of tobacco, chilli, salt or insect repellent. A film canister is a convenient salt container. The wound left by a leech bleeds a great deal, and easily becomes infected if not kept clean. For more on leeches see box on page 53.

Beware of strolling barefoot on damp, sandy riverbeds. This is the way to pick up jiggers (and geography worms). **Jiggers** are female sand fleas, which resemble maggots and burrow into your toes to feed on your blood while incubating their eggs. Remove them, using a sterilised needle, by picking the top off the boil they make and teasing them out (this requires some skill, so it's best to ask a local person to help). Disinfect the wound thoroughly to prevent infection.

Plants

Madagascar has quite a few plants which cause skin irritation. The worst one I have encountered is a climbing legume with pea-pod-like fruits that look furry. This 'fur' penetrates the skin as thousands of tiny needles, which must be painstakingly extracted with tweezers. Prickly pear fruits have the same defence. Relief from the secretions of other irritating plants is obtained by bathing. Sometimes it's best to wash your clothes as well, and immersion fully clothed may be the last resort!

Medical kit

Apart from personal medication taken on a regular basis, it's unnecessary to weigh yourself down with a comprehensive medical kit, as many of your requirements will be met by the Malagasy pharmacies.

Expeditions or very adventurous travellers should contact MASTA (see *Useful addresses*, below). The absolute maximum an ordinary traveller needs to carry (I always carry less) is: malaria tablets; lots of plasters (Band-Aid/Elastoplast) to cover broken skin, infected insect bites etc; antiseptic (potassium permanganate crystals to dissolve in water are best); small pieces of sterile gauze or Melonin dressings and adhesive plaster; soluble aspirin or paracetamol (Tylenol) – good for fevers, aches

MALAGASY HEALTH

Several small charities are working in Madagascar to improve the health education of the local people. Here are reports from just two of them. For details of these charities see page 146.

Blindness in Madagascar
Oliver Backhouse, MOSS

Currently there is just over 1/1,000,000 ophthalmologists in Madagascar and most are based in or immediately around Antananarivo (Europe has approximately 1/60,000). Levels of blindness are predicted to double by the year 2020, mainly due to the increasing number and age of the population. With the WHO 'Vision 2020 – the right to sight' project, which aims to reduce the numbers of needlessly blind by the year 2020, a training programme of eye workers is being undertaken chiefly by a Lutheran organisation SALFA and the Lions Club in cooperation with the Malagasy Ministry of Health.

We found that 60% of adult blindness was due to clouding of the lens (cataract) and this is readily treated with a cheap operation described by the WHO as one of the most cost-effective health interventions. Around 50% of blindness in children was due to scarring of the cornea which was mostly due to a lack of vitamin A in the diet. In reducing the burden of blindness, education must play a key role. One mother we came across had four of her nine children blind from a lack of vitamin A. She earned her income from selling carrots that she grew (a good source of vitamin A) but did not give them to her children to eat as their stomachs were full of rice three times a day. One of the achievements of MOSS was to launch a 'Vitamin A eye game' to help reduce the number of blind children and this has proved very popular and I hope successful. Although 'field trips' are undertaken, many people who could benefit from treatment do not attend due to the familiar reasons of poor communication and transport, lack of or expense of medication, fear of going to an unknown place, difficulty leaving family and work, reliance on local healers, lack of understanding that help is available and services being too few and far away. MOSS hopes to continue reducing these barriers to health care and cut the numbers of needlessly blind.

Childbirth in Madagascar
Samantha Cameron, Feedback Madagascar

With the average Malagasy woman having five or six children, Madagascar's population is growing at rate of 5.3%. However, such population statistics hide great differences, both between and within regions, as well as between people

and for gargling when you have a sore throat. Anusol or Sudocrem or some kind of soothing cream for sore anus (after diarrhoea); also useful in cases of severe diarrhoea where a cough or sneeze can be disastrous are panti-liners or sanitary pads (these are also excellent for covering wounds); Canesten for thrush and athlete's foot; foot powder; Vaseline or Heel Balm for cracked heels. A course of Amoxycillin (or Erythromycin if you're penicillin-allergic) which is good for chest infections, skin infections and cystitis; Cicatrin (neomycin) antibiotic powder for infected bites etc; antibiotic eye drops; anti-histamine tablets; travel sickness pills (for those winding roads); tiger balm or calamine lotion for itchy bites; pointed tweezers for extracting splinters, sea-urchin spines, small thorns and coral.

from different educational backgrounds. Families are much larger in rural areas and for less educated people. Women in the Fianarantsoa region not only have the most children but also suffer from the highest maternal and infant mortality rates in Madagascar, with 12% of children dying before their first birthday.

Risks in childbirth are greatly accentuated in rural areas where education is poor, health services are minimal, reproductive health education is non-existent and only a small proportion of the population have even heard of family planning, let alone use it. Despite most rural women wanting to space pregnancies, many give birth every year, being unaware of how to control their fertility. The majority of childbirths in rural communities are assisted by traditional birth attendants (TBAs): community members, both male and female, who have never had formal training but whose skill was inherited from their predecessors. They are chosen over health centres for various reasons that include distance from the hospital, the cost of services, and their cultural acceptability. Women give birth at home on a woven mat on the floor, with minimal equipment and insufficient hygiene. Often old razor blades are re-used to cut the umbilical cord. Medicinal plant remedies are commonly used to speed up labour, as well as before and after childbirth for the treatment of various conditions.

TBAs are not only employed during childbirth, but are consulted from early in pregnancy right through to childhood, whenever women have concerns or feel unwell. They are therefore respected and much solicited community members, making them ideal health workers. However, numerous traditional practices used are potentially dangerous, such as massaging the womb in pregnancy in order to change the foetus's position, and tugging the umbilical cord after childbirth to force the placenta out. TBAs are also limited in their identification of risk signs, in sanitation and materials. Other harmful traditional practices include the giving of tea to new-born babies, rather than breastfeeding immediately, and confining women to bed for a week or so after childbirth, risking blood circulation problems.

Feedback Madagascar's training programme for TBAs aims to improve maternal and child health through the eradication of such dangerous practices, whilst maximising TBAs' important advisory roles so as to increase community awareness-raising on subjects ranging from prenatal care and nutrition to family planning. The realisation of public health goals is impossible without their participation.

This programme is conducted in partnership with the Ministry of Health in Madagascar.

Useful addresses
UK
British Airways Travel Clinic and Immunisation Service 156 Regent St, London W1; tel: 020 7439 9584. This place also sells travellers' supplies and has a branch of Stanford's travel book and map shop.

Hospital for Tropical Diseases Travel Clinic Capper St (off Tottenham Court Rd), London WC1; tel: 020 7388 9600; web: www.thhtd.org. Offers consultations and advice, and is able to provide all necessary drugs and vaccines for travellers. Runs a healthline (09061 337733) for country-specific information and health hazards. Also stocks nets, water purification equipment and personal protection measures.

MASTA (Medical Advisory Service for Travellers Abroad) Keppel St, London WC1 7HT; tel: 09068 224100. This is a premium-line number, charged at 50p per minute. There are also **MASTA**-run clinics all around Britain. To find your nearest one, phone 01276 685040.

Nomad Travel Pharmacy and Vaccination Centre 3–4 Wellington Terrace, Turnpike Lane, London N8 0PX; tel: 020 8889 7014; email: sales@nomadtravel.co.uk; web: www.nomadtravel.co.uk. As well as dispensing health advice, Nomad stock mosquito nets and other anti-bug devices, and an excellent range of adventure travel gear.

Thames Medical 157 Waterloo Rd, London SE1 8US; tel: 020 7902 9000. Competitively priced, one-stop travel health service. All profits go to their affiliated company InterHealth which provides health care for overseas workers on Christian projects.

Trailfinders Immunisation Centre 194 Kensington High St, London W8 7RG; tel: 020 7938 3999. Also 254–284 Sauchiehall St, Glasgow G2 3EH; tel: 0141 353 0066.

USA

Centers for Disease Control The Atlanta-based organisation is the central source of travel information in the USA with a touch-tone phone line and fax service: Traveler's Hot Line, 404 332 4559. Each summer they publish the invaluable *Health Information for International Travel* which is available from Center for Prevention Services, Division of Quarantine, Atlanta, GA 30333.

Connaught Laboratories PO Box 187, Swiftwater, PA 18370; tel: 800 822 2463. They will send a free list of specialist tropical-medicine physicians in your state.

IAMAT (International Association for Medical Assistance to Travelers) 736 Center St, Lewiston, NY 14092. A non-profit organisation which provides lists of English-speaking doctors abroad.

Australia

TMVC Tel: 1300 65 88 44; web: www.tmvc.com.au. TMVC has 20 clinics in Australia, New Zealand and Thailand, including:

Brisbane Dr Deborah Mills, Qantas Domestic Building, 6th floor, 247 Adelaide St, Brisbane, QLD 4000; tel: 7 3221 9066; fax: 7 3321 7076.

Melbourne Dr Sonny Lau, 393 Little Bourke St, 2nd floor, Melbourne, VIC 3000; tel: 3 9602 5788; fax: 3 9670 8394.

Sydney Dr Mandy Hu, Dymocks Building, 7th floor, 428 George St, Sydney, NSW 2000; tel: 2 221 7133; fax: 2 221 8401.

South Africa

There are many good travel clinics in South Africa eg: *Johannesburg*, tel: 011 807 3132; *Cape Town*, tel: 021 419 3172; *Knysna*, tel: 044 382 6366; *East London*, tel: 0431 43 2359.

SAFETY

Before launching into a discussion of crime, it's worth reminding readers that by far the most common cause of death or injury while on holiday is the same as at home: road accidents. No-one seems to worry about this, however, preferring to focus their anxieties on crime. I have been taken to task by some readers for over-emphasising the danger of robbery, and certainly it is true that most visitors to Madagascar return home after a crime-free trip. However, this is one area where being forewarned is forearmed: there are positive steps that you can take to keep yourself and your possessions safe, so you might as well know about them, while knowing also that the vast majority of Malagasy are touchingly honest. Often you will have people call you back because you have overpaid them (while still unfamiliar with the money) and every traveller can

IDENTIFICATION WARNING

Brett Massoud, who lives and works in Taolagnaro (Fort Dauphin) reports that it is illegal in Madagascar not to carry identification. 'The police have got much tougher about this law, and have been known to imprison (in Fort Dauphin) and to extort money (in Tana and Tuléar) from tourists not carrying proper identification. If you prefer to leave your passport in a safe place in your hotel room when you go out, carrying a photocopy of your passport is no longer sufficient for ID purposes, unless it is an authorised copy, with red stamps all over it, available either from the police (supposedly free) or from the office of the mayor (1,500Fmg per copy). You must provide your passport (photo page and visa page) and as many photocopies of it as you think you might need, and usually it can be done on the spot or at worst overnight. This authorised copy is then valid for the police, for banks, for Western Union, or anyone else who might demand your ID. In Tana this year I have been stopped at least once on every visit (about 10 visits), both in the day and at night.

'Police like to hang around outside the Indra disco, waiting for *vazaha* who have gone out without an ID. In Fort Dauphin they (rarely) do special "round-up" nights, where they collect as many *vazaha* as possible and jam them all in a little insect-ridden cell for the night. This can be an expensive or at best very uncomfortable mistake.'

This is certainly worrying news. In contrast to Brett's experiences I have never been asked for my ID (and never carry my passport in the streets) so suspect that if you are travelling in a group (or, perhaps, appear to be a respectable late-middle-aged lady!) you needn't worry too much. However, independent travellers should take Brett's advice and get some authorised copies of their passport.

think of a time when his innocence could have been exploited – and wasn't. In my experience, too, hotel employees are, by and large, trustworthy. So try to keep a sense of proportion. Like health, safety is often a question of commonsense. Keep your valuables hidden, keep alert in potentially dangerous situations, and you will be OK.

Bear in mind that thieves have to learn their profession so theft is common only where there are plenty of tourists to prey on. In little-visited areas you can relax and enjoy the genuine friendliness of the people.

Before you go

You can enjoy peace of mind by giving some time to making your luggage and person as hard to rob as possible before you leave home. Make three photocopies of all your important documents: passport (information page and visa), airline ticket (including proof of purchase), travellers' cheques (sales advice slip), credit cards, emergency phone number for stolen credit cards, emergency phone number of travel insurance company and insurance documents. Leave one copy with a friend or relative at home, one in your main luggage and one in your handbag or hand luggage.

- Leave your valuable-looking jewellery at home. You do not need it in Madagascar. Likewise your fancy watch; buy a cheap one.
- Lock your bag when travelling by plane or taxi-brousse; combination locks are more secure than small padlocks. Make or buy a lockable cover for your backpack.

- Make extra deep pockets in your travel trousers by cutting the bottom off existing pockets and adding an extra bit. Fasten the 'secret' pocket with velcro.

Crime prevention

Violent crime is still relatively rare in Madagascar, and even in Antananarivo you are probably safer than in a large American city. The response to a potentially violent attack is the same in Madagascar as anywhere: if you are outnumbered or the thief is armed, it is sensible to hand over what they want.

You are far more likely to be robbed by subterfuge. Razor-slashing is very popular (with the thieves) and is particularly irritating since your clothes or bag are ruined, maybe just for the sake of the used tissue that caused the tempting-looking bulge in your pocket. When visiting crowded places avoid bringing a bag (even a daypack carried in front of your body is vulnerable); bring your money and passport or ID (see box on page 117) in a moneybelt under your clothes, or in a neck pouch. Women have advantages here: the neck pouch can be hooked over their bra so no cord shows at the neck and a moneybelt beneath a skirt is safe since it needs an unusually brazen thief to reach for it! If you must have a bag, make sure it is difficult to cut, and that it can be carried across your body so it cannot be snatched (see box on page 160). Passengers in taxis may be the victims of robbery: the thief reaches through the open window and grabs your bag. Keep it on the floor by your feet.

Having escorted scores of first-timers through Madagascar, I've learned the mistakes the unprepared can make. The most common is wearing jewellery ('But I always wear this gold chain'), carelessness with money etc ('I just put my bag down while I tried on that blouse'), and expecting thieves to look shabby ('but he was such a well-dressed young man').

Tips for avoiding robbery

- Remember that most theft occurs in the street not in hotels; leave your valuables hidden in a locked bag in your room or in the hotel safe.
- If you use a hotel safe at Reception, make sure your money is in a sealed envelope that cannot be opened without detection. There have been cases of the key being accessible to all hotel employees, with predictable results.
- If staying in C Category hotels bring a rubber wedge (or Blu-Tack) to keep your door closed at night. If you can't secure the window put something on the sill which will fall with a clatter if someone tries to enter.
- Pay particular attention to the security of your passport.
- Carry your cash in a moneybelt, neck pouch or deep pocket. Wear loose trousers that have zipped pockets. Keep emergency cash (eg: a 100 dollar bill) in a Very Safe Place.
- Divide up travellers' cheques so they are not all in one place. Keep a note of the numbers of your travellers' cheques, passport, credit cards, plane ticket, insurance etc in your moneybelt. Keep photocopies of the above in your luggage.
- Remember, what the thief would most like to get hold of is money. Do not leave it around (in coat pockets hanging in your room, in your hand while you concentrate on something else, in an accessible pocket while strolling in the street). If travelling as a couple or small group have one person stand aside to keep watch while the other makes a purchase in the street.
- In a restaurant never hang your bag on the back of a chair or lay it by your feet (unless you put your chair leg over the strap). When travelling in a taxi, put your bag on the floor by your feet.

- For thieves, the next best thing after money is clothes. Avoid leaving them on the beach while you go swimming (in tourist areas) and never leave swimsuits or washing to dry outside your room near a public area.
- Bear in mind that it's impossible to run carrying a large piece of luggage. Items hidden at the bottom of your heaviest bag will be safe from a grab and run thief. Couples or small groups can pass a piece of cord through the handles of all their bags to make them one unstealable unit when waiting at an airport or taxi-brousse station.
- Avoid misunderstandings – genuine or contrived – by agreeing on the price of a service before you set out.
- ENJOY YOURSELF. IT'S PREFERABLE TO LOSE A FEW UNIMPORTANT THINGS AND SEE THE BEST OF MADAGASCAR THAN TO MISTRUST EVERYONE AND RUIN YOUR TRIP!

...and what to do if you are robbed
Have a little cry and then go to the police. They will write down all the details then send you to the chief of police for a signature. It takes the best part of a day, but you will need the certificate for your insurance. If you are in a rural area, the local authorities will do a declaration of loss.

Women travellers
Things have changed a lot in Madagascar. During my independent travels in the 1980s my only experience of sexual harassment (if it could be called that) was when a small man sidled up to me in Nosy Be and asked: 'Have you ever tasted Malagasy man?'.

Sadly, with the increase of tourism comes the increase of men who think they may be on to a good thing. A firm 'no' is usually sufficient; try not to be too offended: think of the image of Western women that the average Malagasy male is shown via the cinema or TV.

Anne Axel, who travelled solo safely and happily in 1996, has noticed a significant change in male attitudes during her second trip: 'The sexual harassment we experienced was so prevalent and so pervasive that we were forced to be more distant. We didn't freely engage in conversation and were wary of all men who tried to stop us in the street to talk.'

A woman Peace Corps volunteer gave me the following advice for women travelling alone on taxi-brousses: 'Try to sit in the cab, but not next to the driver; if possible sit with another woman; if in the main body of the vehicle, establish contact with an older person, man or woman, who will then tend to look after you.' All women readers agree that you should say you are married, whether or not you wear a ring to back it up.

Sarah Blachford, who travelled courageously off the beaten track, alone, on a very tight budget and with no knowledge of French, adds her comments. 'I would go with most of what was said in the last edition, but have never found a wedding ring a successful ploy. On the couple of times I've tried it elsewhere, it's led to being asked well, where is your husband, and so on, and I'm not a good liar! From my experience, being conservatively dressed does help; I do tend to cover up and dress fairly smartly and I do carry a rape alarm thing, also a cowbell which I hang on the door handle, so it rings if anyone tries the door.

'Really I did have a fantastic time in Madagascar all told. The highlights were the river trip, the food (and I was going to pack tinned sardines in case I got hungry!), the friendliness of the Malagasy people, and the fact the whole time I was away I saw only five other tourists. I also thought the beer was grand. The lows were

A LOSS OF TRUST

Two of my most experienced contributors, Jolijn Greel and Herman Snippe, were involved in a robbery which left them emotionally shattered. 'I had never thought that the theft of our camera could have such an impact on us. It wasn't so much the fact that the camera was gone. It was a professional camera and I like to believe I made good use of it, but a camera can be replaced. The loss of the film was worse. It was a nearly fully exposed film, so we lost around 34 shots of an impressive part of our trip, and they could not be replaced. But the fact that we were cunningly conned into trusting the guys who had every intention of stealing from us, *that* is what hurt the most. We were outraged and disillusioned, embarrassed for not having been able to 'read' the situation; we found it extremely difficult to trust people after this since our gut feeling had obviously failed us. And that was our biggest loss really.'

What had happened was that an ANGAP employee at Ranomafana had flagged down a vehicle to take them to Fianarantsoa. The driver and his companion were chatty and friendly, and offered to take them to their final destination, Antsirabe. During the latter part of the journey, in the dark, one of the men managed to open Jolijn's day pack, while she was dozing, and extract her camera from its case. He then closed the pack and the loss was not discovered until the next day. The full story suggest that the two thieves were professionals who may have been thwarted from their plans of a bigger theft by the fact that valuables such as money and passports were kept out of reach in a money belt, and that their two passengers never strayed far from the car (which could have been driven off with all their luggage inside).

Many experienced travellers will recognise the feeling of anger and shame, and the lurking mistrust that follows such an incident. And we will all agree that you cannot stop trusting people because of one bad incident. The trick is to continue to trust while taking additional precautions to keep your person and valuables safe from the tiny minority of professional criminals. But it's not easy. Jolijn ends her letter ruefully: 'The ethics of tourism are confusing. I think it is much easier to ask provoking questions than to provide answers. I think you'll agree on that.' I do.

Tuléar, the state of some of the loos (my God, and I have lived in Africa!), and my not being able to speak French – it got a bit lonely at times. However, I would say to anyone: go, it's a most magic place.'

Men travellers

To the Malagasy, a man travelling alone is in need of one thing: a woman. Lone male travellers will be pursued relentlessly, particularly in beach resorts. Prostitutes are ubiquitous and very beautiful. And successful. Venereal disease is common. A recent added danger from prostitutes is lacing a tourist's drink with the 'date-rape' drug Rohypnol to render their victim unconscious in his room, then rob him of all his possessions. I have only had one report of this, in Nosy Be, but it is likely to spread.

John Kupiec reports: 'I was constantly fighting off women wherever I went. One night in Fort Dauphin I actually had to run away!' He was also offered the mother of the Président du Fokontany in one village. Saying you're married is considered irrelevant...

In Madagascar

6

MONEY
Cost of travel

By most people's standards Madagascar is not expensive, and if you are prepared for a certain amount of hardship it is cheap. For those travelling mainly by bus or taxi-brousse and staying in Category C hotels, £15/US$23 per day for a couple is about average, and allows for an occasional splurge. Note that couples can travel almost as cheaply as singles, since most hotels charge by the room (with double bed). Sleep cheap and eat well is a good recipe for happy travels.

Costs mount up if you are visiting many national parks or reserves, which cost 50,000Fmg (about £5.50/US$9.00) along with another US$8 or so for the guide.

The easiest way to save money on a day-to-day basis is to cut down on bottled water: a bottle of Eau Vive costs over £1/US$1.45 in smart hotels (but half the price in a shop). Bring a water container and sterilising agent. If you are a beer drinker, be careful where you buy it: from a supermarket it costs 2,500Fmg (about 30p/50c); in a cheap restaurant you could pay 5,000Fmg, and in the best hotels it could be 13,000Fmg or more.

Malagasy francs

Madagascar's currency has always been difficult to cope with. Here is an extract from an account written over a hundred years ago: 'The French five-franc piece is now the standard of coinage in Madagascar; for small change it is cut up into bits of all sizes. The traveller has to carry a pair of scales about with him, and whenever he makes a purchase the specified quantity of this most inconvenient money is weighed out with the greatest exactness, first on his own scales, and then on those of the suspicious native of whom he is buying.'

Ariary confusion

Madagascar's unit of currency is the Franc malgache (Fmg). With recent inflation one rarely sees the small lower-denomination brass coins of 5, 10 and 20 francs (which are practically worthless), but there are silver coins which look, at face value, to be for 10 and 20 francs. Closer inspection reveals that they are *ariary*; one ariary is five francs, so they are worth 50 and 100 francs respectively. For a while the banknotes perpetrated the same deceit on unsuspecting foreigners but now, mercifully, they have returned to the old system of writing the ariary value in words and the francs in figures. Watch out, however, for 2,500Fmg notes, boldly written as 500 (ariary) and the 25,000Fmg one which likewise can be confused with 5,000Fmg.

As a tourist you will always be quoted prices in Fmg, but you will still see ariary prices (in hundreds, rather than thousands) outside shops or market stalls. So if the price of goods look ridiculously cheap, this is the explanation.

The colour of money

Keep the following in mind: big green = 5,000 ariary/25,000Fmg; pink and green = 500 ariary/2,500Fmg; brown = 10,000Fmg; purple = 5,000Fmg; blue = 1,000Fmg. Filthy brown = once green = 500Fmg.

Learn too the approximate value of each colour. At the 2001 exchange rate it was convenient to think of 25,000Fmg (big green) as £2.50/$5 and 10,000Fmg (brown) as the equivalent of a pound, and 5,000Fmg (purple) a bit under a dollar. This is near enough when making quick calculations while bargaining.

Exchange rate and hard currencies

The Malagasy franc floats against hard currencies, but has remained pretty stable during the last few years. In former years all top class hotels and other businesses dealing with tourists quoted prices in French francs (Ff). Now, with the French franc due to give way to the euro (∈) prices are quoted in this currency.

Exchange rate at February 2002

£1 = 9,095Fmg
US$1 = 6,375Fmg
∈1 = 5,790Fmg

Changing money

There are no currency restrictions and you are permitted to make purchases using American dollars – indeed, the tourist-aware vendors in places visited by cruise ships are quite unhappy if offered Malagasy francs.

With the increase of ATMs, travellers' cheques are slipping out of favour, and can be hard to change, especially away from major cities. Cash in US dollars is much more convenient. It is best to change money (including travellers' cheques) at the airport on arrival (see page 152). After that it's simplest to use a hotel, though banks will give a slightly better rate.

Towards the end of your trip change money cautiously. **You cannot change your Fmg back into hard currency, and once you're into the check-in hall at the airport there is nowhere to spend it.** The maximum you are allowed to take out of the country is 25,000Fmg.

Transferring funds

Now that you can draw cash from many BTM banks using your debit or credit card you are less likely to need money transferred from home. If you are staying a long time in Madagascar, however, it's advisable to make the transfer arrangement beforehand. The best bank for this is Banque Malgache de l'Océan Indien, Place de l'Indépendance, Antananarivo. Its corresponding bank in the UK is Banque Nationale de Paris, 8–13 King William St, London EC4P 4HS; tel: 020 7895 7070.

If you need cash in a hurry there are Western Union offices in Madagascar to which money can be transferred from home in a few hours, or in minutes if your nearest and dearest are willing to go to a Western Union office with cash. The fee (in the UK) is £32 if done with a credit card but, for the obliging mum, partner or whatever in your home country, it is a simple procedure which can be done over the phone, saving the journey to a Western Union office. They need to phone Western Union on 0800 833 833 (in the USA: 800 325 6000) and know the town from where you wish to pick up the money. There are Western Union offices in Antananarivo, Mahajanga, Toamasina, Fianarantsoa and Nosy Be. Phone (Tana) 22 313 07 for addresses or further information or check their website: www.westernunion.com.

PUBLIC TRANSPORT

You can get around Madagascar by road, air and water. And – now – by rail. Whatever your transport, you'd better learn the meaning of *en panne*; it is engine trouble/breakdown. During these *en panne* sessions one can't help feeling a certain nostalgia for the pre-mechanised days when Europeans travelled by *filanzana* or palanquin. These litters were carried by four cheerful porters who, by all accounts, were so busy swapping gossip and telling stories that they sometimes dropped their unfortunate *vazaha* in a river. The average distance travelled per day was 30 miles – not much slower than a taxi-brousse today! The *filanzana* was used for high officials as recently as the 1940s. To get around town the locals depended on an earlier version of the current rickshaw, or *pousse-pousse*. The *mono-pousse* was a chair slung over a bicycle wheel. One man pulled and another pushed. The more affluent Malagasy possessed a *boeuf-cheval*: a zebu trained to be ridden. (I've seen a photo; the animal looks rather smug in its saddle and bridle.)

By road

> If I make roads, the white man will only come and take my country. I have two allies – *hazo* [forest] and *tazo* [fever]…
>
> King Radama I

Coping with the 'roads' is one of the great travel challenges in Madagascar. It's not that the royal decree has lasted 180 years but there's a third ally that the king didn't mention – the weather: torrential rain and cyclones destroy roads as fast as they are constructed. But they are being repaired and reconstructed, mostly with foreign aid. At the time of writing many of the most important roads (the *Routes Nationales*) are either paved or in the process of being paved. The others are dreadful, but then…that's Madagascar. Here's a comment from a Belgian traveller: 'A good example of how the Malagasy maintain their roads comes before Rantabe [east coast]. A huge tree fell over the road. Instead of cutting the log in two they made a big hole under the tree in the road!'

Taxi-brousse is the generic name for public transport in Madagascar. Car-brousse and taxi-be are also used, but they all refer to the 'bush-taxis' which run along every road in the country. These have improved a lot in recent years, especially along tourist routes. Even so, stories like those on page 124 are still not unusual.

Taxi-brousse
Vehicles
Taxi-brousses are generally minibuses or Renault vans with seats facing each other so there is no good view out of the window (a *baché* is a small van with a canvas top). More comfortable are the Peugeot 404s or 504s, sometimes known as taxi-be (although some people call the 25-seater buses taxi-be) designed to take nine people, but often packed with 14 or more. A car-brousse is usually a 'Tata' sturdy enough to cope with bad roads. I've even heard of a *tracteur-brousse*, designed to take passengers through the worst road conditions Madagascar can come up with.

Practicalities
Vehicles leave from a *gare routière* (bus station) on the side of town closest to their destination. You should try to go there a day or two ahead of your planned departure to check times and prices, and for long journeys you should buy a ticket in advance (from the kiosk – don't give your money to a ticket tout). The following advice is from Frances Kerridge – a seasoned taxi-brousse traveller: 'Don't be embarrassed to ask to see the vehicle, the Malagasy do. Reserve your seat – they

VIVE LE TAXI-BROUSSE!

Taxi-brousses are improving, especially on the main tourist routes, but I couldn't resist repeating – and adding to – these entertaining stories!

'At about 10 o'clock we (two people) went to the taxi-brousse station. "Yes, yes, there is a car. It is here, ready to go." We paid our money. "When will it go?" "When it has nine passengers." "How many has it got now?" "Wait a minute." A long look at notebooks, then a detailed calculation. "Two." "As well as us?" "No, no including you." It finally left at about 7 o'clock.'

Chris Ballance

'After several hours we picked up four more people. We couldn't believe it – the driver had to sit on someone's lap!'

Stephen Cartledge

'At last we were under way. I had my knees jammed up against the iron bar at the back of the rows in front where sat a very sick soldier, who spent most of the journey with his head out of the window spewing lurid green bile at passers-by like something from a horror-movie… After about 20 minutes we had to stop at a roadside stall to buy mangoes. Since I was now on the sunny side of the vehicle the temperature of my shirt rose to what, had it been made of polyester, would have been melting point. Our next stop was Antsirabe where we were surrounded by about 50 apple vendors and all and sundry went absolutely beserk. I hadn't seen so many apples since…since we left Ambositra. At about 5pm the radio was turned on so we could listen to two men shouting at each other at a volume which would have caused bleeding of the eardrums in Wembley Stadium. When one passenger complained our driver managed to find a few extra decibels. At about 6pm it started to get decidedly brisk, and since the ailing squaddie in front of me showed no sign of having rid himself of toxic enzymes I now had to endure an icy blast in my face. Our next stop was for grapes. We now had enough fruit on board to start a wholesale business in Covent Garden, and I was a bit tetchy.'

Robert Stewart

'We eventually made it after an eventful four-hour taxi-brousse journey which entailed the obligatory trawl around town for more passengers, selling the spare tyre shortly after setting off, a 30-minute wait outside the doctor's as the driver wasn't feeling very well, and all of us having to bump-start the vehicle every time we stopped to pick anyone up.'

H & M Kendrick, 1998

'I woke up nice and early to get my taxi-brousse to Mahamasina from Diego. I clambered on to a nice new minibus, eager to hit the open road. There was one other passenger. We cruised around for three hours, frequently changing drivers, trying to get more customers. In this time our driver got into three fights, one lasting half an hour. There was even a tug-of-war with passengers, which looked quite painful, to persuade them to use their taxi-brousse.'

Ben Tapley, 2001

will write your name on a hand-drawn plan in an exercise book – and get them to write your place on the ticket. Once you have anything written on a piece of paper it is regarded as law and once it is typed it must be gospel! The best seats in a car are in the front, either next to the driver if you have short legs (you'll be sitting where the hand brake should be) or next to the window if you have long legs – but beware of the sun cooking your right arm. In the front you have the added advantage that you can turn down the volume of the stereo when the driver is not looking.

'Never be late for a taxi-brousse. Some of them do leave on time, especially on popular journeys or if the departure time is horrendous, eg: 2am. Get there early to claim your seat, then read your book, write your diary or whatever. Be ready with soap and towel for a bath stop. Follow the women and children to get some degree of privacy.'

On short journeys and in remote areas, vehicles simply leave as soon as they fill up. Or if they have a schedule expect them to leave hours late, and always be prepared (with warm clothing, fruit, water etc) for a night trip, even if you thought it was leaving in the morning.

There is no set rate per kilometre; fares are calculated on the quality of the vehicle, the roughness of the road and the time the journey takes. They are set by the government and *vazaha* are only occasionally overcharged. Ask other passengers what they are paying, or trust the driver. Taxi-brousses are very cheap. It should not cost you more than US$10 for an all-day journey. Faster routes (tarred roads) may be a bit more expensive. Passengers are occasionally charged for luggage that is strapped on to the roof.

Drivers stop to eat, but usually drive all night. If they do stop during the night most passengers stay in the vehicle or sleep on the road outside.

There is much that a committed overland traveller can do to soften his/her experiences on taxi-brousses – see page 91. If you're prepared for the realities, an overland journey can be very enjoyable and gives you a chance to get to know the Malagasy. And before you get too depressed and cancel your trip, remember that on the popular routes there are normal buses with one seat per passenger. The above (and the box) mainly pertains to adventurous journeys.

By air

Air Madagascar started its life in 1962 as Madair but understandably changed its name after a few years of jokes. Most people now call it Air Mad. It serves over 40 destinations, making it the most efficient way – and for some people the only way – of seeing the country. Here are some sample one-way fares from Antananarivo: Mahajanga US$92, Nosy Be US$98, Antsiranana (Diego Suarez) US$98, Toliara (Tuléar) US$98. Remember that you can get a 20–30% discount on domestic flights providing you chose Air Mad as your international carrier.

Air Madagascar has the following planes: Boeing 747 (jumbo) on the Paris to Antananarivo route, Boeing 737 to the larger cities and Nosy Be, the smaller ATR 49-seater turbo props, and the little Twin Otters to the smaller towns.

The recent rise in tourism in Madagascar has brought more passengers than Air Mad can cope with, particularly at peak holiday times. Try to book in advance through one of their agents (see page 87) or through an Antananarivo tour operator. If you are doing your bookings once you arrive, avoid the crush by getting to the Air Mad office when it opens in the morning, or use one of the many very competent travel agents in the capital. Often flights which are said to be fully booked in Antananarivo are found to have seats when you reapply at the town of departure. In any case, you should reconfirm your next flight as soon as you arrive at your destination (at the Air Mad office in town). Rupert Parker, a frequent traveller to Madagascar, reveals his secret: 'Because you are still allowed to make a reservation without payment, flights always appear full, but the trick is to go to the airport two hours in advance and put your ticket on the counter. The *liste d'attente* works on a first come first served basis and half an hour before the flight is due to leave they start filling the empty seats, taking the tickets in order of arrival. We have never, in ten years, been disappointed – it just increases the stress level but we have always got on the plane.' Conversely, passengers with booked seats who check in late will find their seats sold to waiting-list passengers. Always arrive at least an hour before the scheduled departure.

There are no numbered seats on internal flights, which are now non-smoking. It is useful to know that *Enregistrement Bagages* is the check-in counter and *Livraison Bagages* is luggage arrival.

Frances Kerridge gives this advice for flying by Twin Otter: 'The check-in is hilarious – they weigh you as well as your luggage, so a bit of dieting between flights will cover those extra souvenirs you've bought! [Luggage allowance – bags not person! – is usually 20kg.] I recommend getting there early – about an hour before they say – to check in as there will be lots of Malagasy, each trying to cart a market-stall equivalent of whatever goods are a speciality of that region. The smaller your bag, the more popular you will be as other passengers eagerly claim your unused luggage allowance.' She goes on to emphasise that luggage should be locked, but that airport thieves know how to pick locks so keep your luggage in sight for as long as possible. And here's a warning: there are no toilets in a Twin Otter!

Air Madagascar schedules are reviewed twice-yearly, at the end of March and the end of October, but are subject to change at any time and without notice. Air Mad has a website: www.air-mad.com. Their phone number in Antananarivo is 22 22 222.

With a shortage of aircraft and pilots, planes are sometimes delayed or cancelled. Almost always there is a perfectly good reason: mechanical problems, bad weather. Air Mad is improving and on the whole they provide as reliable a service as one can expect in a poor country.

By boat

The Malagasy are traditionally a seafaring people (remember that 6,000km journey from Indonesia) and in the absence of roads, their stable outrigger canoes are used to cover quite long sea distances. *Pirogues* without outriggers are used extensively on the rivers and canals of the watery east. Quite a few adventurous travellers use *pirogues* for sections of their journeys. Romantic though it may be to sail in an outrigger canoe, it can be both uncomfortable and, at times, dangerous.

Ferries and cargo boats travel to the larger islands and down the west coast (see box on page 379).

River rafting is becoming increasingly popular as a different way of seeing the country. This is not the hair-raising white-water variety, but a gentle float down the wide, lazy rivers of the west. For more information see page 395.

By rail

After years of deterioration, Madagascar's railways are up for privatisation. Already the line between Fianarantsoa and Manakara on the east coast has been privatised and is giving a reliable, enjoyable service. The other two lines, from Antananarivo to Toamasina, and to Ansirabe, are set to follow in due course. Enquire at the railway station, tel: 22 205 21.

Transport within cities
Buses
Most cities have cheap buses but few travellers use these because of the difficulty of understanding the route system. No reason not to give it a try, however.

Taxis
Taxi rates have gone up in recent years because of a sharp rise in fuel prices, but they are still reasonable. Taxis have no meters, so you must agree on the price before you get in.

Rickshaws (Pousse-pousses)
Pousse-pousses were introduced into Madagascar by British missionaries who wanted to replace the traditional palanquin with its association with slavery. The name is said to originate from the time they operated in the capital and needed an additional man behind to push up the steep hills. They are now a Madagascar speciality (unlike the pedal rickshaws in other parts of the world, these are pulled by a running man). Most towns have *pousse-pousses* – the exceptions are the hilly towns of the highlands.

Many Western visitors are reluctant to sit in comfort behind a running, ragged, sweating man and no-one with a heart can fail to feel compassion for the *pousse-pousse* pullers. However, this is a case of needing to abandon our own cultural hang-ups. These men want work. Most rickshaws are owned by Indians to whom the 'drivers' must pay a daily fee. If they take no passengers they will be out of pocket – and there's precious little in their pockets. Bargain hard (before you get in) and make sure you have the exact money. It would be optimistic to expect change. For most medium-length journeys 2,000Fmg to 3,000Fmg is reasonable. *Pousse-pousse* pullers love carrying soft-hearted tourists and have become quite cunning – and tiresome – in their dealings with *vazaha*. However, remember how desperately these men need a little luck – and an innocent tourist could make their day!

HIRING (OR BRINGING) YOUR OWN TRANSPORT
Tim Ireland puts it succinctly: 'The great pity is watching so many magnificent landscapes tear past your eyes as you strain your neck trying to get a better view past 15 other occupants of a taxi-brousse.' He goes on to recommend a mountain bike as the perfect means of transport, but a hired vehicle will achieve the same flexibility.

Car hire
More and more visitors have been renting cars or 4WD vehicles in recent years. You would need to be a competent mechanic to hire a self-drive car in Madagascar, and generally cars come with chauffeurs (providing a local person with a job and you with a guide/interpreter). A few days on Madagascar's roads will cure you of any regret that you are not driving yourself. Night-time driving is particularly challenging: headlights often don't work, or are not switched on. Your driver will know that the single light bearing down on you is more likely to be a wide truck than a narrow motorbike and react accordingly. The Merina Highway Code (informal version) decrees that drivers must honk their horns after crossing a bridge to ensure that the spirits are out of the way.

There are car-hire firms in most large towns. A list of the international companies in Antananarivo is below. In addition the Maison du Tourisme has a more comprehensive list, and I have included them in town information outside the capital.

Prices currently work out at about £50/US$75 per day, including fuel and driver, for a small saloon car driving around Antananarivo. For a week's hire of a 4WD you should expect to pay about £750/US$1,125. To give you an idea of an inclusive price, in 2001 Pierrot (see *Fixers*, page 173) charged 3,400,000Fmg (about £380/US$570) for nine days between Tana and Toliara. This included sightseeing in Tana, train tickets from Fianarantsoa to Manakara, hotel bookings and so on.

If you are planning to hire a vehicle, I suggest you consider doing so in Toliara (Tuléar) which has some of the most interesting people and scenery – and the worst roads – in Madagascar. A 4WD vehicle will allow you to get well off the beaten track.

Major car rental firms (in Tana) and prices:

Aventour Tel: 22 317 61/ 22 217 78. Saloon: 189,500Fmg/day + 2350/km + VAT 20% with a driver, without petrol.

Budget Tel: 22 611 11. Clio 386,400Fmg/day with a driver, without petrol; Nissan, 747,600fmg/day with a driver, without petrol.

Europcar Tel: 22 336 47. 4WD: 722,005Fmg to 801,638Fmg/day with a driver, without petrol.

Eurorent Tel: 22 297 66/ 22 621 50; email: intermad@dts.mg. 4WD: 150,000Fmg + 1,500/km + insurance 110,000Fmg + VAT 20%/ day; saloon car: 90,000Fmg + 900/km + insurance 80,000Fmg + VAT 20%/ day.

Hertz Tel: 22 229 61; email: somada@simicro.mg; web: www.madagascar-contacts.com/hertz. 4WD: 602,000Fmg/day; saloon car: 396,000Fmg/day.

Sun and Sea Tel: 22 467 33; email: sun_sea@dts.mg. 4WD (Land Rover): 470,000Fmg/day with a driver, without petrol; Nissan: 550,000Fmg/day with a driver, without petrol.

Motorbike

This is perhaps the very best way of getting round Madagascar: fast enough to cover a lot of ground in this large island, yet flexible enough to deal with the terrible roads. Bringing your own bike will not be easy, but there are a few places that rent out motorbikes.

Marko Petrovic, who used a motorbike to tour remote areas of the southeast, found a small motorbike the most convenient because of the necessity to cross rivers using local *pirogues*. The motorbike was laid across two *pirogues* tied together. He says that 'brand new Yamahas, Suzukis and Hondas are very reasonably priced and available in Tana' so buying a bike is a good option if you are staying a while.

Motorbike rental

Holiday Bikes Auberge du Jardin, Ivato; tel/fax: 441 74. From mopeds to motorbikes, rates range from 100,000Fmg per day to 250,000Fmg, depending on the power. Credit cards accepted.

Madagascar on Bike Tel: 22 484 29; cellphone: 33 11 381 36; email info@madagascar-on-bike.com; web: http://madagascar-on-bike.com. A German company supplying Honda Transalp bikes (600cc 5h/p) for €70 a day or €400 a week.

Mountain bicycle

An increasingly popular means of touring Madagascar is by the most reliable transport: mountain bike. Bikes can be usually hired in Antananarivo, Antsirabe, Taolagnaro (Fort Dauphin), Antsiranana (Diego Suarez) and Nosy Be. Or you can bring your own. You can do a combination of bike and taxi-brousse or bike and plane, or you can set out to cycle the whole way. Don't be overambitious; dirt

COMMERSON

Joseph Philibert Commerson has provided the best-known quote on Madagascar:

> C'est à Madagascar que je puis annoncer aux naturalistes qu'est la véritable terre promise pour eux. C'est là que la nature semble s'être retirée dans un sanctuaire particulier pour y travailler sur d'autres modèles que ceux auxquels elle s'est asservie ailleurs. Les formes les plus insolites et les plus merveilleuses s'y rencontrent à chaque pas.

> Of Madagascar I can say to naturalists that it is truly their promised land. There nature seems to have retreated into a private sanctuary to work on models other than those she has created elsewhere. At every step one encounters the most strange and marvellous forms.

Commerson was a doctor who travelled with Bougainville on a world expedition in 1766, arriving at Mauritius in 1768. He studied the natural history of that island, then in 1770 journeyed on to Madagascar where he stayed for three or four months in the Fort Dauphin region. His famous description of 'nature's sanctuary' was in a 1771 letter to his old tutor in Paris.

roads are so rutted you will make slow progress, and tarred roads can be dangerous from erratic drivers.

People worry, understandably, about the safety aspect. So far I have not heard of anyone being harmed while on a bike, but of course you are vulnerable. You must make your own decisions. All I can recommend is to cycle off the beaten track. Here you will meet only hospitality and curiosity, and will be in no danger – intentional or unintentional – from other road-users. But what I really want to say is 'Go for it – and damn the risk!'.

ACCOMMODATION

Hotels in Madagascar are classified by a national star system – five star being the highest – but in my experience this indicates price, not quality. In this book I have used three categories: A, B and C, which is based on quality as much as price. There is a tourist tax, *vignette touristique*, of between 1,000Fmg and 3,000Fmg per person per night. This is usually absorbed into the price, but may be added separately.

Outside the towns, hotels in the form of a single building are something of a rarity. Accommodation is usually in bungalows which are often constructed of local materials and are quiet, atmospheric and comfortable.

A word about bolsters. Visitors who are not accustomed to the ways of France are disconcerted to find a firm, sheet-covered sausage anchored to the top of the bed. In the better hotels you can usually find a pillow hidden away in a cupboard. Failing that, I make my own pillow with a sweater stuffed into a T-shirt.

Breakfast is rarely included in the room price, and if it is it'll be continental breakfast.

What you get for your money
Category A
There are a few places that compete with anywhere in the world for luxury, and many that are up to international standard in the large towns and tourist areas.

HOTEL: A WARNING

The struggle for presidential power in Madagascar during 2002 caused an almost complete halt to tourism and bankrupted many businesses, including hotels. Publication of this book, scheduled for March 2002, was postponed. To research it all again is obviously impossible, but some of the hotels listed will have closed, others may be struggling and not up to the standard described. Please give them your understanding and support.

Prices may also have changed, but this is the system I used: prices quoted were all checked in late 2001. In cases where the information is over a year old I write 'about' before the price, and prices are omitted when I have no information since the last edition. I often use readers' reports to update hotels and restaurants. 'Recommended' means that more than one reader has praised the place or that I know it personally.

Such hotels are usually foreign-owned. There has been a boom in hotel building during the last few years, and there are now some very good Malagasy-owned hotels in this category, so the difference between A and B has become somewhat blurred. Category A hotels cost between £20/US$30 and £180/US$270 for a double room (there are very few at the top price bracket). The average, even for a really nice hotel, is only about £25/US$38.

Category B

These are often just as clean and comfortable, and have en-suite bathrooms. There will be no TV beaming CNN into your bedroom, but you should have comfortable beds though bolsters are the norm. The hotels are often family-run and very friendly. The average price is about £15/US$22.

Category C

In early editions I described these as 'exhilaratingly dreadful at times' until a reader wrote: 'We were rather disappointed by the quality of the Category C hotels... We found almost all the beds comfortable, generally acceptably clean, and not one rat. We felt luxuriously cheated!' Take heart: the following description from Rupert Parker of a hotel in Brickaville should gladden the masochistic heart, '...a conglomeration of shacks directly beneath the road bridge. The rooms are partitioned-off spaces, just large enough to hold a bed, in a larger wooden building – the partitions don't reach to the ceiling and there is only one light bulb for all the rooms – the hotel manageress controls the switch. Not only can you hear everyone's conversation and what they're up to, but when there is a new arrival, at whatever time of the night, the light comes on and wakes everyone up – that is if you've managed to ignore the rumbling and revving of trucks as they cross the bridge above you, or the banging on the gate which announces a new arrival. Suffice to say the toilet and washing facilities are non-existent.'

Such hotels certainly give the flavour of how Madagascar used to be, and in remote areas you will still find the occasional sagging double bed and stinking hole toilet. Usually you can find the toilet by the smell, but ask for the WC ('dooble vay say'), not *toilette* which usually means shower or bathroom. In these hotels (and some B ones too) used toilet paper should not be thrown into the pan but into the box provided for it. Not very nice, but preferable to a clogged loo.

Most of the C hotels in this book are clean and excellent value, only earning the C because of their price. Almost always they are run by friendly Malagasy who will rustle up a fantastic meal. In an out-of-the-way place you will pay as little as £2.50/US\$3.75 for the most basic room, though £6.50/US\$10 would be more usual.

Hotely usually means a restaurant/snack bar rather than accommodation, but it's always worth asking if they have rooms.

Most B and C hotels will do your washing for you at a very reasonable price. This gives employment to local people and is an important element of responsible travel. In A hotels laundry can be disproportionately expensive!

Camping

Until very recently Madagascar had no official campsites, although backpackers with their own tent were often allowed to camp in hotel gardens. During 2001 several campsites were set up in the south (mainly near Isalo National Park) in the expectation of vast crowds arriving for the solar eclipse. These are still open for business. In addition the NGO Azafady operates several campsites in beautiful situations in the Taolagnaro (Fort Dauphin area), and some of the new national parks (Andringitra, Marojejy) are for camping only. Self-contained backpackers will know the wonderful sense of freedom that comes with carrying their own tent – there is all of Madagascar to explore!

FOOD AND DRINK
Food

Eating well is one of the delights of Madagascar, and even the fussiest tourists are usually happy with the food. International hotels serve international food, usually with a French bias, and often do special Malagasy dishes. Lodges and smaller hotels serve local food which is almost always excellent, particularly on the coast where lobster (crayfish), shellfish and other seafood predominates. Meat lovers will enjoy the zebu steaks, although they are usually tougher than we are used to (free-range meat usually is). Outside the capital, most hotels offer a set menu (*table d'hôte* or *menu*) to their guests. This can cost as little as 30,000Fmg (£3/US\$5). At the upper end you can expect to pay 125,000Fmg (£13/US\$19).

Where the menu is à la carte it is a help to have a French dictionary or phrasebook.

The national dish in Madagascar is *romazava* (pronounced 'roomazahv'), a meat and vegetable stew, spiced with ginger and containing *brèdes* (pronounced 'bread'), tasty, tongue-tingling greens. Another good local dish is *ravitoto*, shredded manioc leaves with fried beef and coconut.

Volker Dorheim adds: 'If you like your food really spicy ask for *pimente verde*. If this isn't hot enough ask for *pimente malgache*.'

Independent travellers will find Chinese restaurants in every town; these are almost always good and reasonably priced. *Soupe Chinoise* is available almost everywhere, and is filling and tasty. The Malagasy eat a lot of rice, but most restaurants cater to foreign tastes by providing chips (French fries). Away from the tourist routes, however, most dishes are accompanied by a sticky mound of rice.

For a real Malagasy meal, eat in a *hotely*. These are often open-sided shacks where the menu is chalked up on a blackboard:

Henan-omby (or *Hen'omby*)	beef
Henan-borona (or *Hen'akoho*)	chicken
Henan-kisoa	pork
Henan-drano (or *Hazan-drano*)	fish

It may end with *Mazotoa homana*. This is not a dish, it means *Bon appétit*!

Along with the meat or fish and inevitable mound of rice (*vary*) comes a bowl of stock. This is spooned over the rice, or drunk as a soup.

Thirst is quenched with *ranovola* (pronounced 'ranoov<u>ool</u>') obtained by boiling water in the pan in which the rice was cooked. It has a slight flavour of burnt rice, and since it has been boiled for several minutes it is safe to drink.

If you don't feel like a full meal, *hotelys* are a great source of snacks. Here are some of the options: *tsaramasy* (rice with beans and pork), *vary sosoa* (rice pudding), *mofo boule* (slightly sweet bread rolls), and *koba* (rice and banana, wrapped in a leaf and served in slices).

For do-it-yourself meals there is a great variety of fruit and vegetables, even in the smallest market. A selection of fruit is served in most restaurants, along with raw vegetables or *crudités*. From June to August the fruit is mostly limited to citrus and bananas, but from September there are also strawberries, mangoes, lychees, pineapples and loquats. Slices of coconut are sold everywhere, but especially on the coast where coconut milk is a popular and safe drink, and toffee-coconut nibbles are sold on the street, often wrapped in paper from school exercise books.

Madagascar's dairy industry is growing. There are some good, locally produced cheeses and Malagasy yoghurt is excellent and available in the smallest shops. Try the drinking yoghurt, *yaourt à boire*.

Vegetarian food

Madagascar is becoming more accustomed to *vazaha* vegetarians and with patience you can usually order meatless dishes even at small *hotelys*. *Tsy misy hena* means 'without meat'. Frances Kerridge reports: 'In more remote places it is actually easier to be accepted as a vegetarian as people are more accepting of *fady* than in the towns.'

Drink

The most popular drink, Three Horses Beer (THB), is wonderful on a hot day. I think it's wonderful on a cold day, too. The price goes up according to the surroundings: twice as much in the Hilton as in a *hotely* and there is always a hefty deposit payable on the bottle. A newish beer is Queens, which is slightly weaker, and there is also Gold. Why does the Star brewery give its beer English names that the Malagasy can't pronounce? And why horses and queens when the country has few of either (and not much gold)? I don't know.

Madagascar produces its own wine in the Fianarantsoa region, and some is very good. L'azani Betsileo (*blanc* or *gris*, *reservé*) is recommended.

A pleasant aperitif is Maromby (the name means 'many zebu') and I have been told that Litchel, made from lychees, is good. Rum, *toaka gasy*, is very cheap and plentiful, especially in sugar-growing areas such as Nosy Be; and fermented sugar-cane juice, *betsabetsa* (east coast), or fermented coconut milk, *trembo* (north), make a change. The best cocktail is *punch au coco*, with a coconut-milk base, which is a speciality of the coastal areas. Yummy!

The most popular mineral water is called Eau Vive, but other brands are now available: Olympiko and La Source. Tiko, which produces Olympiko and cartons of very good fresh juice, also make their own Cola and some very good Classico soft drinks (their lemon-lime is recommended by a reader). It's nice to be able to support a local company rather than the internationals, although Coca-Cola and other popular soft drinks such as Sprite and Fanta are available. Fresh is an agreeable shandy, and Tonic is – you guessed it – tonic water. The locally produced *limonady* sadly bears no resemblance to lemons, and Bon Bon Anglais is revolting (although I do know one *anglaise* who rather likes it!).

Previous page Ring-tailed lemur, *Lemur catta*, on an *aloalo* (Mahafaly tomb carving), Berenty (NG)

Above Beach at Ile aux Nattes off Ile Sainte Marie (HB)

Right Sailing pirogue near Nosy Be (HB)

Below Grandidier's baobabs, *Adansonia grandidieri*, at sunset, near Morondava (NG)

WILD SILK
Angus McCrae

Madagascar has a long tradition of textile weaving, of which silk appears to be one of the oldest and most important. The mulberry or Chinese silkworm, *Bombyx mori*, was first introduced from Mauritius under King Radama I in the 1820s but archaeological evidence suggests that wild silk was probably utilised well before that. Since knowledge of mulberry silk has been extant in China for some 4,500 years and of wild silk for at least 500 years more, it is tempting to think that the earliest immigrants brought the idea with them – in Indonesia, as in Madagascar, wild silk is traditionally reserved for burial shrouds. Whatever the case, Madagascar's wild silk is from the cocoons of the endemic genus *Borocera*, of the worldwide family Lasiocampidae or 'Eggar moths'. Lasiocampidae silk is otherwise known to have been made only by the ancient Greeks and the Aztecs.

Of the six currently recognised *Borocera* species, *B. cajani* (found in all regions of the island but chiefly on the central plateau) is the one most used, gathered from tapia trees in Merina and Betsileo regions. Cocoons of any species, however, might be collected if they occur in sufficient abundance, although none of the three cocoon-making species of Madagascar's 19 emperor moths (often misleadingly referred to as giant silk moths) is utilised. Unlike the mulberry silkworm, *Borocera* is not amenable to domestication and it seems that this silk must remain a fluctuating wild resource.

The caterpillars of *B. cajani* are light grey in colour. Those destined to be females grow up to 10cm in length but males are smaller. They are armed with long, black spines on the back and flanks, and when annoyed they also evert a pair of vicious-looking rosettes of similar spines seated on a velvety blue background from two of their thoracic segments. These spines are shed and incorporated into the cocoon as it is constructed, projecting some 4mm outwards. Despite this the women spin a coarse silk from these cocoons and weave it on home looms into a highly durable fabric which resembles sacking in colour but is softer, finer and of course much more durable. The silk is carded before spinning, like cotton, wool and other fibres, and not reeled like (uniquely) mulberry silk.

Borocera caterpillars and the silk derived from them are called *landibe* ('big caterpillars') as opposed to *landikely* ('little caterpillars') for the mulberry silkworm. *Landibe* commands much the higher prices since demand for the material for burial shrouds far outstrips supply. Burial shrouds are called *lamba mena*: literally 'red cloth' although they can be of any colour, 'red' meaning power. In the past, some truly exquisite *lamba mena* of *landibe* silk were worn by royalty and others of high influence; they could wear grave cloths with impunity because they were considered immortal. Such *lambas* have been copied by entrepeneurs as high-value fashion items for the international market, thus putting further pressure on supply. Yet production remains in villagers' hands whereas mulberry silk is produced by government-backed cooperatives.

When the Malagasy were asked why they build such huge stone tombs when they are content to live in mud and wattle houses, the reply was 'But when you're dead you're dead for a lot longer than when you're alive!'. Similarly, I suppose, as an ancestor you'd appreciate the most durable of clothing – a silk shroud from the *landibe*.

Caffeine-addicts have a problem. The coffee is OK if drunk black, but usually only condensed milk is available. I find that one quickly regresses to childhood and surreptitiously spoons the condensed milk not into the coffee but into the mouth. If you prefer unsweetened white coffee it's best to bring your own powdered milk.

The locally grown tea is very weak, the best quality being reserved for export. A nice alternative is *citronelle*, lemon-grass tea, which is widely available.

Warning If you are travelling on a prepaid packaged tour, you may be disconcerted to find that you are charged for coffee and tea along with drinks. These beverages count as 'extras' in Madagascar.

HANDICRAFTS AND WHAT TO BUY

You can buy just about everything in the handicrafts line in Madagascar. Most typical of the country are wood carvings, raffia work (in amazing variety), crocheted and embroidered table-cloths and clothes, leather goods, carved zebu horn, Antaimoro paper (with embedded dried flowers), and so on. The choice is almost limitless, and it can all be seen in the artisans' market (Marché Artisanal) and other handicrafts markets and shops in Antananarivo and throughout the country.

In the south you can buy attractive heavy silver bracelets that are traditionally worn by men. In Tana, and the east and north (Nosy Be), you will be offered vanilla pods, peppercorns, cloves and other spices, and honey.

Do not buy products from endangered species. That includes tortoiseshell (turtle shell), snake skins (now crocodiles are farmed commercially, their skins may be sold legally), shells and coral and, of course, live animals. Butterflies are farmed commercially so buying mounted specimens is permitted. Also prohibited are endemic plants, fossils and any genuine article of funerary art. To tell turtle shell from zebu horn, hold it up to the light: turtle shell is semi-transparent.

To help stamp out the sale of endangered animal products, tourists should make their feelings – and the law – known. If, for instance, you are offered tortoise or turtle shell, tell the vendor it is *interdit*; and to push the point home you can say it is *fady* for you to buy such a thing.

The luggage weight-limit when leaving Madagascar is normally 20kg – bear this in mind when doing your shopping.

If you want to buy Malagasy craft items after your return home (to Britain) ask for a copy of Discover Madgascar's catalogue (tel: 0208 995 3529 or email: info@discovermadagascar.co.uk).

Semi-precious stones

Madagascar is a rewarding place for gem hunters, with citrin, tourmaline, and beryl inexpensive and easy to find. The solitaire sets using these stones are typical and most attractive. The centre for gems is traditionally Antsirabe but they are for sale in many Highland towns, and now Ilakaka, the town that has sprung up at the centre of the sapphire rush, is the main hub. If you buy uncut stones bear in mind the cost of having them cut at home, and the additional expense of having them made into jewellery.

MUSIC

In recent years Malagasy music has become well known, with several Malagasy groups such as Tarika now touring internationally. Tarika's lead singer, Rasoanalvo Hanitrarivo (known as Hanitra) has many recordings, most recently *Soul Makassar* (Sakay/Rogue Productions) partly inspired by a visit to Sulawesi which shares so many customs with Madagascar, and uses similar musical instruments. Paddy Bush and the *valiha* player Justin Vali have formed a collaboration which has brought Malagasy music to a wider audience through Kate Bush's recording *The Red Shoes* and *The Sunshine Within*. See their website: www.madagascan.net/music/justinvali. For more on Malagasy music see box on pages 166–7.

Finding good local music is a hit and miss affair when travelling. Often your best bet is to look out for posters advertising concerts. These are often put up near the *gare routière*.

COMMUNICATIONS: KEEPING IN TOUCH
Telephone
The phone service has improved enormously in the past two years. You can now buy phonecards for 25, 50 and 100 units, costing from 10,000Fmg to 60,000Fmg and use them for overseas calls from most public phone boxes (Publiphone). Only cream-coloured phones do international calls. Rates are much cheaper in the evenings after 22.00 and on Sundays.

The telephone code for Madagascar is 261 20 (+ town code + the number). Below are the phone codes for all of Madagascar (this information is repeated under relevant town information).

Antananarivo (Tana)	22	Manakara	72
Antsirabe	44	Morondava	95
Antsiranana (Diego Suarez)	82	Moramanga	56
Farafangana	72	Nosy Be	86
Fianarantsoa	75	Sambava	88
Ile Sainte Marie	57	Taolagnaro (Fort Dauphin)	92
Mahajanga (Majunga)	62	Toamasina (Tamatave)	53
Maintirano	69	Toliara (Tuléar)	94

Cellphones
Mobile phones are very popular in Madagascar. Bart Snyers, a GSM engineer, sent me this useful information: 'Before we left, I learned that Madagascar has a GSM network nowadays, so I was eager to find out how well it works there. I also found out that our Belgian GSM operator had a partnership with Madacom, so I would be able to use my own GSM in Madagascar. As you may know, calling with your own GSM in a foreign country is called 'roaming' and is only possible if your own operator has some sort of partnership with the operator from the foreign country. It appeared to work very well. We could phone home, send/receive SMS, check our voicemail in all major cities we visited (Tana, Diego, Fianarantsoa, Antsirabe) and probably some more can be added to this list.

'Strange it works so well in a country where the *Route National* is no more than a dirt road at several places.'

Mail
The mail service is reasonably efficient and letters generally take about two weeks to reach Europe and a little longer to North America. Stamps are quite expensive and postcards do not always arrive (some postal workers prefer to steam off the stamps and chuck the cards). The smaller post offices often run out of stamps, but some hotels sell them. If you want to receive mail, have your correspondent address the envelope with your initial only and your surname in capitals, and send it to you c/o Poste Restante in whichever town you will be in. It will be held at

the main post office. If you are an Amex member the Amex Client Mail Service allows you to have letters sent to their office in the Hilton Hotel. They keep mail for a month. BP in an address is Bôite Postale – the same as PO Box.

Courier service
Colis Express hooks up with DHL. There is an office in Tana (see page 172) and in all the large towns.

Internet
Cybercafés are opening in the capital (see page 172) and all major towns and tourist centres.

MISCELLANEOUS
Tipping
I (and even *vazaha* residents) find this an impossible subject on which to give coherent advice. Yet it is the one that consistently causes anxiety in travellers. The problem is you have to balance up the expectation of the tip recipient – who is probably used to generous tippers – and the knowledge of local wages.

Some tipping is relatively simple: a service charge is added to most restaurant meals so tipping is not strictly necessary though waiters in tourist hotels now expect it. About 10% is ample. Taxi drivers should not expect a tip, though you may want to add something for exceptional service.

The most manipulative people are baggage handlers, because they usually catch you before you are wised up to Madagascar, and are masters at the disappointment act. So before you give a dollar to the doorman for carrying your bag from the taxi to the hotel lobby, bear in mind the average earnings of a Malagasy labourer. As one expat points out: 'Not many Malagasy earn more than 25,000Fmg per week (that's about £3/US$5). A good brick carrier in Tana can manage 18 bricks a time on his head and is paid 5Fmg per brick – so they have to carry 500 bricks before they earn 10 pence.' That said, a dollar is easily found (by you) and easily spent (by them) so in a stressful situation you might as well take the easy way out.

The hardest tipping question is how much to pay guides, drivers… people who have spent several days with you and given excellent service. Here I err on the generous side, because I am coming back, because the tour operator I work for needs to maintain good relations, and because these people are accustomed to generous tips. So I generally tip 25,000Fmg a day.

Where it is essential not to over-tip is when travelling off the beaten track, where you could be setting a very dangerous precedent. It can cause problems for *vazaha* that follow who are perhaps doing research or conservation work and who cannot afford to live up to these new expectations.

Electrical equipment
The voltage in Madagascar is 220. Outlets (where they exist) take 2-pin round plugs. If you use a 3-pin fused plug plus adapter, bring a spare fuse for the plug.

Business hours
Most businesses open 08.00–12.00 and 14.00–18.00. Banks are open 08.00–16.00, and are closed weekends and the afternoon before a holiday.

Television
Posh hotels have CNN but the local station shows BBC World Service news at 09.00

PUBLIC HOLIDAYS

The Malagasy take their holidays seriously. In every town and village there will be a parade with speeches and an air of festivity.

Official holidays

January 1	New Year's Day
March 29	Commemoration of 1947 rebellion
May 1	Labour Day
June 26	Independence Day
August 15	Feast of the Assumption
November 1	All Saints' Day
December 25	Christmas Day
December 30	Republic Day

They also celebrate the movable holidays of Easter Monday, Ascension Day and Whit Monday. When any of these holidays fall on a Thursday, Friday will be tacked on to the weekend. Banks and other businesses often take a half day holiday before the official holiday.

SIX MONTHS OF TURMOIL: THE EVENTS OF 2002

Even in the sometimes bizarre politics of the developing world, the spectacle of two 'presidents' in two 'capitals' with two sets of 'ministers' was unusual. Friends of Madagascar watched appalled as the country unravelled itself, to the indifference of the leaders of the industrialised world and ignored by most of the English-speaking media.

It began in January, when Didier Ratsiraka's claims that the popular mayor of Antananarivo had not won a clear majority in the elections were met by street protests. Every day the people marched peacefully, backed by the Protestant Church of which Marc Ravalomanana is a prominent member. Ratsiraka declared Martial Law, which was countered by Ravalomanana declaring himself president and installing his own ministers in government offices. Ratsiraka retreated to his hometown of Toamasina and established a rival government. All this with the minimum of violence.

But then Ratsiraka's supporters isolated the capital by blocking all roads leading to the city and by dynamiting the bridges. Fuel and food became exorbitantly expensive or disappeared. Air Madagascar was grounded. The army was split behind the two leaders. As the months passed, the blockade caused malnutrition and death to the vulnerable in Antananarivo and hardship to all. Many businesses faced bankruptcy; 150,000 jobs were lost.

In May, the balance of power started to shift. A court-monitored re-count confirmed that Ravalomanana had won the election, and he was sworn in as president. Ratsiraka steadfastly refused to accept this, however. As the army's support for Ratsiraka dwindled and switched to Ravalomanana, it became possible to use force to dismantle the barricades, and to take Ratsiraka's coastal strongholds. The USA, Norway and Switzerland were the first nations to recognise the rightful president, and France was the last. Ratsiraka fled to France on July 5.

As we go to press it looks as though Madagascar has a popular new president with the support and motivation to put the country back on its feet. Time will tell...

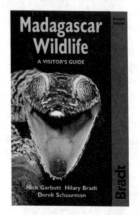

Madagascar and You

7

Tsihy be lambanana ny ambanilantra
'All who live under the sky are woven together like one big mat.'
Malagasy saying

RESPONSIBLE TOURISM

In recent years there has been a welcome shift of attitude among visitors to developing countries from 'What can I get out of this trip?' to 'How can I give something back?' This chapter addresses those issues, and suggests ways in which you can help this marvellous, but often tragic country.

They do things differently there

I once caught our Malagasy guide scowling at himself in the mirror. When I teased him he said: 'As a Malagasy man I smile a lot. I can see that if I want to work with tourists I must learn to frown.' He knew that the group considered him insufficiently assertive. Tolerance and the fear of causing offence is an integral part of Malagasy social relationships. So if a tourist expresses anger in a way that is entirely appropriate in his or her own culture, it may be counter-productive in Madagascar. It is deeply unsettling to the person at the receiving end who often giggles in response, thus exacerbating the situation. If you are patient, pleasant and keep your temper, your problem will be solved more quickly.

Avoid being too dogmatic in conversation (you do not have exclusivity of the truth). Make use of 'perhaps' and 'maybe'. Be excessive in your thanks. The Malagasy are very polite; we miss the nuances by not understanding the language. Body language, however, is easier to learn. For instance, 'Excuse me, may I come through?' is indicated by a stooping posture and an arm extended forward. Note how often it is used.

Part of responsible tourism is relinquishing some of our normal comforts. Consider this statistic: fuelwood demand in Madagascar has far outstripped supply. Wood and charcoal are the main sources of energy, and the chief users are city dwellers. In rural areas, tourist establishments will be the main consumers. Do you still feel that hot water is essential in your hotel?

One of the keys to responsible tourism is ensuring that as much as possible of the money you spend on your holiday remains in Madagascar. Independent travellers should try, whenever possible, to stay at small hotels run by Malagasy; tourists on an organised tour will probably find themselves in a foreign-owned hotel, but can do their bit by buying handicrafts and donating to local charities.

Madagascar's shortcomings can be maddening. Sometimes a little reflection reveals the reasons behind the failure to produce the expected service, but sometimes you just have to tell yourself 'Well, that's the way it is'. After all, you are not going to be able to change Madagascar, but Madagascar may change you.

FARE DEALING

Irene Boswell, a resident of Nosy Be, has observed the behaviour of tourists and locals for many years, and has this to say: 'When you give taxi prices I think it would be better to say that these are the prices in autumn 2001, but increases are to be expected.

'Otherwise you get these unpleasant scenes that I witnessed several times: the tourists, pointing at their book, do not want to pay more than what is written there, and call the Malagasy thieves who take advantage of tourists, and finally everybody feels bad about the other. The Malagasy consider the tourists as cut-throats, who profit by their poverty and need of money to get the prices down, and the tourists think that they get stolen blind by dishonest Malagasy.

'I think you should also advise against too hard bargaining. I always feel ashamed when tourists try to get things for next to nothing, and often get it, just because the seller needs the money, any money, to buy his supper. Worse still when they try to barter an old shabby T-shirt for some beautiful table-cloth. When we first arrived, 20 years ago, the Malagasy didn't barter at all, unlike Africans. Their price was a fixed price and it was justified. Then the tourists introduced the habit of bartering, thinking that in underdeveloped countries that was the fashion everywhere. In my opinion, the tourist should always respect the local people and offer them a fair price, considering the amount of time it takes to make the object and the price of the raw-material.'

Photography

Lack of consideration when taking photos is perhaps the most common example of irresponsible tourist behaviour – one that each of us has probably been guilty of at some time. It is so easy to take a sneak photo without first establishing contact with the person, so easy to say we'll send a print of the picture and then not get round to it, so easy to stroll into a market or village thinking what a wonderful photo it will make and forgetting that you are there to experience it.

The rules are not to take people's photos without permission, and to respect an answer of 'no'. Give consideration to the offence caused by photographing the destitute. Be cautious about paying your way to a good photo; often a smile or a joke will work as well, without setting a precedent. People love to receive pictures of themselves. If you are travelling on an organised tour your guide is sure to visit that area again so can deliver the prints that you send to him. If you are travelling independently write down the addresses and honour your promise.

Philip Thomas writes: 'A Malagasy, for whom a photograph will be a highly treasured souvenir, will remember the taking of the photograph and your promise to send them a copy, a lot longer than you might. Their disappointment in those who say one thing and do another is great, so if you think you might not get it together to send the photograph then do not say that you will.'

A responsible attitude to photography is so much more fun! And it results in better pictures. It involves taking some time getting to know the subject of your proposed photo: making a purchase, perhaps, or practising your Malagasy greetings (if that doesn't draw hoots of laughter nothing will!).

Beggars

Whether or not to give to professional beggars is up to you. I believe that it is wrong to give to the little ragamuffin children who follow you around because it is better to give to the charities (see *How you can help*, page 144) that work with them. Actually, the same applies to all age-groups. My policy is to give to the elderly and I also single out 'beggar days' when I fill my pockets with small change and give to every beggar who looks needy and over school age. And if I make some trickster's day, so be it.

It is important to make up your mind about beggars before you hit the streets so you can avoid standing there looking through a conspicuously fat wallet for a low-denomination bill.

'PLEASE SEND ME A PHOTO'

It is not always easy to keep a promise. Of course we intend to send a print after someone posed cheerfully for the photo, but after we get home there are so many other things to do, so many addresses on torn-out pages of exercise books. I now honour my promises. Here's why.

I was checking my group in to a Nosy Be hotel when the bellboy asked if he could speak to me. He looked nervous, so suspecting a problem with the bookings I asked him to wait until everyone was in their rooms.

When we were alone he cleared his throat and recited what was obviously a carefully prepared speech: 'You are Mrs Hilary Bradt. Ten years ago you gave your business card to the lady at Sambava Voyages and she gave it to a schoolboy who wrote to you. But you were away so your mother answered the letter. She wrote many letters. My name is Murille and I am that boy. And now I want to talk to you about Janet Cross and Brian Cross and Andrew and...' There followed a list of every member of my family. As I listened, incredulous, I remembered the original letter. 'We love England strongly,' he wrote, 'especially London, Buckingham, Grantham, Dover...' I remembered passing it to my mother saying I was too busy for such a correspondence but maybe she'd like to write. She kept it up for several years, answering questions such as 'How often does Mrs Hilary go to Grantham and Dover?' and she sent a photo of the family gathering at Christmas, naming every member on the back of the photo.

This brought an indignant letter from a cousin. 'I have seen your photo. It is a very nice one. I asked Murille if he would lend it for one day only because we all study English so we must have photo of English people more to improve this language, but he refused me strongly because they are only his friends not mine...'

Murille brought out the treasured photo. It had suffered from the constant handling and tropical heat and was peeling at the edges. He wanted to trim it, he explained, 'but if I do I will have to cut off a bit of your mother's beautiful chair and I can't do that.'

Later that year I sent Murille a photo album filled with family photos. I never heard from him again – that's the way it is in Madagascar – but the story has a twist to its tail.

I returned to Sambava 12 years after the original visit, and found myself addressing a classroom of eager adult students of English and their local teacher. Searching for something interesting to say, I told them about the time I was last in their town and the series of letters between Murille and my mother. And I told them about the cousin who also wrote to her. 'I think his name was Patrice,' I said. The teacher looked up. 'I'm Patrice. Yes, I remember writing to Janet Cross...'

HOSTING MALAGASY VISITORS
Lorna Gillespie

Mamisoa and Harimalala, 19-year-old Malagasy girls from the Akany Avoko Centre spent six months with us soaking up Australian life. The vibrant, innovative Akany Avoko Centre hosts a constant stream of international volunteers and visitors but nothing could have prepared Harimalala and Mamisoa for that distinctive Australian accent. What do you do when you've learnt English but cannot understand anyone? Lots of laughter, tears, mimicry and practice coaxed a greater comprehension and this once daunting obstacle was overcome.

Mamisoa and Harimalala were used to setbacks. Everyone involved in this epic journey knew that such an idea was going to be difficult and it was. Malagasy officials initially refused passports, Australian Immigration refused visas and it took months to successfully argue our case. Doggedness remains a prerequisite for such a venture.

Mamisoa loved swimming, particularly in the Murray River, finding kangaroos in their natural habitat and our lovely eucalypts, plus all the consumer goods. Harimalala loved everything particularly the food. She was most delighted by colourful front gardens and Sydney.

We don't know what was gained or what was lost during Harimala's and Mamisoa's time with us. The true benefit may emerge years down the track. Mamisoa now works as communications officer at the Centre and Harimalala returned to complete secondary education.

26,000km later from visiting grandma in the Mallee to tobogganing on Mount Buffalo, swimming at Dromana, steering a paddle steamer at Echuca, rock 'n' roll classes, discos, making paper from reeds, bicycling along river tracks, circuses, magicians and zoos, no wonder they called me Lorna taxi-brousse, or is that taxi-Bruce!

The effects of tourism on local people

The impact of foreigners on the Malagasy was noted as long ago as 1669 when a visitor commented that formerly the natives were deeply respectful of white men but were changed 'by the bad examples which the Europeans have had, who glory in the sin of luxury in this country…'.

In developing countries tourism has had profound effects on the inhabitants, some good, some bad. Madagascar seems to me to be a special case – more than any other country I've visited it inspires a particular devotion and an awareness of its fragility, both environmental and cultural. Wildlife is definitely profiting from the attention given it and from the emphasis on ecotourism. For the people, however, the blessings may be very mixed: some able Malagasy have found jobs in the tourist industry, but for others the impact of tourism has meant that their cultural identity has been eroded, along with some of their dignity and integrity. Village antagonisms are heightened when one or two people gain the lion's share of tourist revenue and gifts, leading in one case to murder, and hitherto honest folk have lapsed into corruption or thievery.

Giving presents

This is a subject often discussed among experienced travellers who cannot agree on when, if ever, a present is appropriate. Most feel that giving presents is appropriate only when it is in exchange for a service. Many tourists to the developing world, however, pack sweets and trinkets 'for the children' as automatically as their sunglasses and insect repellent.

My repeat visits to Madagascar over the course of 25 years have shaped my own view: that giving is usually done for self-gratification rather than generosity, and that one thoughtless act can change a village irreparably. I have seen the shyly inquisitive children of small communities turn into tiresome beggars; I have seen the warm interaction between visitor and local turn into mutual hostility; I have seen intelligent, ambitious young men turn into scoundrels. What I haven't sorted out in my mind is how much this matters. Thieves and scoundrels make a good living and are probably happier than they were in their earlier state of dire poverty. Should we be imposing our cultural views on the Malagasy? I don't know.

But giving does not have to be in the form of material gifts. 'Giving something back' has a far broader meaning. We should never underestimate our value as sheer entertainment in an otherwise routine life. We can give a smile, or a greeting in Malagasy. And we can learn from people who in so many ways are richer than us. See pages 30 and 384 for more thoughts on the subject.

More and more...

Visitors who have spent some time in Madagascar and have befriended a particular family often find themselves in the 'more and more and more' trap. The foreigner begins by expressing appreciation of the friendship and hospitality he or she received by sending a gift to the family. A request for a more expensive gift follows. And another one, until the luckless *vazaha* (white foreigner) feels that she is seen as a bottomless cornucopia of goodies. The reaction is a mixture of guilt and resentment.

Understanding the Malagasy viewpoint may help you to come to terms with these requests. You may be considered as part of the extended family, and family members often help support those who are less well-off. You will almost certainly be thought of as fabulously wealthy, so it is worth dispelling this myth by giving some prices for familiar foodstuffs at home – a kilo of rice, for instance, or a mango. Explain that you don't have servants, that you pay so much for rent, and that you have a family of your own that needs your help. Don't be afraid to say 'no' firmly.

...and the most

I know two couples, one in America and the other in Australia, who have translated their wish to help the Malagasy into air fares to their home country. This is not to be undertaken lightly – the red tape from both governments is horrendous – but is hugely rewarding for all concerned. See box opposite for an account of such a visit.

Dos and don'ts when travelling off the beaten path

Travellers venturing well off the beaten path will want to do their utmost to avoid offending the local people, who are usually extremely warm and hospitable.

Unfortunately, with the many *fady* prohibitions and beliefs varying from area to area and village to village, it is impossible to know exactly how to behave, although *vazaha* and other outsiders are exempt from the consequences of infringing a local *fady*.

Sometimes, in very remote areas, Malagasy will react in sheer terror at the sight of a white person. This probably stems from their belief in *mpakafo* (pronounced 'mpakafoo'), the 'stealer of hearts'. These pale-faced beings are said to wander around at night ripping out people's hearts. So it is not surprising that rural Malagasy often do not like going out after dark – and a problem if you are looking for a guide. The arrival of a pale-faced being in their village is understandably upsetting. In the southeast it is the *mpangalak'aty*, the 'taker of the liver', who is feared.

Villages are governed by the *Fokonolona*, or People's Assembly. On arrival at a village you should ask for the *Président du Fokontany*. Although traditionally this was the village elder, these days it is more likely to be someone who speaks French – perhaps the schoolteacher. He will show you where you can sleep (sometimes a hut is kept free for guests, sometimes someone will be moved out for you). You will usually be provided with a meal. Now travellers have penetrated most rural areas, you will be expected to pay. If the *Président* is not available, ask for *Ray aman-dreny*, an elder.

Philip Thomas, a social anthropologist who has conducted research in the rural southeast, points out several ways that tourists may unwittingly cause offence. 'People should adopt the common courtesy of greeting the Malagasy in their own language. *Salama, manahoana* and *veloma* are no more difficult to say than their French equivalents.

'*Vazaha* sometimes refuse food and hospitality, putting up tents and cooking their own food. But in offering you a place to sleep and food to eat the Malagasy are showing you the kindness they extend to any visitor or stranger, and to refuse is a rejection of their hospitality and sense of humanity. You may think you are inconveniencing them, and this is true, but they would prefer that than if you keep to yourselves as though you were not people (in the widest sense) like them. It may annoy you that it is virtually impossible to get a moment away from the gaze of the Malagasy, but you are there to look at them and their activities anyway, so why should there not be a mutual exchange? Besides, you are far more fascinating to them than they are to you, for their view of the world is not one shaped by mass education and access to international images supplied by television.

'It is perfectly acceptable to give a gift of money in return for help. Gifts of cash are not seen by the Malagasy as purchases and they themselves frequently give them. Rather, you give as a sign of your appreciation and respect. But beware of those who may try to take advantage of your position as a foreigner (and you may find these in even the remotest spot), those who play on your lack of knowledge of language and custom, and their perception of you as extremely wealthy (as of course you are by their standards).'

HOW YOU CAN HELP

There are ways in which you can make a positive contribution. By making a donation to a local project you can help the people – and the wildlife – without creating new problems. Charities based in Tana are described on pages 158–9. All of these welcome visitors and donations.

My favourite (because I've visited many times) is the Streetkids Project, which was started by a couple of English teachers, Jill and Charlie Hadfield. Visiting a charity run by the Sisters of the Good Shepherd in Tana, they could see where a little money could go a long way. The nuns run – amongst other things – a preparatory school for the very poor. When the children are ready to go on to state school, however, the parents can't afford the £15 a year they must pay for registration, uniform and books, so the children were condemned to return to the streets as beggars. The Streetkids Project raises money to continue their education and is administered in Britain through Money For Madagascar.

The organisations and charities listed below are all working with the people of Madagascar, and, by extension, habitat conservation. Most of them are very small, run by dedicated volunteers who would welcome even small donations. Other

SNAKES ALIVE!
Bill Love
The last trip was great! This time I wrote ahead to the two-room school in Ankify, c/o of Le Baobab Hotel nearby, to arrange a cultural visit for my group on a Monday morning. The visit was a huge success! Besides exchanging questions and answers about life in the USA and Madagascar, everyone with me brought a mountain of school supplies to donate, which went a long way even among the 140 kids ranging from 6 to 15 years old.

We also brought in a harmless native snake we found the previous day for a live 'biology lesson' that turned out to be the most memorable part of all! The kids were verging on terror when they first saw the snake. I arranged for Angelin Razafimanantsoa, our local guide, to be the first one seen holding the snake so the kids would see a Malagasy unafraid. This worked perfectly, as we had most students coming forward to touch it within minutes, including most of the girls. The students' reactions and curiosity were unforgettable!

I'll be making this an annual event since I always return to this area. I have approached my hometown elementary school here in Florida to introduce an ongoing cultural exchange relationship with them, kind of like a 'sister' school abroad.

Bill Love is a herpetologist and tour operator (www.bluechameleon.org) who regularly runs 'herping' trips to Madagascar. The northwest around Ambanja is his favourite stopover area. This is how he is 'giving something back' to the region.

charities work specifically for wildlife. What better way to channel your empathy for Madagascar and its problems?

Charities assisting Madagascar
People
Andrew Lees Trust 31b Bassett Street, London NW5 4PG; tel: 020 7482 2731; email: admin@andrewleestrust.org.uk; web: www.andrewleestrust.org.uk. Set up in memory of the Friends of the Earth Campaigns Director who died while researching the possible impacts of a mining project on remaining littoral forests in the southeast of the island, the Trust develops social and environmental educational programmes in the southern province. Working with its local partner of six years, the Libanona Ecology Centre (see box on page 240) the Trust is implementing a number of local development projects including: Projet Radio – disseminating education and information for rural populations via radio broadcast – and Projet Energy – training women to build fuel-efficient wood stoves. For more information and how to contact the Trust visit their website.

Azafady Studio 7, 1a Beethoven Street, London, W10 4LG; tel: 020 8960 6629; fax: 020 8962 0126; email: mark@azafady.org; web: www.madagascar.co.uk. Works mainly in the southeast of Madagascar, aiming to break the cycle of poverty and environmental degradation so apparent in that area. Projects include tree planting and facilitation of small enterprises such as village market gardens, bee farming, basket making, and fruit drying. They fund a Health and Sanitation Programme to improve access to clean drinking water and basic healthcare. To these ends Azafady has built 12 village pharmacies, 10 wells and some 300 latrines, as well as providing associated education and training to 15 village communities in the region. Conservation Projects include studies of the remaining littoral forest in southeast Madagascar and of endangered loggerhead turtle populations.

The Dodwell Trust Christina Dodwell, c/o Madagascar Consulate, 16 Lanark Mansions, Pennard Rd, London W12 8DT; tel: 020 8746 0133; fax: 020 8746 0134. A British registered charity running a radio project designed to help rural villagers, through the production and broadcast of a radio drama series for family health, family planning and welfare. The programmes are in Malagasy, by Malagasy, and based in Malagasy tradition. To enhance this programme The Dodwell Trust also runs a solar radio conversion project, and a clockwork or wind-up radio project which aims to put these radios into rural and rainforest villages. The listeners provide valuable feedback to the programme producers. The Trust is also helping with technical assistance throughout the field of radio production.

Feedback Madagascar Asfield House, by Balloch, Dunbartonshire G83 8NB; tel/fax 01852 500657; email: jamie@feedbackmadagascar.org; web: www.feedbackmadagascar.org. Address in Madagascar: Lot 1B, 65 Isoraka, Antananarivo 101; tel/fax: 22 638 11; email: feedback@simicro.mg. A small but highly effective Scottish charity which bases its activities on feedback from the local Malagasy who identify and agree on development and conservation projects. These have included irrigation dams, the rebuilding of a school and hospital, and a 'school reserve' near Ranomafana. Other schemes have been a project to help communities to manage sustainably 25,000ha of rainforest in Ambohimahamasina, an agricultural training centre and the silk project near Ambalavao. Currently they are working with the Malagasy organisation Ny Tanintsika on women's health (see pages 108–9), traditional medicines from the forest, new silk programmes and computers for all (see page 196).

Money for Madagascar 7 Pinetree Close, Burry Port, SA16 OTF; email: theresa@mfmcar.fsnet.co.uk. This long-established and well-run small charity funds rural health and agricultural projects, and deprived groups in urban areas. It sends funds on a regular basis to the Streetkids Project described on page 158 and to Akany Avoko. I have found this a much easier way of making a donation than transferring the money direct to Madagascar. The staff are all volunteers and they don't even have an office, so the overheads are very low. Thus you can be confident that almost all the money you give will go direct to the project you want to support. Write the cheque to Money for Madagascar but enclose a note saying where you want it to be sent. MFM also provide funds for cyclone relief or other natural disasters.

MOSS Boscawen Cottage, Back Lane, East Clandon, Nr Guildford, Surrey GU4 7SD; email: obackhouse@doctors.org.uk. MOSS (Madagascan Organisation for Saving Sight) was set up in 1993, following a year's work by ophthalmologist Oliver Backhouse and his wife, when a survey showed that, like most other developing countries, 80% of visual impairment was either treatable or preventable by cheap, effective and sustainable means. MOSS was set up to help develop ophthalmic and general health services in Madagascar, where 300,000 people suffer blindness. MOSS is a small, but very active charity with a considerable number of achievements to their credit. The charity has provided one operating microscope for use in opthalmic fieldwork and is seeking funds for a second one. See page 114 for an account of their work.

STARFISH PO Box 18556, Cleveland, OH 44118, USA; tel: 216 382 4297; fax: 216 382 0385. The acronym is for Society Taking Active Responsibility for International Self-help; the aim is to provide the tools and training for local people to do their jobs. The emphasis is on medical help. Projects have included surgery training for student doctors and nurses, village health projects (working in conjunction with the WWF in villages adjoining reserves), the establishment of pharmacies, and the provision of bicycles to allow doctors and nurses to reach remote villages. Jim Sellers, who runs the Madagascar projects for STARFISH, sells Antaimoro paper, greetings cards etc as a means of fundraising. Contact him at the above address.

Valiha High FMS, PO Box 337, London N4 ITW. This is not a registered charity but a project to maintain the musical traditions of Madagascar, instigated by the leader of the

AKANY AVOKO
Lorna Gillespie

Just as you leave Ambohidratrimo on the road to Mahajanga look to your left for a steep driveway bordered by red and yellow splashes of *Euphorbia milii* for here lies the remarkable Akany Avoko Centre, home to 100 kids. Glance over the prickly euphorbia and you'll see a productive terraced vegetable garden and on your right is a dusty basketball court with the Half Way House in the distance. By now your journey will be interrupted by laughing and curious young girls eager to accompany you to the cluster of buildings which make up the administration block, dormitories and work rooms. Welcome to this vibrant, innovative home for children who through every conceivable reason need a place to stay.

Akany Avoko was established by the church as a remand centre for teenaged girls accused of petty crime but over the years destitute boys and girls of all ages have made this home. We became involved after inquiring whether there was anything special happening to help women in Madagascar. This ordinary request led to an extraordinary involvement with staff and children at the Centre. Erase Dickensian images and replace them with laughter, industry (Malagasy crafts), environmental concern (the first bio-gas loo in Madagascar) and wonderful staff including international volunteers and you have some idea as to our continued involvement .

The spontaneous enthusiasm of the Centre's manager, Hardy Wilkinson, together with her spouse Steve and the Half Way House founder Irenee Horne, form a comfortable framework from which staff and kids function. There is magic here, whether it be an impromptu dance party for a *vazaha* guest or a formal visit by Princess Anne. If by now you are wondering what you can do, you could consider sending a package of clothes, sponsoring a child, donating funds. You can also help by buying your Malagasy craft work from the girls at Akany Avoko. To book your visit: email horne@dts.mg or phone 00261 20 22 441 58.

Perhaps one of the most exciting things you could do in Madagascar is to see a traditional dance display at Akany Avoko, Ambohidratrimo. This is only 20 minutes away from Ivato Airport.(25,000Fmg per person for groups of 10 or more and 150,000Fmg per group for groups less than 10). What a lovely way to say hello or farewell to Madagascar!

world-acclaimed Malagasy group, Tarika. Hanitrarivo Rasoanaivo was depressed at the influence of foreign cultures on the young people of Madagascar and the violent or pornographic videos which are now their preferred entertainment. The project, set up in 1997, has been very successful. Students are forming their own *valiha* groups, but their enthusiasm for the instrument is creating its own problem – they are wearing out and need to be replaced! A small donation goes a long way towards the cost of buying the instruments, training teachers and for prizes for competitions.

Wildlife

Conservation International (USA) 1015 18th St NW, Washington DC, 20003, USA. Very active in Madagascar. Among other projects they help fund Ampijoroa Forest Reserve.
Durrell Wildife Conservation Trust Les Augres Manor, Trinity, Jersey JE3 5BP, Channel Islands, British Isles; tel: 01534 860000; fax 01534 860001; email: jerseyzoo@durrell.org. For full details of this non-profit organisation see box on pages 78–9.

World Wide Fund for Nature Av du Mont-blanc, 1196 Gland, Switzerland (International Office); Panda House, Weyside Park, Godalming, Surrey GU7 IXR, UK; 1250 24th St NW, Washington DC 20037-1175, USA; Aires Protégées, BP 738, Antananarivo 101, Madagascar.

Organisations promoting responsible tourism

Center for Responsible Tourism PO Box 827, San Anselmo, CA 94979, USA. Full title: The North America Coordinating Center for Responsible Tourism (NACCRT). 'Exists to change attitudes and practices of North American travelers, to involve North Americans in the struggle for justice in tourism and to work for tourism practices that are compatible with a sustainable global society.'

Tourism Concern Stapleton House, 277–281 Holloway Rd, London N7 8HN; web: www.tourismconcern.org.uk. With the slogan 'putting people back in the picture', Tourism Concern 'promotes tourism that takes account of the rights and interests of those living in the world's tourist areas'. They put pressure on governments or companies which promote harmful tourism, run meetings and conferences, publish an informative and interesting newsletter and distribute the *Community Tourism Guide* (published by Earthscan).

Finally, if on your return to Britain you want to keep connections with Madagascar, how about joining the Anglo-Malagasy Society? The London consulate has information.

Part Two

The Highlands

Golden bamboo lemur

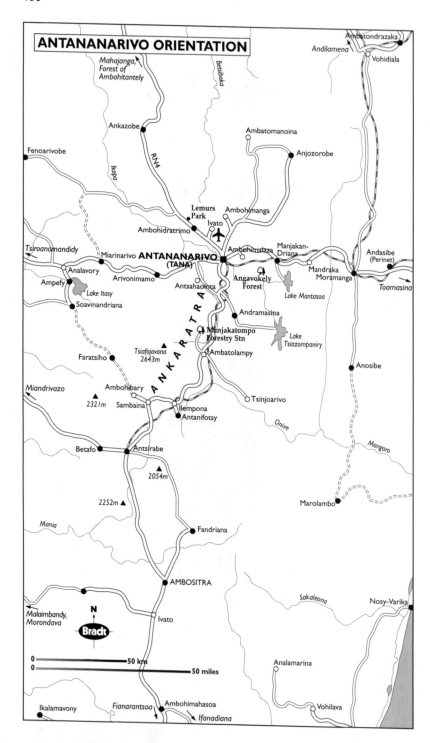

ANTANANARIVO ORIENTATION

Mahajanga,
Forest of
Ambohitantely

Betsiboka

Ambatondrazaka

Andilamena

Vohidiala

Ankazobe

Ambatomanoina

Anjozorobe

Fenoarivobe

RN4

Ikopa

Lemurs
Park

Ambohimanga

Ivato

Ambohidratrimo

Tsiroanomandidy

Miarinarivo   ANTANANARIVO
(TANA)

Ambohimalaza

Manjakan-
Driana

Andasibe
(Perinet)

Analavory

Arivonimamo

Angavokely
Forest

Mandraka
Moramanga

Toamasina

Ampefy

Antsahaointa

Lake Itasy

Lake Mantasoa

Soavinandriana

Andramasina

A N K A R A T R A

Manjakatompo
Forestry Stn

Lake
Tsiazompaniry

Faratsiho

Tsiafajavona
2643m

Ambatolampy

Anosibe

Miandrivazo

Ambohibary

2321m   Sambaina

Ilempona

Antanifotsy

Tsinjoarivo

Onive

Mangoro

Betafo

Antsirabe

2054m

2252m ▲

Marolambo

Mania

Fandriana

AMBOSITRA

Sakaleona

Nosy-Varika

Malaimbandy,
Morondava

N

Bradt

Ivato

0 ───── 50 km
0 ───────── 50 miles

Analamarina

Ikalamavony

Fianarantsoa

Ambohimahasoa

Ifanadiana

Vohilava

Antananarivo and Area

OVERVIEW

Looking down from the plane window as you approach Antananarivo you can see how excitingly different this country is from any of its near neighbours. Clusters of red clay houses and steepled churches stand isolated on the hilltops overlooking a mosaic of green and brown paddy fields. Old defence ditches, *tamboho*, form circles around villages or estates, and dotted in the empty countryside are the white concrete Merina tombs from where the dead will be exhumed in the *famadihana* ceremony.

Most people stay only a day or so in Tana, but there is plenty to see in the city and the surrounding Hauts Plateaux. A week would not be too long to experience the cultural, historical and natural sites which lie within a day's excursion of the capital. The Kingdom of Imerina thrived for over a century before French colonisation, so it is here that the rich and fascinating history and culture of the Merina people are best appreciated.

History

The recorded history of the Merina people (who are characterised by their Indonesian features) begins in the 1400s with a chief called Andriandraviravina. He is widely thought to have started the Merina dynasty that became the most powerful in Madagascar, eventually conquering much of the country.

Key monarchs in the rise of the Merina include Andrianjaka, who conquered a Vazimba town called Analamanga built on a great rock thrusting above the surrounding plains. He renamed it Antananarivo and ordered his palace to be built on its highest point. With its surrounding marshland, ideal for rice production, and the security afforded by its high position, this was the perfect site for a Merina capital city.

In the 18th century there were two centres for the Merina kingdom, Antananarivo and Ambohimanga. The latter became the more important and around 1787 Ramboasalama was proclaimed king of Ambohimanga and took the name of Andrianampoinimerina. The name means 'the prince in the heart of Imerina' which was more than an idle boast: this king was the Malagasy counterpart of the great Peruvian Inca Tupac Yupanqui, expanding his empire as much by skilful organisation as by force, and doing it without the benefit of a written language (history seems to demonstrate that orders in triplicate are not essential to efficiency). By his death in 1810 the central plateau was firmly in control of the Merina and ably administered through a mixture of old customs and new. Each conquered territory was governed by local princes, answerable to the king, and the system of *fokonolona* (village communities) was established. From this firm foundation the new king, Radama I, was able to conquer most of the rest of the island.

Antananarivo means 'City of the Thousand', supposedly because a thousand warriors protected it. By the end of the 18th century, Andrianampoinimerina had taken Antananarivo from his rebellious kinsman and moved his base there from Ambohimanga. From that time until the French conquest in 1895 Madagascar's history centred around the royal palace or *rova*, the modest houses built for Andrianjaka and Andrianampoinimerina giving way to a splendid palace designed for Queen Ranavalona I by Jean Laborde and later clad in stone by James Cameron. The rock cliffs near the palace became known as Ampamarinana, 'the place of the hurling', as Christian martyrs met their fate at the command of the Queen.

There was no reason for the French to move the capital elsewhere: its pleasant climate made it an agreeable place to live, and plenty of French money and planning went into the city we see today.

IVATO AIRPORT

Before describing the intricacies of arrival and departure it is worth mentioning the two restaurants at the airport. In the domestic arrivals/departure area there is a good café which serves tasty food from 06.00. The main restaurant is upstairs in the International section. It's quite smart, with waiter service and good food. As in all airports there are plenty of (expensive) souvenir shops and money changing facilities. The Socimad bank in International Departures gives a better rate of exchange than Bank Africa in Arrivals.

Arriving

In the Good Old Days Ivato was like the cottage of a wicked witch, seducing innocent visitors through its beguiling doors. Once inside, only the good and the brave emerged unscathed. Now (sigh) it is much the same as other international airports in the developing world. On arrival the procedure is as follows:

1 Fill in the Embarkation form. This should be handed to you on the plane, but you may need to retrieve one from an official by the Immigration desk. The questions are straightforward, but be prepared to say where you'll be staying in Tana.
2 If you do not have a visa, fill in the appropriate form and have the required amount (see page 85) ready.
3 Join one of the 'queues' for passport and visa check. (Look at the signs above each desk to make sure you are in the correct queue.)
4 Pick up luggage. There are trolleys to take your bags through customs. If you are carrying a video camera or something of value such as jewellery or a lap-top computer you should pass through the red channel and declare it. Failure to do this may cause problems on departure. Still cameras need not be declared (note that in French *camera* means a video camera; a still camera is *appareil*). If queuing for the green 'Nothing to Declare' channel, try to get behind other tourists who are usually waved through without needing to open their bags. Luggage belonging to Malagasy arrivals is usually thoroughly searched.
  Be warned that the porters at Ivato have become quite aggressive. Be on your guard and, unless you need help, insist on carrying your own stuff. If you do decide to use a porter they will take advantage of the flustered new arrival's tendency to over-tip and complain vociferously if yours does not come up to expectations. A dollar is more than enough.
5 If you can fight off the porters and taxi touts for a while longer, change money at the airport. The banks are always open for international flight arrivals.

Leaving

This has now been streamlined and is an almost normal procedure. Remember that you *must* reconfirm your flight at least 72 hours before your flight departs. At this point you may be able to ask for a seat allocation.

1 Arrive at the airport at least two hours before the flight, with all or most of all your Malagasy money spent. **Remember that you cannot change your Fmg back into hard currency**. The maximum you are supposed to take out with you is 25,000Fmg. The check-in counter is after you leave the main airport area (with shops), so once you have checked in there is nowhere to spend your Fmg. If you find yourself with unspent money, take it home and donate it to one of the charities listed on page 146. There is no longer a departure tax (or rather, it is now incorporated into the price of the ticket).
2 Pick up a departure form and join the queue for the departure gate (with your luggage). When you reach the doorway show your ticket and passport, and pass through baggage security. If the X-ray machine is working you're unlikely to be asked to open your bags but have the keys ready.
3 Proceed to the check-in counter. Any orderly queue will have disintegrated by now as people compete for priority.
4 Passport control. Hand in your departure form.
5 Final passport check, hand-luggage X-ray, and you're through into the departure lounge. There are souvenir shops here (hard currency only) and a bar. It is sometimes possible to change the Malagasy money you've belatedly found in your pocket into hard currency with the ladies who supervise the (very nice) toilets.

Internal flights

The domestic building is separated from the main (international) airport by a long corridor. These flights are no-frills: there are no seat assignments – and no concept of queuing – and no meals (but drinks and sweeties). All domestic flights are now no-smoking.

Lost luggage

Sometimes your luggage doesn't arrive. Most people are on a tight schedule and cannot hang around waiting for the next flight. If you are on an organised tour your guide will handle it, but if on your own it can be a bit of a challenge. For someone else to pick up your luggage you will need to get a proxy form with a signature that is legalised in the town hall. The only alternative is to meet every international flight (assuming it was lost on the way to Madagascar) in the hope that your bag is on it. Unclaimed bags are put under lock and key, and finding *le responsable* may not be easy.

Transport to the city centre (12km)

There is no specific airport bus service. Some of the larger hotels provide courtesy buses. Otherwise official taxis will cost you about 60,000Fmg or 80,000Fmg at night. If you walk purposefully across the carpark you will find some lurking unofficial taxis for around 40,000Fmg. Experienced travellers can go for the local bus which stops at the road junction about 100m from the airport. It costs only 1,000Fmg, and you can pay for an extra seat for your luggage. This bus takes you to the Vasakosy area behind the train station.

ANTANANARIVO (TANA) TODAY

From the right place, in the right light, Antananarivo (Tana for short) is one of the most attractive capitals in the developing world. In the evening sunshine it has the quality of a child's picture book, with brightly coloured houses stacked up the

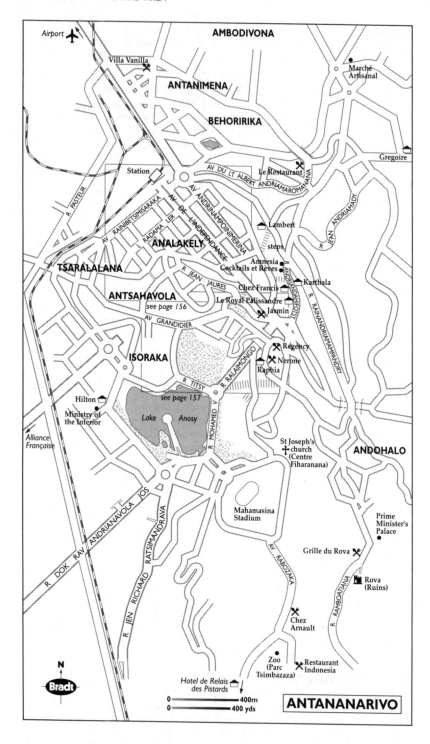

Airport

Villa Vanilla

AMBODIVONA

Marché
Artisanal

ANTANIMENA

BEHORIRIKA

Station

AV DU LT ALBERT ANDRIAMAROMANANA

Le Restaurant

Gregoire

R. PASTEUR

AV. ANDRINAMPOINIMERINA

AV RAINIBETSIMISARAKA

AV DE L'INDEPENDANCE

RADAMA 1ER

Lambert

steps

ANALAKELY

R JEAN JAURES

TSARALALANA

Amnesia
Cocktails et Rèves

Karthala

ANTSAHAVOLA

Chez Francis

RANDRIANDAHOTSY

see page 156

Le Royal Palissandre

RAINANDRIAMAMPANDRY

AV GRANDIDIER

Jasmin

R JEAN ANDRIAMDY

R TITSY

R RALAIMONGO

Regency

ISORAKA

Nerone

Raphia

see page 157

Hilton

R MOHAMED V

Lake

Anosy

Ministry of
the Interior

St Joseph's
church
(Centre
Fiharanana)

ANDOHALO

Alliance
Française

R. DOK RAV ANDRIANAVOLA JOS

R JEN RICHARD RATSIMANDRAVA

Mahamasina
Stadium

Prime
Minister's
Palace

AV RABOZANA

Grille du Rova

R RAMBOATIANA

Rova
(Ruins)

Chez
Arnault

Zoo
(Parc
Tsimbazaza)

Restaurant
Indonesia

N

Bradt

Hotel de Relais
des Pistards

0 ———— 400m
0 ———— 400 yds

ANTANANARIVO

hillsides, and mauve jacarandas and purple bougainvillea against the dark blue of the winter sky. Red crown-of-thorn euphorbia stand in rows against red clay walls, rice paddies are tended right up to the edge of the city, clothes are laid out on the canal bank to dry, and zebu-carts rumble along the roads on the outskirts of town. It's all deliciously foreign, and can hardly fail to impress the first-time visitor as he or she drives in from the airport. Indeed, this drive is one of the most varied and interesting in the Highlands. The good impression is helped by the climate – during the dry season the sun is hot but the air pleasantly cool (the altitude is between 1,245m and 1,469m).

Sadly, for many people this wonderful first impression does not survive a closer acquaintance. Tana can seem squalid and dangerous, with conspicuous poverty, persistent beggars, and a rising crime rate. The population of Tana is over two million and growing fast, but the annual budget for the city is the same as for a village of 2,000 people in France. In 1999 the new mayor of Tana, Marc Ravalomanana (now president-elect), launched a clean-up campaign with fines for a variety of misdemeanours including public drunkenness, urinating in the street, and setting up a market stall without a licence.

The geography of the city is both simple and confusing. It is built on two ridges which combine in a V. On the highest hill, dominating all the viewpoints, is the ruined Queen's Palace or *Rova*. Down the central valley runs a broad boulevard, Avenue de l'Indépendance (sometimes called by its Malagasy name Fahaleovantena), which terminates at the railway station. It narrows at the other end to become Rue du 26 Juin. To escape from this valley means climbing steps, if you are on foot, or driving through a tunnel if you are in a vehicle.

It is convenient to divide Tana into the two main areas most often wandered by visitors: Avenue de l'Indépendance and the side streets to its southwest (districts Analakely and Tsaralalana, or the Lower Town) and the smarter area at the top of the steps leading up from Rue du 26 Juin (districts Antaninarenina and Isoraka, or the Upper Town). Of course there are lots of other districts but most tourists will take taxis there rather than going on foot. This can be a challenging city to explore: streets are often unnamed, or change name several times within a few hundred metres, or go by two different names. When reading street names it's worth knowing that *Lalana* means street, *Arabe* is avenue, and *Kianja* is a square).

Telephone code The area code for Tana is 22.

Analakely and Tsaralalana (Lower Town)

Analakely (which means 'little forest') used to be famous for its large forest of white umbrellas, under which every product imaginable (and many unimaginable) used to be sold. Tana's *zoma* market was famous world wide. Now it has all gone (well, not quite… see box on page 156). In the late 1990s the city authorities, tired of the ever-increasing crime, rubbish, beggars and traffic chaos, called in the Japanese to clean it up. On my first post-cleanup visit I was shocked at the transformation. Instead of smiling ladies trying to sell me a goose or a herbal remedy there were bustling young men with mobile phones pressed to their ears; instead of parasols obstructing the pavement there are parked cars; instead of claustrophobia in the press of humanity, there is agoraphobia in the wide open spaces. Nevertheless, the residents love it and traffic now flows almost smoothly.

Avenue de l'Indépendance is a broad boulevard (grassed in the centre) with shops, snackbars, restaurants and hotels up each side. If you start at the station and walk up the right-hand side you will pass the Tana Plaza and Palace hotels, the city's best bookshop (Librairie de Madagascar), one of the best restaurants (O

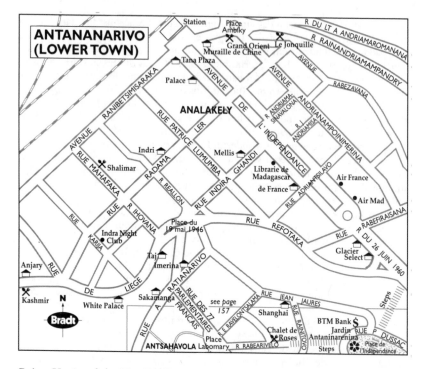

Poivre Vert) and the Hotel de France. Continuing south you reach one of Tana's liveliest bars (Glacier) and then you're at the steps up to Antaninarenina.

This is not a street for strolling – there are too many persistent beggars and souvenir vendors. And thieves. So walk briskly. Shopwise, the north side of the avenue is less interesting, but it does have several excellent snackbars, and the Air Madagascar and Air France office is here.

Tsaralalana is a more relaxing area of side streets to the south of Avenue de l'Indépendance (although maps do not indicate the steep climbs involved if you go too far). Walk down Rue Indira Gandhi (Rue Nice), past the bookshop Tout pour l'Ecole and the Mellis Hotel to the cumbersomely named Place du 19 Mai 1946.

THE SECRET ZOMA

If you stay at the Tana Plaza hotel, have a room overlooking the street at right angles to Avenue de l'Indépendance, and happen to glance out of the window at about 3am, an extraordinary sight will meet your eyes. In the small hours of each morning Rue Rainibetsimisaraka is thronged with rural Malagasy laying out their wares under the street lights amid whispered conversations. Pyramids of polished tomatoes, rows of huge cabbages, ranks of onions, their white bulbs glistening, heaps of rice, piles of pulses. For a few busy hours the people trade and sell, chat and argue, passing the time in the traditional Malagasy way. Soon after dawn they sweep up the remaining grains of rice, return unsold vegetables into their sacks, string the chickens' legs together, and trot off towards their smallholdings.

By the time the authorities arrive, the street is clear.

Beyond it are two mid-range hotels, the Taj and Imerina, and the very popular Sakamanga hotel/restaurant. To avoid a steep (rather dull) climb to Isoraka you can then double back on one of the parallel streets to Avenue de l'Indépendance.

Antaninarenina and Isoraka (Upper Town)

This is the Islington of Tana; or the Greenwich Village. Here are the art shops, the craft boutiques, the atmospheric hotels, the inexpensive guest houses, and a terrific but almost unknown museum. There is also a rose garden where, in October, the jacaranda trees drip their nectar on to the heads below. I love this area. There is no feeling of menace here (which is not to say crime doesn't exist) so this is the district for gentle strolling.

Start at the bottom of the steps, by the Select Hotel on Avenue de l'Indépendance and as you climb up, marvel that so many men can make a living selling rubber stamps. Visit the shopping arcade on the right, near the bottom of the steps, and check out some of the best postcards in Tana. At the top of the steps is Place de l'Indépendance, and Jardin Antaninarenina with its jacarandas and rose bushes. And benches. Nearby is Le Buffet du Jardin where you can sip a fruit juice in the sun. Other landmarks are the Ibis Hotel and the Champion supermarket. Turn left at the Maison and you come to the post office where, if you go through a side door to the philatelic counter, you can buy special-issue Malagasy stamps. If you feel like a coffee, cross the road to the Colbert. The streetside bar/café is where conservationists and other expats meet to discuss their latest challenges.

Now it's time to explore Isoraka. A 30-minute walk will show you the main sights. Start up Rue Rabehevitra, past the Radama Hotel and the good-value Isoraka Hotel. Turn left and you'll pass first the very nice little restaurant, Chez Sucette, then a cobbler's shop with a group of men sitting outside chatting and stitching. If you have anything that needs repairing, this is the place. On a corner is the small and friendly Résidence Lapasoa. At this point look out for a bronze

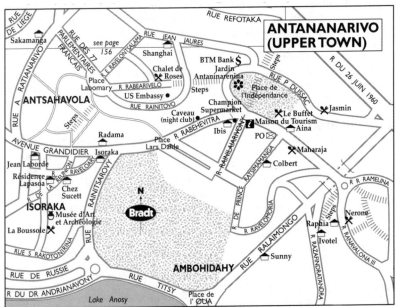

POVERTY IN ANTANANARIVO – WHAT'S BEING DONE?
Janice Booth

The very poor of Tana are known in French as 'les quatre mi' or 'the four mis'. This comes from the Malagasy words miloka (gambling), mifoka (drugs), misotro (drinking) and mijangajanga (prostitution). Some 10% of Madagascar's population of about 14 million are estimated to live in and around the capital, over half of them below poverty level. And it can be grim. However, encouragingly, more and more local organisations are targeting specific sectors.

The Sisters of the Good Shepherd, Centre Fihavanana (Soeurs du Bon Pasteur, 58 Lalana Stephani, Amparibe, 101 Antananarivo; tel: 29981) aim their well-run activities mainly at women and children. There are six sisters: Sri Lankan, French, Lebanese and Malagasy. About 180 children aged 3–12 are taught in four classes and many do well enough to get into State primary school. Undernourished babies (about 70) are fed and their mothers given training. Teenagers come to the centre to learn basic skills and handicrafts. Elderly people (about 150) come twice a month for a little food, company and care. Food is taken weekly to over 300 women, teenagers and children in prison. Finally 72 women do beautiful embroidery at home, while caring for their families, which provides an income both for them and for the centre. Visitors can help with cash, by buying handicrafts, or by donating any unwanted clothes or medicines at the end of their holiday.

Akany Avoko (BP 29, Ambohidratrimo 105, Madagascar; Stephen & Hardy Wilkinson; tel: 441 58) is a remand home for girls, run by the Protestant

'tree' hung with clay pots. This marks the Musée d'Art et Archéologie, which is a super little museum. Last time I visited, it was housing a private collection of traditional musical instruments, beautifully displayed and carefully labelled. One of the attendants was gently playing a *valiha*. Exhibitions change, so the current one may not be so good, but it's worth taking the chance. Entrance is free but a donation is appreciated – and deserved.

On the way back, drop in at one of Tana's best craft shops, Galerie Yerden on Rue Dr Villette, then pick whatever street you fancy to get you back to Place de l'Indépendance.

Getting around
Traffic jams and pollution are a major problem in Tana. Since 1989 the number of cars has increased from 43,000 to 150,000 in 2000: 882 vehicles per kilometre or one vehicle for every metre of road. It therefore makes sense to avoid vehicular transport when possible. Get to know the city on foot during the day (but carry nothing of value); use taxis for long distances, unknown destinations, and always at night.

Taxis should cost about 6,000Fmg for a short trip and 8,500Fmg for longer distances. Prices are much higher after dark, when a 6,000Fmg trip can cost 15,000Fmg. Taxis do not have meters so agree on the price before you get in. Expect to pay more than the locals, but avoid the exorbitant *vazaha* price charged by the taxis serving the big hotels. Battered old vehicles which wouldn't dare go near a hotel will be cheaper and you have the extra bonus of watching the street go by through the hole in the floor, or being pushed by helpful locals when the vehicle breaks down or runs out of petrol.

Federation of Madagascar. Its work began in 1959 when the Church asked the State to allow young girls accused of petty crime to be re-educated rather than sent to prison. The home is designed for up to 75 girls but at present has about 100; two-thirds of them placed there by the Juvenile Court in Tana, mostly for minor offences. The remaining one-third are either abandoned children or else girls placed by their families because of problems. Many of the court referrals are country girls who were sent to the city by their parents to work, but earned pitifully little and were tempted to steal. It may take up to three years for their cases to be heard. Many had little or no schooling so are taught literacy as well as handicrafts and gardening. Others may go to local schools. Girls who had felt rejected regain self-respect.

The State pays about 30c a day for those sent by the courts. Families who place girls in the home are expected to contribute something, but not all can. The World Food Programme provides some rice, cooking oil and beans, and other organisations have helped with specific projects (repairs, construction etc). Individual donations are welcome.

Saomify Stérelle Razafinjato, Lot 2H 127A, Soavimasoandro, Antananarivo 101; tel: 437 29. Recommended by 'vazagasy' reader Claudie Ravoninjatovo, this charity is a group of 25 individuals dedicated to improving the lot of residents in the Soavimasoandro district, which is a suburb of Tana. This is a broad-based organisation, but one of Stérelle's projects is helping aimless youngsters by sponsoring a rugby team. They are therefore always grateful for donations of rugby kit.

Stérelle is also sometimes able to assist in arranging international adoptions.

The great advantage of not having meters is that if the driver gets lost (which frequently happens) you will not pay any more for the extra journey. In my experience Tana taxi drivers are honest and helpful and can be trusted to get you to your destination – eventually. They will also pick you up at an agreed time.

Buses are much cheaper, but sorting out the destinations and districts can be difficult. Good maps of Tana are now available which makes this task much easier.

Safety

Sadly, robbery has become quite common in Tana. Leave your valuables in the hotel (preferably in a safe deposit or locked in your bag) and carry as little as possible. Avenue de l'Indépendance seems particularly risky. One scam is the 'Ballet of the Hats'. Kids carrying wide-brimmed straw hats encircle you and, using the hats to obscure your view, work through your pockets, money-belt, neck pouch or whatever. If you can manage to carry nothing at all – no watch, no camera, no money... not even a paper tissue in your pocket, you will bring back the best souvenirs: memories. But few people (myself included) heed this advice, so just be on your guard and never wander around with something like a passport or your airline tickets which you really can't afford to lose (see box on page 160 but also heed the ID warning on page 117).

Where to stay

New hotels and restaurants are opening all the time in Tana. This selection is by no means complete – be adventurous and find your own!

ALL'S WELL...

Janice Booth

Airline incompetence caused me to arrive in Madagascar for the 2001 total eclipse minus my luggage – so I went off to the Champion supermarket, down in the Faravohitra area near Avenue de l'Indépendance, and then to a nearby street market, to replace basic items. It was good to be back in Tana and the time passed quickly; afternoon sunlight soon turned to dusk.

The theft was carried out with copybook slickness. A hand reached out silently from the deepening shadows and tugged at my small wrist purse, which I had wedged (I thought) securely under my arm. I clutched it with both hands, but the thief was strong – gradually my fingers lost their grip. I chased after him, shouting (in French) 'Stop thief! That man in red! Stop him!' Malagasy passers-by turned and stared – but he ran too fast for them to react. They stopped me from pursuing him up the narrow Escalier Rahoerason, warning me anxiously that it wasn't safe.

The catastrophe was that the bag contained my passport, which I was carrying only because the receptionist had handed it to me just as I was leaving the hotel and I hadn't bothered to take it back to my room.

Luckily I was with an efficient tour company, Za Tours. The director's husband took me to the main police station. He translated for me during the lengthy questioning (no-one seemed to speak much French or English); then we waited while an official typed out a formal 'declaration' in triplicate, with two fingers, on an ancient manual typewriter. If you lose your passport, this 'declaration' is vital – it gives temporary proof of identity and backs up insurance claims.

Next morning, after completing the necessary forms at the British Embassy (for a temporary Travel Document to get me back to Britain I needed 300,000Fmg plus two passport photos), I went to the offices of the newspaper *Midi* to insert an advertisement, giving Za Tours' phone number and offering an unspecified 'reward' for the passport's return. I also asked a journalist to interview me for the next day's edition. Then, one of Za Tours' Malagasy staff came with me to the area where I'd been robbed, to talk to the street vendors. He wrote out a short notice in Malagasy, giving details of the theft and Za Tours' phone number – I had several photocopies made and friendly stallholders agreed to display them.

I rejoined the tour group and continued my trip. Ten days later when we returned to Tana there was no news. I was in Za Tours' office collecting my return air ticket when the phone rang. The director answered it. Amazed, she told me: 'It's a man who says he's found your passport!'

Her driver rattled me off across Tana in a 4WD and located a small mechanic's workshop. Inside, an oil-stained Chinaman wiped his hands on a rag and greeted me with great dignity. My passport was in his safe. He said he had found it in the street, not far from where I'd been robbed, and accepted the reward with just the right level of reluctance.

For security reasons the British Embassy had cancelled the passport's validity, so I phoned to get it re-activated. And tucked it lovingly away into a secure, concealed, inside pocket, well protected from thieving fingers!

Category A

Hilton Hotel Rue Pierre Stibbe, Anosy; tel: 260 60; fax: 260 51; email: sales_madagascar@hilton.com. On the western side of Lake Anosy. €170 double, €145 single. One of Tana's skyscrapers (as you'd expect), with lovely views from the upper floors and comfortable rooms. Its advantages are the offices and shops in the building, including a cybercafé, and the swimming pool. In the pleasantly hot sun of the dry season this is a real bonus. It is some way from the centre of town (though the walk is enjoyable). Most credit cards accepted. Free airport transfers.

Hotel Colbert Rue Printsy Ratsimamanga, Antaninarenina; tel: 202 02; fax: 340 12 or 254 97; email: colbert@dts.mg or colbert@simicro.mg; web: www.madagascar-guide.com/colbert. €83–153 per room (small double to studio apartment). An extension opened in March 2002. Very French, often full, recommended for its good location, nice atmosphere and excellent food. Continental breakfast €7. Most credit cards accepted.

Hotel Le Royal Palissandre 13 Rue Andriandahifotsy (shown on some maps as Rue Romain Desfossés), Faravohitra; tel: 326 14 and 605 60; fax: 326 24; email: HotelPalissandre@simicro.mg. A recommended hotel with all comforts, good food, lovely views, and a pleasant location within walking distance of the centre of town. Rooms: €83 double, €76 single; breakfast €7.5.

Palace Hotel BP 607; tel: 256 63; fax: 339 43. Rooms vary in size, the largest being studio apartments. €55–80. Breakfast €6. Owned by Hotel de France, this is a smart hotel at the lower end of the Av de l'Indépendance. No restaurant, but a short walk to the Tana Plaza.

Tana Plaza 2 Av de l'Indépendance (near the station); tel: 662 60 and 218 65; fax: 642 19; email: hdf-tana@dts.mg. €53 + 3,000Fmg tax. An upmarket hotel with small but good rooms (the ones facing the street are noisy but some have a special view – see box on page 156).

Hotel de France 34 Av de l'Indépendance; tel: 202 93 or 213 04; fax: 201 18; email: hdf-tana@dts.mg. Double room €52; breakfast €6. Large rooms, convenient location and good food.

Hotel Ibis 4 Pl de l'Indépendance; tel: 390 00; fax: 640 40; email: ibistana@simicro.mg. €53 (single), €60 (double), €86 de luxe. Breakfast €6. Convenient, safe location, comfortable, well-run, with a pleasant, small bar and good restaurant.

Radama Hotel 22 Av Ramanantsoa, Isoraka; tel: 319 27; fax: 353 23; email: radama@simicro.mg; web: www.madonline.com/voyages/radama. From €46 (double room to studio apartment); breakfast €4. A very nice small (18 room) hotel in a great location. Rooms vary, so hold out for a good one with a view. Impractical for groups because there is no parking for tour buses, but ideal for business people (there is a conference room) or independent travellers. No lift (elevator). Most credit cards accepted.

Category B

Karib Hotel Av de l'Indépendance; tel: 665 54 or 649 48; fax: 629 32; email: karibotel@dts.mg. From €40 to €47. Two blocks down from Tana Plaza. Clean, safe, comfortable. Credit cards accepted.

Ivotel BP 816, Ambohidahy (near Lake Anosy); tel: 227 16; fax: 249 29; email: ivotel@dts.mg. 20 simple but comfortable rooms including 5 studio apartments. 255,000–350,000Fmg per room. Good restaurant, friendly service, reliable hot water.

Sunny Hotel Rue Ralaimongo (northeast side of Lake Anosy); tel: 263 04; fax: 290 78; email: rasseta@bow.dts.mg. 20 rooms, 3 suites, 350,000–500,000Fmg. A good location (though not sunny) handy for both lower and upper town; friendly staff, good food.

White Palace Hotel 101 Rue de Liège, Tsaralalana; tel: 664 59 or 669 98; fax 602 98. A mid-range hotel conveniently located in the lower town but some rooms reportedly damp in wet weather. Studio rooms with cooking facilities 228,000Fmg; double/twin rooms with bath 123,000–203,000Fmg. All comforts including TV in rooms.

Indri Hotel 15 Rue Radama, Tsaralalana (1½ blocks from Av de l'Indépendance); tel/fax: 209 22. €27 (single) or €35 (double) for the best rooms (TV, minibar, en-suite bathrooms) or 95,000–175,000Fmg for more simple rooms. Comfortable, friendly, medium-sized hotel in a convenient location with a lively cocktail bar.

Hotel Mellis Rue Indira Gandhi; tel: 234 25 or 660 70; fax: 626 60; email: htmellis@dts.mg. 80,000–245,000Fmg. A perennial favourite in a convenient location, but now somewhat rundown.

Taj Hotel 69 Rue de Liège, Tsaralalana (near Place du 19 Mai 1946); tel: 624 9/10; fax: 667 20. 130,000Fmg single/double. Comfortable rooms with hot water.

Résidence Imerina 7 Rue Emile Rajohnson (continuation of Indira Gandhi); tel/fax: 357 04; cellphone: 030 23 820 09. Rooms 126,000Fmg to 201,000Fmg, all with en-suite bathrooms. Good value.

Sakamanga Rue A Ratianarivo; tel: 358 09; fax: 245 87; email: saka@malagasy.com. 10 rooms, 110,000–165,000Fmg, all with en-suite bathrooms. French run, very pleasant (though noisy) but almost always full. There is an excellent, lively French restaurant, also heavily booked.

Hotel Anjary Rue Razafimahandry and Dr Ranaivo, Tsaralalana; tel: 244 09; fax: 234 18. 130,000Fmg double with shower. Clean, large, secure, friendly. Reliable hot water. The rooms on the 4th floor are best but avoid those facing the (noisy) street. Massage for 40,000Fmg per hour.

Hotel Aina 17 Rue Ratsimilaho; tel: 630 51; email: ainahtl@dts.mg. 148,000Fmg. Just beyond the Colbert. No restaurant 'but with the Colbert just around the corner, who cares?' Recommended as efficient and good value.

La Karthala 48 Rue Andriandahifotsy; tel: 248 95; fax: 272 67. Rooms 85,000–95,000Fmg. Not as conveniently located as some, but the chance to be at home with a Malagasy family. Madame Rafalimanana speaks good English.

Hotel Shanghai 4 Rue Rainitovo (near the US Embassy); tel: 314 72. Room rates are highly competitive, with a double room at 115,000Fmg. A good breakfast costs 13,000Fmg.

Hotel Le Jean Laborde 3 Rue de Russie, Isoraka; tel: 330 45; fax: 327 94. Rooms vary in price from 67,000Fmg (shared bathroom) to 175,000Fmg (suite). Once an excellent hotel, in a quiet, safe area, but reportedly becoming rather shabby. Nicknamed by one reader as Labordelle because of the group exodus of prostitutes in the early morning. But the staff are friendly, and there's a good French restaurant.

Résidence Lapasoa 15 Rue de la Réunion, Isoraka; tel/fax: 611 40; email: corossol@malagasy.com. 7 rooms, 180,000Fmg single, 185,000Fmg double, including breakfast. A friendly little B&B in a nice part of town, ideal for lone travellers.

Hotel Raphia Rue Ranavalona III, Ambatonakanga (Upper Town); tel: 253 13. A nice hotel with 7 rooms and a garden, lovely views over Lake Anosy. 110,000Fmg (shared bathroom) and 125,000Fmg (en suite).

Le Relais des Pistards BP 3550, Rue Fernand Kasanga (same road as Tsimbazaza), about 1km beyond the zoo; tel: 291 34. 95,000Fmg (shared facilities) or 120,000Fmg en suite. Price includes breakfast. A friendly, family-style hotel run by Florent and Jocelyn Colney. Pleasant communal dining room, and excellent cooking. Florent Colney is an avid mountain biker, so a stay here is a must for those planning to cycle in Madagascar. His advice will be invaluable.

La Muraille de Chine 1 Av de l'Indépendance; tel: 281 41 or 230 13; fax: 628 82; email: murchine@dts.mg. Rooms from 110,000Fmg to 185,000Fmg, all en suite. One of Tana's longest-established hotels, but is not up to the standard of others in the area.

Hotel Mandana 4 Rue Ratianarivo; tel: 661 15; fax: 649 68. 100,000Fmg and up for rooms with a cold shower and toilet. Breakfast 10,000Fmg. A nice hotel, just down the hill from the Sakamanga. Look for the mural-like doorway.

Category C

Hotel Restaurant Chez Francis Rue Andriandahifotsy (a little way up the hill from the Royal Palissandre); tel/fax: 613 65; email: chezfrancis@vaniala.com. 12 rooms with shower. 2 clean WCs on each landing. 90,000Fmg double, 150,000Fmg treble. A super little place in a good location with lovely views over Tana from the back rooms (could be noisy at the front).

Select Hotel Av de l'Indépendance; tel: 210 01. Rooms 85,000Fmg with en-suite bathrooms. An ugly tower block, but conveniently located near the steps to the Upper Town.

Hotel Isoraka 11 Av Gal Ramanantsoa, Ambatonilita; tel: 355 81; fax: 658 54; cellphone: 032 02 188 99. 55,000Fmg (single), 70,000–80,000Fmg (double). One of the few budget hotels in the Upper Town. Clean, with hot water. Communal bathroom. Extremely friendly and helpful; offers airport transfers (55,000Fmg), snack bar and laundry service. 'I cannot sing its praises enough.' (D Fellner)

Hotel Lambert Tel: 229 92. Up the opposite flight of stairs to those that lead to Place de l'Indépendance. Basic, clean, convenient; 56,000–66,000Fmg. Good value and popular, but be prepared to climb a lot of stairs!

Hotel Glacier 46 Av de l'Indépendance; tel: 202 60; 291 04. Rooms 95,000Fmg. One of the oldest – and shabbiest – hotels in Tana, but it is conveniently located, has a lively bar (full of prostitutes) and excellent music with *salegy* bands from all over Madagascar.

Chambres d'Hôte 'Jim' At intersection of Rues Grandidier and Andrianary; tel: 22 876 37/033 11 827 86. New, clean, balconies with sunset views. En-suite showers, shared toilet. About 40,000Fmg. Only 3 rooms so phone first.

Bed and breakfast

Villa Soamahatony BP 4313, Antananarivo 101; cellphone: 033 110 33 37; email: soamahatony@dts.mg. 3 rooms with shared facilities; 120,000Fmg (double). Breakfast 15,000Fmg; lunch and dinner 40,000Fmg. Stay en famille with Sahondra and Daniel, a very knowledgable French-Malagasy couple who have been helping visitors enjoy Madagascar for many years. Their villa, set in 2ha of grounds, is in Ankadivory (Ankadivory – Ambohijanahary – Ambohibao – Antehiroky), ten minutes by car from Ivato airport. With advance notice they will pick you up from the airport and arrange car rental for short excursions. See their website: http://takelaka.dts.mg/soamahatony.

Soamiandry Sarl BP 11035, Antananarivo; tel: 444 54; fax: 623 45. (16 rooms) Family run (so book ahead). 'Joshua and Fara try to do everything for you; it's one of those places you remember.' Garden, swimming pool. €15 double, with breakfast.

Accommodation near the airport

It can take 45 minutes to get to the airport from the centre of town, so staying nearby is a sensible option, especially when you have an early morning flight.

Hotel/Restaurant Auberge d'Alsace Route d'Ivato 105 Mandrosoa; tel: 446 56; fax: 623 45; email: ratsitoarisoa@dts.mg. 85,000Fmg per room; additional bed 20,000Fmg. Large rooms with desk, en-suite large bathrooms. Good restaurant. This hotel also arranges car-hire for €6.5 per day.

Auberge du Cheval Blanc BP 23, Ivato; tel: 446 46; email: Chevalblanc@dts.mg. Rooms 100,000Fmg single/double. Restaurant. MasterCard and Visa accepted.

Le Manoir Rouge Tel: 441 04; fax: 482 44. Rooms from 40,000Fmg (shared bathroom) to 75,000Fmg (en suite) and 95,000Fmg (bungalow). Camping permitted. Good food. Cybercafé. Recommended by Jim Bond as 'definitely the best value I've come across around Ivato'.

Hotel Ivato Lot K6/28 Imotro, Ivato; tel/fax: 445 10 or 743 05; cellphone: 03311 01 463; email: ivatohotel@dts.mg. Rooms 85,000–145,000Fmg. Friendly, clean, hot showers. Reasonable restaurant.

Résidence Tanikely BP31 Ivato 105; tel: 453 96; fax: 453 97; cellphone: 032 07 101 82. 2 bungalows, 4 rooms. 330,000Fmg double. French-owned, comfortable self-contained units, with cooking facilities, set in a pleasant garden with a swimming pool. Ideal for families.
Hotel Restaurant Farihy ME 475 Mandrosoa, Ivato; tel: 744 62; fax: 307 74. €20 per bungalow; breakfast €4.50. Very pleasant. Recommended.
Auberge du Jardin Lot 57B; tel/fax: 441 74. Down a side road on the left as you approach Ivato (about 10 minutes from the airport). A very nice small place (5 rooms) with a good restaurant. €18 per room; breakfast €3. Airport transfers 12,000Fmg.
Tonga Soa Mandrosoa; tel: 442 88. This pleasant restaurant (see *Where to eat*), only 5 minutes from the airport, has added some rooms. 4 are ready now, and a total of 13 are planned.
Villa Loharanontsoa Lot 316 MD Mandrosa, Ivato; tel: 441 42; email: frazaka@simicro.mg. Rooms 75,000Fmg to 90,000Fmg including breakfast.

Where to eat
Hotel restaurants
Most of the better hotels serve good food. Expats and Malagasy professionals favour the **Colbert**. The 'all you can eat' Sunday buffet is good value (but beware of the health risks of eating cold buffets). There are two restaurants at the Colbert; the Taverne is the smartest and imposes a dress code on its diners. The food and service are excellent – this is the place to go for that special treat. Phone 202 02 for reservations. Bring your French dictionary – menus are not translated.

The **Tana Plaza** has an excellent restaurant with live music (traditional) in the bar.

The **Hilton** does a whole series of buffets which in the past were very good; standards seem to have declined recently, however.

The restaurant at the **Radama** (Tatao) is considered by many to be excellent; others report that its standards have deteriorated. At its best it has very good French and Malagasy cooking.

The **O! Poivre Vert** at the Hotel de France is popular and good.

The **Sakamanga** restaurant is crowded and lively, with excellent food. This is the restaurant of choice for young people, so book ahead: tel: 35 809. It also has internet facilities.

An Indian restaurant on the 7th floor of the **Anjary** hotel is recommended for the good food and super views (no alcohol).

Upper and middle range restaurants
Le Restaurant 65, Rue Emile Ranarivelo, Behoririka; tel: 282 67. A lovely colonial house with a terrace overlooking superb gardens. Excellent food, attentive service. Highly recommended.
Villa Vanille Pl Antanimena; tel: 205 15. A fine old Tana house five minutes by taxi from Tana Plaza, specialising in Creole food. Music (traditional and jazz) every evening. 'Fabulous – it was so good we had to go back. They also have Malagasy art for sale.' (D Simon)
Au Grille du Rova About 100 metres down from the ruins of the Queen's Palace; tel: 627 24; fax: 622 13. Good food, eaten indoors or outside, with a view over the city: about 35,000Fmg. Traditional Malagasy music every Sunday, from midday to sunset. Closed Sunday evening. Good English spoken. Recommended.
Maharaja Round the corner from the Colbert; tel: 686 28. An up-market Indian restaurant serving an excellent selection of dishes.
Le Regency 15 Rue Ramelina, Ambatonakanga; tel: 210 13. French owned, and run with flair and elegance. Lovely atmosphere and super food.

Nerone Rue Ranavalona III; tel: 231 18. A small, up-market Italian restaurant offering a variety of à la carte dishes. Italian wines. Recommended.

La Pradelle Ambatoroka (southeast of the city); tel: 326 51. English spoken, Malagasy and European food, highly recommended by readers and residents.

La Boussole Rue de Dr Villette, Isoraka. A stylish French restaurant with excellent food, a cosy bar and a charming patio for outdoor dining. Especially lively on Friday nights.

La Jonquille 7 Rue Rabezavana, Soarano; tel 206 37. Good, imaginative menu, mainly Chinese. Especially good for seafood. Reasonable prices. Recommended.

Restaurant Jasmin 8 Rue Paul-Dussac; tel: 342 96. Good Chinese food.

Chez Arnault Rue Rabozaka (the road leading from Mahamasina stadium to the zoo). 'Without doubt the best pizza in town!' Also a good French menu and pasta dishes. Quite pricey, however.

Tonga Soa Mandrosoa (about 2km from Ivato airport); tel: 442 88. A small, intimate restaurant run by Mme Nina and husband (and chef) Patrick. 'This is the most pleasant little restaurant I know in Tana and a wonderful place to go for a quiet evening meal or on the way to the airport. The menu is not as extensive as some (because Patrick will only use fresh ingredients) but the food is the best in Tana' (Nick Garbutt). There is another reason to visit: 'The lush gardens are well planted with trees, shrubs and flowers that attract a wide variety of birdlife and there are also upwards of 50 jewel chameleons here. They lay their eggs at the edges of the car park!'

Restaurant le Chateaubriant Mandrosoa, Ivato; tel/fax: 442 69; cellphone: 0331181736. Outstanding cooking from an Paris-trained chef. Conveniently close to the airport.

Le Grand Orient Tel: 202 88. Round the corner from the railways station. One of Tana's long-established restaurants. Chinese, fairly expensive, but an extensive menu, nice atmosphere and piano music every night.

Budget restaurants

Restaurant Chez Sucett 23 Rue Raveloary, Isoraka; tel: 261 00. A pleasant small restaurant in a safe area, serving excellent food. About 19,000Fmg for a meal.

Restaurant Pati Down the road from Tsimbazaza. Very good and economically priced meals. Large portions. Try the Chinese soup.

Restaurant Indonesia Directly across from the zoo entrance. Surprisingly, this is the only Indonesian restaurant in Madagascar. Recommended.

Chalet des Roses 13 Rue de l'Auximad (in the centre of town, opposite the American Embassy); tel: 642 33. 'A fabulous and cheap Italian restaurant.'

Kashmir 5–7 Rue Dr Ranaivo (opposite Anjary Hotel). Muslim, very good and reasonably priced food.

Shalimar 5 Rue Mahafaka, Tsaralalana; tel: 260 70. Good curries and a selection of vegetarian dishes.

Le Muget A cheap and cheerful Chinese restaurant at the bottom of the steps leading to the Lambert hotel.

Hotel Glacier The meals are nothing special, but the decor is! Pure 1930s, with polished wood, huge murals and even larger mirrors.

Snack bars

Le Buffet du Jardin Pl de l'Indépendance. This fast-food restaurant is a convenient place for lunch, a beer or coffee, with pleasant outdoor tables. Ideal for people-watching and meeting other travellers or foreigners living in Madagascar. The food is mediocre, however.

Croissant d'Or Rue Indira Gandhi. Serves great breakfasts and is open at 07.30 all week and 08.00 on Sundays.

THE MUSIC OF MADAGASCAR: A BRIEF INTRODUCTION
Ian A Anderson

The music of Madagascar is like the island itself – owing many things to other parts of the world, but unique.

The Malagasy are very fond of harmony singing, varying from Polynesian style (the Merina) to almost East African on the west coast. Traditional musical instruments include the celebrated *valiha*, a member of the zither family with 21 strings stretched lengthways all around the circumference of a hollow bamboo tube (there's also a box variety called the *marovany*), the *sodina*, an end-blown flute that can work magic in the hands of a master like Rakotofra (find his picture on the old 1,000Fmg note); the *kabosy*, a small guitar with paired strings and partial frets; the *jejy voatavo* with a gourd resonator and two sets of strings on adjacent sides of the neck; the *lokanga bara*, a 3-string fiddle; and a great variety of percussion instruments.

You'll also find most western instruments, successfully adapted to local music. Visit Ambohimanga, for example, to hear one of several generations of blind accordion players. Catch one of the *hira gasy* troupes and they'll be using ancient brass instruments and clarinets. Visit a nightclub or a larger concert and a modern band such as Jaojoby, Mily Clement or Tianjama will have electric guitars, synthesisers, and kit drums and might play one of the wild Malagasy dance styles such as *salegy*, *balesa*, *watsa watsa* or *sega*. Malagasy music has also enjoyed a big explosion of outside interest in recent years. The artists who have gained the most success touring abroad in the

Avenue de l'Indépendance has a growing number of eateries: **Tropique** (good pastries and ice-cream), **Honey** (very good for breakfast and ice-cream, but closed at weekends), **Solimar** for tamarind juice, and **Le Croissanterie** for fresh fruit juice. Also **Bouffe Rapide** and **La Potinerie** (near Air Mad). In the Upper Town both the **Patisserie Suisse** (Rue Rabehevitra) and the **Patisserie Colbert** do good pastries and teas. Patisserie Suisse serves a delicious range of cakes and tarts, but closes at midday for up to three hours.

Do-it-yourself meals can be purchased anywhere. Yoghurt is a particularly good buy and is available even in small towns. Carry your own spoon. Even more convenient – and delicious – is the drinking yoghurt, '*Yaourt à boire*'.

Nightlife
Papillon at the Hilton is a popular nightclub. Also **Le Caveau** (4, Rue Jeneraly Rabehevitra, Antaninarenina; tel: 343 93) which has the **Kaleidoscope** disco on the same premises. Another disco is **L'Amnesia** (8 Rue Andriandafotsy, Ambondrono; tel: 273 41). Next door is **Cocktails et Rêves**, which has a darts board for homesick Brits. The **Indra** nightclub in Tsaralalana is also recommended.

The most popular nightspot is **Piano Bar Acapulco**, near Place de l'Indépendance (14 Rue Ratsimilaho; tel: 232 25), which features local bands, jazz and solo piano. The **Groove Box**, near Tsimbazaza, also draws the crowds. A live band plays jazz on Thursday, international music on Fridays, and dance music on Saturdays.

Finally, it's worth having a drink at the Hotel **Glacier**, on Avenue de l'Indépendance, to admire the wonderful 1930s decor and to observe the more disreputable side of Tana's nightlife!

mid '90s have been Tarika, the Justin Vali Trio, Jaojoby, Njava and guitarist D'Gary.

Finding live music in Madagascar is a hit-and-miss affair; don't expect the real thing to be laid on for tourists in hotels. Keep an eye open for concert posters, and check out clubs used by local people.

The local cassette market has greatly expanded in recent years, though tapes are of variable quality. There are now even a few locally marketed CDs, but Malagasy music on record is still best purchased in Europe or North America where there is now a huge CD selection. A regularly updated Madagascar CD-ography can be found on the Internet at www.froots.demon.co.uk/madaged.html. The following small sample is a good starting point:

Tarika: *Son Egal* (Xenophile XENO 4042) (USA)
The Justin Vali Trio: *Ny Marinal/The Truth* (Real World CDRW51) (UK)
Justin Vali: *The Sunshine Within* (Bush Telegraph Records) (UK)
Jaojoby: *Salegy!* (Xenophile XENO 4040) (USA)
Various: *Big Rd* (Nascente) (UK)
Various: *The Marovany of Madagascar* (Silex Y 225224) (France)
Various: *Madagasikara 2 – Current Popular Music* (GlobeStyle CDORBD 013) (UK)
Various: *Madagaskar 3 – Sounding Bamboo* (Feuer & Els FUEC 712) (Germany)
Various: *Les Grands Maitres Du Salegy* (Sonodisc) (France)

A good source for these Malagasy CDs in London is Stern's African Record Shop, 293 Euston Road, London W1P 5PA.

Entertainment

If you are in Tana for a while, buy a local paper to see what's on or keep an eye out for posters advertising special shows or events. For a truly Malagasy experience go to a performance of *hira gasy* (pronounced 'heera gash'). See box on page 168. There are regular Sunday performances at Andavamamba, in the front yard of a grey concrete three-storey house set back off the street that goes past Alliance Français. A few Malagasy flags fly above the high, red brick wall and the entrance is via a footpath (not signposted). It starts at 10.00 and finishes around 16.00. Tickets cost 4,000Fmg. Part of the seating is under a tarpaulin canopy and the rest is in the open. It's an exciting and amusing day out – have plenty of small denomination notes ready to support the best performers. There are food stalls with drinks. If you miss the Andavamamba *hira gasy* you can arrange to see a performance at Akany Avoko (see pages 147 and 158).

Any entertainment that allows you to join a Malagasy audience will be worth the entrance fee (see box on page 317).

Films are dubbed into French.

WHAT TO SEE AND DO

As if to emphasise how different it is to other capitals, Tana has relatively little in the way of conventional sightseeing, and even less since the Queen's Palace (*Rova*) burned down. However, there's quite enough to keep you occupied for a few days. **La Maison du Tourisme** in theory produces printed lists of hotels, tour operators, car-hire companies etc, and sells good quality T-shirts, handicrafts and postcards. In practice they have little to offer. They may have maps, but better quality ones can be bought in bookshops. Open 09.30–11.30, 15.30–17.30; closed on Sunday, and other times if they feel like it. They have moved from their convenient location in Place de l'Independance to Isoraka.

HIRA GASY

A visit to a session of *hira gasy* provides a taste of genuine Malagasy folklore – performed for the locals, not for tourists.

In the British magazine *Folk Roots* Jo Shinner describes a *hira gasy*: 'It is a very strange, very exciting affair: a mixture of opera, dance and Speaker's Corner bound together with a sense of competition.

'The performance takes place between two competing troupes of singers and musicians on a central square stage. It's an all day event so the audience packs in early, tea and peanut vendors picking their way through the throng. Audience participation is an integral part – the best troupe is gauged by the crowd's response. Throughout the day performers come into the crowd to receive small coins offered in appreciation.

'The most immediate surprise is the costumes. The men enter wearing 19th-century French, red, military frock coats and the women are clad in evening dress from the same period. Traditional *lamba* are carefully arranged around their shoulders, and the men wear straw Malagasy hats. The musicians play French military drums, fanfare trumpets, flutes, violins and clarinets. The effect is bizarre rather than beautiful.

'The *hira gasy* is in four parts. First there are the introductory speeches or *kabary*. Each troupe elects a speaker who is usually a respected elder. His skill is paramount to a troupe. He begins with a long, ferociously fast, convoluted speech excusing himself and his inadequacy, before the audience, ancestors, his troupe, his mother, God, his oxen, his rice fields and so on – and on! Then follows another speech glorifying God, and then a greeting largely made up of proverbs.

'The *hira gasy* pivots around a tale of everyday life, such as the dire consequences of laziness or excessive drinking, is packed with wit, morals and proverbs and offers advice, criticism and possible solutions. The performers align themselves along two sides of the square at a time to address different parts of the audience. They sing in harsh harmony, illustrating their words with fluttering hand movements and expressive gestures, egged on by the uproarious crowd's appreciation. Then it is the dancers' turn. The tempo increases and becomes more rhythmic as two young boys take to the floor with a synchronised display of acrobatic dancing that nowadays often takes its influence from karate.'

Rova

For over a century the Queen's Palace, or *Rova*, the spiritual centre of the Merina people, dominated the skyline of Tana. In November 1995 it was destroyed by fire – an act of arson unprecedented in Madagascar's history.

The ruin still dominates the skyline – in some ways more dramatically than before – but work to repair it has been halted. However, it is worth the walk up to the palace for the view and to imagine its former grandeur.

Prime Minister's Palace (Musée d'Andafiavaratra)

This former residence of Rainilaiarivony (he who married three queens) has been painstakingly restored and now houses the few precious items that were saved from the *Rova* fire. It was built in 1872 by the British architect William Pool. After independence it became in turn army barracks, law courts, a school of fine arts, the presidential palace and (again) the prime minister's palace. It was burned in 1975. The museum is open from 10.00 to 17.00. Closed Mondays. Entry fee 3,000Fmg.

Tsimbazaza

This comprises a museum (natural history and ethnology), botanical garden and zoo exhibiting – with a few exceptions – only Malagasy species.

The zoo and botanical garden

Until 1999 Tsimbazaza (pronounced Tsimbazaz, and meaning 'where children are forbidden', dating from when it was a sacred site) was the centre for the Madagascar Fauna Group, an international consortium of zoos and universities working together to help conserve Madagascar's wildlife. Sadly, the group has withdrawn its financial support, tired of the interminable struggle to bring the zoo up to Western standards. This is disheartening, but gives us a chance to step back and consider the importance of Tsimbazaza to the local people. They *love* coming here, and put on their best clothes for the occasion. As Joanna Durbin of the Durrell Wildlife Conservation Trust (one of the former supporters) comments: 'It is full to overflowing on Sundays and Bank Holidays. I expect that many of those people save up to be able to take their entire family there. You also see lots of school groups during the week'. The chief attraction is the ostrich! And why not? An ostrich is a far more extraordinary animal to a Malagasy child than a lemur.

That said, I no longer bring groups to Tsimbazaza, except to see the aye-aye at night, because too many people find it depressing. As Quentin Bloxam (Zoo Programme Director at the Durrell Wildlife Conservation Trust in Jersey) says: 'It's always hard to come to terms with the place when one has just seen all those wonderful animals in the forests.' But if you are not going to the major reserves, then by all means go to Tsimbazaza because you won't see such a comprehensive collection of Malagasy fauna at any other zoo.

Avoid tipping the 'guides' who should be looking after the animals not trailing after tourists, and hope that the authorities find a compromise between what we in the West expect a good zoo to be, and how the locals want it. A neat example of the difference between the American and the Malagasy view of animal management and life in general was the argument some years ago over a project to have a free-ranging group of lemurs in the park. There was no problem agreeing on the desirability and visitor appeal of this, the conflict was about the components of the group. The American coordinator insisted on single-sex lemurs ('One thing we do *not* want are babies when we have a surplus of lemurs') whilst the Malagasy were holding out for a proper family unit: mother, father and children, because that's what happiness is all about.

Among the animals on display in the zoo are four aye-ayes. Arrangements may be made to visit them after dark when they are active, for a fee of 25,000Fmg per person.

The botanical garden is spacious and well laid out, and its selection of Malagasy endemics is being improved with the help of advisers from Kew (UK) and the Missouri Botanical Garden (USA). It provides a sanctuary for numerous birds – indeed, this is an excellent place for birders – including a huge colony of egrets. There are also some reproduction Sakalava graves.

The museum (Musée Académie Malgache)

This is an excellent museum for gaining an understanding of Madagascar's prehistoric natural history and the traditions and way of life of its inhabitants.

Skeletons of now extinct animals, including several species of giant lemur and the famous 'elephant bird', provide a fascinating glimpse of the Madagascar fauna which the first humans helped to extinction (explanations in French only). There are also displays of stuffed animals, but the efforts of the taxidermist have left little to likeness and a lot to the imagination. It's worth taking a close look at the aye-aye, however, to study its remarkable hands.

The room housing the ethnological exhibits has been modernised, with clear explanations of the customs and handicrafts of the different ethnic groups.

Practicalities

Tsimbazaza is about 4km from the city centre. There are buses from Avenue de l'Indépendance (number 15), but it is easier to take a taxi there and bus back. It is open every day from 09.00 to 17.00. For tourists the entrance fee is 25,000Fmg (5,000Fmg for children aged 6 to 12). This fee goes towards the upkeep of the park, so watch out that a used ticket is not reissued. Sundays are always very busy, so don't anticipate peace and quiet then.

There is a souvenir shop with a good selection of high-quality T-shirts and postcards, but no restaurant or snack bar. And the toilets are difficult to find (ask at the shop).

Museum of Art and Archaeology

This lovely little museum is described under *Isoraka* (page 157). The hours are 09.00–17.00. Closed on Mondays.

Androndra Cultural Centre

This is the brainchild of Hanitrarivo Rasoanaivo, the lead singer of Tarika, who also founded the charity Valiha High (see page 146). Due to open early in 2002, it will comprise a large exhibition space, a performance area, the first professional music studio in Madagascar, and a restaurant serving Malagasy food. There will be comfortable accommodation bookable at the centre, and expert guides on hand to introduce visitors to the Malagasy music, arts and cultural scene. Androndra is about 20 minutes southeast of the city centre. Further information through Rainbow Tours in London or (in Tana) phone Antshow on 22-56547 or email: hmblanche@simicro.mg.

SHOPPING
The handicrafts markets

The Marché Artisanal, which is best reached by taxi, shows the enormous range and quality of Malagasy handicrafts. Most noteworthy is the embroidery and basketry, wood-carving, minerals, leatherwork (stiff cowhide, not soft leather) and the unique Antaimoro paper embedded with pressed flowers. The market is held in the Andravoahangy region of town. This is to the right of the station (as you face it) northeast on Rue Albertini. Open 10.00–17.00, except Sunday.

This market has now been superceded (in popularity) by the more accessible one (also the Marché Artisanal) on the road to the airport. This is quieter, with prices inflated to allow for bargaining; if you accept the asking price here you really are being ripped off!

Serious shopping

The best quality goods are sold in specialist shops. One of the best is **Galerie Le Bivouac**, Antsofinondry – on the road to Ambohimanga – which sells beautiful painted silk items, wood carvings and other handicrafts of a high quality; tel: 429

50. Nearby is the **Atelier Jacaranda** which specialises in batik. The quality here is excellent and the prices low. The Jacaranda workshop is next to Le Bivouac (worth visiting if you have time), but sales are made from the gallery 1km down the road, on the other side of the canal.

Nearer the centre of town, though still a taxi ride away, is **Lisy Art Gallery** on the Route de Mausolée opposite the Cercle Mess de la Police, and near the Hotel Panorama; tel: 277 33. One of the cheapest shops in Tana is **Galerie Yerden** in Isoraka (see page 157). Although the prices are slightly higher than in the market, the peace and quiet, and wide range of arts and crafts, make a visit well worthwhile. An excellent place for wood crafts is **Viva Home** at 23 Rue Ramelina, Antaninarenina, not far from the Colbert; tel: 692 71.

There's a good art gallery, **La Flamant Rose**, at 45–47 Avenue de l'Indépendance; the **Galerie Aquelle** (past the zoo on Route Circulaire opposite Epicerie Tojo) has 'by far the nicest watercolours I found in Tana – really captured the flavour of Madagascar'.

Nice T-shirts and other cheap and cheerful souvenirs are available from the **Baobab** company. Their showroom is opposite the Palissandre Hotel.

For exquisite (and consequently expensive) **weavings** based on traditional *lamba* designs contact British resident Simon Peers; tel: 295 02; fax: 319 56.

The best place in Tana to buy **Antaimoro paper** is at a small 'factory' on the way to the airport (it's a green building on the right) where an enterprising Malagasy, M Mahatsinjo, has a workforce which uses the traditional method of pressing the flowers into the paper pulp. This craft originated in Ambalavao (see page 204 for a detailed description of the paper and how it is made), but you can see all the stages just as easily here. The prices for the finished products are very reasonable, too.

For something a bit different, try the herbal **beauty products** made from Malagasy plants sold under the brand name Phytoline; they seem only to be available from the Hilton shop or in the airport departure lounge.

If you have money to spend and are interested in boats, Jenny Roberts recommends a visit to **Le Village Sarl** (Lot 36F, Ambohibao; tel: 451 97; web: www.madagascar-contacts.com/village) on the way to the airport. 'The manager, Herve Scrive, employs and has trained 54 local people. They make around 30 different scale model boats, some historic (the *Mayflower*, the *Bounty*) based on the original drawings for the boats. Prices range from €115 to €1,507 for a 120cm model of the victory. They can be shipped home but this is very pricey I believe. We chose to have it packed so that we could get it back on the plane/s with us.' If you do this, get a duplicate receipt from Le Village and be prepared to bribe the customs officer when leaving if he claims (wrongly) that you need an export permit.

Best of all, do your shopping at one of the centres that provide work and hope for the disadvantaged girls and women of Tana. **Akany Avoko** (see pages 147 and 158) sells a range of handicrafts at its heart-warming Half Way House. Phone 441 58 to book a visit. And there's my favourite, the **Centre Fihavanana** (see page 158) in Mahamasina, near the stadium, which is run by the Sisters of the Good Shepherd. The centre is in a building set back from the road to the right of an orange-painted church. Ask the taxi driver to take you to the Eglise St Joseph. The women here work to a very high standard, producing beautiful embroidery and greetings cards. The centre is always in need of funds to continue their admirable work with the very poor, and a visit will warm the most resilient of hearts. Judith Cadigan writes: 'We are so glad you suggested visiting the Soeurs du Bon Pasteur in Tana. We bought lots of embroidered linens and were shown around the school, shook hands with what felt like most of the 200 children there, were serenaded by one of the classes, and were altogether greatly impressed by what the nuns are doing. We waited to go there until almost our last day, so that we could take along unused antibiotics, and they were indeed glad to have them. Since I do some embroidery myself, I have a good deal of leftover thread; I asked if they'd like me to send it to them and they sounded as though they'd love it, so I have just sent off a package to them. They use DMC thread.' For an appointment phone Sister Lucy (English-speaking) on 299 81.

Supermarkets

If you don't want handicrafts try some other locally-produced goodies such as chocolate (Chocolat Robert is excellent!) and wine. Both are available from the **Champion** supermarket, beneath the Ibis Hotel in the Upper Town. There is another branch at the lower end of Avenue de l'Indépendance (but avoid this area after dark). Champion also sells very nice souvenir T-shirts. A cheaper supermarket is **Magri**, which is on the way to the airport.

Maps

A large selection of maps (and also old photo prints) can be bought at the **Institut National de Géodésie et Cartographie** (its long Malagasy name is shortened to FTM), Rue Dama-Ntsoha RJB, Ambanidia (tel: 229 35). Hours 08.30–12.00, 14.00–18.00. They produce a series of 12 maps, scale 1:500,000, covering each region of Madagascar. These are most inviting, but sadly not always completely accurate, and some are now out of print. There are also excellent maps of Nosy Be and Ile Sainte Marie. The staff are pleasant and helpful.

FTM maps of the more popular tourist areas can usually be bought in bookshops in the town centre – where you can also buy good maps of Tana.

Bookshops

The best bookshop is **Librairie de Madagascar**, near the Hotel de France on Avenue de l'Indépendance. Another, **Tout pour l'Ecole**, opposite the Hotel Mellis, has a good selection of maps and town plans. Also recommended is **Librairie Md Paoly**, a small Catholic bookshop on the other side of Avenue de l'Indépendance, opposite Sicam and the Banky Fampadrosoana. 'They've got the most amazingly beautiful hand-painted greetings cards. The same cards are sold at the airport for almost double the price.'

Photography

Reliable print film can be purchased and processed in Tana. There are two shops on Avenue de l'Indépendance. There is a useful arcade half-way up the main steps (look for the Kodak sign). This shop also does passport photos.

MEDIA AND COMMUNICATION
Couriers

Colis Express 11, Rue Randrianary Ratianarivo, Ampasamandinika; tel: 272 42.
Midax Madagascar Located at the Auximad office, 18 Rue J J Rabearivelo, Antsahavola; tel: 225 02; fax: 310 98; email: auximad@dts.mg.

Cybercafés

Many of the bigger hotels, including the Hilton, now have internet facilities. There is a cheaper cybercafé on the same road as the post office, near the Colbert. In the same area is Simicro; turn right out of the Colbert, go round the corner, and Simicro is about 20m further, on the same side of the road. 15,000Fmg for 15min. In the Lower Town there's an internet café near the Hotel Sahamanga.

Newspapers and magazines

The main daily newspapers are the *Madagascar Tribune* (in French) which tends to follow the government line and is relatively up-market, and *Midi Madagasikara* (in French and Malagasy), the paper with the highest circulation but little international news. *Express* is a daily newspaper in French and Malagasy, read mainly by intellectuals. *Dans les Média Demain* is an independent weekly magazine, and *Revue de l'Océan Indien – Madagascar* appears monthly.

Post office

The main post office is opposite the Hotel Colbert. There is a separate philately section where you can buy attractive stamps. The post office is open 24 hours a day for outgoing phone calls – useful in an emergency, and much cheaper than phoning from a hotel.

MISCELLANEOUS
Fixers

A local guide/fixer can take a lot of hassle out of planning an independent trip, but bear in mind that anyone recommended here will charge more than newcomers who you have found yourself!

Pierre (S Pierrot Patrick) Lot VT 62E, Ambohibato, Ambohipo, Antananarivo 101; tel: 295 52. Pierrot often meets international flights and will identify himself.
Henri Serge Razafison Lot 1384 Cité 67Ha, Antananarivo 101; tel: 341 90.

Taxi drivers

Christophe Andriamamoinona Tel: 445 08. 'Very knowledgable.'
Joseph Rakotondratsoavina Tel: 782 90.
Charles Razafintsialonina Tel: 238 61. 'Friendly and punctual.'

Vehicle hire

Full details on hiring a car or motorbike are given in *Chapter 6*. If you are dealing with a Tana travel agent they will also be able to arrange car hire. Large hotels will also have car-hire agencies.

Quite a few visitors find their own driver, rather than hiring a car and driver through an agency. Marja and Wim, from the Netherlands, have used the same driver for both their trips to Madagascar: **Justin Randiranarison**; tel: 472 46; cellphone: 032 07 532 19. 'He owns a 1989 (but looks brand new) Peugeot 505 and works independently. He lives 10km outside Tana and is a very pleasant and reliable person, a good driver and speaks some English.'

Information and permits for nature reserves

ANGAP is the organisation responsible for the administration of almost all the protected areas of Madagascar. Permits for the national parks and reserves may be purchased here, although they are now usually available at the town serving the reserve. It is worth visiting the Tana office, however, for the latest information on the reserves that tourists are allowed to visit, and to purchase a National Park Passport for all the parks you wish to visit (cuts down on the hassle and is a nice souvenir). There is also an excellent reference library adjacent to the office. ANGAP is in Antanimena – tell the taxi-driver 'en face de Promodim'. Hours 08.00–12.00, 14.00–16.00. Tel: 319 94. The visitor fee for all ANGAP's parks and reserves is 50,000Fmg.

The address for the World Wide Fund for Nature in Tana is BP 4373; tel: 255 41.

Visa extension

A visa extension can be obtained overnight from the Ministry of the Interior near the Hilton Hotel (see page 85).

Airline offices

Air Madagascar 31 Av de l'Indépendance; tel: 222 22. Hours: 07.30–11.00; 14.30–17.00.
Air France 29 Av de l'Indépendance; tel: 233 21.
Interair The office is at the Hilton Hotel; tel: 211 06/224 52; fax: 624 21.
Air Austral Immeuble Marbour Antsahavola; tel: 359 90.
Corsair 71 Rue Joseph de Villèlle Faravohitra, Mangarivotra; tel: 312 10.
Air Mauritius Immeuble Marbour Antsahavola; 359 90.

Bank and emergency funds

There are now ATMs in Tana, the most convenient being at the Hilton. The BTM bank next to the Champion supermarket will let you draw up to US$200 a day on American Express or MasterCard. Banking hours: 08.00-15.00. Closed on Saturdays. There's a Western Union office on Lalana Generaly Rabehevitra, in Antaninarenina. The American Express office is in the Hilton Hotel.

Medical clinics (private)

MM 24 X 24 Mpitsabo Mikambana, Route de l'Université, tel: 235 55. Inexpensive and very good. Of the government hospitals, the military hospital is better equipped than the civilian one.
Laboratoire d'analyses medicales Pharmacie Hanitra, 172 Route Circulaire, Ankorahotra; tel: 312 81. Blood test for malaria or other nasties: 18,000Fmg.

Church services

Anglican (contact tel: 262 68): Cathedral St Laurent, Ambohimanoro; 09.00 service each Sunday.
Roman Catholic (tel: 278 30): three churches have services in Malagasy, and three in French. Phone for details.

Golf course

There is a good golf course, the **Club de Golf de Rova** at Ambohidratrimo, 20km from town on the road to Mahajanga. It is open to visitors except at the weekend. Good meals are served at the club house and the Wednesday buffet is particularly recommended.

For more on golf in Madagascar contact **Golf Travel Madagascar**, 17 rue Ny Zasindriandiky, Antanimena (BP178, Antananarivo 101); email: golf.tr@dts.mg.

Embassies

British Embassy Lot II I 164 ter, Alarobia Ambohiloha (BP 167), 101 Antananarivo; tel: 493 78/493 79/493 80; fax: 493 81; ukembant@simicro.mg.
American Embassy Antsahavola (BP 620); tel: 200 89/212 57. For visa/passport business it is open Mondays, Wednesdays and Fridays.
Italian Embassy Rue Pasteur Rabary, Ankadivato (BP 16); tel: 212 17.
French Embassy Rue Jean Jaurès (BP 204); tel: 237 00/200 08.
German Embassy Route Circulaire (BP 516); tel: 238 02.

EXCURSIONS
Bus stations (*gares routières*)

The *gares routières* for taxi-brousses are on the outskirts of the city at the appropriate road junctions. Fasan'ny karana, on the road to the airport, is the *gares routière*

THE MARTYR MEMORIAL CHURCHES
Dr G W Milledge

My grandfather, James Sibree, a civil engineer from Hull, was appointed by the London Missionary Society in 1863 to build four memorial churches to commemorate the Malagasy Christians put to death by order of Queen Ranavalona I during the period 1837 to her death in 1861. The sites, mainly within easy walking distance of the palace, were associated with the execution or imprisonment of the martyrs. Mr William Ellis of the London Mission had noted that the sites were suitable for church building, thought of the memorial churches and petitioned King Radama II for the sites to be reserved. This was granted. He also petitioned the mission board who agreed to raise funds in England.

Mention should be made of the difficulties and delays in starting to build large stone churches; quarry men, masons, carpenters all had to be trained. Stone was readily available but other materials were difficult to obtain. Workmen often departed for family functions, government work or military service, and work was held up for weeks. As the spire of Ambatonakangar rose to heights unknown in Malagasy buildings, wives of his workmen pleaded with James Sibree not to ask their husbands to go up to such dangerous heights.

Ambatonakanga is situated at the meeting of five roads in an area given on the map as Ambohidahy. The first church in Madagascar was on this site: a low, dark, mud brick building in which Christians were imprisoned, often in chains before, in many cases, being led out to execution. The first printing press was also on this site and the first Malagasy Bibles were printed here. The present church, opened in 1867, follows the Early English style, with 'Norman' arches. It was the first stone building in Madagascar.

Ambohipotsy is on a commanding site at the southern end of the ridge beyond the Queen's Palace. Its slender spire can be seen for miles around the surrounding plain. On this site the first martyr, a young woman called Rasalama, was speared to death in 1837. Later 11 other Christians suffered the same fate.

Faravohitra Church is on the northern side of the city ridge, built where four Christians of the nobility were burnt to death on March 28 1849. Though not as fine a site as Ambohipotsy, it also commands good views.

Ampamarinana Church is a short way below the Palace on the west side of the ridge on the summit of 'The Place of the Hurling' from where prisoners were thrown to their deaths. Fourteen Christians were killed here on the same day in 1849.

So the four churches stand on historic sites as a memorial to those brave martyrs for their faith, and witness to the interest and concern of Christians in Britain for their fellows in Madagascar.

The late Dr Milledge travelled to Madagascar at the age of 88 to visit the place where he was born. Throughout the trip he was honoured as a descendent of James Sibree, one of Madagascar's major benefactors and perhaps the greatest writer the island has inspired.

serving the south and east of the country. Gare de l'Ouest, Anosibe (Lalana Pastora Rahajason on the far side of Lac Anosy) serves the west and Gare du Nord (at Andravoahangy, behind the Artisan's market) takes care of the north.

East of Antananarivo
Ambohimanga
Lying 21km northeast of Antananarivo, Ambohimanga (pronounced Ambooimanga), meaning the 'blue hill', was for a long time forbidden to Europeans. From here began the line of kings and queens who were to unite Madagascar into one country, and it was here that they returned for rest and relaxation among the tree-covered slopes of this hill-top village. These days tourists find the same tranquillity and spirit of reverence and this recently named World Heritage Site is highly recommended as an easy day's trip.

Ambohimanga has seven gates, though some are all but lost among the thick vegetation. By one of the most spectacular, through which you enter the village, is an enormous stone disc which was formerly rolled in front of the gateway each night. Above the gateway is a thatched-roof sentry post and to the right is a bizarre Chinese pagoda (don't ask me what or why...). The entrance area has recently been 'developed' – for no obvious reason. There are some useful small shops here selling drinks and snacks.

Climbing up the stairs towards the compound you pass some handicrafts stalls with a variety of unique and appealing souvenirs, and in the courtyard are two huge fig trees providing shade for a picnic.

Ambohimanga still retains its spiritual significance for the Malagasy people. On the slope to the left of the door to the compound (where you must pay your 25,000Fmg fee) is a sacrificial stone. Melted candle-wax and traces of blood show that it is still used for offerings, particularly in cases of infertility. Rituals involving the placing of seven small stones in the 'male' or 'female' hole will ensure the birth of a baby boy or girl.

The hours are 09.00–11.00, 14.00–17.00 (closed Mondays).

Inside the compound
The centre-piece here is the wooden house of the great king Andrianampoinimerina (1787–1810). The simple one-roomed building is interesting for the insight it gives into everyday (royal) life of that era. There is a display of cooking utensils (and the stones that surrounded the cooking fire) and weapons, and the two beds – the top one for the king and the lower for one of his 12 wives. The roof is supported by a ten-metre rosewood pole. A visit here can be full of surprises: 'Remember this is not a museum, it is the King's palace: he is there. On all my visits there were always several people asking the King for favours. On one memorable occasion I entered his hut to find what seemed like a party in full flow. A man had been possessed by the spirit of a king from the south, and he had come to the palace to greet, and be greeted by, King Andrianampoinimerina. The man had gone into a trance and a group of mediums were assisting him. They had found an accordion player and the man was dancing to get the King's attention. We were spellbound by all this, but the Malagasy visitors totally ignored what was going on and continued to look round the hut as though nothing was happening!' (Alistair Marshall)

Andrianampoinimerina's son, Radama, with British help, went a long way to achieving his father's ambition to expand his kingdom to the sea. His wife succeeded him as Queen Ranavalona. Three more queens followed and, although the capital had, by that time, been moved to Antananarivo, they built themselves elegant summer houses next to Andrianampoinimerina's simple royal home.

These have been renovated, and provide a fascinating glimpse of the strong influence of the British during those times, with very European décor and several gifts sent to the monarchs by Queen Victoria. French influence is evident too: there are two cannons forged in Jean Laborde's Mantasoa iron foundry. Here also is the small summer house belonging to Prime Minister Rainilaiarivony. Understandably cautious about being overheard (he wielded more power than the queens he married) he chose an open design with glazed windows so that spies could be spied first.

Also within the compound is a mundane-looking concrete pool (the concrete is a recent addition) which was used by the queens for ritual bathing and had to be filled, so they say, by 70 virgins, and a corral where zebu were sacrificed. An enclosing wall built in 1787, and faced with a rock-hard mixture of sand and egg, completes the tour.

From a high point above the bath you can get a superb view of the Haut Plateaux and Tana in the distance, and on an adjacent hill the white mausoleum of the king's *ombiasy*.

Getting there
Ambohimanga is reached on a good road by private taxi or bus/taxi-brousse. The latter takes about 30 minutes and is cheap. To return to Tana, go to the square below the entrance where the taxi-brousses wait for passengers.

Where to eat
Ambohimanga is an ideal place for a picnic, and there is a nice restaurant (tables in the garden) off the palace courtyard. Meals are reasonably priced and there is live music at weekends.

Ambohimalaza (La Nécropole Royale)
Off RN2 which leads to Toamasina is a remarkable cemetery. Ambohimalaza was one of the 12 sacred hills of King Andrianpoinimerina, and only the Merina aristocracy are buried here. Their tombs are topped by a *tranomanara* or 'cold house' resembling a little chalet, which indicates that the deceased was of royal blood, as does the red colour of some of the tombs. Nearby are the tiny graves of uncircumcised children who are not allowed to be buried in the family tombs. Around the perimeter you can see the remains of the deep moat and traces of a retaining wall. There is even one of those huge circular stones for closing off the entrance.

The whole area is resonant with atmosphere. Rupert Parker writes: 'It's difficult not to feel the presence of the ancestors of the royal family. My camera certainly felt them and gave up the ghost in the middle of the film – back in the UK they said it couldn't be fixed and my Malagasy friends gleefully pointed out that the ancestors had had their revenge. They also stole a shoe from one of my young nephews – that was his excuse anyway!'

Getting there
The easiest way is by private taxi, but taxi brousses run every day except Sunday from Ambasapito, on the east of Tana to the village of Ambohmalaza, then it's a 2km walk to the site.

Lake Mantasoa
Some 70km east of Antananarivo is Mantasoa (pronounced Manta<u>soo</u>) where in the 19th century Madagascar had its first taste of industrialisation. Indeed, historians now claim that industrial output was greater then than it ever was during

THE TWO-MAN INDUSTRIAL REVOLUTION

Technology was largely introduced to Madagascar by two remarkable Europeans: James Cameron, a Scot, and Jean Laborde, a Frenchman.

James Cameron arrived in Madagascar in 1826 during the country's 'British' phase when the London Missionary Society (LMS) had attempted to set up local craftsmen to produce goods in wood, metal, leather and cotton. Cameron was only 26 when he came to Madagascar, but was already skilled as a carpenter and weaver, with wide knowledge of other subjects which he was later to put to use in his adopted land: physics, chemistry, mathematics, architecture and astronomy. Cameron seemed able to turn his hand to almost anything mechanical. Among his achievements were the successful installation and running of Madagascar's first printing press (by studying the manual – the printer sent out with the press had died with unseemly haste), a reservoir (now Lac Anosy) and aqueduct, and the production of bricks.

Cameron's success in making soap from local materials ensured his royal favour after King Radama died and the xenophobic Queen Ranavalona came to power. But when Christian practice and teaching were forbidden in 1835, Cameron left with the other missionaries and went to work in South Africa.

He returned in 1863 when the missionaries were once more welcome in Madagascar, to oversee the building of stone churches, a hospital, and the stone exterior to the *Rova* or queen's palace in Antananarivo.

Jean Laborde was even more of a 'renaissance man'. The son of a blacksmith, Laborde was shipwrecked off the east coast of Madagascar in 1831. Queen Ranavalona, no doubt pleased to find a less godly European, asked him to manufacture muskets and gun-powder, and he soon filled the gap left by the departure of Cameron and the other artisan-missionaries. Laborde's initiative and inventiveness were amazing: in a huge industrial complex built by forced labour, he produced munitions and arms, bricks and tiles, pottery, glass and porcelain, silk, soap, candles, cement, dyes, sugar, rum ... in fact just about everything a thriving country in the 19th century needed. He ran a farm which experimented with suitable crops and animals, and a country estate for the Merina royalty and aristocracy to enjoy such novelties as firework displays. And he built the original queen's palace in wood (in 1839), which was later enclosed in stone by Cameron.

So successful was Laborde in making Madagascar self-sufficient, that foreign trade was discontinued and foreigners – with the exception of Laborde – expelled. He remained in the queen's favour until 1857 when he was expelled because of involvement in a plot to replace the queen by her son. The 1,200 workmen who had laboured without pay in the foundries of Mantasoa rose up and destroyed everything – tools, machinery and buildings. The factories were never rebuilt, and Madagascar's Industrial Revolution came to an abrupt end.

He returned in 1861 and became French consul, dying in 1878. A dispute over his inheritance was one of the pretexts used by the French to justify the 1883–85 war.

the colonial period. It was thanks to Jean Laborde that a whole range of industries was started, including an iron foundry which enabled Madagascar to become more or less self-sufficient in swords, guns and gunpowder, thereby increasing the power of the central government. Jean Laborde was soon highly influential at court and he built a country residence for the queen at Mantasoa.

Many of the buildings remain, and a day's visit to Mantasoa is most rewarding. A stay of a few days would be even better, to give you a chance to walk the quiet, leafy tracks and enjoy the unspoilt small village.

Getting there
Mantasoa can be reached by taxi-brousse from Tana. The village and its attractions are quite spread out, but it is a very pleasant area for walking.

What to see
Beside the school playing field is a chimney, once part of the china factory. The cannon factory still stands and part of it is lived in, and the large furnace of the foundry remains. All are signposted and fascinating to see; you can just imagine the effort that was required to get them built.

Jean Laborde is buried in the cemetery outside the village, along with 12 French soldiers; there is an imposing mausoleum with a strikingly phallic monument.

The very active *Les Amis de Jean Laborde* have started developing the area for tourism. If you have a special interest in this fascinating man you can phone them on 402 97 or email: topoi@dts.mg.

The first project has been to restore Laborde's house which is now a very interesting museum set in a lovely garden. All the labels are in French but a guide may be available to translate. It is worth making the effort to follow Laborde's remarkable story and achievements (see box).

Where to stay/eat
Domaine de l'Ermitage BP 16, Mantasoa; cellphone:030 23 836 09. The rooms are so-so but the meals and old-fashioned atmosphere make is well worth a stay. Rooms cost from 150,000Fmg to 250,000Fmg. Meals (*very* slow service) are 55,000Fmg, 65,000Fmg on Saturday nights.The Sunday buffet is excellent value for 60,000Fmg with a small band playing songs from the 1950s. The Ermitage is set up as a country club and offers all sorts of recreational activities such as riding, tennis, boating on the lake, country walks etc.
Motel le Chalet/ Le Chalet Suisse BP 12, Mantasoa; tel: 42 66 005. The Swiss owner, Mme Verpillot, seems to have been around since Jean Laborde's day, and has now handed over the running of the place to her son Adrian. There are five bungalows costing between 85,000Fmg and 115,000Fmg, and a restaurant serving good food. Meals (which must be eaten there) cost 45,000Fmg (50,000Fmg Sunday lunch). The walk here from the taxi-brousse drop-off point is a pleasant 1½ hours.

Angavokely Station Forestière
Clare and Johann Herman recommend this day trip from Tana. 'At Carion, 30km from Tana on the RN2, you follow the track to Angavokely which takes about 30 minutes down a rutted track which had once been cobbled. It ends at an extraordinary turreted barrier which will be opened after you have applied at the offices a ten-minute walk away. They are located in a large set of buildings amongst a defunct sawmill. A permit costs 20,000Fmg. Faded direction signs and a map indicate the way to the Arboretum with picnic tables and parasols, and you can camp. Mt Angavokely is a fair climb up past the eucalyptus plantation and takes about 30 minutes. Thoughtfully, steps with railings are built in the rock face so that

you can enjoy the splendid views from the top of the Ankaratra mountains and Lake Mantasoa. A wide track leads back down through the Arboretum to the offices.'

Mandraka (Pereyras Mandraka Reptile Farm)

This is usually visited en route to Périnet, but can also be done as a day trip from Tana. If you take RN2 towards Toamasina (Tamatave) the 'Reptile Farm' is situated opposite the hydro-electric power plant, just west of Anjiro. It is owned by one of Madagascar's prominent naturalists, André Pereyras.

The centre provides the opportunity to see and photograph some of the island's most extraordinary reptiles and invertebrates, but at a price: the animals are kept in crowded and stressful conditions, and are often roughly handled by the 'guides'. The main purpose of the centre is the breeding (for export) of various butterflies and moths, but the demand for reptiles for the pet trade is also satisfied by illegal collecting from the wild.

All in all, I can no longer recommend a visit here with a clear conscience, but there's no denying that the photographic opportunities are wonderful. Visitors pay 25,000Fmg to tour the collection with a guide who costs an additional 15,000Fmg.

West of Antananarivo
Antsahaointa

John Kupiec recommends a visit to this hilltop village which is a bus ride southwest of Tana. 'There are many royal tombs, a museum (small fee), wonderful views and a small house for visitors to sleep in. The guide speaks English.'

Lake Itasy

Off the road to Tsiroanomandidy (access town Analavory) this lake and its surrounding area are particularly beautiful and easily reached by taxi-brousse or private car (although the road is now in a poor state). 'We could have walked for days through the hamlets which offered an insight into the day-to-day life of these exceptionally welcoming people.' (P Crawford) The nearby village of **Ampefy** is full of once splendid French colonial mansions. There is a choice of accommodation: the Kavitaha, (not what it was – now reportedly unfriendly with mediocre food) and the humble Bungalows Administratifs. A better bet is the Village Touristique between the lakes: spacious but basic bungalows.

It is an 8km walk from Ampefy to **Ilôt de la Vièrge** on Lac Itasy. 'From the Ilôt there are fantastic views over the lake and surrounding hills. One of my abiding memories is descending the hill and hearing the beautiful singing at the Sunday service in the church at the bottom.' (PC) West of the road are the **Chutes de la Lily** (waterfalls) and about 45 minutes' drive northwest of Ampefy are some hot springs with spectacular mineral deposits (this road was impassable in 2001 so check whether it has been repaired).

Tsiroanomandidy

Lying about 200km to the west of Tana, on a surfaced road (four hours), this town is a pleasant and attractive place to spend a day or two. Its main attraction is the large cattle market, held on Wednesdays and Thursdays. The Bara people of the south drive huge herds of cattle through the Bongolava plateau to sell at the market.

There are two hotels. Chez Marcelline, north of the market and near the airport, seems to be the best.

Tsiroanomandidy is linked to Maintirano and Majunga by Twin Otter, and also to Morondava. You can also travel west on river trips as far as the Manambolo gorges (see *Chapter 16*).

Above Lowland rainforest, Mantadia National Park (NG)

Above right Male crowned lemur, *Eulemur coronatus*, clambering on *tsingy*, Ankarana (NG)

Below left Milne-Edwards sportive lemur, *Lepilemur edwardsi*, in its tree hole, Ampijoroa (NG)

Below right Adult male red-bellied lemur, *Eulemur rubriventer*, in rainforest canopy, Ranomafana National Park (NG)

Above Helmet vanga, *Euryceros prevostii*, on its nest in Marojejy National Park (NG)

Above right Male Madagascar paradise flycatcher, *Terpsiphone mutata*, on its nest in Ampijoroa Forest (NG)

Right Madagascar harrier hawk, *Polyboroides radiatus*, Ifaty spiny forest (NG)

Above Colony of shield bugs (Pentatomidae) on a leaf, Ampijoroa Forest (NG)

Right Male comet moth, *Argema mittrei*, resting on its egg case (NG)

Below Giant day gecko, *Phelsuma madagascariensis grandis* (NG)

Northwest of Antananarivo
The forest of Ambohitantely

The name means 'Where honey is found' and is pronounced 'Ambweetontel'. This is the last remnant of natural forest in the province of Ankazobe and there are hopes that it will shortly become a protected area. This report is by Dr Graham Noble and Sandra Baron of South Africa. 'It takes at least 2½ hours to get to the forest which lies 150km northwest of Tana off the road to Mahajanga. The access village is Ararazana. The forest is 10km from the road and you do not see a tree until you reach the site.

Estimates of its size vary from 1,400 to 3,000ha. It is surrounded by a barrier of burnt trees, but as you go two metres into the forest the leaf-litter is already 10-15cm deep. There is a network of paths through the forest. The University of Antananarivo has a right to a part of it as a study site and refers to that section as the Botanical Garden. The forestry director is very keen to receive tourists into the area for day walks and will also organise provisions for overnight stays. Good birding and lots of orchids.'

Derek Schuurman adds: 'This is actually a very beautiful little rainforest, with rufous mouse lemurs and common brown lemurs as well as tenrecs. Birds found there include the Madagascar blue pigeon, long-billed greenbul, forest rock thrush, blue vanga and, en route, the Réunion harrier.' However, he adds that it is only really worth visiting if you are driving north to Mahajanga so pass nearby. You will see nothing here that can't be found (more easily) in Périnet.

Check with ANGAP on the current status of the forest (and to buy a permit), and make a further visit to the Direction des Eaux et Forêts in Ankazobe, 106km from Tana. Because of a problem with bandits in the area, you are advised to check with the Eaux et Forêts people about where to stay/camp, and always travel with a reliable guide.

Lemurs Park

This large zoo makes a good day trip from Tana for those on a quick visit who are not able to see lemurs in their natural habitat. Seven species of lemur live free in the 4ha park; many of them are confiscated pets, and this is the first step towards rehabilitation. The park is 25km northwest of Tana, on the road to Mahajanga (RN 4). The entry fee is 50,000Fmg. There is a good restaurant here, plus a boutique for souvenirs.

The baboon grows to an enormous size ... at least seven feet high when standing on its hind legs. It is a very savage and untractable animal and its imperfect and hideous resemblance to the human form gives it an horrific appearance.

Samuel Copland, *History of the Island of Madagascar*, 1822

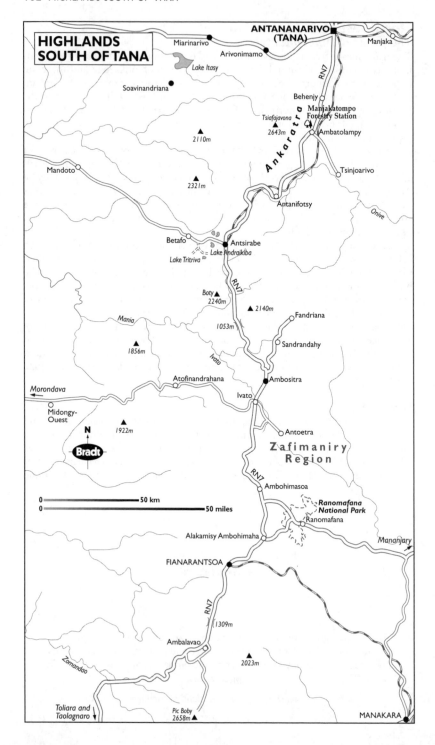

Highlands South of Tana

OVERVIEW

Now that Route Nationale 7 (RN7) has been improved, many visitors drive its full length to Toliara, either by hired car or by public transport. It is a delightful journey, providing an excellent overview of the Hauts Plateaux and Merina and Betsileo culture, as well as spectacular scenery, especially around Fianarantsoa.

FROM TANA TO ANTSIRABE

All along this stretch of road you will see Merina tombs, and can watch the labour-intensive cultivation of rice paddies.

About 15km from Tana look out for a huge, white replica of the *Rova* across the paddy fields on the right. This is President Ratsiraka's palace, funded by North Korea. When he briefly became ex-president and fled to France he stripped it bare. Now he is back in power and presumably the furnishings are back too.

Ambatolampy and region

Ambatolampy lies some two hours/68km from Tana and has a colourful market as well as a very good hotel/restaurant. It is also the starting point for two interesting excursions to Tsinjoarivo, with its summer *rova*, and the forestry station of Manjakatompo.

South of the town, near the Manja Ranch, is an insectarium set up by a Frenchman, Jean-Baptiste Cornet (admission about 25,000Fmg). He is hoping to use the revenue to provide financial support to entomology students.

Telephone code The area code for Ambatolampy is 42.

Where to stay/eat

Hotel au Rendezvous des Pecheurs Tel: 492 04. 8 rooms, 70,000Fmg (single), 90,000Fmg (double). Albanian-owned and renowned for its 'quite glorious' food (meals are 55,000Fmg). The rooms are simple but comfortable, mostly with shared bathrooms (with a big bathtub) and hot water; some have en-suite WC. Recommended

Manja Ranch BP 36, Ambatolampy 104; tel: 492 34; email: ManjaRanch@hotmail.com. Rooms (shared bathrooms, unreliable water) are about 50,000Fmg, but 4 new bungalows have en-suite bathrooms for 90,000Fmg. Camping: 10,000Fmg or free if you eat at the ranch. Good meals for 30,000Fmg. About 2km south of Ambatolampy and owned by Doug Cook, an American, and his Malagasy wife Bijou. Horses and bikes for hire.

Tsinjoarivo

From Ambatolampy a road leads southeast to Tsinjoarivo. Johan and Clare Hermans write: 'Check conditions before setting out; although only about 50km it takes a good three to four hours by car and is not an all-weather road (there is an

DISTANCES IN KILOMETRES

Antananarivo–Ambatolampy	70km
Antananarivo–Ampefy	135km
Antananarivo–Antsirabe	170km
Antananarivo–Ambositra	330km
Antananarivo–Fianarantsoa	408km
Antsirabe–Ambositra	70km
Antsirabe–Fianarantsoa	240km
Antsirabe–Miandrivazo	225km
Ambositra–Ranomafana	331km
Fianarantsoa–Mananjary	204km
Fianarantsoa–Manakara	264km
Fianarantsoa–Ihosy	206km

alternative road on higher ground which bypasses some of the boggiest stretches of the main road). The journey is worthwhile for the series of waterfalls and the *Rova* of Queen Rasoherina; in her time it took three days to get there from Tana by palanquin. There is a guardian who will show you round the buildings, one for the queen with the remains of some fine wooden carving from her bed, and others for the prime minister, the chancellor and the guard. Situated on a promontory overlooking the falls, the site has spectacular views and an incredible atmosphere. There are stone steps down from the *Rova* to the viewpoint at the falls, complete with spray.'

Manjakatompo Forestry Station
A road leads west, and then north from Ambatolampy to Manjakatompo, an hour's drive (17km). 'The road passes through aluminium smelting villages – worth a stop to watch them making cutlery and cooking pots. Permits for the Manjakatompo Forest are obtainable at the gate: 20,000Fmg. Guides not obligatory (ours was not worth the money). Well signposted walks, sights include a small waterfall, and an interesting lichen forest with two royal tombs, circa 1810 near the encampment. It is a four-hour hike to Tsiafajavona, tallest peak of the Andringitra range.' (Johan and Clare Hermans)

Merina tombs
About 15 minutes beyond Ambatolampy are some fine painted Merina tombs. These are on both sides of the road, but the most accessible are on the right.

Antanifotsy
This small town, some 40km south of Antsirabe, has a wonderful market on Mondays.

ANTSIRABE
Antsirabe lies 169km south of Antananarivo at 1,500m. It was founded in 1872 by Norwegian missionaries attracted by the cool climate and the healing properties of the thermal springs. The name means 'the place of much salt'.

This is an elegant city, and with its top-class hotels and interesting excursions merits a stay of a few days. A broad avenue links the handsome station with the amazing Hotel des Thermes; at the station end is a monolith depicting Madagascar's 18 main tribes.

Antsirabe is the agricultural and industrial centre of Madagascar, best known as the centre for beer. You can smell the Star Brewery as you enter the town.

This is the *pousse-pousse* capital of Madagascar. There are hundreds, perhaps thousands of them. The drivers are insistent that you avail yourself of a ride, and why not? But be very firm about the price. Now that lots of tourists come to Antsirabe, the drivers have found they can make a dollar just by posing for pictures. To actually have to run somewhere towing a large *vazaha* for the same price must seem very unfair.

On a promontory overlooking the baths stands the Hotel des Thermes: an amazing building in both size and architectural style. There is nothing else like it in Madagascar – it would not be out of place along the French Riviera and is set in equally elegant gardens (see *Where to stay*).

If you are travelling between May and September you will need a sweater in the evening. It gets quite cold.

Telephone code The area code for Antsirabe is 44.

Getting there and away
By rail
The train now only runs spasmodically, the journey from Tana taking from four to ten (!) hours. In theory there are trains twice a week, leaving Tana at 08.00 on Tuesdays and Thursdays, and returning (also at 08.00) on Wednesdays and Fridays. Check at the railway station in Tana or Antsirabe for the latest information.

By road
Antsirabe is generously served by buses and taxi-brousses. These leave from Anosizato station in Tana, the 170km journey taking about four hours. Continuing south to Ambositra takes two hours and costs 7,000Fmg. Travelling from Antsirabe to Fianarantsoa (non-stop) by private car takes five hours.

Note that there are two taxi-brousse stations in Antsirabe – one in the north of the town and one in the south.

Where to stay
Many new hotels have opened in Antsirabe – and others have closed. I am only listing those I know are open; there will be plenty others in the C category, so look around. For the best value try the rooms in private houses, which are a special feature of Antsirabe.

Category A
Aida Tel: 492 98. 173,000Fmg (double room with breakfast) or 300,000Fmg (suite). A large hotel on the northern side of town, near the taxi-brousse station. Comfortable, and competitively priced.

Arotel Rue Ralaimongo, Antsirabe 110; tel: 481 20/485 73/485 74; fax: 491 49; email: arotel@sinergic.mg. 39 rooms, 6 suites, 2 apartments. Rooms 295,000Fmg, breakfast 25,000Fmg, dinner 50,000Fmg. A well-situated, comfortable and overpriced hotel. Luxurious full-sized bathtubs. Variable food. There is a lovely secluded garden at the back with a swimming pool that is open to non-residents, at 4,000Fmg.

Hotel des Thermes BP 72; tel: 487 61/2; fax 492 02. 350,000Fmg (double) including breakfast. An amazing place from the outside, and done up inside for its 100th birthday in 1997. 'But still only enough hot water for one small bath.' There is a cosy bar and reasonably good food is served in the restaurant (dinner 50,000Fmg). In the warmer months the large garden and swimming pool (open to non-residents) makes this a very pleasant place to relax. Visa and MasterCard accepted.

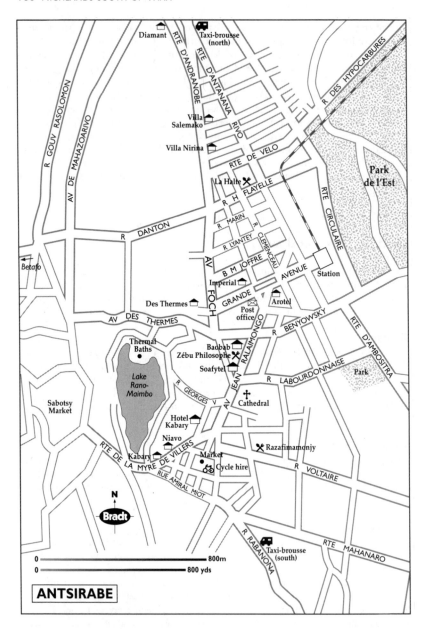

La Casa Lot 27 C 120 Mahazoarivo, 110 Antsirabe; tel: 492 03. 137,000Fmg (double) to 275,000Fmg (suite). All rooms have en-suite bathrooms and TV. Breakfast 16,500Fmg. Comfortable, but 'you need to like brown if you stay here'.

Category B
Villa Salemako BP 14, Antsirabe; tel: 495 88. A good-value private home with five rooms for visitors, run by Julia-Brigitte Rakotonarivo. Rooms vary in size and facilities and

therefore price. The range is from 75,000Fmg for a small double room with shared bathroom and toilet, to 100,000Fmg for a family room with en-suite facilities. Beautiful garden. To find the house look for the Malagasy motif on the chimney.

Au Geranium Route du Velodrome; tel: 497 31; cellphone: 032 07 045 44. 5 nice rooms, with or without shower. 55,000Fmg.

Villa Nirina Route d'Andranobe (BP 245), Antsirabe; tel: 485 97 or 486 69. 85,000Fmg (single), 95,000Fmg (double). Larger rooms 130,000Fmg to 160,000Fmg. Fairly basic rooms. Owned by Mrs Zanoa Rasanjison, who speaks fluent English as well as French and German.

La Caleche Rue Jean Ralaimongo; cellphone: 032 07 44 491 18; email: verodes@simicro.mg. 115,000Fmg (single), 127,000Fmg (double). 4 beautiful double rooms (shared bathroom) in a restored colonial villa owned by Eddy Marzel and Veronique Descheyer. Restaurant and bar. Terrific food! Menu 55,000Fmg.

Residence Camelia One block east of Rue Marechal Foch; tel: 488 44. 70,000–115,000Fmg for various sized rooms. A converted villa set in lovely gardens in the French part of town. The small rooms, in the main house, are a bit dark and small, but the two in the annexe are spacious, with en-suite bathrooms and their own veranda overlooking the garden.

Imperial Hotel BP 74 (Grande Av), Antsirabe; tel: 483 33. All rooms have en-suite bathrooms. From 88,000Fmg (single) to 138,000Fmg (family room). Chinese run. Comfortable but noisy. Very good food.

Category C

Hotel Diamant 110 Route d'Andranobe; tel: 494 40; fax: 493 72; email: diamant@hdiamant.com; web: www.hdiamant.com. Rooms 64,000–94,000Fmg; new room with TV and phone: 129,000Fmg. A well-established, medium-sized hotel offering a good selection of rooms but be warned: the cheaper ones are dreadful: dirty, buggy and noisy. Internet facilities (English keyboard) for 1,500Fmg/min.

Hotel Soafytel Tel: 480 55. 55,000Fmg for a room with a shared toilet, 75,000Fmg for a three-bedded room with toilet. Large room 100,000Fmg. This hotel has slipped from B to C, because it needs renovating, but it has hot water and it's cheap!

Hotel Kabary Antsenakely, 110 Antsirabe; tel: 496 07; email: kabary@compro.mg. Rooms 30,000Fmg to 65,000Fmg. This is a charming new backpacker's hotel just down the road from the Niavo. Serves good breakfasts, has live music at night, friendly staff. 'A very hip, cheerful place.' (DF)

Hotel Niavo (The full name is Hotel/Restaurant Fitsangantsanganana Niavo!) Rue Rakotondrainibe Daniel; tel: 484 67. 70,000Fmg (double). A once-popular family-run hotel with a garden on the far side of the lake. A great setting and view, but now so run down it cannot be recommended.

Hotel Baobab Tel: 483 93. Seems to be on the decline but it's cheap! One of their rooms is, alarmingly, for 'one double bed for three people' (35,000Fmg pp) but other more conventional ones with shared facilities are 30,000Fmg to 50,000Fmg, and 60,000Fmg en suite.

Where to eat

Le Zébu Philosophe Av Jean Ralaimongo; tel: 498 09. A popular coffee bar with good food. Worth the visit for its extraordinary and appealing (or appalling, depending on your taste) décor.

Restaurant la Halte Tel: 489 94. Once the best restaurant in Antsirabe this has recently disappointed several readers. This trend has continued through 2001. Don't go there.

Bar-Restaurant Razafimamonjy Antsenankely; tel: 483 53. Opposite the market on Av de l'Indépendance. 'The best restaurant in Madagascar! Super service from elderly waiters,

RICE

The Malagasy have an almost mystical attachment to rice. King Andrianampoinimerina declared: 'Rice and I are one,' and loyalty to the Merina king was symbolised by industry in the rice paddies.

Today the Betsileo are masters of rice cultivation (they manage three harvests a year, not the normal two) and their neat terraces are a distinctive part of the scenery of the central highlands. However, rice is grown throughout the island, either in irrigated paddies or as 'hill rice' watered by the rain. Rice production is labour-intensive. First the ground must be prepared for the seeds. Often this is done by chasing zebu cattle round and round to break and soften the clods – a muddy, sticky job, but evidently great fun for the boys who do it. Seeds are germinated in a small plot and replanted in the irrigated paddies when half grown. In October and November you will see groups of women bent over in knee-deep water, performing this back-breaking work.

The Malagasy eat rice three times a day, the annual consumption being 135kg per person (about a pound of rice per day!) although this is declining because of the availability of other foods and reduced productivity. Rice marketing was nationalised in 1976, but this resulted in such a dramatic drop in the amount of rice reaching the open market that restrictions were lifted in 1984. By that time it was too late to reverse the decline in productivity, which was mainly due to the decay of irrigation works. Despite a steady increase in acreage at the expense of the precious forest, production is continuing to fall: from 150kg per head of population in 1973 to an estimated 113kg in 1998.

Small farmers grow rice only for their own consumption but are forced to sell part of their crop for instant cash. Richer families in the community store this grain and sell it back at a profit later. To solve this small-scale exploitation, village co-operatives have been set up to buy rice and sell it back to the farmer at an agreed price, or at a profit to outsiders if any is left over.

a nice mix of Malagasy and tourists, and Saturday night entertainment.' Another reader adds: 'Don't skip the fresh, homemade yoghurt for desert.' Mainly Chinese; reasonable prices.

Restaurant Manambina Malagasy dishes.

Auberge Danielle Roughly opposite the Hotel Diamant. This little *hotely* serves well-prepared, cheap meals. Try also the *hotelys* on the left of the petrol station as you enter town from Tana.

Salon de Thé Moderne A pleasant snack bar opposite the Pharmacie Mahosa.

Mirana (formerly Helena Patisserie) Cellphone: 032 02 069 41. Near the Zébu Philosophe, and opposite BNI bank. Good for breakfast and take-away meals. 'Pizza, quiche, and the first apple turnovers I've tasted in Madagascar; OK, so they were made from strawberries but one can't be too fussy when travelling!' (F Kerridge)

Wheels and hoofs

In the first street (south) behind the daily market is a **bicycle hire** shop. Good mountain bikes for about 50,000Fmg per day. Bikes can also be hired from Soafytel and Villa Nirina (40,000Fmg per day). **Horses** may be hired at the Villa Nirina hotel: 40,000Fmg per hour, 120,000Fmg per half day.

What to see and do

Saturday is **market** day in Antsirabe, an echo of Tana before they abolished the *zoma* but with an even greater cross-section of activities. It's enclosed in a walled area of the city on the hill before the road to Lake Tritriva. 'The entire back wall of the market is a row of open barber stalls. Each has a small mirror, a chair and a little peg for one's hat. There are a few local gambling places nearby, too. They're hard to find, and the stakes can get pretty high.' (Maggie Rush)

It is worth paying a visit to the **thermal baths** (*thermes*). There is a wonderfully hot swimming pool full of laughing brown faces that laugh even harder at the sight of a *vazaha*. But it's friendly laughter. You can also take a none-too-clean, 4,000Fmg private bath here (but there's a 20-minute limit) and have a massage. Only open to the public in the morning.

If you are in a group, an interesting organised excursion is to the homes of various **craft workers**, using a horse-drawn *calèche* (Malagasy stagecoach). Touristy, but fascinating, and the chance to see craft workers in their homes – and to buy direct from them. My favourite was 'Miniature Mamy', where a soft-spoken man makes exquisite models of bicycles, *pousse-pousses*, cars etc, from scrap materials. His knowledge of engineering and painstaking eye for detail is admirable. The tour takes three hours and costs 71,000Fmg. Enquire at the Hotel Calèche.

If you are looking for a different souvenir of Antsirabe try the honey shop opposite the Hotel Calèche. 'Here you can buy different sorts of Malgache honey and jam, for example lychee and eucalyptus honey.'

Excursions from Antsirabe

Lake Andraikiba

This large lake 7km west of Antsirabe is often overlooked in favour of the more spectacular Lake Tritriva. 'One of the few moments when you stepped back into another world. Very laid back, very few people. Tranquil and picturesque.' Volker Dornheim.

Taxi-brousses heading for Betafo pass close to the lake, or you can go by hired bicycle. The new **Hotel Deka** (chalets 85,000Fmg) overlooks the lake.

Lake Tritriva

The name comes from *tritry* – the Malagasy word for the ridge on the back of a chameleon (!) – and *iva*, deep. And this emerald-green crater lake is indeed deep – 80 metres, some say. It is reached by continuing past Lake Andraikiba for 12km on a rough, steep road (4WD only) past small villages of waving kids. You will notice that these villages are relatively prosperous-looking for Madagascar – they grow the barley for the Star Brewery.

Apart from the sheer beauty of Lake Tritriva (the best light for photography is in the morning), there are all sorts of interesting features. The water level rises in the dry season and debris thrown into the lake has reappeared down in the valley, supporting the theory of underground water channels.

Look across the lake and you'll see two thorn trees growing on a ledge above the water with intertwined branches. Legend says that these are two lovers, forbidden to marry by their parents, who drowned themselves in Tritriva. When the branches are cut, so they say, blood, not sap, oozes out. You can walk right round the lake for impressive views of it and the surrounding countryside.

The local people have not been slow to realise the financial potential of groups of *vazahas* corralled at the top of a hill. There is an 'entrance charge' of 10,000Fmg, and once through the gate don't think you will be alone at the lake.

Getting to Tritriva without a 4WD vehicle is difficult. The best ways are to take a bus to Lake Andraikiba and then walk or to rent a bike and make it a day trip. If you are self-sufficient you can stay in the village of Belazao, midway between the two lakes (no hotel), or camp at the lake.

Betafo

About 22km west of Antsirabe, off the tarred road that goes as far as Morondava, lies Betafo, a town with typical highlands red-brick churches and houses. Dotted among the houses are *vatolahy*, standing stones erected to commemorate warrior chieftains. A visit here is recommended. It is not on the normal tourist circuit, and gives you an excellent insight into Merina small-town activities. Monday is market day. There is no hotel in Betafo, but you should be able to find a room by asking around.

At one end of the town is the crater lake Tatamarina. From there it is a walk of about 3km to the Antafofo waterfalls among beautiful views of ricefields and volcanic hills. You will need to find someone to show you the way. 'It's very inviting for a swim but they told me there are ghosts in the pool under the falls. If you go swimming they will pull at your legs and pull you to the bottom.' (Luc Selleslagh)

On the outskirts of Betafo there are hot springs, where for a few francs you can have a hot bath with no time limit.

Continuing south on RN7

Leaving Antsirabe you continue to pass through typical highland scenery of rice paddies and low hills. About 45 minutes beyond the town you'll cross a river and pass one of the nicest rural markets I've seen. There are strange fruit and vegetables, lots of peanuts, and fascinating grey balls that turn out to be soap made from the fat from zebu humps. At the back of the market is a makeshift barber-shop, and behind the men with the scissors are rolling green hills.

About 2½ hours (70km) after leaving Antsirabe you reach Ambositra.

AMBOSITRA

Ambositra (pronounced 'Amboostr') is the centre of Madagascar's wood carving industry. Even the houses have ornately carved wooden balconies and shutters. There is an abundant choice of carved figures and marquetry, in several shops, and the quality is improving, although there are occasional lapses into pseudo-Africana. In an earlier edition I complained that I've yet to see a carved lemur. I've now seen some but sadly the carver obviously has yet to see a lemur... For carvings of people, however, one artist stands out. 'Jean' carves exquisite scenes from Malagasy life, many in a fine-grained, creamy wood known locally as *fanazava*. Jean has now opened a shop on one of the minor roads that joins the RN7 just south of the town. Look for the signs 'Société Jean et Frère'.

The best woodcarving shop (and workshop) is Chez Victor, opposite the Grand Hotel. It has a huge selection at very reasonable prices. Clare Hermans recommends 'Mr Randrianasolo's workshop at Ilaka Centre, just north of Ambositra. He has 25 apprentices working for him and has some artifacts that are different from the usual run-of-the-mill stuff.'

Sadly, several readers have complained that this town has more persistent beggars than anywhere else in Madagascar. Probably because it's small, and many tour groups stop here.

Telephone code The area code for Ambositra is 47.

Where to stay

Prestige Andrefan' i Vinani, Ambositra; tel: 711 35. 12 large, comfortable rooms with shared bathrooms. 80,000Fmg (single), 150,000Fmg (double). Now considered the best hotel in Ambositra: 'A beautiful, charming *auberge*. The owner, Francis Rakotonisa, couldn't have been more thoughtful and helpful. When I mentioned I had an interest in crafts he took me all around town, into narrow houses, stores and we spoke to all sorts of people.' (Sharon Giarratana)

Hotel Violette Tel: 710 84. There are two hotels, the original Violette and its annexe. The old (and atmospheric) Violette is up the hill and to the left. 90,000Fmg (double), 110,000Fmg (single). The Annexe is on the south side of town about 200m past the Grand Hotel. It's a little more expensive, but has a terrace on which to sip a drink while you admire the view.

Hotel Mania Malagasy-owned, in the centre of town. 11 rooms. 95,000Fmg . 'The entrance is pedestrian only via a gate off the main street, locked at night so you have to ring the bell to get in.' The owners can organise tours to Zafimaniry villages.

La Source Tel: 711 96. Opposite Le Tropical, in the centre of town. 82,000Fmg for double room with shared bathroom and toilet.

Le Tropical Tel: 712 77. Simple rooms (shared facilities); single 41,000Fmg, twin 56,000Fmg, family room 80,000Fmg. French-Malagasy owned, this used to be the best accommodation in Ambositra. Now a bit run down.

Grand Hotel This non-grand hotel has been around a long time and has a loyal clientele among frequent Mad travellers. 'A beautiful old place, very woody.' Rooms have basin, bidet and screen, and are very good value at 45,000Fmg. Reports on the food vary from 'good' to 'gone down the pan'.

Where to eat

Hotely ny Tanamasoandro Good and cheap. Also has rooms.

Hotely Gasy 'The best restaurant on our entire trip.' Amazing Scottish décor, huge portions, low prices.

Places of interest near Ambositra

Royal Palace

On a hill east of the town is a ruined royal palace. It takes about 1½ hours to walk up (there's no shortage of guides to show you the way). 'At the palace an official guide introduced himself. The 'palace' consisted of two houses, two flagpoles, two tombs and a rock on which the king stood to make his speeches. One of the buildings houses a little museum which contains the story of the place in some detail. There's a brilliant view of the surrounding hills and valley.' (Volker Dornheim)

Zafimaniry villages

The Zafimaniry people follow a traditional way of life in the forests southeast of Ambositra. This is not an area to attempt without an experienced guide, however. The danger is not so much in getting lost, but in the detrimental effects uncontrolled tourism has already had on the villagers nearest the road.

If you decide to go it alone, you should at least know that taxi-brousses only make the journey to Antoetra, the nearest Zafimaniry village to the road, on market days, Saturdays and Tuesdays. On other days, if you can't afford a taxi, you are stuck with a 23km hike from Ivato on RN7.

If you want to see the results of catastrophic deforestation this is as good an area as any. The impact is heightened by the beauty of the untouched forest and the simple way of life practised by the inhabitants of the more remote villages, where the picturesque houses show that wood carving is still the main industry. Sharon Giarratana reports: 'We walked many hours through beautiful, rolling hills and

DEFORESTATION AND CLIMATE – A HISTORICAL PERSPECTIVE

Concern about deforestation and its effects on climate is not new. Here are two observations, one from a 19th-century Russian playwright and one from an observant traveller in Madagascar a century earlier.

> There are fewer and fewer forests, the rivers are drying up, the wild creatures are becoming extinct, the climate is ruined, and every day the earth is growing poorer and more hideous ... I realise that the climate is to some extent in my power, and that if, in a thousand years man is to be happy, I too shall have had some small hand in it. When I plant a birch tree and see it growing green and swaying in the wind, my soul is filled with pride...'

> Anton Chekhov, *Uncle Vanya*, 1899

> When this island was first inhabited the ground was all cleared by means of fire. It would, however, have been prudent to leave rows of trees here and there at certain distances. Those rains, which in warm countries are so necessary to render the earth fertile, seldom fall on ground after it has been cleared; for it is the forests that attract the clouds and draw moisture from them ... cultivation without measure, and without method, has sometimes done much more hurt than good.

> Abbé Rochon, *A Voyage to Madagascar and the East Indies*, 1792

deep valleys, pretty challenging in some places. In the remote Zafimaniry villages, you'll find small wooden dwellings, dark and smoky inside with corn hung from low ceilings to dry. Catholic village so tons of kids hanging around. The Zafimaniry tombs look like large square heaps of tightly-packed stones, topped with obelisks. I haven't seen anything like it elsewhere in Madagascar.'

Guided tours of the Zafimaniry countryside are advertised in hotels in Ambositra or Fianar (the Tsara Guest House, for instance). Dany and Sahondra, a French-Malagasy couple running Villa Soamahatony, a B&B in Tana (see page 163) do trekking trips there and are extremely knowledgeable. Contact them by email: soamahatony@dts.mg.

Sandrandahy and Fandriana

A rough road northeast of Ambositra leads to Fandriana, well known for its raffia work, hats and so on. It takes about three hours or so to reach here. Roughly half way is Sandrandahy which holds a huge Wednesday market. This is also a silk weaving centre, where exquisite *lambas* are made.

South from Ambositra on RN7

From Ambositra, the scenery becomes increasingly spectacular. You now pass remnants of the western limit of the rainforest (being systematically destroyed). The road runs up and down steep hills, past neat Betsileo rice paddies interspersed with eucalyptus and pine groves. The steepest climb comes about two hours after Ambositra, when the vehicle labours up an endlessly curving road, through thick forests of introduced pine, and reaches the top where stalls selling oranges or baskets provide an excuse for a break. Then it's down through more forest, on a very poor stretch of road, to **Ambohimahasoa**. Hotel Nirina serves good snacks. If heading for Ranomafana, enquire here about the short cut, bypassing Fianarantsoa.

Leaving Ambohimahasoa you pass more forests, then open country, rice paddies and houses as you begin the approach to Fianarantsoa.

FIANARANTSOA

The name means 'Place of good learning'. Fianarantsoa (Fianar for short) was founded in 1830 as the administrative capital of Betsileo. It is one of the more attractive Malagasy towns, built on a hill like a small-scale Antananarivo. Fianar is an ideal base from which to do a variety of excursions (organised by the excellent Tsara Guest House): Andringitra, Ranomafana and even Isalo are within easy(ish) reach.

There is quite a contrast between the charming Upper Town and the dreary Lower Town. Travellers making only a brief stop tend to see only the Lower Town, dominated by a huge concrete stadium, and are not impressed. The Upper Town, with its narrow winding streets and plethora of churches, should be visited for the wonderful views, especially in the early morning when the mist is curling up from the valley. It's quite a way up: take bus number 3 or a taxi, and walk back.

Telephone code The area code for Fianar is 75.

Getting there and away
By road
For a tranquil journey the company KOFIAM, which operates buses between Fianar and Tana with a lunch stop in Ambositra, has been recommended. There is also the Jumbobus which runs between Tana and Toliara. See page 222.

For the onward journey to Toliara, a taxi-brousse takes around 14 hours.

By rail
See page 197.

By air
The 2001 Air Mad schedule shows Twin Otter flights on Wednesdays and Sundays. I wouldn't bank on it.

Where to stay
Category A
Hotel Soafia BP 1479; tel/fax: 503 53. This large hotel (74 rooms, 135,000–150,000Fmg) has all sorts of unusual features. 'Looks like a cross between Disneyworld, a Chinese temple and a gigantic doll's house' (J Hadfield). 'A veritable rabbit warren…walking around the spartan corridors made me feel I was going to round a corner and meet Jack Nicholson wielding an axe! A bizarre place' (Jerry Vive). 'The hotel has lost any semblance of civility. The tackiness which once charmed, now grates. The reception staff are off-hand and unfriendly to the extreme – rare attributes for Malagasy, they must hand-pick them specially' (Clare Hermans). However, its patisserie sells wonderful bread, croissants and pastries, and there are all sorts of useful goodies for sale in the shop, such as phone cards and stamps, and the photo shop next door sells very high quality postcards. Just don't stay in the hotel unless you're desperate!

Hotel Soratel BP 1335; tel: 516 66; fax: 516 78; email: soratel@dts.mg; web: soratel.free.fr. 26 rooms, 120,000–170,000Fmg including breakfast. A new hotel located near the train and taxi-brousse station which seems to be just what Fianar needs: 'Double rooms with wonderful huge bath, hot water, minibar, fridge stocked with cold drinks; extremely helpful, friendly staff.' (Debbie Fellner)

I. T. COMES TO 'THE PLACE OF GOOD LEARNING'

Feedback Madagascar is launching a new project sourcing 'waste' computers in Europe and sending them to Madagascar, then installing them in schools and public institutions. Aimed at giving disadvantaged people access to computers and a chance to learn new skills, this project also highlights the huge amount of technological material that gets thrown away in the West. Fianarantsoa's schools have virtually no computers and the only computers available at a couple of places in town are unaffordable. Even printing out a CV is beyond the possibility of most. The poor are always at a disadvantage for jobs.

Given a room in the Fianarantsoa library by the town council, the project is starting with a basic range of services available at a price which serves to cover just the running costs. Patrice de la Victoire, who is designing the project, hopes eventually to provide internet access as well.

Radama Hotel Tel: 507 97; fax: 513 76; email: radama@hotels.online.mg. €25 (double). On Fahaleovantena, about 200m from the Plazza Inn. 32 rooms (14 rooms plus 18 studios) all with TVs, and en-suite facilities.

Tsara Guest House BP 1373, Fianarantsoa 301 (Ambatolahikosoa, New Town); tel: 502 06; fax: 512 09; email: tsaraguest@dts.mg; web: www.tsaraguest.com. The best rooms, with beautiful views over the rice paddies and en-suite bathrooms are 220,000Fmg; those in the main house are 80,000Fmg. For over a decade the Tsara has been the most popular *vazaha* place in Madagascar, universally praised by readers. It is located in an old house that began its life as a church, with a terrace from which you have a wonderful view of the town. The owners, Jim Heritsialonina and his Swiss wife Natalie, deserve their success – they have worked unstintingly to provide all the comforts and atmosphere that travellers desire, making them feel part of a large family. The more expensive rooms have en-suite bathroom. Excellent restaurant. Wide variety of tours offered. The profits from this place go to support a small school at the edge of the rainforest.

Hotel Mahamanina Tel: 521 11. Double about 100,000Fmg; triples 135,000Fmg. Very pleasant rooms with good views from the balcony. Excellent restaurant.

Hotel Moderne du Betsileo BP 1161; tel: 500 03. 12 rooms, 60,000Fmg to 80,000Fmg. Part of the Papillon restaurant, located near the station. Clean, en-suite bathroom, hot water. 'Great value – spotless, safe ad friendly' (S Blachford).

Category B

Hotel Cotsoyannis 4 Rue Ramaharo; tel: 514 72; fax: 514 86. 90,000Fmg (double), 100,000Fmg (twin). This long-established hotel has had its ups and downs. Improved by a recent extension: pleasant rooms with en-suite bathrooms, good views. Old rooms may be available at a cheaper price. Good pizzas served in the restaurant. Note, however, that conscientious *vazaha* are boycotting this hotel because the owner is currently serving a prison sentence for serious sexual assaults on children. He is likely to buy his release before his full sentence is served. This hotel owns Camp Catta, in Andringitra.

Hotel Lanohy Conveniently located next to the taxi-brousse station. 70,000Fmg for a room with a hot shower. 'No meals except for the bed bugs.'

Lac Hotel 518 73; fax: 519 06. Outside town, a set of bungalows in a quiet, lake-side location. 100,000–120,000Fmg (family bungalow). Very friendly (no English spoken).

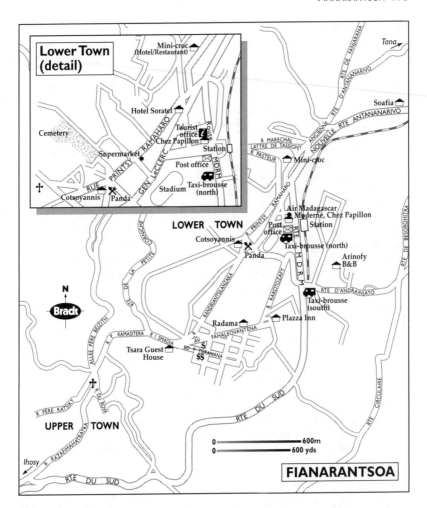

Mini Croq Hotel-Restaurant Tel: 505 87; email: minicroq.hotel@dts.mg. A popular restaurant now offering a few rooms. 76,500Fmg en-suite double. 'To locate it follow the road from the service station up the hill one block; it is near the large pharmacy on the top of the hill. Off-street, secure parking, clean, bright and cheerful. A delightful young waiter makes the restaurant fun.' (L Gillespie)

Category C

Arinofy B&B BP 1426, Fianarantsoa 301; tel: 508 38. A clean and very friendly place, up the hill from the taxi-brousse depot. By far the best of the cheaper hotels. A twin-bedded room is about 50,000Fmg, and a four-bunk one considerably less. You can eat in a communal dining room (excellent meals), and there is a laundry service. Camping is also permitted in the garden, either with your own tent (25,000Fmg) or using one supplied by the hotel (40,000Fmg).

There are other cheap places in Fianar, especially around the station. Avoid the **Hotel Ideal**. '55,000Fmg for the worst room I have ever had' (Sarah Blachford).

Where to eat

Chez Papillon Tel: 500 03. Back in the 1980s and 1990s this restaurant basked in its reputation of being the best restaurant in Madagascar. Now there are many better places, but the service is good and English is spoken.

Anofy B&B. A better, more friendly alternative to the Papillon. 'Great menu, reasonable prices, and quaint dining room.' (DF)

Panda Across the street from the Hotel Cotsoyannis. Very good Chinese meals, and game dishes (bat, frog and pigeon, according to one reader!) for around 35,000Fmg and attractive décor.

Estmill Grill Directly behind the Hotel Sofatel on Rte MDRM. 'Absolutely fantastic! I had the *romozava*. A slightly up-scale locals' joint.'

Resto Blue Very good, inexpensive food. Friendly.

Tiki dairy shop Across from the train station. Great yoghurt and cheese.

La Case The menu – and décor – gets its inspiration from North Africa. Dishes include savoury tajines and *yassa* of rabbit.

Nightlife

Moulin Rouge 'A fantastic nightclub on the outskirts of town. The place to be at the weekend. Varied music: Malagasy, African, Reggae, funny Euro-pop disco.'

Chez Tantine By the taxi-brousse station. Very Malagasy and fun.

What to see and do

This is a good town for strolling around. Take your time to explore the Upper Town and then check out the market. This is best on Friday, so is called *Zoma* (which means Friday).

Lorna Gillespie recommends an Antaimoro paper-making business she found particularly interesting. 'From the left-hand side of the taxi-brousse station follow the sign to the Arinofy Hotel, go over the bridge and take the road to your right, following the power lines. You will see the paper drying on frames. This is a family concern and they are most happy to show you the process. The prices are very reasonable and the product more interesting than most.' **Maurice Razafimahaleo**, Lot 1B 241/3611 Tanambao-Zoara 301, Fianarantsoa.

Excursions

Tea estate

The Sahambavy Tea Estate is situated on one side of a very pretty valley beside Lake Sahambavy, 25km by road from Fianar, or by rail to the Sahambavy station on the way to Manakara. Although tea-growing was encouraged in Madagascar in precolonial times, this is a relatively new estate and is now managed by a Dutch company, HVA, and run by a Scot. The company employs 700 people and 75% of the tea produced must by law be exported.

Visitors are welcome at the estate which is a beautiful place for picnics. Aim to get there before 15.00 since work finishes at 15.30. The estate is closed at weekends.

Wineries

Although the Famoriana wine estate mentioned in previous editions has reportedly closed (at least to visitors), Debbie Fellner persevered: 'Travelling north on the main road into town, you hit Madagascar's wine country. There are about four wineries between Ambalavao and Fianar. We stopped at Soavita, 3km from Ambalavao, in hopes of touring the winery. Silly us expecting to find something organised! We wandered around the property until we found what appeared to be the front entrance. A few young men were playing soccer nearby in the cleared vineyards. After an hour or so, one of the men came to unlock the factory doors and led us into the cellars. He proceeded to give us a 'tour' of sorts in Mala-French-Charades. He scooped out glassfuls of wine from various ageing vats for us to taste (then poured the remaining wine back into the vats!), showed us the labelling process (an old, toothless woman slapping labels on wine bottles with coconut paste) and showed off the 'high-tech' cork-insertion apparatus. It was the best wine tour I've ever been on, even if I only understood a fraction of what was going on.'

Train to Manakara

The seriously good news for rail buffs is that this line has been privatised and is running on schedule. It leaves for Manakara on Tuesday, Thursday and Saturdays, at 07.00 and the spectacular journey takes ten hours. The ticket office opens at 06.00 and you should get there shortly after it opens to secure the best seats. Ticket prices are 44,000Fmg first class and 39,000Fmg second class.

In the recent past the 163km trip had taken up to 48 hours, with sometimes one or two nights spent on the stationary train. This state of affairs could return, of course (as any Briton knows, privatising the railway does not guarantee punctuality!) but the future of this lovely railway looks rosy. There has been substantial investment by USAID and LDI, donations by a Swiss railway company, and even the King of Thailand got involved with advice on an erosion-preventing plant.

You can buy a nice little booklet, produced by the ADI-FCE (railway users' association), which describes the history of this railway, the villages on the way, and various statistics about the line (it was constructed between 1926 and 1936, there are 67 bridges and 48 tunnels, the longest of which is 1,072m long). The train stops frequently, for ten minutes at a time, allowing ample time for photography and for buying fruit, snacks or drinks from vendors. 'Most of all it is the people on the railway stations and in the villages that make this trip unforgettable, and as a bonus the landscape is beautiful...and as you near Manakara the railway crosses the airport runway! One last comment: on arriving at Manakara one should be prepared to deal with at least 100 *pousse-pousse* men waiting for you at the railway station.' (Marja van Ipenburg)

RANOMAFANA

The name Ranomafana means 'hot water' and it was the waters, not the lemurs, which drew visitors in the colonial days and financed the building of the once-elegant Hotel Station Thermale de Ranomafana.

These days the baths are often ignored by visitors anxious to visit the Ranomafana National Park which was created in 1991. This hitherto unprotected fragment of mid-altitude rainforest first came to world attention with the discovery of the golden bamboo lemur in 1986 and is particularly rich in wildlife.

Ranomafana has experienced a welcome explosion of accommodation in recent years (for nearly a decade after it opened there was just one, dire hotel) so now pleases almost everyone. I have always loved it! First you have the marvellous drive down, with the dry highland vegetation giving way to greenery and flowers. Then there are the views of the tumbling waters of the Namorona river, and the relief when the hillsides become that lovely unbroken, knobbly green of virgin forest and you know you are near the reserve. Hidden in these trees are 12 species of lemur: diademed (Milne-Edwards) sifaka, red-bellied brown lemur, red-fronted lemur, black-and-white ruffed lemur and three

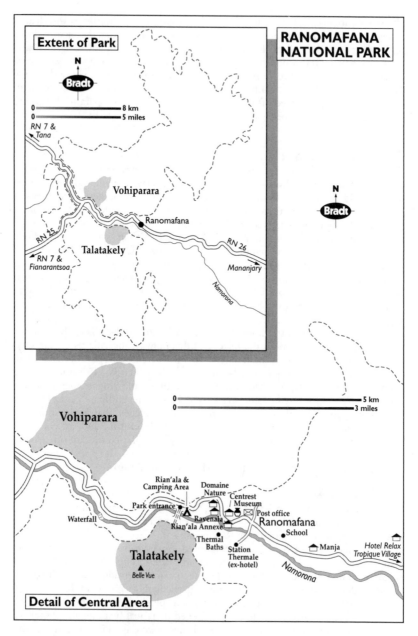

species of bamboo lemur. At night you can add mouse lemur, woolly lemur (avahi), lepilemur, greater dwarf lemur, and even aye-aye. Then there are the birds: more than 100 species with 36 endemic. And the reptiles. And the butterflies and other insects. Even if you saw no wildlife, there is enough variety in the vegetation and scenery, and enough pleasure in walking the well-constructed trails, to make a visit worthwhile. And – I nearly forgot – in the warm summer months you can swim in the cold, clear water of the Namorona while a malachite kingfisher darts overhead. Some negative things: the trails are steep and arduous, and few of the guides have reached the Périnet standard. It often rains, and there are leeches.

Getting there and away

In your own transport the journey is about three hours from Fianar or four hours from Ambositra. There are two roads leading there from RN7: a little-known short cut from Ambohimasoa (via Vohiparara) which is often closed, and an all-weather but potholed one which starts at Alakamisy Ambohimaha, about 26km north of Fianar. By taking a tour organised by the Tsara Guest House in Fianar (450,000Fmg) you can cut out a lot of the hassle of getting to Ranomafana.

Public transport has always been a problem since it is so often full. The trick is to leave early in the morning: be at the Fianar *gare routière* at 06.00 to ensure a good seat. At least two taxi-brousses leave between 07.00 and 09.00. The journey takes three to four hours. A similar service used to run from Ambositra (at the PNR Garage) but it seems to have been discontinued. Check locally.

Coming from Manakara or Mananjary you should be at the taxi-brousse station as early as possible in the morning.

Where to stay
Category A

Centrest Sejour Beyond the museum, on the left as you enter Ranomafana. 225,000Fmg double (high season); 185,000Fmg (low season) for comfortable, light, airy rooms, 65,000Fmg for lovely thatched bungalows with shared facilities. This is the comfortable hotel that Ranomafana has been waiting for. Well run, with a good restaurant and craft shop.

Category B

Hotel Domaine Nature A very well-managed, friendly and popular hotel with 14 bungalows overlooking the river, halfway between the village and the park, and some new ones on the hillside on the other side of the road. 195,000Fmg (double), breakfast 20,000Fmg, dinner 35,000Fmg, picnic 30,000Fmg. Bookings (Tana) through Destinations Mada; tel: 22 310 72, fax: 22 310 67.

Hotel Manja 10 bungalows and some rooms. 60,000Fmg (bungalows), 60,000Fmg to 180,000Fmg for rooms, depending on facilities. On the road to Mananjary (RN 26), 5 minutes' walk east along the river. 'One of those places that made me consider tearing up my return airline ticket and staying forever!' says reader Bradley Rink.

Category C

Gîte Jardin Reservations (Tana) tel: 22 223 51 or cellphone: 033 1146096. Four bungalows for 60,000–80,000Fmg with shared bathrooms and hot water. Breakfast in the lovely garden for 7,500–15,000Fmg. In town, opposite the *navette* stop for transport to the park. Recommended.

Rian'ala Dormitory accommodation near the park entrance for only 28,000Fmg. Meals around 18,000Fmg. The food is excellent, and the moths 'the size of frisbees' which are attracted to the lamps are an added bonus!

Rian'ala Annexe Three rooms with hot water: 65,000Fmg (double), 90,000Fmg (triple).Good value accommodation opposite the museum.

La Palmeraie 9 rooms for 32,500–62,500Fmg. Dormitory (4 beds) for 26,500Fmg per bed.

Hotely Ravenala 10 rooms, all 30,000Fmg; breakfast 7,500Fmg; lunch and dinner from 5,000Fmg (Malagasy cooking), more for something fancy. Located opposite the museum. Basic, funky, very friendly, beautiful views, good food.

Out of town

For those with their own transport there are a couple of quiet hotels on the way to Mananjary which are recommended.

Hotel Relax 5km from Ranomafana. 120,000–130,000Fmg. It, and its restaurant, Le Terrace are highly recommended. 'Lovely setting, away from the bustle of Ranomafana.' **Tropique Village** 180,000–250,000Fmg. A new (2001) upmarket hotel in Mahatsynosorano, about 9km from Ranomafana.

Camping

Camping is no longer permitted in the park, but there is a campsite at the park entrance: 10,000Fmg with your own tent, or you can rent a large one for 15,000Fmg a night and pay an additional 10,000Fmg per person. There are six covered tent sites, with open-sided A-frame thatched shelters giving shade as well as protection from the rain, and one centrally located covered picnic table. A tap provides drinking water and there is a bungalow with kitchen facilities.

This campsite was built by the villagers and the money goes directly to the community.

Where to eat

Chez Roger (Tsilavintsoa) Just up the road from the taxi-brousse stop. 'It has great food for about 15,000Fmg, including Malagasy specialities such as *Ravitoto sy hena kisoa* (pork and crushed casava leaves) and *akoho rony sy sakamalao* (chicken soup and ginger) and also spaghetti and so on. Amazing home-made ice-cream and crepes.' (Julia Jones)
Resto Bamboo Between the post office and the museum. Good food, convenient location.

Three *hotely*s opposite the market serve basic, but tasty food for 5–6,000Fmg.

Ranomafana and conservation

The Ranomafana National Park Project, set up by Dr Patricia Wright, established a large range of activities, from education and health care for the villagers on the periphery of the park, and an ecological monitoring team which works at several sites within the park. ANGAP and NGOs have continued this good work. The national park is one of the country's flagship conservation projects, with the involvement of the local communities playing an important role.

Much scientific research takes place in the park and there have been some clashes between researchers and tourists. Tourists have been known to push researchers aside in order to get a better photo, and to encourage guides to shake or bang on trees to persuade a lemur to move. It goes without saying that this is irresponsible behaviour and is counter-productive since some researchers withhold information on the whereabouts of the rarer lemurs for fear of being disturbed in their work.

At present an international consortium from countries including Finland and Italy, along with UNESCO and Stoney Brook University, New York, is building a new research centre near the park entrance.

Visiting the national park
Getting there from your hotel

The entrance to the park is some 6km west of the now defunct Hotel Station Thermale, on the main road. A *navette* (minibus) run by ANGAP leaves Ranomafana village at 07.00 to take visitors and guides up to the park entrance. It returns at 16.00 and costs 5,000Fmg.

Permits and guides

Permits (50,000Fmg) are obtainable from the National Park Office. You are not allowed into the park without a guide. Most only speak French, but they usually know the animals' names in English. There are some knowledgeable guides in Ranomafana, but the standard is still far removed from the courteous, informative guides of Périnet. This is now the only popular national park which provokes readers to complain regularly about the laziness and even rudeness of their guides.

The official fees are posted at the park entrance: currently 75,000Fmg for a long day tour and 50,000Fmg for a night visit. Groups of more than four must have two guides. Try to check the posted rate before hiring a guide, and confirm your intentions – and interests – with him or her before you set out. Guides will expect a tip in addition to the set fee – but don't feel you have to give one unless they deserve it!

In the forest

The paths in the forest have been improved in recent years. There are standard routes, most taking a few hours, but if you are fit, you should opt for the longer tours taking 6–8 hours. You will see primary forest, and it will be quieter. Even for the shorter walks you need to be reasonably fit – the paths are moderate to steep, and sometimes slippery. Your guide will assume that it is lemurs you have come to see; so, unless you stress that you are interested in other aspects such as botany or insects, he will tend to concentrate on mammals and birds. You are most likely to see red-fronted brown lemurs and the rarer red-bellied lemur. Greater bamboo lemur and even the star attraction, golden bamboo lemur are now fairly frequently seen. The most memorable of the easily-found lemurs is a subspecies of the diademed sifaka, Milne-Edwards' sifaka. Unlike the more familiar Verreaux's sifaka from the dry forests of the south, which is largely white, this is dark brown with cream-coloured sides.

A delightful, if strenuous, walk is along the river to Cascade Riana. This circular walk shouldn't be missed. Allow at least two hours for the round trip plus time to swim in the pool at the base of the falls.

Another trail system has been established on flatter ground at Vohiparara, near the boundary of the park 12km west of Ranomafana on the main road. It only takes about three hours to do all the trails here with a guide. 'Vohiparara is good for birders. Among many others you may see the brown emutail, Madagascar snipe, Meller's duck and the extremely rare slender-billed flufftail. The song of the cryptic warbler was first recorded here in 1987' (Derek Schuurman). According to Nick Garbutt this is also the best place for the rufous-headed ground-roller and yellow-bellied sunbird-asity.

A new path has recently been opened in *Parcelle II*, back up the road past the falls and in a boggier area of the reserve. 'The forest there is more varied, wetter with a lower canopy. We saw some Milne-Edwards' sifakas quite easily. We also arranged a half-day walk in another part of the forest through the official guide. Starting at the village of Ambatolahy, we hiked up behind the village into the reserve. accompanied by a local guide-villager. The track followed ridges and criss-crossed streams. A nice example of how money is going from the visitors to the locals directly.' (Clare & Johan Hermans)

ANGAP are planning an even more ambitious (and exciting-sounding) two-day circuit with a night camped at the village of Bevohajo. This community is near a spectacular waterfall and perform the traditional *tombolo* dance of the local Tanala people. Enquire at the ANGAP office for information.

A nocturnal visit to Belle Vue, a popular viewpoint, is recommended for the habituated mouse lemurs which come for bananas, along with greater dwarf lemurs and the civet or fanaloka which is attracted by meat. A viewing platform and

CRAYFISH
Julia Jones

Visitors to Ranomafana, and other eastern rainforest areas, will probably come across people selling platefuls of tasty looking crayfish. These have been boiled and seasoned in salt to make a delicious fast-food snack. On the road to Ranomafana, passing through Betsileo villages Sahavrondronan and Vohiparara, you may see them being sold in another form. Many travellers wonder what is in the small cylindrical bamboo cages held up by smiling children, closer inspection would show each is packed with live crayfish.

Madagascar's crayfish maybe less charismatic than other aspects of her fauna but like most of the animals and plants in this fascinating country they are unique and biologically very exciting. Six species have been described from Madagascar, all are found nowhere else on earth. No crayfish are native to Africa or India so the origins of Madagascar's crayfish are a mystery to biologists.

For as long as anyone can remember people in the eastern highlands have harvested crayfish from the forest streams for food. They are a great source of protein to people whose main diet is rice and beans. However, now that the human population has grown, road access increased, and the demand for crayfish from specialist markets in towns opened up, crayfish have become increasingly important as a source of income. This increased pressure on wild populations may not be sustainable under current harvesting practices and some communities are worried about the effect on their crayfish stocks.

Crayfish are relatively fecund and fast-growing, meaning that with careful management, sustainable harvests should be achievable. Some villages are investigating the possibilities of crayfish culturing to reduce pressure on wild populations while others are discussing introducing a Dina (village law) to prevent females with eggs from being harvested. Hopefully these changes will mean visitors to the Ranomafana area and local people will continue to enjoy this wholesome, tasty snack.

If you are a tourist remember: crayfish are a good source of income for local people and since crayfish need forest this industry can indirectly help in forest protection. It is a meal you can enjoy with a good conscience.

---

shelter have been built here. There are good photo opportunities, and the steep paths have been made as safe as possible, but even so negotiating them by torchlight can be tricky. And Nick Garbutt reports that 'at times it becomes a real circus, with far too many people – 40 or 50 – there are one time.'

Museum/gift shop

This is part of the Ranomafana National Park Project to improve visitor understanding of the area. The museum is still being added to, but there is now quite a comprehensive collection labelled in English and Malagasy.

When shopping for gifts – here or in other places – look out for soft-toy lemurs and chameleons made from old *lambas*. What a great idea!

Thermal baths

These are close to the former Station Thermale hotel. It costs only 5,000Fmg for a wonderful warm swim in the pool or 2,500Fmg for a private bath ('in a grotty little room where the door doesn't close all the way'). You can even have a massage for 25,000Fmg. Open 07.00–12.00, 14.00–17.00; closed Wednesday afternoons for cleaning. On Thursday to Saturday nights you can have a nocturnal swim with poolside beers and barbecue.

THE ROAD TO MANAKARA

The journey by car takes about five hours, passing several interesting small towns all of which have shops and *hotelys*. This road would repay a more leisurely journey on foot or by bike. Bjørn Donnis points out that after Irondo, as you near the coast, the landscape becomes bone-dry – quite unexpected in the 'eastern rainforest'. This is due (you guessed it) to deforestation and overgrazing.

Manakara and other eastern towns are covered in *Chapter 13*.

Continuing south on RN7

The next leg of the journey, to Ihosy, is 206km. Coming from Fianar the landscape is a fine blend of vineyards and terraced rice paddies (the Betsileo are acknowledged masters of rice cultivation), then after 20km a giant rock formation seems almost to hold the road in its grasp. Its name is, appropriately, *Tanan'Andriamanitra*, or Hand of God. From here to Ihosy is arguably the finest mountain scenery in Madagascar. Reader Bishop Brock who cycled the route writes: 'Those three days were the most rewarding of my career as a bicycle tourist. I pity people who only pass through that magnificent landscape jammed inside a taxi-brousse.'

It is worth noting that taxi-brousses from the north continue south in the afternoon. This may be the best time to get a place if you're pushed for time.

AMBALAVAO

Some 56km southwest of Fianarantsoa is my favourite town, Ambalavao. RN7 does not pass through the attractive part of town, and I strongly urge people to stop here for a few hours. 'Nowhere in Madagascar have I seen a town so resembling a medieval European village as here. Although the main street was not narrow, the wooden balconies with their handsomely carved railings leaned into the street, giving them that look of a fairytale book tilt. The roofs were tiled, and, lending that final touch of authenticity, pails of water were emptied on to people passing too near the gutter.' (Tim Cross)

A worthwhile visit is to the silk project at Ankazondandy, about 3km south of Ambalavao. This is an easy walk and a representative of CCDN, who run the project, may be found at the paper factory and will show you the way. You get a tour of the project and there is a shop selling the silk items made by the trainee women.

Getting there and away

Although Ambalavao is on RN7, southward-bound travellers may prefer to make it an excursion from Fianarantsoa, since vehicles heading to Ihosy and beyond will have filled up with passengers in Fianar.

Where to stay

Hotel Snackbar Aux Bougainvillées BP 14, Ambalavao 308; tel 01 (!). Next to the Antaimoro paper shop. 26 simple bungalows with solar-powered hot water, and a restaurant serving good, plain food. Reasonably priced at 86,000Fmg for rooms with shared facilities, and about 106,000Fmg for bungalows. Good breakfasts. The hotel owns an orchid garden on the outskirts of town, but with an entrance fee of 25,000Fmg plus 35,000Fmg for a guide, they probably don't get many takers.

Stop Hotel Five double rooms with communal WC and washing facilities. Basic but adequate. They expect you to eat at least one meal a day in the restaurant and to order it in advance.

La Notre Similar in price and quality to Stop Hotel. Cockroaches an added bonus.

Frances Kerridge adds: 'NB: in both these hotels the beds are small so you need to be good friends or Malagasy sized.'

Camping
If you have a tent you can camp at Ankazondandy.

What to see
Antaimoro paper
Ambalavao is the original home of the famous Malagasy 'Antaimoro' paper. This papyrus-type paper impregnated with dried flowers is sold throughout the island as wall-hangings and lampshades. The people in this area are Betsileo, but paper-making in the area copies the coastal Antaimoro tradition which goes back to the Muslim immigrants who wrote verses from the Koran on this paper. This Arabic script was the only form of writing known in Madagascar before the LMS developed a written Malagasy language nearly 500 years later using the Roman alphabet.

Antaimoro paper is traditionally made from the bark of the *avoha* tree from the eastern forests, but sisal paste is now sometimes used. After the bark is pounded and softened in water it is smoothed on to linen trays to dry in the sun. While still tacky, dried flowers are pressed into it and brushed over with a thin solution of the liquid bark to hold them in place. The open-air 'factory' (more flowerbeds than buildings) where all this happens is to the left of the town (signposted) and is well worth a visit. It is fascinating to see the step-by-step process, and you get a good tour (in French with a smattering of English) from the manager. A shop sells the finished product at reasonable prices.

Cattle market
Held Mondays and Thursdays on the outskirts of town. It gets going at about 3am, so you need to be an early riser! The herdsmen take a month to walk the zebu to Tana.

Beyond Ambalavao
The scenery beyond Ambalavao is marvellous. Huge granite domes of rock dominate the grassy plains. The most striking one, with twin rock towers, is called *Varavarana Ny Atsimo*, the 'Door to the South' by the pass of the same name. Beyond is the 'Bonnet de l'Evêque' (Bishop's Hat), and a huge lump of granite shaped like an upturned boat, with its side gouged out into an amphitheatre; streams run into the lush vegetation at its base. This dramatic landscape begs to be explored on foot and now, with the opening of Andringitra National Park, you can do just that.

You will notice that not only the scenery but the villages are different. These Bara houses are solidly constructed out of red earth (no elegant Merina pillars here) with small windows. Bunches of maize are often suspended from the roof to dry in the sun.

Shortly after Ambalavao you start to see your first tombs – some painted with scenes from the life of the deceased.

The next town of importance is Ihosy, described in *Chapter 10*.

ZEBU

The hump-backed cattle, zebu, which nearly outnumber the country's human population, produce a relatively low yield in milk and meat. These animals are near-sacred and generally are not eaten by the Malagasy, other than at ceremonies of social or religious significance. Zebu are said to have originated from northeast India, eventually spreading as far as Egypt and then down to Ethiopia and other parts of East Africa. It is not known how they were introduced to Madagascar but they are a symbol of wealth and status as well as being used for burden.

Zebu come in a variety of colours, the most sought-after being the *omby volavita*, which is chestnut with a white spot on the head. There are 80 words in the Malagasy language to describe the physical attributes of zebu, in particular the colour, horns and hump.

In the south, zebu meat is always served at funerals, and among certain southern tribes the cattle are used as marriage settlements, as is done in Africa. Whenever there is a traditional ritual or ceremony, zebu are sacrificed, the heads being given to the highest ranking members of the community. Blood is smeared on participants as it is believed to have purification properties, and the fat from the hump of the cattle is used as an ingredient for incense. Zebu milk is an important part of the diet among the Antandroy; it is *fady* for women to milk the cows but it is they who sell the curdled milk in the market.

While zebu theft in the past was considered an act of bravery, it is now confined mainly to the Bara. The traditional penalty for cattle-rustling was the *dina* whereby the culprit and his family were reduced to slavery. Among the Antandroy and Mahafaly a fine of ten zebu would have to be paid by the thief: five for the family from whom the cattle were stolen and five for the king.

To the rural Malagasy a herd of zebu is as symbolic of prosperity as is a new car or a large house in our culture. Government aid programmes must take this into account; for instance improved rice yields will indirectly lead to more environmental degradation by providing more money to buy more zebu.

The French colonial government thought they had an answer: they introduced a tax on each animal. However, local politicians were quick to point out that since Malagasy women had always been exempt from taxation, the same rule should apply to cows!

ANDRINGITRA MOUNTAINS

These spectacular granite peaks and domes have entranced me since I first travelled the length of RN7, so I am thrilled that they can now form the focus for a trekking holiday. Part of this range has been gazetted as a national park (see page 207) but the tour operator Boogie Pilgrim has its **Tsara Camp** outside the park's boundaries on the northwest side of the range. It is not always made clear to visitors that the camp is not in the park so does not offer the same trekking possibilities.

Nevertheless the Tsara Camp is an imaginative use of the wilderness, being a tented-camp similar to those used to accommodate tourists in Africa. Clare and Johan Hermans sent the following report: 'The approach road to Tsara camp is an unsignposted track off the RN7 before the village of Tanambao, 37km south of Ambalavao; in all it takes about two hours from the main road. It is not an all-

SOME ANDRINGITRA LEGENDS
Debbie Fellner
The story of the waterfalls
These falls, named Riandahy (the male) and Rianmbavy (female), plunge dramatically off the edge of the Andringitra plateau, and supply the villages of Ambalamonandray (village of the son) and Namoly (weavers) below. The falls are said to be the natural embodiments of the old king and queen of the weaver people. According to local legend, the king and queen could not conceive a child, so they met at the falls with an *ombiasy* (spiritual healer) and sacrificed a white-faced zebu to satisfy the gods. They were successful: now the waterfalls and streams that feed them are considered highly sacred, and are ruled by strict codes of conduct. For example, it is *fady* to wash a pig in the waters. The power of this *fady* was demonstrated in 1993 when a group of Christian missionaries washed their Easter pig in the sacred waters. It hailed all the next day, ruining the rice fields. It is also *fady* to speak of one's boat as it crosses the water – any such utterance would cause the boat to capsize and sink.

Pic Boby
The name of Madagascar's second highest mountain derives from a more prosaic story. The summit was named after the dog of a French botanist who conducted research in Andringitra in the 1920s. The tale goes that one night a heavy fog enveloped the scientist's encampment and his dog, Boby, went out wandering and got lost. The researcher tried desperately to find Boby, and followed the dog's barks through the mist to the top of the mountain. It is not known if he ever found his dog. Today, the stone shelter where the botanist worked is still partially standing in the cradle below the summit.

weather track and so the camp closes in the rainy season for three months. It passes through a delightful village, Vohitsoka, where the kids are curious and so far not contaminated by gifts. Walking down the main street was like the Pied Piper of Hamlyn, with 30 kids in tow.

'The camp consists of ten tents under thatched shelters, set in a spectacular plain bounded by the Andringitra massif to the east. It was only opened in October 2000. It is a hybrid between safari and basic camping with wooden floors to the canvas tents. Chemical toilets are set behind the tents. The shower is refreshingly cold, with the surrounding thatch giving privacy up to *vazaha* mid-riff. Candles and paraffin lamps are provided. The eating area is in a bigger tent; food basic, and at present rather reliant on tinned goods. However there is refrigeration so cold drinks are available and welcome. The woman who runs it is friendly, efficient and has a sense of humour.

'There is not much to do once you get there except enjoy the spectacular views, sunsets, moon and star gaze and do some walking. There's a half-day walk to the private reserve in the Tsaranoro valley to see ring-tailed lemurs if you are lucky. What they omit to say beforehand is that there is a 30,000Fmg fee for it. This walk can be extended to an all-day hike up the hill the locals call the Chameleon, 1,500m. In the dry season they provide gaiters for your legs as there is a vicious grass whose seeds penetrate straight through two socks and implant into the skin. The walks involve clambering over boulders so some sensible footwear is a must: we witnessed one twisted ankle and a lot of bruises in the two day stay there.'

Camp Catta up the road is run by the Cotsoyannis Hotel in Fianar. It has established itself as a centre for climbing and paragliding. Basic brick-built huts and a generator.

Your decision on whether to stay at Tsara Camp or the National Park will be dictated by your interests. Tsara camp is ideal for non-hikers who want to enjoy the scenery; the National Park is designed for walkers and the accommodation is more basic.

Andringitra National Park

Created in 1999, this park protects the flora and fauna around Madagascar's second highest peak, Pic Boby (2,400m), and is already delighting visitors who relish the fantastic scenery, good infrastructure, and lack of crowds. Andringitra (pronounced Andringtra) has some wildlife, but landscape, vegetation and trekking are the chief attractions.

Here's a description of the Andringitra experience from Debbie Fellner: 'Our visit to Andringitra was, by far, the highlight of our Madagascar adventure. While in Fianar, the Tsara Guest House arranged for us to meet Lolo – a local guide who leads trips to the park and other areas throughout the central highlands. He spoke perfect English, was highly organised, prepared and professional (even to our lofty Western standards). Plus, Lolo is just a great guy and it was fun to get to know him. We paid him top dollar – US$150 per person – to arrange the trip. He took care of food, transportation, hiring local guides and porters – the works – for a two-night, three-day backpacking trip.

'The park is just stunning with waterfalls, rivers, flower-filled valleys, sheer rock escarpments and lunar-like summits. On the second day, we hiked to the summit of Pic Boby – the highest accessible peak in Madagascar at 2,658m. The trails are exceptionally well maintained – laboriously crafted by local guides and porters under the direction of the WWF. Our local guide was Hyllarion. Employing Lolo, a driver, three guides and porters (plus another local who carried our firewood the first day), the enormity of our team at first seemed like a joke, "How many Malagasy does it take to get two *vazahas* up a mountain?" But, in the end, their help was invaluable and we had wonderful interactions with everyone, learned a ton about local traditions and expanded our Malagasy vocabulary a thousand-fold.'

Getting there and away

The entrance to the park is 46km south of Ambalavao – but you should allow at least an hour (it often takes two) for the journey by private vehicle. The road can be treacherous if it's raining – it gets extremely slippery – and there are four toll booths (5,500Fmg per vehicle) which may, or may not, be manned. 'The road to the *gîte* is awesome. Picturesque churches, usually with free-standing clock towers. In the rocks high above the road are tombs, decorated with zebu skulls.' (Volker Dornheim)

Travelling here by public transport is problematic. Committed visitors can usually find a taxi-brousse to take them at least part of the way, but they should be prepared for a lot of walking.

Local guides

'There are few, if any, English-speaking local guides. For language-challenged travellers like us, hiring an English-speaking guide and translator such as Lolo was essential. I wouldn't have wanted to miss all that Hyllarion had to teach us! For instance he explained the traditional uses of the local flora from stopping urination to curing gout. One even provided fire for making gravestones, the xerophite, which can carry heat just as well as coal. Hyllarion's favourites were *vaxinim*, a plant that bears a sweet, peach-like fruit, and *fandramana*, wild Malagasy tea, which he gathered for our dinner that night. My favourite was the *dombya*, graced with flowers similar to red roses, that had no apparent use. I saw several flowering *dombya* bushes along the trail to Pic Boby.

'Our English-Malagasy dictionary was the key to our interaction with the local guides. Each night, we'd teach each other words from our surroundings – rain, thunder, lightning, mountains, waterfalls. A deck of playing cards was also a great icebreaker. One night, the six of us sat around the campfire playing blackjack and chewing bubble gum. The Malagasy are quick learners when it comes to cards! I still chuckle when I recall their cries of "heet!" and "boosted!" as they tried to score 21.'

Lolo Voyages BP 1183, Ambalapaiso Ambony, Fianar; tel/fax: 520 80. 'Lolo is the best! Find him through the Tsara Guest House. Tell him Debbie and Brian sent you.'

Where to stay/eat

If you want a fixed base, rather than a backpacking trip, there is a WWF *gîte* at Ambolamandary, 7km from the park entrance. No meals are provided, but if you shop for meat and vegetables in the local village (with a guide), one of the *gîte* staff will cook them for you. There are also campsites below the sacred waterfalls and on the trekking route to Pic Boby.

Trekking

There are three trails: a three-hour hike up to the sacred waterfall, the Diavolana Trail which is a seven-hour circuit giving the best views and most varied scenery, and the climb up Pic Boby – highly recommended if you are fit. It is about 24km, so although I know a loony who did it in one day, it really takes two or three days, camping en route.

Part Three

The South

Sifaka

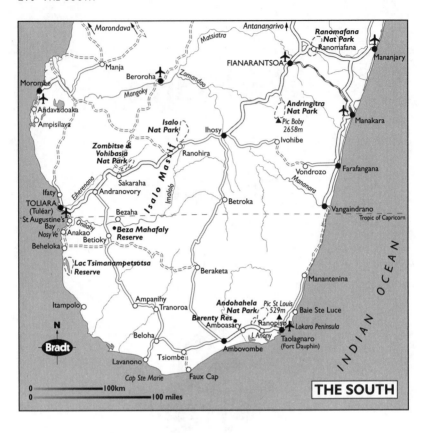

THE SOUTH

ANDROY: LAND OF THORNS

Pays où l'on a soif
où souvent l'on a faim
où les hommes sont forts et fiers.

A land where one goes thirsty
Where one often goes hungry
Where the people are strong and proud

The South

OVERVIEW
This is the most exotic and the most famous part of Madagascar, the region of 'spiny desert' where weird cactus-like trees wave their thorny fingers in the sky, where pieces of 'elephant bird' shell may still be found, and where the Mahafaly tribe erect their intriguing and often entertaining *aloalo* stelae above the graves. Here also is one of the country's most popular nature reserves (Berenty), and its best beaches and coral reefs. No wonder the south features on almost all tour itineraries.

History
Europeans have been coming to this area for a long time. Perhaps the earliest were a group of 600 shipwrecked Portuguese sailors in 1527. Later, when sailors were deliberately landing in Madagascar during the days of the spice trade in the 16th and 17th centuries, St Augustine's Bay, south of the modern town of Toliara (Tuléar), became a favoured destination. They came for reprovisioning – Dutch and British – trading silver and beads for meat and fruit. One Englishman, Walter Hamond, was so overcome with the delights of Madagascar and the Malagasy, 'the happiest people in the world', that fired by his enthusiasm the British attempted to establish a colony at St Augustine's Bay. It was not a success. The original 140 settlers were soon whittled down to 60 through disease and murder by the local tribesmen who became less happy when they found their favourite beads were not available for trade and that these *vazaha* showed no sign of going away. The colonists left in 1646. Fifty years later St Augustine was a haven for pirates.

The people today
Several ethnic groups live in the south: the Vezo (fishermen), Mikea and Masikoro (pastoralists) are subclans of the Sakalava. The Mahafaly, Antanosy, Antandroy and Bara all have their regions in the interior. These southern Malagasy are tough, dark-skinned people, with African features, accustomed to the hardship of living in a region where rain seldom falls and finding water and grazing for their large herds of zebu is a constant challenge. The **Bara** are particularly known for their association with cattle – this warlike tribe resisted Merina rule and were never really subdued until French colonial times. Cattle rustling is a time-honoured custom – a Bara does not achieve manhood until he has stolen a few of his neighbour's cows.

In contrast to the highland people, who go in for second burial and whose tombs are the collective homes of ancestors, those in the south (with the exception of the Bara) commemorate the recently dead. There is more opportunity to be remembered as an individual here, and a **Mahafaly** or **Masikoro** man who has lived eventfully, and died rich, will have the highlights of his life perpetuated in the form of wooden carvings (*aloalo*) and colourful paintings adorning his tomb.

DISTANCES IN KILOMETRES

Ihosy–Toliara	327km
Ihosy–Taolagnaro	506km
Ihosy–Betroka	132km
Ihosy–Ranohira	75km
Ranohira–Toliara	244km
Toliara–Anakao	50km
Toliara–Andavadoaka	325km
Toliara–Andranovory	70km
Toliara–Ejeda	304km
Toliara–Bezaha	125km
Toliara–Ampanihy	290km
Toliara–Bevoay	206km
Toliara–Morombe	284km
Bezaha–Ampanihy	195km
Bezaha–Ejeda	145km
Betroka–Ihosy	132km
Ampanihy–Berenty	267km
Ampanihy–Taolagnaro	334km
Taolagnaro–Betroka	374km
Taolagnaro–Manantenina	110km
Taolagnaro–Amboasary	110km
Taolagnaro–Ambovombe	145km
Ambovombe–Tsiombe	67km
Tsiombe–Faux Cap	30km
Tsiombe–Lavanono	92km
Faux Cap–Cap Sainte Marie	40km
Lavanono–Androka	250km
Androka–Itampolo	61km
Itampolo–Anakao	134km

Formerly the *aloalo* were of more spiritual significance; but just as we, in our culture, have tended to bring an element of humour and realism into religion, so have the Malagasy. As John Mack says (in *Island of Ancestors*), '*Aloalo* have become obituary announcements when formerly they were notices of rebirth'.

Antandroy tombs may be equally colourful. They are large and rectangular (the more important the person the bigger his tomb) and, like those of the Mahafaly, topped with zebu skulls left over from the funeral feast. A very rich man may have over 100 skulls on his grave. They usually have 'male and female' standing stones (or, in modern tombs, cement towers) at each side. Modern tombs may be brightly painted with geometric patterns or imaginative paintings (unlike those of the Mahafaly these do not represent scenes from the life of the deceased).

In Antandroy country, burial sometimes takes place several months after the day of death, which will be commemorated by the sacrifice of cattle and ritual mourning or wailing. A few days later the body is placed in the coffin – and more zebu are sacrificed. Meanwhile finishing touches will be made to the tomb, before the internment ceremony which takes place over two days or more. The tomb is finally filled in with stones, and topped with the horns of the sacrificed zebu. Then the house of the deceased is burnt to the ground. The burial ceremonies over, the family will not go near the tomb again.

The **Antanosy** have upright stones, cement obelisks, or beautifully carved wooden memorials. These, however, are not over the graves themselves but in a sacred and secret place elsewhere.

Getting around

Road travel in the south can be a challenging affair, but some of the roads are being improved, and most of RN7 to Toliara (Tuléar) is now paved. Apart from this and the road between Taolagnaro (Fort Dauphin) and Ambovombe, the 'roads' that link other important towns are terrible, so most people prefer to fly. In addition to the regular flights to the main towns of Taolagnaro and Toliara there are occasional small planes to Ampanihy, Bekily and Betioky as well as Ihosy. Check the current schedule with Air Mad.

IHOSY

Pronounced 'Ee-oosh', this small town is the capital of the Bara tribe. It is a medium-sized town which had its moment of glory in June 2001, when it was one of Madagascar's eclipse centres. Few people stop for long, but Patrick Blackman sent this report: 'It's a nice town, lots of shops, spread out on a sandy plain. Lots of dust. Almost maddeningly friendly. A useful man to know is Alexandre Ralainandrasana, who is a *Guide Touristique Regional* with an office at Lot IM14 Andrefantsena, Ihosy. This is on the right, on the road towards Tuléar.'

Ihosy is about five hours from Fianar by taxi-brousse and lies at the junction for Toliara and Taolagnaro. The road to the former is good; to the latter, bad. A now impassable road also runs from Ihosy to Farafangana, on the east coast. Drivers expecting to refuel at Ihosy, though, should be warned that they may be disappointed.

Telephone code The area code for Ihosy is 75.

Where to stay

Zaha Motel BP 67; tel: 740 83. Pleasant, comfortable bungalows, cold water (hot if you ask them to turn on the gas heater). 110,000Fmg.
Hotel Relais-Bara 'Good for drugs and prostitutes.'
Hotel Bienvenue On the outskirts of town on the road to Toliara (left-hand side). If you have your own vehicle there is nowhere to park, however.
Hotel Revaka About 400m from the taxi-brousse station, on the road from Fianar. There is road parking here and camping is permitted in the garden.

Where to eat

Evah's Restaurant Brand new (in anticipation of eclipse visitors) and reportedly 'up to Western standards' with very good Chinese and Malagasy food. It is quite a walk from the centre of town, however – about 500m down the road to Toliara (on the right-hand side).

In town there is a nice little square of open-sided *hotelys* serving good Malagasy food. The **Hotely Dasimo** is recommended for its excellent *tsaramasy* (rice with beans and pork).

FROM IHOSY TO FARAFANGANA

According to Marko Petrovic this road (which looks promising on the map) has been impassable by car for almost 20 years. From Ihosy it is possible to go as far as **Ivohibe** and from Farafangana you can get to Vondrozo by 4WD. However, between Ivohibe and Vondrozo all the bridges decayed a long time ago and the road has become overgrown with trees, making it difficult even for a motorbike.

FROM IHOSY TO TAOLAGNARO (FORT DAUPHIN)

RN13 is in very poor condition. Adventurous travellers will enjoy the consequent lack of tourist development but don't underestimate the time it takes to travel even short distances.

The first town is **Betroka**, a friendly little place with a basic hotel and restaurant, Des Bons Amis, with a loo-shed outside. If you don't want to eat in the hotel there are plenty of *hotelys*. Next comes **Beraketa** which has the even more down-to-earth Herilaza Hotel. This seems to be the last accommodation (except in private houses) before Ambovombe and the paved road to Taolagnaro.

FROM IHOSY TO TOLIARA (TULEAR)

After leaving Ihosy, RN7 takes you for two hours across the Horombe Plateau, grasslands dotted with termite hills. As you approach Ranohira, *Medemia* palms enliven the monotonous scenery. Henk Beentje of Kew Gardens writes: 'The palms are properly called *Bismarckia*, but the French didn't like the most common palm in one of their colonies to be called after a German so changed the name, quite illegally according to the Code of Botanical Nomenclature!'

RANOHIRA AND ISALO NATIONAL PARK

The small town of Ranohira lies 97km south of Ihosy and is the base for visiting the popular Isalo National Park. It is also the nearest established town to Ilakaka, the new settlement that is the base for the sapphire trade. When sapphires were first discovered in the region in 1998, conservationists were alarmed that Isalo was threatened. Tim Ireland, a geologist, assures me this is not so: 'It is clearly understood by everyone in the field that the stones do not exist further north, and Isalo National Park is not in any physical danger. One miner told me the stones continue all the way to Toliara (which I consider characteristic Malagasy resource optimism), but he was adamant there's nothing to be found to the north. His view, at least with regard to the northern boundary of the gem-bearing deposits, is correct and is supported by the evident geology.'

Many readers have commented on the transformation of previously sleepy Ranohira. 'It has the feel of the Wild West… full of buyers from the Far East who go around with briefcases stacked with money, and the prospectors who dress like small-time gangsters with their wide-brimmed hats, dark glasses and money belts.' (Rupert Parker)

Getting there and away

Getting to Ranohira is usually no problem: it's 75km –about two hours– from Ihosy. If leaving from Toliara note that the taxi-brousses and buses depart early in the morning; it is best to book your seat the night before. If time is short it's worth considering hiring a car and driver in Toliara.

Where to stay
Category A

Relais de la Reine BP 01, 313 Ranohira. This lovely French-run hotel is not in Ranohira but at Soarano, 9km further south, on the edge of the park. It has been thoughtfully designed to blend as much as possible into the surrounding landscape. There are blocks of six rooms grouped round a courtyard, and solar panels provide hot water. The water is drawn from their own stream and fans cool the rooms in the hot season. A twin-bedded room with bathroom costs ∈55; breakfast ∈2.5; dinner: 58,000Fmg. Bookings must be made through Madagascar Discovery Agency in Tana; tel/fax: 351 65 or 351 67; email: mda@bow.dts.mg. Other agencies in Tana will also make the booking. The hotel keeps horses and runs riding tours; €46 half day, €77 full day. It even has a landing strip if you decide to splash out and book their private plane.

Category B

Motel d'Isalo Opened spring of 2001, so likely to be better than the Orchidée. Good food.

Hotel Orchidée d'Isalo The once good rooms have deteriorated and the place is overrun with sapphire dealers. However, it does have hot water and an extension is being built. En-suite double about 60,000–80,000Fmg.

Isalo Ranch BP 3, 313 Ranohira. A group of 8 bungalows, a few kilometres south of Ranohira. Shared facilities, but solar-powered hot water. 60,000Fmg per bungalow. The food is reportedly superb. Transport is provided to and from the National Park.

Category C

Hotel les Joyeux Lémuriens 14 rooms, about 80,000Fmg. The most popular backpacker hotel in Ranohira, but the rooms are small and noisy and the toilets have seen better days. Well run and friendly, however.

Hotel Berny In the centre of town, next to the ANGAP office. An assortment of rooms round a courtyard. Basic; about 40,000Fmg.

Camping

Claire Graham reports on a new campsite: '**Momo Trek** is situated next to the ANGAP office. It's basically a field, with a bar where you can buy drinks and hot food. It also has showers and toilets. It is run by a very friendly Malagasy man who speaks excellent English. 5,000Fmg per person per night.'

Bart Snyers is lyrical about the campsite **Les Etoiles d'Isalo** (also new, built for the eclipse hordes who never came). 'Les Etoiles d'Isalo is a few kilometres before Ranohira next to the RN7. The main building serves as restaurant and bar. The two sanitary buildings are spotlessly clean (I was almost embarrassed to walk in with my dirty trekker's outfit) and the showers even have warm water! It was three days of pure luxury. The kitchen is absolutely great, and besides the usual stuff, you can eat some very delicious Malagasy dishes. You can hire a tent or pitch your own. There's also a big terrace with wooden benches and a marvellous view of the Isalo 'rockies'. It's a bit expensive (40,000Fmg per tent if you pitch your own) but worth it considering the luxury they offer.'

Isalo National Park

The combination of sandstone rocks (cut by deep canyons and eroded into weird shapes), rare endemic plants and dry weather (between June and August rain is almost unknown) makes this park particularly rewarding. For botanists there is *Pachypodium rosulatum* or elephant's foot – a bulbous rock-clinging plant – and a native species of aloe, *Aloe isaloensis*; and for lemur-lovers there may be sifakas, brown lemurs and ring-tails. 'Isalo is fantastic! It is not just the abstract sculpturing and colours of the eroded terrain or the sweeping panoramas which so impressed, but also the absolute and enveloping silence. No birds, insects or other animals, no wind, no rumbling of distant traffic and no other people,' wrote a reader some years ago. These days you have to get off the beaten track to escape from other visitors but… it's a big area.

Isalo is also sacred to the Bara tribe. For hundreds of years the Bara have used caves in the canyon walls as burial sites. There is one for a king in Canyon des Singes, high up in the cliff wall, but there are others scattered everywhere. Ask your guide about this but it is wise not to push the issue. Their beliefs and traditions need to be preserved.

Tourists who do not wish to hike (and this should not be undertaken lightly – it can be very hot) or to pay the park fee have various options. Simply driving past the sandstone formations which can be seen from the road is exciting enough, and you can visit the Oasis, an idyllic palm-shaded grotto (although after a dry season this can be waterless and disappointing). The track leading here is about 10km south of Ranohira, on the left just before a 'milestone' ('Tuléar 230km').

Another popular visit – perhaps too popular at times – is to the Fenêtre, a natural rock formation providing a window to the setting sun. The president commandeered this spot for the total eclipse in 2001; and a solitary cloud hid the sun… Walk behind the rocks for the proper Isalo feeling of space and tranquillity.

Permits and guides

For an excursion in the park you will need a permit (50,000Fmg) which must be purchased at the ANGAP office in Ranohira, next to Hotel Berny. You must take an accredited guide with you. Toussaint has been recommended as 'young, keen and knows a lot.' (R Bowkers). Charles has been similarly praised. Charges (standard for most parks) are posted on the wall of the office. In 2001 it was 125,000Fmg for a whole day's hiking, visiting both canyons and the Piscine Naturelle. Plus you should provide your guide with food. Schematic maps of the park are available from ANGAP.

Isalo Interpretation Centre

Well worth a visit to learn more about the people who live around the park, as well as the wildlife in the national park itself. Apparently, to reach manhood the Bara have not only to steal some cattle, but also to pass a test in epizooty, or the study of parasites and disease in zebu!

Hiking in the park

The two most popular hiking excursions are to the Piscine Naturelle, a natural swimming pool; and to the Canyon des Singes (sometimes more correctly called Canyon des Makis) and its neighbour, Canyon des Rats. With the help of a vehicle you can do the canyons and the Piscine in one day, but a circular tour lasting two or three days is more rewarding. Another canyon has been added: Namaza. Frances Kerridge warns: 'At one point it involves a choice of inching along a narrow ledge or swimming along a channel below and being hauled out at the other end.' But this is also one of its attractions: there are few other tourists. There is also an additional *piscine* – the Piscine Noire.

Budget travellers with only a day in hand should opt for the **Piscine Naturelle**. It is less distance to walk (6km/2hrs each way, if the shortest route is taken); and it provides the best viewpoints with a wonderfully cool swim at the end. But be warned – you won't be alone in such a perfect place. The walk there is pleasant and varied. 'First you have a fairly steep ascent and after about 10 to 20 minutes you get on to a rocky plateau with just a little bit of bushy vegetation left and right of the path between the rocks plus the odd tree. The rock formations have been given names by the guides: 'The Turtle', 'The African Woman', 'The Skull' and 'The Crocodile'. For some of it you need a lot of fantasy.

'After walking for about 20 minutes on this plateau, you arrive at a point where your guide will make you climb up a rock (very easy) and suddenly you overlook a valley that resembles Death Valley or Colorado. The valley is rocky and barren except for a line of green through its middle that indicates the flow of the stream. Take a few minutes break and enjoy!

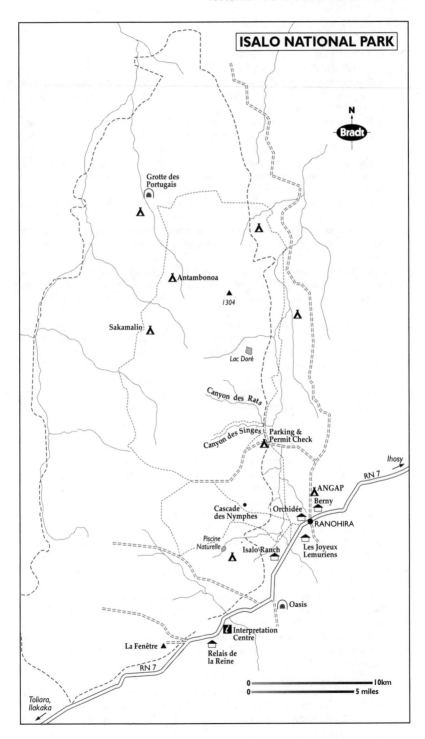

GEMSTONES

Tim Ireland

As a geologist and a gemologist I spent a good part of my trip explaining to other travellers how the gemstones occur, why they occur where they do, and what the significance of the local geology is. It seems appropriate to describe that here to future readers.

The crystalline rocks that comprise most of Madagascar are similar in age and type to those of southern India and Sri Lanka in which gemstones are also abundant. Broadly these are termed 'high grade metamorphic' rocks, alluding to the fact that they have been changed dramatically, through recrystallisation without complete melting, from some precursor rocktype. The current mineralogy and texture of the rocks indicates the conditions under which recrystallisation occurred; the entire region has been exhumed from an original depth of 10-30km, and cooled from an original temperature of around 700°C. This is not to say that the rocks were that distance below their present position, but rather that they were somewhere in the core of an ancient collisional mountain belt not unlike the Himalaya. Erosion has stripped material from those ancient mountains to expose their crystalline interiors, and at the same time the land has flexed upward in response. These processes have combined to leave rocks at the surface today that formed under the weight of tens of kilometres of other rock.

The younger flat-lying rocks of the west are made up largely of marine sediments that lap on to this crystalline core of Madagascar. Within the massive volume of rock, worn down over the millennia, gemstones formed only in comparatively minute units in which certain chemical and physical conditions prevailed for sufficient time. As erosion slowly dismantled the mountains, it first uncovered, and then destroyed the gem-bearing units of rock. As precious stones by their nature are dense and physically durable, they collected in major

'From here it's about 20 minutes or so to some rocks and suddenly you are a few metres above the pool. Getting down to the pool is like going through one of the glass houses in Kew Gardens, only you can walk between the plants and it's much bigger' (Volker Dornheim). 'It was really strange, trekking the whole day through dry grass and arid landscapes and then to find this small pool, surrounded by greenery, perfect in every way. It looked as though it was man-made for a shampoo advertisement or something!' (Claire Graham)

Those with a vehicle can drive along a track (with one ford) from Ranohira for 30 minutes to the base of the rocks where the hiking trail starts. From there it is about 90 minutes to the pool. The Relais de la Reine has vehicles for guests, and they can sometimes be hired in Ranohira.

If you are continuing on foot to the canyons, your guide will take you by way of the **Piscine Noire**. The *piscine* here is really a shower – water dribbles out of the high pool providing relief from the hot sun.

The **Canyon des Singes** and **Canyon des Rats** can also be reached directly from Ranohira, either on foot (9km/3hrs each way) or part of the way by car. In the dry season any vehicle can take you most of the way; in the rainy months you need a 4WD. The car park is about 30 minutes from the canyons.

Hikers make the trek direct from the Ranohira church, striding across a flat plain with the Canyons des Singes and des Rats tantalisingly in view the whole time. The hot sun should be taken very seriously: carry two litres of water (and river channel deposits adjacent to the weathering mountains while other components of the rock were more completely broken down. As finer, lighter particles, these were carried further by the rivers to be deposited further downstream or even reach the sea. There are few in-situ occurrences of the true precious stones (sapphire, ruby etc) in Madagascar, and the majority of mining involves searching for and chasing the old river channel deposits.

To retrieve the gemstones in Ilakaka, an exploratory shaft is sunk until the miners recognise a particular combination of rocktypes in the boulders of the gravel; certain rocks were being shed from the mountains and accumulated in the gravels contemporaneously with deposition of the gemstones. At this stage a few bags of gravel are washed and, if the results are good, a pit is sunk on the site down to the level of the rich gravel layer. The numbers quoted to me by one miner testify to astonishing richness of the good gravel at Ilakaka. Just half a dozen bags of gravel from an exploratory hole might yield 20 million francs worth of sapphires. The catch is that that payload layer is often around 15m deep, yet only 1m thick, and that demands a very large hole for a small yield. Curiously, the government has precluded the use of heavy machinery by Malagasy people, while outsiders are free to mine in whatever fashion they wish. So while small syndicates of Malagasy miners break their backs shifting dirt with shovels, Thai and Sri Lankan miners use earth-moving equipment to dig the efficient way. Money floods out of Madagascar by way of gemstones at a rate beyond anyone's wildest dreams – incalculable because of the shady nature of the industry. At the end of the day, a few thousand Malagasy are securely employed in Ilakaka for the duration of the rush (2 years, 10 years, 100 years?), while a small number of foreigners make enough to retire in style several times over. The smartest Malagasy I met at Ilakaka weren't digging stones…they were providing security to the foreign buyers with their suitcases of money and their pockets of jewels.

purifying tablets for the canyon water), wear a hat and apply liberal quantities of sunscreen. The contrast between the space and yellowness of the plain and the ferny green of the canyon makes the effort well worthwhile; though when we arrived, sweat-soaked, at the first pool we were taken aback to find an elderly couple and their grandchild sitting in deckchairs at the water's edge. That was when I learned about vehicle access. Although a 4WD is recommended, a saloon car can manage the trip in about an hour – an impressive drive through rolling grass steppe. Around the entrance of the Canyon des Singes is a forest where ring-tailed lemurs may be seen, especially in the mornings. You can get very close to the animals, so this is an excellent photo opportunity.

The walk up the canyon is highly recommended. A path goes over rocks and along the edge of the tumbling river; and there are pools into which you can fling yourself at intervals, and, at the top, a small waterfall under which to have a shower. The sheer rocks hung with luxuriant ferns broaden out to provide views of the bare mountain behind, and trees and palms provide shade for a picnic.

The Canyon des Rats is very green with lots of vegetation, but no lemurs. At the canyon entrance you can see Bara tombs in the rock face. With each reburial after the traditional washing of the bones, the deceased are buried higher up in the rock wall.

For the real Isalo experience you should trek for a few days. The combined Piscine/Canyon des Singes circuit is the most popular and usually done in three days. The first day to the campsite at the swimming pool is only two or three hours, then five or six rugged hours the next day to the canyon. It is then a three-hour walk back to Ranohira.

The less visited parts of the park are even more rewarding. Bishop Brock took a five-day hike: 'The forest of Sakamolia... is one of the most beautiful places I have ever camped in, perhaps not in absolute beauty but in contrasts. In the middle of the dry, grassy plain, surrounded on two sides by massive rock walls, a small crystal-clear river runs over a clean, sandy bottom supporting a 20-metre-wide luxuriant green-belt. Paradise!'

Ilakaka

This new settlement has sprung up as a centre of the sapphire trade and is worth a visit: 'The atmosphere is incredible. Like an American gold rush town! The activity was frenetic, with people carrying heavy bags of sediment to the river for panning, men trying to sell us bits of quartz etc, women washing their clothes, mini fast-food stalls, amazing hardware stands, and lots of police/military with guns' (J & V Middleton). Tim Ireland writes: 'Ilakaka is a vibrant town which is becoming an indelible part of the Malagasy psyche... If you don't know about gemstones don't spend any serious money. All the quality sapphires and rubies are bought by dealers and nothing of quality will be offered to you. In general Malagasy faceting (stone polishing) is poor and if you insist on buying stones buy uncut ones. Ask to be shown a lapidary workshop (*maison d'un lapidaire*) where you can see the process and the atmosphere for making a purchase will be more relaxed.'

CONTINUING SOUTH

The drive from Isalo to Toliara (244km) takes a minimum of four hours. After you pass the landscape scars and shanty town of the sapphire mine, the rugged mountains give way to grasslands, and following the rains there are many flowers – the large white *Crinum firmifolium* and the Madagascar periwinkle – but in the dry season it's quite monotonous. It is the people aspect that makes this final stretch so rewarding. First there are some charming villages – Bara, Mahafaly and Antandroy – and, once you pass Sakaraha, there are some wonderful tombs with *aloalo* near the road. As you get closer to Toliara you'll see your first baobabs and pass through a cotton-growing region. Look out for the enormous nests of hammerkop birds in roadside trees.

Twenty-five kilometres northeast of Sakaraha is **Zombitse and Vohibasia National Park** which is popular with birders. See *Excursions*, page 225. About half an hour beyond **Sakaraha** (Hotel Eden – basic) you will pass the first Mahafaly tombs on your right. There are groups of tombs all the way into Toliara, and they merit several stops (the group nearest Toliara are described under *Excursions*).

About two hours beyond Sakaraha is the small village of **Andranovory** which has a colourful Sunday market. Another hour and Toliara's table mountain, La Table, comes into view on the right; half an hour later you pass the airport and head for the town.

TOLIARA (TULEAR)

The pronunciation of the French, Tuléar, and the Malagasy names is the same: 'Toolee-ar'. Toliara's history is centred on St Augustine's Bay, described at the beginning of this chapter, although the name of the town is thought to derive from an encounter with one of those early sailors who asked a local inhabitant where he might moor his boat. The Malagasy replied: *Toly eroa*, 'Mooring down there'. The town itself is relatively modern – 1895 – and was designed by an uninspired French

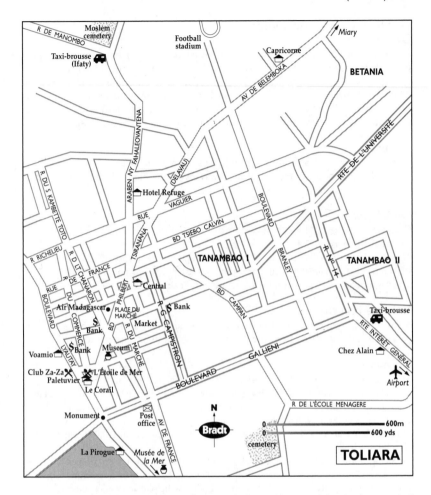

architect. His tree planting was more successfully aesthetic, and the shady tamarind trees, *kily*, give welcome respite from the blazing sun.

There are three good reasons to visit Toliara: the rich marine life with excellent snorkelling and diving, the Mahafaly and Masikoro tombs and a museum which puts it all in context, and the remarkable spiny bush in places north and south of the town (although this is being destroyed at an alarming rate).

The beaches north and south of the town have fine white sand, and this whole area is opening up to tourism (fortunately the poor or non-existent roads are an effective deterrent to overdevelopment). Beyond the sandy beaches is an extensive coral reef but this is too far from shore to swim out to – a *pirogue* (for hire at the beach hotels) is necessary. Toliara itself, regrettably, has no beach, just mangroves and mud flats.

Telephone code The area code for Toliara is 94.

Warning In the cool season (May to October) the nights in Toliara are very cold. The cheaper hotels rarely supply enough blankets. And in the hot season (November to April) everything closes for siesta between 13.00 and 15.00.

Getting there and away
By road
Route Nationale 7 (RN7) is now a well-used road served by a variety of quite comfortable vehicles. There are two special tourist buses. One, operated by Mad Voyages (tel: 94 42 729), leaves Tana on Tuesdays, returning from Toliara on Thursdays at 07.00. The other is the Jumbobus, operated by Montana Voyage in Tana (tel: 22 25 861). The bus leaves Muraille de Chine (near the station) every Tuesday at 07.30 and makes several stops so you don't have to go all the way to Toliara.

By air
There are daily flights from Tana and Taolagnaro, but in the high season these tend to be fully booked. However, it's always worth going to the airport whatever they say in the office.

Vehicle hire
Car hire
Joshua Calixte Tel: 427 47.
New Horizon Bd Gallieni, about 200m east of the post office; tel/fax: 427 73. Recommended. Italian owner Guiseppe (Jimmy) Castelluccio rents out reliable 4WD vehicles for about ∈ 85 per day, plus ∈ 3 per day for the driver.

Where to stay
Most visitors spending any time in the Toliara area stay at the beach resorts (see pages 226–30) but there are some good-value hotels in or near the town.

Category A
Motel Le Capricorne BP 158; tel: 414 91/431 12/426 20; fax: 413 20. 10 rooms. 230,000Fmg (with fan) to 260,000Fmg (air-conditioned), including breakfast. About 2km from the town centre on RN7. Considered the best of the Toliara hotels. It has a lovely garden and is well run with a good restaurant.
Hotel Paletuvier A good hotel opposite L'Etoile de Mer restaurant. 120,000Fmg double, 150,000Fmg triple.
Le Sax'aphone Villa Soarimanga, Besakoa, (BP 591 Toliara); tel: 440 88. 4 3-person bungalows, 135,000Fmg; 4 rooms, 65,000–150,000Fmg. Described as 'a charming guesthouse run by Alain and Michèle who are both very helpful and can organise excursions. There is a very nice atmosphere, the food is excellent and the manager plays the piano in the evenings. They have this ability to make people feel at home.' (Nivo Ravelojaona) North of Toliara (Besakoa), on the road to Ifaty.

Category B
Chez Alain BP 89; tel: 415 27; fax: 423 79; email: chez.alain@simicro.mg. From 60,000Fmg (double room with shared toilet) to 350,000Fmg (suite). One of the most popular *vazaha* hotels (bungalows) in Madagascar. Well run, friendly, good food. Mountain bikes available for hire. The diving centre L'Ancre Bleue is based here.
Chez Soi BP 545; tel/fax: 411 82. A nice Belgian-owned hotel near Chez Alain. Large, quiet rooms with en-suite facilities. About 55,000–70,000Fmg. Restaurant.
Le Refuge A very pleasant, medium-priced hotel near the centre of town. Good food.
Saphir Hotel Tel: 436 79. A centrally located hotel with air-conditioned rooms and hot water.

Category C
Hotel Central Bang in the centre of town, so convenient for the market and museum. Hot water and en-suite WC for 75,000Fmg, or shared facilities for 35,000Fmg. Recommended.

Le Pousse-Pousse Rue de l'Eglise; tel: 438 75. 60,000Fmg. Two minutes from the market square, this is a new, friendly, French-owned hotel. Rooms are very clean, with a shower and sink. 'The only disadvantage is the tin roof. There's a central courtyard, a good bar and the best peppered zebu steak with chips in all of Madagascar.' (D Simon)

Le Corail Bungalows near the restaurant L'Etoile de Mer. Clean, with en-suite shower and sink, for about 45,000Fmg. Only one shared toilet, and very hot during the day (or cold at night, depending on the season) because of the tin roofs. 'A funky, friendly place, very Malagasy, with a lovely terrace restaurant from which to have a beer and watch the sunset.' (S Giarratana)

La Pirogue Tel: 415 37. 57,000Fmg double with fan; 75,000Fmg double with en-suite bathroom and hot water. Clean, but can be noisy.

L'Hotel Analamanga Tel/fax: 415 47. Double room 50,500Fmg, bungalow 45,000Fmg. Located on the outskirts of Toliara as you arrive on RN7. Some rooms plus five neat, small bungalows on stilts; clean communal bathrooms. Nice quiet setting out of town, cool under trees, but within easy walking distance of town.

Where to eat
L'Etoile de Mer Tel: 428 07. This unpretentious restaurant located in a wooden building on the seafront, between the Plazza Hotel and the Voamio, has maintained its high standards since I first visited Toliara in 1982, and deserves its success. It specialises in seafood.

Club Za Za Serves particularly good fish.

Corail Excellent pizza and other dishes, and a pleasant bar.

Internet Café Rue du Commerce.

Good places for snacks are the three rival Salons de Thé, situated in a row next to each other, opposite the Hotel Central. They are **Le Gourmet**, **Glace d'As** (popularly known as 'frozen arse') and **Le Maharaja**.

Nightlife
'The Za Za Club has a following across the world. You have not been to Tuléar unless you have been to Za Za!' So wrote a reader a decade ago, and the Za Za still has many fans plus a few doubters: '*What* a disappointment! Full of old *vazaha* men buying cokes for their beautiful, scantily-dressed Malagasy "girl friends". And the music was poor' (F Kerridge). The Za-Za has a dress code (!): no flip-flops.

Watersports
Diving and snorkelling
For many people the main reason to visit Toliara is for the coral reefs. The WWF recognises the importance of these in developing ecotourism in the area and a conservation programme is under way, centred at the University of Toliara. The goal of the project is 'to ensure that the coral reefs and coastal zone are effectively conserved through the establishment of a multiple-use marine park and sustainable economic development'. Certainly there is potential for marine ecotourism, although dead or dying coral is disturbingly evident on the reefs. See boxes on pages 234 and 248 for information on marine conservation in the south. The following is a summary of diving centres in the Toliara region.

Deep Sea Club BP 158, Toliara; tel: 426 20.
Bamboo Club BP 47, Toliara; tel: 427 17.
Club Nautique (Dunes Hotel); tel: 339 00.

Club Nautique (Lakana Vezo Hotel); tel: 426 20.
Gipsy Club (Hotel Nautilus); tel: 418 74; email: nautilus@simicro.mg.
L'Ancre Bleue (Hotel Chez Alain); tel: 415 27; email: chez.alain@simicro.mg.
Alizee Dive In Hotel Safari Vezo, Anakao.

Sailing
Location Catamaran (tel: 433 17) organise catamaran trips to the Barren Islands, Belo Sur Mer, Andavadoka, Ifaty, Anakao and Itampolo.

Surfing
Toliara, Anakao and Itampolo are all places served by the surfing project set up by Yves Jousseaume in Taolagnaro. See page 245.

Medical clinic
The Clinique Saint-Luc (tel: 421 76) is run by Dr Noel Rakotomavo who speaks excellent English. The profits from his paying beds go towards providing free treatment for the poor.

Sightseeing and excursions
In town
Toliara has more 'official' sightseeing than most Malagasy towns. Some places are worth the trip, others are not. In town the most interesting place to visit is the small **museum** on Bd Philbert Tsiranana, run by the University of Toliara. The entry fee is 25,000Fmg. There are some remarkable exhibits, including a Mikea mask (genuine masks are rare in Madagascar) with real human teeth. These are well-displayed and labelled in Malagasy and French, and include some Sakalava erotic tomb sculptures. Marine enthusiasts should visit the **Musée de la Mer**, also run by the university, on Route de la Porte (tel: 41 612). The main attraction here is a coelacanth – the only one now on view in Madagascar. The **market** is lively and interesting. This is one of the best places in all of Madagascar for *lambas*. You can also find the mohair rugs that are made in Ampanihy, a terrific selection of herbal remedies (*fanafody*), and a wide range of fruit.

Tombs
The most spectacular tombs within easy reach of the town are those of the Masikoro, a sub-division of the Sakalava. This small tribe is probably of African origin, and there is speculation that the name comes from *mashokora* which, in parts of Tanzania, means scrub forest. There are also Mahafaly and Bara tombs in the area.

The tombs are off RN7 a little over an hour from Toliara, and are clearly visible on the right. There are several large, rectangular tombs, flamboyantly painted with scenes from the distinguished military life of the deceased, with a few mermaids and Rambos thrown in for good measure. These are known as the **Tombs of Andranovory**.

Another tomb, on the outskirts of town beyond the university, is **King Baba's Tomb**. This is set in a grove of Didierea trees and is interesting more for the somewhat bizarre funerary objects (an urn and a huge, cracked bell) displayed there and its spiritual significance to the local people (you may only approach barefoot) than for any aesthetic value. This King Baba, who seems to have died about 100 years ago, was presumably a descendant of one of the Masikoro kings of Baba mentioned in British naval accounts of the 18th century. These kings used to trade with English ships calling at St Augustine's Bay and gave their family and courtiers English names such as the Prince of Wales and the Duke of Cumberland. On the way to King Baba's Tomb you may visit a little fenced-off park of banyan trees, all descending from one 'parent'. This is known as 'the sacred grove' and in theory would be a place for peaceful contemplation, but the hordes of tourist-aware children are a deterrent.

Day excursions from Toliara
Tour operators
Most excursions can be made by taxi but for something more ambitious where a guide is advisable the following tour operators are recommended.

Madagascar Airtours Office in the grounds of the Plazza Hotel.
Air Fort Services BP 1029; tel/fax: 426 84.
Hotel Capricorne Many excellent tours are run by this hotel.

Arboretum d'Antsokay
This botanical garden of rare southwestern flora makes an excellent day trip from Toliara. It costs 25,000Fmg for a day visit with the option of a delicious lunch. Simple accommodation may be available here.

The turn-off to the hotel/arboretum is on the right, just north of the track to La Mangrove hotel and St Augustine on RN7. It is clearly signposted. The Swiss-born botanist and founder, Hermann Pétignat, sadly died in 2000, but his influences lives on. A trained guide takes you on a two-hour tour of the 'improved' area (7ha) of the 50ha arboretum. Here you will see the rare plants nurtured by the late M Pétignat, including 100 species of euphorbia and 60 species of kalenchoe. You will also see an abundance of birds and reptiles: 'We followed a running coua about for 15 minutes while it noshed on locusts, and saw a button quail nest on one of the flowerbeds. And we watched a large snake catch a frog.' (Derek Schuurman)

Try to arrive as early as possible in the morning to miss the heat of the day. Or, if still available, stay overnight in one of the basic bungalows.

Zombitse and Vohibasia National Park
This pocket of forest (21,500ha) straddling RN7 some 25km northeast of Sakaraha is of major importance to birdwatchers. The forests are an important example of a boundary zone between the western and southern domains of vegetation and so have a high level of biodiversity. Zombitse offers the chance to glimpse one of Madagascar's rarest endemics, Appert's greenbul, which is confined to this forest. Many other species may be seen. There are no official paths, only zebu trails, and tree felling in this vulnerable area is sadly evident. Nevertheless, a visit here is most rewarding. We were there at the worst possible time of day, noon, yet the forest was alive with birds and had we had more time I am sure we would have seen many species. This is also a wonderful place for invertebrates, particularly butterflies.

It takes two to three hours to reach Zombitse from Toliara, so serious birdwatchers should leave as early as possible in the morning. The WWF administration office is by the Zombitse forest on the left hand side of the road (travelling towards Sakaraha) at about the 18km roadmark. It is unsignposted, so unless you are with an official guide you may not find it! Best to buy a permit in Tana.

Adventure tours
Trajectoire BP 283, Toliara 601; tel/fax: 433 00; email: trajectoire@simicro.mg. Run by Bernard Forgeau, who owns a secluded hotel in Madiorano (see page 228). He runs small

group adventure tours throughout remote areas of the southwest, including the Makay massif by motorbike and the descent of the Mangoky River by canoe.

BEACH RESORTS NORTH OF TOLIARA

Ifaty has long been established as Toliara's main beach resort, but hotels are now being built on beach areas further north.

Ifaty

Ifaty offers sand, sea and snorkelling, and has several sets of beach bungalows. The village lies only 27km north of Toliara, but the road is terrible (though very scenic) so it can take as much as three hours by taxi-brousse. The normal price (2001) is 10,000Fmg but *vazaha* may be charged up to 25,000Fmg.

The bad state of this road – and others in the southwest – is the consequence of deforestation. With all the trees gone, there is nothing to hold the sandy topsoil, and no repair is going to last more than a few months. The poor road suits the hotel owners quite well; they can (and do) charge what they want for transfers from Toliara. 80,000Fmg each way is average.

You should also know that cellular phones often don't work in Ifaty; hotel radios are the only means of contacting the outside world. There are no money-changing facilities in Ifaty.

When selecting a hotel bear in mind that only those in the north of Ifaty, and in Mangily, have sandy beaches.

Birding

Ifaty is a popular place for birdwatchers, having a fast-dwindling area of spiny forest where some of the southern endemics can be seen. The best guides are undoubtedly Madindraka and his son Mosa who have, to the relief of birding groups, returned to Ifaty after an unsuccessful venture into sapphire mining. Hotels know where to find them, or provide someone who knows the way.

Keen birders should come here soon while there is still some forest left. Lyn Mair, who leads birding groups, reports: 'It is *so* distressing to see and hear how the spiny forest is being cut down day by day. There were chopped down trees and evidence of charcoal-making everywhere. While we were watching the glorious long-tailed ground-roller all we could hear was the hollow ringing of busy woodcutters' axes.'

Where to stay/eat
Category A
Hotel Paradisier BP 490; tel: 429 12; email: paradisier@paradisier.com. The most expensive hotel in Ifaty, with a luxury suite costing 505,000Fmg, but worth the price. 'Staff friendly and obliging, bungalows very comfy with huge mozzie net and coil provided. Veranda with cooling sea breezes. Food good, too.'
Nautilus Cellphone: 03207 41874; email: nautilus@simicro.mg. 15 bungalows near Lakana Vezo. Double 148,000Fmg per person; single 295,000Fmg. Up-market new hotel on a nice beach. Excellent restaurant, especially for seafood. The Gipsy Club diving centre is located here.
Hotel Lakana Vezo c/o Capricorne, Ifaty, BP 158; tel: 462 20. One of the best hotels in Ifaty; one hour's walk south of the Dunes hotel. 10 bungalows; €53 double; rooms €60. The Club Nautique is probably the best in Ifaty, run very professionally by Denis and Natalie Guillamot. A wide variety of activities are available, though snorkelling and scuba-diving are favourites. The hotel also offers powerboat excursions to Nosy Ve and Anakao.
Hotel de la Saline BP 456; tel: 417 03; fax: 413 84. 10 two-person bungalows, 5 with air-conditioning (300,000Fmg). Facing the salt pans, rather than the beach, this French-

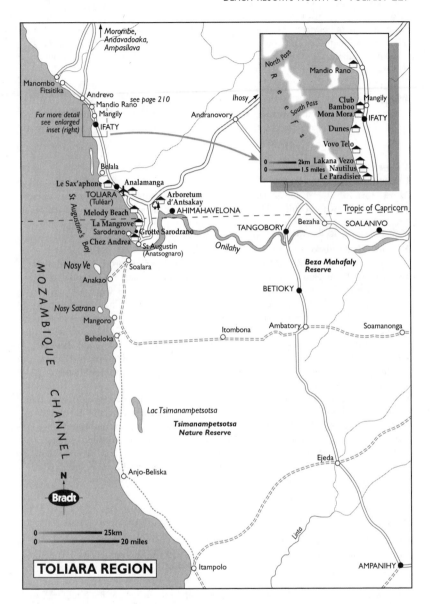

TOLIARA REGION

managed hotel has a particularly good dining room, with terrific views over the lagoon and superb food. 'The *poisson au sauce vanille* was the best I've ever eaten' (Judith de Witt). But the décor isn't to everyone's taste: 'It's from a different planet – the modern bungalows look like flying saucers, the beds are futon on a concrete base, and the rooms are high, white and sterile. Built to attract Westerners.' (V Dornheim)

Category B
Dunes Hotel BP 285; tel: 428 85. In the southern part of Ifaty (rocky beach), this is a set of concrete bungalows with two adjoining bedrooms: 62 rooms in all. Some of the

bungalows are in poor conditions but others have been renovated and offer better value. The Club Nautique des Dunes is located here: snorkelling 66,000Fmg, whale-watching 90,000Fmg. About 150,000Fmg per bungalow; breakfast 18,000Fmg. Transport from Toliara arranged.

Mangily

Recommended as being cheaper and more friendly than Ifaty, this small village just to its north is easily reached by taxi-brousse from Toliara or you can walk up from Ifaty.

Where to stay/eat
Category B

Mora Mora BP 282; tel: 434 32; fax: 437 38. The longest-established of this region's beach resorts. French-owned, comfortable, friendly, with a large choice of activities. Bungalows at 130,000Fmg (half board). Free transport from outside the internet/video store in Toliara (but 50,000Fmg per person to return).

Hotel/Club Bamboo BP 47; tel/fax: 427 17; cellphone: 00873 761 294 355. Five minutes' walk north of Mora Mora, so convenient for the spiny forest. 150,000Fmg for a twin-bedded bungalow – good value, but rather hot in summer. There's a diving club (but more geared to snorkelling) – 40,000Fmg for snorkelling trips. For bookings enquire at the Bamboo shop opposite the Hotel Central in town. Their transfers cost 75,000Fmg (from the airport). There are varying levels of enthusiasm from readers for the meals and service but Volker Dornheim loved it: 'Very nice, simple bungalows with toilets and showers, three bordering the beach. A little army of employees makes sure the place is clean and tidy. Small swimming pool. Very good food, especially the fish. We thought the setting was much better than the other places and the bamboo huts blend in to the environment.'

Hotel Vovo Telo Tel: 439 69. A newish set of 12 bungalows between Mora Mora and the Dunes Hotel which is receiving rave reviews from independent travellers (it does not take groups). 'We thought this place had the best food in Ifaty – great steaks and wonderful pizzas' (FK). 'A super little establishment; it's about time Ifaty had something like this' (JM). 'Much better than our hotel (Dunes) restaurant and one night had live music and dancing.' (CG) 'Wide choice of food, good atmosphere. Heaving with customers so come early if you haven't booked a table.' (VD)

Category C

Note: I haven't received recent information on these places, so no prices.

Chez Deka Good, basic and right on the beach.

Chez Thomas 'Another cheap, basic, friendly place. Relaxed atmosphere, there is nothing Thomas and family would not do to make you feel welcome; tasty food (caters for vegetarians). Very basic facilities, exposed washing/toilet area, pigs wandering around, but perfectly comfortable. Most taxi-brousse drivers will drop you right at the gate if you ask.' (Anna Dudziec)

Madiorano

Jim Bond recommends **Chez Bernard** at this village 35km north of Toliara. 'Ideal for the discerning independent traveller – no tour groups. Five peaceful, comfortable bungalows for about 130,000Fmg (full board) near a quiet stretch of beach. Not far to walk to PK32 (the road). Excellent food, huge portions. Rustic douche facilities. Bernard Forgeau is a very pleasant and interesting Breton bush-hand and explorer.' He can be contacted through Trajectoire (see page 225) in Toliara.

Above Market day in the village of Sendrisoa near Andringitra (NG)

Left Malagasy child, Antananarivo (HB)

Below Villagers travelling by river canoe to market at Marovoay (CP)

Above Local bands play at weddings, bone-turning ceremonies (*famadihana*) and other festive occasions (HB)

Above right Detail of *The Tomb of Ranonda*, an Antanosy commemorative carving near Taolagnaro (photographed in the 1980s) (HB)

Below Famadihana. The bones of the ancestors are wrapped in a fresh burial shroud (HB)

CONTINUING NORTH TO MOROMBE AND MORONDAVA

See page 393 for information on getting to Morombe. If you want to continue to Morondava, there is a choice of sea (by *pirogue*, risky) or road. A vehicle known as the 'Bon Bon Caramel' used to leave Toliara at 06.00 on Thursdays, spending the night at Manja (good food and bungalows) and arriving in Morondava Friday evening. I have no recent information on whether it is still running, however.

An easier overland option is to take the transport offered by Lakana Vezo to service their new bungalow complex in Morombe. More information – on the bungalows as well as the transport – from the Lakana Vezo in Ifaty.

As a much simpler alternative to travelling overland there are flights between Toliara and Morondava via Morombe.

BEACH RESORTS SOUTH OF TOLIARA

New beach hotels are opening up in the very attractive region south of Toliara, but they still cannot compete with Ifaty for comfort.

St Augustine's Bay (Baie St Augustin)

St Augustine is full of natural wonders and history. This was the site of an ill-fated British colony, abandoned in 1646, and later frequented by pirates. St Augustine's Bay was mentioned by Daniel Defoe in *The King of Pirates*.

The natural wonders include dramatic sand dunes, a cave swimming pool, bottle trees, and some good birding.

The hotels in the region will arrange transfers from Toliara, but there is a regular taxi-brousse to Sarodrano, costing about 7,500Fmg. A private taxi will charge around 200,000Fmg (negotiable).

Grotte Sarodrano and Sarodrano village

Don't miss this lovely swimming hole. Under a rocky overhang is a deep pool of clear blue water. Swimmers will find the top layer of water warm is only mildly salty, while the cooler lower layer is saline. Fresh water flows from the mountain into the pool, on top of the warmer, heavier layer of salt water from the sea. In the area of the pool are some surealistic bottle trees or moringas. You may find yourself paying a local 5,000Fmg to go to the pool.

Grotte Sarodrano is a 4km walk south from La Mangrove hotel (along an easy road). Kids with *pirogues* hang around there to take you back for about 30,000Fmg. Well worth it!

Another 4km south is the village of Sarodrano which is located on the tip of a peninsula. In the area there are some impressive sand-dunes and spectacular cliffs (but the beach is dirty). For naturalists a track leads up through spiny forest where you can find wild ring-tailed lemurs and southern endemic birds. John and Valerie Middleton write: 'There are several narrow, but good walks in the hills between La Mangrove and St Augustine's Bay, all botanically and ornithologically rich, with superb views. These walks can be continued along the equally spectacular rocky peninsula at the point where the river merges.'

Volker Dornheim checked out the Grotte des Lemurien which is accessed via an unsignposted trail off the road leading to La Mangrove from Toliara. 'We took up position near the cave entrance and waited. As the sun went down we heard a little rustling and a few moments later we saw them: on top of the crater-like cave entrance a group of ring-tailed lemurs. One of them climbed down to an overhanging rock in the cave wall which seemed to be his favourite spot as he stayed there for as long as we were there. Unfortunately we only had about 15-20 minutes before we had to leave as it was approaching nightfall.' This place is difficult to find without a guide.

Where to stay

Hotel Melody Beach Tel: 445 38; fax: 418 70; email: mouktar@dts.mg; web: www.ifrance.com/melody-beach. 15 bungalows from 50,000–295,000Fmg (depending on size and quality). This is an excellent hotel serving delicious food (breakfast 25,000Fmg; dinner 50,000Fmg). Overlooking a sandy beach with good swimming, it is just 5km from the main road so is more easily accessible by public transport than St Augustine's Bay itself or Anakao. The Indian co-owner runs a shop in the market called Remi and may be able to provide transport, but it is easy enough to walk in providing you have good footwear for the rough, rocky road.

La Mangrove 8km from RN7 (the turn-off is signposted). A French-run hotel under the same ownership as Chez Alain. Ten bungalows for 80,000–100,000Fmg, depending on whether they have en-suite WC or shared. Good meals at 45,000Fmg. There's no beach, but a rocky access to the sea for swimming. This is a diving centre, and boat excursions to Nosy Ve and Anakao can be arranged. Free transfers from Chez Alain in town. If you want to hike it, avoid the heat of the day and keep to the road; the whole area is laced with confusing tracks.

Chez Andrea An Italian-owned hotel near Sarodrano. Thoughtfully designed, very friendly, excellent food and service. Book through Boogie Pilgrim in Tana.

ANAKAO AND REGION

Anakao is a pretty little Vezo fishing village, with colourful boats drawn up on to the sands. It is the centre for some excellent diving or snorkelling, and trips to the small islands of Nosy Ve and Nosy Satrana. Sadly, tourism here has created child beggars who pursue their goals with single-mindedness. It is an example of the harm that tourists can inadvertently cause by giving out sweets or other small gifts to an impoverished community (see page 142). Ben Tapley, who spent some time in the village as part of a marine research group, reported that their work was hampered by villagers' expectations: 'Tourists giving out presents made our work with the villagers in Anakao very difficult, as they would not allow us to examine their catch without first giving them a gift. Please refrain from giving out presents indiscriminately. If you want to make a difference give a donation of money or medicine to the medical centre situated behind the village.' There is also a new women's project (see box in page 232) where you can help the villagers in a far more constructive way by buying their handicrafts.

Anakao is accessible from Toliara via a 50km dirt road, or by boat. Most tourists go by sea, either with Safari Vezo (see below) or another motorised boat. Attractive though a *pirogue* trip may seem when you bargain with the fishermen, bear in mind that there is almost always a very strong head wind. The 'three-hour trip' can take up to nine hours. Even motorised *pirogues* are unreliable, breaking down with regularity.

Where to stay/eat

Safari Vezo BP 427, Toliara 601; tel: 413 81 or 426 20. An unpretentious set of beach bungalows. Swiss-run. Bungalows are €29 double; breakfast €4.5. Good restaurant. The Club Nautique is Anakao's diving centre. Boat transfers from Toliara cost €26 per person.

Chez Clovis Small bungalows, more economically priced than Safari Vezo. Simple food eaten round a communal dining table.

Chez Emile Two bungalows, but no toilet (ie: use the bushes). But it is a friendly, lively place with a cheerful bar popular with the locals. Emile and his wife have a little shop which sells snacks and a limited selection of postcards.

Chez Monica These bungalows are further up the beach so give some respite from begging children. Very good buffet lunch for 40,000Fmg.

A new Italian restaurant and bungalows is being built in the next bay south of Anakao. This may well be open by the time you read this.

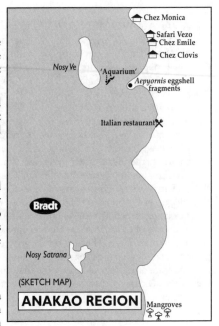

Excursions
In addition to trips to Nosy Ve and Nosy Satrana there are other worthwhile excursions and places to explore on your own. All the hotels listed above run excursions to the main places of interest.

The 'Aquarium'
Ben Tapley reports that this is an area of protected shallow reef, with abundant fish species including an inquisitive grouper known as George. Great for snorkelling.

Diving
'Spectacular diving, with many surgeon, angel, butterfly fish, groupers and rays. You will also find enormous rock lobsters. The coral is fantastic. Shark sightings are not common here. The reef is huge and much of it is still unstudied and has not been dived. The best time for diving is during the dry season when the water is clear of river sediment' (BT). Most hotels will organise diving trips for about 250,000Fmg per person.

Tombs, wildlife and aepyornis eggshells
Take the track behind the village heading south. On the outskirts of Anakao you will find some interesting tombs, and will then come to a small peninsula jutting into the sea. This is littered with fragments of eggshell from the long-extinct *aepyornis*. Please keep your collecting instincts under control so that others can enjoy this extraordinary glimpse of the past.

Once you are well clear of population areas you should start to see wildlife. Ring-tailed lemurs are occasionally seen, and tortoises are quite common along with other reptiles such as chameleons, day geckos, and other lizards. There are some wonderful didierea trees here. Wildlife is much more visible in the wet season.

Three bays south of Anakao is a large area of mangroves with accompanying wildlife. Ben Tapley reports: 'This area is very interesting and when the tide is out it is fascinating to snorkel down the tannin-stained channels. It is probably too far and hot to walk here, but a boat trip could be organised through one of the hotels. It is a good spot for birds: Madagascar plovers, flamingos, hoopoes, bee eaters and vasa parrots.'

ANAKAO WOMEN AND SUSTAINABLE DEVELOPMENT

A new women's organisation has been formed in Anakao to improve the quality of life. The environment (and tourism) will also be a beneficiary if the group achieves its aims. L'Association Feminine d'Anakao and the Coastal Communities Foundation (CCF) have joined together to assess the needs of the village. A sewing and embroidery project has created an alternative source of income for village women, and helped take pressure off the octopus fishery (their primary means of generating income). At the time of writing, 32 women are participating in Projet SoaVezo. One of their tasks has been to help build six toilets in the village, as an alternative to using the beach, and have led Anakao and Madagascar in its first participation in International Coastal Clean-up Day.

The women congregate at the Centre Sociale, located behind the village, each morning and afternoon to use the four manual sewing machines to produce shirts embroidered with marine species. Visitors are encouraged to visit the centre and speak with the women and learn more about their lives. These women are responsible for taking care of the children, cooking, cleaning, selling the fish that their husbands catch, and generate all additional income needed to care for their families.

By purchasing their work you can make a positive contribution to the village.

Nosy Ve and Nosy Satrana

Nosy Ve (the name means 'Is there an island?'!) lies 3km west of Anakao, and is a sacred site for the Vezo people who annually sacrifice zebu at its northern point. It has a long history of European domination: the first landing was by a Dutchman in 1595, and Nosy Ve was officially taken over by the French in 1888 before their conquest of the mainland although it is hard to see why: it is a flat, scrub-covered little island.

What makes Nosy Ve special to modern-day invaders is the excellent snorkelling on its fringing reefs and the breeding colony of red-tailed tropic-birds which are gradually increasing in number. During the first few months of the year you will see them at their nest sites under bushes at the southern tip of the island, as well as flying overhead: a thrilling sight.

Camping is no longer allowed on the island, and visits are dependent for their success on wind and tide (strong wind makes snorkelling difficult). With no natural shade on the island, make sure your boatman erects a sail on the beach to provide respite from the burning sun. And at low tide be prepared to push the boat through the shallow water!

If you are not a snorkeller there is endless pleasure to be had searching for shells and poking around in rock pools on the exposed part of the reef. Take care – a member of our party found a poisonous stone fish.

The island is illegally exploited (see box on page 234–5) by the local Vezo people but they do not harm the tropic-birds, the result of a *fady* originating in a great fire which destroyed much of the island's vegetation – except for the tropic-bird colony and the ancestors' tombs. Another (fortunate) *fady* is against defaecating on the beach. A boy angered an ancestor and went missing for doing just that. Tourists should also respect the ancestors and keep away from the tombs.

Nearby Nosy Satrana offers equally good snorkelling but no tropic-birds.

A day's excursion to Nosy Ve, with snorkelling equipment provided, will cost around 150,000Fmg.

Lake Tsimanampetsotsa

This large, shallow soda lake, about 40km south of Anakao, is a haven for waterfowl, notably flamingos, and other rare endemic birds. It is a Strict Nature Reserve and as such is not normally accessible to tourists (although some tour operators include it in their itineraries).

FURTHER SOUTH

The two isolated resorts of Beheloka and Itampolo are normally accessed from RN10, the (poor) road that links Toliara with Taolagnaro (Fort Dauphin) although a barely motorable, sandy road does run down the coast from Anakao (140km). Beaches in this area are littered with fragments of *aepyornis* eggshell.

Beheloka

Thirty kilometres down the coast from Anakao, this village is developing into a low-key resort. A palm-thatched hotel, **Relaise la Canne à Sucre**, has been built by the owner of Chez Alain. Four rooms for about 80,000Fmg. Book through Chez Alain in Toliara (tel: 415 27).

Itampolo

This small town, about 150km south of Toliara, is said by some to have the most beautiful beach in Madagascar with pinkish-coloured sand. It also has the best surfing (see page 245 on how to enjoy surfing while helping Malagasy youngsters to learn the sport). The hotel here, also a Chez Alain establishment, is called **Sud Sud**.

BEZA MAHAFALY SPECIAL RESERVE

This reserve is the model for the WWF's integrated conservation and development efforts. It was established at the request of local people who volunteered to give up using part of the forest. In return they have been helped with a variety of social and agricultural projects; for example by the provision of a school and the building of irrigation channels.

The government has designated the reserve as its number one priority from ten sites in the Environmental Action Plan. Agroforestry is being developed under the guidance of Tana's School of Agronomy and the Direction des Eaux et Forêts, and many research projects take place there. The goal has always been to integrate conservation and rural development projects around the reserve, and to support the sustainable use of natural resources.

The reserve protects two distinct types of forest: spiny forest and gallery (riverine) forest. In this it mirrors Berenty, but there the comparison ends. Tourism is not discouraged, but at present the Malagasy locals and researchers come first. This is an enormously rewarding place for the serious naturalist, however. In addition to lemurs, the forest has four species of tenrec including the rare large-eared one, *Echinops telfairi*, three species of carnivores including the fosa, and lots of reptiles. About 90 species of birds have been recorded.

Practical information

Beza Mahafaly is 35km north of Betioky along a very rough road. To get there you need a 4WD vehicle, a zebu cart, a bicycle or a strong pair of legs.

Like other protected areas in Madagascar, permits can be obtained at the site or in Tana through ANGAP. Since the reserve is a research centre, permission to visit should be requested through the University in Antananarivo (tel: 323 19) or by writing to Beza Mahafaly Project, BP 10, Betioky Sud (612). A programme to

THE CORAL REEFS OF ANAKAO
Ben Tapley

The author was part of a group of young volunteers organised by the conservation organisation, Frontier, to evaluate the coral reefs of Anakao prior to the possible establishment of a marine reserve.

The reef system extending down the west coast of Madagascar is extremely important to the local coastal communities in the area. However, with increasing exploitation by an increasing population how is the reef ecosystem coping, and is it in need of protection? This is what Frontier decided to look at, working with a local research institute, the IHSM.

Because it is the local people who depend on and use the reef, much of our work was with them. We went to the small local villages daily. These are Vezo settlements which use traditional methods of fishing out of *pirogues*. When these returned early in the afternoon we went along to the villages and measured the size, weight and species of the catch so we could see if, over time, the fish stocks are depleting as the more mature breeder fish are taken. We also questioned the men on where they fished, time spent fishing and equipment used.

Another programme was Bay Watch where we monitored all the human activity in the sea and shore from a vantage point every 15 minutes for the daylight hours. This gave us an insight on how the people use the reef system.

The Vezo women also gather sea cucumbers for export to the Far East and sea urchins in vast numbers for food: each meal needs hundreds, so these species are going to be under threat eventually because more are being taken out of the system than are being naturally replaced. The local people, when we interviewed them, could not comprehend that their food resources were not infinite. The collection of sea cucumbers for export to the Far East is an important part of the women's life. By collecting all day she may get up to 35p. They even hunt at night at low tides far out on the reefs using lanterns.

Both men and women collect shells to sell to tourists. We found that the most highly prized shells such as cowries, triton trumpets and horned helmets, are the predators of the crown of thorns starfish, which decimate coral populations. There has been a small explosion in numbers of these starfish along some parts of the reef, which could seriously degrade the ecosystem so we carried out surveys on these.

improve the facilities for visitors is under way. At present you should be self-sufficient and well prepared with camping gear, food and cooking equipment.

Beza Mahafaly Reserve is reached within 45 minutes with a 4WD from Betioky during the dry season. The access is difficult and sometimes impossible during the rainy season, so check at the Beza Mahafaly Project office in Betioky, located near the Département des Eaux et Forêts. Whether driving or walking (ten hours), you should take a guide from Betioky to the reserve since the road there has many branches.

THE ROAD TO TAOLAGNARO (FORT DAUPHIN)

A taxi-brousse from Toliara to Taolagnaro takes two to three days. The fastest public vehicle is the Besalara truck, a Mercedes; the slowest is the Bienvenue. It's a shame to pass straight through such an exciting area, however. Much more interesting is to rent a vehicle and driver, or to do the trip by taxi-brousse in stages,

It was our suspicion that the reptile life, consisting of Ridley, green and hawksbill turtles, may be under threat from local people. On questioning them, we found that the turtles are widely exploited for food and tourist souvenirs. Nosy Ve is a known and protected nesting site, but this is not really enforced and the people dig up and take all the turtle eggs and any adults they can find. The egg raiding takes place every day in the nesting season. They can sell a large turtle for £15: an enormous amount of money to these impoverished people. The other species include whales and dolphins. Unfortunately the dolphins are hunted for food, whole shoals being illegally speared, and the locals tell officials they found them stranded and so escape the legal consequences. The right whale is safe from the local populous, as it is feared due to its large size. In previous years dugongs were a feature of the area and grazed on the extensive sea grass beds, but unfortunately these have been hunted to extinction.

The adjacent islands of Nosy Ve and Nosy Satrana are also important areas for some species of birds and reptiles. Nosy Ve has the only population of breeding red-tailed tropic-birds in Madagascar, and every month we went and counted the birds and the chicks to see how they were getting on. Rats were, up till last year, present on the island and it was feared they posed a threat to the tropic-birds by eating the eggs. So Frontier helped to co-ordinate a rat eradication plan which as been successful.

The region south of Anakao has an extensive mangrove system. We mapped it using GPS, and recorded bird, fish, reptile and tree species and, via transects, looked at the amount of trees the local people have been cutting down.

The research in the Anakao region is still on going and it is a vital procedure if this rich ecosystem is to get the protection it needs, and most importantly the local people are to live off the reef in a sustainable manner.

More information about this research from www.frontierprojects.ac.uk. Or contact Frontier, 50-52 Rivington St, London EC2A 3QP; tel: 020 7613 2422.

Frontier is involved in a project in the southwest. In 2001, an agreement was signed with the Institut Halieutique et des Sciences Marines (IHSM) of Toliara, part of the Ministry of Higher Education in Madagascar, to initiate the Wilderness Project in the Mikea region, proposing to contribute to the establishment of a reserve as part of the UNESCO 'Man and Biosphere' reserve designation.

staying at Betioky, Ampanihy and Beloha or Ambovombe, or – most interesting of all – by a combination of walking and whatever transport comes along, taking pot luck on where you'll spend the night.

Bezaha

A side trip to this town, which lies east of the road to Betioky, is worth it if you have your own vehicle: 'A road full of botanical and scenic wonders' and there are some good Mahafaly tombs along the road. The best hotel is the clean and friendly **Hotel Teheza**. A half hour's walk east are some hot springs.

Betioky to Ampanihy

Betioky is a day's taxi-brousse ride from Toliara. The first 70km are on paved road, then it's a very dusty 70km or so, but worth it for the Mahafaly tombs alongside the road. In Betioky the best hotel is **Chez Claudia**, 1km before the town, which is family-run with good food. In town are the **Mamyrano Annexe** and the **Hotel Mahafaly**.

Some 20km south of Betioky is the small village of **Ambatry**, with good Mahafaly tombs. Next comes **Ejeda**, about 2½ hours from Betioky on a reasonable dirt road. In the dry season you can watch the activity on the dry riverbed. Holes are dug to reach the water: upstream for drinking, midstream for washing, and downstream for clothes. The hotel here is 'good value for money: almost no value but also almost no money'. About 10km south of Ejeda are a few big Mahafaly tombs, one with over 50 zebu horns. Look for them on the right, on a hill.

Ejeda to Ampanihy takes about five hours by truck on a very bad, rocky road.

Ampanihy

The name means 'the place of bats', but now it is set to become the place of the goats. The weaving of mohair carpets was a thriving business in the 1970s and 1980s but the careless cross-breeding of the Angora goats reduced the quality of the wool until the industry collapsed. In 1994 a Frenchman, Eric Mallet, built a new carpet factory and trained local women to work the looms. The wool, however, was imported from France and New Zealand. Thanks to EU funding, 1999 saw the first pure-bred angora goats born in Ampanihy for decades and the industry seems set for a good future. These rugs are very beautiful, incorporating traditional Mahafaly motifs. Only natural colours and vegetable dyes are used.

It's worth a couple of days' stay so you can visit the carpet 'factory'. There is a WWF nursery for endemic plants, near the Protestant church. Walk 2km south to some good Mahafaly tombs.

Where to stay/eat

Motel Relais d'Ampanihy A touch of luxury in the desert! No hot water. Excellent food. The owner, Luc Vital, can organise excursions to the forest adjoining the river Menarandra (lemurs), and to see baobabs and Mahafaly tombs.

Hotel Tahio About 300m from the big market. Very friendly, economically priced. Good meals. Showers.

Ampanihy to Ambovombe

After Ampanihy you enter Antandroy country and will understand why they are called 'people of the thorns' (Androy means 'the land of thorns'). The road deteriorates (if you thought that possible) as you make your way to **Tranoroa** (the name means two houses) in about five hours. This is one of the main weaving towns in the south. There's an interesting Antandroy tomb here crowned by an aeroplane which moves in the wind. Another five hours and you approach Beloha on an improving road (much favoured by tortoises, which thrive in the area since it is *fady* to eat them) and with tombs all around.

Beloha is probably the best place to spend the night on this leg of the journey. It has a basic hotel, **Mon Plaisir**, with a restaurant, and elsewhere there is a bar, **Les Trois Frères**, which serves ice-cold drinks. Take a look at the new Catholic church with its beautiful stained glass, made by a local craftsman.

Between Beloha and Tsiombe is the most interesting stretch of the entire journey. There are baobabs, tortoises (sadly it is not *fady* for the local Antanosoy to eat them) and some wonderful tombs about 33km before **Tsiombe**. 'If "be" means "big" then "Tsiom" must mean "cockroach"!' Luc Selleslagh had reservations about his hotel, but there *is* a choice of simple *hotelys*. Two roads lead from here to Faux Cap (see next page) and Cap Sainte Marie (see page 239).

From Tsiombe it is 67km to Ambovombe. The next place you come to is **Ambondra**, the main centre for weaving in the region. Here you may be able to buy woven cloth from the makers. You are now not far from Ambovombe and the main tourist beat.

Ambovombe to Amboasary and Taolagnaro

With the end in sight, most travellers prefer to push on to Taolagnaro, but there are several hotels in **Ambovombe**: the **Relais des Androy** (no running water; good food), the **Oasis** (running water), and the Fanantenana (very basic, but cheap). Ambovombe has a good Monday market. This town is interesting as a centre for sustainable development projects overseen by the Peace Corps, involving the local people. At their request, for example, the town now has 20 new wells.

About 30km from Ambovombe is Ambosoary, the village that marks the turn-off to Berenty. If you decide to drop in to Berenty, thus saving the very high transfer fee from Taolagnaro (Fort Dauphin), think again. Transport from Taolagnaro is part of the package and you may not be admitted on your own (although with your own car this is less of a problem). Budget travellers should visit the reserve of Amboasary Sud instead (see page 000).

From Amboasary to Taolagnaro is less than two hours on a paved road.

Amboasary

This thriving town with a bustling market makes a worthwhile stop if you are visiting Lake Anony or Amboasary Sud. Don't stay too long, though; 'without charm, like a Mexican border town and full of street kids.'

Where to stay/eat

Hotel-Restaurant Mandrare A complex of small bungalows constructed from *Alluaudia procera* [ouch!]. 'A bargain at 18,000Fmg [1998 price]. The price excludes breakfast, but this is available; dinner is 10,000Fmg. Mary, the owner, has taught herself English and efficiently manages both the hotel and adjacent store. We arrived late at night and her welcoming smile and friendly manner were priceless. We appreciated the bucket of hot water and other homely touches.' Ken and Lorna Gillespie were in a hired vehicle, so welcomed the secure parking here.

THE FAR SOUTH

If you are in a 4WD vehicle or are a strong hiker, you should consider taking a side trip to the southernmost point of Madagascar. From Tsiombe a road runs south (30km) to Faux Cap and southwest to Cap Sainte Marie. Road conditions are very poor, but in the dry season an ordinary saloon car can make it in about six hours.

Hotels and tour operators in Taolagnaro offer this trip.

Faux Cap

I made my first visit to this dramatic, lonely place in 1997, and then predicted that it would soon be developed for tourism. Fortunately for adventurers, but sadly for the local people, the road to Faux Cap is, if anything, worse and visitors here remain a rarity.

Faux Cap is a small community, isolated from the outside world not only by the terrible roads, but by wild seas and a treacherous coral reef. The huge, shifting sand-dunes are littered with fragments of *aepyornis* shell. It is an extraordinary place which is worth making considerable effort to visit (see box on page 238).

LANDFALL AT FAUX CAP
Janice Booth

On an 'expedition cruise', coast-hopping round Madagascar on *MV Professor Khromov*, we were due to sail overnight from Fort Dauphin (southeast) to Tuléar (southwest). The captain agreed to pause en route so we could try to visit Faux Cap, at the island's remote southernmost tip. A sand-dune there contains fragmented fossil eggs of the *aepyornis* (elephant bird), extinct for around 800 years.

We didn't know whether tide, currents and the surrounding reef would allow us to land. *Khromov* dropped anchor far offshore at 1am. At dawn, the recce zodiac was launched, carrying expedition staff – and me, because I speak French and some Malagasy. As we bounced across oily swell the white girdle of waves on the reef appeared unbroken. Our zodiac veered sideways, searching for a gap.

Then we saw a wooden outrigger from the beach put to sea and steer for the reef. Suddenly there were two black heads in the water, sleek as seals, and two boys scythed through the waves towards us. We waved a welcome. They slithered wetly aboard the zodiac and, grinning proudly, piloted us ashore.

People were streaming down the cliff on to the beach. The village holds about 500 and it seemed few were absent! They stood on the sand, waiting. The zodiac scraped to a standstill and we clambered out; then it roared back to *Khromov* – boys determinedly still aboard – to collect the other passengers.

The villagers were tense and uncertain. I gave the traditional Malagasy greeting: '*Inona no vaovao?*' (What news?). There was a ripple of relief. At least the strangers knew how to behave correctly! Faces relaxed into smiles.

Some chatted in French. They'd seen the *Khromov* anchor but hadn't known why. 'As you can imagine, we didn't get much sleep last night,' one man admitted. Apparently we were the first visitors ever to arrive from the sea. A rumpled policeman introduced himself and politely requested passports, then waived his request as long as we didn't go inland.

The zodiac returned and was quickly surrounded by fascinated children. Stefan, our expedition leader, gestured 'OK' and they hurtled aboard, in a tangle of arms, legs and grinning faces. He zoomed them off on a quick loop of the lagoon (to the dismay of some parents!), their squeals of delight and excitement almost drowning the engine.

Meanwhile I asked carefully about the *aepyornis* eggs. Might we perhaps go to see them? A guide was found for the longish walk to the dune – which probably had been some huge midden, the fragments of fossilised shell lay so thickly on the ground. We could stroll and photograph (and, guiltily, collect) to our hearts' content. Two boys brought 'reconstructed' eggs for sale: diverse fragments stuck together to make unconvincingly lopsided wholes.

As we returned along the beach, children pattered beside us. A girl aged about eight touched my blouse curiously. In Malagasy I asked her name and told her mine. She stretched out her sandy little brown hand and shook my much larger white one, smiling shyly.

The midday sun poured gold on the sea as the zodiacs bounced us back to *Khromov*, wet, burnt, windswept – and happy, feeling like pioneers. It was an 'expedition' cruise indeed!

Getting there and away

The starting point for a trip to Faux Cap is Tsihombe. Stay at one of the *hotelys* and ask around for ongoing transport. Faux Cap is 30km from here and there is no water en route. If you decide to hike, be prepared to carry all that you need. There is a good chance that you will catch a lift, however. The village at Faux Cap is called Betanty.

Where to stay/eat

Hotel Cactus 18 basic bungalows. No running water or electricity but beautifully located and run by the very friendly Marie Zela. Good food with huge portions. A great place to relax for a few days.

Cap Sainte Marie

Cap Sainte Marie is as spectacular as its neighbour, with high sandstone cliffs and dwarf plants resembling a rock garden. It is also possible to get here without a vehicle. Andrew Cooke wrote: 'I suppose the highlight for me was taking a taxi-brousse to Beloha and then taking a *chavette* to Lavanono (on the coast) and then walking to Cap Sainte Marie (the distance is 30km which took us two days). All the way we met great hospitality. Water is in very short supply.' Note that since Cap Sainte Marie is a reserve, a permit must be purchased, and this should be arranged in Tana. Visitors arriving without a permit have been turned away.

This is a good area to see humpback whales; between September and November they can be observed quite close to shore with their calves.

TAOLAGNARO (FORT DAUPHIN)
History

The remains of two forts can still be seen in or near this town on the extreme southeast tip of Madagascar: Fort Flacourt built in 1643; and one that dates from 1504, thus the oldest building in the country, which was erected by shipwrecked Portuguese sailors. This ill-fated group of 80 reluctant colonists stayed about 15 years before falling foul of the local tribes. The survivors of the massacre fled to the surrounding countryside where disease and hostile natives finished them off.

A French expedition, organised in 1642 by the Société Française de l'Orient and led by Sieur Pronis, had instructions to 'found colonies and commerce in Madagascar and to take possession of it in the name of His Most Christian Majesty'. An early settlement at the Bay of Sainte Luce was soon abandoned in favour of a healthier peninsula to the south, and a fort was built and named after the Dauphin (later Louis XIV) in 1643. At first the Antanosy were quite keen on the commerce part of the deal but were less enthusiastic about losing their land. The heavily defended fort only survived by use of force and with many casualties from both sides. The French finally abandoned the place in 1674, but their 30-year occupation formed one of the foundations of the later claim to the island as a French colony. During this period the first published work on Madagascar was written by Pronis's successor, Etienne de Flacourt. His *Histoire de la Grande Île de Madagascar* brought the island's amazing flora and fauna to the attention of European naturalists, and is still used as a valuable historical source book.

Taolagnaro/Fort Dauphin today

The town itself is unattractive, but it is the most beautifully located of all popular destinations in Madagascar. Built on a small peninsula, the town is bordered on three sides by beaches and breakers and backed by high green mountains which dwindle into spiny forest to the west. One eye-catching feature of the bay are the shipwrecks. A romantic imagination associates these with pirates or wreckers of a

LIBANONA ECOLOGY CENTRE

The Libanona Ecology centre was set up in 1995 to create a local environmental education resource and training centre for Malagasy students, researchers and development professionals. The Centre was founded by Mark Fenn of WWF and Raoul Mulder of the University of Melbourne, and launched with funds sent by the Andrew Lees Trust, its UK partner of six years.

The Centre is managed by Sylvain Ebrooke (Director) and Maka Robinson (Administrator) and provides courses in environmental and social disciplines, training facilities for visiting students and researchers, and a networking base for many national and international organisations visiting and/or working in the south of Madagascar.

The Centre links environmental field training programs for Malagasy students with the universities of Antananarivo and Toliara and aims to increase the capacity of local people to create, develop and implement their own environmental and social development solutions for the country.

For further information contact Mark Fenn on cel@dts.mg or the Andrew Lees Trust in London (see page 145).

bygone era. In fact they are 'all unfortunate insurance scams with boats that should have been out of use years ago'. Pity!

More geared to tourism than any other Malagasy mainland town, Taolagnaro is a very lively place offering a variety of restaurants and nightlife, as well as exceptionally interesting excursions and some fine beaches. Independent travellers would do well to plan a stay of a few days here.

Most people (myself included) still use the French name, Fort Dauphin, but to be consistent with the rest of the book I shall stick to Taolagnaro in the text.

I am grateful to Brett Massoud, of Azafady (see page 145) and his team of volunteers, and Yvonne Orengo of the Andrew Lees Trust (see page 145) for extensive updates to this section.

Telephone code The area code for Taolagnaro is 92.

Warnings Taolagnaro is prone to strong winds in September and much of October. Muggings and sexual assaults have been reported on some of the beaches.

Getting there and away
By road
The overland route from Tana (bypassing Toliara) is reportedly best done with the companies Sonatra or Tata which operate three times a week from the taxi-brousse station on the far side of Lake Anosy. These buses go via Ihosy, Betroka and Ambovombe. You should book your seat as far in advance as possible. For the journey overland from Toliara, see page 234.

By air
There are flights to Taolagnaro from Tana and Toliara every day (but check the latest Air Mad schedule). Sit on the right for the best views of Taolagnaro's mountains and bays. Flights are usually heavily booked. Airport transfers from the de Heaulme hotels (see opposite) are expensive. Take a taxi (fixed rate) for the 4km ride into town.

Where to stay

Much of Taolagnaro belongs to M Jean de Heaulme, the owner of Berenty Reserve. His hotels are the Dauphin and the Miramar, with a new one being built. You are expected to stay in one of these if you want to visit Berenty.

Category A

Hotels Le Dauphin and Le Galion PO Box 54; tel: 212 38. The Dauphin is the main hotel and Galion its annexe. Meals are taken in the Dauphin which has a lovely garden. Prices are € 48 single or double, plus breakfast: € 4.5. A new de Heaulme hotel is being built next to the Dauphin, which is likely to be a higher standard (and more expensive). **Hotel Miramar** 310,000Fmg per room. Nicely situated on the cliff road overlooking Libanona Beach. There are a limited number of rooms costing the same as the Dauphin, through which bookings must be made. About 50m down the road is its restaurant, one of the best in Taolagnaro, superbly located on a promontory with wonderful views over two beaches; a rough walk in the dark (bring a torch).

Category B

Libanona Bungalows BP 70; tel: 213 78; fax: 213 84. Its location vies with the Miramar as the best in Taolagnaro, but the bungalows vary in quality. 100,000Fmg. Breakfast 17,000Fmg, dinner 40,000Fmg.
Petit Bonheur BP 210; tel: 211 56/212 74. Bungalows 80,000Fmg or rooms at 100,000Fmg. Another very friendly hotel on Libanona beach. Single/double rooms with a shared shower, and bungalows. The hotel runs tours in 4WD vehicles, including Le Grand Sud (Cap Ste Marie and Faux Cap). They also operate boat trips to Lokaro (see *Excursions*).
Hotel Kaleta BP 70; tel: 212 87; fax: 213 84. Rooms 240,000Fmg (for rooms facing the sea) or 160,000Fmg. En-suite bathrooms. A 32-room hotel in the centre of town offering a good alternative for those looking for comfort and lemurs (they operate Amboasary Sud Reserve) but unable to afford the de Heaulme/Berenty prices. Airport transfer 10,000Fmg.
Motel Gina BP 107; tel: 212 66; fax: 217 24. Pleasant bungalows with en-suite bathrooms on the outskirts of town, ranging from 80,000–220,000Fmg, depending on the season. Excellent restaurant. Unlike many other hotels, the Gina accepts Visa credit cards. Bike hire and excursions offered. An annexe has opened across the road.
Hotel Panorama Situated behind the Panorama disco, above Shipwreck Bay. 62,000Fmg double with en-suite shower. Also bungalows with a sea view.
Hotel Nepenthes New bungalows, hotel and restaurant set in quiet spacious grounds in Ampasikabo on the road that leads to the WWF. Rooms 70,000Fmg per night (single) or a bungalow for 4 at 120,000Fmg. Plus 1,000Fmg tax.
Soavy Hotel Down the road from Nepenthes, providing similar accommodation and restaurant. Pleasant surroundings. Prices from 35,000Fmg per night (single), 50,000Fmg (double) and 60,000–70,000Fmg for a bungalow.
Tournasol (See under *Where to eat*). 10 new rooms for 75,000Fmg.

Category C

Hotel Mahavoky Annexe Most rooms have a balcony with dramatic views of the shipwrecks in the bay. Nice friendly manager and staff, and centrally located, but the restaurant is no longer recommended.
Hotel Mahavoky Tel: 213 32. Situated in the town centre opposite the Catholic cathedral. Inexpensive rooms with communal (outside) shower and WC. Occupies an old missionary school which gives added interest. There's a helpful, English-speaking manager and a good restaurant.
Maison Age d'Or Readers' praise has been heaped on this establishment, not for its comfort but for its hugely hospitable owner, Krishna Hasimboto. 6 rooms, all but one with

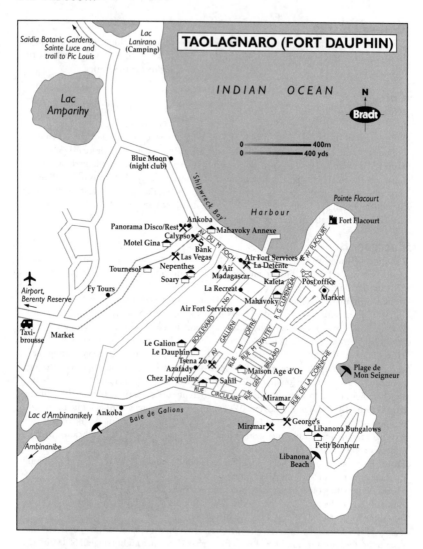

TAOLAGNARO (FORT DAUPHIN)

Saidia Botanic Gardens, Sainte Luce and trail to Pic Louis

Lac Lanirano (Camping)

INDIAN OCEAN

Lac Amparihy

0 ——— 400m
0 ——— 400 yds

Blue Moon (night club)

'Shipwreck Bay'

Harbour

Pointe Flacourt

Fort Flacourt

Ankoba
Panorama Disco/Rest Calypso — Mahavoky Annexe
Motel Gina
Bank
Las Vegas
Tournesol — Nepenthes — Air Fort Services & La Détente
Soary — Air Madagascar
Kaleta — Post office
La Recreat
Airport, Berenty Reserve
Fy Tours
Mahavoky
Market
Air Fort Services

Taxi-brousse — Market

Le Galion
Le Dauphin
Tsena Zó
Azafady
Chez Jacqueline — Sahil
Maison Age d'Or

Plage de Mon Seigneur

Miramar

Lac d'Ambinanikely — Ankoba
Baie de Galions
Miramar — George's — Libanona Bungalows
Ambinanibe
Petit Bonheur
Libanona Beach

shared bathroom. Bring your own mosquito net. The Age d'Or is best reached via the Kaleta Hotel bus from the airport.

Chez Anita 50m from the Age d'Or. Rooms for 37,000–42,000Fmg. Good food.

Hotel Chez Jacqueline Tel: 211 26. A family-run hotel in Bezarikely (the cliff road) in a nice location beyond the Miramar restaurant (Ampasimasay). Good value at 50,000Fmg for 4 clean rooms with en-suite bathroom.

Sahil Hotel Indian-owned, new and immaculate. 65,000Fmg for double room with telephone, en-suite shower and hot water. Recommended.

Libanona Ecology Centre bungalows Mark Fenn writes: 'We also have several guest bungalows complete with kitchen facilities. These bungalows are especially handy for people with small children or school groups (for which we can organise meals). We are not in the tourism business but it helps us to pay bills and upkeep on the buildings. The bungalows are simple, yet are older and have character. They are also situated on a peninsula with breathtaking ocean views (and whale-watching from July to November). People should contact us in advance via email: cel@dts.mg.

Camping
Azafady have set up several campsites in the beautiful area to the northeast. The nearest one to the town is Lake Lanirano, 2km away from Taolagnaro. See page 248.

Where to eat
In Taolagnaro eating is taken seriously. All the Category A hotels serve very good food with an emphasis on *fruits de la mer*. If you are dining away from your hotel, the following are recommended:

Serious eating
Miramar A contender for one of the best restaurants in Madagascar. Go for lunch, so you can enjoy the marvellous view. Not cheap, but worth every penny.
Gina's restaurant (Motel Gina) Again, not cheap but excellent food.
Restaurant Las Vegas Opposite Motel Gina. A lively and deservedly popular place run by Gabriella. 'The only place to eat, drink and meet people. Happy, friendly atmosphere, cheap tasty food. A brilliant place – I miss it and everyone there!' (Ania Dudziec)
Tournesol Tel: 216 71. 'A new restaurant offering a bright, clean and crisp atmosphere, good food and service. Often has calamari on the menu when no-one else in town does! Situated just up from the Gina Motel and Las Vegas restaurant, with garden. About 70,000Fmg for three courses.' (YO)
Mirimirana 'A small unassuming restaurant in the same road as the Mahavoky hotel, whose main attraction is that it is run by Honore, a superb guitar player who attracts other local musicians to play with him at this venue. There are frequent musical soirées and everyone is encouraged to participate – singing, playing or just enjoying themselves. A family business, the cuisine is very good and clients are truly welcomed. About 40,000Fmg.' (YO) 'They like it if you come in the afternoon and order your food, then it arrives quickly. Very highly recommended by the Azafady team: 'it is "our" restaurant'(BM).
George's Beach Restaurant and Gym 'Extraordinarily, and as if it wasn't enough exercise just getting round and about in Fort Dauphin, a large gym has now opened on Libanona beach. The gym provided full muscle-building facilities as well as ping-pong tables for the less ambitious. There is also a round restaurant which looks across the Libanona Bay and boasts some excellent cuisine. You can order lunch, or dinner in advance (advisable, as it's slow!), bathe in the sea and return an hour later for a fresh chilled fruit juice before your meal. Approx 55,000Fmg for three courses' (YO). 'Great grilled fish but they don't start peeling the potatoes until they get your order...' (BM).
Restaurant Pub Bar Calypso A brand new very slick looking restaurant opposite the Panorama. It has a very well-equipped cocktail bar, a nice terrace plus indoor seating, and good but slow-to-arrive food. Extremely friendly staff and a lovely place to spend some time.

Snacks
Mahavoky Escale Buvette Near the Panorama disco. 'Claude and his wife Mamanina always are hospitable and friendly for those who want to get to know the locals better' (Mark Fenn).
Tsena Zo 'Serves cheap beer and drinks, and the very best brochettes and sambos in Fort Dauphin. This little family-run bar is highly recommended for a quick pre-dinner snack. It is in Bazarikely on the steep road that leads down to Avenue Gallieni. Service is quick, the place is always busy (high turnover means fresh food?) and the snacks are really very good, all served with home-made tomato sauce and home-made sakay' (BM).

La Recreat Beer, coffee and light meals. Very nice outdoor café almost opposite the BFV bank. Friendly service and excellent *Mi Sao* and sandwiches.

Nightlife

Panorama Disco This is very popular with the locals. On the road to the airport, not far from Motel Gina, it is open every night except Mondays and used to be enjoyed by *vazaha*. But a recent traveller reports: '...resembles a building site, seedy, very assertive prostitutes of both sexes – can be intimidating for females'. Some still enjoy it, however. 'Much of its appeal is in its location, perched on the edge of the bay. When you get too hot and sweaty from dancing you can take a stroll outside to cool off in the ocean breeze and watch the waves roll in' (RM). Panorama now has a new restaurant, La Terrace, facing the sea.

The Blue Moon 'A new bar set up by Yvon and Bambi on the far side of the port, Blue Moon provides a welcome new alternative for night life in Taolagnaro, with varied entertainment from local live Malagasy bands every week-end, to a full-scale pool table, and the fastest food you can find in the south – burgers, pizza and fries alongside the more traditional Malagasy sambosas and brochettes. With views over the bay of Fort Dauphin and a friendly staff, it offers an enjoyable, relaxed evening out' (YO).

Saloon Billiards About as sophisticated (and European) as it gets in Fort Dauphin, this cool pool hall has four pool tables (charged by the hour), a bar serving rum cocktails and a clay oven for tasty Italian pizzas. This is a popular venue situated in the old Chambre de Commerce above the port. If lost ask for Radio Josvah and follow the signs downstairs. 'It's a very good bar in the basement of the building to the right of the post office. There's a great music selection, Scrabble and billiard tables. After two weeks in taxi-brousses it hit the spot...' (Daniel Simon)

Shopping

Taolagnaro has some distinctive local crafts. Most typical are the heavy (and expensive) silver bracelets worn traditionally by men. These are often offered for sale outside the main hotels. The best souvenir shop in town is **Au Bout du Monde** boutique, on the left-hand side of the road to the airport.

If you go to Libanona Beach you will be offered shells or necklaces for sale by charming local girls who have expertly sussed out the guilt factor prevalent in most *vazaha* dealings. When you refuse to buy their goods they insist on giving you a simple shell necklace as a gift. There are no strings attached – they know that the next day you will be prepared to buy anything!

Vehicle hire/tour operators

Air Fort Services Located on Avenue Gallieni. Postal address: BP 159; tel/fax: 212 24; email: air.fort@dts.mg. The main tour operator in the region. They hire out vehicles (from cars to buses, but no longer do bicycles) and even small planes, as well as offering a variety of tours.

Safari Laka Tel: 212 66. Situated in the Hotel Gina, and offering adventure trips ranging from mountain biking to trekking and canoeing.

Fy Tours Tel/fax: 216 31. New, on the road between Tanambao market and the Gina. 'They can organise just about any tour you could imagine and we have found them to be highly competitive price-wise' (BM). Fy also rent out 4WD vehicles (with driver).

Bike hire Opposite the BFV Bank and next door to La Recreat Restaurant (and with the same proprietor) is a motor bike and bicycle hire business (with no name). Motor bikes in general in Fort Dauphin are around 250,000Fmg per day and bicycles are between 25,000Fmg and 50,000Fmg per day.

Watersports

Club Vinanibe Another de Heaulme enterprise, this water sports club is situated half an hour by road out of Taolagnaro in Ambinambibe. The club offers windsurfing and waterskiing, paddle boats and sun loungers with a view over the lake. Lunchtime restaurant. Membership available (150,000Fmg) or visit through a de Heaulme hotel.

Ankoba Sports Based in two locations, one (their office) is in the same building as the Panorama disco, and the other (their beach bar) is on the beach at the Baie de Galions. 'They hire everything that you could need for a water based holiday, from a surfboard (75,000Fmg per day or 25,000Fmg per hour) to a motor boat (700,000Fmg per day for the biggest and 350,000Fmg for the smallest, both including petrol and skipper) and at their beach location they have a really wonderful tree-fringed hideaway with direct beach access. There they serve cold drinks, hire wind-surfers, surfboards, snorkelling and diving gear etc. This beach near Ankoba and heading south to Ambinanibe is much more popular with tourists these days as you can usually avoid the shell necklace sellers, it is much quieter in general, it is clean, the water is shallow for safe frolicking, and due to Ankoba having a manned lookout tower for their windsurfers, it has a little security. Can be very windy at some times of the year.' (BM)

Surfing

With some of the most superb coastline of the Indian Ocean, the south of Madagascar offers fantastic and, as yet, relatively unexplored surfing opportunities. A local surfing project has been set up in the bay of Monseigneur, on the other side from Libanona beach, to help develop a surf school for Malagasy youngsters and launch the first surf federation on the island (Surf Development Federation – SDF). The organiser, Yves Jousseaume, has been training young Malagasy surfers for several years. An experienced surfer, he takes internationals to some of the best 'surf spots' along the southern coastline. Surfers are then invited to leave boards, wetsuits or any other surf equipment, which helps to support the school and the training of these local children.

Yves can organise surf trips to four main safe surf sites in Taolagnaro, Lavanona, Itampolo, Anakao and Toliara for approximately US$50 per day per person depending on location (including camping and food, but excluding cost of 4WD and petrol). You will be taken into fishing villages where camping or local style bungalows provide adequate accommodation and fresh lobster is served over BBQs on the beach. Trips can be tailored to your ability and/or your travel schedules. Other local tours can also be organised. The best months for surf are June–August (Taolagnaro) and September–November (Anakao). It is important to note that there have been no accidents with sharks along this coast whose waters are safely fished up to 17km out.

For information contact Yves Jousseaume, c/o BP42, Taolagnaro 614; tel: 92 217 54.

Sightseeing and excursions
In and around town

Taolagnaro offers a choice of beach and mountain. The best easy-to-reach beach is **Libanona**, with excellent swimming (but beware the strong current) and superb tide-pools. Admirers of the weird and wonderful can spend many hours poking around at low tide. The pools to the left of the beach (as you face the sea) seem to be the best. Look out for a bizarre, frilly nudibranch or sea-hare, anemones and other extraordinary invertebrates, as well as beautiful little fish. Local hotels recommend that you visit in groups because of the danger of muggings. There is another beach below the Hotel Dauphin, but this is dirty (turdy) and there have also been muggings there.

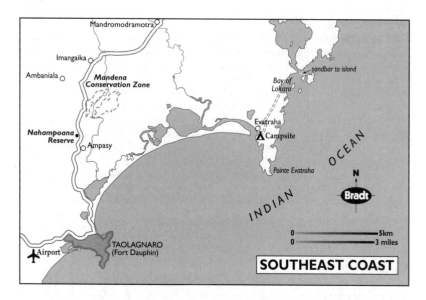

Pic Louis, the mountain that dominates the town, is a straightforward though strenuous (and hot) climb up a good path and offers nice views. The trail starts opposite SIFOR, the sisal factory about 3km along the road to Lanirano. It takes 1½–2 hours to get to the summit, so allow at least a half day to get up there and back – or better still take a picnic. The view from the top is spectacular: on a clear day you can see as far as Baie Sainte Luce. Apart from birds there is not much wildlife to be seen, though Nick Garbutt reports: 'I was once up there with a group when someone called out "Oh look, a monkey!" A grey bamboo lemur leapt over the rocks and into the nearby bushes.'

Another arm of the de Heaulme empire is the **Saidia Botanical Gardens** situated about 16km out of town towards Sainte Luce. Clare Hermans reports: 'A private garden complete with crocodile pen. Planting of local flora has been attempted and the trees have been untouched for 30 years. It may soon be the only place to see the local flora if the rate of cutting and burning continues. There are a few lemurs on islands in the lake – apparently an overspill from Berenty where some over-habituated ones had become aggressive.'

Day trips
There are numerous places to visit as a day trip in this beautiful part of Madagascar. If you haven't a car you will probably need to join an organised tour, though the energetic could reach most places by hired bike.

Portuguese Fort (Île aux Portuguais)
The tour to the old fort, built in 1504, involves a *pirogue* ride up the river Vinanibe, about 6km from Taolagnaro, and then a short walk to the sturdy-looking stone fortress (the walls are one metre thick) set in zebu-grazed parkland. This is the oldest building in Madagascar, and worth a visit for the beautiful surroundings.

Réserve de Nahampoana
This is a new, readily accessible zoo cum reserve owned by Air Fort Services (tel: 92 212 24). The 67ha park is just 7km (15 mins) from Taolagnaro, on the way to

Sainte Luce. It provides the usual tame lemurs (both local species and introduced), reptiles (again, some chameleon species do not really belong here) and regional vegetation. The price for a permit and guide is ∈ 10, and ∈ 9 for a picnic lunch. This is the ideal lemur-fix for those on a tight budget.

Further afield
Baie Sainte Luce (Manafiafy)
About 65km northeast of Taolagnaro is the beautiful and historically interesting bay where the French colonists of 1638 first landed. There is a superb beach and a protected area of humid coastal forest here, owned by M de Heaulme, and also some bungalows (usual de Heaulme price). It is possible to reach Manafiafy by taxi-brousse but most people will opt for the organised tour run by Air Fort Services, among others.

Evatraha
This is a very attractive coastal village to the north of Taolagnaro, situated on the mouth of a small river just south of Lokaro. Day trips here, by boat, can be organised through many tour operators, or a longer stay through the operator Tour Laka, based at the Mahavoky Annexe, and run by Fy. 'He has two beautiful bungalows on the lake edge at Evatraha, a fast boat to get you there, and great staff at the bungalows to look after you. They can arrange for fish or lobsters to be delivered by fishermen, and the prices are very reasonable. The bungalows (each with double bed only but en-suite bathroom) are 35,000Fmg per night. The boat trip is 500,000Fmg for the return journey and easily handles a group of four plus baggage. Some captive lemurs detract from the experience' (BM). There is also the Azafady campsite here (see page 249).

Security warning Serious sexual assaults, violent robbery and a rape have occurred on the beach between Taolagnaro and Evatraha in recent times (2001). It is inadvisable to walk to Evatraha without a Malagasy guide or at the very least in a group. The culprits are still at large.

Lokaro
The isolated Bay of Lokaro is perhaps the most beautiful spot on the southeast coast. Alasdair Harris and his team of underwater researchers spent six weeks there studying the coral reef, and his report (see box on page 248) makes mouth-watering reading. Most visitors can only see Lokaro as part of a day's excursion, but Al makes a strong case for spending more time there, which is no problem if you stay at Evatraha (camping or bungalows). There is no public transport to either Lokaro or Evatraha, but Evatraha can be reached from Taolagnaro either by *pirogue* (a peaceful sail downriver), by road in a sturdy 4WD or mountain bike, or on foot – a three-hour, 10km walk along the beach running north from Taolagnaro. 4WD vehicles can be rented in Taolagnaro at the steep cost of US$80 per day (journey time around two hours). From Evatraha, it is an hour's walk through hills and forest to the beach at Lokaro.

The essential requirement for a stay of a few days is self-sufficiency. Preferably you should have your own tent, stove and supplies – although you can buy almost everything you need in Evatraha, from eggs to beer and bottled water 'and plenty of the best shellfish I've ever tasted'. If you organise your stay through Azafady (see page 248) the logistics will be taken care of.

In conclusion Al writes: 'The best way by far [to reach Lokaro] is to stroll up on the spectacularly long beach that heads out north of Fort Dauphin [but do heed the security warning above]. It's an awesome stretch of fine white sand with enormous

Alasdair Harris, Eucare Research Co-ordinator

SNORKELLING AND DIVING IN LOKARO

The spectacularly beautiful Baie de Lokaro lies some 20km north of Fort Dauphin. Visitors to this remote tropical paradise cannot fail to be struck by the stunning scenery of the region: pristine littoral and tropical forests, rushing streams, meandering rivers and palm-fringed, emerald lakes. All these stretch from the mountains on the horizon down to the long stretches of fine white sand that fringe the shore. Exposed rocky islets protect the bay's turquoise waters from the wild ocean beyond, and help explain why Lokaro boasts the only substantial coral habitat in the southeast of Madagascar – in fact the only coral habitat south of Toamasina, some 500km further north.

The coral can be found in an idyllic lagoon sheltered by one of the bay's islands. This offers great snorkelling opportunities and can be reached from Lokaro's main beach. Travel to the northern point of the beach and head out a few hundred metres across the sandy spit that connects the beach with Lokaro Island, a favourite haunt for local fishermen. At various times of year the spit is partially covered by the sea, but the water depth is never so great that the journey cannot be made on foot. The lagoon itself is situated between the two rocky outcrops that make up Lokaro Island.

A short swim out into the shallow lagoon is sufficient to see the thriving colourful communities of coral, fish and invertebrates. At least two species of sea turtle are known to use the lagoon's beach as a regular nesting ground. Visitors to the area should respect the uniqueness of the habitat, by exercising caution when swimming in order to avoid damaging the fragile coral, and also when walking on the beach to avoid disturbing turtle nests.

For those wanting to dive, primitive (but adequate) SCUBA equipment and dive boats can be hired at Ankoba Sports in Fort Dauphin, although with no up-to-date diving facilities available in the town, most diving visitors opt to bring their own equipment. No public boat services run north from Taolagnaro, and

breakers crashing down every few seconds. As for campsites, there are some of the most mind-bendingly beautiful spots I've ever visited that would be just perfect to pitch a tent. Or try getting a *pirogue* there and then walking back – the silent sail down the meandering river through the forest to Evatraha is not to be missed. It makes you feel as though you're in a Conrad novel set in southern Madagascar.' Makes you ache to do it, doesn't it?

Azafady campsites

The following information is provided by the organisation Azafady. Their campsites give you the chance of staying in some of Madagascar's most beautiful places and helping out in a community project (if you want). 'Prices vary according to whether you are a student, a researcher or a tourist, and we welcome enquiries at our main office in Avenue Gallieni in Fort Dauphin or by email to azafady@dts.mg.'

Lake Lanirano A lake-front site 2km from Fort Dauphin, with full kitchen facilities and a huge dining/recreation room in a large stone house. Showers and toilets are provided and the house has mains electricity. The Lanirano site is home to several Azafady projects, and campers can witness or volunteer to assist with the conservation tree nursery, the medicinal plants garden, or can learn to build bee-hives or solar fruit dryers through the 'sustainable livelihoods' training programmes. The site, close to the foot of Pic St Louis, and local the cost of hiring a power boat to visit Lokaro (approximately 1.5hours each way) remains high, at around US$75 per day.

In addition to Lokaro, other smaller patch reefs can be found on the coast closer to Taolagnaro, the best of these being between Taolagnaro and Lokaro, running along the more sheltered sections of the southern side of Evatraha point, west of the lighthouse. However, owing to the dangerous and unpredictable swells and currents in the area, diving here should only be attempted from the safety of a boat, and not from shore. Diving in these more exposed waters offers excellent opportunities for viewing larger pelagic species such as barracuda, kingfish, trevallies and sharks. In addition to being ideally situated for viewing humpback whale migrations, the region also offers rare sightings of schooling hammerhead sharks.

The Eucare Project

Lokaro's isolation and communication difficulties (in particular the often impassable roads) make organising any form of research expedition to the region a logistical nightmare. These problems are increased considerably when the research in question is to be carried out underwater. In July/August 2001 a team of divers from Eucare launched an expedition to explore, survey and chart Lokaro's unique underwater environment. Prior to this, the marine habitat in the region was completely unknown and no base-line data existed. The data collected by the team are currently contributing to a feasibility study for a national protected coastal area for Lokaro. Eucare is involved in similar research on reefs around Toliara and the southwest, and also further north on the west coast at Belo sur Mer.

EUCARE (Edinburgh University Coral Awareness and Research Expeditions) organises teams of divers working with local personnel to survey and chart unexplored coral reefs around Madagascar and the Western Indian Ocean. (www.eucarenet.com)

dugout canoes can be hired and paddled through the many kilometres of lakes and rivers that lead you to Evatraha.

Evatraha An 11ha site a couple of minutes walk from the village, with two bungalows, each sleeping three or four, and sufficient space for up to 50 campers easily. Camp-fire, an outdoor shower room, an outdoor (covered) cooking room, and clean latrines. All catering equipment is provided. An ideal base for exploring Lokaro.

Evatraha Beach Camp About 1km from the village, near a white sand beach. An excellent place for observing the activities of local fishermen, but large enough for privacy too. No facilities (except a latrine toilet) and all equipment (including water) must be carried to the site. Catering equipment can be provided.

Sainte Luce Forest Camps Sainte Luce is about 70km by road from Fort Dauphin. Both camps are 3–4km walk from the village, and are convenient for biological research or hiking in the littoral forests. Camp S9 Limit is on the border of the forest closest to the village (suitable for up to 30 campers), and the other camp, Camp S9 Central is an easy 15 minute hike into the forest. In both cases wildlife is abundant: Camp S9 Central has a habituated troop of collared brown lemurs, and three other species of lemur are present. Both of these camps are based inside locally protected forest, and are therefore simple and relatively undeveloped. All Sainte Luce forest camps are managed between Azafady and the local forest management committee (VOI) and revenue raised from campers here goes directly to the committee to help fund ongoing conservation activity.

Sainte Luce Beach Mission Situated on a 60ha headland, the site of a former missionary school, about 3–4 km from the forest camps. It is fringed by coconut palms, and is two minutes' walk into the beautiful and totally traditional Antanosy village of Manafiafy (Sainte Luce). At present only camping is available, but by the end of 2002 rooms will also be available in the102 year-old ex-missionary house which is being restored. Facilities include shower rooms and toilets at the camp-site and a separate kitchen/dining house. This is our second base for village development activities and plenty of work is available for groups or individuals ready to participate in community projects.

Spiny Forest or Rain Forest Camping Azafady can arrange camping for groups in several other places where we currently have no facilities but are still well known because of our community projects. We highly recommend the stunning rainforest at Farafara Vatambe (40km north of Fort Dauphin) for incredible waterfalls, magnificent primary forests and palm jungles. The site can be reached by car but we recommend the adventurous hike through villages, across (and in) rivers, past waterfalls and along the side of the mountain forests, from Belavenoka to Vatambe. Spiny forest camping can be arranged in several sites, all with intact forest, for those with an interest in dry forest. Please contact us for further details.

THE WILDLIFE RESERVES

The southwest of Madagascar gives the best opportunity in all of Madagascar for wildlife viewing to suit all budgets and all levels of energy. Whilst Berenty is rightly world famous, adventurous visitors should give equal consideration to Andohahela, whilst those on a tight budget can consider Amboasary Sud, and the new Mandena Conservation Zone.

Berenty Private Reserve

This is the key destination of most package tours and I've never known a visitor who hasn't loved Berenty (well, there was one...). The combination of tame lemurs, comfortable accommodation and the tranquillity of the forest trails makes this *the* Madagascar memory for many people. The danger is that Berenty is already becoming overcrowded, and too many groups bring problems. Fortunately there is only a limited amount of accommodation, so if you can arrange to spend a night or two you can still have the reserve to yourself in the magic hours of dawn and dusk.

Visits to the reserve must be organised through the Hotel Dauphin (or the Capricorne in Toliara). Accommodation is full board only, and the same price as the de Heaulme hotels: €60 single, €75 double (with breakfast). Meals are an additional €20. Transport from Taolagnaro (three or more people) costs €58, so one night in Berenty will set you back about US$130. If you are lucky you will end up with Jean Benoit Damy as a guide for the trip to Berenty. I found him exceptionally knowledgeable and interesting, especially on the people of the area.

The road to Berenty

The reserve lies some 80km to the west of Taolagnaro, amid a vast sisal plantation, and the drive there is part of the experience. For the first half of the journey the skyline is rugged green mountains, often backed by menacing grey clouds or obscured by rain. Traveller's trees (*ravenala*) dot the landscape, and near Ranopiso is a grove of the very rare triangular palm, *Neodypsis decary*. (To see an example close up, wait until you arrive in Berenty where there is one near the entrance gate.)

Your first stop used to be a visit to some **pitcher plants** – *Nepenthes madagascariensis* – whose nearest relatives are in Asia. Sadly, this area has been destroyed by fire.

An optional stop before reaching the spiny forest is at an **Antanosy 'tomb'** (actually the dead are buried elsewhere) known as the tomb of Ranonda. It was carved by the renowned sculptor Fiasia. The artistry of this unpainted wooden memorial is of a very high standard though the carvings are deteriorating in the frequently wet weather. There's a girl carrying the Christian emblems of Bible and cross; someone losing a leg to a crocodile; and the most famous piece, a boatload of people who are said to have died in a *pirogue* accident. On the far side there used to be a charming herd of zebu, portrayed with unusual liveliness (a cow turns her head to lick her suckling calf). In 1990 the cow and her calf were ripped away by thieves. To add to the poignancy, a row of cattle skulls indicate the zebu that had to be sacrificed to counteract this sacrilege. One hopes the revenge of the Ancestors was terrible.

The very reasonable response by the villagers to this desecration has been to fence off the tombs, which can now be viewed only through binoculars.

In the area are other memorials, but without carvings. These cenotaphs commemorate those buried in a communal tomb or where the body could not be recovered, and look like clusters of missiles lurking in the forest.

Shortly after **Ranopiso**, and the turn-off to Andohahela National Park, there is a dramatic change in the scenery: within a few kilometres the hills flatten and disappear, the clouds clear, and the bizarre fingers of *Didierea* and *Alluaudia* appear on the skyline, interspersed with the bulky trunks of baobabs. You are entering the spiny forest, making the transition from the Eastern Domain to the Southern Domain. If you are on a Berenty tour your guide will identify some of the flora. If on your own, turn to page 72.

The exhilaration of driving through the spiny forest is dampened by the sight of all the **charcoal sellers** waiting by their sacks of ex-*Alluaudia*. These marvellous trees are being cut down at an alarming rate by people who have no other means of support. While condemning the practice, give uneasy thought to the fact that your sumptuous meals in Berenty will be cooked on stoves fuelled with locally produced charcoal. And that it is city-dwellers who consume the most charcoal in Madagascar: on average two sacks a month.

One enterprising community is now selling **wood carvings** of subjects that hitherto have been hard to find in Madagascar: the local fauna. These are carved from a light-weight *Burseraceae* wood known locally as *daro*. For a dollar or so you can buy primitive but delightful lemurs, tortoises and chameleons – a world better than the pseudo-African carvings found elsewhere.

If you pass through the village of **Ankaraneno** (25km from Taolagnaro) on a Thursday, do stop for the zebu market. Fascinating.

Amboasary (for accommodation see page 237), which also has a terrific market, is the last town before the bridge across the river Mandrare and the turn-off to Berenty. The rutted red road takes you past acres of sisal and some lonely-looking baobabs, to the entrance of the reserve.

The reserve

The name means 'big eel' but Berenty is famous for its population of ring-tailed lemurs and sifakas. Henri de Heaulme and now his son Jean have made this one of the best-studied 260ha of forest in Madagascar. Although in the arid south, its location along the river Mandrare ensures a well-watered habitat (gallery or riverine forest) for the large variety of animals that live there. The forest is divided into two sections, Malaza (the section near the tourist bungalows) and Ankoba to its northwest.

The joy of Berenty is the selection of broad forest trails that allow safe wandering on your own, including nocturnal jaunts. Remember, many creatures are only active at night and are easy to spot with a torch/flashight; also the eyes of

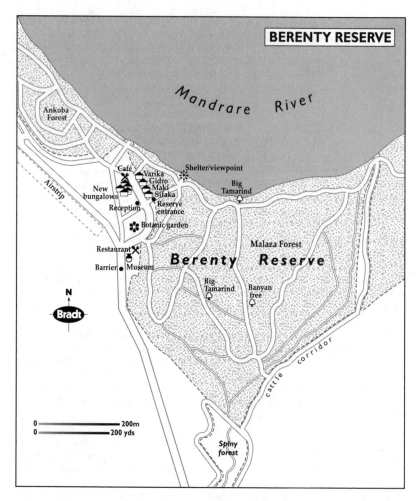

moths and spiders shine red, and all sorts of other arthropods and reptiles can be seen easily. A dusk visit (with a guide) to the reserve's area of spiny forest is a must: you'll observe mouse lemurs, but just seeing those weird, giant trees in silhouette and hearing the silence is a magical experience.

Next day get up at dawn; you can do your best birdwatching, see the sifakas opening their arms to the sun, and enjoy the coolness of the forest before going in to breakfast.

Berenty wildlife: an overview

Lemurs are what most people come here for, and seeing the following species is guaranteed: brown lemur, ring-tailed lemur and sifaka. The lemurs here have been fed bananas by tourists for decades and, although this is no longer allowed, they have not lost their trust in people. Disappointed that an outstretched hand no longer offers food, they will also try to sneak into your cabin to find it for themselves. **Ring-tailed lemurs** have an air of swaggering arrogance, are as at home on the ground as in trees, and are highly photogenic with their grey, black

THE LEGEND OF THE SIFAKA

The name 'sifaka' comes from the animals' alarm call which sounds like: 'She-fahk!'. Or, to some ears, 'Froo-trahk!'. Here's why the sifaka swears at humans.

Once upon a time the sifaka was human (you can tell that by looking at its hands and feet). Then a wicked woman hit her stepdaughter in the face with a sooty cooking spoon and sent her flying into the trees where she stayed, with a black face. Now, when the sifaka's descendants see humans they threaten them with the cry 'Aforotrako!' – 'I'm going to get you!'

and white markings and waving striped tails. These fluffy tails play an important part in communication and act as benign weapons against neighbouring troops which might have designs on their territory. Ring-tailed lemurs indulge in 'stink fights' when they scent their tails with the musk secreted from wrist and anal glands and wave them in their neighbours' faces; that is usually enough to make a potential intruder retreat. They also rub their anal glands on the trunks of trees and score the bark with their wrist-spur to scent-mark their territory.

There are approximately 350 ring-tailed lemurs in Berenty, and the population has stayed remarkably stable considering that only about a quarter of the babies survive to adulthood. The females, which like most lemurs are dominant over the males, are receptive to mating for only a week or so in April/May, so there is plenty of competition amongst the males for this once-a-year treat (April is also the best time to observe 'stink-fighting' among males). The young are born in September and at first cling to their mother's belly, later climbing on to her back and riding jockey-style. Ring-tails eat flowers, fruit and insects – and the occasional chameleon.

Attractive though the ring-tails are, no lemur can compete with the **Verreaux's sifaka** for soft-toy cuddliness, with its creamy white fur, brown cap, and black face. Sifaka belong to the same family of lemur as the indri (seen in Périnet). The species here is *Propithecus verreauxi verreauxi* and there are about 300 of them in the reserve. Unlike the ring-tails, they rarely come down to the ground but when they do the length of their legs in comparison with their short arms necessitates a comical form of locomotion: they stand upright and jump with their feet together like competitors in a sack race. The best places to see them do this are on the trail to the left at the river and across the road by the aeroplane hangar near the restaurant and museum. Sifaka troop boundaries do not change, so your guide will know where to find the animals. The young are born in July. Like the ring-tails, sifaka make a speciality of sunbathing – spreading their arms to the morning rays from the top of their trees. They feed primarily on leaves and tamarind fruit so are not interested in tourist-proffered bananas.

The **red-front brown lemurs** (*Eulemur fulvus rufus*) were introduced from the west and are now well established and almost as tame as the ring-tails. These are the only sexually dimorphic lemurs in Berenty – in other words you can tell the males from the females by their colour: males have a fluffy orange cap; females' heads are greyish and bodies are a more chestnut brown than the males. Both sexes have long, black noses and white 'eyebrows'.

There are other lemurs which, being nocturnal, are harder to spot although the **lepilemur** (white-footed sportive lemur) can be seen peering out of its hollow tree nest during the day. **Grey mouse lemurs** (*Microcebus murinus*) may be glimpsed in the beam of a flashlight, especially in the area of spiny forest near the reserve, a popular destination for night walks.

Apart from lemurs there are other striking mammals. **Fruit bats** or flying foxes live in noisy groups on 'bat trees' in one part of the forest. You are not permitted to approach closely, but you will still have a rewarding view of these appealing animals.

Birdwatching is rewarding in Berenty, and even better in Bealoka ('Place of much shade') beyond the sisal factory. Nearly 100 species have been recorded. You are likely to see several families unique to Madagascar, including the hook-billed vanga, and two handsome species of couas – the crested coua and the giant coua which have dramatic blue face-markings. The cuckoo-like coucal is common, as are grey-headed lovebirds and the beautiful paradise flycatcher with its long tail feathers. These birds come in two colour phases: chestnut brown, and black and white. Two-thirds of the Berenty paradise flycatchers are black and white. If you visit from mid-October to May you will see a variety of migrant birds from southeast Africa: broad-billed roller, Malagasy lesser cuckoo and lots of waders (sanderlings, greenshank, sandpiper, white-throated plover).

Then there are the **reptiles**. Although Berenty's chameleons are somewhat drab-coloured (two species are found here, *Furcifer verrucosus*, or warty chameleon, and *Furcifer lateralis*, often called jewel chameleon but in Berenty most un-gem like), they are plentiful. There is also a good chance of seeing Dumeril's boa (a huge, placid snake). In captivity there is a sulky-looking crocodile (its companion escaped after its enclosure was damaged in a cyclone) and some happy radiated and spider tortoises.

Finally, don't forget the **insects**. One of my favourite activities in Berenty is visiting the 'cockroach tree', a large tamarind on the left of the main trail to the river. This is pockmarked with small holes, and if you visit at night and shine your torch into the holes, you will see pairs of antennae waving at you. These belong to giant hissing cockroaches. If you are able to catch one of these 6cm insects it will give a loud, indignant hiss. (I have kept them as pets in England; they brought me endless enjoyment!) Another equally entertaining insect is the ant-lion (see box on page 52). Look for their conical holes on the sandy paths, then find an ant as a drop-in gift.

Berenty has been welcoming tourists longer than any other place in Madagascar, and all who fall in love with it will want to do what they can to preserve it and its inhabitants. The ban on feeding the lemurs is a sensible conservation measure. As long as visitors continue to behave responsibly they will be allowed to wander in the forest unaccompanied – a real treat for those who value solitude and the time to sit quietly and observe this unique piece of nature. However, don't miss out on the tours with the excellent English-speaking guides, who will greatly increase your knowledge and understanding. Their fee is paid by the reserve but a tip is appropriate.

Where to stay/eat

There are 12 bungalows (sleep two, comfortable, fairly reliable hot water) and six older buildings with pairs of twin rooms. Accommodation is also available in Ankoba. Generators are switched off at 22.00, after which there is no electricity. Without the electric fans it can get very hot. Rooms are screened, but in the older bungalows you should burn a mosquito coil (provided).

There is a snack bar near the bungalows where breakfast is served, and the bar/restaurant (near the museum) offers good fixed-menu meals, and cool outdoor seats for your pre-dinner drink. Near the restaurant is quite a good souvenir shop.

There are no telephones at Berenty. An efficient and reasonable laundry service is available – ask at Reception.

SISAL

This crop was introduced to Madagascar in the inter-war years, with the first exports taking place in 1922 when 42 tons were sent to France. By 1938, 2,537 tons were exported and 3,500ha of sisal were planted in the Tuléar and Fort Dauphin region. By 1950 production reached 3,080 tons. In 1952 a synthetic substitute was developed in the US and the market dropped. The French government stepped in with subsidies and bought 10,000 tons.

The Tuléar plantations were closed in 1958 leaving only the de Heaulme plantations in Fort Dauphin. In 1960 these covered 16,000ha, and by the mid 1990s 30,000ha of endemic spiny forest (that's about 100 square miles!) had been cleared to make way for the crop, with plantations under the ownership of six different companies. Workers earn 160,000Fmg per month (1999 figure). There is no sick pay or pension provision. The de Heaulme plantation alone employs 15,000 people who cut 300,000 leaves per day.

And here's something to think about: in the late 1990s there has been a resurgence of demand for sisal, with exports predicted to reach 5,000 tons by the year 2005, putting more spiny forest at risk. Why? Because we 'green' consumers in the EU are demanding biodegradable packaging. What is the best biodegradable substance? Sisal!

Excursions

Tourists staying more than a day should take the two excursions offered. The area of **spiny forest** here is superb (though hot) and may be your only chance to see mature *Alluaudia* trees. Some tower over 15m – an extraordinary sight. A visit to the **sisal factory** may sound boring but is, in fact, fascinating – and, for some, disturbing. On the natural history front, this used to be one of the best places in Madagascar to see and photograph the enormous *Nephila* spiders on their golden webs. But in 2001 I was horrified to find that my beloved spiders had been cleared away; however, I have faith that *Nephila* persistence will overcome this temporary setback.

Museum of the Androy

This is undoubtedly the best ethnological museum in Madagascar, and if your interest in the region extends beyond the wildlife, you should allow at least an hour here. Several of the rooms are given over to an explanation (in English and French) of the traditional practices of the Antandroy people, illustrated by excellent photos. There are some beautiful examples of handicrafts and a small but interesting natural history section including a complete *aepyornis* egg. This museum should be seen in conjunction with the replica Antandroy 'village' near the botanical garden, where you can step inside a small house, very similar to those you pass on the road to Berenty.

All credit to M de Heaulme for celebrating the lives of the human inhabitants of the region in this way. Don't miss this opportunity to learn more about the People of the Thorns.

Amboasary Sud (Kaleta Park)

The private reserve, set up in competition with Berenty, is adjacent to that reserve and a good option for those who cannot afford the de Heaulme prices. The forest here is degraded (ie: not in its natural state) and has been browsed by domestic animals. That said, most visitors find the wildlife viewing as satisfying as at Berenty.

The reserve is run by Rolande Laha, who for many years worked in Berenty, and is geared to independent travellers rather than groups. Hitherto most people came just for the day, but three new bungalows have been built (as yet with no water supply) and camping is allowed so overnight stays may soon become the norm.

One of the attractions here is the sifakas which are more approachable than in Berenty and even accept food from visitors. Whether this is a good thing for the sifakas, I'm not sure. The usual Berenty extras along the road to Ambovombe – tombs and pitcher plants – are also visited.

The entrance fee is about 50,000Fmg. If you also need transport it goes up to around 500,000Fmg per person or 150,000Fmg for a group of three or more. Arrangements are best made through the Kaleta Hotel (tel: 212 87).

Mandena Conservation Zone

This new (2001) reserve has been established by QMM (see box opposite) to protect 230ha of rare littoral forest in the region that is the centre of their controversial ilmenite mining project. This conservation area includes 160ha of the least degraded fragments of forest. Twenty-two species of flora are endemic to this region, with about 200 species of large trees. Littoral forest is similar to coastal rainforest, but with a 2% or 3% difference.

I visited Mandena the week before it was officially open and was entranced! It is completely different from the Berenty experience, has been thoughtfully conceived to give tourists as much variety as possible, and the local Antanosy people are involved. At present this is primarily a botanical experience. The lemurs are still shy, but no doubt will become habituated in time, but you'll see plenty of birds and reptiles. There is a standard circuit which takes three to four hours and includes level paths (the walking is easy) and a canoe trip. Our pioneering group paddled their own canoes (not very competently!) and I suspect that once the reserve is receiving a regular supply of tourists, local people will do the job. The canoes take you down a waterway fringed with pandanus palms (there are three species in Mandena). It is an experience straight out of *Walking with Dinosaurs* – completely otherworldly. Then it's a walk back along another forest trail to the visitor centre and tree nursery.

Mandena Conservation Zone will be run by local villagers (with guidance), and all proceeds will go into the local communities. Already the local Antanosy are taking pride in their new reserve and patrolling the forest on the lookout for illegal logging activity.

Visiting Mandena

The main hotels and tour operators in Taolagnaro will be running day trips, but independent travellers can just turn up. The reserve is about 10km from Taolagnaro (a beautiful drive) so within cycling distance. Bikes can be hired in town near the Kaleta hotel. A taxi costs around 75,000Fmg. There is a campsite just outside the boundary of the reserve, and in this area you can walk around without a guide so are free to look for wildlife at your own pace.

The fee to visit the reserve is 40,000Fmg per person, which includes the canoe trip. Guides are paid an additional 10,000Fmg.

Lac Anony

About 12km south of Amboasary is a brackish lagoon, Lac Anony. There are flamingos here and a large number of other wading birds in a lunar landscape. There is a village, Antsovelo, and accommodation and food are available. Nearer the main road is the Hotel Bon Coin, which also has a restaurant.

MINING IN THE SOUTH: AN ENVIRONMENTAL AND SOCIOLOGICAL DILEMMA

The dry south of Madagascar has large deposits of ilmenite used to produce titanium dioxide, which is used as a base for paint. The Canadian company QMM (owned by Rio Tinto), in partnership with the Malagasy government, plans to exploit this mineral resource. The mine would be active for some 60 years, would be the largest such venture in Madagascar and would involve an investment of US$350 million for the mine, a separation plant, a port and roads.

The project could bring 600 direct new jobs plus more indirect jobs to a severely depressed area of the country. Jobs would create prosperity which would reduce the pressure on the environment caused by *tavy* and the felling of trees for charcoal. The project would involve clearing some of the remaining coastal littoral forest with its endemic flora and fauna.

An RT representative writes: 'Rio Tinto and our Malagasy partner are well aware of the unique natural environment of Madagascar and the worldwide concern that it should be preserved and protected. That is why, since 1987, two sets of social and environmental studies have been carried out: an initial program from 1987 to 1992 and a comprehensive Social and Environmental Impact Assessment (SEIA) which was submitted to the Government of Madagascar in May 2001. At the time of writing (September 2001), the Government is conducting a review of the SEIA in order to decide on the environmental acceptability of the project. An international team of specialists was drawn from Madagascar, Canada, the United States, Britain, Australia and France. One of the key issues is the special botanical interest of the littoral forest that occupies some of the area to be mined. The expert studies have concluded that with the appropriate conservation and rehabilitation programs, the mining could proceed with virtually total conservation of fauna values and protection of most floral endemic species including all types of representative forest. Rio Tinto is publicly committed to a conservation and a rehabilitation program and to plantations of fast growing species that will provide the local population an alternative source of charcoal, fuel and lumber. If environmental authorisations are issued by the Government, further feasibility studies and project financing will be required before an investment decision can be made.'

The government of Madagascar issued the required environmental permit in November 2001.

Andohahela National Park

This national park (pronounced Andoowah<u>e</u>la) opened to tourists in 1998, and is a model of its kind. Much thought and sensitivity has gone into the blend of low-key tourist facilities and the involvement of local people, and all who are interested in how Madagascar is starting to solve its environmental problems should try to pay it a visit.

The reserve spans rainforest and spiny forest, and thus is of major importance and interest. A third component is the east/west transition forest which is the last place the triangulated palm (*Neodypsis decaryi*) can be found. These three distinct zones, or 'parcels' (from the French *parcelle*, meaning plot or area of land), make Andohahela unique in its biodiversity.

Andohahela Interpretation Centre (Centre d'Interpretation Andohahela)

Even if you are not able to visit Andohahela itself, do spend some time in this beautifully organised centre. It is a green building on the left-hand side of the road as you leave Taolagnaro. The centre was set up with the help of the Peace Corps and the WWF, for both tourists and – more importantly – the local people. Through clear exhibits, labelled in English, French and Malagasy, it emphasises the importance of the forest and water to future generations of Malagasy, and explains the use of various medicinal plants. Local initiatives include the introduction of fuel-efficient cooking stoves that burn sisal leaves. Wind power is also being investigated. Schools are being built in the area, with educating the next generation on the importance of preserving the environment one of the priorities.

Visiting Andohahela

At the time of writing a visit to most of the National Park requires the use of a 4WD vehicle and full camping gear (all provided by tour operators). Fit and properly equipped hikers or cyclists can make it independently, however. Tour operators such as Air Fort Services offer packages to Andohahela. Contact them (page 244) for the latest details and prices.

The national park
Malio (Parcel I – rainforest)

The rainforest area has a trail system and campsites. It has lagged behind the other two 'parcels' because most tourists have visited a rainforest reserve (Périnet or Ranomafana) by the time they reach Taolagnaro. This is part of its appeal... there will be no crowds. The area has all the rainforest requisites: waterfalls, orchids and lemurs (*Lemur fulvus*). It is also popular with birders who come here looking for the rare red-tailed newtonia. To get there (dry season only) you take the paved road out of Taolagnaro for approximately 15km, turn north on a dirt road before the town of Manambaro and go 6km to the nice little village of Malio. Independent travellers can buy a permit at the ANGAP office in Taolagnaro and reach the trail head by taxi.

Ihazofotsy and Mangatsiaka (Parcel 2 – spiny forest)

Visitors should remember that spiny forest is very hot, so camping/walking here can be quite arduous. That said, for the committed adventurer this is a wonderful area for wildlife, birding and botany. Even if you were to see no animals, the chance to walk through untouched spiny forest – the real Madagascar – gives you a glimpse of how extraordinary this land must have seemed to the first Europeans.

Apart from the fascinating trees and plants unique to this region, you should see sifaka (this is one of the areas where you can observe them leaping on to the spiny trunks of didierea trees without apparent harm), small mammals such as tenrecs (if you're lucky) and plenty of birds endemic to the south, such as running coua and sickle-billed vanga; also many reptiles. Equally you may see nothing! Remember that this is not Berenty; the wildlife tends to be shy, and is inactive during the heat of the day. Be patient.

Of the two spiny forest parcels, Mangatsiaka is the easiest to visit, being only 6km off the main Taolagnaro–Amboasary-Sud road, so ideal for self-sufficient independent travellers. There is a well laid-out trial system and a good campsite. Ihazofotsy is more popular with groups because you need a 4WD to tackle the two-hour access track. Camping is permitted near the village and there is a good trail system through the superb Alluadia trees. An added bonus is the view from a huge domed rock, which is crawling with *Oplurus* lizards.

Tsimelahy (Parcel 3 – transition forest)

I *loved* this place! Apart from reptiles (lizards and snakes), we saw little wildlife but the scenery and plants are utterly wonderful! This region is the only area in which the triangular palm is found; it says something for the rest of the botany that seeing this was not the highlight of our stay. The campsite for Tsimelahy is within a stone's throw of a large deep pool, fed by a waterfall, and fringed with elephant-ear plants. You can slip into the cool water from the smooth rocks and swim to your heart's content.

You can take a 4WD to within a few kilometres of the campsite, then you have a marvellous walk. A choice of two trails run along both shores of the river Taratantsa, affording super views of white flowered *pachypodium lamerii*, and green forest. My favourite plant was the 'celebrity tree' (*Lazar* in Malagasy or *Cyphostema vitaceae*). It seems to start as a tree, then change its mind and become a true liana (it belongs to this family), draping its droopy top over neighbouring plants. Young Malagasy seeking popularity or success will ask the *mpanandro* (soothsayer) to ask the tree for help.

Another highlight for us was the visit to the little village of Tsimelahy. This is an inspiring example of how a newly-established protected area can involve and benefit the local people. There are well-made handicrafts for sale and you will be treated to a rousing song about the forest and its animals from the children in the tiny school room.

Tsimelahy is accessible for independent travellers who are prepared to hike the 12km trail (or 15km road) from Ranopiso. A permit and directions are obtainable from the Interpretive Centre.

Part Four

The East

Indri

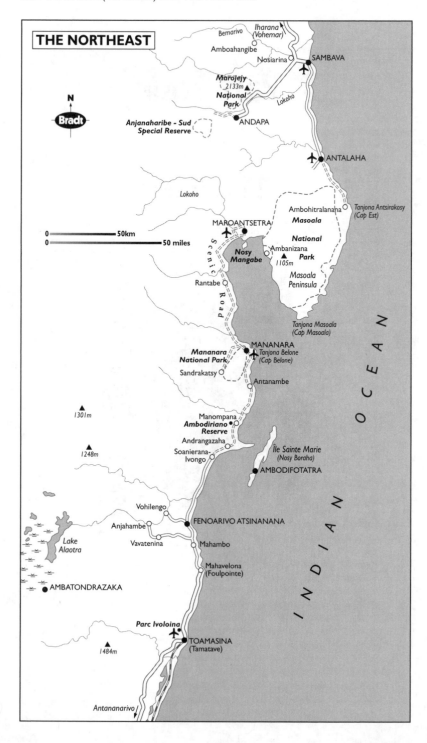

Toamasina (Tamatave) and the Northeast

OVERVIEW

Punished by its weather (rain, cyclones), eastern Madagascar is notoriously challenging to travellers. In July 1817 James Hastie wrote in his diary: 'If this is the good season for travelling this country, I assert it is impossible to proceed in the bad.' With this in mind you should avoid the wettest months of February and March, and remember that June to August can be very damp as well. The driest months are September to November, with December and January worth the risk. April and May are fairly safe apart from the possibility of cyclones. The east coast has other problems: sharks and dangerous currents. So although there are beautiful beaches, swimming is safe only in protected areas.

Despite – or perhaps because of – these drawbacks, the northeast is perhaps Madagascar's most rewarding region for independent travellers. It is not yet on the itinerary for many groups, yet has a few beautifully situated upmarket hotels for that once-in-a-lifetime holiday, or wonderful exploratory possibilities for the intrepid backpacker. Much of Madagascar's unique flora and fauna is concentrated in the eastern rainforests and any serious naturalist will want to pay a visit. Other attractions are the rugged mountain scenery with rivers tumbling down to the Indian Ocean, the friendly people, abundant fruit and seafood, and access to the lovely island of Nosy Boraha (Ile Sainte Marie).

The chief products of the east are coffee, vanilla, bananas, coconuts, cloves and lychees.

History

This region has an interesting history dominated by European pirates and slave traders. While powerful kingdoms were being forged in other parts of the country, the east coast remained divided among numerous small clans. It was not until the 18th century that one ruler, Ratsimilaho, unified the region. The half-caste son of Thomas White, an English pirate, and briefly educated in Britain, Ratsimilaho responded to the attempt by Chief Ramanano to take over all the east coast ports. His successful revolt was furthered by his judiciously marrying an important princess; by his death in 1754 he ruled an area stretching from the Masoala Peninsula to Mananjary.

The result of this liaison of various tribes was the Betsimisaraka, now the second largest ethnic group in Madagascar. Some (in the area of Maroantsetra) practise second burial, although with less ritual than the Merina and Betsileo.

Getting around

Although the map shows roads of some sort running almost the full length of the east coast, this is deceptive. Rain and cyclones regularly destroy bridges so it

DISTANCES IN KILOMETRES

Toamasina–Mahambo	90km
Toamasina–Soanierana Ivongo	163km
Toamasina–Mahavelona	60km
Iharana–Sambava	163km
Sambava–Antalaha	89km
Sambava–Andapa	119km

is impossible to know in advance whether a selected route will be usable, even in the 'dry' season. The rain-saturated forests drain into the Indian Ocean in numerous rivers, many of which can only be crossed by ferry. And there is not enough traffic to ensure a regular service. For those with limited time, therefore, the only practical way to get to the less accessible towns is by air: there are regular planes to Nosy Boraha (Ile Sainte Marie), and flights between Toamasina (Tamatave) and Antsiranana (Diego Suarez). Planes go several days a week from Toamasina to Maroantsetra, Antalaha and Mananara, and to Sambava.

For the truly adventurous it is possible to work your way down (or up) the coast providing you have plenty of time and are prepared to walk.

TOAMASINA (TAMATAVE)
History

As in all the east coast ports, Toamasina (pronounced 'Tourmasin') began as a pirate community. In the late 18th century its harbour attracted the French, who already had a foothold in Ile Sainte Marie, and Napoleon I sent his agent Sylvain Roux to establish a trading post there. In 1811, Sir Robert Farquhar, governor of the newly British island of Mauritius, sent a small naval squadron to take the port of Toamasina. This was not simply an extension of the usual British/French antagonism, but an effort to stamp out slavery at its source, Madagascar being the main supplier to the Indian Ocean. The slave trade had been abolished by the British parliament in 1807. The attack was successful, and Sylvain Roux was exiled. During subsequent years, trade between Mauritius and Madagascar built Toamasina into a major port. In 1845, after a royal edict subjecting European traders to the harsh Malagasy laws, French and British warships bombarded Toamasina, but a landing was repelled leaving 20 dead. During the 1883–85 war the French occupied Toamasina but Malagasy troops successfully defended the fort of Farafaty just outside the town.

Theories on the origin of the name Toamasina vary, but one is that King Radama I tasted the seawater here and remarked '*Toa masina*' – 'It's salty'.

Toamasina today

Toamasina has always had an air of shabby elegance with some fine palm-lined boulevards and once-impressive colonial houses. Every few years it's hit by a cyclone, and spends a time in a new state of shabbiness before rebuilding. As you'd expect, it's a spirited, bustling city with a good variety of bars, snack bars and restaurants (updated here by residents Charlie Welch and Andrea Katz with insiders' knowledge). Nearby is the excellent Parc Ivoloina, which is the ideal place to spend a day (or night, if you have your own tent).

Telephone code The area code for Toamasina is 53.

Getting there and away
By road
Route Nationale 2 (RN2) is one of the country's best roads, and thus attracts dangerous drivers. Nevertheless, this is the fastest and cheapest way of reaching Toamasina from Tana. Vehicles run only twice a day, morning or night, and take from six to 12 hours. There is a wide choice of vehicle: bus (auto-car), minibus, and Peugeot station wagon. The large buses are the most comfortable (MAMI is a popular bus company); a night bus may seem like a good option but it is impossible to sleep because of the radio turned up to top volume. It's also more dangerous. Minibuses and Peugeots are faster, and a little more expensive (35,000Fmg).

Book your seat at least a day in advance at the taxi-brousse departure point, Fasan'ny karana, on the road to the airport.

Warning: Even if you've never suffered from motion sickness, take precautions on this trip. The macho drivers and winding road are a challenge to any stomach.

By air
There are daily flights between Tana and Toamasina.

By rail
The once-famous train from Tana to Toamasina sadly no longer takes passengers. For the time-being, at least, it is for cargo only.

By sea and river
Toamasina's Port Fluvial is in the south edge of the town (separate from the harbour). This is where you can look for boats to take you down the Pangalanes (see pages 306–7).

Where to stay
Note: Bd Ratsimilaho was mostly washed away in the 1994 cyclone Geralda so is not continuous. It now ends just after the crossing of the Pangalanes Canal. To reach the beach hotels in the north of the city you must first go west to catch the road through Tanamakoa then cut back eastward towards the ocean. Best just to take a taxi!

Category A
Neptune 35 Bd Ratsimilaho (on the seafront); tel: 336 30; fax: 324 26. E65 double. The poshest hotel in town. Swimming pool, excellent food, good bar. Credit cards accepted.
Hotel Miramar Tel: 332 15. Comfortable chalets and bungalows in a good location (to the north, near the beach). Chalets 155,000Fmg, simple bungalows 210,000Fmg, family bungalows 255,000Fmg. The pool is open to the public, and the hotel is convenient for the airport. Credit cards are not accepted.
Hotel Joffre 30 Bd Joffre; tel: 323 90. 150,000–210,000Fmg for air-conditioned rooms with en-suite bathroom. An atmospheric old hotel with all facilities and very good restaurant. Credit cards accepted.
Hotel Le Toamasina Rue Reine Betty; tel: 335 49; fax: 336 12. 135,000–227,000Fmg, depending on facilities. Comfortable and efficient. Reasonable food. Visa cards accepted.
Hotel Sharon Tel: 304 20; email: sharon@dts.mg. A high rise concrete building on Bd de la Liberation, 100m west of Hotel Plage. €61.5. All rooms with air-conditioning. Restaurant that serves Indian food. No alcohol. Small swimming pool, exercise room etc; mostly a business person's hotel.
Noor Hotel At intersection of Bd Mal Foch and Rue du Mal de Lattre de Tassigny (north side); tel: 338 45. 112,950Fmg (air conditioned), 92,500Fmg (with fan). No restaurant, but

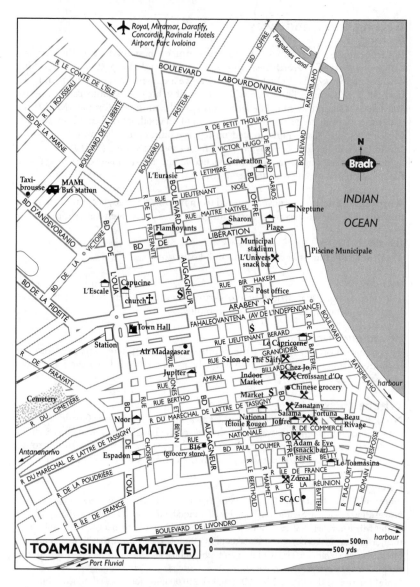

TOAMASINA (TAMATAVE)

Jade is round the corner and Vesuvio Pizza across the street. Credit cards accepted.

Hotel Generation 129, Bd Joffre; tel: 321 05/328 34. 99,750Fmg double with fan, 173,750Fmg with air-conditioning and TV. A nice hotel serving good food.

Hotel les Flamboyants Bd de la Libération; tel: 323 50. About 85,000Fmg for room with fan, 98,000Fmg with air-conditioning. En-suite bathrooms. Good value. Credit cards accepted.

Category B

Espadon Hotel Bd de l'OUA; tel: 303 86. A concrete highrise building beyond the Noor Hotel). 85,000Fmg with fan, 135,000Fmg with air-conditioning and TV. Mostly used by business people.

Royal Hotel Route d'Ivoloina; tel: 311 15/312 81. A concrete highrise without much character, but clean and relatively new. 112,000Fmg (shared toilet) to 152,000Fmg (TV and fridge). Restaurant. Located on a busy street away from centre of town.

Salama Tel: 307 50, on a side street behind Hotel Joffre. 66,000–101,000Fmg all with fan, hot water, and en-suite toilets and showers. Clean and simple.

Hotel National (formerly Etoile-Rouge) 13 Rue du Mal de Lattre de Tassigny; tel: 322 90. 60,000Fmg to 85,000Fmg (single, with en-suite bathroom) or 110,000Fmg with air-conditioning. A popular, friendly hotel. Most of the cheaper rooms are cell-like, but have fans or barred windows which can be left open. No restaurant.

Eurasie Bd Augagneur; tel: 306 00; cellphone: 033 11 408 02. 85,000–105,000Fmg breakfast included. 4 rooms in a nicely renovated old building in a quiet location away from the business district but not far from town centre. Fan, hot water. Private toilet outside room in 2 rooms, and shared WC for the other two rooms. Nice restaurant serving Chinese, European and Malagasy dishes. Airport transfers.

Capricorn 33 Rue de la Batterie; tel: 336 51. Large rooms, some with balconies, and en-suite bathrooms; 59,000Fmg (with fan) to 98,500Fmg with air-conditioning.

Darafify Tel: 326 18. In the north of the town, with a good beach location about 2km beyond the Miramar. 75,000–125,000Fmg. Basic bungalows with cold showers and en-suite WC. Good restaurant.

Ravinala (formerly Mandibule) Tel: 308 83; email: fgbaril@dts.mg. On Bd Ratsimilaho on the beach, about 200m north of Hotel Miramar. 9 rooms with fans and hot water, nicely decorated with bamboo. 50,000–115,000Fmg (85,000–115,000Fmg with en-suite WC and shower). Quiet and peaceful;, Good restaurant serving European and Malagasy food, and pizza. Friendly people, recommended.

Category C

Hotel Jupiter Bd Augagneur; tel: 321 01. 63,500Fmg (shared WC) to 83,500Fmg. Hot water and fan. Restaurant with Friday cabaret downstairs. Concrete building in business district close to the market. Night club next door.

Concordia Tel: 317 42. The closest hotel to airport (within walking distance) on the road towards town. 72,000–82,000Fmg for very nice bungalows with fans and hot water, in a compound which includes a restaurant.

Hotel Eden Cellphone: 030 55 850 93: fax: 312 90. Appropriately situated near the Adam & Eve Snack Bar on Bd Joffre, opposite the BMOI bank. 51,000Fmg for room with shared bathroom to 61,000Fmg for en-suite shower (but shared WC). Fans and hot water in rooms.

Hotel Plage Bd de la Libération (round the corner from the Neptune); tel: 320 90. From 55,000Fmg for double room with cold water to 95,000Fmg to a triple with en-suite bathroom and hot water. Quite clean and comfortable, but the disco is murder and appears to go on seven nights a week.

Hotel Capucine Near the railway station (off Bd Poincaré, opposite the Hotel de Ville). 41,000Fmg for shared shower and WC; 48,000Fmg for en-suite shower (but shared WC). Clean, friendly, but very hot – though you can pay 5,000Fmg for a fan.

Hotel Capucine Annexe Near taxi-brousse station so convenient for late arrival or early departure, but hot; 39,000Fmg.

Hotel Beau Rivage Rue de Commerce; tel: 330 85. 12 clean rooms, some with fan and balcony. From 25,000Fmg (shared toilet, but shower in room) to 60,000Fmg (fan, shower and toilet in room). Good value.

Where to eat
The following hotels have exceptionally good restaurants: **Neptune** – especially recommended is its all-you-can-eat Sunday buffet (lunch). **Joffre** and

Flamboyants are two other Category A hotels, but also recommended are the restaurants at the less posh **Darafify**, **Ravenala** and **Eurasie**.

Jade Next door to the Noor Hotel. This is an upmarket Chinese restaurant with good food but quite expensive.

Restaurant Fortuna A very good Chinese restaurant (but slow service). Next to it, under the same management, is **Soupe Chinoise** which opens at 17.00 (as against 19.00) and serves tasty Chinese soup and noodle specialities.

La Pacifique Rue de la Batterie. A popular and good-value Chinese restaurant just across the road from the Fortuna and serving very good meals at reasonable prices.

La Récrea A trendy place on the beach, north side. Under new management, serving good food. A nice place to stop for a drink; piano bar in the latter part of the week.

Bella Italia (part of the Hotel Beau Rivage) Rue de Commerce 'A great selection of Italian food, including pizzas, and good desserts.'

Adam & Eve Snack Bar 13 Rue Nationale; tel: 334 56 (near Hotel Joffre). 'Best cuppa in Madagascar.' Other star features are good prices, strong, hot coffee and delicious samosas (sambos). Always busy, slow service.

Croissant d'Or Recommended for breakfast. Operates a small grocery with hard-to-find *vazaha* items.

Bateau Ivre. Adjoins the old municipal swimming pool on the east side of the stadium on Bd Ratsimilaho. A bar and restaurant with character. Owners have done a very nice job of fixing up the old municipal pool complex, so you can go there to swim and eat. Moderately priced European food, with seafood a speciality. Live music in the evenings (piano and singer).

Vesuvio pizzeria. Good pizza convenient to the Noor hotel (right across the street). They deliver!

Zanatany The name is a Malagasy word for a *vazaha* who has come to Madagascar and ended up staying! Bd Joffre across from BNI bank. In an old Creole house with a nicely decorated interior – full of character. European, Malagasy and Chinese food.

Zoreal Bd Joffre, north of the BMOI bank. A local hangout with 2 billiard tables, darts, and bar. French, Creole and Malagasy food, plus pizzas.

Perroquet Bleu On a side road across from the BNI bank that runs on the side of Zanatany. An open air bar and small restaurant which is a local hangout. Pizza and Italian food.

Hans Burger Adjoins the Hotel Capricorne. A Korean-run restaurant that serves hamburgers. A nice fix for a burger craving!

Dragon de Mer Chinese restaurant on side road off Bd Joffre, across from the BMOI bank. Usually lots of trucks parked around. Very good Chinese food at reasonable prices.

L'Univers. Incorporated into the stadium on its west side. Serves *grillades* and simple plates. Only restaurant open 24 hours.

Internet

Butterfly Network Company Bd Joffre, one block north of Hotel Joffre. Inexpensive internet access.

Western Union

There are two offices, one at the BFV Bank on the corner of Av de l'Indépendance and Bd Joffre, and the other on Bd Augangeur.

Shopping

B16 Supermarket, Bd Augagneur, in the south part of town has an excellent selection of goods. The new Champion supermarket on the eastern end of Av de l'Indépendance sells everything. The *Librairie* near the market is very good and sells CDs of Malagasy music as well as books and nice postcards.

Car hire
Note: renting a car in Toamasina is more expensive than in Tana.

Aventour Rue Bir Hakeim; tel: 322 43.
LCR Bd Joffre; tel: 334 69; 339 04.
Rabarijaona Rue Victor Hugo; tel: 339 58/301 52; email: gracetours@simicro.mg.
SICAM Bd d'Oua; tel: 321 04; email: sicam.tamatave@simicro.mg.

Nightlife and entertainment
Pandora Station Near the Hotel Miramar. 'An interesting night club. Fun place to go dancing without hassles from night ladies (for men). Safe place for women to dance unhassled as well. Used to serve meals as well but they seem to be moving away from that. Décor is imaginative' (Charlie Welch).
Minigolf 18 hole course at the end of Rue de Commerce down from the port entrance. 'Sounds corny but is nicely laid out and kept up with bar and *grillade* restaurant' (CW). If you're looking for something completely different to do...
Swimming pool (Piscine Municipal). Already mentioned along with its Bateau Ivre restaurant. A nice place for a dip if you are not staying at the Neptune, Miramar or Sharon. Eat poolside or in the restaurant.

Parc Ivoloina
This began life in 1898 as a rather grand Botanical Garden but is now a conservation centre and zoo. It is funded by the Madagascar Fauna Group, a consortium of 30 or so zoos from around the world with a special interest in Madagascar.

In total there are 13 species and subspecies of lemurs here, including four species that are free-ranging. These include black-and-white ruffed lemurs, white-fronted lemurs, red-bellied lemurs and grey bamboo lemurs. These offer great photo opportunities, as well as the pleasure of seeing 'zoo animals' living in freedom.

There are also reptiles (tortoises, chameleons and boas) and they hope soon to have some tomato frogs which are unique to the Maroantsetra area.

An interpretive trail leads you through the forest, and a 1½km trail has just been completed which runs around the perimeter of the lake. In the zoo itself is a botanical tour, with labelled native trees, and a guide-booklet in French and English. There's a snack bar (which also sells souvenirs) and you can even go on a *pirogue* trip on the lake!

Backpackers with their own tents can camp for 10,000Fmg per night. The park can provide a stove and charcoal but campers should bring their own food.

Visitors who are keen to see what aid organisations are doing to help Madagascar with its environmental problems should pay a visit to Ivoloina. In addition to the attractions of the zoo, there is an excellent new education centre with some beautiful displays, aimed particularly at local people and schoolchildren. The aim is to create a model station which will demonstrate to local cultivators the techniques of sustainable land use, as opposed to slash-and-burn. Vegetables, fruit trees, rice paddies etc will be part of the demonstration. This is on the forest station road, just before you arrive and the zoo, and is open to all, though it targets the locals.

Ivoloina is 12km north of town, and is open daily from 09.00 to 17.00; the entrance fee is 20,000Fmg. The MFG has an office in Toamasina, next to the

Miramar Hotel, so it is worth calling in to learn about any new developments. The Technical Advisors for the park, Charles Welch and Andrea Katz, have exciting plans for its future.

THE ROUTE NORTH

The road is tarred and in good condition as far as Soanierana-Ivongo. Beyond that it is usually passable as far as Maroantsetra. Then you have to take to the air or journey on foot across the neck of the road-free Masoala Peninsula.

Mahavelona (Foulpointe)

The town of Mahavelona is unremarkable, but nearby is an interesting old circular fortress with mighty walls faced with an iron-hard mixture of sand, shells and eggs. There are some old British cannons marked GR. This fortress was built in the early 19th century by the Merina governor of the town, Rafaralahy, shortly after the Merina conquest of the east coast. There may now be a charge to visit the fortress.

Where to stay/eat

Hotel Manda Beach Located on the Toamasina side of town. Bungalows and safe swimming. Can be booked in Tana (tel: 22 317 61) as well as locally (322 43).
Au Gentil Pêcheur. Next door to Manda Beach. Bungalows and excellent food.

Mahambo

A lovely beach resort with safe swimming (but nasty sandfleas, called *moka fohy* in Malagasy).

Where to stay/eat

Hotel Le Recif Tel/fax: (57) 300 50. Bungalows for about 90,000Fmg (facing the sea) or 80,000Fmg for others. Under new (French) ownership. Well-run, friendly, good food.
Le Gîte About 250,000Fmg per bungalow. Set menu for 25,000Fmg. Two-storey bungalows with hot showers and en-suite WC. Your stay will be enlivened by the four free-ranging lemurs (three black-and-white ruffed, and one crowned) and by the herds of zebu on the beach.
Le Dola Spanish owned, dilapidated (cyclone damage), but with good food and mosquito nets.

Heading west

Between Mahambo and Fenoarivo Atsinanana is a road leading inland to **Vavatenina**, where there is basic accommodation in bungalows, and on to **Anjahambe**. This town marks the beginning (or end) of the Smugglers' Path to Lake Alaotra (see page 314).

Fenoarivo Atsinanana (Fénérive)

Beyond Mahambo is the former capital of the Betsimisaraka empire. There is a clove factory in town which distils the essence of cloves, cinnamon and green peppers for the perfume industry. They are not geared up for tourist visits but will show you round if you ask.

There are several basic hotels, including **Belle Rose** bungalows on the road leading to the hospital. Dolphins can sometimes be seen swimming offshore.

West to Vohilengo

From Fenoarivo a road leads west to Vohilengo. This makes a pleasant diversion for those with their own transport, especially during the lychee season. 'We arrived at the start of a six-week lychee bonanza... Along the road to Vohilengo were prearranged pickup points where the pickers would bring their two ten-kilo panniers. Vohilengo is a small village, perfumed with the scent of cloves laid out to dry; the local *hotely* sells coffee at amazingly cheap prices.' (Clare Hermans)

Soanierana-Ivongo

Known more familiarly as 'Sierra Ivongo', this little town is one of the starting-points for the boat ride to Sainte Marie. It is also the end of the tarred road. Daniel Simon saw it at its best: '...we found ourselves in S-Ivongo just in time for the Police Nationale disco. This appears to be held every few months and this one coincided with the lychee harvest when everyone had some available cash. A fantastic night dancing away to Malgache music with lots of incredibly happy and possibly drunken Malgache.'

Where to stay/eat

Hotel Espece Basic bungalows for 20,000Fmg. The best budget option. Near the boat departure point for Ile Ste Marie. Well run by Emile, friendly, with excellent food.
Relais Sainte Marie Nice bungalows for 35,000Fmg.

Tour operator

Look out for **Nord-Est Nature**, run by Pascal Bonneton, a Frenchman, who is planning to develop tourism in the area. Contact details (although I have not succeeded in contacting him): BP 9; tel/fax: 53 333 80.

CONTINUING NORTH (IF YOU DARE!)

From Soanierana-Ivongo the road is unreliable, to say the least. As fast as bridges are repaired they wash away again. You may have a fairly smooth taxi-brousse ride with ferries taking you across the rivers, or you may end up walking for hours and wading rivers or finding a *pirogue* to take you across. You should get local advice before setting out, especially if you have a lot of luggage to carry or are on a tight schedule.

Rupert Parker, who drove from Mananara to Toamasina in 1998, reports on the conditions then: 'There are many ferries and bridges to cross. The last but one ferry (ie: the second one if driving north from S-Ivongo) is also dependent on high tide to work so you can have to wait up to six hours. The other problem is that ferries are only supposed to work in the hours of daylight, so you have to bribe the ferry men if you are travelling outside these hours, as well as having to send a boy in a *pirogue* to find them, as they're always on the opposite side of the river to you.' I have had no recent reports but have no reason to believe that the situation has changed much.

Andrangazaha

There is just one reason to stop at this little place midway between S-Ivongo and Manompana: Madame Zakia. 'Madame runs the best place north of Tamatave. All vehicles going north stop there to eat. Why? Because Madame feeds the drivers for free, passengers pay. Her food is excellent, bungalows clean with mozzie nets, away from the noise and bustle of town in the bush where you can wait for a lift in quiet comfort.' (Paul and Sarah McBride). Note: this report dates from several years ago so don't make the journey specially!

Manompana

For many years this village, pronounced 'Manompe', was *the* departure point for Nosy Boraha/Ile Sainte Marie. Because of a spate of recent accidents there are no longer scheduled services to Sainte Marie, but you can find a private boat to take you over. Beware of *pirogues*, however, which are too small to cross the reef safely.

Around Manompana there is good surfing and swimming, and a small reserve, run by ADEFA, who have an office in the village. As well as guiding you in the reserve, they will take you on a tour of the village, showing a number of interesting things: the bakers oven, coffee being dried on mats, vanilla pods drying in glass coca-cola bottles, sea cucumbers drying on mats before being shipped over to Japan to end up in sushi. You also see how they make their very bitter local drink, *betsa-betsa*, which is made in a week using sugar cane juice and has about the same alcohol percentage as wine. A team from Edinburgh University went there in 2001 to study the effects of deforestation on chameleons; I am grateful to Andrew Willis for the new information incorporated here.

Where to stay/eat
Chez Lou Lou Central; 6 beachfront A-frame bungalows, very clean, good toilets, good seafood.

Chez Wen-ki's Far end of town; 5 spacious beachfront bungalows for only 25,000Fmg. Bucket shower (cold water). Secluded, superb food. Laundry service. Mountain bikes for hire.

Mahle Hotel On Mahle Point, 1km from the village. 'Run by an incredibly friendly brother and sister team, the punch coco was the best we tried!' The food is also excellent. This is a very beautiful, oceanfront place with good diving and lovely nearby forest.

Ambodiriano reserve
This was set up by two school teachers from Réunion in the mid 1990s, and is now run by the local community, ADEFA (Association de Défense de la Forêt d'Ambodiriano). The small (65ha) reserve incorporates three dramatic waterfalls, above which shelters have been set up for picnics or overnight camping. If you have your own tent it's worth spending the night in order to search for chameleons (always easier by torchlight) and to get the best dawn birdwatching. You may also see lemurs.

MANOMPANA TO MAROANTSETRA
Antanambe
Some 35km north of Manompana, on the edge of the UNESCO biosphere project, is this pretty little town and a French-owned hotel (four bungalows) which has everything: gas cooking, filtered running water, pressure showers and flushing toilets with soft paper, comfortable beds with mozzie nets; all this plus a superb restaurant with Creole and French cooking and fresh fish daily! Not surprisingly, it's already very popular, and being expanded. Alain and Céline Grandin arrange tours in the Mananara biosphere reserve, and diving and fishing excursions to a vast reef 1km from the hotel. The 1998 price (I have no up-to-date reports) was 60,000Fmg per bungalow and 25,000Fmg for a three-course meal. There is no way to contact Alain and Céline in advance, but it's worth taking pot luck and simply turning up.

There is just one problem with this otherwise idyllic place: 'When we were there we were attacked by tiny black sandflies which leave nasty red spots which take weeks to go away – they can cover your body in these in a matter of minutes and it's wise to be careful (we weren't...!) Apparently it is a seasonal problem so you might be lucky.' (Rupert Parker)

Permits to visit the reserve can be bought for 50,000Fmg in the ANGAP office adjacent to the hotel and it takes about two hours to walk to the entrance. It's

A SACRIFICE TO THE ANCESTORS
Andrew Willis

We were invited to a *Fête de Zebu* in Manompana one weekend. Apparently one of the men in the village had cut down a sacred tree and built his house nearby. This had offended the ancestors, and he was obliged to hold a large party and invite as many members of the village as he could afford. When we arrived at about 9am, several hundred people were already sitting around a zebu, lying on its side with its legs tied together, in the owner's sandy back garden, drinking *betsa-betsa* from banana leaf 'cups'.

The village elders stood in a semicircle behind the zebu and the man who had cut down the sacred tree was gently hitting the cow with a stick and chanting something. Presumably he was asking for forgiveness from the ancestors. Then the zebu's throat was slit and its head cut off. This was pointed to the east, with a glass of honey and a glass of *betsa-betsa* placed in front of it for the ancestors. While the rest of the zebu was cooking in oil drums, women started to dance and people kept on drinking till the early hours of the next day.

possible to stay overnight in the park in huts but you will need a guide from the town. A nice day excursion is to walk to the edge of the park and skirt round it to a spectacular waterfall which has cold clear pools for swimming.

Mananara-Nord

Mananara, 185km north of Soanierana-Ivongo at the entrance to the Bay of Antongil, is the only place in Madagascar where one can be pretty much assured of seeing an aye-aye in the wild, on Aye-Aye Island. The hotel of choice is **Hotel Aye-Aye** on the beachfront opposite the airport, which has bungalows with shower but shared WC. The Malagasy owner, Oliver, offers island tours and other excursions.

Other hotels include the once recommended **Chez Roger** (for which I have no recent reports) or **Ton-ton Galet**, a friendly, modest set of bungalows located near the hospital.

Transport is usually advertised in the big Chinese shop in the square.

What to do in and around town

There is more to do in Mananara than Aye-Aye Island and a visit to the biosphere reserve. There's a lively market, a good disco at weekends and the ocean for relaxation. Three kilometres south of the town is a beautiful bay protected by a reef, with shallow, safe swimming.

Aye-Aye Island

Visitors who imagine Aye-Aye Island to be a chunk of pristine forest are in for a shock: 'Sharing the island with the aye-ayes are the warden and his family, dogs, chickens, pigs and a pet lemur. But seeing an aye-aye is almost guaranteed. On the night we visited we saw a mother and her baby. The warden was very entertaining and obviously very fond of, and proud of, his aye-ayes. It was a wonderful experience.' (R Harris and G Jackson)

Visits to the island are best organised by the Aye-Aye Hotel. The cost is around 40,000Fmg.

Mananara National Park and Biosphere Reserve

This example of eastern rainforest has been described by John Dransfield of Kew Gardens as 'The Biosphere's Botanical Paradise'. To visit it you need a permit from the Biosphere office in Mananara-Nord or from ANGAP in the access town of Antanambe. And a lot of enthusiasm. The most interesting parts of the park are in the interior, and there are no good trails.

It is quite challenging to do the park on your own. The most interesting part of the park is inland. You drive to **Sandrakatsy** by taxi-brousse (the first one leaves at 08.00 and the journey takes about two hours) and then walk for 1½ hours to **Ivavary** where there is accommodation for park (Biosphere) visitors. From here to the park is a further 1½ hours.

Mananara to Maroantsetra

To continue the journey north is an adventure, but that's part of the attraction.

In the early 1990s the intrepid Luc Selleslagh set out in a small boat: 'On the way the sea got rougher and rougher, the waves twice as high as the boat... I thought we were going to end between the sharks. The five other passengers were all sick. I was too afraid to be sick. Finally the captain decided to return!' After that Luc set out on foot. The bridges across the rivers sounded almost as dangerous as the sea but at least he was master of his fate. After two days and one lift he reached **Rantabe** from where there is at least a vehicle a day heading for Maroantsetra. Luc warns that even in ideal conditions it takes at least eight hours to go the 110km.

In 1998 Rupert Parker did the trip by 4WD vehicle. 'The road is the worst I've ever experienced but also the most spectacular. It hugs the coast climbing up and down through virgin forest right down to the sea, affording stunning glimpses of cliffs and deserted bays if you can divert your attention from holding on for dear life. It took us four hours to do the 40km. There are ferries, broken-down bridges and some sections of the route which are like giant's staircases – huge boulders haphazardly scattered over steep inclines. Definitely mission impossible, but because of that the forest is largely uncleared and it's one of the most beautiful areas in Madagascar.

I have had no reports since then – where have all the adventurous backpackers gone?

MAROANTSETRA AND THE MASOALA PENINSULA

Despite difficulty of access and dodgy weather, this is perhaps the leading destination for ecotourists who want to see Madagascar's most important natural habitat in terms of biodiversity – the eastern rainforest, exemplified by Nosy Mangabe and the Masoala Peninsula.

These places require fitness and fortitude but the rewards, for nature-lovers, are great. Fitness is needed for the hills and mud which are an aspect of all the reserves, and fortitude because this is the wettest place in Madagascar, with the annual rainfall exceeding 5,000mm. The driest months tend to be November and December.

Maroantsetra

Nestled at the far end of the Bay of Antongil, Maroantsetra is Madagascar at its most authentic. Well away from the usual tourist circuits, it is a prosperous, friendly and sleepy little town, with enough comfortable hotels to make a visit a pleasure for both packaged and independent travellers.

Getting there and away
By air
Most people fly. Consequently flights tend to be booked well in advance. At present flights go on Tuesdays, Thursdays, Fridays and Saturdays, but check latest schedules/availability with Air Mad. The airport is 8km from town.

By land and sea
You can come on foot (and occasional vehicle) from Mananara or hike from Antalaha (see page 279). The cargo boat from Ile Sainte Marie no longer serves Maroantsetra.

Where to stay
Relais du Masoala Bookings: cortez.expeditions@simicro.mg. 300,000Fmg. 15 spacious, palm-thatched bungalows set in 7ha of gardens and coconut groves overlooking the Bay of Antongil. Described proudly as 'Malagasy huts with American bathrooms', the rooms contain beds which are extra long to accommodate large *vazahas*, the showers work, and the covered verandas overlook the bay. There is a swimming pool and the food, including picnic lunches, is excellent. The Relais runs tours to Nosy Mangabe (with optional camping overnight), birdwatching in the Masoala Peninsula, *pirogue* excursions up river, whale-watching, and many other trips including a newly set up visit to the village women of Navana (see page 276). Near the hotel is a small forest where aye-aye are occasionally seen. The guide Julien (brother of Maurice and Patrice of Périnet) takes guests on night walks and other excursions here.

Motel Coco Beach BP 1; tel: 18. Bungalows on the outskirts of town. En-suite with cold water 90,000Fmg, shower but no WC 70,000Fmg. Meals in the spacious dining room are of variable quality. The former owner, Patrice, died in 2000 but his wife, 'Madame Patrice', continues to run the place. One attraction of Coco Beach are the striped tenrecs running about in the garden at night. A 'fixer' who calls himself Rakoto Vazaha can be found here and is highly recommended by Helen Ranger: 'Rakoto organised a boat and permits for Nosy Mangabe, and took me shopping in the market for food, and helped us get to Masoala.'

Hotel Vatsy Newish bungalows and older rooms at a reasonable price. Small restaurant. Recommended.

Hotel du Centre Across from the market offering inexpensive rooms and bungalows. 'I rather like this place. The bungalows are modest but well-kept and in a tidy garden. The

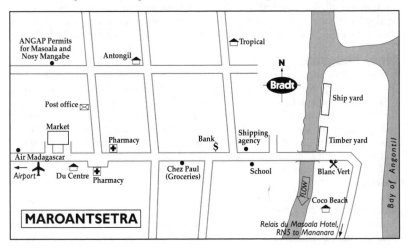

MAROANTSETRA

location is excellent and I would recommend it without hesitation to travellers on a tight budget.' (MR). This hotel has the added bonus that the manager is president of the Maroantsetra hoteliers.

Hotel Maroa Nice bungalows with showers etc. Excellent food, but slow service. Good value at about 65,000Fmg per room.

Eating and making merry

Readers recommend the **Chinese restaurant** across from the gas station which serves wonderful seafood. **Pagode de Chine**, near the market, is also good. 'Must recommend the **Blanc Vert** restaurant over the river bridge towards Hotel Coco Beach. Excellent prawns au poivre vert' (Helen Ranger). Also look for 'a particularly good bakery' by Coco Beach near the gas station.

'There's a brilliant disco called the Calypso. Very friendly. Should be 2,500Fmg entrance but *vazahas* get charged 5,000Fmg. Great atmosphere. The people still do a couple of the traditional dances as well as jive' (Katie Bloxam).

Excursions
Andranofotsy and Navana

This very worthwhile tour is a *pirogue* trip up the Andranofotsy river to the village of the same name. The vegetation and riverlife viewed on the way are fascinating, and the unspoilt (so far) village, with its inquisitive inhabitants, is delightful. This excursion can be arranged through the Relais du Masoala, or independently.

Equally worthwhile is a visit to Navana. Follow the coast east along a beach backed by thickets, through waterways clogged with flowering water-hyacinth and past plenty of forest. You need to cross a lot of water on a *pirogue*, a regular local service. It takes an hour through little canals and costs very little.

You can also enjoy an insight into local village life by joining a tour called 'A day in the life of the Malagasy Women', set up by the Relais de Masoala hotel. 'In the morning we take our group (or individuals for that matter) by boat across the bay to Navana where they join the women fishing along the shore, teaming up a Malagasy and a *vazaha*. We then walk through the village to the coffee plantations, cloves, vanilla or rice fields depending on the time to the year and the activity taking place at the time. In June we go to the coffee fields, pick the coffee and then go through all the stages that coffee goes through until it becomes a cup of Starbucks. Visitors seem to greatly enjoy the entire experience, being in touch with the local women and contributing directly to the economy of the village.'

Nosy Mangabe

In fine weather the island of Nosy Mangabe is superb. It has beautiful sandy coves, marvellous trees with huge buttress roots and also strangler figs. And it's bursting with wildlife including, of course, its famous aye-ayes which were released here in the 1960s to prevent what was then thought to be their imminent extinction. If aye-ayes are what you're after, there's little point in coming here just for the day (they are nocturnal) but there is plenty to see on a day visit, including the weird and wonderful leaf-tailed gecko, *Uroplatus fimbriatus*.

There is no accommodation on the island – you must camp in the thatched shelters.

Getting there and away

To visit the island you must have a permit. They are available from the Projet Masoala office near the market in Maroantsetra. A guide is mandatory. Information

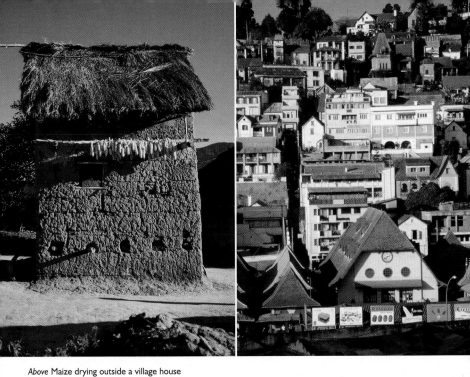

Above Maize drying outside a village house
near Toliara (HB)

Above right Antananarivo (HB)

Below Aerial view of a Merina fortified
village on the approach to Antananarivo (CP)

Above Rice paddies near
Andringitra (NG)

Below Trekking in Andringitra
National Park (BS)

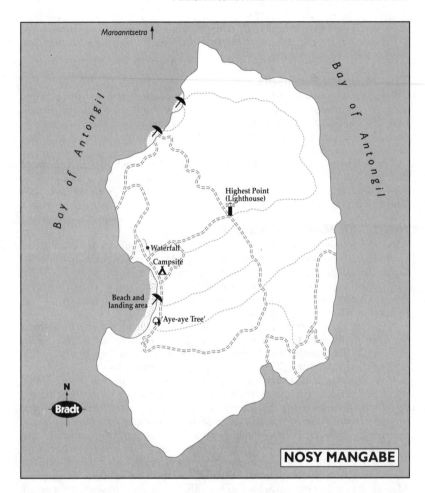

on boat hire may be available from the Motel Coco Beach. However, there is also the option (risky) of going by *pirogue*. All boats leave early in the morning when the Bay of Antongil is calm. It takes 45 minutes (by motorised launch) to Nosy Mangabe. Don't forget to bring sunscreen and drinking water. It is not easy to find a safe, affordable boat. Ask at the ANGAP office.

Exploring the island

Not everyone sees aye-ayes; the best time to view them is between June and September, when they come right down to the trees by the shore to feed. But there is a wealth of other creatures: white-fronted brown lemurs, black-and-white ruffed lemurs – these are quite difficult to see, but you will hear them – green-backed mantella frogs, and reptiles such as the marvellous *Uroplatus*, chameleons and snakes. The trails have recently been upgraded and walking, though strenuous, is not difficult.

To complete your experience of Nosy Mangabe climb the hill to the lighthouse. En route you will have the chance to see all sorts of reptiles, invertebrates, as well as other sights, sounds and smells. It's a magical island. In rain, though, the paths are slippery and it's pretty unpleasant. And it rains often.

As you leave Nosy Mangabe the boatman will often take you to see some old (15th-century) inscriptions carved on some rocks on the shore. Fascinating! And there is also a recent shipwreck.

The Masoala Peninsula

The peninsula (pronounced 'Mashwahl') is one of the largest and most diverse areas of virgin rainforest in Madagascar, and probably harbours the greatest number of unclassified species. Any scientific expedition here hits the jackpot – for example a Harvard biologist identified 100 species of ant in Masoala alone, many of them new to science.

The peninsula's importance was recognised by the French back in 1927 when they gave it reserve status, but independent Madagascar was swift to degazette it in 1964. However, in the 1990s it received protection and finally National Park status. The park now covers 410,000ha.

How to visit Masoala National Park

Masoala can only be reached by boat, which takes 3–4 hours from Maroantsetra. For independent travellers, finding a safe but affordable boat is the main difficulty. Up to 1,600,000Fmg has been quoted, and that's just for the boat. Go to the ANGAP office and ask for the president of the ecotourist guides in Maroantsetra, Armand Marozafy. He may be able to provide the *Serendipity*, donated by the City of London School in 1999, at a much lower cost.

If you are a keen naturalist and can afford an organised tour, take the one offered by Relais de Masoala to Lohatrozona, currently the best site for wildlife on the peninsula. Other hotels may also offer tours. At Motel Coco Beach you can find Rakoto Vazaha (see page 275) who will organise the trip for you.

Even the most ardent supporters of Masoala will agree that protection within the park has not been entirely successful. Sadly, this means that **Ambanizana** (pronounced Ambani<u>zan</u>) the gateway village, has spread its cultivation – and hunting activities – so far that now much of the day is spent just hiking the 7km to the forest. Once there, the wildlife is quite shy. The preferred centre is now **Andranobe**, 7km further along the coast, but even this is not safe from the logger's axe: 'During our afternoon walk south of Androbe, we heard someone cutting down a tree. All our guide could do was report the incident. Tragic place. Man's gotta eat, but does man have to bribe the government minister for a permit to cut down the ebony trees, leaving the local peasants wondering why they can't cut down the trees too?' (Helen Ranger)

Andranobe is the centre for the research organisation, the Peregrine Fund, and has a more extensive system of trails. Even better than Andranobe is **Lohatrozona**, about 5km to the south. There is a trail from Andranobe or you can reach it in 20 minutes by canoe. The forest a short walk behind the beach is wonderful – very good for red ruffed lemur, helmet vanga and ground-rollers. Even Bernier's vangas can be seen. Nocturnal walks are also rewarding.

If you opt to go to Ambanizana, you can still have a rewarding time. There are palm-thatched shelters here which provide extra protection from the frequent torrential rain. There is room to pitch tents under these. There are beds, and providing you have a good mozzie net you won't need a tent. But there are *lots* of mosquitoes! The village of Ambanizana is a peaceful collection of bamboo and palm-thatched huts and, although my former description of it being hassle-free is, sadly, no longer true, it's still a lovely example of a peaceful, car-free village.

There are snorkelling possibilities around the coral reefs off Masoala but never go into the water without checking on safe areas with your guide; the Bay of

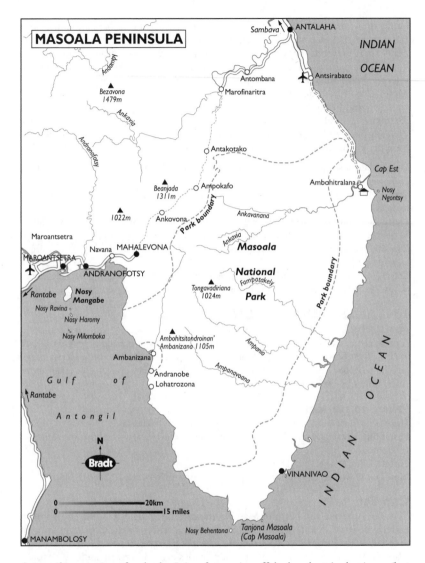

Antongil is notorious for sharks. It is safe to swim off the beach at Ambanizana (but there is no coral).

Walking from Maroantsetra to Antalaha

I have heard mixed reports of this five-day hike. The distance is 152km, and in the heat it is very strenuous. Considering that you are mainly passing through secondary forest and cultivated areas, it doesn't attract me as much, say, as hiking the scenically marvellous road from Mananara to Maroantsetra. However, many people want to do it, and will be faced with the choice of going it alone or hiring a guide and porters.

Luc Selleslagh walked alone in the early 1990s. He says the path is well used by local Malagasy and if you become confused you should just wait for someone to come. Abandon any idea of keeping your feet dry. A tent is useful in emergencies (and a mosquito net, or at least mosquito coils, essential) but there are houses you can stay in and meals will be cooked for you for a reasonable charge. The villagers may expect presents. They may also expect medicines. Be cautious of introducing – or perpetuating – expectations here. Independent walkers should buy the relevant FTM map, *Antalaha*. If you failed to buy it in Tana there is one in the Motel Coco Beach which you can trace.

Angus and Philippa Crawford, who did the trip in 1999, point out good reasons for taking a guide and porters: 'If you take neither guide nor porters you lay yourself open to hustlers who insist on accompanying you, and you also deprive local people of work. And the route is by no means obvious…'

Day 1 Maroantsetra to Mahalevona, the village beyond Navana, which is described under *Excursions*. A pleasant 5km walk.

Day 2 Mahalevona to Ankovona. The track climbs into the mountains and there are rivers to cross.

Day 3 Ankovona to Ampokafo. A long trek to Ampokafo which marks the halfway point. Very hilly and very beautiful, with lots of streams and orchids. The village has a small shop.

Day 4 Ampokafo to Analampontsy. Less wild, but still orchids along the way. Most villages en route have shops.

Day 5 Analampontsy to Antalaha. You emerge on to the road at the village of Marofinaritra, about 30km from Antalaha. From here you can get a taxi-brousse to Antalaha.

ANTALAHA AND BEYOND
Antalaha
A prosperous, vanilla-financed town with large houses and broad boulevards. There are excellent beaches nearby, making this a very pleasant place to spend a day or so.

The road to Sambava is rough in places, with one ferry crossing. It takes about three hours by taxi-brousse.

Where to stay/eat
Hotel Florida Tel: 813 30. The best hotel, with air conditioning and hot water.
Hotel du Centre Tel: 811 67. In the centre of town, European run, comfortable with good meals.
Hotel Ocean Plage Tel: 812 05.
Hotel Le Cocotier Tel: 811 77.

Cap Est
South of Antalaha and north of Masoala, the coastline bulges to Madagascar's most easterly point, Cap Est. An upmarket hotel, **La Résidence du Cap**, consisting of seven thatched bungalows, has received much praise from readers. Run by George, a South African, and his wife Magali, it provides everything you could wish for in Madagascar: rainforest, beach and wonderful food. 'A delightful spot… George organises fishing and snorkelling trips in his boat and it's safe to swim because it's protected by a reef.'

The hotel costs €37 per person per night (full board) single, or €30 double. Boat transfers from Antalaha are €137 round trip'.

The postal address is BP 206, Cap Est, Antalaha. Reservations can be made in Antalaha at the hotel's office, tel: 813 27. In Tana book through Eco-Tour; tel/fax: 22 262 81; or Silver Wings; tel/fax: 22 210 79 or tel: 22 200 92.

Getting there the hard way
Rupert Parker stayed at Cap Est in 1998 and reports: 'There is a boat to Ambohitralanana (the nearest village to Cap Est) once a week which takes the locals –

ANTALAHA AND BEYOND 281

VANILLA IN MADAGASCAR
Clare and Johan Hermans

Vanilla is the major foreign currency earner for Madagascar, which together with Réunion and the Comoros grows 80% of the world's crop. Its cultivation in Madagascar is centred along the eastern coastal region, the main production centres being Andapa, Antalaha and Sambava.

The climbing plants are normally grown supported on 1.5m high moisture-retaining trunks and under ideal conditions take three years to mature. When the plants bloom, during the drier months, the vines are checked on alternate days for open flowers to hand-pollinate. The pod then takes nine months to develop; each 15–20cm pod will contain tens of thousands of tiny seeds.

The pods are taken to a vanilla processing plant to begin the long process of preparing them for the commercial market. First they are plunged into a cauldron of hot water (70°C) for two minutes, and are then kept hot for two days. During this time the pods change colour from green to chestnut brown. At this stage they are exposed to the sun (mornings only to avoid over-cooking) for three to four weeks.

After maturing, the pods are sorted by size; the workers sit in front of a large rack with 'pigeonholes' for the different lengths. The bundles of sorted pods, approximately 30 to a bunch, are tied with raffia. They are checked for quality by sniffing and bending before being packed into wooden crates with 90% of the product going to the USA for use in the ice-cream industry.

The vanilla used in cultivation in Madagascar is *Vanilla planifolia* which originates from Mexico. It was brought to Madagascar by the French once the secret of hand pollination had been discovered – the flower has no natural pollinator in its foreign home. The culinary and pharmaceutical use of vanilla dates back to pre-Aztec times when it was used as a drink or as an ingredient of a lotion against fatigue for those holding public office. Similarly a native Malagasy vanilla stem can be found for sale in the *zoma* in Tana as a male invigorator.

Four different species of vanilla orchid occur naturally in Madagascar, most of them totally leafless. One species can be seen on the roadside between Sambava and Antahala resembling lengths of red-green tubing festooned over the scrub, another is to be found in the spiny forest near Berenty in the south. Most of the native species contain sap that burns the skin and their fruits contain too little vanillin to make cultivation economic.

Uses for vanilla pods

Although conventionally used for cooking, vanilla is also an insect repellent or the wonderful-smelling pods can be put in drawers instead of the traditional pomander to scent clothing or linen.

When cooking with vanilla you can reuse the pods for as long as you remember to retrieve them – wash and dry them after each use. Vanilla does wonders to tea or coffee (just add a pod to the teapot or coffee filter, or grind a dried pod with the coffee beans) and can be boiled with milk to make a yummy hot drink (add a dash of brandy!) or custard. If you take sugar in tea or coffee put some beans in your sugar tin and the flavour will be absorbed. Vanilla adds a subtle flavour to chicken or duck, rice or… whatever you fancy.

a sort of marine taxi-brousse – with all the same risks and this costs 20,000Fmg per person. Enquire in Antalaha. There is also a Project Masoala research boat which makes the trip – enquire at their office in town. The other alternative is to walk from Antsirabata, south of Antalaha – it takes around 12 hours – or hire bikes. We did the bike trip and the track is very rough; we ended up pushing the bikes most of the way, but you pass through many villages where you can get basic supplies – even beer. We left Antalaha around noon and it took about six hours – it was very hot and I would not recommend doing it at this time of day. We came back with the local boat which was piled high with people, cases, supplies and our bikes on the top. The boat journey takes about four hours and can be rough. Because the boat is piled so high, it is a potentially dangerous situation – George from the hotel provided us with life jackets, just in case.'

SAMBAVA

The centre of the vanilla and coconut growing region, and an important area for cloves and coffee production, Sambava merits a stay of a few days. The town is charming, the people are friendly and easy-going, and there is plenty to see and do.

Telephone code The area code for Sambava is 88.

Getting there and away

Sambava has air connections with Tana, Toamasina and Antsiranana, and is accessible by good road from Iharana (Vohemar), taking approximately two hours. The airport is not far from town: you can even walk it if you are a backpacker. Be warned, however, that Sambava is a sprawling town with long distances between most places. The taxi-brousse station is on the northern outskirts, 30 minutes from the centre (shops, post office) and beach hotels are 10–15 minutes beyond that.

Where to stay/eat
Category A
Hotel Carrefour BP 53; tel: 60. Situated near the beach, with all mod cons (hot water, air conditioning). Good food.
Le Club Plage (bungalows) BP 33; tel: 44. A posh hotel (two-person bungalows) overlooking the sea with a swimming pool. Also **Hotel Le Club** with conventional rooms. Hotel Le Club offers a choice of several tours, including trekking; they provide transfers to and from the airport, 4WD vehicles with driver, and mountain bikes.
Las Palmas BP 120; tel: 87. Nicely situated by the beach, well run with conscientious and friendly staff. €28 (double), €25 (single). Hot water but poor water pressure. Good food. Air-conditioned rooms and bungalows. The hotel offers a variety of excursions, such as the Bemarivo river.

Category B
Hotel Esmeralda BP 113; tel: 128. This is the backpackers' favourite Sambava hotel, pleasantly located with rooms and bungalows overlooking the ocean. Cold water only; en-suite WC.
Hotel Cantonnais Tel: 124. A hotel rather than beach bungalows, but in a quiet part of town and most rooms have balconies. There are five rooms with toilets; hot water (with good pressure). Good value. The Chinese owner also sells precious stones.
Nouvel Hotel Good value and recommended for its food.

Category C
Chez M Jaoravo Six rooms on the left side of the cemetery, on the main road. Rooms very hot but clean. Cold water.

Hotel Pacifique Tel: 124. Three rooms, also bungalows.
Hotel Calypso BP 40; tel: 108. An unassuming, reasonably priced hotel in town.
La Romance North of the taxi-brousse station.

All the restaurants at the above hotels serve good meals. Specialist restaurants include **Cantonnais** and **Mandarin** (Chinese) and the **Etoile Rouge** and **Etoile Rouge Annexe**. The latter is said to serve the better food.

For do-it-yourself meals head for the *épicerie* to the right of the cemetery. Prices and staff are more user-friendly than in the supermarket.

Things to do
In and around town

Sambava itself is one long main street with parallel dirt roads, so you won't get lost. There is a good **market** which is known as **Bazaar Kely**, not because it's small or *kely* (it isn't – and certainly not on Tuesdays, market day) but because there used to be two markets and no-one thought of changing the name when they amalgamated them.

As this is one of the main vanilla-producing areas in Madagascar, a tour of the **vanilla factory**, Lopat, is interesting and teaches you a lot about the laborious process of preparing one of Madagascar's main exports. Likewise a visit to the **coconut plantation** (*germoir pépinière*), some 3km south of the airport, is more rewarding than it sounds. You need a permit and a guide so it's easiest to go on an organised tour arranged by one of the hotels.

The highlight for us, however, was a visit to CLUE, the Center for Learning and Understanding English. This lively place was set up by the Peace Corps and welcomes visits from tourists to help the (adult) students practise their spoken English and understanding of a variety of accents. For the visitors it's an excellent chance to learn from the people of the east coast. CLUE is on the main street (you can't miss it) and you should look for Patrice, the Malagasy English teacher. Don't miss this opportunity to do something for cross-cultural understanding. 'A wonderful experience.' (Anne Axel)

North of Sambava is a beautiful beach with safe swimming, and marvellous *Nephila* spiders on their golden webs between the branches of the shady trees.

Excursions further afield

The tour operator Sambava-Voyages (BP 28a; tel: 110) offers a variety of excursions including Marojejy National Park and the trek from Sambava to Doany. The manageress, Mme Seramila, speaks some English.

River Bemarivo

A pleasant do-it-yourself excursion is up the Bemarivo, though this won't be possible at the end of the dry season – the river is very shallow. Take a taxi-brousse to Nosiarina, on the road north, and look for a *pirogue* to take you the five-hour journey up-river to Amboahangibe. Anne Axel paid 25,000Fmg for five people plus gear. 'It's a beautiful river trip. The river is wide and there are some small villages that you pass periodically. However, the land by the river has been deforested.'

It is also possible to find a cargo boat to Amboahangibe. This is quite a large village with several grocery stores and some houses with rooms. Look for the sign 'Misy Chambres'. These fill up with vanilla-pickers during the harvest. Anne Axel found the last room in town, at the **Hotel Fandrosoana**. 'It had a captive crocodile in the yard next to the WC.' As an alternative to taking a boat back, it is a pleasant hike along the river, with some interesting above-ground coffins and groves of shady giant bamboos.

CONTINUING NORTH

The road to the next town of importance, Iharana (Vohemar), is excellent and transport is no problem (about two hours). For a description of this pleasant town see *Chapter 14*, page 340.

ANDAPA AND AREA

Andapa lies in a fertile and beautiful region, 108km west of Sambava, where much of Madagascar's rice is grown. This is also a major coffee-producing area and it was to facilitate the export of coffee that the EEC provided funding for the building of an all-weather road in the 1960s (see box). This remains one of the best roads in Madagascar. The journey to Andapa is most beautiful, with the jagged peaks of the massif of Marojejy (now a thrilling new national park) to the right, and bamboo and palm-thatch villages by the roadside. The journey takes about three hours by taxi-brousse.

Where to stay

Hotel Vatasoa (pronounced 'Vats') BP 46; Andapa 205; tel: 39. Comfortable (but sometimes noisy) rooms with hot water cost around 80,000Fmg. The food is amazing (but a set meal and not good for vegetarians) and the hotel has all sorts of pluses. There is a large detailed map on the wall of the lounge which shows footpaths and tracks in the area (actually, a reproduction of the FTM 1:100,000 which can be purchased in Tana). For hikers this is invaluable for planning (see *Excursions*). The Chinese owner, Mr Tam Hyok, is 'Mr Andapa'. This dynamic man likes to take a personal interest in his guests and their plans, and will accompany those whom he feels will most benefit from his attentions.

Chez Tam Hyok About 15 minutes' drive towards Sambava is Mr Tam Hyok's pièce de résistance: his own house and some bungalows under construction overlooking arguably the most beautiful mountain view in Madagascar. Free-range lemurs (white-fronted and crowned lemurs) leap around the trees, and flowering shrubs blaze against the dark green of the Marojejy massif. Bureaucratic problems have slowed down the work on these bungalows. For information enquire at the Hotel Vatasoa in town.

Hotel du Centre Basic clean rooms, but a 'less than pleasing WC. Wear sturdy shoes; not for the weak of heart or poor of bowels'. No shower, but acceptable overall.

Where to eat

Mini-Restaurant On the opposite side of the street to the Vatasoa, about a block down the road. Popular with locals and WWF employees.

Restaurant au Bon Plaisir One block away from the taxi-brousse station, on the same street as Hotel du Centre. 'Our favourite *hotely*. We would place an order for a vegetarian meal several hours in advance and they would have it ready at the appointed hour. They never baulked at our requests although they became more bizarre as the weeks went by.' (Anne Axel)

Services

There is a good **pharmacy** with a reliable supply of antibiotics. The **post office** cannot really cope with *vazaha* mail. 'It helps if you know the basic cost of mailing letters and postcards home. Buy the biggest envelope you can to accommodate the numerous, small-denomination stamps – and don't forget the glue stick.' The two **banks** won't change travellers' cheques, only cash. There's an **airport**, but no planes; and there's an Air Mad office.

FOREIGN AID IN ANDAPA

Before 1963, Andapa's only link with the rest of the island was through Air Madagascar's flights to Sambava and Antalaha. This made the export of its cash crops, vanilla and Robusta coffee, prohibitively expensive. The newly-independent government, under President Tsiranana whose tribal roots (Tsimihety) were the same as those of the people of Andapa, applied to the EEC for funding to build a road to the coast. Also at the request of the government, a European team carried out a thorough agronomic survey and census of the region in the early 1960s, which led to 20 years of agricultural development overseen by a Belgian agency.

The initial achievements were considerable. Traditional hill rice (dependent on rain so with low productivity) gave way to irrigated rice paddies, served by a pumping station and irrigation channels. Thus 3,000ha of land were brought under cultivation. The hand-plough was replaced by more efficient zebu-hauled ploughs, and fertilisers and improved seeds were introduced. The same expertise was put into improving coffee production, and after ten years the previous yield of 300–450kg per hectare had risen to over 2,000kg/ha for some farmers.

In modern times Andapa has retained some of this prosperity, but the high yields have fallen victim of Madagascar's malaise: deforestation. The once-verdant forests that encircled the Andapa Basin have been depleted and smoke rises from the new areas of *tavy* hacked out by land-hungry peasants. Topsoil has poured into the rivers which feed the pumping station, clogging the machinery and causing the closure of the station. Less rice means more poverty which means more deforestation. The story of Madagascar.

Excursions

This is a wonderful area for wandering. At every step you see something interesting from the people or wildlife perspective (in the latter category butterflies, snakes and chameleons) and the scenery is consistently beautiful.

Mr Tam Hyok will have suggestions for more organised sightseeing, including the local **cemetery** where the dead are interred in coffins above the ground or in the trees.

Hiking

By using the map in the Hotel Vatasoa you can plan a variety of day hikes. Almost any dirt road through villages would bring you the pleasures we experienced on our hike a few years ago. Here are some of the highlights: chameleons in the bushes, coffee laid out to dry on the ground, an entire school of shrieking kids surging up the hill towards us, a village elder matching his stride with ours in order to converse in French, little girls fishing with basket-nets in the irrigation channels, home-made musical instruments, smiles, laughter and stares. It helped that we had our local guide with us who could interpret the village activities. In one place we experienced the power of Malagasy oratory (*kabary*) at full throttle. The theme was communal work. The 20 or so men of the village listened respectfully as the Président du Fokontany exhorted them to contribute their labour towards the building of a new fence. Some young men demurred: they would rather pay the let-out fee of 2,500Fmg. The Président discussed the issue with them, explaining the importance of the community working together. By the end of the discussion the young men had started stripping the leaves of a raffia palm to bind up the bamboo poles and begin fence-making.

If you explore off the beaten path, just remember the enormous power you have to change things irreversibly. Your gift or payment will certainly be received with delight and will make you feel warm inside; but will it benefit the village in the long run?

PROTECTED AREAS

In the last decade the area around Andapa has opened two of its most exciting reserves to visitors. The recently gazetted Marojejy National Park and Anjanaharibe-Sud Special Reserve are at the heart of one of WWF's main Integrated Conservation and Development Projects. For the first five years these areas are being administered by the WWF regional office in Andapa, but soon ANGAP will take over the reins. WWF are very keen to develop ecotourism in this infrequently visited part of the country. Both places lack the well-made paths and tourist infrastructure found in the popular parks and reserves: the few paths are narrow and often very steep – these are some of the most remote and pristine rainforests remaining on the island – and visitors need to be fit and willing to put up with a fair degree of discomfort.

Anjanaharibe-Sud Reserve

The Anjanaharibe-Sud Special Reserve/Befingotra Forest region, some 20km southwest of Andapa, is an easier option than the magnificent but challenging new national park of Marojejy. Anjanaharibe-Sud can be equally rewarding for naturalists with sufficient time to seek out the shy wildlife. This is the most northerly range of the indri which here occurs in a very dark form – almost black. The silky sifaka is also found here, but you are more likely to see the troops of white-fronted brown lemurs. Birders will be on the lookout for four species of ground-roller.

Even without seeing any mammals it is a most rewarding visit, with an easy-to-follow (though rugged) trail through primary forest to some hot springs. The reserve is also a vital element in the prosperity of the area. The Lokoho River, which rises in Anjanaharibe-Sud, is the *only* source of water for the largest irrigated rice producer in the country.

Befingotra and Andasibe

If you are making your own way to the reserve you will spend some time in these two gateway towns looking for ongoing transport. Befingotra has a couple of *épiceries* with basic supplies (rice, beans etc) and there is a small restaurant. Andasibe is the larger town with several *épiceries* and *hotelys* offering a reasonable range of food.

Visiting the reserve

A permit to visit the reserve can be obtained from the Hotel Vatosoa. Mr Tam Hyok can arrange a day visit to Anjanaharibe-Sud, or you can look for another private vehicle for hire in Andapa but it is possible and rewarding to visit it on your own. Camping is permitted and allows you to get the most out of your stay. Anne Axel, who made four lengthy visits to the reserve in 1998, recommends two tough, but inexpensive ways of getting there: 'one is to take a taxi-brousse to Andasibe, the last town on the decent road, from where it's a steep two-to-three-hour hike to Befingotra, then another two to three hours to the trailhead; or from Andapa or Andasibe wait for a truck heading for Bealanana and have them drop you off at the reserve'. A guide is not mandatory, but these days the trailhead is very hard to find,

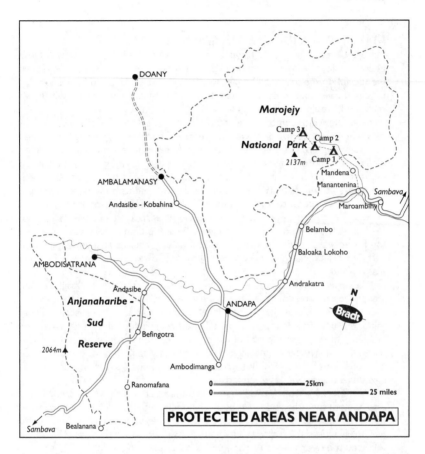

PROTECTED AREAS NEAR ANDAPA

so you will probably need to be shown where to enter the forest, and where to find water near the campsite.

If you merely need to be shown the way, and get help carrying gear, look for a guide and/or porters in Andasibe or Befingotra. Be warned, however, that they are unlikely to speak French. Serious naturalists should seek out Gaston Rabemanana, who works for the WWF and is being trained by them as a tourist guide. The Hotel Vatasoa should know where to find him. Gaston will also arrange for transport to the trailhead.

When I was there in 1997 the trailhead was indicated with a nice WWF board: 'Piste Touristique de Ranomafana Source Thermal à 4,260m' giving the time needed for the return trip as being five hours which is roughly right, although it does not allow much time for examining, watching and listening. Or photography. I don't know if the sign is still there.

The path is clearly marked – the trees are tagged with coloured tape: orange indicates the route to the hot springs, and other colours, with metres written on them, show the distance to the campsite – it takes about an hour of brisk walking. The hot springs are an hour beyond the campsite. From the road the trail follows an up-and-down route, slippery at times, but full of interest. On our rather fast day trip we saw no mammals, but campers should see brown lemurs and perhaps indri. John Kupiec reports: 'When you get to the river area it is hard to find the springs

MAROJEJY – A JUNGLE EXPERIENCE, 1976

Marojejy was to be the highlight of my first visit to Madagascar. I had fallen deeply in love with the country, and here was a reserve that looked so wonderful on the map – all brown swirling contours and green forest, with no roads for miles and miles. The map showed a path running across it which, we reckoned, would take two days to walk.

As we flew into Sambava we could see the green peaks of Marojejy poking up through a covering of cloud. But there was something strange: it looked as though a box of matches had been strewn over the soft crumpled landscape. There had been a cyclone the previous week which had felled numerous huge trees as well as destroying much of Sambava. Unperturbed, we hitched towards Marojejy. A shopkeeper offered us his floor for the night and an introduction to a representative from the Département des Eaux et Forêts. To our relief we now had the required permit but we had mixed feelings when he said he was coming with us. He didn't really seem dressed for a two-day backpacking trip: he had no luggage apart from a briefcase carrying his official papers, a clean shirt and three hats. He was wearing plastic sandals.

We would never have found the way ourselves. The narrow trail climbed steeply up the mountain to a large stone which marked the edge of the reserve. Our Man then told us that he had never actually walked in the reserve. Never mind, the trail was clear and we made good progress, until the first fallen tree blocked our way. For the rest of the day we scrambled over or crawled under trees. Our heavy packs unbalanced us, the heat debilitated us, and sweat ran into our eyes. That night we cooked a sumptuous supper. It had been a strenuous day so we deserved a treat.

Next morning we followed the path to the river, which we crossed. There was no path the other side. We boulder-hopped after Our Man as he followed the river upstream. With a heavy pack this was very tiring, and we asked plaintively where the trail was. He didn't know. Should we turn back? No, if we followed the river we would soon find another path. We didn't.

The river entered a canyon, impossible to boulder-hop or even to wade. We climbed the steep, slippery clay sides, hanging on to lianas and hauling ourselves up to the overhanging jungle. I learned later that the high-altitude rainforest in Madagascar is the densest in the world. I believe it. Without a machete to slice away the vegetation we could only move very slowly. The forest floor – what we could see of it – was composed of moss-covered logs and spongy leaves. Each step was a false step, the rotting matter giving way and plunging us into hidden holes. When we grabbed at plants or branches they hit back. There were plants that stung, plants that stabbed and plants that sliced. Blood soon mixed with the sweat that ran down our bodies. Huge trees, toppled by the cyclone, blocked our passage. Their overhanging branches harboured fire-ants which dropped down our necks when we crawled underneath. I started to cry.

Back at the river, we sat down to consider our situation. We were lost. The map didn't make sense, Our Man was silent. We turned our attention to our blotched and blood-streaked arms and legs. Fat leeches were fastened to our ankles and between our fingers. Since I refused to turn back and repeat the cliff and jungle trek, the only course was to follow the river. The map showed it winding towards Ambatobe, our destination. We no longer cared about wet boots nor safety when we crossed the river on moss-slippery tree trunks. Your sense of balance seems much better when you don't much care whether you live or die.

After 12 hours of unmitigated effort we stopped for the night. Wordlessly we set up the tent and cooked the last of our food: soup followed by tea and raisins. We were up at dawn. Knowing the rigours ahead, we drank our tea and ate our three raisins in even deeper gloom. The first six hours were the same as the previous day: slither, trip, sweat and push our way through water and jungle with no lunch to give us renewed energy. Then, in the early afternoon, Our Man shouted in delight. He was pointing to a human footprint in the damp sand by the river. Robinson Crusoe's heart cannot have lifted as did ours at this sign that our ordeal could be coming to an end. A few hours later we saw the sight we had long dreamed of – a solitary hut on the mountainside above the river.

The climb up was one of the hardest yet and we were bitterly disappointed to find the hut had long been abandoned. Still, there were some edible plants growing in the garden and Our Man was thrilled to find tobacco. He also found some other tasty food, collecting a bag full of large weevils. They were delicious roasted, he said. Supper was an almost cheerful occasion. We ate boiled leaves, Our Man coughed happily over his home-made cigars, and we found one last teabag at the bottom of my pack. We didn't roast the weevils.

Our mood was shattered again the following morning when we topped the hill above the hut and saw, not a village, but miles and miles of unbroken jungle. Six hours later we reached a trail but felt none of the anticipated elation. We were too tired. We just trudged onward until a voice greeted us from behind. We sat down and let Our Man and the woman chatter away. 'She knows my family,' he told us excitedly. 'My wife is wondering where I am!'

The woman led us to her hut and we lay down on the palm-leaf mats while the family regarded us with gratifying respect and sympathy as Our Man told our story. Each newcomer was entertained with an ever lengthier version. Then a huge bowl of rice was brought in, along with several kinds of vegetables. Feeling almost human we set off along the path to Ambatobe. With Civilisation at hand we realised the appearance we presented: our clothes had been wringing wet with rain and sweat for four days, we were covered in dried blood from scratches and leech bites, and we stank. When we came to a stream we motioned to Our Man to go ahead. With clean bodies and fresh clothes we approached the village. The inhabitants were all lined up on each side of the path, hands outstretched, shouting 'Salama! Salama!' 'Salama!' we grinned, shaking the outstretched hands. It seemed a huge population for such a small village. Then we realised that the people at the the back of the line were running to the front for a second go.

Reverently we were guided to the biggest hut where we found Our Man already enthroned and talking. The room filled with people and we smiled and nodded as the epic journey was described. It had the audience enthralled. Our Man was evidently a master of the art of storytelling. Then supper arrived. They had killed a chicken in our honour, so we had not only rice and greens, but chicken stew. Then came a plate of what looked like large peanuts. The weevils! They had a pleasant nutty flavour. The next day two youths were enlisted to carry our packs and we almost floated along the trail to the road. We arrived in under two hours, having covered about the same distance that we'd achieved in the previous three days.

without someone to show you. There are three: one is too hot to keep your feet in; another is shallow but it meets a stream which makes it easier to take; the third is a pool to swim in which also merged with stream water.'

Marojejy National Park
This stunningly beautiful national park was established in 1998. It is not for the faint-hearted but the rewards are high – there are few other areas in Madagascar to compare with Marojejy for awesome splendour and the feeling of ultimate wilderness. Imposing mountains and craggy cliffs are surrounded by lush rainforests full of wildlife.

Visiting the park
The tour operator Sambava-Voyages (see page 283) will organise excursions to Marojejy, complete with tents, porters and guides, food etc. Independent travellers should arrange their visit through the WWF in Sambava.

Once only open to self-sufficient campers, Marojejy now has basic accommodation – simple huts with bunk beds – at the first two camps, but you must bring your own food. There are three campsites at different altitudes, so with their own distinctive flora and fauna. Nick Garbutt, who has spent an enviable amount of time in Marojejy, has provided the following report.

'Access is via the village of Manantenina on the Sambava to Andapa road, from where it takes about two hours to walk to the park boundary through rice paddies and cultivated areas, with a further two hours to Camp Mantella (Camp 1), situated in the heart of superb lowland rainforest. Here you stand a good chance of seeing helmet vanga (*Euryceros prevostii*) and various ground-rollers. You may also see white-fronted brown lemurs. Camp Mantella (400m) has washing cubicles and a proper flushing loo. There is a communal dining area.

'Camp 2 (750m) is a further hour's walk and lies at the transition between lowland and mid-altitude rainforest. It sits opposite an amazing outcrop of rock cloaked in rainforest. This is one of the most spectacular views you could ever imagine waking up to. Above this campsite the trail becomes very steep and continues right through all the altitudinal zones to the peak of the Marojejy Massif at 2,137m. The areas above Camp 2 are best for silky sifaka (*Propithecus diadema candidus*). The trail has been improved and there is now a viewing platform at 1,300m, just before Camp 3.

'Camp 3 (1,380m) is nothing more than a handful of cleared tent pitches on a ridge top. The forest here is more stunted because of the altitude, but is still good for silky sifaka, and birds such as rufous-headed ground-roller and yellow-bellied sunbird-asity. The frogs in the nearby stream are diverse and abundant.

'The camp is used to facilitate walks to Marojejy peak (2,137m) – a four to five-hour climb It's one of the most spectacular walks I've ever done – fantastic views over rainforest-clad ridges, amazing mountains and above the tree line bizarre moorland-type habitat. There are dwarf palms (30cm high) with little chameleons in them. The view from the top is awesome and the feeling of space and wilderness is the greatest I've experienced. But it's very tough and only for those who are extremely fit.'

291

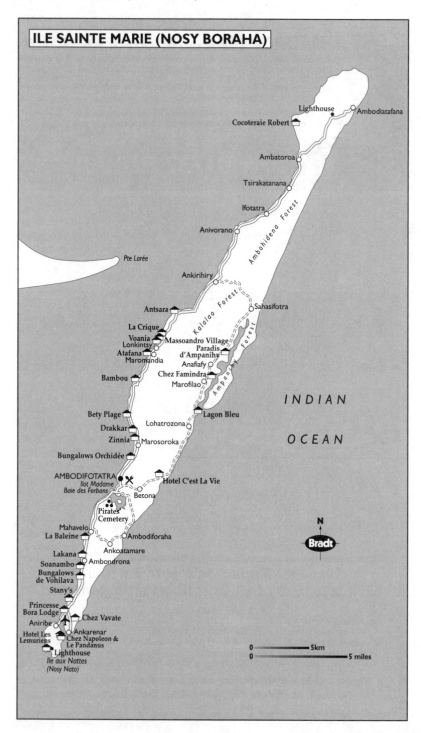

ILE SAINTE MARIE (NOSY BORAHA)

Lighthouse
Ambodiatafana
Cocoteraie Robert
Ambatoroa
Tsirakatanana
Ifotatra
Anivorano
Ambohidena Forest
Pte Larée
Ankirihiry
Antsara
Sahasifotra
Kalalao Forest
La Crique
Voania
Massoandro Village
Lonkintsy
Paradis
Atafana
d'Ampanihy
Maromandia
Anafiafy
Bambou
Chez Famindra
Marofilao
Ampanihy Forest
INDIAN
Bety Plage
Lagon Bleu
Drakkar
Lohatrozona
OCEAN
Zinnia
Marosoroka
Bungalows Orchidée
AMBODIFOTATRA
Ilot Madame
Hotel C'est La Vie
Baie des Forbans
Betona
Pirates
Cemetery
N
Mahavelo
La Baleine
Ambodiforaha
Bradt
Ankoatamare
Lakana
Soanambo
Ambondrona
Bungalows
de Vohilava
Stany's
Princesse
Bora Lodge
Chez Vavate
Aniribe
Ankarenar
Hotel Les
Chez Napoleon &
Lemuriens
Le Pandanus
Lighthouse
Ile aux Nattes
(Nosy Nato)

0 ————— 5km
0 ————— 5 miles

Ile Sainte Marie (Nosy Boraha)

OVERVIEW

Ile Sainte Marie is 50km long and 7km at its widest point. The only real town is Ambodifotatra (pronounced 'Amboodif<u>oo</u>tatr'). Other small villages comprise bamboo and palm huts. The island is almost universally known as Sainte Marie – few people use its Malagasy name. Here is a cliché of a tropical island with endless deserted beaches overhung by coconut palms, bays protected from sharks by coral reefs, hills covered with luxuriant vegetation, and a relative absence of unsightly tourist development. Most travellers love it: 'As soon as we saw the island from the air, we were ready to ditch our travel plans and spend the rest of our trip nestled in paradise. Everything about the island is intoxicating: the smell of cloves drying in the sun, the taste of coco rum and the warmth of the sea.'

Sainte Marie unfortunately – or perhaps fortunately, given the dangers of overdevelopment – has a far less settled weather pattern than its island rival, Nosy Be. Cyclones strike regularly and you can expect several days of rain and wind all year round, but interspersed with calm sunny weather. The best months for a visit seem to be June and mid-August to November, although a reader tells me she twice had perfect weather in January, and another reports that in July most days were sunny and hot, but with frequent light rain overnight or in the morning, and fairly strong winds from the south.

For an all-inclusive package to Sainte Marie, with various options for excursions and transport by boat from Soanierana-Ivongo, contact Sainte-Marie Loisirs, BP 3650, Isoraka, Antananarivo; tel/fax: 22 611 40; email: corossol@malagasy.com. Bookings can also be made through soanambo.tana@simicro.mg.

Telephone code The area code for Ile Sainte Marie is 57.

History

The origin of the Malagasy name is obscure. It means either 'Island of Abraham' or 'Island of Ibrahim', with probable reference to an early Semitic culture. It was named Ile Sainte Marie by European sailors when the island became the major hide-out of pirates in the Indian Ocean. From the 1680s to around 1720 these pirates dominated the seas around Africa. There was a Welshman (David Williams), Englishmen (Thomas White, John Every and William Kidd) and an American (Thomas Tew) among a Madagascar pirate population which in its heyday numbered nearly one thousand.

Later a Frenchman, Jean-Onésime Filet ('La Bigorne'), was shipwrecked on Sainte Marie while escaping the wrath of a jealous husband in Réunion. La Bigorne turned his amorous attentions with remarkable success to Princess Bety, the daughter of King Ratsimilaho. On their marriage the happy couple received Nosy

Boraha as a gift from the king, and the island was in turn presented to the mother country by La Bigorne (or rather, put under the protection of France by Princess Bety). Thus France gained its first piece of Madagascar in 1750.

GETTING THERE AND AWAY
By air
Air Madagascar flies every day from Tana and Toamasina to Sainte Marie, using either ATR42 or Twin Otters. All flights are heavily booked, especially in July and August, and you should try to make your reservations well in advance. Make sure your hotel reconfirms your return flight (or do it yourself at the Air Mad office in the north part of Ambodifotatra).

By boat
A motor launch runs between Soanierana-Ivongo, at the end of the surfaced road north of Toamasina, and Ambodifotatra. The service is daily (not Sundays), except when the weather is bad when you may have to wait up to a week. The boat leaves Ambodifotatra (Ilot Madame) at 08.00 and S-Ivongo at about 10.30. The trip takes 2½ hours.

In 2000 the *Samsonette* sank, with the loss of 27 lives. When it is back in service it is fast and usually reliable. A more basic boat is *Le Dugong* (but like its namesake it may now be extinct). Find out if it's still running at the restaurant Le Barachois in Ambodifotatra, Sainte Marie, or in S-Ivongo. This boat waits to fill up with passengers, so the schedule is erratic.

You can usually get a private boat (not a *pirogue* – too risky) to Manompana.

Getting around the island
There is a taxi-brousse service, at least up the west coast. Prices are higher than on the mainland (about 10,000Fmg from the airport to Ambodifotatra) but they will sometimes pick you up at a pre-arranged time. Look out for the cheaper *taxi asaka*, yellow taxi-brousse. Once or twice a week it goes as far as Cocoterie Robert (about 120,000Fmg). It's worth flagging down any vehicle. Most will stop and charge the standard rate.

Most hotels have bikes for rent (the French for mountain bike is VTT). You'll pay around 50,000Fmg per day. Bikes are cheaper at Ambodifotatra. You can see quite a lot of the island by bike, but don't reckon on covering much ground – the roads are very rough and most bikes in poor condition (check the brakes!).

You can hire motorbikes opposite the Hotel Soanambo and mopeds are also available in Ambodifotatra.

WHERE TO STAY AND EAT
Almost all Ile Sainte Marie's hotels are ranged along the west coast of the island, with only a few in the east or on Île aux Nattes in the south. Prices here are for high season; almost all hotels offer reduced rates – as much as half price – during the low season.

Note: Most hotels have their own vehicles and meet the incoming planes. If you are not pre-booked you will need to make a quick decision: once the vehicles have departed you may be stuck at the airport. But check with the driver that there is room at their hotel before climbing aboard.

If you are on a tight budget beware of staying at one of the distant hotels. You will be obliged to buy their (often pricey) meals and transport will be expensive.

West coast hotels

These hotels are listed in geographical order, from south to north. Their price/quality category is given in brackets.

Chez Vavate (*Category C*) BP21; tel: 401 15/16. 6 rooms/bungalows. On first appearance an unprepossessing collection of local huts built on a ridge overlooking the airstrip. Don't be taken in by first impressions, the food here is wonderful (the *punch coco* also ensures that you spend your evenings in a convivial haze) and the relaxed family atmosphere makes this a very popular place with young travellers. The only catch is you must walk 1½km from the airport. There is no road, and the 'courtesy vehicle' is a man with a wheelbarrow! If you miss him take the wide grassy track which runs parallel to the airstrip then veers to the left up a steep hill.

Princesse Bora Lodge (*Category A*) BP13, 515 Ile Sainte Marie; tel/fax: 40 147; email: bora@dts.mg; web: www.princesse-bora.com. Half-board prices per person from 270,000Fmg (4 people sharing, low season) to 550,000Fmg (single, high season). Within walking distance of the airport, but transfers are usually through zebu-cart. Owned by François-Xavier Mayer, whose family has been on Ste Marie for over two centuries, this beautifully designed new hotel with bungalows for two or four people has been recommended by several readers. 'Can't recommend this place enough. The food (3-course set dinner) is superb. François is passionate about conserving whales in this part of the Indian Ocean and runs serious whale-watching trips (100,000Fmg each)' (F Donovan & A Callow). The hotel runs a private plane service from Tana in the high season (700,000Fmg one way). Mountain bikes for hire. Credit cards accepted.

Bungalows de Vohilava (*Category B*).Tel/fax: 401 40; email: vohilava@malagasy.com. Bungalows about 3km from the airport. 135,000Fmg (single), 225,000Fmg (double). There is a restaurant but these are mainly self-catering with fully-equipped kitchens; suppliers come daily to sell fresh food. For bookings contact: Sainte-Marie Loisirs in Tana.

Stany's Bungalows/Bungalows Mayer (*Category C*). About 10km south of Ambodifotatra, 20 minutes up the road from the airport. Adequate bungalows. Nice view looking out to sea. Bush showers and toilet. Very helpful and friendly owner.

Soanambo (*Category A*) BP 20; tel: 401 37; fax: 401 36; email: soanambo@dts.mg. 3km from airport, 10km from Ambodifotatra. €43 (single), €61 (double) for a comfortable bungalow; €51 or €68 (single/double) for de luxe rooms. Lovely garden with *Angraecum* orchids and a terrace bar/restaurant from which you can watch the whales. Swimming pool. Bicycles available for hire. Credit cards accepted.

Lakana (*Category B*) BP 2; tel: 401 32; fax: 401 33; email: lakana@fyd.mg; web: www.lakana.com. 5km from the airport. 6 simple but very comfortable wooden bungalows, including 4 perched along the jetty; From 130,000Fmg to 195,000Fmg; breakfast 12,000Fmg. Mountain bikes for hire. Visa cards accepted.

La Palourde (*Category C*) Tel: 403 07. 4 clean bungalows on the beach with en-suite cold shower; hot water on request. 60,000Fmg. The Malagasy/Mauritian owner is a great cook, especially if meals are ordered in advance.

Hotel La Baleine (*Category C*) Tel: 401 34. About 7km from the airport, 8 rustic bungalows owned by Albert Lanton. Communal bathroom with cold water. Very good food. With the proceeds of the hotel, Albert sponsors a youth football club and other local projects The only negative point is that the beach is not particularly nice here… but who cares?

Bungalows Orchidée (*Category A*) Tel: 400 54. Located 3km south of Ambodifotatra, 12km from the airport. 10 bungalows, 4 double rooms. €38 double; breakfast €4; dinner €9. Hot water, air conditioning, water sports, excursions. Bookings may be made in Tana, tel: 237 62/270 15; fax: 269 86. Also in Tamatave: tel: 333 51/337 66. Credit cards accepted.

Manaus Gargotte (*Category C*) 3 basic bungalows (home-made) with outside toilets; located between Vanilla Café and Orchidée. 20,000Fmg. Clean, friendly, with terrific food for 27,000Fmg.

Hotel Zinnia (*Category C*) Tel: 400 09; fax: 400 32. Right by the harbour wall at Ambodifotatra. 6 bungalows at about 25,000Fmg for a double, with hot water, fans and outside flushing toilet. Good, neat and pleasant restaurant with excellent food and 'the best coffee on Sainte Marie'. Mountain bikes for hire at 25,000Fmg a day.

Hotel La Bigorne (*Category C*) Tel: 401 23. About 200m south of the Air Madagascar office in Ambodifotatra. A good bar/restaurant which also has one room and two bungalows in the back garden. Friendly, recommended.

La Falafa (*Category C*) Tel: 400 50. This restaurant in Ambodifotatra (good food) also has a few inexpensive rooms. 'The walls were paper thin and I heard everything within a one block radius, including the disco across the street. Additionally, I heard rats scurrying around all night.' (Anne Axel)

Le Drakkar (*Category C*) Tel: 400 22. 1km north of Ambodifotatra. Simple bamboo bungalows with cold shower. Rooms from about 25,000Fmg. The main building is an old colonial house with lovely décor and a sitting/dining room on the water's edge. Convenient for an early morning boat departure.

Ilot Mouettes (*Category B*) Tel: 401 00; cellphone: 032 02 369 37. 4km north of Ambodifotatra. 4 bungalows set in 24ha including its own beach. 5-person bungalow 125,000Fmg, 2-person bungalows 50,000Fmg. Prices do not include meals. Family-run by Françoise and Renée, a local couple; very friendly (but no English spoken!), terrific food.

Hotel Bety Plage (*Category A*) 6km north of Ambodifotatra. Beautifully landscaped, but the position right by the road is not perfect. Noisy generator. From ∈ 15; breakfast ∈ 3, dinner ∈ 8.

Hotel Bambou (*Category C*) Between Ambodifotatra and Loukintsy. Inexpensive beach huts, with a superb view of the sunset over a pristine sandy bay – and friendly. Recommended.

Atafana (*Category C*) BP 14; tel: 401 54. Two sets of bungalows, about 15 minutes from each other, about 4km south of La Crique, well run by the Noel family. Described by some as having the best location, on a private bay, with good food and very friendly. Rooms with baths (hot water) are 100,000Fmg; cold-water shower and wash basin are 80,000Fmg. Camping is permitted for 10,000Fmg. Communal flushing toilets. Power comes from a generator until about 21.00. Excellent swimming at the northern beach. Residents can rent two mountain bikes and a rowing *pirogue*. 'Best budget hotel on the island.'

Hotel Voania (*Category C*) Roughly 200m from the Atafana. On a clean beach, raked every morning to get rid of rocks and flotsam. 18,000Fmg for a basic double bungalow; more for those with a cold shower. Next to the local village, but the newest part is private and secluded. No electricity, but equipped with powerful pressure lanterns. The restaurant is slightly cheaper than Atafana's. The delicious large *crevettes* are recommended, but must be ordered in advance.

Hotel Bon Coin (*Category C*) This hotel at Lonkintsy, with rooms at about 15,000Fmg, is described as 'OK' by Rick Partridge. It's 1km before La Crique, and the last place easily reached by road going north. The only minus point is 'an unhygienic beach'.

Hotel Masoandro Village (*Category A*) Tel/fax: 401 03; email: masoandro@simicro.mg. 12 bungalows, local style, each with a sea view. A lovely location opposite Pointe Larée (just south of La Crique). About 100,000Fmg (double); meals cost 75,000Fmg. Italian-owned. Diving and snorkelling. Excursions to the Forêt d'Ampanihy or camping on Pointe Larée. Mountain bikes for hire. Good English spoken.

La Crique (*Category B*) BP 1. Tel/fax: 401 60 (mornings only); email: lacrique@dts.mg. ∈ 23 single, ∈ 28 double. Deservedly popular, these are bungalows with shared facilities in one of the prettiest locations, 1km north of Lonkintsy, with a wonderful ambience and good (but expensive) food. In September you can watch humpbacked whales cavorting offshore. Often full, so try to book ahead. Electricity from 18.00 to 20.00 only. Transport to/from the airport costs about 40,000Fmg, and there is a regular minibus to town. Mountain bikes available.

Hotel Manga (*Category C*) Manga Gargota, Sainte Therese (BP 515). This recommended budget hotel is about 900m north of La Crique, at the end of the paved road.

Hotel Antsara (*Category B*) 300m north of La Crique. 5 beach bungalows, plus 8 more on a slope further from the sea. Rooms from about 35,000Fmg, with or without WC or bathroom. Excellent Réunionnaise-French hosts. Snorkelling gear available. Has a noisy disco, but only at weekends.

La Cocoteraie Robert (*Category A*) BP 29. In the extreme north of the island, described by one who knows as 'the most beautiful beach in the world', and has recently added 40 more bungalows. ∈ 14 (double). Breakfast ∈ 2, dinner ∈ 6. Transport from the airport is expensive, but a boat goes there from Soanambo (it's run by the same French family). It even has its own airstrip.

East Sainte Marie

Restaurant Bungalows Paradis d'Ampanihy (*Category B*) On the river close to Anafiafy, opposite the Forêt d'Ampanihy. Run by Helène, a Malagasy woman, and her family. A basic bungalow with mosquito net is about 30,000Fmg, more for those with shower. Four-course meals in a beautiful dining room with outside tables and several tame lemurs. A *pirogue* trip across the river to the Forêt d'Ampanihy and back is only about 4,000Fmg per person. Ten minutes' walk to the sea. Recommended by several readers.

Chez Famindra (*Category C*) This is not really a hotel (I've made up the name) but a family enterprise run by a friend of Madophile Rick Partridge. 'Clébert Famindra is a tourist guide (he speaks only French) who lives near Anafiafy on the other side of Sainte Marie in a really peaceful location by the Bay of Ampanihy. I would suggest staying with him and his family for a few days; it's an excellent way to get to know Malagasy people. His prices are inexpensive and negotiable. M Famindra has extra accommodation in the form of two beach-hut type houses a few hundred metres from the sea and river. Conditions are hygienic but not developed (eg: earth privy). He is gradually developing a hotel/restaurant business in addition to his tourist guide activities.

Hotel Lagon Bleu (*Category C*) On the east coast, near Marofilao, 7km from Anafiafy. A smallish cosy site, but clean and peaceful. Complimentary daily *punch coco*.

Hotel C'est La Vie (*Category B*) Nord Ilampy (east coast, more or less opposite Ambodifotatra). A new, South-African run set of bungalows with 'the best views on the island'.

Mora Mora Hotel (*Category A*) Ambodiforaha; tel: 401 14; fax: 400 48. 13 bungalows, 9 with en-suite bathrooms. Half-board 200,000Fmg per person; lunch 50,000Fmg. This Italian-owned place specialises in boat trips to watch whales (US$30) or for watersports including diving. Some visitors have been disappointed that it does not have a beach and is a bit isolated. Airport/town transfers 25,000Fmg.

Boraha Village (*Category A*) Tel/fax: (33) 05 56 68 06 50; email: boraha-village@wanadoo.fr; web: www.boraha.com/index/html. A French-owned hotel with 10 bungalows (doubles). No beach. Specialises in deep-sea fishing.

Ile Aux Nattes
There are several places to stay here – see page 299.

Where to eat
Ambodifotatra
Restaurant La Jardine serves good, inexpensive food and is recommended for breakfast. Home-made hot croissants with hot chocolate, and friendly people. The

Hotel Antsara is recommended for its inexpensive set dinner. **Bar-Restaurant Le Barachois** is across the road from the harbour, next to the ferry booking office, and has 'the most comprehensive menu encountered anywhere'. Quite inexpensive, and the tables on the porch are fine for people-watching.

Anafiafy
Restaurant Bar Bleu gets rave reviews!

Maromandia
Chez Charles 'Very cheap, plentiful food beautifully served by candlelight' (S Blachford). Order in advance.

Ile Aux Nattes
A tradition is a day trip to this little island for lunch. A variety of hotels now serve good food. See page 299.

AMBODIFOTATRA
The town is growing and has several boutiques and a patisserie which runs out of bread in the late morning. The **market** is on Tuesdays and Thursdays. There's a **bank**, open 07.30–10.30, and 13.30–15.00, which will change travellers' cheques. There are **fax and email** facilities at Safan Baleine.

Of the **boutiques**, the Swedish-owned Vohibaranto has been recommended as selling 'the best material for lambas that I saw anywhere' (Robert Bowker).

Sightseeing
There are some interesting sights around Ambodifotatra and the Baie des Forbans which are an easy cycle ride from most of the hotels. In the town itself there is a **Catholic church** built in 1837, which serves as a reminder that Ile Sainte Marie had been owned by France since 1750. As a further reminder of French domination there is a **war monument** to a French-British skirmish in 1845.

The **Pirates' Cemetery** is just before the bay bridge to the town (when coming from the south). A signposted track, not usable at high tide, leads to the cemetery. It takes 20 minutes and you don't need a guide (though it may be hard to shake off the pestering kids). This is quite an impressive place, with gravestones dating from the 1830s, one with a classic skull and crossbones carved on it, but not many graves. There is a 1,000Fmg charge to visit the cemetery.

The **town cemetery** is worth a visit, though it lacks the story-book drama of the pirates' final resting place. The graveyard is about 6km north of Ambodifotatra, at Bety Plage on the right side of the road.

EXPLORING THE ISLAND
The best way to explore Ile Sainte Marie is by bike (hard work), motorbike or on foot. In the low season, if you are fit and energetic, you could walk or cycle around most of the island and take your chance on places to stay. During peak seasons most of the hotels would be full.

Crossing from west to east
Although possible to do on your own, it's easy to get lost so many young men have made a lucrative business of guiding visitors to the Indian Ocean side of the island. Many overcharge and have no information except for the route.

Anne Axel recommends two guides from the village of Maromandia: Lapace and Augustine (who runs a restaurant on the east side so eating there is part of the arrangement). Both are polite, knowledgeable and charge a reasonable amount for their services. Lapace speaks good English and knows many of the plants and birds – and some folk stories. He can also arrange a *pirogue* ride to Anafiafy. The walk across the island takes about 2½ hours. Another starting point for the walk across the island is Antsara. If you take a guide for the island crossing, be sure to agree on the price first.

It is well worth taking a *pirogue* trip to explore the coast around the northeastern peninsula with its Forêt d'Ampanihy: 'The beach was the most beautiful I have ever seen. The colour of the water was a mixture of deep blue and emerald green. There weren't any other tourists – in fact I saw only three other people, fishermen, the whole time I was there. I ate a leisurely lunch then walked along the beach for miles. I would hate to see this place spoiled by tourism – it's so pristine!' (AA). 'A quite dramatic *pirogue* trip along the river, as the trees met overhead to form a tunnel. The *pirogue* will take you to an inlet where the peninsula is at its narrowest, and it's a five-minute walk to the sea on the other side. The coral reef is several hundred metres offshore, so you need another *pirogue* to dive there – diving from the shore is too dangerous because of the tidal flow. Absolutely deserted, with huge trees on the shore and here and there a lone fisherman.' (Jeremy and Lindie Buirski)

The far north
About one hour's walk from La Cocoteraie Robert is a beautiful and impressive *piscine naturelle*, with a waterfall, a big pool and enormous basalt rocks.

Ile Aux Nattes (Nosy Nato)
To many people this little island off the south coast of Ile Sainte Marie is even better than the main island. 'If I were to do the trip again, I'd split my time equally between both islands. Nosy Nato is about as fantasy-islandesque as it gets. Pristine beaches, quiet villages, hidden bungalows, excellent restaurants' (Debbie Fellner). The circumference of the island is 8km, and it takes at least three hours to walk round it. Don't try this at high tide – there are some tricky bits to negotiate past often rough seas.

There is much to see during a short walking tour, including the island's unique – and amazing – orchid *Eulophiella roempleriana*, known popularly as l'orchidée rose. It is two metres high with deep pink flowers.

The best beach is at the north of the island: 'crystal clear, shallow water, calm tide, soft sand – absolute paradise!'

A *pirogue* transfer here from near the airport on Sainte Marie costs about 12,000Fmg round trip.

Where to stay/eat
Maningory (*Category A*) BP 22; cellphone: 032 07 090 05/06; fax: 401 25; email: lem.sces@simicro.mg; web: www.madagascar-contacts.com/maningory. Well-equipped bungalows built in the local style on a nice beach, some facing the sea. 150,000–200,000Fmg; meals in the large, pleasant bar-restaurant 50,000Fmg. Diving school.
Chez Napoléon (*Category A*) Tel: 401 26/7; fax: 401 36. Or (Tana) tel: 22 207 20; fax: 22 677 70. Napoléon, who died in 1986, was a charismatic character who 'ruled' – in various guises – this little island and enjoyed entertaining *vazaha*. Bungalows with en-suite bathrooms are 200,000Fmg (double) and with shared facilities 146,000Fmg. Family rooms are also available. There are no fans, but mosquito nets are provided. There's a restaurant, where Napoléon's famous *poulet au coco* is still served to appreciative diners, even if taped pop music has replaced the sound of wind in the palm trees. Meals are 60,000Fmg. An upgrade is scheduled for 2002.

Le Pandanus (*Category B*) Tel/fax: 401 28; email: lem.sces@simicro.mg. A double bungalow is 70,000Fmg with shared bathrooms. Food a little pricey for what you get.
Bungalows (name not known!) (*Category C*) This budget place is between Chez Napoléon and Pandanus and is very good value for 30,000Fmg with an excellent restaurant.
Hotel Les Lemuriens (*Category B*) 10 comfortable A-frame huts, many with bay views and balconies, at the southern end of the island, about an hour's walk from the Pandanus. Shared bathrooms. There's a nice restaurant here enlivened by a troop of tame ruffed lemurs dedicated to stealing your lunch (meals cost 35,000Fmg).
Chez Regine Readers Nicholas Robson and Juliette Enser rave about this place, well off the beaten track on the western beach of the island. 'Chez Regine consists of three wooden bungalows with no electricity but plenty of candles and on most nights plenty of stars. No hot water, no television, no fridge. Every day Regine cooked us three-course meals of exquisite fresh food. From the dining table we could watch humpbacked whales. The place is hard to find: head west along the beach from the Hotel Pandanus. Once out of the lagoon and around the corner of the island walk south for about ten minutes along the white sand beach until you come to the hexagonal bungalows just before the football pitch. Nine days at Chez Regine cost us 2,000,000Fmg full board!' There seems to be no way of contacting Regine except just to turn up! Worth the risk.

WATERSPORTS AND ACTIVITIES
Snorkelling and diving
The shallows around Sainte Marie are ideal for snorkelling and diving, although the island's inshore waters are overfished by local Malagasy. Lobsters (crayfish) are very much in evidence in and around the reefs, of which there are many, six to ten metres down in clear water and close to Atafana and La Crique. There are also several huge coral 'tables', some nearly two metres wide, but unfortunately a number have been broken off by fish traps.
Bathers should watch out for the vicious spines of sea urchins.

Balenottero Dive Centre Tel/fax: 400 36 (Ambodifotatra) or tel: 22 450 17 (Tana); email: ilbalenottero@simicro.mg; web: www.ilbalenottero.com. Italian owned. Very good equipment, organised dive trips to wrecks off Sainte Marie as well as the coral reefs. Whale-watching, and swimming with the whales! Prices: whale watching €31, diving €31 (10 dives €230).
Maherybe Tel/fax: 401 48; cellphone: 032 07 532 51/906 39; email:maherybe@hotmail.com; web: http://maherybe.cpw.net. Diving instruction at all levels.

The following hotels offer diving:

Club Nautique Princesse Bora Tel: 401 47; email: bora@dts.mg.
Maningory (Île aux Nattes) Tel: 402 20.
Mora Mora Tel: 401 14.

Whale-watching
July to September seems to be the best time to see humpbacked whales; you can watch them from the beach at La Crique or Atafana, or take a boat excursion (offered by many of the hotels and diving clubs).

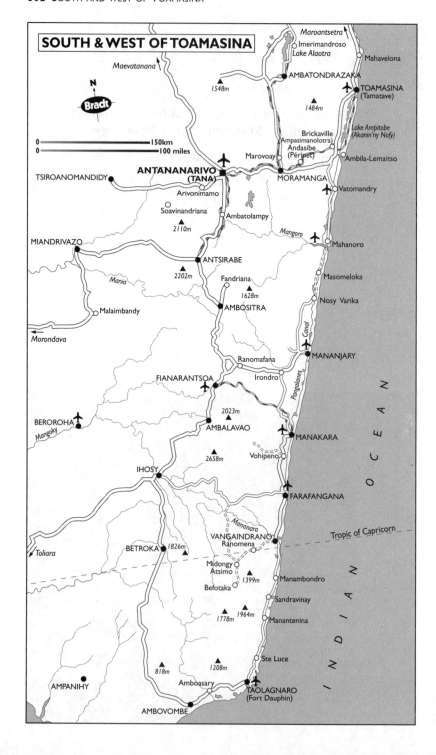

SOUTH & WEST OF TOAMASINA

Bradt

N

0 ———————————150km
0 ———————————100 miles

Maevatanana

Maroantsetra
Imerimandroso
Lake Alaotra
Mahavelona

AMBATONDRAZAKA

1548m

1484m

TOAMASINA
(Tamatave)

Lake Ampitobe
(Akanin'ny Nofy)

Brickaville
(Ampasimanolotra)
Andasibe
(Périnet)

Marovoay

Ambila-Lemaitso

**ANTANANARIVO
(TANA)**

MORAMANGA

Vatomandry

TSIROANOMANDIDY

Arivonimamo

Soavinandriana

2110m

Ambatolampy

Mangoro

Mahanoro

MIANDRIVAZO

ANTSIRABE

2202m

Fandriana

1628m

Masomeloka

Mania

Nosy Varika

Malaimbandy

AMBOSITRA

Morondava

Canal

Ranomafana

MANANJARY

FIANARANTSOA

Irondro

Pangalanes

2023m

BEROROHA

AMBALAVAO

MANAKARA

Mangoky

2658m

Vohipeno

IHOSY

FARAFANGANA

O
C
E
A
N

Mananara

VANGAINDRANO
Ranomena

Tropic of Capricorn

Toliara

BETROKA

1826m

Midongy
Atsimo

1399m

Manambondro

Befotaka

Sandravinay

I
N
D
I
A
N

Manantenina

1778m

1964m

818m

1208m

Ste Luce

AMPANIHY

Amboasary

TAOLAGNARO
(Fort Dauphin)

AMBOVOMBE

South and West of Toamasina

13

OVERVIEW

This chapter incorporates the increasingly visited Pangalanes lake resorts to the south of Toamasina and the most popular national park in Madagascar, Andasibe-Mantadia (still known by most people as Périnet). Also included is Lake Alaotra, shunned by tour groups but quite popular with independent travellers.

The coastal area around Manakara and Mananjary is here, as is the road south to Taolagnaro (Fort Dauphin) which is for the seriously adventurous only.

PANGALANES

This series of lakes was linked by artificial canals in French colonial times for commercial use, a quiet inland water being preferable to an often stormy sea. Over the years the canals became choked with vegetation and no longer passable, but studies are being undertaken on the feasability of re-establishing the unbroken waterway which stretched from Toamasina to Vangaindrano (see box on pages 306–7).

The quiet waters of the canal and lakes are much used by local fishermen for transporting their goods in *pirogues* and for fishing. The canal and ocean are separated by about a kilometre of dense bush, so it is not easy to go from one to the other.

In recent years Pangalanes has been developed for tourism, with lakeside bungalows and private nature reserves competing with the traditional ocean resorts for custom. There's even a shallow-draught canal cruiser, the *M/V Mpanjakamena*, which has six double cabins, sundeck, dining saloon and cocktail bar. The cruiser is operated by Softline, 25 Boulevard Joffre, BP 532 Toamasina (tel: 329 75). They have a contact in Tana, too (tel: 341 75). Although Softline's brochure implies that all 420km of the Pangalanes are navigable, this shouldn't be accepted as fact.

The centre for Pangalanes tourism is **Lake Ampitabe**, which has broad beaches of dazzlingly white sand, clean water for swimming (and only a few crocs which prefer dogs to people!), and a private nature reserve with several introduced species of lemur. The three hotels are in a small village called Ankanin'ny Nofy, which means 'House of Dreams'. Lake Ampitabe is 25km by boat from the village of Manambato on RN2, or there is a 35km track (negotiable by 4WD vehicles) linking the lake and RN2.

Getting there and away
The normal way
Each hotel provides its own transport for booked-in guests. Reaching the lodges on Lake Ampitabe (Ankanin'ny Nofy) from RN2 involves a drive to Manambato, at the edge of Lake Rasoabe, 7km south of Vohibinany, followed by a 45-minute boat

DISTANCES IN KILOMETRES

Toamasina–Vatomandry	190km
Vatomandry–Mahanoro	125km
Mahanoro–Nosy Varika	86km
Manakara–Farafangana	109km

journey along Pangalanes. You can also take a motor launch from the Port Fluvial in Toamasina. The ride takes 1½ hours and is most enjoyable, giving a good flavour of the lakes and connecting canal, and the activities of the local people. It's nice to see the speed boats slow down to a crawl when they pass the laden *pirogues*, to avoid capsizing them in the wash.

The adventurous way

Independent travellers can take a taxi-brousse to Manambato where there is a hotel, and the possibility of hiring a boat or *pirogue* to take them further. Alternatively, take a taxi-brousse to Brickaville and walk along the railway track to Ambila-Lemaitso, which is 60km south of Toamasina and the nearest seaside resort for Tana bourgeoisie.

In 2000 Taco Melissen made his own way to Ampitabe: 'I got dropped off at the intersection just outside Brickaville. You have to know where it is, because it's just a mud track. I walked with a local who showed me the way along the railroad-track. This was nice and only about 12km to Ambila. I wanted to hitch rides through the Pangalanes, but I found this very difficult. I waited for almost a day, but not one boat or *pirogue* was going that way. So I decide to walk. I walked along the beach, which is really beautiful, but you have to bring enough water.

'I thought it would be quite easy to hop across to the Pangalanes canal, but that is very hard because the rainforest is so thick. After about 17km you will find a small village. They even sell water and have a train station. I walked on all the way to Lake Ampitabe. There are plenty of camping possibilities and the beach is beautiful and wild. When I reached the lake I met the owner of Bush House. She was very friendly and let me camp there (which is normally not allowed). It was nice.

'Sonja told me that traffic on the channel hardly exists. It can happen that a freight boat will pass by if building is going on somewhere, and crossing the lakes that lay ahead is very hard work in a *pirogue*. She told there has been an East German guy who canoed 400km along the channel in his own kayak. This was ten years ago.

'Having developed some blisters I accepted the offer to get in the fast

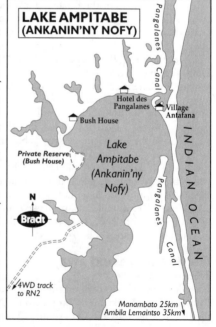

LAKE AMPITABE (ANKANIN'NY NOFY)

Pangalanes Canal

Hotel des Pangalanes
Village Antafana
Bush House

Lake Ampitabe (Ankanin'ny Nofy)

Private Reserve (Bush House)

Pangalanes Canal

INDIAN OCEAN

N
Bradt

4WD track to RN2

Manambato 25km
Ambila Lemaintso 35km

speedboat that was leaving next day to Tamatave. Being on this boat at 60km/h and seeing the local fishermen in their *pirogues*, in the rain with hardly any protection... I felt like an alien.'

Brickaville and Ambila-Lemaitso
Brickaville
Brickaville is one those Malagasy towns which has resisted changing its name, despite the efforts of mapmakers. Rupert Parker offers this clarification: 'Brickaville is the last and only major town before you hit the coast on the way from Tana to Tamatave. You know you've past it when you go over a large iron bridge over the Rongaronga river. It's also got a railway station, which is the last station before Ambila Lemaitso. Everyone, Malagasy included, knows it as Brickaville, but I see from my map that the name is Ampasimanolotra, 134km south of Tamatave.' No one would stay in Brickaville out of choice, but you may get stuck there.

Where to stay
Hotel des Amis 'You wouldn't put your worst enemies there...' (Rupert Parker). But it's cheap.
Hotel Florida 'Near the railway station; at least half-decent but often full.' Bungalows for about 50,000Fmg.
Chez Luigi Manambato (BP8), Brickaville; tel: 56 720 20 This is an upmarket beach resort at Manambato, about 8km north of Brickaville, comprising bungalows, rooms and a good restaurant. Manambato can only be reached on foot or in a private vehicle (on a reasonably good dirt road).

Ambilo-Lemaitso
This is a seaside/canalside resort town, where you can happily get stuck for a day or so. But now the trains are not running it is harder to reach by public transport.

Where to stay/eat
Hotel Relais Malaky Good situation close to the station and overlooking the ocean. Reasonable food. About 100,000Fmg, shared facilities, 150,000Fmg en suite.
Ambila Beach About 3km from the station, overlooking the Pangalanes. Nice bungalows, some with cooking facilities. Good value restaurant, friendly staff. About 60,000Fmg upwards.
Hotel les Cocotiers About 90,000Fmg for self-contained bungalows. Good, but about 3km from the station so a bit isolated.

Lakeside resorts
There are three sets of beach bungalows at Ankanin'ny Nofy (Lake Ampitabe). Quoted prices usually include a double bungalow, plus transfers and meals. Phone the agencies in Tana or Toamasina (details below) for latest prices and availability.

For those wanting a cheaper look at the Pangalanes, there is an additional lodge at Lake Raoabe, near RN2.

Village Atafana Lake Ampitabe; reservations in Tana through the agency MTB, 20 Rue Ratsimilaho (Isoraka, near the Colbert); tel: 22 223 64; postal address: BP 121. 2- to 3-person bungalows on a lovely stretch of beach; excellent meals and excursions.
Hotel Pangalanes Lake Ampitabe; bookings: BP 112, Toamasina 501; tel: 53 334 03 or 53 321 77. 10 2-person bungalows for 181,500Fmg; breakfast 17,500Fmg.
Bush House Lake Ampitabe; book through Boogie Pilgrim, 40 Av de l'Indépendance, Tana; tel: 22 258 78; fax: 22 625 56; email bopi@dts.mg. German-run, comfortable, and in a beautiful situation. 10 rooms. Single 256,000Fmg full board, double 393,800Fmg.

CANAL DES PANGALANES – THE WATER HIGHWAY OF THE EAST COAST

Colin Palmer

I was fortunate enough to go to Madagascar to study the potential for increasing the use of the waterways. Water transport is generally far better from an environmental point of view, yet experience from many countries (Thailand is a prime example) has shown that waterways are all too often overlooked in the rush for 'development' through road building.

A prime place for our study was the Canal des Pangalanes, which offers an exceptional opportunity to provide communications and access for many of the coastal communities of the east coast. That was how I came to be exploring the extraordinary and unexpectedly beautiful waterways of eastern Madagascar. To the south of Toamasina a wild expanse of natural lagoons and waterways fill the low plains behind the surf-pounded beach.

The Canal des Pangalanes was created in colonial times to provide a safe means of transport along the east coast. The shore is surf beaten and the few harbours are shallow and dangerous. The inland water passage provided a safe alternative and around the turn of the century regular ferry services were in operation. The canal interconnected the natural rivers and lagoons, where necessary cutting through the low-lying coastal plain. At intervals it crosses rivers which flow to the sea, providing access for fishermen and ensuring that the level is stable.

The waterways fell into disuse, but in the 1980s a grand project to rehabilitate them was carried out. Silted canals were dredged, new warehouses built and a fleet of modern tug barge units purchased to operate a cargo service. That may once have worked, but now the warehouses and quaysides are empty and the tug barge units lie in a jumbled array in the harbour at Toamasina.

Meanwhile, local people make good use of the waterways. Mechanised ferries run from Toamasina and every house along the way seems to have its wooden *pirogue*. The communities face the water and for many people it is the only reliable means of transport, especially in the wet season. It is also a vital source of livelihood and the stakes of fish traps almost fill the channels, while fields of cassava line the banks. Piles of dried fish, wood and charcoal stand in heaps awaiting collection by the returning ferries. Coming from the town, they

Hotel Rasoa Beach Lake Raoabe, near Manambato; for bookings tel: 22 252 35 in Tana. A friendly hotel offering a good taste of the Pangalanes without the expensive transfers. Accommodation varies from 2-person and 4-person bungalows to a 'Tarzan' hut on stilts. Good food.

Bush House Reserve

This small reserve is no longer owned by Bush House. It is an hour's walk along the beach and well worth the 35,000Fmg entrance fee. Although it's more a zoo than a real reserve in that most of the lemurs have been introduced, they are free-ranging but tame enough to make photographing normally rare species easy and rewarding. There are crowned lemurs, red-bellied lemurs (and a fascinating hybrid of the two), ring-tailed lemurs, black-and-white ruffed lemurs, and Coquerel's sifaka.

In a separate area you'll see chameleons and radiated tortoises, and there is a well-tended garden of succulents.

are overflowing with people competing for space with beer crates, bicycles, sacks of food and all the other paraphernalia of life.

Nowadays, navigation on the canal starts at the Port Fluvial in Toamasina, but it once ran further north. There is a loop that runs around behind the town and connects to the sea, and from there another channel runs north at least as far as the first river, and to Mahavelona according to the map.

From Toamasina, navigation is said to be possible as far as the stretch between Masomeloka and Nosy Varika, where it is blocked by siltation. This may just mean 'blocked' for commercial vessels and perhaps *pirogues* would have no problems. Beyond Nosy–Varika it opens up again as far as Mananjary. The *Cartographia* map shows it continuing almost as far as Farafangana, but there are references that say it goes further, to Vangaindrano. Either way, that's a total distance of more than 600km from Mahavelona. What an adventure to explore the full length!

To travel on the Pangalanes is a joy – well most of it is. Start at Toamasina and you get the worst bit over and done with quickly. Boats leave from the bleak Port Fluvial, with its empty warehouses and jumble of discarded tug barge units.

The first, man made, cut of the canal runs south from the town, past the oil refinery. The air is thick with the smell of hydrocarbons and greasy black outfalls show all too clearly the source of the grey slime that coats the water hyacinth, the only thing that seems to be able to grow. But persevere and soon you start to pass family canoes tied to the bank and the slender, deeply loaded ferry boats pushed by struggling outboard motors. As the water starts to clear, the vegetation recolonises the river bank and the pervasive odour of industrialisation slips away.

The artificial straightness of the first sections gives way to twisting channels and the wider expanses of lagoons and lakes – a world where communities of thatched wooden houses cluster around small landing places, grey rectangles in a canvas of green and blue, delineated here and there by the stark white of sandy beaches.

Those planning an exploration of the Pangalanes in their own canoe should buy maps no 6 and 8 of the 1:500,000 series published by FTM (see page 172). French sea charts also show the canal.

Lac aux Nepenthes

A few kilometres from Bush House. Here there are literally thousands of pitcher plants – a terrific sight!

ANDASIBE-MANTADIA NATIONAL PARK (PÉRINET)

Although still almost universally known as Périnet, this is the new name given to the amalgamation of Analamazaotra Special Reserve and the more recently created Mantadia National Park. Because of its proximity to Tana and its exceptional fauna, Andasibe-Mantadia is now Madagascar's most popular reserve, receiving up to 300 visitors a day. This block of moist montane forest (altitude: 930–1,049m) is exceptionally rewarding for its variety of lemurs, birds, reptiles and invertebrates and – some experts say – a higher number of frog species than any comparable rainforest on earth (although I never manage to see them!). It is also the reserve closest to Tana and consequently the most visited in Madagascar.

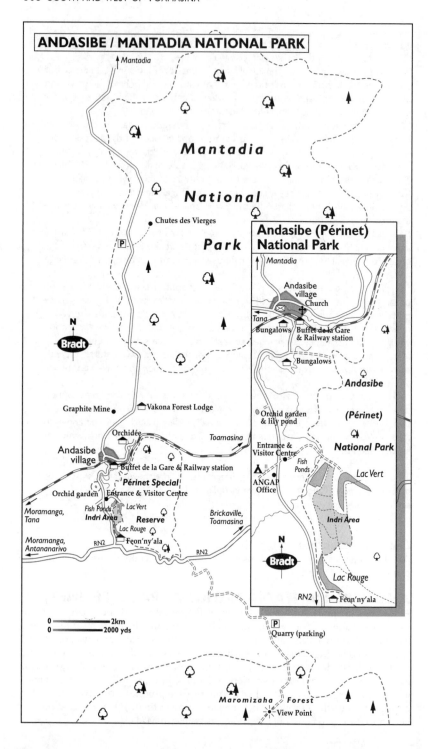

Warning: In the winter months of May to August it can feel very cold here, especially when it rains (as it does at that time of year). Hotels without heaters can be quite an ordeal. Bring warm clothing, adequate waterproofs, and be prepared to sleep in long-johns!

Andasibe village

Few visitors bother to cross the river to look at the village. It's a shame that so little of the tourist revenue has found its way here; you can do your bit by shopping for fruit etc there.

Getting there and away
By train

This railway is set for privatisation, and by the time you read this a train may, once again, be running to Andasibe. At the time of writing it runs intermittently to Moramanga, but beyond that is for freight only. Check with a tour operator or at the station in Tana for the latest information.

By road

The taxi-brousses used on this route tend to be quite comfortable. You will pay less from Tana if you take a taxi-brousse to Moramanga (a regular stop) and a local taxi-be 25km to the Andasibe turn-off from RN2. These, however, tend to be very crowded.

Where to stay/eat

Vakôna Forest Lodge BP 750, Antananarivo; tel: 22 213 94; fax: 22 230 70; email: izouard@bow.dts.mg; web: www.madagascar-contacts.com/vakona. 280,000Fmg (low season) to 330,000Fmg (high season). American breakfasts 28,000Fmg. This is Andasibe's luxury hotel, and is only accessible with your own vehicle. Its location near the graphite mine (same ownership) is not idyllic, but the hotel itself works to perfection. The main building has been thoughtfully designed as an octagonal reception area, bar and lounge-dining room with a huge log-fire in the middle (very welcome in the cold season). The upper storey has a shop. The 14 bungalows are quiet and comfortable and there is a swimming pool. The management is efficient and courteous, and the food delicious. It really is quite something, and deserves longer than the normal couple of days so you can relax and enjoy the swimming pool and some horse-riding, as well as the usual lemur-viewing. By wandering around on the roads near the hotel you will see quite a bit and have the rare pleasure of doing it on your own. To reach Vakôna from Andasibe, cross the bridge into the village, and take the left fork. The hotel is signposted. The Vakôna has its own 'reserve' with black-and-white ruffed lemurs, among others. There's no doubt about the appeal of very tame lemurs jumping on your shoulder, but before you decide to visit, bear in mind that this is in reality a zoo, and eucalyptus trees are not the proper habitat for these animals – which is one reason they are so tame; they have to be fed. There are also unsubstantiated rumours that the lemurs there were trapped in the wild.

Hotel Feon' ny ala Tel: 56 832 02. A total of 30 bungalows, 18 with en-suite bathrooms for 90,000Fmg double, 7 with shared facilities for 60,000Fmg double; continental breakfast 12,000Fmg. Meals 36,000Fmg. Camping area, 10,000Fmg. The name means 'Voice of the Forest'. This popular place is on the right side of the road that runs from RN2 to Andasibe and is favoured by serious naturalists since it's right by the reserve – close enough to hear the indri call (hence its name). The location is superb – overlooking the river with an orchid garden and resident chameleons. The only drawbacks are the lack of heaters in the cold, winter months, and noise: some people complain that the 'voice of the forest' is, at night, the snores of the guests in nearby bungalows. Bring earplugs! The Chinese owners, M and Mme Sum

Chuk Lan, are very helpful and the meals are usually excellent. If you don't want to eat at the hotel you are only a shortish walk from the good snack bar at the entrance to the reserve. **Hotel Buffet de la Gare** Next to the station. Until 1993 this was the only place to stay in Andasibe, and its list of distinguished guests includes Prince Philip, Gerald Durrell and David Attenborough. Built in 1938 it must once have been appropriate for its role of housing the Great and the Good who wished to visit Périnet, but rooms in the main hotel have deteriorated so much that I believe it is now closed. However, the more recently-built bungalows are fine: there are five in a lovely meadow close to the forest about 75m towards the reserve, each has three to four beds and hot water and – what joy! – fireplaces. Less luxurious but perfectly adequate are the seven chalet-type bungalows opposite the Buffet. The dining room in the main Buffet is truly elegant – fresh flowers on the tables and a marvellous rosewood bar. Good food, too. A nice little feature of the dining room is the *phelsuma* gecko which stuck to the new paintwork near the door; the enthusiastic workman simply applied another coat of paint over the little body and there it remains.

Camping
You can camp at the entrance to the park or at Hotel Feon' ny ala . Camping is also permitted by the road in Mantadia.

Permits and guides
You can get your permit from ANGAP in Tana, or at the park entrance (50,000Fmg). The Périnet guides are the best in Madagascar and an example to the rest of the country for knowledge, enthusiasm and an awareness of what tourists want. The Association des Guides Andasibe (AGA) ensures that standards are maintained. All the guides know where to find indri and other lemurs. Those who I can particularly recommend are Maurice and his brothers Luke and Patrice, and sister Marie, along with Lala, Désiré, Eugene, Nirinha, Zac and Jean; but there are other rising stars. The fee is 60,000Fmg for three hours during the day (group of three); 80,000Fmg for four to six hours; 40,000Fmg for a night walk. A visit to Mantadia costs 120,000Fmg. On top of the fee guides expect a tip of around 50,000Fmg per person for two days.

Information and souvenirs
At the entrance to the reserve is a shelter with some information and maps, and nice souvenirs such as T-shirts. There is also a very good snack bar here and a rather splendid toilet.

Andasibe National Park (Périnet)
This 810ha reserve protects the largest of the lemurs, *Indri indri*. Standing about a metre high, with a barely visible tail, black-and-white markings and a surprised teddy-bear face, the indri looks more like a gone-wrong panda than a lemur. The long back legs are immensely powerful, and an indri can propel itself 10m (30 feet), executing a turn in mid-air, to hug a new tree and gaze down benevolently at its observers. And you will be an observer: everyone now sees indris in Périnet, and most also hear them. For it is the voice that makes this lemur extra special: whilst other lemurs grunt or swear, the indri sings. It is an eerie, wailing sound somewhere between the song of a whale and a police-siren, and it carries for up to three kilometres as troops call to each other across the forest. The indris are fairly punctual with their song: if you are in the reserve between one and two hours after daybreak and shortly before dusk you should hear them. They call periodically throughout the morning before settling down to their noontime siesta in the tops of trees.

Indri are monogomous, living in small family groups of up to five animals, and give birth in June. Births usually occur every two years.

In Malagasy the indri is called *Babakoto* which means 'Father of Koto'. It is *fady* to kill an indri, the legend being that the boy Koto climbed a tree in the forest to collect wild honey, and was severely stung by the bees. Losing his hold, he fell, but was caught by a indri which carried him on its back to safety.

There are nine species of lemur altogether in Périnet (including aye-aye), although you will not see them all. You may find the troop of grey bamboo lemurs which are diurnal and sometimes seen near the concrete bridge at Lac Vert, brown lemurs, and perhaps a sleeping avahi (woolly lemur) curled up in the fork of a tree. It is worth going on a nocturnal lemur hunt (the guides are experts at this) to look for mouse lemurs and the greater dwarf lemur that hibernates during the cold season.

Lemurs are only a few of the creatures to be found in Périnet. There are tenrecs, beautiful and varied insects and spiders, as well as reptiles. Sadly the latter are becoming very scarce, as the illegal reptile trade takes its toll. In the old days boys would bring some spectacular Parson's chameleons (bright green and half a metre long) to the trees by the entrance. Now even this artificial display has gone. If you're lucky your guide will leave you while he 'looks' for a chameleon ('I expect he was flipping through the Yellow Pages for the nearest branch of *Chameleons-R-Us*' commented one of my group this year as she viewed his 'find'). However, tree boas are common here and quite placid.

This is also a great place for birdwatching (keen birders should ask for Patrice or Maurice to be their guide). Specials to look out for include the velvet asity, blue coua and nuthatch vanga.

Leeches can be an unpleasant aspect of Périnet if you've pushed through vegetation and it's been raining recently. Tuck your trousers into your socks and apply insect repellent. If a leech gets through your defences a handy supply of salt will persuade it to let go.

Mantadia National Park

This recently created national park is 20km to the north of Périnet. It varies more in altitude (between 800m and 1,260m) than the more popular reserve and consequently harbours different species providing a wonderful addition to Périnet for fit and energetic visitors.

What is so special about Mantadia is that, in contrast to Périnet, it is virtually untouched primary forest. There are 10,000ha with just a few constructed trails – visitors must be prepared to work for their wildlife – but this is a naturalist's goldmine, with many seldom-seen species of mammals, reptiles and birds.

The forest is bisected by the road. On the left is the area for black-and-white ruffed lemurs (*very* hard scrambling) and to the right, if you are lucky, you may see the beautiful golden-coloured diademed sifaka or *simpona* and almost certainly some indri (curiously much darker in colour than in Périnet). Both these lemur species are getting easier to see as they become habituated to humans. This section of Mantadia has some good, if steep, trails with gorgeous views across the forest and super birdwatching possibilities, including specials such as the scaly ground-rollers, pitta-like ground-roller, and red-breasted coua. It really is a terrific place, but you must be in good shape.

There are three main trail areas; the one at km14 is the best for wildlife, but there's an easy, two-hour trail which leads up through the forest to a waterfall and lake (*Cascade* and *Lac Sacré*). Bring your swimsuit for a cooling dip in the pool beneath the waterfall.

To do justice to Mantadia you should spend the whole day there, bringing a picnic, and leave the hotel at dawn. You will need your own transport and, of course, a guide. If you stay until dusk you will find a nocturnal walk up to the waterfall very rewarding.

Torotorofotsy and Ampasipotsy

Torotorofotsy Marsh is being added to the itineraries of birding groups, for the rare endemics such as Meller's duck, Madagascar snipe, Madagascar rail, Madagascar crested ibis, Madagascar flufftail, grey emutail and even the very rare slender-billed flufftail. This is also the only known habitat for the golden mantella frog.

An excursion to Torotorofotsy takes all day – it involves a three-hour walk down the railway track from Périnet. A shorter option, where you will see most of the above birds, is Ampasipotsy, which is only 45 minutes' walk from the main road.

OTHER PLACES OF INTEREST ON RN2

Quite a few hotels and eateries have sprung up in recent years along RN2, so if you have your own vehicle you have a range of possible stopping places.

Antsampanana

If you are driving up RN2 from Toamasina this is a popular place to stop to buy fruit. The little town is bursting with stalls offering all sorts of goodies. Nice for photography, too. If you want to dally longer there is the basic **Hotel Espérance** and some restaurants. From here it is about 1½ hours' drive to Andasibe.

Moramanga

The name means 'Cheap mangos'(!) and this formerly sleepy town is about a half-hour drive from Andasibe. It gained a new lease of life with the completion of the Chinese road (there is a memorial here to the Chinese workers) and, during the 1980s and early '90s, from the absence of comfortable hotels in Andasibe. Moramanga is a lively town and still a popular lunch stop when driving to Andasibe from Tana. There's quite a bit of Moramanga beyond the main road.

Try to make a visit to the **Museum of Gendarmerie**. 'Surely the most comprehensive collection in Madagascar, not only police, but cultural, with excellent original exhibits. A must!' (K & L Gillespie)

Telephone code The area code for Moramanga is 56.

Where to stay/eat

Grand Hotel Tel: 620 16. Helpful, friendly; hot water, but reportedly not very clean.
Emeraude Tel: 621 57. Hot showers. Probably the best value in town.
Mirasoa A newish hotel on RN2 about 1km from the centre on the Tana side of town. Simple but clean.
Restau-Hotel Maitso an'Ala, the **Hotel Fivami**, and **Hotel au Poisson** are other basic hotels.
Guangzou restaurant (tel: 62 089) serves good Chinese food. Almost as popular is the **Au Coq d'Or**; tel: 62 045.

Mandraka (Pereyras Mandraka Reptile Farm)

Described on page 180.

Marovoay

This is the first stop on the railway line north towards Lake Alaotra, and the name means 'Many Crocodiles'. Appropriately, there is a commercial crocodile farm which is open to visitors. There are over a thousand *Crocodylus niloticus*, some over two and a half metres in length, living in semi-wild conditions. The best season to visit is January, when the eggs are hatching. For a visit contact: Reptel Madagascar, 50 Av Grandidier, BP 563, Isoraka, Antananarivo; tel: 22 348 86, fax: 22 206 48.

Manjakandriana

This largish town 46km from Tana has a good choice of *hotelys* so make a good breakfast stop if you have made a pre-dawn start from Tana. There is also a bank and a hospital. About 5km towards Tana (on the left) is the recommended **Pizza Nina**.

LAKE ALAOTRA

This is the largest lake in Madagascar and looks wonderful on the map: one imagines it surrounded by overhanging forest. Sadly, forest has made way for rice, and this is one of the most abused and degraded areas in Madagascar. Half a million people now live around the lake, and deforestation has silted it up so that its maximum dry-season depth is only 60cm. Introduction of exotic fish has done further damage. However, all is not lost. The area has been designated a Site of Special Biological Interest by the WWF because of its endemic waterfowl, though it is too late to save Delacour's grebe (Alaotra little grebe) which is now extinct, and the Madagascar pochard may have gone the same way. Work done by the Durrell Wildlife Conservation Trust has ensured that the Alaotran grey bamboo lemur has a future. Not only are these animals breeding happily at Jersey Zoo (see box pages 78–9) but the human inhabitants of the area have cooperated fully with the WWF and DWCT's programmes to introduce conservation measures – another example of how sensitively organised projects can benefit both the local people and the wildlife.

Getting there and away
By rail
A spur of the railway runs from Moramanga and, when trains are running, they leave Tana early in the morning, and end at Ambatondrazaka near the southeast side of the lake. It takes 12 hours (to go 300km!). Check at the station in Tana.

By road
The dirt road (RN44) from Moramanga is being improved and bridges are being built. It is still a challenging route, however.

Ambatondrazaka
The main town of the area, and a good centre for excursions, with a couple of Category B/C hotels.
Where to stay/eat
Hotel Voahirana BP 65, Côte Postale 503. Most rooms have mosquito nets; no en-suite facilities but hot water available. Good restaurant. Quite a walk from the station. Next door is the restaurant **Cantonnais**; very good value.
Hotel Max Near the station. 14 rooms. The restaurant **Fanantenana** is next door.

Excursions
Probably the best reason to come to Lake Alaotra is to meet the guide Jean-Baptiste Randrianomanana and join him for one of his excursions. 'He speaks excellent English, studied sociology and philosophy and is extremely knowledgeable about all aspects of Madagascar. His wife is a geographer. He will take you on a tour of the lake which involves a taxi drive to a traditional village on the shores of the lake, a night with a local family at Imerimandroso, a *pirogue* crossing on the lake to another village called Vohitsara to meet the medicine man and the school teacher etc, and a taxi-ride back to Ambatondrazaka.' (J and R McFarlaine)

Jean-Baptiste can give you detailed information for hiking the Smugglers' Path to the coast – a four- or five-day hike (see below). He can usually be contacted through the Hotel Voahirana.

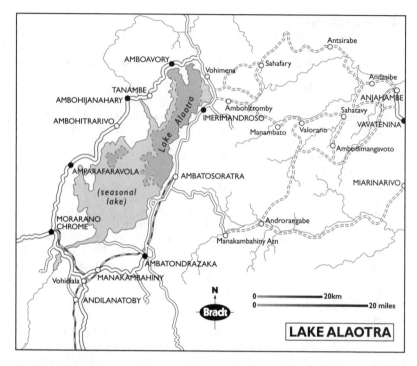

Imerimandroso
A small town near the lake; half an hour's walk to the south is a village from where you can take a *pirogue*.
There is one basic hotel, the **Bellevue**.

The Smugglers' Path

John Kupiec – an exceptionally adventurous and independent traveller – decided to do this trail on his own. In 1996 he wrote: 'From the following story you will see what happens when an out-of-the-way path in Madagascar gets touristed.' It is quite a long story. The core of it is that John's contact with the local people was almost entirely negative (in sharp contrast to his experiences elsewhere), he was cheated out of money at almost every stage (despite speaking some Malagasy), and the uncertainty of what would happen each day spoiled the walk anyway. John's conclusion is that even with the FTM map it is not possible to follow this path without a guide, and that it would be better to seek out the services of Jean-Baptiste. In the years that have elapsed since that letter I have had no feedback about this trail. In my view there are other, nicer, areas to hike in.

For the record, John's journey took him from the train station at Vohidiala then by taxi-brousse to Tanambe where there is a basic hotel. Next day he walked to Vohitsara and took a *pirogue* across the lake to Andromba where the Smugglers' Path begins. In Ambohitromby he picked up one of a series of guides to take him to Manambato. Three days and several villages later he reached the end of the trail at Anjahambe. From there it was a short taxi-brousse ride to Vavatenina, where he stayed in some hotel-bungalows, and thence to the east coast road.

THE SOUTHEAST COAST

For most people this begins with Mananjary, which is linked to the Highlands by both air and road. Adventurous souls, however, can slowly make their way south, leaving RN2 after Brickaville.

The route south from Toamasina to Mananjary

The following report is from Helena Drysdale, and was written at least ten years ago. The journey she describes formed the basis of her book *Dancing with the Dead* (see *Appendix 4, Books*). I have had no recent reports on what should be an exciting and do-able trip.

> We travelled from Tamatave to Mananjary over two weeks. Generally people assured us it was impossible, that there were no roads, that all the bridges were down in the cyclone, and the ferries were *en panne* (that familiar phrase). But with luck and ingenuity we made it. One taxi-brousse per week from Tamatave to Mahanoro (two days), otherwise river boats available at Tamatave's river port for hitching (we went on boats travelling south to a graphite mine in Vatomandry – a very uncomfortable three days).
>
> In Vatomandry we stayed in the Hotel Fotsy; thatched bungalows. Good food here and some Chinese restaurants in town. From there to Mahanoro, one day by taxi-brousse, two by boat. Hotel Pangalanes, full of ladies of the night and noisy revellers but a nice atmosphere. Boat from Mahanoro to Masomelika one day; very simple hotel but friendly people (I asked for the toilet and was pointed to a bucket. This was the shower – the toilet was in the bushes). From Masomelika to Nosy Varika took half a day hitchhiking. There's a relatively expensive Chinese hotel here. Then on to Mananjary, one night by boat.

The Chinese-owned hotel described by Helena is **Hotel Petite Oasis**, which 'serves excellent food, is clean and light and has rooms as well as little bungalows at the back' (Maggie Rush). Another nearby is the **Hotel de la Saraleona**.

MANANJARY AND MANAKARA

These two pleasant seaside towns have good communications with the rest of Madagascar and are gaining in popularity among discerning travellers, especially now the super railway from highlands to coast has been rehabilitated.

Getting there and away

Mananjary is usually reached by road from Ranomafana, and Manakara is the end (or beginning) of the railway journey from Fianarantsoa (see page 197). The road between the two towns is surfaced, but badly potholed. Even so, the journey by taxi-brousse takes only four hours. Mananjary and Manakara are linked by air with Tana and Taolagnaro several times a week (ATR42 and Twin Otter). The Air Mad office in Manakara is in the Hotel Sidi.

Mananjary

This is a very nice small town accessible by good road and taxi-brousse (lovely scenery) from Ranomafana, and famous for its circumcision ceremony which takes place every seven years. The next one will be in the year 2007.

There is a long beach with terrific breakers (dangerous swimming – and there are sharks) and the Pangalanes Canal, plus all the attractions of people-watching. 'The men go out early (4am) in a tremendous surf and row or sail back into the river. Shrimps are sold to wholesalers. Other fish (some very pretty ones) are eaten. Some fishermen's *fady*: Wives are not allowed to look at another man until 12pm or something will happen to the husband at sea; a man who eats pork cannot go to sea.' (C and J Hermans)

Where to stay/eat

Jardin de la Mer A very pleasant set of beach bungalows; 120,000Fmg per bungalow (two beds); single 103,000Fmg. Hot showers and WC en suite. Disappointing restaurant.

Sorafahotel (formerly Solimotel) Bd Maritime. The second best hotel (87,000Fmg). Best food.

Hotel aux Bons Amis Proprietor friendly and accommodating. Inexpensive.

Chez Stenny About a kilometre north of town. Friendly and clean small guesthouse with two rooms (40,000Fmg) and three bungalows (50,000Fmg).

Route des Epices Good restaurant on R25 just before the cathedral. English spoken. Tours organised.

Manakara

Now that the railway has been privatised, this town at the end of the line is bound to gain in popularity. It already has its fans: 'The Allée des Filaos running between ex-colonial buildings and the ocean makes the waterfront a very attractive part of town. The new town and station are across the river bridge and of no interest. *Pousse-pousses* provide the best local transport' (Andrea Jarman). The taxi-brousse station is some way from the centre of town; take a *pousse-pousse* if your bags are heavy.

You should not swim in Manakara because of dangerous currents and sharks. But the sea is infinitely rewarding anyway: 'We absolutely fell in love with the beach (except for trash piles and human excrement). The combination of the offshore reef, the breakers, the wide sand strip, the grass and other foliage, then the

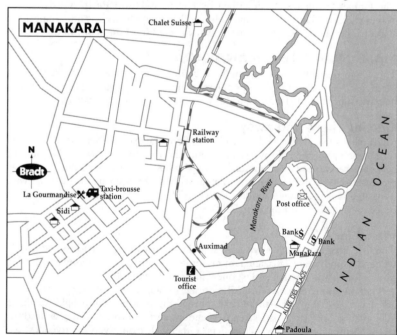

THE MAGIC SHOW
Chris Ballance

We saw a poster in Manakara for a Magic Show so bought tickets. The magician was quite good in a relaxed way. The audience were brilliant. About 120 people in a dingy youth centre hall without lights. He began with a couple of simple disappearing tricks that drew rounds of applause. It was the lesser tricks that were applauded; the better ones left the audience too spell-bound to think of clapping. His magic wand was a flute-sized rod which he empowered by touching a plastic skull with a red robe hanging from it. He used few other props – two or three magic boxes, a few packs of cards and a glass. He filled this with flour, wrapped it in a 'magicked' newspaper and turned it into a glass of bon-bons which he threw into the audience. From this moment the audience were his, body and soul. There was no 'willing suspension of disbelief'. These people had eaten the proof of his powers.

He repeated the trick later, turning coffee powder into cigarettes. He put one of the cigarettes into a guillotine and cut it. Then he put a volunteer boy's finger into the guillotine. Another boy had to hold a hat to catch the finger. Down came the guillotine, the hand was hidden in the hat and then magicked better. As the boy left the stage he was mobbed. All we could see was a heap of every child in the audience. Suddenly a finger shot up from the centre of the heap, triumphantly showing everyone it was attached to its hand. And when the conjuror got a girl in the audience to lay an egg, everyone – but everyone – had to see it, touch it, and marvel at it.

The show ended with a draw in which names were put into a hat (we prayed we wouldn't win). There were prizes of 1,000, 5,000 and 10,000Fmg notes. Each winner was given the note to put into an envelope which was put into a magic box, magicked, and then given back. We suspected they got a message to the effect of 'You've been had'. The girl next to me goggled – that's the only word – at the sight of the money. 'Cinq mille francs!' she kept repeating over and over in an ecstasy of hope. The sight of the 10,000Fmg note shut her up entirely.

Next day we changed £40 to last us for three days. We received 138,000Fmg (this was in 1996). The obscenity of international finance, beside that girl, shamed us.

first line of pine trees… gave the place a park-like atmosphere. The breakers alone proved fascinating, partly because of the endless interplay between the incoming and outgoing surf.' (John Robertson)

Telephone code The area code for Manakara is 73.

Where to stay/eat
Padoula Chambres d'Hôtes Lot 1B 132 Manakare-Be 316, Manakara; tel: 216 23. New, locally run by Perline, basic but very clean. Prices vary from 40,000–66,000Fmg, and there is also a campsite. This beach-side hotel comes highly recommended by two separate readers for its friendliness, food, and efforts to make guests as comfortable as possible. The owner grows orchids and other plants and is happy to guide you through his collection.

Ampilao Beach Hotel 8 nice bungalows with shower and toilet, on the beach just outside Manakara. 230,000Fmg. Excellent seafood in the restaurant.

Parthenay Club Tel: 211 60 A club for the locals with some tourist bungalows. About 95,000Fmg (double).

Hotel Sidi Tel: 212 85. A few years ago this was the best hotel, but now 'it should be renamed Seedy.' 125,000Fmg for a double room. Breakfast 12,000Fmg. Not recommended.

Hotel Manakara A friendly, once-pretty hotel, but now very run-down and shabby.

Le Chalet Suisse BP 31 Manakara; tel: 213 89. An excellent place to eat *grillades*, Swiss specialities including *raclette* and *macaroni à la crème*, and a variety of other well-prepared dishes. It is easy to spot its large red and white sign on the right side of the road to the airport, on the edge of town a short distance after you pass the railway station.

La Gourmandise This restaurant and cake shop is a few minutes walk from Hotel Sidi, opposite the taxi-brousse stop. 'Good value, yummy food and quite a lot of imported products to buy.'

Manakara to Fianar by train

This is the most interesting – and, let's face it, the only – train ride in Madagascar. Since 1995 I've been describing the heroic experiences of adventurous rail-buffs, waiting in town for an eternity while the train plucked up courage to make the journey, then stuck on the stationary train for days... Now all that is finished: the line has been privatised, the trains run on time, and there is even a booklet describing the attractions en route (see page 197).

The train leaves Wednesday, Friday and Sunday at 07.00. Get to the ticket office at 06.00 so you can select your seat. Ticket prices are 44,000Fmg first class and 39,000Fmg second class. There is little difference in comfort, but first class is less crowded. The journey takes ten hours.

CONTINUING SOUTH
Vohipeno

Situated some 45km south of Manakara, this small town is the centre of the Antaimoro tribe who came from Arabia about 600 years ago, bringing the first script to Madagascar. Their Islamic history is shown by their clothing (turban and fez, as well as Arab-style robes). They are the inheritors of the 'great writings', *sorabe*, written in Malagasy but in Arabic script. *Sorabe* continue to be written, still in Arabic, still on 'Antaimoro paper'. The scribes who practise this art are known as *katibo* and the writing and their knowledge of it give them a special power. The writing itself ranges from accounts of historical events to astrology, and the books are considered sacred.

Farafangana

On the map this appears to be a seaside resort, but its position near the mouth of a river means that the beach and ocean are not easily accessible. The town is a prosperous commercial centre, with well-stocked shops and a busy market. According to Frankie Kerridge, the locals do not swim – they say the sea is full of monsters – so they watch football instead. The Farafangana team frequently comes top in the Madagascar league.

Telephone code The area code for Farafangana is 72 – but phones rarely work here!

Getting there and away

Air Madagascar flies from Tana to Farafangana and on to Taolagnaro about twice a week.

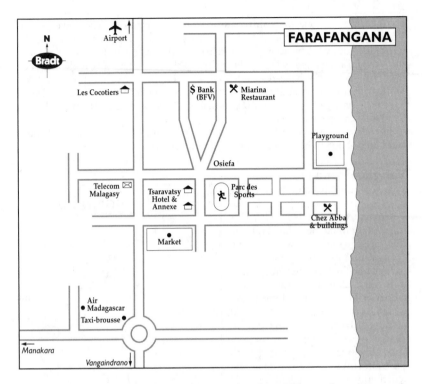

A taxi-brousse from Tana to Farafangana takes about 24 hours, but most people will arrive here via Manakara. Farafangana is only two or three hours away on a good road.

Where to stay/eat
Hotel Les Cocotiers BP 135, Fenoarivo, Faranfangana; tel: 911 87/8; fax: 911 86. Near the post office, this is an upmarket hotel with en-suite bathrooms and hot water. 110,000Fmg. Good restaurant.

Chez Abba Tel: 911 85. About 40,000Fmg for a seafront bungalow with a simple bucket shower.

Miarina (formerly Les Tulipes Rouges) The rooms are all called after different shades of red! Now primarily a restaurant but it still has some rooms. Good food and safe parking.

Tsaravatsy Hotel Tel: 910 36. Popular with Malagasy; good restaurant (Malagasy and Chinese specialities). Cold water, shared facilities. 30,000Fmg.

Le Croustillant bakery Good selection of breads and croissants across the road from Les Cocotiers.

Les Mimosas Salon de Thé Opposite Les Cocotiers. Lots of imported goodies available (at a price).

To the west or south
Looking at a map, onward travel from Faranfangana seems to present few problems, but be warned: most of the roads in this region are in a terrible state!

If you are seriously adventurous and want to try to reach Ihosy (which looks entirely practical on the map) you will need to go on foot, with a guide. You can do the first section, to **Vohitranambo**, by taxi-brousse. The next goal is **Vondrozo**, about 50km away, which is passable by vehicle but has no public transport. You will have to hope to hitch a ride. You can continue by car as far as the **Vevembe** region at which point the passable road ends and jungle has taken over. You will probably need a guide to proceed on foot (or with a mountain bike) to the next stretch of passable road at **Ivohibe** because of the numerous trails that have been created by the locals. If you make it to Ivohibe you're home and dry – there are taxi-brousses to Ihosy.

In contrast, the road to Vangaindrano is 'one of the best in Madagascar' and it takes only about an hour to cover the 70km by taxi-brousse.

Vangaindrano

Very few tourists come here which gives it a certain appeal! Marko Petrovic, who stayed with his missionary uncle here and explored the area (see below) reports: 'Vangaindrano itself is not a particularly interesting place, but as it is only 12km from the sea it is worth making this trip along a road which has been beautifully repaired because Madagascar's minister in charge of roads comes from that area. The road runs parallel with the enormous river Mananara, which flows past Vangaindrano. It is interesting to watch the fishermen who live by the sea going out into the 10ft waves in their narrow wooden *pirogues*. I swam there many times enjoying the amazing power of the waves, but was always careful not to go too far out because currents can very quickly take you in the direction of Australia! Sharks, too, are a

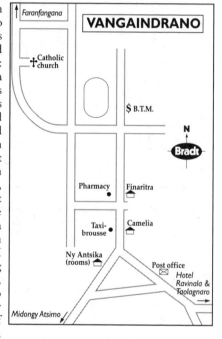

possible danger although I never saw any. The beach is beautifully sandy but beware of rocks under the water.'

Marko says his adventure-loving uncle (Mompera (Father) Klemen) would probably be happy to meet and advise (in French) travellers wishing to explore the area. He is based at the Catholic church in Vangaindrano.

Where to stay/eat

There are several small *hotelys*. Marko recommends:

Zorah About a half kilometre from the town centre, on the left-hand side as you enter town from the north. Very good food, but the quality of the rooms is unknown.

From Vangaindrano to Taolagnaro (Fort Dauphin)

Vangaindrano is the end of the road for most people, but you can continue further. The seriously adventurous make it all the way to Taolagnaro, 230km away. I am grateful to Marko Petrovic who explored the southeast by motorbike in 2000, in company with his uncle, and provided the following information. 'From Vangaindrano to **Midongy Atsimo** a 4WD vehicle is essential. As far as **Ranomena** the road is not too bad, but can be very muddy in the rainy season. The 50km stretch from Ranomena is without doubt the worst road I saw in Madagascar. I travelled there (by car) in March when it was still wet and it took us an incredible nine hours at an average speed of 5km/h! We got stuck at least five times, on one occasion having to use the winch which actually uprooted the tree we had fixed it to. Luckily a nearby metal pole, which had formerly served as an electricity pylon, proved a stable anchor. In colonial times apparently this road was so well maintained that Citroen 2CVs could do it.

'At the end of my stay my uncle and I decided to tackle the RN12 from Vangaindrano to Fort Dauphin with small (50cc) motorbikes because bigger ones would have been awkward crossing rivers by dugout canoes. We set off one Sunday afternoon, laden with food, spare clothes, tools and carrying extra fuel because there would be no petrol station until Fort Dauphin. The first hurdle was crossing Lake Masianaka, which would have been straightforward if the ferry hadn't been *simba* (broken down). We persuaded the ferry operators to tie two canoes together so we could lay the motorbikes across them. The rowers, my uncle and I, squatted in what space was left, doing our best to keep as still as possible. After some haggling we paid 50,000Fmg for the crossing.

'After that the road became a mud bath fit for a hippo. As light waned we just ploughed straight through the mud – an incredible thrill! We spent that night in **Manambondro**. The next day we had to cross another river, again using canoes. Several dozen zebu swam with us, only their horns, nose and humps protruding above the water. The next obstacle was a bridge that looked so rickety we carried the bikes across gingerly, one by one. The road became a roller-coaster ride, winding its way up and down and round the hills that separate the sea from the mountains that run parallel to the coast. It was raining, and my bike began to stall with annoying regularity. We solved this by tying a rope between the two bikes so I was towed by my uncle. We reached **Sandravinanay** by early afternoon and decided to call it a day. We spent the night sheltering in the wooden church, listening to the rain pattering on the roof.

'Next morning we were advised by the locals to take the bikes by canoe down the River Sandra as far as the sea, where we followed tracks left by lobster-merchants' trucks on the beach and later rejoined RN12, which is really no more than a rough dirt track. Before we reached **Manantenina**, the largest town between Vangaindrano and Fort Dauphin, we crossed two rivers which actually had functioning ferries, although we had to bribe the ferrymen to take us across. The final stretch, from Manantenina to Fort Dauphin (110km), took us a whole day but the road was marginally better and all five ferries were operating. Some ferries are operated by pulling on a rope which is stretched across the river. A constant hazard was the numerous streams crossing the road which in places are deep enough to drown a motorbike. We reached Fort Dauphin after four days on the 'road' exhausted but happy.'

This is a route for the true adventurer with a small motorbike or mountain bike. Or a sturdy pair of legs and a backpack. Go for it!

Part Five

The North and West

Giant jumping rat

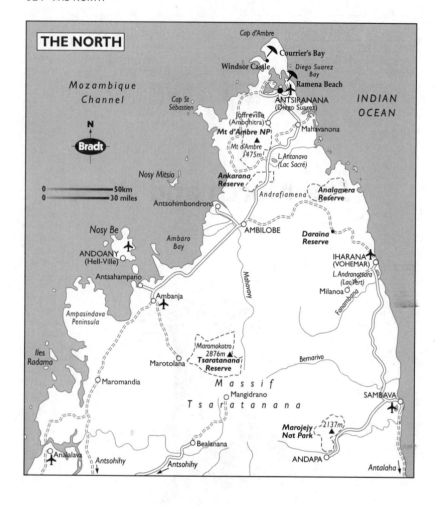

THE NORTH

Cap d'Ambre

Courrier's Bay

Windsor Castle

Diego Suarez
Bay

Ramena Beach

Mozambique
Channel

Cap St
Sébastien

ANTSIRANANA
(Diego Suarez)

INDIAN
OCEAN

Joffreville
(Ambohitra)

Mt d'Ambre NP

Mahavanona

N

Bradt

Mt d'Ambre
1475m

L.Antanavo
(Lac Sacré)

Nosy Mitsio

Ankarana
Reserve

Andrafiamena

Analamera
Reserve

0 ——— 50km
0 ——— 30 miles

Antsohimbondrona

AMBILOBE

Daraina
Reserve

Nosy Be

Ambaro
Bay

ANDOANY
(Hell-Ville)

IHARANA
(VOHEMAR)

L.Andranotsara
(Lac Vert)

Antsahampano

Milanoa

Ampasindava
Peninsula

Ambanja

Mahavavy

Fanambana

Iles
Radama

Maromandia

Maromokotro
2876m
Tsaratanana
Reserve

Marotolana

Bemarivo

SAMBAVA

M a s s i f

T s a r a t a n a n a

Mangidrano

Analalava

Bealanana

Marojejy
Nat Park

2137m

Antsohihy

Antsohihy

ANDAPA

Antalaha

The North

14

OVERVIEW

The north of Madagascar is characterised by its variety. With the Tsaratanana massif (which includes Madagascar's highest peak, Maromokotro, 2,876m) bringing more rain to the Nosy Be area than is normal on the west coast, and the pocket of dry climate around Antsiranana (Diego Suarez) which has seven months of dry weather with 90% of the 900mm of rain falling between December and April, the weather can alter dramatically within short distances. With changes of weather go changes of vegetation and its accompanying fauna, making this region particularly interesting for botanists and other naturalists.

This is the domain of the Antankarana people. Cut off by rugged mountains, the Antankarana were left to their own devices until the mid-1700s when they were conquered by the Sakalava; they in turn submitted to the Merina King Radama I, aided by his military adviser James Hastie, in 1823.

Getting around

Roads in the area are being improved and Antsiranana is losing its isolation. Distances are long, however, so most people prefer to fly between the major towns.

ANTSIRANANA (DIEGO SUAREZ)
History

Forgivingly named after a Portuguese captain, Diego Suarez, who arrived in 1543 and proceeded to murder and rape the inhabitants or sell them into slavery, this large town has had an eventful history with truth blending into fiction. An often-told story, originated by Daniel Defoe, is that pirates in the 17th century founded the Republic of Libertalia here. Not true, say modern historians.

Most people still call the town Diego. The Malagasy name simply means 'Port' and its strategic importance as a deep-water harbour has long been recognised. The

DISTANCES IN KILOMETRES	
Ambondromamy–Antsiranana	737km
Antsohihy–Ambanja	218km
Antsiranana–Ambilobe	131km
Antsiranana–Ankarana	120km
Antsiranana–Ambanja	240km
Antsiranana–Anivorano	75km
Antsiranana–Daraina	247km
Antsiranana–Vohemar	294km

MADAGASCAR OPERATIONS IN WORLD WAR II

Peter La Niece (who was there)

After the fall of Singapore in 1942 a Japanese Strike Force bombed Colombo and sank three major British warships in the vicinity. At the time Madagascar was in the hands of the Vichy French sympathetic to the Axis Powers. Churchill and the War Cabinet feared that if Japan or Germany were afforded facilities in Madagascar the vital supply routes round the Cape through the Mozambique Channel to Egypt and India could be threatened and cut off. The capture of the strategic harbour of Diego Suarez was ordered.

The assault took place on May 5 1942 on three beaches on the northwest corner of Madagascar. There was some opposition but the advance towards Diego Suarez proceeded satisfactorily until it reached the outskirts of the town where it was halted with fairly heavy casualties at a fixed defence line. It was decided to break the stalemate by despatching the ship's detachment of 50 Royal Marines from the battleship *Ramillies* to take the French defences from the rear. They were embarked in the destroyer *Anthony* which proceeded at 30 knots through the night round the northern tip of Madagascar and succeeded in entering Diego Suarez harbour undetected, landing the very seasick Royal Marines. All they had in the way of maps was a page torn from a 15-year-old tourist guide. They set off in the dark and soon came to a large barracks building. Inside they found all the French soldiers asleep and their firearms piled neatly in the entrance to their dormitories. The French were called upon to surrender which they did. The Royal Marines then set off again towards their objective. Very soon they arrived at the telephone exchange where an enterprising French-speaking Royal Marine officer phoned the commander of the French defences, informed him that his colleagues in the barracks had surrendered and requested him to do the same. He complied and Diego Suarez was in British hands.

The following month a Japanese submarine dropped two human torpedoes off the entrance to Diego Suarez and succeeded in sinking a tanker and heavily damaging the *Ramillies*. There were also indications that the town of Majunga on the west coast of Madagascar was being used as a base by Vichy French and probably German U-boats. It was therefore decided to launch two further operations and occupy Madagascar completely.

The second assault took place at Majunga on September 10 1942 which, after incurring some casualties, was successful. Elements of an East African brigade started their march on the capital. The assault force was re-embarked and all ships went round and anchored in Diego Suarez Bay to finalise plans for the third operation.

On September 18 the whole force appeared off the east coast town of Tamatave. An ultimatum was signalled to the French commander to the effect that unless he surrendered, his positions would be bombarded by the *Warspite* and her escorting cruisers as well as air strikes from the carrier *Illustrious*. He capitulated and the landings were unopposed. Troops of the East African brigade set off immediately for Tananarive which fell on September 23. The Governor-General escaped southwards with 700 troops but was overtaken later in October which ended the campaign.

French installed a military base here in 1885, and the town played an important role in World War II when Madagascar was under the control of the Vichy French (see box opposite). To prevent Japanese warships and submarines making use of the magnificent harbour and thus threatening vital sea routes, Britain and the allies captured and occupied Diego Suarez in 1942. There is a British cemetery in the town honouring those killed at this time.

Antsiranana today

This is Madagascar's fifth largest town (population about 80,000) and of increasing interest to visitors for its diverse attractions. Traditionally rated second in beauty after Rio de Janeiro the harbour is encircled by hills, with a conical 'sugar loaf' plonked in one of the bays to the east of the town. From the air or the top of Montagne des Français, Antsiranana's superb position can be appreciated but the city itself is in the usual state of decay, though with a particular charm. The port's isolation behind its mountain barrier and its long association with non-Malagasy races have given it an unusually cosmopolitan population and lots of colour: there are Arabs, Creoles (descendants of Europeans), Indians, Chinese and Comorans.

Almost everyone enjoys Diego. It is colourful, compact, has some great eateries, and of course the excellent nearby reserves. Women report feeling very safe here. This is a pleasant town for wandering; take a look at the market – one of the largest and most colourful in Madagascar – poke around the harbour, and investigate a few souvenir shops. If you want to relax on a beach for a few days, stay at Ramena.

The name 'Joffre' seems to be everywhere in and around the town. General Joseph Joffre was the military commander of the town in 1897 and later became Maréchal de France. In 1911 he took over the supreme command of the French armies, and was the victor of the Battle of the Marne in 1914.

Telephone code The area code for Antsiranana is 82.

Getting there and away
By air
There are flights from Tana (returning the same day) via Mahajanga on most days, also regular flights from/to Nosy Be. Twin Otters link Antsiranana with the east coast towns of Iharana (Vohemar), Sambava and Toamasina.

There are taxis waiting at the airport but they set their own price: an extortionate 50,000Fmg for the 6km to the town centre. A cheaper alternative is to walk to the main road and wait for a taxi-brousse.

By road
The overland route between Ambanja (nearest town to Nosy Be) and Antsiranana is popular. Tougher, less interesting, but possible is the road to Iharana (Vohemar). Both routes are described later in this chapter. The company Anila Transport (see page 346) will also provide comfortable road transport to Ambilobe for 20,000Fmg.

Where to stay
Category A
King's Lodge 8km east of Antsiranana. Well designed, set on a gentle slope backed by a hill, with a shaded terrace and sea view. Good restaurant. €31–38, depending on the season; meals €5. Book through Le King de la Piste (see page 331); tel: 225 99; fax: 235 60.
Hotel Colbert 51 Rue Colbert; tel: 232 89; 232 90; email: hicdiego@dts.mg. 27 air-conditioned rooms with en-suite bathrooms. Safe deposit boxes in each room. 230,000Fmg. Recommended.

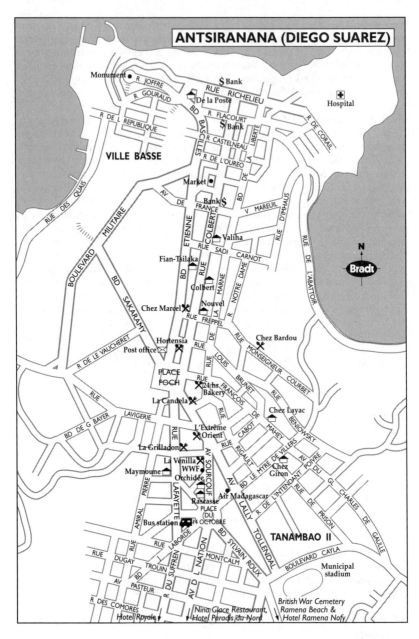

ANTSIRANANA (DIEGO SUAREZ)

Category B

Hotel Escale On the road to the airport; tel: 223 82. From about 100,000–115,000Fmg for a double bungalow. I have no reports on its quality but it's worth checking out.

Hotel Paradis du Nord Rue Villaret Joyeuse, across from the market; tel: 214 05. 82,000Fmg (single), and 92,000–140,000Fmg double. All en suite. Good value since everything works – air-conditioning, hot water… The rooms themselves are cell-like except for No 1 which is marvellously spacious and overlooks the colourful market. There is a pleasant balcony dining room (with good food), a laundry service, and a secure garage if you are driving (you can rent cars from here, including 4WD).

Hotel de la Poste BP 121; tel: 214 53. Near Clémenceau Sq, overlooking the bay. A superb location but few other redeeming features.

Hotel Maymoune 7 Rue Bougainville. About 140,000Fmg. It may have improved since the last report: 'Decidedly seedy, with music from the nightclub opposite thumping through the walls until 3am.' However, a big plus for some people is that it has CNN on television!

Hotel Valiha 41 Rue Colbert (BP 270); tel: 215 31. 127,000Fmg for clean rooms with air conditioning and hot water.

Hotel Orchidée Rue Surcouf; tel: 210 65. 75,000Fmg for double room with fan (en suite), and 100,000Fmg with air-conditioning. Friendly, helpful, Chinese-run hotel with a small restaurant and a few rooms for around 50,000Fmg.

Category C

Chez Layac 35 Rue François de Mahy; tel: 210 21. 41,000–56,000Fmg for double room with shared toilet, 75,000Fmg for en-suite double. Very good value.

Hotel Royale Rue Suffren, around the corner from the Paradis du Nord. About 50,000Fmg per person; breakfast about 7,000Fmg. Cell-like rooms but clean, and with fans. Lockers with padlocks. The interior rooms are quieter. Friendly, some English spoken. Good value.

Hotel Fian-tsilaka 13 Bd Etienne; tel: 223 48. 52,000Fmg for a basic room with washbasin and shared toilet. 82,000–102,000 for en-suite rooms. Good restaurant.

Hotel la Rascasse Rue Surcouf, opposite Air Mad; tel: 223 64. Good value rooms from 85,000Fmg (shared toilet) to 100,000Fmg for en-suite facilities, but the place is pretty seedy: 'The restaurant and the terrace are mostly occupied by lonely men and easy-going girls.' (CH)

Chez Yvette Giron Villa Elise, 0512D0110, Polygone III route de la SIM, Diego Suarez 201; tel: 220 89. Not a hotel, but rooms in a private house for 50,000Fmg per night; breakfast 18,000Fmg. Recommended by Debbie Fellner: 'Yvette Giron's home is beautiful, safe and clean, within walking distance of downtown, and she provides an excellent breakfast.'

Where to eat

Balafomanga A French-run, expensive restaurant, with excellent food. Try the marinated zebu or coco shrimp.

La Venilla Up the road from the Hotel La Rascasse and opposite the WWF office. Arguably the best restaurant in town, yet still keeps its prices reasonable. Especially recommended for breakfast, when little else is open.

La Grilladon Av Sourcouf (not far from the WWF office). An up-market restaurant with a pool table and outdoor bar; excellent food. Try the fish with mushroom and aubergine.

La Candela North of La Venilla (next to the Alliance Française). Once popular with travellers, with a good menu (excellent pizzas), but service is slow.

Halmah Resto Rue Roi Tsimiaro. Where the locals eat, and always busy. Good value.

Restaurant Libertalia Next to La Candela. Offers a few good, low-priced meals on the first floor. There's also a lovely garden restaurant. 'This has to be the best for a Friday night! We had a full moon, good food, great music, prostitutes dancing for their ex-pats.'

L'Extrème Orient A popular restaurant near Air Mad; inexpensive, good food.

La Rosticceria Rue Colbert; an excellent Italian restaurant with veranda. 'The owner makes her own lemon/cream liqueur and will ply you with it despite protestations!'

Chez Marcel Bd Etienne, across the street from the Nouvel Hotel. Good food; recommended.

Snacks and fast food are easy to find. The **Hortensia**, near the post office, does fast food at all times of the day. If your hotel does not serve breakfast, go to the

Boulangerie Amicale, between La Rascasse and the cinema. Excellent hot rolls and *pain au chocolat*. **Glace Gourmande**, on Rue Colbert, probably serves the best ice-cream in town, and is recommended for breakfast. The **bakery** on rue François de Mahey, around the corner from the Libertalia, sells baguettes day and night. And ice-cream.

Nightlife
Vahinée Bar Rue Colbert, opposite BNI-CL bank. Great for people-watching.

Cybercafés
There are a couple in the centre of town.

Ramena
This beach resort is growing fast and provides a pleasant alternative to staying in Diego. Ramena is about 18km from the town centre, 45 minutes from the airport. Get there by taxi-brousse or by private taxi (about 75,000Fmg round trip). It's a beautiful drive around the curve of the bay, with some fine baobabs en route. The road down to the beach is just after the Fihary Hotel.

As well as a selection of hotels and restaurants, there is a disco along the beach.

Where to stay/eat
Residence du Nosy Lonjo Tel: 294 00. On the way to Ramena, overlooking the island of Nosy Lonjo.
Fihary Hotel Tel: 228 62/294 15; fax: 294 13. 15 chalets with modern bathrooms, hot water, mosquito nets, a large restaurant (super food, only they often run out!) with a terrace. About 125,000Fmg.
Badamera Near the beach, friendly, wonderful food. Huts or rooms for 50–80,000Fmg with communal bathrooms.
Ramena Nofy. Bungalows about 180,000Fmg. Very clean and quiet, with working fans. Two minutes from the beach. Delicious food, especially fish.
Restaurant Emeraude 'Walk down the road to the beach from Hotel Fihary. Turn left on to the beach at the pier. This is the first restaurant you'll come to. Excellent.'
Hotel Oasis Poor location in the middle of the village; rooms 60,000Fmg. Good restaurant.

Excursions around Ramena
Angela Slater and David Pollard recommend the following walk to the **Baie des Dunes** 'The walk is best done early in the morning or late afternoon because of the heat, also carry plenty of water. It starts from the village of Ramena (if you are staying at the Ramena Nofy bungalows you can obtain a pass to walk through the military camp). Walk along the metalled road towards the headland – straight on from the bungalows rather than down to the beach – which will take you to the military installation where you will have to show your pass to the gatehouse. Once in the camp follow the signs to the lighthouse or dunes past the barracks then along an open stretch to the hillside and follow the obvious track along the contour. Bird life is very good: two species of vanga (sickle-billed and Chabert's), bee-eaters and kestrels.

'The track continues past some ruined buildings and there is a signpost to the lighthouse. Carry on along the track, which can be hard going at times in the soft sand, and then the view opens up seaward. A word of caution at this point: if you leave the track to look at the view (which I can recommend as there are white-tailed tropic-birds) be careful of the cliffs. All along the walk there are numerous animal tracks, mainly land crabs but some reptiles also. Then you arrive at the Baie des Dunes; the bay itself is overlooked by an old gun emplacement. On the beach to the right of this there is a stretch of white sand gently sloping to the sea; to the left there is a remnant reef with pools, then a steep drop off into the water, excellent for snorkelling. In front of the emplacement there is a small island which is accessible from the beach.

'The whole area is excellent for wildlife, especially the pools, and there is the potential to spend the whole day here exploring if you bring a packed lunch. Further over in the same woodland we found crowned and Sanford's brown lemur.

Boat trips
You can arrange to be taken by boat to 'a wonderful small island. Two hours in a choppy sea, but worth it. Fish caught by boatmen cooked on the beach. About 100,000Fmg per person.'

Sightseeing and half-day excursions
British Cemetery
On the outskirts of town on the road that leads to the airport, the British cemetery is on a side road opposite the main Malagasy cemetery. It is well signposted. Here is a sad insight into Anglo-Malagasy history: rows of graves of the British troops killed in the battle for Diego in 1942, and the larger numbers, mainly East African and Indian soldiers serving in the British army, who died from disease during the occupation of the port. Impeccably maintained by the Commonwealth War Graves Commission, this is a peaceful and moving place.

Montagne des Français (French Mountain)
The mountain gets its name from the memorial to the French and Malagasy killed during the allied invasion in 1942. Another sad reminder of a war about which the locals can have had little understanding. There are several crosses but the main one was laboriously carried up in 1956 to emulate Jesus's journey to Calvary.

It is a hot but rewarding climb up to this high point with splendid views and some nearby caves. Go early in the morning for the best birdwatching (and to avoid the heat of the day). Take a taxi 8km along the coast road towards Ramena beach, to the start of the old road up the mountain. This is 50m before the King's Lodge. The footpath is marked with red paint about 300m along the track on the left. 'In the area of *tsingy* just before the high cliffs we spotted Sandford's brown lemurs. Many more small footpaths extend from left to right and make enjoyable walking including some which lead to the obvious large cave high above King's Lodge. Since early 2000 these cliffs and the interior of the cave have become a mecca for rock climbers where French groups have put up many bolted routes. Full details of these can be found at the Kings Lodge.' (V & J Middleton)

Apparently the flora and fauna are much more rewarding on the Indian Ocean side of the mountain.

EXCURSIONS FROM ANTSIRANANA
Getting organised
Tour operators
Nature et Océan 5 Rue Cabot, BP 436, Antsiranana. They run 4WD vehicles to places of interest such as Montagne d'Ambre, Ankarana, Antanavo, Windsor Castle, Courriers Bay and Ambilobe. They also run sea trips and fishing expeditions. Madagascar Airtours also has an office here.

Le King de la Piste Bd Bazeilles (near Hotel de la Poste), Antsiranana; tel/fax: 225 99. This agency, run by Jorge Pareik (German), is recommended as the best in town for trips by 4WD (minimum two people) to hard-to-reach places such as Windsor Castle, Cap d'Ambre and Analamera. Jorge and his Malagasy wife also organise excursions by motorbike or mountain bike. Prices are quite high (and you must pay in cash – credit cards are not accepted) but worth it: this tour operator continues to receive (mostly) top marks from readers. Highly recommended.

Zanatany Tours BP 475, Antsiranana; tel: 237 88; fax: 224 44. Run by one of Madagascar's best guides to the north: Hyacinthe (Luc Hyacinthe Kotra) and his team which includes Angelin and Angelic who are known by many visitors for their outstanding knowledge of Ankarana. They specialise in natural history tours to reserves such as Ankarana, Analamera and Daraina, providing all necessary camping equipment and 4WD vehicles. A highly recommended, slightly cheaper alternative to King de la Piste.

Many of Diego's hotels can organise tours so if your budget is limited it is worth shopping around.

Car and bike hire

ADA Location (Batiment SICAM), Bd Duplex; tel: 224 98; email: sicam.diego@simicro.mg. A Peugeot 106 costs 241,000Fmg per day including a driver.

Hotel Paradis du Nord Sometimes has cars plus drivers.

The Blue Marine 67 Colbert (near the Nouvel Hotel). Bike hire.

Windsor Castle and Courrier's Bay

A half-day drive (4WD) or full-day bike excursion takes you to the fantastic rock known as Windsor Castle. This monolith (visible from Antsiranana and – better – if you arrive by ship) is steep-sided and flat-topped, so made a perfect lookout point during times of war. The views from there are superb. It was fortified by the French, occupied by the Vichy forces, and liberated by the British. A ruined staircase still runs to the top (if you can find it). There is some *tsingy* here, and many endemic water-retaining plants including a local species of pachypodium, *P. baronii windsori*.

To get there take the road that runs west towards Ampasindava, where you turn right (north) along a rocky road, then left towards Windsor Castle. The road continuing north is the very rough one to Cap d'Ambre. The stone staircase to the top of Windsor Castle is not easy to find, and alternative routes sometimes bring you to dense forest or an impassable rock face. Sven Oudgenoeg, who also initially failed to find the staircase, enlisted the help of a local fisherman who acted as a guide and showed him the path. He gives these precise instructions: 'Drive exactly 28.2km from Diego Suarez towards Cap d'Ambre; here you come to a fork in the road. The 'main' road (once metalled, now potholed) continues towards Cap d'Ambre, the left branch goes to Windsor Castle. After 4.2km the road passes through a clump of mango trees where it divides into two paths. Take the one to the left which leads along a steep ridge to the foot of the ruined staircase. The way up the staircase is not always clear, so you have to apply a little logic, but it can be done, and takes about an hour to the top.' A more recent description comes from John and Valerie Middleton (2001): 'A much easier and more interesting ascent route is to follow the less steep ridge to the one mentioned until it is possible to traverse leftwards beneath the large rock face. This leads directly to the steps to the top. The northwest side of Windsor Castle is reported to be superior for its flora and fauna but requires a camp en route from the Courrier's Bay road. Incidently, this road is cut off for around five hours at high tide for about 60 metres.'

This is a hot, dry climb. Take plenty of water and allow yourself enough time. Courrier's Bay, half an hour beyond Windsor Castle, is an exceptionally fine beach.

Cap d'Ambre

To reach the northernmost tip of Madagascar you need a 4WD vehicle or motorbike and nerves of steel. Or a mountain bike and plenty of time. If you can carry enough water this area merits exploration; it is seldom visited and is particularly interesting for its flora. I have yet to hear of a traveller who has reached the Cape, however. This is a very difficult and potentially dangerous trip and should not be undertaken lightly.

LAC ANTANAVO (LAC SACRÉ)

The sacred lake is about 75km south of Antsiranana, near the small town of Anivorano. It attracts visitors more for its legends than for the reality of a not particularly scenic lake and the possibility of seeing a crocodile. The story is that once upon a time Anivorano was situated amid semi-desert and a thirsty traveller arrived at the village and asked for a drink. When his request was refused he warned the villagers that they would soon have more water than they could cope with. No sooner had he left than the earth opened, water gushed out, and the mean-minded villagers and their houses were inundated. The crocodiles which now inhabit the lake are considered to be ancestors (and to wear jewellery belonging to their previous selves. So they say).

The crocodiles are sometimes fed by the villagers, so you may do best to book a tour in Diego; the tour operator should know when croc feeding day is.

There are two smaller lakes nearby which the locals fish cautiously – often from the branches of a tree to avoid a surprise crocodile attack.

THE NORTHERN RESERVES
Montagne d'Ambre (Amber Mountain) National Park

This 18,500ha national park was created in 1958, the French colonial government recognising the unique nature of the volcanic massif and its forest. The park is now part of the Montagne d'Ambre Reserves Complex which also includes the Special Reserves of Ankarana, Analamera and Forêt d'Ambre. The project, initiated in 1989, is funded by USAID, the Malagasy government and the WWF; it was the first to involve local people in all stages of planning and management. The aims of conservation, rural development and education have largely been achieved. Ecotourism has been encouraged successfully with good information and facilities now available.

Montagne d'Ambre National Park is a splendid example of upland moist forest, or montane rainforest. The massif ranges in altitude from 850m to 1,475m and has its own micro-climate with rainfall equal to the eastern region. It is one of the most visitor-friendly of all the protected areas of Madagascar, with broad trails, fascinating flora and fauna, a comfortable climate and readily available information. In the dry season vehicles can drive right up to the main picnic area, giving a unique opportunity (in Madagascar) for elderly or disabled visitors to see the rainforest and its inhabitants.

The name comes not from deposits of precious amber, but from the amber-coloured resin which oozes from some of its trees and is used medicinally by the local people.

Warning Antsiranana is now firmly on the itinerary of cruise ships, with Montagne d'Ambre the focus of the day's excursion. This means that upward of 100 passengers will pour into the park. Independent travellers may wish to visit the port to check if a ship is due before planning their visit.

Permits and information

Permits (50,000Fmg) and a very good information booklet are available at the park entrance. The ANGAP office is on the outskirts of town towards the airport. Permits are also available here.

It is compulsory to take a guide.

Getting there

The entrance to the park is 27km south of Antsiranana, 4km from the town of Ambohitra, or Joffreville as almost everyone still calls it. Taxi-brousses leave Antsiranana at 07.00 for Joffreville, and return at 14.00. The journey takes about an hour (the road is tarred). A private taxi is cheaper than organising the trip through a tour operator.

Where to stay

There are shelters and bunk beds in the park for visitors equipped with their own sleeping bags (bring your own food). From the wildlife point of view, staying in the park is far preferable to making a day trip, so if you have a tent bring this in case the shelters are occupied by a group. If you have no tent, there is accommodation at the **Auberge Maréchal Joffre,** at Joffreville.

There is a **campsite** (often crowded) at the car park/picnic area (known as Station de Rousettes) where a visitor centre is being built.

Weather

The rainy season (and cyclone season) is from December to April. The dry season is May through August, but there is a strong wind, *varatraza*, almost every day, and it can feel very cold. The temperature in the park is, on average, 10°F cooler than in Antsiranana, it is often wet and muddy, and there may be leeches. So be wary of wearing shorts and sandals however hot and dry you are at sea-level. Bring rain gear, insect repellent and even a light sweater.

The most rewarding time to visit is during the warm season: September through November. There will be some rain, but most animals are active and visible, and the lemurs will have babies.

Flora and fauna

Montagne d'Ambre is as exciting for its plants as for its animals. A very informative booklet gives details and illustrations of the species most commonly seen. All visitors are impressed by the tree-ferns and the huge, epiphytic bird's-nest ferns which grow on trees. The distinctive *Pandanus* is also common, and you can see Madagascar's endemic cycad. Huge strangler figs add to the spectacle.

Most visitors want to see lemurs and, as the two diurnal species become habituated, this is becoming easier. The park is home to a subspecies of brown lemur, Sanford's brown lemur and the crowned lemur. Sanford's lemur is mainly brown, the males having white/beige ear-tufts and side-whiskers surrounding black faces, whilst the females are of a more uniform colour with no whiskers and a grey face. Crowned lemurs get their names from the triangle of black between the ears of the male; the rest of the animal is reddish brown. Females are mainly grey, with a little red tiara across the forehead. Both sexes have a lighter-coloured belly; in the female this is almost white. Young are born from September to November.

Other mammals occasionally seen are the ring-tailed mongoose and – if you are really lucky – the fosa. And there are five species of nocturnal lemur.

Take time to look carefully at the forest floor; this is the place to find the leaf-mimic *brookesia* chameleon, little more than 2cm long, pill millipedes rolled into a perfect ball, frogs, lizards, butterflies, mysterious fungi and a whole host of other living things. At eye-level you may spot chameleons – although the drive up from Antsiranana is a better hunting ground for these reptiles.

Even non-birders will be fascinated by the numerous species here: the Madagascar crested ibis is striking enough to impress anybody, as is the paradise flycatcher with its long, trailing tail feathers. The forest rock thrush is tame and

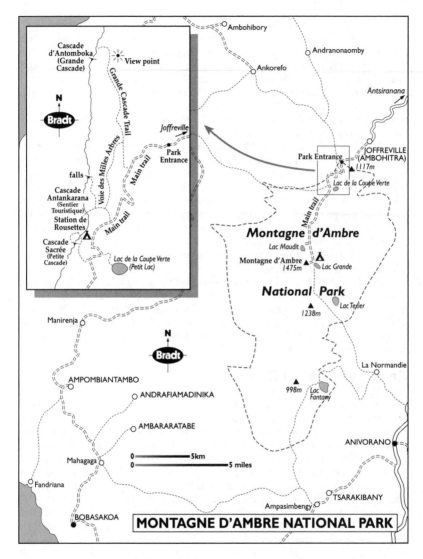

MONTAGNE D'AMBRE NATIONAL PARK

ubiquitous, and the black-and-white magpie robin is often seen. The jackpot, however, is one of Madagascar's most beautiful birds: the pitta-like ground-roller.

Trails, waterfalls and lakes

The park has, in theory, 30km of paths, but many of these are overgrown although they are gradually being cleared and renamed. The best, and most heavily used, trails lead to the Petit Lac, the Jardin Botanique, and two waterfalls, Cascade d'Antomboka (Grande Cascade) and Cascade Sacrée (Petite Cascade). There is also a Sentier Touristique with another lovely waterfall at the end.

The three waterfalls provide the focal points for day visitors. If time is short and you want to watch wildlife rather than walk far, go to the **Cascade Sacrée**. This is only about 100m along the track beyond the picnic area (Station de Rousettes) and on the way you should see lemurs, orchids and birds galore. Take a small path on your left to the river for a possible glimpse of the white-throated rail and the malachite kingfisher. The Cascade Sacrée is an idyllic fern-fringed grotto with waterfalls splashing into a pool. In the hot season there is a colony of little bats (I don't know the species) twittering in the overhang to the right of the pool.

The **Sentier Touristique** is also easy and starts near the Station de Rousettes (walk back towards the entrance, cross the bridge and turn left). The path terminates at a viewpoint above **Cascade Antankarana**: a highly photogenic spot and a good place to find the forest rock thrush and other birds.

The walk to the **Cascade d'Antomboka** is tougher, with some up and down stretches, and a steep descent to the waterfall. There is some excellent birdwatching here, some lovely tree-ferns and a good chance of seeing lemurs – especially if you bring a picnic which includes bananas… On your way back you'll pass a path on the right (left as you go towards the waterfall) marked **Voie des Mille Arbres** (formerly Jardin Botanique); don't be misled into thinking this will lead you to the rose-garden. It's a tough roller-coaster of a walk, but very rewarding, and eventually joins the main track.

Another easy walk from Station de Rousettes is the viewpoint above the crater lake, **Lac de la Coupe Verte**.

A full day's walk beyond Station de Rousettes takes you to a crater lake known as **Lac Maudit**, or Matsabory Fantany, then on for another hour to **Lac Grand**. Beyond that is the highest point in the park, **Montagne d'Ambre** (1,475m) itself. Unless you are a fit, fast walker it would be best to take two days on this trek and camp by Lac Grand. That way you can wait for weather conditions to allow the spectacular view.

Analamera Special Reserve

This 34,700ha reserve is in remote and virtually unexplored deciduous forest some 20km southeast of Montagne d'Ambre, and is the last refuge of the very rare Perrier's black sifaka which few people have been fortunate enough to see. The reserve is now open to visitors and, for the enthusiast, easily merits between two and four nights' camping. There are no facilities of any kind, so visitors must be totally self-sufficient.

To reach the reserve from Antsiranana you drive 50km south on a good road, and are then faced with a further 11km on a dreadful stretch which is impassable in the rainy season. Guides and porters can be organised in the nearby village of Menagisy, but it is more sensible to arrange the visit through an operator in Antsiranana, such as Le King de la Piste or Zanatany Tours. In addition to the black sifaka, you may also see the white-breasted mesite and Van Dam's vanga, which are also seriously threatened species.

Ankarana Special Reserve

About 108km south of Antsiranana is a small limestone massif, Ankarana. An 'island' of *tsingy* (limestone karst pinnacles) and forest, the massif is penetrated by numerous caves and canyons. Some of the largest caves have collapsed, forming isolated pockets of river-fed forest with their own perfectly protected flora and fauna. Dry deciduous forest grows around the periphery and into the wider canyons. The caves and their rivers are also home to crocodiles, some reportedly six metres long. The reserve is known for its many lemur species, including crowned and Sanford's brown lemur, but it is marvellous for birds, reptiles and insects as well. Indeed, the 'Wow!' factor is as high here as anywhere I have visited.

After a preliminary look in 1981, an expedition led by Dr Jane Wilson (Bradt's very own medical consultant) spent several months in 1986 exploring and studying

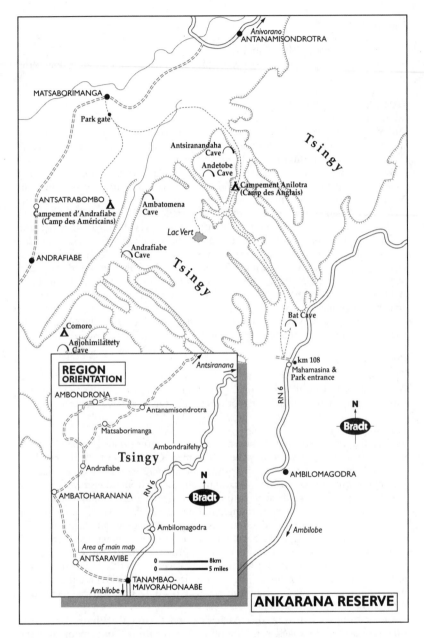

the area. Their findings excited considerable scientific interest, a TV film and a book (see *Appendix 4, Further Information*).

Ankarana is a Special Reserve (18,220ha) which is included in the WWF's Montagne d'Ambre Reserves Complex. It is rightly becoming the western reserve most people want to visit, although at present it is a hiking and camping trip only.

Permits and guides

A permit for Ankarana should be purchased from the WWF (or ANGAP) in Antsiranana or from ANGAP in Tana.

A guide is compulsory. Most live in Matsaborimanga, but are available at the ANGAP office at Mahamasina.

Getting there and away

With a 4WD vehicle you can drive all the way to the main campsite, Campement Anilotra (Camp des Anglais), in the dry season. Most drivers approach from the north, turning off at Anivorano and heading for the village of Matsaborimanga. Allow five hours for this drive from Antsiranana.

By far the best way to get there, however, is to hike in from RN6, a good tarred road which runs between Ambanja and Antsiranana The journey to the village of Mahamasina takes about three hours from Ambanja or 2½ hours from Antsiranana and is easily made by taxi-brousse or ordinary taxi. Anila Transport (see page 346) will take you to the entrance point in comfort. There is an ANGAP office near the trailhead at the 108km sign on the road. It's a super walk of about 11km in to the reserve; allow 2½ to 3 hours. The first part is down a wide track, then, after about 20 minutes, you turn right down a gully and cross a river. Shortly after that the trail levels out, enters some beautiful forest (you are now in one of the wide canyons). A huge ficus marks the halfway point and a steep gully indicates that you are arriving at Campement Anilotra.

On the way back, if you use the same route, your guide will take you along an alternative trail to visit the bat caves – a tough scramble, but well worth it.

Organised tours

The easiest way of doing Ankarana is through a local tour operator. Recommended in Antsiranana is Le King de la Piste or Zanatany; it is worth paying a little more for their superb organisation (2,300,000Fmg for two people, three days/two nights in 2000).

Campsites

The main campsite, formerly known as Camp des Anglais (following the Crocodile Caves Expedition), has recently been renamed **Campement Anilotra**. It is equipped with long-drop toilets and picnic tables. There are three separate areas, so although it tends to get crowded you can usually escape from other travellers. Note that the camp offers considerably more shade than Campement d'Andrafiabe, as well as a chance to bathe in the river running through the cave. However, as the reserve becomes more popular, so does the likelihood of finding this campsite fully occupied. The water supply is a good ten minutes' walk away down a slippery slope.

The usual alternative campsite is **Campement d'Andrafiabe** (Camp des Américains), which is handy for the Andrafiabe cave. It now has a water supply and toilets, but can get very crowded. Recent reports (October, 2001) are that the two main campsites are in 'a disgusting state'. Hopefully this will be rectified if Ankarana is to continue to delight visitors.

Other camps are **Camp des Africains** and **Camp de Fleur**. Camp des Africains is near the caves, some four hours' walk from Campement Anilotra. Camp de Fleur is about two hours from Campement Anilotra and is a good base for visiting Lac Vert and some of the best *tsingy*.

What to bring

If you are doing it independently, you'll need strong shoes or boots, a rucksack, food for the duration of your stay and food for your guide (rice can be bought in

Matsaborimanga), a two-litre water bottle, insect repellent, torch (flashlight) for the caves plus batteries. Plus, of course, a tent. A light sleeping bag or sheet plus blanket is enough for the hot season. Oh, and bring earplugs. The lepilemurs and cicadas of Ankarana are highly vocal!

What to see

Ankarana reminds me of J-P Commerson's famous quote: 'There one meets the most strange and marvellous forms at every step!' Everything is strange and marvellous: the animals, the birds, the plants, the landscape. The main things to see are *tsingy* and caves.

Tsingy

If staying at Anilotra camp, the best *tsingy* is about two hours away, over very rugged terrain, just beyond the beautiful crater lake, Lac Vert. This is a very hot, all-day trip (start early, in the cool of the day, bring a picnic and plenty of water) and is absolutely magnificent. Board walks have been constructed to allow safe passage over the *tsingy*, protecting the fragile rock while you admire the strange succulents such as *Pachypodium* which seem to grow right out of the limestone. Lac Vert is as green as its name, and if you are crazy enough you can hike down a steep, slippery slope to the water's edge. An easier alternative is recommended by the Middletons: 'An interesting site not mentioned is that of the small *tsingy* to be found just 15 minutes from the campsite. For those who may consider the walk to Lac Vert too hard the *tsingy* is just as good although smaller, there are similar plants and there are lemurs.'

Caves

From Andrafiabe camp you can explore the gigantic passageways of Andrafiabe Cave. 'We don't believe that even the most claustrophobic person could get claustrophobia here! This is well worth a visit with an exit half way through into one of the spectacular canyons from where an interesting return can be made. The Crocodile Caves in the southern end of the reserve seem to be little visited but are well worth the effort – the situation is spectacular and the passageways are huge. We went in for almost a kilometre to the first lake but did not find any crocodiles (the rest of the cave is more or less dry at this time of year [September]).' (V & J Middleton)

Don't miss the wonderful bat caves, especially Crystal Cave. 'This is an underground fairytale land of sparkling stalagmites and stalactites. Bring a headlamp or flashlight – hiking over such delicate terrain can be tricky and dangerous. You'll feel like a mouse in the Bat Cave with its towering walls pocked with bat and swift nests. The ground crawls with cockroaches and is littered with bat carcasses.' (D Fellner)

OVERLAND FROM ANTSIRANANA TO SAMBAVA

The first section of road is poor, transport erratic, and breakdowns frequent. Once you reach Iharana, however, it is plain sailing down one of the best roads in Madagascar. A taxi-brousse from Antsiranana (Diego) to Ambilobe (on RN6) takes about three hours. Then you head east, on a poor road, to the coastal town of Iharana (still usually known by its old name, Vohemar). The whole trip, from Antsiranana to Sambava, should be accomplished in one long day.

Ambilobe
Where to stay/eat

The following hotels are no doubt still open and others will have joined them: **Hotel Golden Night**, **Hotel Mahavavy**, and (bungalows) **Rêve d'Or**. Then, near the excellent market, there's the **Hotel Bagdad**, the **Hazar** and the **Amical** which is near the taxi-brousse station.

Daraina

Daraina is a small town around 70km northwest of Iharana; the road is bad to very bad (impossible in the wet season) and the journey takes about three hours in a taxi. There is only one reason to stop here: you can see one of the rarest species of sifaka. Nick Garbutt sent the following report:

> There's not a lot in Daraina except a couple of hotelys serving regular hotely fare and it's often murderously hot, but the nearby forests are home to the beautiful golden-crowned Sifaka (*Propithecus tattersalli*) – one of the rarest of all lemurs and listed as one of the 25 most threatened primates in the world.
>
> A Malagasy NGO called FANAMBY has set up a project to work with the local communities and try to preserve the forests and the sifaka. One of their aims is to establish a network of protected areas in the region (currently none of the forests where the sifakas live is protected). The region has deposits of gold and is rich in semi-precious stones which is one of the factors causing conflict with the establishment of a park.
>
> Visitors are required to pay a fee of 40,000Fmg to the Mayor of Daraina to go and see the sifakas – 25,000Fmg of this goes to Daraina, and 15,000Fmg to the village near where the sifakas can be seen.
>
> The village is called Andranotsimaty and is accessible by 4WD (45 minutes from Daraina) or by walking (1½ hours). The people here scrape a living by mining for gold and the forests near the village are scarred with deep pits that have been excavated. However, the sifakas in the forests adjacent to the village are common and very easy to see. It is possible to camp in the forest near Andranotsimaty.

For more information contact Serge Rajaobelina or Astrid Vargas at FANAMBY, BP 8434, Antananarivo 101; tel/fax: 261 20 22 288 78; email: fanamby@fanamby.org.mg; web: www.fanamby.org.mg.

Iharana (Vohemar)

I'm convinced by Peace Corps volunteer Bronwen Eastman that this pleasant beach resort town is *the* place to recover from some rough travelling. It has all the right ingredients: a comfortable (but not expensive) hotel and some wonderful food. And a beach. There are enjoyable walks to be taken in the area too. It is also still something of a Cinderella in tourist terms: often gets ignored in favour of better-known resorts.

Getting there and away

The easiest way to get here is to fly to Sambava then take a taxi-brousse for the two-hour road journey. It takes about 12 hours by taxi-brousse from Antsiranana.

The alternative is to fly (by Twin Otter) from Antsiranana or Nosy Be (note that even Air Mad uses the old name, Vohemar). The Air Mad office is hard to find; it's tucked away in the Star Breweries yard!

Where to stay

Sol y Mar Excellent bungalows in a beautiful setting by the shore with shower and WC. Prices from 70,000Fmg for a basic bungalow to 160,000Fmg for one facing the ocean, with hot water. 'Just a few paces from my room into the sea for a splendid swim. Also had good food' (Philip Jones). 'The *punch coco* is out of this world, and the lychee punch isn't bad either. The meals, when the French co-owner is cooking, are really superb!' (BE). Recent reports (2001) confirm this place is still the tops.

Poisson d'Or Basic, with a good restaurant.

Railouvy Across from the Poisson.

Where to eat

Hotely Kanto A terrific place for meals, run by Madame Elizabeth, who as well as being very friendly is a tremendous cook. Her speciality is *ravitoto* with coconut.

La Florida You can order almost anything in this restaurant: calamari, shrimp coco, *soupe Chinoise* etc, all for a very reasonable price.

OVERLAND FROM ANTSIRANANA TO AMBANJA AND NOSY BE

RN6 has recently been improved, and this route is popular with travellers heading for Nosy Be but there is plenty to see in the area so it is a shame to rush. The journey from Antsiranana to Ambanja at present takes about five hours for the 240km journey.

The first place to break your journey is Ambilobe (see page 339). Then on to Ambanja (two hours), which merits a stay of a day or two.

Ambanja

This is a pleasant little town set amid lush scenery. 'I took a nice walk along the river Sambirano. The path goes up and down/to and from the river, and at one high point there's a good view of the bridge in Ambanja. I saw lemurs high up in bamboo trees.' (J Kupiec)

Telephone code The area code for Ambanja is 86.

Getting there and away

Most people stopping at Ambanja are on their way to or from Nosy Be. Josephine Andrews offers these hints for the trip to Antsiranana. 'There are some fixed-time taxi-brousses which leave at 11.00 and 13.00 (those big nine-place Peugeots) for Diego. There is a little office near to the main market in the north of the town. Otherwise there are always vehicles of every description heading north from the same market, or south from the little market at the far south of town.'

Where to stay/eat

Hotel Palma Nova Probably the best hotel in Ambanja, and close to the town centre. 70,000Fmg for a clean, en-suite, air-conditioned room. Excellent breakfasts.

Hotel Patricia A perennial *vazaha* favourite. Run by M Yvon and his wife (Chinese/Malagasy) who go out of their way to be helpful. Rooms vary in quality and price, so there is something to suit everyone. Usually shut in the afternoon (for siesta) so be prepared to wait. There is an excellent Malagasy cookbook for sale here, written by M Yvon's sister.

Hotel Bougainvilleas Rooms have a shower and WC. Similar to the other two.

Ankify

This beautiful area of coast is being developed as a resort. It is the departure point for ferries and water taxis (*kinga*) to Nosy Be and has two lovely (*Category A*) hotels.

Where to stay

Le Dauphin Bleu BP 33, Ambanja; tel: 320 235 083; email: info@ledauphinbleu.com; web: www.ledauphinbleu.com. 250,000Fmg including breakfast. 7 stone bungalows with hot water

and breakfast served on its beach terrace. A lovely hotel a few kilometres beyond the Baobab, with a view of Nosy Komba. German-owned, with a large garden and a private beach..
Le Baobab BP 85, Ambanja; tel: 65. Located about 2km northwest of the dock area, nestled between rocky cliffs and a beach that overlooks Nosy Komba. Very pleasant bungalows with separate bathrooms, hot water, table fans, mosquito nets (but reportedly with unhelpful staff). About €23. Bill Love, who stays here regularly, writes: 'The grounds are beautifully planted in bougainvillea, palms, ylang-ylang etc, with paved paths between cottages. The restaurant/bar is located on top of another hill, is open-air under a huge thatched roof, and is very comfy and with a great view of the bay... Crowned lemurs pass over the trees over the road nearby, and lower lifeforms abound on evening flashlight walks down the road outside the hotel.' Bill adds: 'The panther chameleons residing locally are among the most beautiful of all – greenish bodies with brilliant blue bands.'

Tsaratanana

Adventurous travellers look at a map of Madagascar and long to climb its highest mountain. However, Tsaratanana is not open to tourists and those who have tried to penetrate it for scientific research have had a rough time. In a nutshell, this mountain is largely deforested, waterless, trailless and hot.

Continuing south from Ambanja to Mahajanga

For a description of this journey see *Chapter 16*.

BAYS AND INLETS ACCESSIBLE TO YACHTS

The bays below could be reached by adventurous hikers or cyclists (many are near villages) but are visited mainly by yachties (lucky devils!).

Russian Bay (Helondranon Ambavatoby)

This is a beautiful and remote place opposite the Nosy Be archipelago. It provides excellent anchorages, all-round shelter and is a traditional 'hurricane hole'. The marine life in the bay itself is terrific, offering wonderful snorkelling and diving, especially in the reefs outside the entrance. There is excellent fishing too. In the right season (October to December), whales are commonly sighted in the bay. This is one of the best spots in which to seek the very rare whale shark. The beaches are known turtle-nesting sites. The sambirano and moist tropical deciduous woods there harbour abundant birdlife, reptiles and lemurs, and there is a choice of trails for day hikes.

The bay's name dates back to an incident in 1905, during the Russo-Japanese war, when a Russian warship, the *Vlötny*, anchored there. The order was to attack any passing Japanese ship, but the crew took one look at life in Madagascar to realise that they did not wish to wage war nor to return to Russia. They had barely organised a mutiny before their officers gave in, having taken one look at the lovely Malagasy women. The ship was hidden in the reaches of Russian Bay and twice emerged to trade with pirate vessels in the Mozambique Channel before they ran out of fuel for the boilers. The Russians were decimated by malaria, but the survivors quickly adapted to their new home, living by fishing. The last one died in 1936. The Russians sold anything they could remove from the ship, but the remains can still be seen at low tide.

Baramahamay Bay (Maroaka)

The Baramahamay river is navigable for about 3km inland and provides a beautiful, well-sheltered anchorage with verdant hills behind sunny, white beaches. The wide bay is conspicuous as a large gap in the coastline. Yachties should approach on the north side of the bay and anchor near the villages in 8m over sand and mud. These villages are known also for their blacksmiths, who make large knives and *pangas*. One of the small villages here is known for its wild honey, and there is a pool with good drinking water.

Your chances of seeing the (very rare) resident Madagascar fish eagles here are good.

Berangomaina Point

The bay inside this headland is an attractive, well-sheltered anchorage. Good visibility is needed to access the bay, however, as there are many scattered reef patches. The channel is at its deepest on the north side, where the depth exceeds 15m right up to the reef. Anchor off the beach before the village, in 10m over a mud bottom. This place is for self-sufficient travellers only, no provisions are available.

HAINTENY
Reflect on regrets, Andriamatoa.
They do not look in at the door to be told 'enter!'
They do not sit to be told 'May I pass?'
They do not advise beforehand,
but they reproach afterward.
They are not driven along like sheep,
but they come following like dogs;
they swing behind like a sheep's tail.

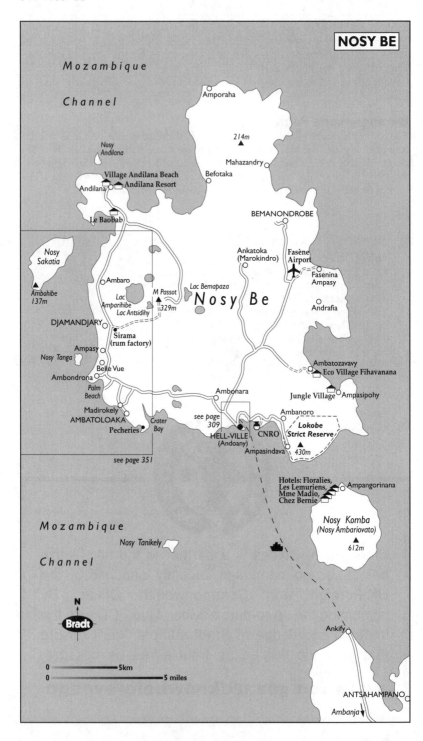

NOSY BE

Mozambique

Channel

Amporaha

214m ▲

Nosy
Andilana

Mahazandry

Village Andilana Beach
Andilana Resort

Befotaka

Andilana

Le Baobab

BEMANONDROBE

Nosy
Sakatia

Ankatoka
(Marokindro)

Fasène
Airport

Ambaro

Fasenina
Ampasy

Ambohibe
137m ▲

Lac
Amparihibe

M Passot
▲
329m

Lac Bemapaza

Nosy Be

Lac Antsidihy

Andrafia

DJAMANDJARY

Sirama
(rum factory)

Ampasy

Nosy Tanga

Belle Vue

Ambondrona

Palm
Beach

Ambatozavavy
Eco Village Fihavanana

Ambonara

Jungle Village   Ampasipohy

Madirokely
AMBATOLOAKA

Ambanoro

Pecheries

Crater
Bay

see page
309

Lokobe
Strict Reserve
▲
430m

HELL-VILLE
(Andoany)   CNRO

Ampasindava

see page 351

Mozambique

Nosy Tanikely

Channel

Hotels: Floralies,
Les Lemuriens,
Mme Madio,
Chez Bernie

Ampangorinana

Nosy Komba
(Nosy Ambariovato)
▲
612m

N

Bradt

Ankify

0 ———5km
0 ————— 5 miles

ANTSAHAMPANO

Ambanja ▼

Nosy Be

OVERVIEW

The name means 'Big Island' and is usually pronounced 'Nossy Bay' although 'Noos Bay' is nearer the Malagasy pronunciation. Blessed with an almost perfect climate (sunshine with brief showers), fertile and prosperous, with sugar, pepper and vanilla grown for export, and the heady scent of ylang-ylang blossoms giving it the tourist-brochure name of 'Perfumed Isle', this is the place to come for a rest – providing you can afford it. Compared with the rest of Madagascar, Nosy Be is expensive.

Nosy Be developed tourism long before mainland Madagascar, so inevitably the island seems touristy or 'commercialised' to adventurous travellers. However, Nosy Be provides a taste of everything that is special to Madagascar, from wonderful seafood to beaches, from chameleons to lemurs, so for this reason is ideal for those with very limited time, who are looking for a hassle-free holiday.

Most of the easily accessible beaches on Nosy Be have been taken over by hotels. None is perfect for swimming – they shelve too gradually so the water is shallow at high tide and a long walk out at low tide.

Those determined to find an undeveloped area should study the FTM map of Nosy Be (scale 1:80,000), which is readily available in Tana and Hell-Ville. It is very detailed and marks beaches.

Telephone code The area code for Nosy Be is 86.

History

Nosy Be's charms were recognised as long ago as 1649 when the English colonel, Robert Hunt, wrote: 'I do believe, by God's blessing, that not any part of the world is more advantageous for a plantation, being every way as well for pleasure as well as profit, in my estimation.' Hunt was attempting to set up an English colony on the island, at that time known as Assada, but failed because of hostile natives and disease.

Future immigrants, both accidental and intentional, contributed to Nosy Be's racial variety. Shipwrecked Indians built a magnificent settlement several centuries ago in the southeast of the island, where the ruins can still be seen. The crew of a Russian ship that arrived during the Russo-Japanese war of 1904–5 (see *Russian Bay* page 342), are buried in the Hell-Ville cemetery. Other arrivals were Arabs, Comorans and – more recently – Europeans flocking to Madagascar's foremost holiday resort.

When King Radama I was completing his wars of conquest, the Boina kings took refuge in Nosy Be. First they sought protection from the Sultan of Zanzibar, who sent a warship in 1838, then two years later they requested help from Commander Passot, who had docked his ship at Nosy Be. The Frenchman was only too happy to oblige, and asked Admiral de Hell, the governor of Bourbon Island (now Réunion), to place Nosy Be under the protection of France. The island was formally annexed in 1841.

GETTING THERE AND AWAY
By air
There are regular flights from Tana, Mahajanga and Antsiranana, and international flights from Réunion.

Taxis from the airport currently cost 60,000–70,000Fmg, but may well rise with fuel prices.

By boat from Mahajanga
Finally, there is a comfortable sea connection to Nosy Be! The *Jean-Pierre Calloc'h* leaves Mahajanga on Thursdays at 18.00, arriving in Nosy Be the following day at 13.00. It returns at 18.00 on Sundays. This is more a cruise than a ferry, with a first and second class lounge, a bar, a disco, televisions and comfortable airline seats. It costs 300,000Fmg first class, 250,000Fmg second class, and 150,000Fmg third class. Cars cost 1,300,000Fmg plus tax. Contact details, tel: 0320 221686; fax (Mahajanga): 62 226 86. This ferry is also the main supplier of fresh fruit and vegetables to Nosy Be.

From Ankify or Antasahampano
Nosy Be's nearest mainland town of any size is Ambanja; taxis leave from outside the Hotel de Ville for Ankify or Antsahampano, the departure points for the ferry. There are two ferries a day; the sailing times (and port) depend on the tide, and the trip takes 2½ to 3 hours and costs 7,500Fmg. This ferry can take two vehicles (240,000Fmg). You have the alternative of going by steam boat (*vedette*). Being smaller, these are less tied to the tides, and often call first at Nosy Komba. Avoid the afternoon, when the sea tends to be rough. Best of all are the speedboats. These leave as they fill up (so you may wait 30 minutes or so) and cost 20,000Fmg for the half-hour journey.

If you are taking the ferry back from Nosy Be to Ankify, check the board outside the ferry office in Hell-Ville (*A M Hassanaly et fils*) a few doors up from Air Madagascar. If you have a vehicle, book it on the ferry here.

By road and boat from Antsiranana
Anila Transport offers a daily vehicle/speedboat combination for 100,000Fmg. The trip takes 5½ hours, and tickets can be purchased from at the main port in Hell-Ville (mornings only) or in front of the Hotel Orchidée in Antsiranana (evenings). 'One of the most comfortable trips I've experienced in Madagascar. It costs a bit more because they only take one passenger per seat!' (Karl Lehmann)

GETTING AROUND THE ISLAND
The roads are good (for Madagascar) and transport around the island is by taxi-be or private taxi (of which there are plenty).

Taxi
Shared taxis are inexpensive, costing around 2,500Fmg for anywhere in town; to Ambataloaka about 7,000Fmg.

Private taxis operate on a fixed rate, but these are usually negotiable.

Car, bike, motorcycle and plane hire
Many of the hotels rent out mountain bikes and mopeds/motorbikes. If you hire a motorbike, check your insurance policy: many companies will not insure you

PET LEMURS

In recent years an insidious new tourist attraction has emerged in Nosy Be. Tourists pay to be photographed with a 'pet' lemur on their shoulder. These animals have usually been trapped in the wild, and are tethered during their short lives in captivity. It's unlikely that any reader of this book would consider contributing to this cruel business, but do make a stand and point out (politely) that it is illegal and that tourists do not like it. Try to dissuade other, less well-informed, tourists from encouraging this practice and point out that a trip to Nosy Komba will allow them to have the same experience with lemurs that live free in the forest.

Hotels that keep pet lemurs should be boycotted.

against motorbike accidents! Prices vary according to power: about 100,000Fmg for a 125cc (half day) to 200,000Fmg for a 350cc.

Nos Autos Car Hire (Hell-Ville) BP 48; tel: 611 24/ 611 51. 5 minibuses, 12 cars, 2 4WD vehicles.

Société Aeromarine (Hell-Ville); tel/fax: 611 25; cellphone: 0331 14 44 44. Cessna 206 and 207. Tours of the island by plane.

Boat trips

Soconet (Daniel) Camp Vert, Hell-Ville; tel: 610 79; fax: 615 92. The leader in cheap and cheerful day-trips to Nosy Komba and Nosy Tanikely.

WATERSPORTS
Yachting

Madavoile (also known as **Blue Planet**) BP 110, Ambatoloaka; tel: 614 31; cellphone: 03 207 207 00. Well-run sailing trips; efficient and helpful.

Nosy Be Croisière (sailing trips) BP 52, Hell-Ville; tel: 613 51. Two sloops (13.4m and 12.2m).

Alefa (round-island luxury *pirogue* trip) BP 89, Madirokely; tel/fax: 615 89. Trips last from two to 22 days, camping with cooks, tents etc provided.

Diving

The once-lovely coral around Nosy Be itself has sadly been destroyed, but the pristine little islands of the region offer excellent diving. May to October are the recommended months. The average cost, including all equipment, ranges from about €54 for 2 dives to €252 for 10 dives.

Madagascar Dive Club Tel: 614 18. Behind the Marlin Club Hotel. Member of PADI International Resort Association. First-class equipment.

Oceane's Dream BP 173, Ambatoloaka, Nosy Be 207; tel/fax: 614 26; cellphone: 03 207 127 82; web: www.oceanesdream.com. Organises diving trips to many of the outlying islands and even to the Comoros. Run by Laurent Duriez.

Tropical Diving (Centre International de Plongée) Annexe Coco Plage, Ambatoloaka, BP 212; tel: 614; cellphone: 03 207 127 90 02; fax: 610 91; email: tropical.diving@simicro.mg. Specialise in night-diving (€32 per dive) and underwater photography. Swiss owned.

Blue Dive BP 250, Hell-Ville (Madirokely); tel: 616 31; email: Celine.b@dts.mg; website: www.bluedive-madagascar.com. Contact Celine Barondeau.

Manta Dive Club BP 326, Hell-Ville (Madirokely); cellphone: 03 207 207 10; email: manta@dts.mg or madiro.h@dts.mg; web: www.mantadiveclub.com. Contact Gianluca.

Forever Dive (Mandirokely). Cellphone: 03 207 125 65; email: forever.dive@simicro.mg.
Contact Sylvia Jacquin.
Sakatia Dive Inn BP 186, Hell-Ville; tel: 610 91 or 615 14; fax: 613 97. See Nosy Sakatia
(page 359).

Deep-sea fishing
This is increasingly popular in Nosy Be. The recommended centre is at the **Hotel
Espadon**, in Ambataloaka. Jean-Charles Taifin takes clients fishing for marlin,
swordfish, wahoo, barracuda etc. He has several world-class boats.

SOUVENIR SHOPPING
The large number of tourists visiting Nosy Be has made this one of Madagascar's
main centres for souvenir production, and provides a unique chance to buy direct
from the makers and benefit the local people.

Handicraft sellers frequent the road to the port and there are some high quality
goods in Hell-Ville's many boutiques. The best shops in town are **Chez Abud**,
which has the widest variety of goods, along with **Maison L'Artisanat**, at the
north end of town (near the airport junction), **Pok Pok** next door, and **Arts
Madagascar** – each shop has its own speciality. Also take a look at **Parfum de
Mangues**, near the Oasis snack bar.

HELL-VILLE (ANDOANY)
The name comes from Admiral de Hell rather than an evocation of the state of the
town. Hell-Ville is quite a smart little place, its main street lined with boutiques
and tourist shops. There is a market selling fresh fruit and vegetables (which may
also be purchased from roadside stalls) and an interesting cemetery neatly arranged
according to nationality.

The BFV bank here only opens from 07.30–11.00 and 14.00–15.00.

Where to stay in Hell-Ville
There is a good choice of budget hotels in Hell-Ville; staying here will save money
while you firm up your plans for making the most of the island.

Category B
Chez Houssen Ben Amad Tel: 613 25; fax: 615 64. Opposite the market. The owner has
a degree in English literature and is recommended by a reader as being particularly helpful.
Room rates are negotiable, depending on how long you want to stay. Great food!
Hotel Abud Tel: 610 55. A 5-storey building centrally located above Chez Abud souvenir
shop. 30 comfortable small rooms, with or without en-suite toilet, 82,000–132,000Fmg.
Some rooms have balconies overlooking the street. Restaurant.
Hotel Diamant 10 La Batterie (near Hotel de la Mer); tel: 614 48. 16 comfortable air-
conditioned rooms; 131,000Fmg.

Category C
Hotel de la Mer Bd du Docteur Manceau; tel: 613 53. The once infamous 'Hotel de
Merde' is now a respectable and pleasant place to stay in town. 15 rooms:
35,000Fmg–100,000Fmg. There's a great view from the restaurant.
Hotel Diana Off the main street near Hotel Abud; tel: 615 73/617 22. 55,000–70,000Fmg.
Some en-suite rooms, others with shared WC/shower.
Hotel Victoria Tel: 613 25; fax: 615 64. Behind Chez Abud, on first floor of ONE office.
50,000–85,000Fmg. 8 airy rooms with fans and shared bathrooms. Recommended for
budget travellers.

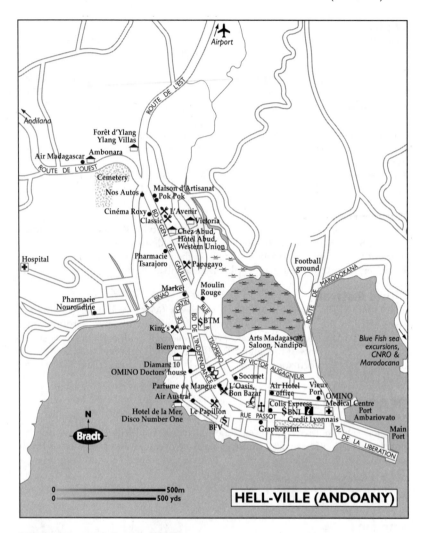

HELL-VILLE (ANDOANY)

Where to eat in Hell-Ville

Le Papillon Tel: 615 82. On the right (as you walk towards the harbour) just before the Catholic church, where Bd de l'Indépendance becomes Rue Passot. Good food, especially pizzas.

L'Oasis Tel: 615 75/611 78. Opposite the Papillon. An excellent and low-priced snack bar on the main road, opposite BFV bank. Fresh croissants and *pain au chocolat* daily. Good cakes and ice-cream and a terrace where you can eat them and watch the world go by.

King's Restaurant La Batterie (not far from Hotel Diamant 10). Medium-priced, offering Chinese and international cuisine.

Restaurant l'Avenir Malagasy-run small restaurant opposite the Roxy Cinema near to Classic Restaurant on the main street. Cheaper than the other restaurants but can still provide a good shrimp sauce and chips!

Saloon On main street. 'Very casual bar/restaurant with some rather awful but cheap rooms.'

Nightlife

Vieux Port A popular place at the old port. 'Wild nights, usually gets going around 22.00, with live music. Great *salegy* and reggae music. 5,000Fmg to get in but drinks expensive.' (JA)

Moulin Rouge Discotheque Not far from the market; tel: 610 36. Serves pizzas during the day and disco every night from 21.30 until dawn.

Disco Number One In a basement beneath the Hotel de Mer. Thursdays and Saturdays.

Bar/Restaurant Papagayo Near the main taxi rank close to the market, geared to tourists. Terrace-style bar/restaurant with potted palms. Has live music on Tuesdays. Popular.

Bar Nandipo Tel: 613 52. French-run bar in the centre of Hell-Ville (near the town hall), popular with expats. Pool table and darts. The best place for a Happy Hour cocktail.

Warning I have been told of a case of the 'date-rape' drug, Rohypnol, being put in a tourist's drink by a 'lady of the night' who then robbed the unconscious victim in his room. This may be an isolated incident (a resident of Nosy Be said he hadn't heard of this before – 'normally they rely on the guys drinking too many beers!'). However, it pays to be wary, especially in Hell-Ville.

Music festival

The Donia music festival is held each Pentecost (May). A four-day celebration takes place in the Hell-Ville football ground southeast of town. Groups come here from Mauritius, Réunion and Seychelles as well as all parts of Madagascar. Lots of events and lots of fun, all for 5,000Fmg. Hotels get very booked up at this time. For more information contact Philip Hardcastle at the Ylang Ylang hotel (Ambataloaka).

BEACH HOTELS

Most visitors prefer to stay in beach hotels located along the sandy western coast. Hoteliers separate these into seven zones, including Hell-Ville and Nosy Komba. For simplification I have used (mostly) the same divisions, but note there is beach accommodation in other areas such as Lokobe and some of the outlying islands. These are listed under the appropriate headings.

The prices are for high season (mid-July to mid-September, and over the Christmas holiday). Low-season rates are cheaper.

Andilana

Northern Nosy Be is the most beautiful part of the island, but is succumbing to development. It is 45 minutes' drive from Hell-Ville.

Category A

Hotel Village Andilana Beach Tel: 615 23/33. A huge new hotel complex (200 rooms) with shops, swimming pool, and other 'no-need-to-leave-the-hotel' facilities. Italian-owned. Expected to open in 2002.

Le Baobab BP 45, Hell-ville; tel: 614 37; fax: 612 93. Closed at the time of writing.

Category B

Andilana Resort Hotel BP 301 Andilana, Nosy Be 207; tel: 614 25. Malagasy owned. 4 rooms for 252,000Fmg; 4 bungalows with shower and fan for 150,000Fmg (double). Breakfast 20,000Fmg, dinner 65,000Fmg. Lovely situation, good restaurant; Sunday all-you-can-eat buffet (75,000Fmg).

Belle Vue (Djamandjary area)

Djamandjary is an ugly small town with some strange igloo-shaped cement structures which, long ago, were provided by a relief organisation as cyclone-proof housing. They are, indeed, indestructible, and have mostly been abandoned by the villagers who have tired of waiting for them to fall down in the time-honoured Malagasy way. Opposite the town is a sugarcane and rum processing factory. Although the beach here is uninspiring (it shelves too gradually for good swimming) it is shaded by coconut palms, and a chain of hotels stretches down the coast. Each hotel rakes away the dead seaweed that the high tide deposits daily on the beach.

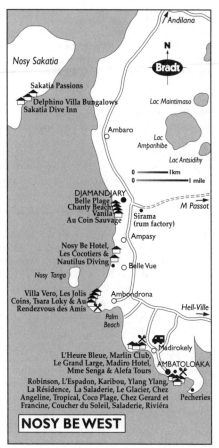

Category A

Hotel Vanila BP 325; tel: 615 23; fax: 615 26; email: vanilahotel@simicro.mg; web: www.vanila-hotel.com. 3km north of Dzamandzar. 30 airy rooms. €64–135. Probably the best hotel in Nosy Be; very well managed, with a lovely swimming pool and excellent food.

Chanty Beach BP 172; Tel: 614 73; fax: 614 74; web: http://travel.to/Chanty-Beach. 2 luxury two-person self-catering apartments with spacious veranda, equipped with air conditioning/fans and telephones, near a good beach north of Hotel Vanila. €37.5 including breakfast. Dinner €13. Also cheaper (Category B) double rooms for €30 per person. Airport transfers €13.

Au Coin Sauvage Tel: 612 85 (Tana: 22 228 54); email: coinsauvage@nosybevillas.com; web: www.nosybevillas.com. 10 rooms in two 4-room villas and one 2-room villa. 363,000Fmg per room, including breakfast. South of the Vanila in a beautiful location on a hill overlooking the sea. Free airport transfers.

Les Cocotiers BP 191; tel/fax: 613 14; email: cocotier@dts.mg; web: http://lescocotier.nemo.it. Italian/Malagasy owned. 26 pleasant bungalows, and very good Italian food. High season: about €177 per person (double) half board. Less than half those prices low season. Airport transfers about 60,000Fmg.

Nosy Be Hotel Tel: 614 30; fax: 614 06. Italian/French owned. The most popular mid-range hotel in the area; 7 bungalows, 36 rooms, some with air-conditioning, others with fans. Swimming pool. Prices range from €72.5 to €145, depending on the room and season. Breakfast an additional 30,000Fmg. Some visitors have complained that the food is overpriced and monotonous and transfers from the airport are expensive (€10).

Category B
Belle Plage (formerly L'Ampasy Village) BP 19, Djamandjary; tel: 614 77; fax: 611 58. 16 bungalows with air conditioning and WC. Restaurant. €40 (low season) and €55 (high season) per two-person bungalow per day including breakfast. Fixed menu meals: 60,000Fmg. Despite the name, the beach is dirty.

Category C
Nautilus Diving BP 139, Plage Belle Vue; tel: 613 43. 3 rooms at 130,000Fmg without breakfast. Meal: 45,000Fmg. Diving, sea excursions.

Ambondrona
South of Djamandjary; some prefer it to the busier, noisier Ambataloaka. If you don't want to eat at your hotel it's close enough to walk to Ambataloaka through the sugarcane fields and get a taxi back.

Category B
Villa Vero (Formerly Villa Blanche) BP 79; tel/fax: 620 28; cellphone: 032 02 171 30/34. (In Tana: 3207 508 42.) Email: villavero@hotmail.com. 150,000Fmg single, 200,000Fmg double or triple; breakfast 15,000Fmg. 17 bungalows in a nice location by one of the rare clean beaches of Nosy Be. No air-conditioning, but hardly necessary in this breezy location. Well-run by Mme Portos; good value, especially for families or friends who are willing to share a triple room. Good restaurant with mainly Malagasy dishes.
Les Jolis Coins BP 220, Ambondrona Avaratra. 8 bungalows, 11 rooms. Comfortable; varied menu in restaurant.

Category C
Tsara Loky BP 160; tel: 610 22. Malagasy run. 6 simple bungalows with fans, showers and WC. 180,000Fmg. 6 rooms with shared bathroom: 40,000–70,000Fmg double. Family bungalow sleeping 4-6: 250,000Fmg. Prices do not include breakfast. Open-air restaurant.
Au Rendezvous des Amis 5 simple bungalows by the sea. Reasonably-priced restaurant.

Madirokely
The name means 'little tamarind' or 'few tamarinds'. Lying just north of Ambatoloaka, this is a quieter option but is becoming quite developed. It now has a good pharmacy called TOKO.

Category A
Marlin Club BP 205; tel: 610 70/613 15; fax: 614 45; email: marlin.club@simcro.mg. 16 rooms plus a few bungalows. From 540,000–950,000Fmg. Very comfortable, price includes breakfast. A good beach-restaurant. Water sports and deep-sea fishing.

Category B
L'Heure Bleue (formerly Chez Zou) Three 2-storey family bungalows for 350,000Fmg and 8 simple bungalows for 250,000Fmg. Breakfast 20,000Fmg. Set meals, must be ordered in advance, 60,000Fmg. Swimming pool. Beautiful view of Ambataloaka Bay.
Madiro Hotel BP 218, Madirokely; tel/fax: 614 18; email: madiro@simicro.mg. 15 comfortable bungalows set round the swimming pool. All have fans and fridges. About €74 high season, €54 low season. Tours offered include camping trips to other islands, water-skiing, parasailing. Also a scuba-diving centre.
Le Grand Large BP 89 Madirokely; tel/fax: 615 84. 14 rooms with air conditioning and hot water. Excellent location. Double room from about €45 (low season) to €54 (high season). Restaurant with patisserie. Water scooters; three boats for excursions.

Category C
Chez Madame Senga 3 simple bungalows with WC, shower and fan; very good value at about 80,000Fmg; breakfast 10,000Fmg; other meals 30,000–80,000Fmg.

Ambatoloaka
This is a fast-growing tourist centre (formerly a charming fishing village) which offers the best options for inexpensive places to stay as well as luxury accommodation. It is the liveliest place on the island so if you're looking for nightlife, this is where it's at.

Where to stay
Category A
Hotel l'Espadon Tel: 614 28; fax: 614 27. Swiss-owned. 11 bungalows, 9 rooms. Very comfortable with air conditioning, TV etc. 320,000–560,000Fmg, depending on location of room. Excellent restaurant, with a Sunday barbeque. Breakfast 25,000Fmg. Specialise in deep-sea fishing.
Hotel Coco Plage BP159; cellphone: 03 207 76 964. 11 rooms for 242,000Fmg and 2 suites for 400,000Fmg. Breakfast 15,000Fmg. About 1km south of the village.

Category B
Hotel L'Ylang Ylang BP 110; tel: 614 01; fax: 614 02; web: www.hotel-lylangylang.com. 12 rooms, 8 with fans, 4 with air-conditioning. All rooms en-suite with wall safe and mini bar. The best hotel in this category; British owned and very good value at €40 double (room with fan) or €55 (air-conditioning) including breakfast. Good restaurant. Airport transfer 55,000Fmg. Visa cards accepted.
La Résidence Ambatoloaka BP 130; tel: 610 91; fax: 616 43. This popular place had become a bit run-down, but is now under new management. 12 air-conditioned en-suite rooms and a good terrace/lounge. Double rooms are 200,000Fmg (low season) and 240,000Fmg high season.
Chez Gérard et Francine BP 193; tel: 614 09. Comfortable family house, at a good, quiet location at the southern end of Ambataloaka; nine rooms, some with en-suite shower. Deservedly popular so usually full. €31 (double) including breakfast. The owners are strongly opposed to sex tourism so do not accept single men.
La Saladarie Tel: 614 52. A pleasant hotel/restaurant with 16 basic but clean and spacious rooms.125,000Fmg en-suite, or 100,000Fmg shared facilities. Very good, economically priced meals. Specialise in salads.
Hotel Tropical BP 198; tel: 614 16. 7 bungalows with shower and WC; 110,000Fmg with breakfast.
La Riviéra (formerly Hotel Caraval) Route d'Ambatoloaka; tel: 614 05 or 612 26. 5 bungalows with en-suite bathrooms; hot water; fans. 130,000Fmg without breakfast.
Hotel Robinson Tel: 614 36. On the junction of the road to Madirokely. 6 bungalows with shower, WC and fan. 130,000–150,000Fmg, depending on the location. 100,000Fmg low season.

Category C
Coucher du Soleil Hotel & Restaurant BP 134; tel/fax: 616 20. 7 very clean and comfortable bungalows with en-suite bathroom (basic showers, new toilets). Not on the beach, but sea view; 80,000Fmg; breakfast 12,000Fmg.

Where to eat
Most of the main hotels have good restaurants, with **L'Ylang Ylang** particularly recommended, but Ambataloaka has always been renowned for its little restaurants

serving delicious food. Look out for the food stalls and snackeries not listed here, where you can often eat a marvellous meal very cheaply.

Chez Angeline Tel: 616 21. Before the arrival of big-time tourism in Nosy Be, this was its most popular little restaurant, famous for its seafood and *poulet au coco*.
Karibou Tel: 616 47. Excellent Italian food, including pizzas.
La Saladerie Tel: 614 52. Salads and sandwiches.
Le Glacier Drinks, snacks and ice-cream.
Soleil A lively bar/restaurant.
Au Fin Gourmet (Chez Edith) Very tasty, inexpensive food.

Nightlife

Le Djembe 'The best-equipped night club in the whole of Mada: air-conditioning, high-tech lighting and special effects, mirrored walls … even a waterfall behind the bar' (S Edghill). Price fluctuates. 5,000Fmg at the time of writing, but may revert to its former 10,000Fmg.
Karibou Restaurant Dinner dancing with local band every Thursday. Free if you have a meal, 5,000Fmg for the band only.
Glacier Snack Bar Live music on Friday nights.
Le Jackpot A gambling place next to the Djembe night club. More down-market than Le Casino.
Le Casino Set on a hill-side like an old plantation house, diagonally opposite on the right as you leave Ambataloaka. Fruit machines, roulette, blackjack etc. Live music on Saturday nights.

PRACTICALITIES
Medical care

There is always a doctor on call at the main Nosy Be hospital in Hell-Ville and people to patch you up in an emergency. However, if you can avoid the hospital you are advised to do so. There is a good clean hospital/clinic in Ambanja which has better facilities. In case of serious emergency you should plan to be flown out to Réunion or home. For minor problems go to one of Nosy Be's GPs, and pay around 10,000Fmg for a consultation including prescription.

Pharmacies

There are two well-stocked pharmacies in Hell-Ville. One of them is always open as a *Pharmacie de Garde* for emergencies (this changes each week but the taxi drivers usually know as there are announcements on the radio). **Pharmacie Tsarajoro** is on the main street north of the market, almost opposite Chez Abud; tel: 613 82. **Pharmacie Nouroudine** is in Andavakatoko not far from the small market to the west of town down the road from the main market; tel: 610 38. There is also a good new pharmacy in Mandirokely, near Ambataloaka.

Money

Very few hotels take credit cards. Banks are open 07.30–11.00; 14.30–16.30 weekdays only. Banks usually only work a half day before a holiday.

Banks

BNI (Credit Lyonnais) On the road down to the port, it often has the best exchange rates.
BTM Closest bank to the market, also on the main drag. Gives cash advances on MasterCard. Expect to wait at least an hour.
BFV Close to Oasis, almost opposite the post office. Gives cash advances on Visa .

Western Union

Of interest to people needing cash sent in a hurry! There's an office for Western Union in the foyer of Chez Abud Hotel: you get a friend to deposit the money at a Western Union office in the UK (tel: 0800 833 833) or another country (eg: USA tel: 800 325 6000), they then get a code number which they fax, email or phone to you, you take this and some ID to the office, and collect your money in Fmg within minutes!

Photo shop

Graphoprint in Hell-Ville (opposite the Catholic church) do next-day service for developing prints, and sell film and camera batteries. Also photocopying service.

Yacht supplies and repairs

A new supermarket, **Leader Price**, has opened in Hell-Ville which has a wide range of goods for yachtsmen at prices comparable to those in France. **Mécabe**, in Hell-Ville, sell spare parts and will facilitate repairs.

EXCURSIONS
Mont Passot

A popular excursion is the trip to the island's highest point, Mont Passot. There are good views of a series of deep-blue crater lakes, which are said to contain crocodiles (though I have never seen one) and to be sacred as the home of the spirits of the Sakalava and Antakarana princes. It is *fady* to fish there, or to smoke, wear trousers or any garment put on over the feet, or a hat, while on the lakes' shores. It is, in any case, difficult to get down to the water since the crater sides are very steep.

The road to the peak runs from Djamandjary, and can be hiked or cycled. Tour groups come to Mont Passot to see the sunset, but in the clear air of Nosy Be this is generally less than spectacular, so it is better to make a day excursion of it and take a picnic. Souvenir sellers have discovered the joys of having captive *vazahas* waiting for the sun to dip, and have set up tables for their wares. This is not a hill of solitude.

Lokobe

Nosy Be's only protected area, Lokobe, is a Strict Reserve and as such is not currently open to visitors (plans for it to become a national park seem to have been shelved). However, it is possible to visit the buffer zone on the northeast side of the peninsula where permits are not required. The two little villages here, Ambatozavavy and Ampasypohy, have embraced tourism with enthusiasm and the whole area does not bear comparison with the unspoilt place I so delighted in over a decade ago. However, a visit here still offers a glimpse of village life in Nosy Be and is an informative and enjoyable excursion.

Before the opening of small hotels here, the excursion to Lokobe was the sole preserve of Jean-Robert who still runs day-trips from the main Nosy Be hotels to Ampasipohy, 45 minutes by *pirogue* from Ambatozavavy. This trip is still a good option for those who cannot spend the night (see *Where to stay*). During the course of the day you are served a traditional lunch and taken on a tour of the forest (now sadly very degraded) where Jean-Robert, who speaks excellent English and is a natural showman, explains the traditional uses of various plants and points out a variety of animals. You are bound to see a lepilemur which, unlike the species in Berenty, spends its day dozing in the fork of a favourite tree rather than in a hole (Jean-Robert likes to 'please' tourists by shaking the tree to make the animal jump: visitors should say a firm 'no' to this cruelty.) You should see black lemurs (shyer, but in better condition than those on Nosy Komba) and a carefully placed boa and chameleons. The chameleons here are the panther (*pardalis*) species and in the breeding season (November to May) the male is bright green and the female a pinkish colour. The villagers grow vanilla and peppers, and a wide range of handicrafts can be bought direct from the maker.

Jean-Robert meets most planes, but if you miss him your hotel will know where he is. His tours cost around 150,000Fmg.

Where to stay
Eco-village Fihavanana BP 203, Ambatozavavy; tel/fax: 614 75. Designed for ecotourists rather than beach fanatics; Swiss-managed. 9 very comfortable, spacious palm-thatched bungalows with hot showers and solar-powered. About 195,000Fmg (high season). Transfer from Hell-Ville costs about 25,000Fmg for two people. The manager can organise trips with local fisherman, but they also have their own Zodiac. An excellent feature is the Lokobe Nature Trail, which can be walked at night so is of particular interest to those devoted to reptiles and nocturnal fauna of all kinds.
Jungle village BP 208, Hell-Ville. 6 lovely basic bungalows in Ampasypohy, run by Marc Dehlinger. Beautifully located, and excellent value at around 90,000Fmg per bungalow, or 500,000Fmg for the main house (5–6 people). Dinner 35,000Fmg.

Ambanoro and the CNRO Museum
Ambanoro was formerly the site of the Black Lemur Forest Project set up by Josephine Andrews, but sadly no longer functioning. The closure of this centre reduces the interest in a visit to this area but it is still a pleasant walk with enough to see to make it worth a half day excursion. The area was once an important Indian community, and there are the ruins of an ancient mosque, half-hidden by enormous sacred fig trees, and the elaborate Indian cemetery. Ambanoro was once the capital of Nosy Be (its other name, Marodokana, means 'many shops') and was a thriving port and trading centre up until the rise of Hell-Ville in the early 1800s.

The CNRO (Oceanographic Research Institute) museum is about 2km from town on the road to Ambanoro. Here you can see amazing examples of preserved fish (including a baby hammerhead shark) and a very good local seashell collection (weekday mornings only).

NOSY KOMBA AND NOSY TANIKELY
No visit to Nosy Be is complete without an excursion to these two islands. Nosy Komba's main attraction is the black lemurs, and the marine national park of Nosy Tanikely lures snorkellers and bird enthusiasts.

Getting there and away
All the Nosy Be hotels do excursions to Nosy Komba which is usually combined with Nosy Tanikely. Most will let you do the sensible thing of taking an overnight break in Nosy Komba, then rejoining the boat the following day for Nosy Tanikely. For Nosy Komba alone it is much cheaper to go by *pirogue*. Go to the small *pirogue* port (Port Ambariovato, to the east of the main port in Hell-Ville). The *pirogues* leave at around 11.00 each day after the morning's shopping in Hell-Ville. The trip should cost from 5,000 to 15,000Fmg. If you are a group of six or more, you can find a fast boat from the main port for around 25,000Fmg per person to Nosy Komba.

Yachties approaching from Nosy Be should wait until Nosy Verona (the island with the old lighthouse) then bear 020 degrees. Good anchorage in 3–7m over sand and mud.

Nosy Komba (Nosy Ambariovato)

Once upon a time Nosy Komba was an isolated island with an occasional boat service, a tiny, self-sufficient village (Ampangorinana), and a troop of semi-tame black lemurs which were held to be sacred so never hunted. Now all that has changed. Tourists arrive in boat-loads from Nosy Be and from passing cruise ships which can land over 100 people.

Komba means 'lemur' (interestingly it is the Swahili word for bushbaby which of course is the African relative of the lemur) and it is the lemurs that bring in the visitors. During the 1980s the villagers made nothing out of these visits apart from the sale of clay animals which they glazed with the acid of spent batteries. Then they instigated a modest fee for seeing the animals and increased the variety of handicrafts. Now that Nosy Komba is on some cruise-ship itineraries they have taken on the works: 'tribal dancing', face decoration, escorted walks... anything that will earn a dollar or two.

With all the demands on your purse, it sometimes takes a bit of mental effort to see the underlying charm of Ampangorinana, but it is nevertheless a typical Malagasy community living largely on fishing and *tavy* farming (witness the horrendous deforestation of their little island; when I first visited in 1976, it was completely covered with luxuriant trees) but it is the black lemurs that provide the financial support (and probably prevent further degradation of their environment). The ancestor who initiated the hunting *fady* must be pleased with himself. If you want the lemurs-on-your-shoulders experience and the chance to see these engaging animals at close quarters you should definitely come here. Only the male *Eulemur macaco* is black; the females, which give birth in September, are chestnut brown with white ear-tufts.

Nosy Komba also provides an excellent opportunity for observing lemur behaviour, although the troop size here is much higher than normal, leading to aggression and fighting. Female lemurs tend to be dominant, but here it is a general free-for-all. Note the way the males rub their bottoms on branches to scent-mark them and gain some authority. Take a look at a lemur's hands: you will see the four flat primate fingernails (such wonderfully human hands!) and the single claw which is used for grooming. Be careful when feeding the lemurs: an accidental nip with their razor-sharp canines can give a nasty wound (although this usually heals very quickly).

A small fee (about 2,500Fmg) is charged to see the lemurs, and en route to Lemur Park everyone in the village will try to sell you something. Since you are buying direct from the grower/maker, this is the best place to get vanilla and handicrafts (carved *pirogues*, clay animals and unusual and attractive 'lace' tablecloths, curtains and bedspreads). The handicrafts here are unlike any found on the mainland, so it is worth bringing plenty of cash (small change). If you intend to buy a bedspread (and this is the best place to do so) you will need at least 200,000Fmg for a double-bed size.

One of the former glories of Nosy Komba, its coral, has sadly almost completely disappeared so snorkelling is no longer rewarding. The sea and beach near the village are polluted with human waste, but there is a good swimming beach round to the left (as you face the sea).

The best way to visit Nosy Komba is by yourself, or in a small group, and avoid the 'rush hour' (09.30–10.30). When there are few other tourists, Nosy Komba is a tranquil place, so consider an overnight stay or a stay of a few days. The available accommodation is comfortable enough and cheaper than beach options on Nosy Be. Given time to explore, it is possible to find and watch lemur groups away from 'Lemur Park' or to take a hike up the hill for spectacular views of the whole of Nosy Be (the top of Nosy Komba, at 630m, is higher than any point on Nosy Be), but start early before it gets too hot and bear in mind that there is little left of the primary forest; just secondary growth with lots of bamboo.

Warning: Do not drink the supposedly potable water from public taps along the front of the village. It may be contaminated.

Where to stay
Chez Bernie Mrs Bernie and Remo, who run Albatros (see *Cruising*), have 4 luxury bungalows. €69 full board (which includes unlimited boat hire). They also organise hiking trips across Nosy Komba and can provide camping equipment. Recommended.

Les Floralies BP 107, Nosy Be, fax: 613 67. 7 French-run bungalows and one beach house beautifully situated at the end of the quietest beach, with en-suite shower and toilet. 100,000–150,000Fmg including breakfast. Bar and restaurant. An additional series of backpacker bungalows, Les Bungalows de la Gare, have been added. These cost only 25,000Fmg! This surely must be one of the best bargains in Madagascar.

Hotel Lémuriens BP 185, Nosy Be. Good bungalows run by Martin (German) and Henriette (Malagasy), about 100,000Fmg per bungalow (with shower and WC), 35,000Fmg shared facilities. This hotel deserves your support. Martin was responsible for the construction of water reservoirs, the school and a clinic for the islands' inhabitants. Can be prebooked by fax: 613 71 (Hell-Ville).

Hotel Madame Madio BP 207. 8 simple bungalows for about 30,000Fmg (shared facilities); 3 bungalows with en-suite bathrooms: 50,000Fmg. Breakfast 12,500Fmg. Order other meals in advance. Mme Madio shares some of her guests with her neighbouring cousin Mme Yvonne, an excellent cook.

Chez Alexandre Simple bungalows near the Buvette des Vahinys; about 30,000Fmg.

Nosy Tanikely
Although now much visited, this is still pretty close to Paradise. Nosy Tanikely is a tiny island with a lighthouse and… a rumour of planning permission to build a hotel there. The island is a marine reserve and it is for the snorkelling that most people visit it. And the snorkelling is excellent (even if too many ships dropping too many anchors are beginning to take their toll on the coral). In clear water you can see an amazing variety of marine life – coral, starfish, anemones, every colour and shape of fish, turtles, lobsters…

With this new world beneath your gaze there is a real danger of forgetting the passing of time and becoming seriously sunburnt. Even the most carefully applied sunblock tends to miss some areas, so wear a T-shirt and shorts.

Don't think you have finished with Nosy Tanikely when you come out of the water; at low tide it is possible to walk right round the island. During your circumambulation you will see (if you go anticlockwise): a broad beach of white sand covered in shells and bleached pieces of coral, a couple of trees full of flying foxes and – in the spring – graceful white tropic-birds flying in and out of their nests in the high cliffs. At your feet will be rock pools and some scrambling, but nothing too challenging.

Then there is the climb up to the lighthouse at the top of the island for the view.

Sadly, Nosy Tanikely has a problem with years of rubbish left by visitors, though the local Platform for the Environment, Nosy Be (a group of environmental organisations and interested individuals), is trying to get this removed through a series of volunteer clean-up days. The best time to visit is out of the main tourist season. If you can afford it, hire your own boat and take a picnic or arrange for the boat crew to grill a fish on the beach. Boats running trips to Nosy Tanikely may provide snorkelling gear, but it's safer to bring your own.

OTHER ISLANDS IN THE NOSY BE ARCHIPELAGO

Nosy Sakatia

This rather bare island lies off the west side of Nosy Be. Sakatia means orchid island, but a more remarkable aspect of its flora are the baobabs. There are some well-run hotels here catering for divers.

Where to stay

Sakatia Passions BP 295; tel: 61 462; fax: 61 435. 12 bungalows run by fishing specialists Jacques Toussaint and Jean-Claude Clement who own six boats fully equipped for deep-sea fishing. Also windsurfing, and kayaking.

Sakatia Dive Inn BP 186, Hell-Ville; tel: 61 514; fax 61 367. 6 rustic bungalows with mosquito nets, basins and WC, 195,000Fmg per day; 5 *huttes Canadiennes* (A-frame tents) 95,000Fmg. Communal facilities. Family-style dining; lunch 55,000Fmg, dinner 70,000Fmg. As the name implies, this place offers diving courses and excursions.

Delphino Villa Bungalows Tel: 61 668. 4 charming, rustic traditional Malagasy bungalows. 45,000Fmg per night (without breakfast) with refreshingly inexpensive drinks.

These places welcome visitors from boats. The channel between Nosy Be and Nosy Sakatia provides safe anchoring some 150m off the beach at 5m over a sandy bottom, if you don't wish to anchor off Hell-Ville – but beware strong tidal currents.

Nosy Mitsio

The archipelago of Nosy Mitsio lies some 60–70km from Nosy Be and about the same distance from the mainland. This is the Maldives of Madagascar, with two exclusive (and expensive) fly-in resorts on stunningly beautiful small islands.

La Grande Mitsio

The largest island is populated by local Malagasy – Antakarana and Sakalava, who survive on their denuded island through farming, cattle and goats. 'Main mode of transport: *pirogues*, some very big – able to do shopping/selling trips to mainland (Port St Louis) and Nosy Be, even with the odd cow in the boat!' (JA). Overgrazing has devastated the island but some forest remains in the southern part. Huge basalt columns are a prominent feature on the northwest tip, used as an adventure playground by enterprising goats.

The island attracts yachties to its coral reefs and good anchorages. Maribe Bay provides good anchorage, protected between two hills. This is a good area for seeing manta rays.

Tsara Banjina

The name means 'good to look at' and this is a small but incredibly beautiful island, made famous by British actress Joanna Lumley who was 'cast away' here. The red, grey and black volcanic rocks, rising quite high at its centre, have a mass of lush, green vegetation clinging to them, from baobabs and other large trees to pachypodium and tiny rockery plants. But its real glory are the pure white beaches of coarse sand, along which lap a crystal-clear green/indigo sea. Turtles and rays rest near the beaches. Divers can be kept busy for a couple of days, and there are walking trails.

Yachties can anchor off the southwest, at 6m over a sandy bottom.

Where to stay

L'Hotel Tsarabajina Contact details: main office (Tana); tel: (261) 285 14; fax: 285 15; email: Groupe.Hotel@simicro.mg. Built by an ex-South African, Richard Walker, and his partners, this is beautifully designed, constructed predominantly of natural materials and accommodating just a few people at a time. The building containing the bar/restaurant is

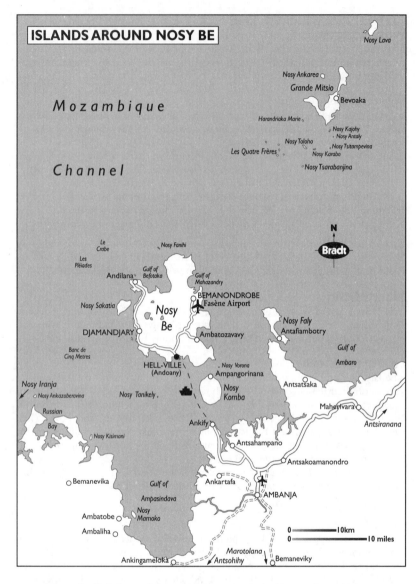

ISLANDS AROUND NOSY BE

Nosy Lava

Nosy Ankarea
Grande Mitsio
Bevoaka

Harandriaka Marie

Nosy Kajohy
Nosy Antaly
Nosy Toloho
Nosy Tsitampevina
Les Quatre Frères
Nosy Karabo

Nosy Tsarabanjina

M o z a m b i q u e

C h a n n e l

N

Bradt

Le Crabe
Nosy Fanihi
Les Pléiades
Gulf of Befotaka
Andilana
Gulf of Mahazandry
Nosy Sakatia
BEMANONDROBE
Fasène Airport
Nosy Be
Nosy Faly
Antafiambotry
DJAMANDJARY
Ambatozavavy
Gulf of Ambaro
Banc de Cinq Metres
HELL-VILLE
(Andoany)
Nosy Vorona
Ampangorinana
Antsatsaka
Nosy Iranja
Nosy Ankazoberavina
Nosy Tanikely
Nosy Komba
Mahenivara
Russian Bay
Nosy Kisimani
Ankify
Antsiranana
Antsahampano
Antsakoamanondro
Bemanevika
Gulf of Ampasindava
Ankartafa
AMBANJA
Ambatobe
Nosy Mamoko
Ambaliha
0 ══ 10km
0 ══ 10 miles
Ankingameloka
Marotolana
Antsohihy
Bemaneviky

separate from the 20 A-frame chalets which have en-suite bathrooms. Rates: high season €185 double; €115 single; low season: €148 double, €92 single. There is an additional tourist tax of 3,000Fmg per day. 'What a perfect ending! Superb snorkelling, dolphins feeding close to the shore, turtles hatching out by our bungalow… a piece of paradise!' (J Dudley). Transfers by speedboat (€123 per person round trip). This is also a world-class scuba-diving centre, and offers a wide range of watersports such as windsurfing.

Nosy Ankarea

Another beautiful place to spend a few luxurious days. There are some gorgeous, sun-drenched beaches and the low hills make for pleasant walking excursions. 'The island is superb. Fabulous pachypodiums, flamboyants etc. Surrounded by coral reefs in an azure sea. The forest on the island is relatively undisturbed, due to numerous *fadys* and the fact that no one lives there except Marlin Club tourists. It is possible to climb up the highest hill (219m – quite steep but well worth it) to reach a plateau covered with pachypodiums and lots of wierd and wonderful other succulents. From here you can see all of Nosy Mitsio and the surrounding reefs.' (Josephine Andrews)

Here is the **Marlin Club Ecohotel Annex** with 6 luxury tents, with beach parasols, showers and toilets. About €140 per day inclusive. First-class meals in a thatched restaurant built around a huge baobab tree. Contact Marlin Club Hotel (page 352) for details.

Les Quatre Frères (The Four Brothers)

These are four imposing lumps of silver basalt, two of which are home to hundreds of nesting seabirds, including brown boobies, frigate birds and white-tailed tropic-birds. A pair of Madagascar fish eagles nest on one of the rocks. The sides drop vertically to about 20–30m, and divers come here because three of the boulders can be circumnavigated during one vigorous dive. Yachties can anchor to the southeast of Nosy Beangovo, roughly 100m from the mouth of a cave, at a depth of about 10m. Currents reach up to one knot. The best marine life is in the lee. There are huge caves, spectacular overhangs and rockfalls in the area.

Nosy Iranja

About two hours by boat from Nosy Be (€92 per person), or transfer by helicopter can be arranged. Until a few years ago this was a peaceful island inhabited by fisherfolk, and an important breeding reserve for hawksbill turtles. When news broke that planning permission had been granted for a luxury hotel there was consternation – and outrage – among conservationists. However, now the hotel is open the reports, such as the following from a tour operator, are very favourable: 'This is a hit – even though it should never have been built. The accommodation is really attractive, the food is very good indeed, the staff are absolutely charming, the site is fantastically beautiful, the specialists know their stuff, very well equipped – and the management is dead keen to please and make sure things work well. The English spoken is limited, but someone with no French could get by. Emanuel is a scientist from Nosy Be working on the turtle monitoring project, very proud of it, and eager to show visitors both the turtle project and the reptiles and amphibians on Iranja Be. Everyone has awarded it full marks.' €113 per person half-board. Book through their operations centre on Rue Raimbault (BP 56, Nosy Be 207; tel/fax: 86 616 90; cellphone: 261 32 07 068 30.

Nosy Kivinjy

Otherwise known as Sugarloaf Rock, this is a great basalt boulder with 'organ pipes' formations on one side. Not recommended for diving (poor) or anchorage (very insecure). There are strong northeast-flowing currents around the islet.

Nosy Mamoko

This little island is at the southwest end of Ampasindava Bay. Known among the yachting fraternity for its exceptional shelter in all weather, it is a lovely, tranquil spot for a few days' relaxation. Nosy Mamoko is on the itineraries of two or three operators, based in Nosy Be, who organise lengthy trips into the region. There is good fishing here and whale-watching from October to December. Good anchorage is found in the channel between the island and the mainland, in 15m over a sandy bottom.

Nosy Radama

The Radama islands, which lie to the far south of Nosy Be and thus are only really accessible to yachties, compete with the Mitsios for the best diving sites in the northeast of Madagascar. They are set in a breathtaking coastline of bays backed by high mountains. Most of these high sandstone islands are steep-sided above and below water and covered with scrub, grass and trees. Sharp eroded rock formations, however, render the remaining forest rather difficult to explore.

Nosy Kalakajoro

The northernmost island, featuring dense, impenetrable forest on the south side. There are good beaches on the southern side and snorkelling is worthwhile off the southeast. Yachts should anchor 100m off the southeast side in 10–12m over good holding sand and mud, to get protection from the north-to-west winds.

Nosy Ovy (Potato Island)

This is the largest of the group, but the environmental degradation is terrible. Nearly all the trees have been cut and goats have completed the destruction of its flora. Red soil weeps from gaping scars into the surrounding water. If you still want to visit, boats can anchor off the east side, near a protected rocky outcrop.

Nosy Valiha

A small island which is privately owned so you should not visit without permission.

HAINTENY

The *dingadingana* has borne fruit without coming into leaf,
the *hazotokana* has borne fruit without coming into flower,
and the fishing has been uncertain this year.
Why have these changes occurred, my elder brother?
– Have you forgotten, perhaps, the sayings of our ancestors?
Consider, children, the conditions here on earth:
the trees grow, but not unceasingly,
for if they grew unceasingly, they would reach the sky.
Not only this,
but there is a time for their growing,
a time for their becoming old,
and a time for their breaking.
So it is, too, for man: there is a time for youth,
a time for old age,
a time for good,
a time for evil,
and a time for death.

HAINTENY

It is through his subjects that the sovereign reigns,
It is the rocks that cause the stream to sing.
It is its feathers that make the chicken large.
The palm-trees are the feet of the water.
The winds are the feet of the fire.
The beloved is the tree of life.

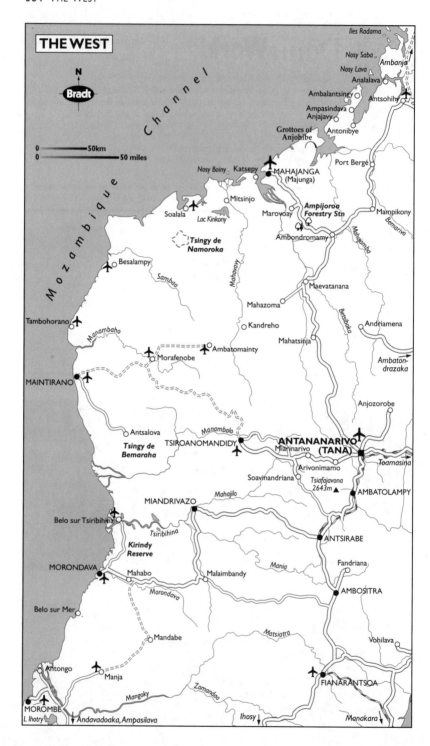

THE WEST

N

Bradt

0 ___ 50km
0 ___ 50 miles

Iles Radama

Nosy Saba

Nosy Lava Ambanja

Analalava

Ambalantsingy

Ampasindava Antsohihy

Anjajavy

Antonibye

Grottoes of
Anjohibe

Nosy Boiny Katsepy Port Bergé

Mitsinjo MAHAJANGA
(Majunga)

Soalala Lac Kinkony

Marovoay *Ampijoroa
Forestry Stn* Mampikony

Mozambique Channel

Bemarivo

Ambondromany

*Tsingy de
Namoroka*

Mahavavy

Maevatanana

Besalampy

Sambao

Mahazoma

Mahajamba

Tambohorano

Manambaho

Kandreho

Mahatsinja

Andriamena

Betsiboka

Ambaton-
drazaka

Morafenobe Ambatomainty

MAINTIRANO

Anjozorobe

Antsalova

Manambolo

*Tsingy de
Bemaraha*

TSIROANOMANDIDY ANTANANARIVO
(TANA)

Miarinarivo

Arivonimamo Toamasina

MIANDRIVAZO *Mahajilo*

Soavinandriana *Tsiafajavona
2643m* ▲ AMBATOLAMPY

Belo sur Tsiribihina

Tsiribihina

*Kirindy
Reserve*

ANTSIRABE

MORONDAVA Mahabo Malaimbandy *Mania* Fandriana

Morondava

Belo sur Mer

AMBOSITRA

Mandabe *Matsiatra* Vohilava

Antongo

Manja

Mangoky *Zomandao*

MOROMBE

L. Ihotry ↓Andavadoaka, Ampasilava Ihosy↓ FIANARANTSOA

Manakara↓

The West

OVERVIEW

The west of Madagascar offers a dry climate, deciduous forest (with some excellent reserves to protect it), and endless sandy beaches with little danger from sharks. The region is the fastest-growing in Madagascar in terms of tourist development, the poor roads doing little to deter the building of new beach hotels, some of which depend on fly-in tourism. Because of the lack of roads and agreeable climate this is the ideal area for mountain bikers or walkers. Adventurous travellers will have no trouble finding a warm welcome in untouristed villages, their own deserted beach and some spectacular landscapes.

This is the region to see one of Madagascar's extraordinary natural wonders: the *tsingy*. Pronounced 'zing' this is exactly the sound made when one of the limestone pinnacles is struck by a small stone (they can be played like a xylophone!). Limestone karst is not unique to Madagascar, but it is rare to see such dramatic forms, such an impenetrable forest of spikes and spires. The endemic succulents that struggle for a foothold in this waterless environment add to the unworldly feeling of a *tsingy* landscape.

Opposite major rivers the sea water along the west coast is a brick red colour: 'like swimming in soup', as one traveller put it. This is the laterite washed into the rivers from the eroded hillsides of the highlands and discharged into the sea: Madagascar's bleeding wounds.

History

The west is the home of the Sakalava people. For a while in Malagasy history this was the largest and most powerful tribe, ruled by their own kings and queens. The Sakalava kingdom was founded by the Volamena branch of the Maroserana dynasty which emerged in the southwest during the 16th century. Early in the 17th century a Volamena prince, Andriamisara, reached the Sakalava river and gave its name to his new kingdom. His son, Andriandahifotsy (which means 'white man'), succeeded him around 1650 and, with the aid of firearms acquired from European traders, conquered the southwestern area between the two rivers, Onilahy and Manambolo. This region became known as the Menabe. Later kings conquered first the Boina, the area from the Manambolo to north of present-day Mahajanga, and then the northwest coast as far as Antsiranana.

By the 18th century the Sakalava empire occupied a huge area in the west, but was divided into the Menabe in the south and the Boina in the north. The two rulers fell out, unity was abandoned, and in the 19th century the area came under the control of the Merina. The Sakalava did not take kindly to domination and sporadic guerrilla warfare continued in the Menabe area until French colonial times.

KING RADAMA II

The son of the 'Wicked Queen' Ranavalona, King Radama II was a gentle ruler who abhorred bloodshed. He was pro-European, interested in Christianity (although never formally a Christian) and a friend of William Ellis, missionary and chronicler of 19th-century Madagascar. After Radama's death, Ellis wrote: 'I have never said that Radama was an able ruler, or a man of large views, for these he was not; but a more humane ruler never wore a crown.' With missionaries of all denominations invited back into Madagascar, intense rivalry sprang up between the Protestants sent by Britain, and the Jesuits who arrived from France. Resentment at the influence of these foreigners over the young king and disgust at the often rash changes he instigated boiled over in 1863, and only eight months after his coronation he was assassinated, strangled with a silken sash so that the *fady* against shedding royal blood was not infringed.

The French-British rivalry was fuelled by the violent death of the king, even to the extent that Ellis was accused of being party to the assassination. But was Radama really dead? Both Ellis and Jean Laborde believed that he had survived the strangling and had been allowed to escape by the courtiers bearing him to the countryside for burial. Uprisings, supposedly organised by the 'dead' king, supported this rumour. In a biography of King Radama II, the French historian Raymond Delval makes a strong case that the ex-monarch eventually retreated to the area of Lake Kinkony and lived out the rest of his life in this Sakalava region.

The Sakalava kingdom bore the brunt of the first serious efforts by the French to colonise the island. For some years France had laid claims (based on treaties made with local princes) on parts of the north and northwest, and in 1883 two fortresses in this region were bombarded. An attack on Mahajanga followed. This was the beginning of the end of Madagascar as an independent kingdom.

The Sakalava people today

The modern Sakalava have relatively dark skins. The west of Madagascar received a number of African immigrants from across the Mozambique Channel and their influence shows not only in the racial characteristics of the people, but also in their language and customs. There are a number of Bantu words in their dialect, and their belief in *tromba* (possession by spirits) and *dady* (royal relics cult) is of African origin.

The Sakalava do not practise second burial. The quality of their funerary art (in one small area) rivals that of the Mahafaly: birds and naked figures are a feature of Sakalava tombs, the latter frequently in erotic positions. Concepts of sexuality and rebirth are implied here. The female figures are often disproportionately large, perhaps recognising the importance of women in the Sakalava culture.

Sakalava royalty do not require an elaborate tomb since kings are considered to continue their spiritual existence through a medium with healing powers, and in royal relics.

Getting around

Roads are being improved, but driving from town to town in the west can still be challenging and in much of the area the roads simply aren't there. There are regular flights to the large towns and a Twin Otter serves many of the smaller ones.

MAHAJANGA (MAJUNGA)
History
Ideally located for trade with East Africa, Arabia and western Asia, Mahajanga has been a major commercial port since 1745, when the Boina capital was moved here from Marovoay. One ruler of the Boina was Queen Ravahiny, a very able monarch who maintained the unity of the Boina which was threatened by rebellions in both the north and the south. It was Mahajanga which provided her with her imported riches and caught the admiration of visiting foreigners. Madagascar was at that time a major supplier of slaves to Arab traders and in return received jewels and rich fabrics. Indian merchants were active then, as today, with a variety of exotic goods. Some of these traders from the east stayed on, the Indians remaining a separate community and running small businesses. More Indians arrived during colonial times.

In the 1883–85 war Mahajanga was occupied by the French. In 1895 it served as the base for the military expedition to Antananarivo which established a French Protectorate. Shortly thereafter the French set about enlarging Mahajanga and reclaiming swampland from the Bombetoka river delta. Much of today's extensive town is on reclaimed land.

Mahajanga today
A hot but breezy town with a large Indian population and enough local colour and interesting excursions to make a visit of a few days well worthwhile.

The town has two 'centres', the town hall (Hotel de Ville) and statue of Tsiranana (the commercial centre), and the streets near the famous baobab tree. Some offices, including Air Madagascar, are here. It is quite a long walk between the two – take a *pousse-pousse*, of which there are many. There are also some smart new buses, and taxis which operate on a fixed tariff.

A wide boulevard follows the sea along the west part of town, terminating by a lighthouse. At its elbow is the **Mahajanga baobab**, said to be at least 700 years old with a circumference of 14 metres.

Telephone code The area code for Mahajanga is 62.

Getting there and away
By air
There is an international flight into Mahajanga from Moroni, Comoros Islands. The town is served by regular flights from Tana on Tuesdays, Wednesdays, Fridays and Saturdays, with back-up flights by Twin Otter.

The airport is near the village of Amborovy; 6km northeast of the town. If you don't want to take a taxi, taxi-brousses pass close to the airport.

By road
Mahajanga is 560km from Tana by the well-maintained RN4. Taxi-brousses and the comfortable MAMI minibus usually travel overnight, taking 15–18 hours. It's a lovely trip (at least until it gets dark) taking you through typical Hauts Plateaux landscape of craggy, grassy hills, rice paddies and characteristic Merina houses with steep eaves supported by thin brick or wood pillars. 'Try to be awake for crossing the Betsiboka: a huge red river with big rocks tossed about. Concentrate on the scenery, not the strength of the bridge supports.' (F Kerridge)

This is a popular drive for those with their own vehicle, with the option of a stop at the forest of Ambohtantely at the Tana end, and Ampijoroa near Mahajanga. You should allow about 14 hours for the trip.

The taxi-brousse station in Mahajanga is on Avenue Philbert Tsiranana.

DISTANCES IN KILOMETRES

Antananarivo–Ampijoroa	466km
Ampijoroa–Mahajanga	110km
Antananarivo–Mahajanga	572km
Antananarivo–Morondava	665km
Miandrivazo–Morondava	274km
Morondava–Belo sur Tsiribihina	106km

By sea

The *M/S Sam-Son* is a motor vessel belonging to the JAG Group, which owns several hotels in this part of Madagascar, running from Mahajanga to the Comoro Islands. Prices range from about €69–85 and include all meals and non-alcoholic drinks.

You can access Mahajanga from Nosy Be with the comfortable ferry, the *Jean-Pierre Calloc'h*, which sails weekly and takes 20 hours. Tel (cellphone): 0320 221686, or tel/fax: 62 226 86. It is operated by Malagasy Sambo Ligne, Quai Barriquand. Details on page 346.

For the truly adventurous, why not try to hitch a ride on a cargo boat? Colin Palmer writes: 'We spent a lot of time in the harbour and saw a number of sailing cargo boats that serve the northwest and west... What better way to access Maintirano, Belo and Morondava?'

Where to stay

Category A

Le Tropicana This incorporates the Hotel Gatinière and the Restaurant Oasis; tel: 220 69. This fine hotel-restaurant is up the hill from the Don Bosco school behind the cathedral, in a 1930s French colonial house. 10 rooms with satellite TV and hot water for 190,000Fmg (double), also bungalows for 190,000Fmg. Swimming pool, excursions to the Anjohibe caves etc. French and Malagasy cuisine. 'The dining is superb. Even on an oppressively hot day you can escape from the dust of urban Mahajanga and sit on the terrace with friends over lunch... telling stories of exotic places and pretending you are Joseph Conrad.' (Mark Ward)

Hotel de France Rue de Maréchal Joffre. BP 45; tel: 237 81/223 27; fax: 223 26; email: h.france@dts.mg. 20 air-conditioned rooms with en-suite bathrooms. 250,000Fmg (single), 275,000Fmg (double). Convenient location in the centre of town. Tours organised.

Zaha Motel Tel: 225 55/237 20; fax: 237 11; email: zahamotel.mjn@malagasy.com. At Amborovy beach (not far from the airport, and 8km from Mahajanga). Rooms 233,000Fmg, bungalow 423,000Fmg, including breakfast. This is a slightly vulgar, large hotel complete with activities such as tennis, volley ball and so on. In 2001 it was under new management and the food/service had deteriorated – perhaps only temporarily. It offers a cool alternative to staying in Mahajanga, but you need your own transport. Nice beach with blue, not red, sea.

Sunny Hotel Route d'Amborovy; tel: 235 87; fax: 235 89; email: sunnymaj@dts.mg. Double €68 pp, single €137. 30 well-equipped rooms, some with air-conditioning; safe, minibar. Good swimming pool; tennis courts. Excellent food. Excursions; car hire. The only negative is the caged lemurs.

Category B

New Hotel Rue Henri Palu; tel: 221 10; fax: 293 91. Room with fan 120,000Fmg, with air-conditioning 152,000Fmg. Clean rooms with bathrooms en suite, hot water, TV and phone, and a very good restaurant.

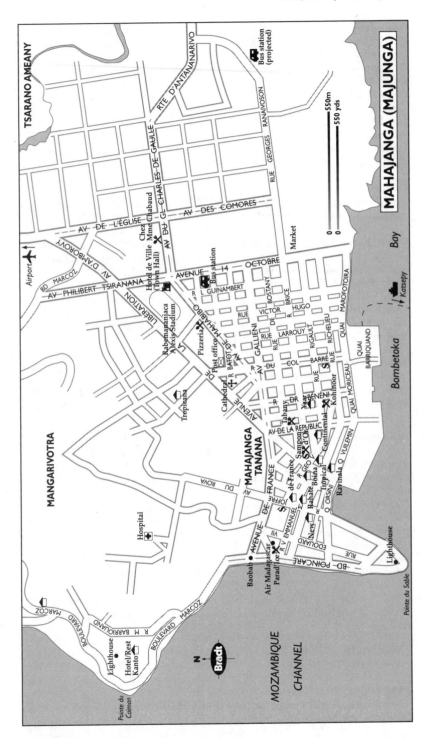

MAHAJANGA (MAJUNGA)

New Continental Av de la République; tel: 225 70; fax: 241 19. Double room with fan, 140,000Fmg, air-conditioning 150,000Fmg. TV, phone, en-suite bathrooms. Town centre hotel, Indian-owned, well run.

Le Nouveau Baobab Rue du Maréchal Joffre, just off Av de France. 152,000Fmg for air-conditioned en-suite rooms.

Boina Beach Bd La Corniche, tel: 238 09. 9 rooms from 60,000Fmg (single) to 125,000Fmg (double).

Hotel Voanio Tel: 238 78. 75,000Fmg (with fan) to 126,000Fmg (double, air-conditioned). All rooms en suite. In a quiet part of town; clean and friendly.

Hotel Ravinala Quai Orsini; tel: 229 68. From 92,000Fmg (fan, en-suite facilities) to 117,000Fmg (TV, phone, air-conditioning).

Category C

Hotel Tropic 22 Rue Flacourt (near the port); tel: 236 10. 8 rooms; the most basic have en-suite cold shower and shared WC. Clean and comfortable, but avoid the lower storey rooms which have no windows; about 95,000Fmg.

Kanto Hotel Tel: 229 78. Overlooking the sea about 2km north of the town. 47,000Fmg (double, shared toilet) to 82,000Fmg (en-suite double, air-conditioning). There's an annexe near the central market: corner of Av de la République and Rue Henri Palu.

Hotel Boina Tel: 224 69. About 60,000Fmg with shower.

Yaar Hotel Tel: 230 12. Near the New Hotel. Single room with en-suite toilet, 40,000Fmg.

Chez Chabaud (see *Katsepy*) Tel: 233 27. Mme Chabaud's daughter runs a basic hotel near the Hotel de Ville. Rooms 65,000Fmg. The restaurant opposite is run by another daughter, Christiane. All the family speak English.

Where to eat

'Specialities include chapatis (*pakopako*), coconut sweetmeats, and *khimo* (minced meat in gravy with chili, lime and bread (not rice), as well as delicious yoghurt, milkshakes, ice-cream and fruit juice. There are milkshake bars everywhere!' (F Kerridge)

Snack le Grilladin 32 Ave Galleni Ampasika. A new, above-average Indian restaurant with an extensive menu. Tandoori and vegetarian specialities. 10,000–15,000Fmg for the main dish. The owner, Georges, was born in Farafangana and can organise tours in Madagascar's southeast.

Kohinoor Restaurant Indian restaurant with good food and kitsch décor. One of the few places to do a vegetarian dish of the day.

Pizza restaurant On Av de Mahabibo. 'Strange, but good pizzas…'

Pakiza Av de la République, near the New Continental. Name may be missing but easy to recognise: 'Zebu heads and horns sticking out everywhere.' A great variety of ice-creams and milkshakes, also good for breakfast. Terrific tamarind juice.

Bar Tabany A popular meeting place in the west part of town, near the market.

Salon de Thé Saify Near the post office and cathedral. A perennial favourite for breakfast and snacks.

Parad'Ice Next to the Air Madagascar office off Bd Poincaré. 'The best ice-cream in Madagascar – the passionfruit ice-cream is out of this world!' They also serve wonderful breakfasts.

Cybercafé

Near the Hotel de France.

Maps

The Librairie de Madagascar (on Avenues de Mahabido and Gallieni) reportedly has a good selection of maps including the FTM one of the Mahajanga region.

Sightseeing and excursions
Recommended driver
Ibrahim Soumalla; tel: 230 12 (home); 220 35 (office). 1999 rates: Ampijoroa 200,000Fmg; Cirque Rouge 20,000Fmg; Marovoay 50,000Fmg.

Tour operator
For tours to Ampijoroa etc, try the Sunny Hotel.

Sightseeing in and around town
Museum
Mozea Akiba is situated about 2km from the centre of town, near the Plage Touristique (take a *pousse-pousse* or taxi). The rewarding result of cooperation between the universities of Mahajanga and Gotland, Sweden, it has a display showing the history of the region, as well as an exhibition of paleontology and ethnology, and photos and descriptions of some of Mahajanga's tourist sights such as the Cirque Rouge and Grottes d'Anjohibe. Signs are in English and French. Hours: 09.00–11.00, 15.00–17.00.

Fort Rova
This impressive fort was built on the highest point in Mahajanga in 1824 by King Radama I. The entrance has now been restored, and it is worth a visit for the views and sense of history. The fort is reached via Rue du Maréchal Joffre.

Day excursions
Cirque Rouge
About 12km from Mahajanga and 2km from the airport (as the crow flies). This is a canyon ending in an amphitheatre of red, beige and lilac-coloured rock eroded into strange shapes – peaks, spires and castles. The canyon has a broad, sandy bottom decorated with chunks of lilac-coloured clay. It is a beautiful and dramatic spot and, with its stream of fresh water running to the nearby beach, makes an idyllic camping place.

As a day trip a taxi will take you from Mahajanga and back, but make sure the driver knows the way: there are no signposts. A cheaper alternative is to take a taxi-brousse from the street west of Chez Chabaud (opposite the BTM bank). This will take you to the intersection of the Zaha Motel and airport, from where you can walk the final 6km. Give yourself at least one hour to look around. Late afternoon is best, when the sun sets the reds and mauves alight.

Katsepy
Katsepy (pronounced 'Katsep') is a tiny fishing village across the bay from Mahajanga which is reached in 45 minutes by ferry. This runs twice a day: 07.30 (08.30 Sundays and holidays) and 15.30, returning an hour later (so the last ferry back is 16.30). The trip takes just under an hour.

Until recently there was only one reason to go to Katsepy: to dine Chez Chabaud. I still go weak at the knees remembering my meal there in 1984. However, I understand that this place is not what it was and there is really not much point in visiting Katsepy any more, especially now the extremely rare crowned sifaka in the garden of Madame Chabaud have reportedly all been killed and eaten by the local people.

However, the very fact that a place is no longer recommended is an attraction to some – so I look forward to some readers' reports.

FURTHER AFIELD
Nosy Boiny (Nosy Antsoheribory)
This is a small island, about a kilometre long, in Boina Bay, with some fascinating ruins of an Arab settlement established around 1580 after a Portuguese raid on the mainland. The settlement thrived until 1750, when the Sakalava conquered the area. In its heyday the town, known as Masselage, probably supported a population of about 7,000. The ruins include several cemeteries, houses and mosques. 'The surface of the island is scattered with pottery. There are also many baobabs.' (Dan Carlsson)

To reach the island start from Katsepy and continue by road to the village of Boeny-Ampasy on the west side of the bay. There are some bungalows here. A 1½-hour boat journey brings you to Nosy Boiny. **Patrice Kerloc**, tel: 236 62 (address: BP 376, Mahajanga), can arrange trips here and to the Grottes de Anjohibe.

Anjohibe caves
The Grottes de Anjohibe are 82km northeast of Mahajanga and accessible only by 4WD vehicle, and then only in the dry season. There are two places to visit, the caves themselves and a natural swimming pool above a waterfall. The caves are full of stalactites and stalagmites (and bats), and have 2km of passages.

To reach the caves turn left at the village of Antanamarina, from where it is another 5km. Then, to cool off, return to the village and take the road straight ahead to the waterfall and pools. There is a troop of sifaka here, and natural pools both above and below the waterfall. To add to the excitement there may be crocodiles in the lower pool.

Dan Carlsson of Project Madagascar (Sweden) excavated these caves in 1996. 'It seems as though the caves have been used for normal living but also as a place of sacrifice. We found…pottery with ash, charcoal and animal bones… also several hippopotamus bones believed to be some million years old.'

The best person to organise a tour here is probably Patrice Kerloc (see above). He can also arrange trips to Nosy Boiny.

Birding trips in the Betsiboka Delta
Keen birders will want to go out into the Betsiboka Delta to visit islets which are the breeding grounds of the very rare Bernier's teal and white ibis. For this four-hour excursion the Zaha Motel charges an outrageous 1,800,000Fmg for two people and 2,500,000Fmg for four. There is no shade on the boat and it can be extremely hot. You are very likely to see the birds, however.

A much cheaper option is to find a local *pirogue* owner to take you.

BEACH RESORTS NORTH OF MAHAJANGA
If you look on a map of Madagascar, you'll see a glorious expanse of nothingness along the indented coastline between Mahajanga and Nosy Be. This is where two entrepeneurs have established fly-in resorts which come (in my opinion) as close to perfection as you could hope for.

Antanimalandy
About 100km from Mahajanga, and 25km south of Anjajavy (see page 373) this is a wilderness area where the former owner of Anjajavy has set up a 'bush camp'.

Lodge des Terres Blanches Owner Jackie Cauvin can only be reached by phone: 032 023 7543. There are six large bungalows in this pristine area which cost €92 per night; the price includes all meals, with wine or beer, and excursions; €68 without excursions. Transfers are by private plane (there is no road access) €122 round trip from Mahajanga.

RURAL LIFE AROUND ANJAJAVY
Angus Carpenter
While studying the reptiles around l'Hotel, Angus Carpenter did a survey of the social structure of three coastal villages near the hotel: Anjajavy, Ambohidrapsy and Ansangabe.

Most men have more than one 'wife' but may cohabit with only one. In one village, Antsangabe, the priest appears to have decreed that men and women should live in different halves of the village, with the church as the dividing line. Men pay for the upbringing of their children. Wives are expected to be monogamous, and several generations of women may live in one house. The workers brought in by the hotel are accommodated at Anjajavy, but there is no integration with the local villagers.

Land belongs to the first person to fell an area of forest for cultivation. All the family help with cultivation and on the death of the male head of the household, his land is divided between his offspring. There is little thought to the future – this is true subsistence farming, just taking care of each day's needs.

All three villages have *fady*. In Antsangabe the priest has decreed that it is *fady* to raise zebu or goats within the village. Special paddocks have been built for these animals outside the village. It is *fady* to light a fire outside the hut after sunset. In all villages there are *fady* attached to days of the week: In Antsangabe it is *fady* to sell anything on a Monday (market day is on Sunday) and to build anything on a Tuesday, unless there is a full moon. In Ambohidrapsy and Anjajavy, the two fishing villages, it is *fady* to catch fish on a Thursday, and to tend to crops on Tuesday or Sunday.

Anjajavy

This luxury hotel really does have it all: isolation, coral reefs, *tsingy*-like limestone outcrops, pristine beaches, extensive mangrove forests, a dramatic bat-filled cave, a private reserve bustling with birds and lemurs, sifakas gambolling on the villa roofs... not to mention total comfort, brilliant service and superb food! Anjajavy is under the same ownership as Tsarabanjina, so visitors are encouraged to stay at both hotels (though this is not insisted on).

Anjajavy l'hôtel Tana office: Lot VW 105, Ambohimitsimbina (BP 876), Antananarivo; tel: 22 285 14; fax: 22 285 15; email: Groupe.Hotel@simicro.mg. Paris office: 23 rue Truffaut, 75017 Paris; tel: 01 44 69 15 00; fax: 01 44 69 15 55; email: lhotelparis@prat.com. 25 villas sleeping up to 60 guests. One villa is adapted for disabled travellers. Price €165 per person per night; €92 for a 3rd and 4th person. 20% higher over Christmas holiday. Includes all meals, excursions that do not involve motor transport, and a full range of sports activities. To further shield clients from the realities of Madagascar, the 10-seater Anjajavy plane meets international flights (from Paris) and whisks you north for €185 each way.

Because of the expense of getting to Anjajavy, and the choice of activities while you're here, a minimum of three days is required; five would allow you to relax as well.

AMPIJOROA FORESTRY STATION

This is part of the Réserve Naturelle Intégrale d'Ankarafantsika. Ampijoroa (pronounced Ampijeroo) is one of the few areas of protected western vegetation.

ANJAJAVY

A few years ago Dominique Prat, a wealthy and widely travelled Parisian businessman, went to his travel agent and told her that he'd heard a lot about Madagascar and wanted to go there. The girl smiled and said. 'Sorry monsieur, but Madagascar's not for you!' She went on to explain that there was very little luxury accommodation and that the tourist infrastructure was inferior to what he was accustomed to. So Monsieur Prat set out to build a hotel in Madagascar for people like him. Luxurious, yes, but isolated and in harmony with nature. This sounded like the perfect place to bring my exhausted group after the Total Eclipse. It was.

The seaplane (now, sadly, discontinued) circled a bay so perfect that if it were in a holiday brochure you'd mutter about computer touch-up. Thick, bobbly forest ended abruptly at yellow sand. This in turn was lapped by the clearest sea I've seen in Madagascar. A lone baobab stood on the beach, its red trunk bright against the dark of the rock cliffs. The hotel itself is lovely, but the point of Anjajavy is *not* that it's just another luxury sea-side hotel, it's that Monsieur Prat is in charge of a large area of Madagascar's dwindling dry deciduous forest. This is what makes it special – it's the only protected area between Mahajanga and Nosy Be, and the hotel management has every incentive to ensure that the fauna and flora not only survive, but flourish, for this is what brings tourists to Madagascar.

Wildlife viewing here is effortless. At 3.30 each day a troop of Coquerel's sifaka visits a fruiting tree near one of the villas and a few metres from the beach. Sometimes they are joined by common brown lemurs and at night our torch beam picked out the eyes of perhaps a dozen mouse lemurs. Then there are the birds – flocks of bright green grey-headed love-birds. sickle-billed vangas, crested couas and vasa parrots, to name just a few. Reptiles are common. You may see ground boas and hog-nose snakes and plenty of chameleons – most common is Oustalet's chameleon, Madagascar's largest species. We were particularly impressed with the local guide, Matoary, a gentle, mature man who has a wealth of experience to share. It was he who told us about the *kononono* (see box on page 386). This sort of knowledge cannot be taught – English and scientific names can.

There's a cave, too, spectacular enough with its stalactites and stalagmites to be worth a visit, but with the addition of countless Commerson's leaf-nosed bats. Another cave has the skulls of extinct lemur species embedded in the rocks.

There is just one flaw to this perfect place: the beautiful wooden buildings are constructed from one of Madagascar's rarest hardwoods, palissandre. I shudder to think of how many trees were felled for its construction. But it has been done and there is no undoing it. To its credit, the hotel management is working with local communities to provide schools and medical clinics and to encourage sustainable agriculture (there is a policy to buy *all* fruit and vegetables that the villagers bring to them).

Anjajavy only opened in December 2000, so it is too early to know if they will achieve their aim of combining luxury accommodation with social responsibility. If they do, then one's normal reservations about supporting a foreign-owned and foreign-run hotel will disappear. As long as the local environment and communities benefit we should be able to enjoy it without guilt.

Its administration is shared by ANGAP and the Direction des Eaux et Forêts, with funding from the German organisation KfW.

This is a super reserve. It is easy to get to, thrilling to visit with an abundance of wildlife of all kinds, and with many clear, level or stepped paths which make hiking a pleasure.

Ampijoroa straddles RN4 from Mahajanga. The main part of the reserve is on the southern side of the road (on your right coming from Mahajanga), with Lac Ravelobe to the north.

Getting there and away
From Mahajanga
The reserve is 120km from Mahajanga. It takes a little over two hours to make the journey by car, and if you are in a private vehicle it is worth stopping at Lac Amboromalandy, a reservoir which is an excellent place to see waterfowl. Taxibrousses leave town early in the morning heading for Tana, so this is a much cheaper option (about 10,000Fmg).

From Tana
RN4 from Tana is now in good condition and the journey by taxi-brousse should take no more than 12 hours, costing around 40,000Fmg. Coming from Tana it is easy to miss Ampijoroa, so look out for **Andranofasika**. This little town lies on a T-junction; you will recognise it by the triangle of grass with blue-painted concrete benches and map of Madagascar. Ampijoroa is 4km further on. There is a basic, but excellent hotel here (see page 376) so it is no longer essential to camp at the reserve.

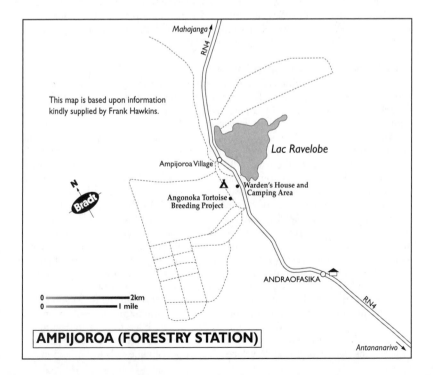

Where to stay/eat

If at all possible you should stay overnight at (or near) Ampijoroa. Wildlife is much more active in the cool of the day so you will see far more at dawn and dusk. Several tour operators in Mahajanga, including the Zaha Motel, organise luxury **camping** trips to Ampijoroa. If you have your own tent, it costs 20,000Fmg per night under thatched shelters. The facilities have been improved and there is an ablution block with three toilets (one even flushes!) and two showers. To be on the safe side bring your own food, but usually someone will cook a meal for you. There is also a tiny 'shop' with a freezer that sells cold beers and other basic necessities.

The alternative to camping is the **Dila Hotel** in Andranofasika. This super place was my best find in 2001: it serves wonderful food at rock bottom prices, and the attention and courtesy given our group put many international hotels to shame. There are 10 new bungalows costing 25,000–30,000Fmg, and the Indian owner is talking about providing a shuttle service to the reserve. Certainly he will make sure that those arriving by taxi-brousse will not be stranded – although it's only a 4km walk to Ampijoroa.

Permits and guides

Ampijoroa is administered by ANGAP and permits (50,000Fmg) are available at the reserve or in the ANGAP office in Mahajanga.

Most guides at Ampijoroa are very enthusiastic and knowledgeable. Sadly one of the best guides, Izo, was attacked and killed by a crocodile at Lake Ravelobe in 2000, but Jacky Ratiantsiharana has literally been calling the birds from the trees for a decade or more. Another up-and-coming birding guide is Guy. Hari (female) is also recommended. When you arrive, a guide 'bags' you and remains with you for your stay. Keen birders may want to try to reserve Jacky or Guy in advance. You can write to them c/o Ankaranafantsika Reserve, Andranofasika 403, Madagascar, or ask around in the village and someone will find them. There is a standard charge: day walk: 25,000Fmg; night walk 40,000Fmg.

Flora and fauna of Ampijoroa

This is typical dry, deciduous forest with sparse understorey and lots of lianas. In the dry winter season many of the trees have shed their leaves, but in the wet months the forest is a sea of bright greens. Conspicuous is the tree with menacing spines, the *Hazom-boay*, or *Hurac crepitances*.

Wildlife viewing in Ampijoroa starts as soon as you arrive. Right beside the parking area is a tree that Coquerel's sifaka use as a dormitory. They are extremely handsome animals with the usual silky white fur but with chestnut-brown arms and thighs. On your walks you may also see mongoose lemur, woolly lemur and the sportive lemur if the guide shows you its tree. This is the only place in the world where you might see the recently discovered (1998) golden-brown mouse lemur, *Microcebus ravelobensis*, named after Ampijoroa's Lake Ravelobe. There are always lots of reptiles (two new species of *Brookesia* chameleons were discovered there recently), and this is a birder's paradise. 'Within minutes we found sicklebill, Chabert's and hook-billed vangas all nesting round the campsite… and then the highlight: white-breasted mesites which walk just like clockwork toys' (Derek Schuurman). John and Valerie Middleton recommend a walk to the 'Canyon'. 'Perhaps the finest walk we did here. It's a 4km walk through the forest and across the savanna to an amazing multi-coloured erosion feature. On this route we pretty well saw all the bird, animal and plant life that this park has to offer in daytime.'

After seeing the main reserve you should (if permitted) cross the road to the lake. A path runs right round Lake Ravelobe (7½km) providing excellent birding: lots of waterfowl and the very rare Madagascar fish eagle. However, at the time of writing this circuit is closed, crocodiles having killed five people in recent years. The boldness of the crocs may partly be attributed to the fact that they are sacred, and a zebu is slaughtered for them once a year (on New Year's Day). Don Reid points out that a more likely reason that the crocodiles have turned to human prey is the overfishing of the lake, so their natural food has gone. Derek Schuurman adds: 'Pity, I remember swimming in that lake and the crocs surfacing about 15ft away and leering at us with beady eyes. One came up later with quite a big fish thrashing in its jaws.'

A small part of the lake shore, affording views of the fish eagles, is open to visitors.

Ampijoroa is also home to the Angonoka Tortoise Programme, but tourists are no longer encouraged to visit this area. This is one of Madagascar's most successful captive breeding projects. After many years of research and much trial and error, the ploughshare tortoise – the world's rarest tortoise – is now breeding readily and it is now being reintroduced to the Baly Bay area – its original habitat. Equally rare, the attractive little flat-tailed tortoise (*kapidolo*) is also being bred here.

The latest project is to try to breed the Madagascar big-headed (also known as side-necked) turtle.

KATSEPY TO MITSINJO, LAKE KINKONY AND SOUTH
Mitsinjo and Lake Kinkony

Taxi-brousses sometimes meet the ferry at Katsepy for the onward journey to **Mitsinjo** (and vehicles taking the ferry are almost certainly bound for that town). The journey takes about three hours.

'Mitsinjo is a lovely town with a wide main street, trees with semi-tame Decken's sifakas, a general store that has a few rooms available, and Hotely Salama which serves wonderful food and cold beer!' (Petra Jenkins). Not far from Mitsinjo is **Lac Kinkony** (a protected area). Petra reports: 'About once a week in the dry season the fishermen of Lac Kinkony do a supply run to Mitsinjo and you may be able to get a lift. The lake is wonderful. It boasts fish eagles, flamingoes, sacred ibis ... need I say more? It is free from bilharzia but the northeast end is a bit silty for swimming. Cadge a lift by *pirogue* and you've got paradise! Crocodiles are friendly and don't bother swimmers (!).'

John Kupiec enjoyed a *pirogue* and walking trip with Patrick, the English-speaking son of the owner of Hotely Salama. They stayed away for five days and saw plenty of wildlife as well as the lovely lakeside scenery. On the southern part of the lake is the little village of **Antseza** which has a Thursday market where you may be able to reprovision if you are camping. In the lake is a small island, Mandrave. The legend is that this island rose up in the lake after the boats of the invading Merina had been sunk by the Sakalava. It is a sacred island with many *fady*: you may not wear gold jewellery on the lake and if you have gold teeth you must not speak while on the lake! No-one can live on the island, nor urinate there, nor approach too close to the sacred tamarind tree that grows there (although prayers may be offered to it). A Sakalava king is buried beneath the tree.

An alternative hard way to reach Mitsinjo is to attempt it by *boutre* or cargo boat (see box on page 379) or you can take the soft(er) option of rafting the River Mahavavy with the specialist river-runners, Remote River Expeditions. See page 397.

Soalala and beyond

From Mitsinjo you may be able to make your way to Soalala although there is no longer any road transport there. Perhaps you can catch a motor *vedette* from Mahajanga. These go (irregularly) to Soalala to collect prawns, crabs and fish. John and Valerie Middleton write: 'This is a fascinating port and well worth visiting. It contains several very large African baobabs and impressive Pachypodiums. It was previously a French fort and at least two ancient cannons can be seen on the sea front. There are many good eating places but nowhere to stay unless camping. We managed to stay in the compound of the Forestry and Water Department where there was a good water supply, albeit shared by a constant stream of ever-friendly locals. Across the bay is a new, massive French shrimp farm and if it is intended to take a vehicle across written permission needs to be obtained to cross the farm's land. The old village vehicle ferry no longer crosses to the old road although passenger ferries do make the crossing. From here are occasional taxi-brousses.'

There is an air service (Twin Otter, once a week) out of Soalala, or you can go on to **Besalampy**, which is also served by Twin Otter. Then you can continue to make your way down the coast, taking cars, *pirogues* or whatever transport presents itself. This route is only practical in the dry season and for rugged and self-sufficient travellers. You can fly out of Tambohorano and Maintirano (and other towns – check the Air Mad timetable). Good luck!

Tsingy de Namoroka

This is a Strict Nature Reserve, and as such is not generally open to tourists so make your arrangements through a tour operator; the Middletons organised their trip through Madagascar Air Tours. This is their report: 'The route south to **Vilanandro** takes about three hours by vehicle and passes through some magnificently varied landscapes. One 10km section in the middle contains evergreen forest and swampland with a multitude of different ferns and dense stands of raffia palms. In other sections small lakes provide excellent birdwatching. Vilanandro is a delightful village; we found one bar which only sold beer, about four small shops, nowhere to stay, and very, very friendly people. One family allowed us to camp in their compound from where we made daily forays into the reserve. To do this we carried an ANGAP guide from Soalala, the ANGAP representative in Vilanandro, a local guide, and three villagers with tools to build/rebuild the road as we went along! We spent three days exploring Namoroka and would definitely say that the *tsingy*, the bird life, the plants and the scenery are amongst the best we had seen in Madagascar. Places visited include the almost 5km long cave of Anjohiambovonomby and its amazing associated canyons, the stunningly beautiful sacred spring of Mandevy with its scented water-flora of white Aponogetons, and the many large dolines, washed pure white by the winter rains and surrounded by superb *tsingy* and flora.'

CONTINUING BY ROAD FROM MAHAJANGA
Marovoay

About 50km from Mahajanga a road branches off the RN4 and leads to Marovoay (12km). Formerly the residence of the Boina kings, the town's name means 'many crocodiles'. When the French attacked the Malagasy forces assembled in Marovoay in 1895 in their successful drive to conquer Madagascar, it is reported that hundreds of crocodiles emerged from the river to devour the dead and dying. Malagasy hunters have since got their revenge, and you would be lucky to see a croc these days. And in all six editions of this book I've written that I'd yet to hear of a tourist going there – until this year! Colin Palmer, a self-confessed 'boat anorak', reports: 'Marovoay is just a nice place to hang out. It has warm, friendly people and a port to wander in. This was evidently quite important in French times, but is now silted up and disused by large vessels. However, local people still make use of it as a market for their produce from the delta. An exuberant lady

THE SAILING CARGO BOATS OF THE NORTHWEST
Colin Palmer

The hot, dry plains northwest of Madagascar are cut by the mighty Betisboka and Sofia rivers, which deposit their red silt into sprawling deltas lined with mangrove forests. The Indian Ocean surf of the east coast is replaced by the gentler waters of the Mozambique Channel. Water transport can make safe use of the sea – the deltas provide protection for fleets of fast outrigger fishing boats while larger sailing cargo boats ply their trade along the coast.

A huge area of the country between Mahajanga and Maintirano is devoid of roads and things are not much better as far south as Morondava. For many places in this remote region, the only way to move goods and people is by boat.

Almost uniquely in the modern world, the ports along this coast are served by non-mechanised sailing cargo boats, owned and operated by the Vezo people – primarily fisherfolk from the south west who have diversified into the ownership and operation of cargo boats.

Two quite different designs operate side by side. The 'Arab' lateen-rigged (one large triangular sail) *boutres* and the 'European' gaff-rigged *bateaux*. The *boutres* are built in a time-honoured tradition that relies on the eye of the builder to get the shape right, while the *bateaux* are built to plans and templates most probably introduced by the French. Perhaps this was an attempt to 'improve' the local *boutres*, but if so the improvement seems to be lost on the locals. New boats being built in Mahajanga (and probably elsewhere) are almost exclusively in the *boutre* tradition.

This clash of boatbuilding techniques is an example of east meeting west, or at least east meeting modern west. The eastern approach to building boats is to think of the planking as the hull of the boat and build it first. The ribs are added later, simply as something to stiffen the hull. In the west we once did things the same way, as the Viking ships show. But there is another approach that may have been introduced by the Romans, where the ribs are set up first to get the shape, and the planks bent round them to keep the water out.

In Madagascar, the result of either method is a stout, flat bottomed boat that can find its way into the silting creeks of the northwest deltas as well as hold its own in the open seas of the Mozambique Channel. Business seems to be thriving and the boats are well cared for and expertly sailed. Facilities on board are basic, but it ought to be possible for intrepid travellers to hitch a ride along the coast. Those who do will be fortunate indeed to experience some of the last seagoing cargo boats to earn their livings under sail.

called Seraphine has just opened **Hotel Standard** in the main street. Her food was good and she showed us round the rooms – which looked clean, if simple. She speaks expressive, voluble French and a little English.'

Rejoining RN4 you pass through the reserve of **Ampijoroa** (see page 373) to meet RN6, the road to Antsiranana, at Ambondromamy. Here you have the choice of the easy road south or the deceptively short route north to Ambanja and Nosy Be.

THE ROUTE NORTH
The 'road' to Antsohihy

It would be lunacy (but I have some loony readers!) to do this route by taxi-brousse, but drivers of 4WD vehicles report their adventures with some relish. The following are from Colin Palmer and Stuart Edgill. 'At Ambondromamy the road forks and you turn left on to the RN6, marked as a red road on the map. This was presumably a good metalled road in colonial times, but this is certainly not the case now. It immediately became a heavily rutted track with the occasional glimpse of a crumbling fragment of tarmac giving a hint of its former glory. There were many deviations off the main route into the scrub to avoid the most badly rutted sections obviously caused by lorries during the rainy season. Our average speed on this 84km section to Mampikony was 15km/hr!

'As we approached **Mampikony** I saw what at first I took to be paddy fields, but I found to my surprise these were fields of onions. Mampikony is the centre of onion production in Madagascar, even exporting them to Réunion.' Accommodation is limited **to Hotel La Mampikony** 'rooms at 25,000Fmg; best deal of the trip, but basic!' (CP) or **Les Cocotiers** '40,000Fmg with cold shower, loo down the corridor, palissander wood floors, and a terrace by the road where we ate and watched the world go by. Everywhere there were onions, on the stalls, on lorries, loose being sorted or in sacks waiting to be transported…. you have got to know your onions in Mampikony!' (SE)

The next town of importance is **Port Bergé** (Boriziny), 82km away on a road just as poor. Onions give way to tobacco and cotton. This is a pleasant town with at least two hotels, the **Zinnia** ('filthy, smells, rats') and **Le Monde** ('immaculate, friendly'. Family rooms for 60,000Fmg; good value). The road improves from Port Bergé to Antsohihy, so the 133km stretch can be done in about five hours.

Antsohihy

Pronounced 'Antsooee', this town is a good centre for exploration, and accessible by Twin Otter as well as taxi-brousse. Like many towns in Madagascar it is built on two levels. 'I am afraid we all found the place a bit depressing, it having passed from the stage of splendid decay to being truly rundown. We visited the 'port', basically a creek, eventually leading out to sea, capable of taking very small cargo ships.' (SE)

Where to stay/eat

Hotel Blaina Thatched bungalows with en-suite bathrooms, about 70,000Fmg. By far the best accommodation in town.

Hotel de France In the upper town, by the main square.

Hotel La Plaisance On the opposite side of the square to Hotel de France. 'It had fewer squashed and flying mosquitoes in the rooms than the Hotel de France. 40,000Fmg, cold shower, loos on the second floor landing (some rooms are on the opposite side of the road). All ground floor rooms in effect open on to the street. It also had a bar and small dance floor downstairs where there is a Friday disco' (SE).

Getting there and away

If you are using a taxi-brousse, approach from the north rather than the terrible road to the south. It takes about 10 hours from Ambanja. Twin Otter flights between Mahajanga, Analalava, Antsohihy and Ambanja (Tuesday and Thursday).

Excursions from Antsohihy

Antsohihy is situated on a fjord-like arm of the sea which becomes the River Loza. There is a regular boat service to **Ananalava**, an isolated village accessible in the dry season by taxi-brousse but otherwise only by boat or plane (Twin Otter). The **Paradise Hotel** is inexpensive, and the owner of the *épicerie* across the road from the Paradise has a few rooms to let.

'I loved the maze of paths on both sides of the village. There is a *fady* in effect on one stretch of the river. At one time this area was ruled by a queen and many trees may not be cut down and there are other taboos. In the boat everyone removed their hats when we passed. There is still a powerful queen in the area who occasionally grants an audience. In her presence you must ask your question to the guard who repeats it to the queen. Her answer is made the same way.' (J Kupiec)

Nosy Saba

From Ananalava you may be lucky enough to find a sturdy boat to take you to this almost perfect island for a few days. I have been here twice and doubt if any island comes closer to paradise. There is fresh water, a few fishermen's huts (abandoned in the rainy season), coconut palms, curving bays of yellow sand, a densely forested section with clouds of fruit-bats, coral, chameleons…

If arriving by yacht, the anchorage south of the eastern tip gives good shelter from the north to northwest winds. Anchor 100m off the beach over a sand shelf 1.5–4m deep. The edge of the shelf drops off steeply. Close to the shore are shallow coral patches. But further out, watch the strong tidal currents: the northwest-flowing ebb makes a rolling swell. The water is very clear and a remarkable number of large game fish can be seen even when snorkelling along the island's edge southwest of the anchorage. The coral is excellent, and rewarding scuba-diving can be had along the drop-off.

Nosy Lava

The large island of Nosy Lava (Long Island) lies temptingly off Ananalava. *Don't go there!* Why not? It's Madagascar's Devil's Island, a maximum security prison housing the country's most vicious murderers. By all accounts the prisoners lead pretty enjoyable lives: women from nearby Ananalava are said to cross over by *pirogue* to fraternise with the prisoners. They've also been provided with electricity and other mod cons not available to ordinary folk. One Malagasy informant commented that 'Nosy Lava is more like a holiday camp than a prison'. Nosy Lava had a brief moment in the international spotlight in 1993 when two notorious convicts boarded the yacht *Magic Carpet* and murdered its South African/German occupants.

From Antsohihy into the interior

Two roads run from Antsohihy in an easterly direction into the lush and mountainous interior: a lovely area for the adventurous to explore.

A tarred road runs southeast to Mandritsara, a small town set in beautiful mountainous scenery. Taxi-brousses leave every morning, passing through **Befandriana Nord** where there is a hotel, the **Rose de Chine**.

Mandritsara

The name means 'peaceful' (literally 'lies down well'), and was reportedly bestowed on it by King Radama I during his campaigns. There are several hotels here including **Hotel Pattes**, a nice little place with excellent food.

Mandritsara is linked with the outside world by Twin Otter.

Bealanana

An alternative (paved) road from Antsohihy runs northeast to Bealanana, 'a muddy, scruffy highland town with friendly people'. The town is quite high, and the temperate climate with ample rainfall allows the cultivation of potatoes and a great variety of fruit.

Hotel Ramagasy is family-run and friendly; basic rooms around 20,000Fmg. **Hotel La Crête** has double rooms with basin and shower (but probably cold water).

The hotels will arrange for a taxi-brousse to pick you up for the return trip (four hours) to Antsohihy or Abatoriha. The road is good; the vehicles are not.

West from Antsohihy

Just to show that nothing is beyond my more adventurous readers, here is an account from Valerie and John Middleton, whose interest is limestone karst and the plants that grow there. 'From Ansohihy we drove quickly to Marovantaza where we hired a local guide to show us the way westwards to **Antonibe**. This is a true wilderness route with few people, many challenges, some good deciduous forest, many birds and many Coquerel's sifaka. Antonibe is a large, hot, friendly town close to Narinda Bay. There is nowhere to stay and the few *hotelys*, bars and shops are difficult to find. After obtaining permission from the mayor to proceed further we collected yet another guide and headed for **Amboaboaka**, an even friendlier village situated amongst some superb cone karst scenery. Much to the villagers' interest we camped within the village. The following day we were taken by the headman and several village elders to view the karst where we found many interesting succulent plants and visited four previously unexplored and very beautiful caves including one, Ampahito Valakely, some 800m in length. This karst is reasonably close to Anjajavy and as such is a possible excursion from there.

From Amboaboaka we returned to Antonibe and then headed up Narinda Bay to **Ampasindava**. This route is very spectacular and for its final 3-4km involves driving along the beach. This is only passable for two hours either side of low tide and even then we had waves coming in through the window! And we have photos to prove it! We again camped in the centre of the village which has superb views across the bay. Our route then took us across the peninsula and through more cone karst to **Ambalantsingy**, a beautiful sleepy fishing village on the edge of some massive mangrove swamps. Our purpose here was to visit, with the aid of a local *pirogue* (25,000Fmg) the karstic islands in the very beautiful Morambe Bay. These islands, which were probably originally land-formed cones, had become even more eroded with some undercutting at low tide of up to 6m. The *tsingy* is good, the plants almost primeval, and the setting breathtaking.'

Antsohihy to Ambanja

Stuart Edgill continues his saga: 'The next day, after croissants and coffee at the taxi-brousse station, we set off on the road to Ambanja, 217km away, marked white on the map. Be careful not to continue on the RN31: you need, in effect, to turn left at a rain barrier (a barrier which is closed when the road is impassable during the rainy season) about 15km from Antsohihy. This road turned out to be no worse, and in some places better, than the road before. Although unmetalled, the road was flat and firm; also here the terrain was more open, making it easier to drive around the heavily rutted parts. Children ran away from us here. Our friend says it was because they have been told that *vazaha* drink their blood to gain strength or kidnap them. Another thing was that all the way along this route the children called out for empty mineral water bottles, presumably to collect water in.

'As we began to near Ambanja after **Maromandia** we began to climb and suddenly the scrub land gave way to tropical vegetation and cashew trees. We left Ansohihy at 6am and arrived at Ambanja at about 5pm.'

MAINTIRANO AND REGION

Maintirano, a small port due west of Tana, has been somewhat out on a limb, with very few foreign visitors. Bishop Brock, the indefatigable cyclist, provided most of the following information in 1996.

The road from Tsiroanomandidy to Maintirano

'I cycled from Tana to Maintirano, thence to Morondava, a distance of about 1,100km, of which only about 250km was tarred. The ride from Tsiroanomandidy to Maintirano is a difficult trek through a rugged, arid wilderness, that requires a large degree of self-sufficiency. Although there is ample water, it's not always conveniently located and at times I carried up to eight litres. There is no formal accommodation, and only one shop and *hotely* in Ambaravaranala, Beravina and Morafenobe. I camped in the bush, stayed in villages and with a family in Morafenobe. Crossing the Bangolava between Ambaravaranala and Beravina was difficult, and crossing the northern tip of the Plateau du Bemaraha east of Maintirano was brutal riding. The scenery was magnificent and varied, however, at times being so wide open that the sense of isolation was almost overwhelming. It took me eight days to cover this 438km.'

This road is also travelled by trucks and 4WD taxi-brousses. Bishop recommends that you look for a vehicle in Tsiroanomandidy, rather than Tana. The journey should take two to three days.

Maintirano

This small western port is attractive for people who want to get off the beaten track. Nothing much happens here. Bishop points out that although it appears to be a seaside town on the map, 'it's as though the town has turned its back on the sea: virtually nothing in Maintirano overlooks the ocean.' However, he found it one of the friendliest towns in Madagascar (no doubt its isolation has something to do with this). 'I was constantly entertained by local families (and the Catholic missionaries) and one man insisted that I take all my meals with his family during my stay there.'

The best hotel is the **Laizama**.

Maintirano is one of the places served by Air Mad (Twin Otter) on its Tana–Mahajanga run, so there is an alternative to the overland journey. You can also float down the Mambolo River (see page 396).

Telephone code The area code for Maintirano is 69.

From Tsiroanomandidy to Ankavandra, via Belobaka

Jolyjn Geels and Herman Snippe made their way by road and trail to the head of the Manambolo river and thence to Belo Sur Tsiribihina. For a synopsis of this wonderfully adventurous trip, see page 396.

FROM MAINTIRANO TO MORONDAVA

Continuing by bicycle, Bishop Brock writes: 'This is somewhat easier than the Tsiroanomandidy to Maintirano stretch, and there are major towns/villages every day or two. Some self-sufficiency is still required, though, and water was a problem south of Bekopaka (all the rivers were dry; I had to get water from village wells). Although this route gives free access to the Tsingy de Bemaraha, in my opinion it is not a very interesting bike ride.'

Again, there is an alternative to cycling this route: 'The road is currently being served by a 6WD taxi-brousse that passes each way about once a week.'

MOONLIGHT IN BELOBAKA
Jolyjn Geels

From Tsiroanomandidy we went to Belobaka by taxi-brousse, and that is where the road ends. In a small town with no electricity, no toilets and no hotels. After presenting ourselves to the *maire* and the *gendarmerie*, we were offered a room in the newly built 'city-hall' which was not yet in use. The room was on the first floor, and it was completely empty. Water was provided in a bucket, and the 'toilet' was 'past the *gendarmerie* to the left behind the bushes'. From Belobaka we would have to walk to Ankavandra, the starting point of our Manambolo river trip.

Most of the time Belobaka is very dark at night, with only candles and oil lamps to provide a little light. However, on a clear night when the moon is full, a bluish light, casting sharp shadows, shines over Belobaka and the streets that otherwise are so quiet come alive. In this remote town, the children sing and dance to a full moon!

It was our first night in Belobaka. After our evening meal and a bucket shower in a hidden corner, we retreated to the balcony on the first floor where we sat and talked for a while. Then we heard singing, clapping, drumming and a lot of laughter! On the square just next to our 'hotel' many children of all ages and some adults were dancing, clearly visible in the light of the full moon. Running up and down the street, challenging a second group of kids to improve on their performance, they seemed to make up their game as they went along. All of a sudden they were chanting '*Vazaha! Vazaha!*' and the whole spectacle moved towards our balcony where they put up a real show for us. Of course we sang along as best as we could when they started singing some well known French songs. Did we understand Malagasy? they asked. Well, not really, but we told them what words we knew, and every attempt we made to say something

Tsingy de Bemaraha National Park

Until *National Geographic* magazine published photos of the *tsingy* in 1987, very few people – even the Malagasy – knew of this impenetrable wonderland. Until 1998 it was closed to tourists; only scientists could visit the Réserve Naturelle Intégrale du Tsingy de Bemaraha. Now it is a national park, and well worth the effort of getting there. The scenery rivals anything in Madagascar and it's a treasure house for botanists. At 152,000ha it is one of Madagascar's largest protected areas. It lies to the south of Maintirano, with the river Manambolo forming the southern border of the park, cutting a spectacular gorge through the limestone.

The main point of access is at **Bekopaka** on the north bank of the Manambolo river. Here is the main park entrance and from it leads a network of well-constructed paths and walkways through the best areas of the reserve's southern extremity. Some of the paths take you through and up on to the *tsingy*, where boardwalks have been constructed for safer access. However, some of the terrain is still tough going and is really only suitable for those who are reasonably fit (and thin – there are some tight squeezes through gaps in rocks).

Adjacent to the park entrance is a lake which has a pair of highly endangered Madagascar fish eagles. Other water birds include Madagascar jacana, white-faced whistling duck, Humblot's heron and purple heron.

Some 25km further to the north are the famous areas of *grande tsingy* – imposing limestone pinnacles up to 50m in height, with equally impressive canyons and gorges. There are now paths leading to this area and constructed walkways allow in their language triggered outbursts of laughter. It was just wonderful! At times we felt a bit silly, like a king and queen being cheered by a crowd, but what a happy crowd it was!

Then, without warning, the party was over and the children dispersed. Within minutes the streets of Belobaka were completely empty and silent.

The following day we had plenty of things to do: we made enquiries about the walk to Ankavandra, we started to look for a guide, we had agreed to meet a few people, and we wanted to buy some supplies for the walk. We had many visitors enjoying tea and cold drinks on our balcony. While we were sitting there, the singing and dancing started again. One of our visitors explained that these spontaneous celebrations occur every four weeks if the sky is clear and the streets of Belobaka are moonlit.

The show went on. The children invited us to join them in the streets to sing and dance and clap with them. It seemed as if the whole world revolved around the children of Belobaka, as if time stood still while we shared songs and laughter. How much time had passed I really couldn't tell, but like the night before all of a sudden the party seemed to come to an end. However, this time the children didn't leave in silence. We shook many hands and wished them 'tafandria mandry!', which is Malagasy for 'good night' or 'sleep well'. They wished us 'tafandria mandry' too, and as they walked away in small groups, they happily chanted 'tafandria mandry!' again and again until they had reached their homes. Then there was silence.

When we woke up next morning we heard, below our window, 'tafandria mandry, vazaha!', and then laughter. Of course we replied, and there was more laughter. That day we were leaving for Ankavandra. As we walked the streets to do our last bit of shopping, it still echoed 'tafandria mandry!' in a shy but conspiratorial way. It made us smile from ear to ear.

limited access into the area. Reaching the area, however, remains a real challenge – from Bekopaka it's a full day trek and all camping gear and supplies must be taken.

Naturalist and photographer Nick Garbutt, who has just made his second visit to Bemaraha, writes: 'Bemaraha is undoubtedly a very special place and well worth visiting, but it's not without its frustrations. After my first visit in 1998 I reported on the inflexibility of the ANGAP administration – something I hoped would relax once the new park found its feet. Sadly this has not proved to be the case. Although some improvements are evident, the ANGAP attitudes remain intransigent – this is a park run by a rule-book which can be problematic for those with wildlife as their major interest.

'There are set circuits to walk, lasting between 1½ and 8 hours and different rates are charged according to the length of the circuit. Most of these circuits run through a combination of forest areas and *tsingy*. However, if for instance, your principle interest is the wildlife, the system doesn't allow you to concentrate in the forest areas and miss out the other bits, or combine the forest portions of different set circuits. The park official at the gate is adamant that each circuit has to be completed before the next can begin. There are no nocturnal walks allowed either. The official line is that 'the guides have not been trained'. This is hugely disappointing as the forests of Bemaraha undoubted harbour some spectacular nocturnal lemurs and other wildlife. Frankly the set-up remains utterly infuriating and may spoil the experience of the park.' Nick is not alone in his criticisms, but all visitors report the helpfulness of the guides and staff, so once the bureaucracy

ANT-LIONS (KONONONO)

In the reserves of the south and west – or anywhere that trails are sandy rather than muddy – one of the most enjoyable pursuits for sadists is feeding the ant-lions. Look for a small, conical pit in the sand, find an ant or other small insect, and drop it in. There'll be a flurry of activity at the bottom of the pit – grains of sand will be thrown up to smother the ant – and it will either be pulled dramatically down into the depths of the pit or manage to escape with its life. For full details of this extraordinary animal see page 52.

Children in the northwest of Madagascar have recognised the decorative potential of these creatures and call them *Kononono* which means 'nipple-badge'. Once you persuade one to grasp a soft piece of skin (ie: a nipple) it will hang on for hours! The name teaches you another Malagasy word: *nonono* which means nipple. Think of the sound of a baby sucking, and you'll recognise the onomatopoeia!

allows them to run the park for the benefit of its visitors, it should be a superb experience for all.

Pirogue rides on the Manambolo river up through the adjacent gorge are also available – but only in the morning. These are highly recommended. There are spectacular cliffs and wonderful forest on either side, and it's possible to see groups of Decken's sifaka and red-fronted brown lemurs basking in the early morning sun.

Flight of fantasy

Charter flights from Morondava (either returning to Morondava or landing in Belo sur Tsiribihina) over the *Grand Tsingy* are spectacular. The flight up from Morondava takes about 35 minutes; the pilot will then fly back and forth over the best areas of *tsingy*. 'The views and spectacle are utterly amazing – massive needles of rock interspersed with pristine forest. When the pilot drops down low, it's even possible to see brilliant white Decken's sifaka sitting in the trees. I was so engrossed in taking photos I was violently sick at the end of the flight!' (Nick Garbutt)

Getting there

Bekopaka is reached in about 10 hours from Morondava, if you have your own 4WD vehicle. Access is not easy by public transport, even in the dry season. From the north, the park can be reached from Antsalova, which has an air service. Most people, however, approach from the south, where the nearest town accessible by taxi-brousse from Belo Tsiribihina is Ankilizato (not to be confused with the town of the same name east of Morondava) which is 57km north of Belo. From there you must either walk (porters can be hired) or take a zebu-cart the 24km to Bekopaka.

Organised tours

Hotel **Bouganvilliers** and Hotel **Morondava Beach** in Morondava both organise tours by 4WD to the Bemaraha.

Where to stay in Bekopaka

Auberge chez Ibrahim Simple 2-person bungalows, shared facilities, for 40,000Fmg. Adequate meals for 35,000Fmg. Tours of the park are organised by the hotel.

Hotel Relais de Tsingy Web: www.relaisdestsingy.mg. A beautifully situated set of 6 bungalows (total capacity 20) with en-suite bathrooms and hot water, overlooking the lake. Double rooms 200,000Fmg; good meals (full board) 100,000Fmg. The owner's collection of caged animals (including lemurs) spoils an otherwise perfect place.

Camping A camp ground has been set aside on the north shore of the Manambolo, right next to the park entrance. There are groves of mango trees that provide good shade and a basic toilet. It's very picturesque. There is also an adjacent snack bar (Annex de Chez Ibrahim) with basic meals and cold drinks.

Belo sur Tsiribihina

Apart from being the town at the end of the river Tsiribihina (see *River trips*, page 395), this place has little to offer. The famous Avenue of Baobabs is nearer Morondava and an easy excursion from there. Likewise Kirindy, though travellers coming from the north can visit both attractions on their way to Morondava. Tsiribihina means 'where one must not dive', supposedly because of the crocodiles. Be warned!

Arriving from the north you have to cross the river by ferry to get to the taxi-brousse station for Morondava. There is no timetable and the journey takes half an hour.

Where to stay/eat

Grande Lumière Opposite the Menabe. 8 bright, clean rooms with cold shower.
Restaurant Pacifique Near the market. Good food, especially the crevettes.

MORONDAVA

The Morondava area was the centre of the Sakalava kingdom and their tombs – sadly now desecrated by souvenir hunters – bear witness of their power and creativity.

This was evidently a popular stopping place for sailors in the past and they seem to have treated the natives generously. In 1833, Captain W F W Owen wrote of Morondava: 'Five boats came alongside and stunned us by vociferating for presents and beseeching us to anchor.'

Today Morondava is the centre of a prosperous, rice-growing area (and has successfully introduced ostrich farming to Madagascar!). For tourists it is best known as a seaside resort, with a laidback atmosphere.

This is the centre for visiting the western deciduous forest, the famous baobabs, and the Tsingy de Bemaraha National Park.

Telephone code The area code for Morondava is 95.

Getting there and away
By road

Morondava is 700km from Tana and served by a once-good road. A MAMI minibus leaves the Anosibe depot in Tana in the afternoon, arriving the following morning. The road is not bad until the 120km stretch between Miandrivazo and Malaimbandy, which can take nine hours. See also *Travelling between Morondava and Toliara*, page 392.

If you are driving, note that there is no diesel between Antsirabe and Morondava.

By air

There is a regular service from Tana or Toliara, and the Twin Otter calls here after visiting small west-coast towns.

By sea

There may be a weekly boat from Morondava to Morombe, from where you can (maybe) get a taxi-brousse to Toliara (see *Travelling between Morondava and Toliara*, page 392).

Where to stay

Most hotels are clustered along the beach on the peninsula known as Nosy Kely. Erosion is causing major problems and some are in danger of falling into the sea.

Category A

Baobab Café BP 77, Nosy Kely, Morondava; tel: 520 12; fax: 521 86; email: baobab@dts.mg. 18 rooms with en-suite facilities and hot water. 150,000–490,000Fmg depending on quality and facilities. Superb food: 'The fresh fish and seafood are sensational; there's none finer in Madagascar' (Nick Garbutt). The hotel backs on to the river opposite Sun Beach restaurant. Good pool which is open, for a small fee, to non-residents. Airport transfer 15,000Fmg pp.
Chez Maggie BP 73; tel: 523 47. 8 comfortable two-storey chalets in a lovely location on the beach. 200,000Fmg per room; extra bed 50,000Fmg. Swimming pool, excellent food. British-owned (Maggie MacDonald).
Royal Toera Hotel Up the beach from Chez Maggie. 14 beautifully built A-frames by the sea, with a large, clean swimming pool. €58 single, €70 double. Meals 55,000Fmg; breakfast 35,000Fmg.
Hotel Les Philaos Tel: 521 02. 18 rooms, including one self-catering. 120,000Fmg per room. A very nice, secluded hotel beyond Chez Maggie. Under the same ownership as the Hotel Central.
Renala au Sable d'Or BP 163; tel: 520 89. 14 large, solid wooden bungalows in Nosy Kely (next to Chez Maggie)

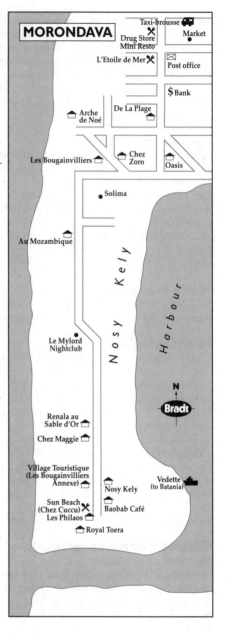

surrounded by landscaped gardens and grass. No restaurant.

Category B

Les Bougainvilliers BP 78; tel: 521 63. Double bungalows with en-suite facilities, hot water and fan, 100,000Fmg. Simple room with double bed, hot water, shared bathroom, 50,000Fmg. Good food. Visa cards accepted. The hotel can organise a variety of excursions.

Arche de Noé An architecturally striking hotel on the waterfront, praised by many. 60,000–120,000Fmg. Meals must be ordered in advance.

Hotel les Piroguiers BP 206; tel: 526 19; email: piroguiers@yahoo.fr. 4 bungalows on stilts in Betania; about 85,000Fmg. Menu about 54,000Fmg. This one of Jim Bond's 'best discoveries in recent years' and Jim knows the area well. Betania is 'a delightful Makoa fishing village across the river, famous for its fabulously large, sun-bathing pigs.' Take a *taxi-pirogue* (500Fmg) or a *vedette* (2,500Fmg). The hotel is owned by Pascal and Bodo Boisard, who are involved members of the Betania community. 'The food is excellent – particularly recommended is Bodo's wonderful fish in saffron and coconut sauce. They also have 12 horses on which you can do trips further south along the coast.

Au Mozambique Beach bungalows near Les Bougainvilliers.

Les Paletuviers de Matanito Beach bungalows near the village of Avaradrova, 1km south of Morondava. Quiet and comfortable.

Category C

Chez Zoro 4 beach bungalows plus tent site (15,000Fmg for your own tent or 25,000Fmg if provided by the hotel) behind Hotel Bougainvilliers. About 45,000Fmg for shared facilities; one en suite for around 70,000Fmg. Quiet, friendly, clean and cheerful.

Hotel Central BP 50; tel: 523 78. On the main street, newish and recently renovated. Hot shower and WC. No restaurant but breakfast served.

Hotel Oasis Route de Batellage, Morondava; BP 232; tel: 522 22; email: vazahabe@dts.mad. A near-beach hotel (100m from the shore); family-run and very friendly. Some bungalows have air-conditioning. Good restaurant and bar and often live music performed by the owner and local musicians. Mountain bikes available here.

Hotel Menabe 23 spacious rooms with en-suite bathroom (cold water) but reportedly (2000) buggy and not very clean. Also noisy: a church bell next door tolls all night. About 32,000Fmg.

Where to eat

Jonathan Ekstrom, a biologist, has compiled a comprehensive listing and evaluation of restaurants in Morondava. Email me at Hilary_Bradt@bradt-travelguides.com for a free copy.

Le Sun Beach (formerly Chez Cuccu) BP 22; tel/fax: 522 38. Near Les Bougainvilliers in Nosy Kely. Good, varied menu.

Renala On the seafront and specialising in seafood.

L'Etoile de Mer A very good value open-air restaurant by the beach serving superb seafood. 'My absolute favourite; I'd marry the owner just to eat there every day!' (SB)

Port au Prince Excellent, but relatively expensive food.

Drug Store Mini Resto Across from the market. Best value snack bar in town.

Tour operator and guides

Baobab Tours Located at the Baobab Café (same contact details), they offer a large selection of vehicle and boat trips, including excursions to Kirindy and deep-sea fishing trips, the Tsingy de Beharaha National Park, and flights over the *tsingy*.

Michael Golfier Recommended English-speaking guide/fixer. BP279, Morondava; tel: 52 140.

Jean le Rasta (Rasta Jean) Recommended by several travellers as being 'efficient, reliable and charismatic'. Speaks some English. Contact through the Hotel Oasis.

Excursions from Morondava
Baobabs

This is the region of the splendid Grandidier's baobab, *Adansonia grandidieri*, best seen at the Avenue of the Baobabs. Also popular are Les Baobabs Amoureux (two entwined baobabs), and there's a Sacred Baobab as well.

Mountain bikes are available at some of the hotels and are an excellent way to see the baobabs. Beware of the heat, flies and thorns on the road.

By car or taxi, the **Avenue of the Baobabs** is 45 minutes from Morondava. Try to get there shortly before sunset (or – better – sunrise) for the best photos. **Les Baobabs Amoureux** are another half hour or so away. Nearby is a lake which is very good for birdwatching. There are two **Baobabs Sacrés** (sacred baobabs), one near the Swiss Forest and one near the turn-off from the main road to Belo. Both are the chunky *Adansonia rubrostipa* not the stately *A. grandidieri*. The former has signs of offerings nearby and *lambas* tied to the branches. The one near the main road also shows signs of offerings. This is its story: a woman medium or healer was unable to pass her powers on to an heir since her only child, a son, was a Christian and had rejected the traditional beliefs. So the woman was buried under the baobab with her amulets, and the tree became her heir, taking on her powers. So now the people come to the baobab to ask for good crops, a son or healing – just as they would have come to the woman during her lifetime.

Namahora

If you arrive by air you will pass through this small town on the way to Morondava from the airport. There is a very lively Friday market, and the place is of historic interest, being the site of the Sakalava defeat of the Merina back in the 19th century. The name means 'Place where they were tied' (ie: the captive Merina). If you want to stay, there is a small hotel on the edge of town, nearest the airport.

Zebu market

If you are in Morondava on Friday it's worth visiting the Marché des Zebus, held at **Analeiva**, the first village outside Morondava on the road to Tana.

Sakalava tombs: a warning

Although the Menabe region is famous for its tombs, some things of obvious interest to tourists should be left alone. This applies particularly to the famous erotic carvings on tombs in the area around Morondava.

These carvings are fertility symbols, and often depict figures engaged in sexual activities which the Sakalava consider *fady* to practise. One example is oral sex. Erotic carvings of this kind can nowadays be seen in cultural museums in larger towns such as Tana or Toliara, and small replicas are often carved and sold as souvenirs – erotica always has a ready market. In the early 1970s unscrupulous art dealers pillaged the tombs around Morondava, removing nearly all the erotic carvings. As a result, the Sakalava now keep secret the location of those tombs which still have carvings. As one guide reported: 'Some of the graveyards are for the tourists, but most are secret – for the people.'

RESERVES NORTH OF MORONDAVA

The dry deciduous forests between the rivers Morondava and Tsiribihina are of great biological importance. Indeed, this is one of the most threatened forest types in the world. Many endemic species of flora and fauna are found here; the area is particularly rich in reptiles such as turtles, snakes and a variety of lizards. The fosa is common in these forests and seven species of lemur are found, including white sifaka and the rare pale fork-marked lemur and pygmy mouse lemur, the world's smallest primate. The giant jumping rat, Madagascar's most charming rodent, is unique to this small area.

DIVING CENTRES IN THE SOUTHWEST
There are coral reefs down much of the west coast, and whilst the Toliara region remains the most popular for diving, other specialised centres are being developed in the Morodava-Morombe stretch of coast.
Menabe Plongée (Belo Sur Mer) BP 384, Morondava; tel: 95 524 51; email: Mena.belo@ad.com.
Laguna Blu/Manta Diving Centre (Ampasilava-Andavadoaka, near Morombe); web: lagunabluresort.com.

There are three protected areas between the two rivers: Andranomena, Analabe and Kirindy. Heading north from Morondava, the first one you come to is **Andranomena**, a Special Reserve now under the control of ANGAP which has an office in the village of Andranomena, where permits may be purchased and a guide hired (compulsory) to take you on the trails.

Analabe is a private nature reserve owned by M Jean de Heaulme, of Berenty fame. There are, as yet, no facilities for tourists. Analabe lies 60km north of Morondava, to the west of Kirindy by the village of Beraboka. In addition to forest it contains some mangrove areas as well as marshes and lakes typical of coastal plain.

Kirindy

This is one of the most rewarding natural areas in Madagascar, but it is not a reserve. Until a few years ago its sole purpose was the sustainable 'harvesting' of trees, but despite this the wildlife is abundant. Indeed, it is probably the best western reserve for seeing Madagascar's endemic dry-forest species such as the giant jumping rat, which is found only in this area. It is also the best place to see fosa, especially between November 5–20 when they are mating.

There are some warnings, however: giant jumping rats are seldom seen during the coldest months and tend to keep out of sight when there is a full moon; likewise tenrecs and tortoises will be less active (or in aestivation) in the winter; and, sadly, with the departure of the efficient Swiss corporation which used to manage the area, both protection and facilities have declined. It may be that by the time you read this, Andranomena (see above) offers a better experience. The best months to visit these forests are September to November.

Getting there/staying there

Kirindy is about 65km northeast of Morondava – about 2½ hours by poor road (in a taxi or private vehicle) or three tedious hours plus a long, hot walk, by taxi-brousse.

Facilities are fairly basic: there is no electricity and just one smelly long-drop toilet. There are four 2-person bungalows (with mosquito nets, but bring your own sleeping bag) for around 50,000Fmg, or you can camp for 20,000Fmg. There is also a small restaurant (cold beer!); simple meals cost about 20,000Fmg. Even if you normally dislike roughing it, you should stay the night here. Day visitors see far less than those able to observe wildlife at the optimum time of dawn and dusk, and a night-time stroll to look for the giant jumping rat is part of the experience.

Information, permits and guides

At the time of writing (2001) the management of Kirindy is changing and facilities and information are unreliable. At present visits are arranged through the Hotel Continental in Morondava, but if you turn up there you will find a guide. Cyrille and Remi are the best.

TRAVELLING BETWEEN MORONDAVA AND TOLIARA

There are two slow routes, road and road-and-sea. Or you can fly between the two main cities via Morombe.

By road

In the dry season, from April to the end of November, the venerable *Bon Bon Caramel*, a 28-year-old green Mercedes truck, may still make the journey between Morondava and Toliara. If running, it leaves Morondava on Monday at 06.00, arriving Tuesday at about 17.00. The return from Toliara is Thursday at 06.00, arriving Friday evening. The night is spent in **Manja** (where there are bungalows and good food), or at the river some 80km from there (where you can sleep on the beach). If the truck is not running you are in for a long and adventurous trip. 'We endured a three-day, three-night journey on a truck called *OK Zaza* for 100,000Fmg. Went from Morondava via Miandrivazo, Antsirabe, Fianar, Ihosy and Tuléar. A trip that could only be described as legendary... by the third day the three of us [*vazaha*] had lost the plot and so all got rottenly drunk on rum and warm coke. Suddenly the music was fab, the truck was great, and we ended up having a very funny night...' (S Blachford)

By road and sea

One couple spent 60 hours just getting from Morondava to Morombe! In theory there is a weekly boat, or you can hire a *pirogue*. Once in Morombe you can get a taxi-brousse for the onward journey. Failing this you can find road transport between Morondava and Belo Sur Mer, and between Morombe and the Ifaty road-head north of Toliara. The sea stretch in the middle can be done (adventurously!) by *pirogue*.

My advice is to fly!

Belo Sur Mer

Not to be confused with Belo Sur Tsiribihina, this Vezo village 70km south of Morondava is a place you either love or hate. To enjoy it you need to be there in the coolest time of year. 'In the hot season Belo is a hell-hole of inescapable heat and insufficient drinking water.' A well has just been built now in the village and so drinking water is less of a problem.

The village itself is a collection of small houses and huts, on the border of a small lagoon, shrouded in palm trees; each family keeps a pig which is allowed to forage at night – Belo's mobile garbage disposals. There are huge cargo vessels (*boutres*) among the coconut palms at the Belo lagoon, and these are still built using exactly the same designs as the pirates used centuries back (see box on page 379). Belo is also the base for visiting a cluster of nine interesting offshore islands. The largest island is Nosy Andravano, but there are numerous islets. Those to the north are mere sandbanks, but the islands to the south have vegetative cover. Nomadic Vezo fishermen live on the northerly islands for six months of the year. There are shark carcasses and turtle shells left to dry on the sand, and fish and shark fins are salted in troughs. Each of the islands is fringed by coral reefs, although to view the healthy coral you may have to snorkel out up to 2km off the coast. You can hire a *pirogue* from Belo Sur Mer, from 25,000Fmg per day, to take you around the islands. Remember to bring your own drinking water and enough food for yourself and the *piroguers* if you intend to camp on the islands. Rob Conway, Eucare researcher who updated this section, warns 'Those islands south of Nosy Andravano are infested by rats that have a remarkable ability to chew through anything'.

The area is being developed fast. There are already two discos in Belo and small restaurants are being opened. The crab here is highly recommended and available all year round.

Getting there and away

Adventurers can go by *pirogue*, but 'Watch out for some flash English-speaking guides who will try to charge 600,000Fmg for this trip'. It should cost around 125,000Fmg, but most *vazaha* settle for 400,000Fmg. It takes about eight hours to sail to Belo from Morondava. Another option is to hitch from Morondava to the intersection for Belo Sur Mer and then hitch again to the village itself. A taxi-brousse also runs, temperamentally, from Morondava.

Where to stay

Marina de Belo Sur Mer Once highly recommended, this hotel has changed ownership and now receives less enthusiastic reports, mainly because 'the prices are now much higher, without the organisation that one would expect'. However, if you want to see Belo in comfort, with transport laid on, this is the only option. You can book the hotel (and find out the latest prices) through Espace Océan, next to Hotel de La Plage in Morondava. This hotel runs some excellent tours, taking you to see baobabs and a lake of flamingoes (if they're there), then snorkelling. This tour costs about 780,000Fmg.

Menabe Another up-market, well-run hotel which also has a diving school which offers courses and (expensive) tours from Belo Sur Mer to the fringing reefs of the islands.

There are now numerous other hotels open in Belo Sur Mer, which start from about 50,000Fmg. Also there's a report that bungalows are being developed on **Nosy Andravano** by the owner of Hotel Zoom in Morondava. Problems, however, have been encountered as no drinking water is available on the island.

If you have your own tent, you can arrange for a *pirogue* to take you to one of the islands and pick you up a couple of days later. If you do this, make sure you bring enough drinking water!

For more information on the Eucare marine conservation project check their website: www.eucarenet.com.

Morombe

Until now the only description of Morombe in this book was Chris Ballance's comment in 1996: 'Morombe clearly died when the French left, but 9,000 souls remain and they spend their time walking up and down the only street, very slowly, shaking hands with each other and discussing the possibility that someone might build a proper road to them someday.' Now I – and several thousand other tourists – have visited Morombe for the total eclipse and the town will never be the same again. The citizens now walk briskly up and down the street, shaking hands, and lamenting that the tourists have gone and there is still no decent road to their town.

Morombe deserves a visit. We very much liked this unpretentious seaside town, with its pleasant beach, active fishing village and mangroves. There is ample accommodation (none luxurious) and tourists are still a bit of a novelty.

Getting there and away
By road
Morombe is usually accessible by taxi-brousse from Ifaty, north of Toliara. The road is sandy and in very poor condition, and the 200km journey takes about 22 hours. In a private 4WD vehicle, however, it is a worthwhile prospect because of the breathtaking scenery en route. 'On your left is the blue sea and white sand, and

on your right is the incredible spiny forest, where the Mikea people live. This is a paradise for birders, and for baobab lovers. Normally it takes 8–10 hours to drive from Ifaty to Andavadoaka or Ampasilava. It is only practicable between the end of June and early November. The car can get stuck in the sand forever without the help of villagers to pull you out.' (Nivo Ravelojaona)

By air

Morombe airport can only take Twin Otters but it is a short hop from Morondava. The Air Mad service runs twice a week.

Where to stay/eat

Hotel Baobab 16 concrete bungalows on the beach on the south side of the town. With fan 150,000Fmg, with air-conditioning 175,000Fmg. Good restaurant. The best hotel in Morombe. Bookings (Tana): 22 427 01.

Lakana Volamena BP 30 Morombe; tel: 618. New, but basic rooms grouped round a central courtyard, some with bathrooms. 80,000–150,000Fmg without shower, 200,000–250,000Fmg with shower (prices may come down now the eclipse tourists have gone). Finished just in time for the eclipse, this is a very pleasant new hotel, right on the beach just north of the Baobab, French managed, serving good food.

Other hotels include the **La Croix du Sud** and the **Hotel Crabe** (in the northern part of town).

Sightseeing

Morombe rewards those with time to stroll. It's quite a prosperous-looking little town, with some spacious houses in the north and a bustling fishing village of wooden huts to the south. Like so many Malagasy seaside towns, it is very spread out with no obvious sign of a centre.

If you continue south along the beach beyond the Baobab hotel you will come to a rewarding group of mangroves where you can watch mud-skippers. Behind this area are some local tombs; we did not investigate these, respecting the local *fady* against such visits.

Andavadoaka and Ampasilava

These two villages are adjacent to each other by 'one of the best beaches in Madagascar' some 45km to the south of Morombe. Coming south from Morombe, you first reach Andavadoaka then, 5km further on, Ampasilava, described as 'a sweet little village'. The drive there is varied and very beautiful. It takes around two hours. If you travel here independently it is best to take a *pirogue* from Morombe, which takes about five hours, and hitch a lift back with one of the vehicles owned by the Catholic Mission.

Where to stay/eat

Hotel Coco Beach Andavadoaka. Basic bungalows at 100,000Fmg; meals 50,000Fmg, breakfast 15,000Fmg. Under the same management as Hotel Baobab, Morombe. Described by an exasperated tour operator as 'an absolute dump!'. Diving/snorkelling available.

An enterprising man who calls himself **Monsieur Coco** has inexpensive rooms in the village.

Laguna Blu Resort, Ampasilava; tel: 00 816 21 01 20 75; email: lagunabluresort@lagunabluresort.com; web: lagunabluresort.com. Classy, Italian-owned bungalows for €46 single, €92 double. Very little English spoken. This is a scuba diving/snorkelling centre. At the time of writing, the manager is an Italian doctor who also runs a clinic for local people.

Miandrivazo

Said to be the hottest place in Madagascar. The town lies on the banks of the Mahajilo, a tributary of the Tsiribihina, and is the starting point for the descent of that river. 'The name comes from when Radama was waiting for his messenger to return with Rasalimo, the Sakalava princess of Malaimbandy with whom he had fallen in love. He fell into a pensive mood and when asked if he was well replied *"Miandry vazo aho"* – I am waiting for a wife.' (Raniero Leto)

It's a ten-hour journey from Morondava by car or taxi-brousse, with one infamously bad stretch of road between Miandrivazo and Malaimbandy.

Where to stay/eat

Hotel Chez la Reine Rasalimo Tel: 95 438. Concrete bungalows on a hill overlooking the river. Good restaurant. Double room 90,000Fmg; triple 100,000Fmg.

Le Relais de Miandrivazo BP 22. On the main square. Comfortable rooms with mosquito nets. Reasonable food, good atmosphere. Intermittent water.

Hotel Laizama 'A simple but homely hotel – we often found ducks in the shower – with very helpful management. We ate at the Buvette Espoir in town. Meals must be booked in advance; great value.' (R Harris and G Jackson)

Descending the Tsiribihina River

This is a popular trip (see below) and can easily be set up from Miandrivazo. The guides have organised themselves into the Association Guide Piroguier Miandrivazo (AGPM) which seems very professional. Wherever you are staying, someone from AGPM will find you.

José Rakotomamonjy and his wife Soul are warmly recommended by Thomas Feichtinger of Austria, not only for the canoe trip down the Tsiribihina but for other excursions. José is knowledgable about wildlife and speaks good French and some English. Soul comes along as the cook. José can be found at the Bar Amical in Miandrivazo.

RIVER TRIPS

Trips down the lazy western rivers of Madagascar are becoming increasingly popular, and can be done as an organised tour or independently. Tour operators use fast (but noisy) motor boats, local people use canoes.

The four rivers that are navigable are the Tsiribihina, the Mangoky, the Manambolo and the Mahavavy. The former is quite easy to do independently, but the others are more challenging and you are advised to go with the specialist tour operators.

Tsiribihina River

This is a three- to five-day trip, with the starting point in Miandrivazo. The birdlife viewed from the river is excellent, and there is a good chance of seeing lemurs, chameleons and snakes. Nights are spent camping on the river bank. Some river-goers report it too hot to sleep in a tent, in which case a mosquito net is absolutely essential. At the end of the wet season the trip changes dramatically: camping on the beach is impossible due to the high river so you walk to the nearest village, and the trips are much shorter due to the faster-flowing river.

The trip should not be undertaken lightly: 'Long, long days paddling in the searing heat... I got sunburnt in spite of Factor 15 sunblock, and chewed to death by mosquitoes, despite extra-strong repellent. But I'm glad I did it...' (Sarah Blachford).

This is an easy trip to arrange independently. Opinions vary on whether it should be organised locally or before you arrive in Miandrivazo. 'It is significantly cheaper to book through AGPM than through agents in Tana. The problem is that communication with Tana is very difficult, so you have to wait until you get to Miandrivazo to book' (Colin Palmer). 'I suggest that organisation of a river trip in Tana or Antsirabe is preferable to organisation in Miandrivazo, and that travellers discuss all aspects of their trip in detail. When staying in local villages during our descent, our guide didn't ever make the attempt to bridge the communication gap between us and the villagers when we would have loved to, indeed would have paid to, be shown how they weave raffia fibre so effectively. An enthusiastic guide would have organised that and broken the ice between mute hosts and guests. As a traveller approached by a guide, be assertive enough to say no to an inadequate or unenthusiastic guide even if the trip sounds good. There will be plenty of enthusiastic, friendly guides around if you are patient' (Tim Ireland). Desiré Rabemanantsoa, in Antsirabe, has been recommended as being just that. Expect to pay around ∈154 for the trip.

Other readers who have organised their own trips on the Tsiribihina add the following points:

- Find out the language of your paddler. Ours did not speak much French.
- Look at the *pirogue* before agreeing to anything, and go for a test run. We didn't. Three minutes into our trip and we were back on shore – the *pirogue* was so unstable we would certainly have gone over. The paddlers found another one which worked out fine.
- Don't assume the paddlers are guides and know about the wildlife.
- Do your own food shopping or tell your paddlers exactly what you want. You should also pay for the food for your paddlers.
- A mosquito net is essential; a tent advisable.

Manambolo River

The descent of the Manambolo can be arranged through the tour operator Mad'Cameleon (see page 100) or through Remote River Expeditions (see advert on page 000). On an organised tour the trip takes three days (though five allows for some rest and sightseeing), beginning at Ankavandra. This is a spectacular trip, through the untouched homeland of the Sakalava. On the third day you pass through the dramatic Manambolo gorge between towering limestone cliffs, and through the Tsingy de Bemaraha reserve. The chances of seeing the area's special wildlife, such as Decken's sifaka and the Madagascar fish eagle, are high.

It's rare for anyone to do the Manambolo independently, but Herman Snippe and Jolyjn Geels achieved it in 1999. They took a variety of taxi-brousses from Tana to Tsiromanomandidy and on to Belobaka. From here they hired a guide to take them on foot to Ankavandra along the Route de Riz used by rice porters. This walk took three days and was 'wonderful' although they warn of a shortage of drinking water in the dry season. Ankavandra is pretty much owned and run by a Mr Nouradine, who owns the only hotel and river-worthy *pirogues*. The trip down river cost Herman and Jolyjn about US$125 (a high price for Madagascar). The price included two piroguiers and their food. In April, after rain, the two and a half day descent of the river was thrilling and spectacularly beautiful.

Getting from Bekopaka to 'civilisation' at Belo sur Tsiribihina was an adventure in itself! Herman and Jolyjn walked for a day before finding a tracteur-brousse – a tractor towing a trailer crowded with passengers – to take them the final stretch.

Mangoky River

This is a new expedition river, but it happened to run right through the zone of totality for the total eclipse, so was the main focus of Remote River Expeditions' June 2001 tour. The group spent nine days on the river, and reported that probably its most outstanding feature is that it passes through an area with perhaps the highest number of baobab trees on the planet. The group saw a great variety of endemic birds, lemurs, chameleons, and found some of the most beautiful camping sites anywhere.

Mahavavy River

Another 'special' from Remote River Expeditions, this river was first explored in 1998. The rafting team put in at Kandreho and ended in Mitsinjo. The area was extremely rich in both lemurs and birds, with large expanses of beautiful forest. Lemur-viewing was far superior to the other western rivers. 'For sheer numbers, proximity, and ease of viewing, the Mahavavy was superb, mainly for the two subspecies of Verreaux's sifaka (*deckeni* and *coronatus*) and *Eulemur fulvus rufus*. The outstanding areas for these species were around the Kasijy forest and the riverine tamarind gallery forest between Bekipay and Ambinany. To give some ideas of densities in both the Kasijy area and also the forest between Bekipay and Ambinany, I can say that a short foray into the forest, moving maybe 2–300 metres, staying one hour, would produce five to six families of sifaka, which were remarkably unconcerned by our presence. Red-fronted brown lemurs were very numerous, especially in Kasijy. The Mahavavy is very rich in birds; the most exciting sightings of the trip were of Madagascar fish eagles (a total of six)' (Conrad Hirsh).

Tour operators running river trips

Most of the main ground operators listed in *Chapter 4* organise river trips on comfortable vessels with good food and camping equipment, and experienced guides.

There are some specialist operators such as **Mad'Cameleon** (BP 4336, Antananarivo 101; tel: 630 86; fax: 344 20; email: madcam@dts.mg) who run canoe trips on the Manambolo river, allowing you to see the *tsingy*. **Remote River Expeditions**, now based in the USA, take groups on all the main rivers and regularly pioneer new trips. Check their website:www.remoterivers.com.

MEASUREMENTS AND CONVERSIONS

To convert	Multiply by
Inches to centimetres	2.54
Centimetres to inches	0.3937
Feet to metres	0.3048
Metres to feet	3.281
Yards to metres	0.9144
Metres to yards	1.094
Miles to kilometres	1.609
Kilometres to miles	0.6214
Acres to hectares	0.4047
Hectares to acres	2.471
Imperial gallons to litres	4.546
Litres to imperial gallons	0.22
US gallons to litres	3.785
Litres to US gallons	0.264
Ounces to grams	28.35
Grams to ounces	0.03527
Pounds to grams	453.6
Grams to pounds	0.002205
Pounds to kilograms	0.4536
Kilograms to pounds	2.205
British tons to kilograms	1016.0
Kilograms to British tons	0.0009812
US tons to kilograms	907.0
Kilograms to US tons	0.000907

5 imperial gallons are equal to 6 US gallons
A British ton is 2,240 lbs. A US ton is 2,000 lbs.

Temperature conversion table

The bold figures in the central columns can be read as either centigrade or fahrenheit.

°C		°F	°C		°F
−18	**0**	32	10	**50**	122
−15	**5**	41	13	**55**	131
−12	**10**	50	16	**60**	140
−9	**15**	59	18	**65**	149
−7	**20**	68	21	**70**	158
−4	**25**	77	24	**75**	167
−1	**30**	86	27	**80**	176
2	**35**	95	32	**90**	194
4	**40**	104	38	**100**	212
7	**45**	113	40	**104**	219

Appendix 1

HISTORICAL CHRONOLOGY

Adapted from Madagascar, Island of the Ancestors with kind permission of the author, John Mack

AD500	Approximate date for the first significant settlement of the island.
800–900	Dates of the first identifiable village sites in the north of the island. Penetration of the interior begins in the south.
1200	Establishment of Arab settlements. First mosques built.
1500	'Discovery' of Madagascar by the Portuguese Diego Dias. Unsuccessful attempts to establish permanent European bases on the island followed.
1650s	Emergence of Sakalava kingdoms.
Early 1700s	Eastern Madagascar is increasingly used as a base by pirates.
1716	Fénérive captured by Ratsimilaho. The beginnings of the Betsimisaraka confederacy.
1750	Death of Ratsimilaho.
1787	The future Andrianampoinimerina declared King of Ambohimanga.
1795/6	Andrianampoinimerina established his capital at Antananarivo.
1810–28	Reign of Radama I, Merina king.
1818	First mission school opened in Tamatave.
1820	First mission school opened in Antananarivo.
1828–61	Reign of Ranavalona I, Merina queen.
1835	Publication of the Bible in Malagasy, but profession of the Christian faith declared illegal.
1836	Most Europeans and missionaries leave the island.
1861–63	Reign of Radama II, Merina king.
1861	Missionaries re-admitted. Freedom of religion proclaimed.
1863–8	Queen Rasoherina succeeds after Radama II assassinated.
1868–83	Reign of Queen Ranavalona II.
1883	Coronation of Queen Ranavalona III.
1883–85	Franco-Malagasy War.
1895	Establishment of full French protectorate: Madagascar became a full colony the following year.
1897	Ranavalona III exiled first to Réunion and later to Algiers. Merina monarchy abolished.
1917	Death of Ranavalona III in exile.
1942	British troops occupy Madagascar.
1947	Nationalist rebellion suppressed with many dead.
1958	Autonomy achieved within the French community.
1960	Madagascar achieves full independence.
1972	General Ramanantsoa assumes power.
1975	Didier Ratsiraka first elected president.

1991	Demonstrations and strikes. Ratsiraka steps down.
1991	Albert Zafy elected president.
1993	The birth of the Third Republic.
1996	Albert Zafy impeached.
1997	Didier Ratsiraka re-elected president.
2002	Disputed presidential elections lead to six-month power struggle. Marc Ravalomanana declared president.

Cymbidiella

Madagascar only requires the advent of railways and roads to make it one of the most prosperous commercial countries of the world.

Capt E W Dawson,
Madagascar: its Capabilities and Resources, 1895

Appendix

THE MALAGASY LANGUAGE
Some basic rules
Pronunciation

The Malagasy alphabet is made up of 21 letters. C, Q, U, W and X are omitted. Individual letters are pronounced as follows:

a	as in 'father'
e	as in the a in 'late'
g	as in 'get'
h	almost silent
i	as ee in 'seen'
j	pronounced dz
o	oo as in 'too'
s	usually midway between sh and s but varies according to region
z	as in 'zoo'

Combinations of letters needing different pronunciations are:

ai	like y in 'my'
ao	like ow in 'cow'
eo	pronounced ay-oo

When k or g is preceded by i or y this vowel is also sounded after the consonant. For example *alika* (dog) is pronounced Aleekya, and *ary koa* (and also) is pronounced Ahreekewa.

Stressed syllables

Some syllables are stressed, others almost eliminated. This causes great problems for visitors trying to pronounce place names, and unfortunately – like in English – the basic rules are frequently broken. Generally, the stress is on the penultimate syllable except in words ending in na, ka and tra when it is generally on the last syllable but two. Words ending in e stress that vowel. Occasionally a word with the same spelling changes its meaning according to the stressed syllable, but in this case it is written with an accent. For example, *tanana* means 'hand', and *tanána* means 'town'.

When a word ends in a vowel, this final syllable is pronounced so lightly it is often just a stressed last consonant. For instance the Sifaka lemur is pronounced 'She-fak'. Words derived from English, like *hotely* and *banky*, are pronounced much the same as in English.

Getting started

The easiest way to begin to get a grip on Malagasy is to build on your knowledge of place names (you have to learn how to pronounce these in order to get around) and to this end I have given the phonetic pronunciation in the text. As noted in the text, most place names mean something so you have only to learn these meanings and – hey presto! – you have the elements of the language! Here are some bits of place names:

An-, Am-, I-	at, the place where	Manga	blue or good
Arivo	thousand	Maro	many
Be	big, plenty of	Nosy	island
Fotsy, -potsy	white	Rano, -drano	water
Kely	small	Tany, tani-	land
Kily	tamarind	Tsara	good
Mafana	hot	Tsy, Tsi	(negative)
Maha	which causes	Vato, -bato	stone
Mainti	black	Vohitra, vohi-,	hill
Maintso	green	bohi-	

In Malagasy the plural form of a noun is the same as the singular form.

Vocabulary
Social phrases
Stressed letters or phrases are underlined.

English	Malagasy	Phonetic pronunciation
Hello	Manao ahoana	Mano own
Hello	Salama	Salaam
(north & east coast)	Mbola tsara	M'boola tsara
What news?	Inona no vaovao?	Inan vowvow?
No news	Tsy misy	Tsimees

These three easy-to-learn phrases of ritualised greetings establish contact with people you pass on the road or meet in their village. For extra courtesy (important in Madagascar) add *tompoko* (pronounced 'toomp'k') at the end of each phrase.

Simple phrases for 'conversation'

English	Malagasy	Phonetic pronunciation
What's your name?	Iza no anaranao?	Eeza nanaranow?
My name is	Ny anarako	Ny anarakoo
Goodbye	Veloma	Veloom
See you again	Mandra pihaona	Mandra pioon
I don't understand	Tsy azoko	Tsi azook
I don't know	Tsy haiko	Tsi haikou
Very good	Tsara tokoa	Tsara t'koo
Bad	Ratsy	Rats
Please/Excuse me	Aza fady	Azafad
Thank you	Misaotra	Misowtr
Thank you very much	Misaotra betsaka	Misowtr betsak
Pardon me		
(ie: may I pass)	Ombay lalana	M'buy lalan
Let's go	Andao andeha	Andow anday
Crazy	Adaladala	Adaladal
Long life! (Cheers!)	Ho ela velona!	Wellavell!

If you are pestered by beggars try:

I have nothing	Tsy misy	Tsimeess
(there is none)		
Thank you, I don't need it	Misoatra fa tsy mila	Misowtr, fa tsi meel
Go away! Mandehana!	Man day han	

Note: The words for yes (*eny*) and no (*tsia*) are hardly ever used in conversation. The Malagasy tend to say '*yoh*' for yes and '*ah*' for no, along with appropriate gestures.

Market phrases

How much?	*Ohatrinona?*	*Ohtreen?*
Too expensive!	*Lafo be!*	*Laff be!*
No way!	*Tsy lasa!*	*Tsee lass!*

Basic needs

Where is…?	*Aiza…?*	*Ize…?*
Is it far?	*Lavitra ve izany?*	*Lavtra vayzan?*
Is there any…?	*Misy ve…?*	*Mees vay…?*
I want…	*Mila … aho*	*Meel … a*
I'm looking for…	*Mitady … aho*	*M'tadi … a*
Is there a place to sleep?	*Misy toerana hatoriana ve?*	*Mees too ayran atureen vay?*
Is it ready?	*Vita ve?*	*Veeta vay?*
I would like to buy some food	*Te hividy sakafo aho*	*Tayveed sakaff wah*
I'm hungry	*Noana aho*	*Noonah*
I'm thirsty	*Mangetaheta aho*	*Mangataytah*
I'm tired	*Vizaka aho*	*Veesacar*
Please help me!	*Mba ampio aho!*	*Bampeewha!*

Useful words

village	*vohitra*	*voo-itra*
house	*trano*	*tran*
food/meal	*hanina/sakafo*	*an/sakaff*
water	*rano*	*rahn*
rice	*vary*	*var*
eggs	*atody*	*atood*
chicken	*akoho*	*akoo*
bread	*mofo*	*moof*
milk	*ronono*	*roonoon*
road	*lalana*	*lalan*
town	*tanana*	*tanan*
river (large)	*ony*	*oon*
river (small)	*riaka*	*reek*
ox/cow	*omby/omby vavy*	*oomby/omb varve*
child/baby	*ankizy/zaza kely*	*ankeeze/zaza kail*
man/woman	*lehilahy/vehivavy*	*layla/vayvarve*

One of the great evils arising from [slavery] is the dignifying of idleness as belonging to freedom, and the degrading of labour by making it the badge of slavery.

Rev W Ellis, *The Martyr Church*, 1869

Appendix 3

MADAGASCAR'S MAMMALS AND WHERE TO SEE THEM

Nick Garbutt

Although there are relatively few species (compared with mainland Africa), Madagascar is an exceptional place to watch mammals. Of course, everyone wants to see lemurs but for those with time, patience and a little luck, there is far more to see. Listed below are the best places to try and see Madagascar's mammals. Species marked with an asterisk (★) are nocturnal.

Lemurs

Common name	Scientific name	Distribution/Where to see
Grey mouse lemur	*Microcebus murinus*★	The dry forests of the west and spiny forests of the south. Best sites Ampijoroa Forestry Station, Kirindy Forest and Berenty Reserve.
Brown mouse lemur	*Microcebus rufus*★	Throughout the eastern rainforest belt. Andasibe-Mantadia National Park Ranomafana NP.
Pygmy mouse lemur	*Microcebus myoxinus*★	Currently known only from the Kirindy Forests area.
Golden-brown mouse lemur	*Microcebus ravelobensis*★	Currently known only from the forests of Ampijoroa. Ampijoroa Forestry Station.
Hairy-eared dwarf lemur	*Allocebus trichotis*★	Central and northeastern lowland rainforests. Analamazaotra Reserve.
Greater dwarf lemur	*Cheirogaleus major*★	Eastern rainforests. Ranomafana National Park and occasionally seen in Andasibe-Mantadia NP
Fat-tailed dwarf lemur	*Cheirogaleus medius*★	Dry forests of the south and west. Ampijoroa Forestry Station and Kirindy Forest.
Coquerel's dwarf lemur	*Mirza coquereli*★	Dry forests of the west and moist forests of the Sambirano region. Kirindy Forest and secondary forests near Ambanja in the northwest.
Eastern fork-marked lemur	*Phaner furcifer furcifer*★	Rainforest centred around the Masoala Peninsula. Ambanizana and Andranobe on the Masoala Peninsula.

404

Pariente's fork-marked lemur	*Phaner furcifer parienti*★	Sambirano region in the northwest. Ampasindava Peninsula and the forests around the village of Beraty.
Pale fork-marked lemur	*Phaner furcifer pallescens*★	Dry forests of the west. Kirindy Forest.
Amber Mountain fork-marked lemur	*Phaner furcifer electromontis*★	Montagne d'Ambre, Ankarana and Analamera region of northern Madagascar. Montagne d'Ambre National Park and Ankarana Reserve.
Weasel sportive lemur	*Lepilemur mustelinus*★	Northern half of the eastern rainforest belt. Marojejy National Park, Anjanaharibe-Sud Reserve and Masoala National Park.
Small-toothed sportive lemur	*Lepilemur microdon*★	The southern half of the eastern rainforest belt. Andasibe-Mantadia National Park and Ranomafana National Park.
Northern sportive lemur	*Lepilemur septentrionalis*★	Forests of the extreme north. Ankarana Reserve and Montagne d'Ambre National Park.
Grey-backed sportive lemur	*Lepilemur dorsalis*★	Sambirano region and offshore islands in the northwest. Lokobe Reserve on Nosy Be.
Milne-Edwards sportive lemur	*Lepilemur edwardsi*★	Dry forests of the west, north of the Manambolo river. Ampijoroa Forestry Station.
Red-tailed sportive lemur	*Lepilemur ruficaudatus*★	Dry forests of the west, south of the Manambolo river. Kirindy Forest.
White-footed sportive lemur	*Lepilemur leucopus*★	Spiny and gallery forests of the south and southwest. Berenty Reserve, Hazafotsy and Beza-Mahafaly Reserve.
Eastern grey bamboo lemur	*Hapalemur griseus griseus*	Eastern rainforest belt. Andasibe-Mantadia National Park and Ranomafana National Park.
Western grey bamboo lemur	*Hapalemur griseus occidentalis*	Sambirano region in the northwest, Namoroka, Soalala and Tsingy de Bemaraha regions in the west. Sambirano river valley near the village of Benavony.
Lake Alaotra reed lemur	*Hapalemur griseus alaotrensis*	Reed and papyrus beds and surrounding marshes of Lake Alaotra. Southwest shore of Lake Alaotra.
Golden bamboo lemur	*Hapalemur aureus*	Rainforests of Ranomafana and Andringitra in the southeast. Ranomafana National Park.
Greater bamboo lemur	*Hapalemur simus*	Rainforests of the southeast. Ranomafana National Park.

Ring-tailed lemur	*Lemur catta*	Spiny forests and gallery forests of the south and southwest and the Andringitra Massif. Berenty Reserve, Beza-Mahafaly Reserve and Isalo National Park.
Mongoose lemur	*Eulemur mongoz*	Dry forests of the northwest. Tsiombikibo forest near Mitsinjo and Ampijoroa Forest Station.
Crowned lemur	*Eulemur coronatus*	Forest of the extreme north. Ankarana Reserve, Montagne d'Ambre National Park and Analamera Reserve.
Red-bellied lemur	*Eulemur rubriventer*	The eastern rainforest belt (mid to high elevations). Ranomafana and Marojejy National Parks.
Common brown lemur	*Eulemur fulvus fulvus*	Dry forests of the northwest and central eastern rainforests. Ampijoroa Forest Station and Andasibe-Mantadia National Park.
Sanford's brown lemur	*Eulemur fulvus sandfordi*	Forests of the far north. Montagne d'Ambre National Park and Ankarana Reserve.
White-fronted brown lemur	*Eulemur fulvus albifrons*	Rainforests of the northeast. Nosy Mangabe and Anjanaharibe-Sud Reserves, Marojejy and Masoala National Parks.
Red-fronted brown lemur	*Eulemur fulvus rufus*	Dry forests of the west and rainforests of the southeast. Kirindy Forest and Ranomafana National Park.
White-collared brown lemur	*Eulemur fulvus albocollaris*	Rainforest between the Manampatra and Mananara rivers in the southeast. Manombo Reserve and the forests to the west of Vondrozo.
Collared brown lemur	*Eulemur fulvus collaris*	Rainforests of the extreme southeast. Andohahela National Park and St Luce Private Reserve.
Black lemur	*Eulemur macaco macaco*	Sambirano region and offshore islands in the northeast. Lokobe Reserve on Nosy Be and the neighbouring island of Nosy Komba.
Blue-eyed black lemur	*Eulemur macaco flavifrons*	Forests just south of the Sambirano region in the northwest. Forests to the southwest of Maromandia and the vicinity of Marovato-Sud.
Black-and-white ruffed lemur	*Varecia variegata variegata*	Eastern rainforests. Nosy Mangabe Reserve, Ranomafana and Mantadia National Parks.
Red ruffed lemur	*Varecia variegata rubra*	Rainforests of the Masoala Peninsula. Andranobe and Lohatrozona in Masoala National Park.

Eastern avahi	*Avahi laniger*	Throughout the eastern rainforest belt. Andasibe-Mantadia National Park and Ranomafana National Park.
Western avahi	*Avahi occidentalis*	Western and northwestern Madagascar. Ampijoroa Forest Station.
Diademed sifaka	*Propithecus diadema diadema*	Central and northeastern rainforests. Mantadia National Park.
Milne-Edward's sifaka	*Propithecus diadema edwardsi*	Southeastern rainforests. Ranomafana National Park.
Silky sifaka	*Propithecus diadema candidus*	Northeastern rainforests (at higher elevations). Marojejy National Park.
Perrier's sifaka	*Propithecus diadema perrieri*	Dry forests in the extreme north between the Lokia and Irodo rivers. Analamera Reserve.
Verreaux's sifaka	*Propithecus verreauxi verreauxi*	Dry forests of the west, south of the Tsiribihina river and spiny forests of the south and southwest. Berenty Reserve, Beza-Mahafaly Reserve, Hazafotsy and Kirindy Forest.
Coquerel's sifaka	*Propithecus verreauxi coquereli*	Dry forests of the northwest. Ampijoroa Forestry Station.
Decken's sifaka	*Propithecus verreauxi deckeni*	Western Madagascar, between the Manambolo and Mahavavy rivers. Tsiombikibo forest near Mitsinjo and Tsingy de Bemaraha National Park near Bekopaka.
Crowned sifaka	*Propithecus verreauxi coronatus*	Dry forests between the Mahavavy and Betsiboka rivers. The Bongolava Massif and areas south of the Manambolo river. Near the lighthouse north of Katsepy and the forest around Anjamena on the banks of the Mahavavy river.
Golden-crowned sifaka	*Propithecus tattersalli*	Forest fragments between the Manambato and Loky rivers in northeast Madagascar, 6km northeast of Daraina.
Indri	*Indri indri*	Central eastern and northeastern rainforests. Andasibe-Mantadia National Park and Anjanaharibe-Sud Reserve.
Aye-aye	*Daubentonia madagascariensis*★	Eastern rainforests and western dry forests. Nosy Mangabe Reserve and Île mon Désir (Aye-aye Island) near Mananara.

Other mammals
Carnivores

| Fanaloka or striped civet | *Fossa fossana*★ | Rainforest of the east and north, the Sambirano in the northwest and the dry forests of the extreme north. Ranomafana National Park and Ankarana Reserve. |
| Falanouc | *Eupleres goudotii*★ | Eastern rainforests and dry forests of the northwest and extreme north. Montagne d'Ambre and Ranomafana National Parks. |

Fosa	*Cryptoprocta ferox*	All native forests. Kirindy Forest and Ankarana Reserve.
Ring-tailed mongoose	*Galidia elegans*	Native forests of the east, north and west. Ankarana Reserve and Ranomafana National Park.
Narrow-striped mongoose	*Mungotictis decemlineata*	Dry forests of the west, south of the Tsiribihina river. Kirindy Forest.

Tenrecs

Common tenrec	*Tenrec ecaudatus*★	All native forest areas. Andasibe-Mantadia National Park, Ranomafana National Park, Kirindy Forest and Ampijoroa Forestry Station.
Greater hedgehog tenrec	*Setifer setosus*★	All native forest types. Andasibe-Mantadia National Park and Nosy Mangabe Reserves and Ranomafana National Park.
Lesser hedgehog tenrec	*Echinops telfairi*★	Dry forest of the west and spiny forest and gallery forests of the south. Ihazafotsy, Berenty, Ifaty and Beza Mahafaly Reserve.
Lowland streaked tenrec	*Hemicentetes semispinosus*	Eastern rainforests. Andasibe-Mantadia National Park and Ranomafana National Park. Dry forests of the west and the spiny forest and gallery forest areas of the south and southwest. Kirindy Forest and Beza Mahafaly Reserve.
Large-eared tenrec	*Geogale aurita*★	

Rodents

Giant jumping rat	*Hypogeomys antimena*★	Western dry forest between the Andranomena and Tsiribihina rivers. Kirindy Forest.
Red forest rat	*Nesomys rufus*	Eastern rainforests. Ranomafana National Park.
Lowland red forest rat	*Nesomys audeberti*	Lowland eastern rainforests. Ranomafana National Park.

Bats

| Madagascar flying fox | *Pteropus rufus*★ | Eastern rainforests, western dry forests and southern gallery forests. Berenty Reserve, Nosy Tanikely off Nosy Be. |
| Commerson's leaf-nosed bat | *Hipposideros commersoni*★ | Anjavy caves. Ankarana. |

Appendix 4

FURTHER INFORMATION
Books
Madagascar's historical links with Britain and the current interest in its natural history and culture have produced a century of excellent books written in English. This bibliography is a selection of my favourites in each category.

General – history, the country, the people

Bradt, H *Madagascar* (World Bibliographical Series), Clio (UK); ABC (US) 1992. An annotated selection of nearly 400 titles on Madagascar, from the classic early works to those published in the 1990s.

Brown, M *A History of Madagascar* D Tunnacliffe, UK 1996. The most accurate, comprehensive and readable of the histories, brought completely up to date by Britain's foremost expert on the subject.

Covell, M *Madagascar: Politics, Economics and Society* Frances Pinter, UK (Marxist Regimes series) 1987. An interesting look at Madagascar's Marxist past.

Crook, S *Distant Shores: by Traditional Canoe from Asia to Madagascar* Impact Books, UK 1990. The story of the 4,000-mile Sarimanok Expedition by outrigger canoe across the Indian Ocean from Bali to Madagascar. An interesting account of an eventful and historically important journey.

Dodwell, C *Madagascar Travels* Hodder & Stoughton, UK 1995. An account of a journey through Madagascar's most remote regions by one of Britain's leading travel writers.

Drysdale, H *Dancing with the Dead: a Journey through Zanzibar and Madagascar* Hamish Hamilton, UK 1991. An account of Helena's journeys in search of her trading ancestor. Informative, entertaining and well-written.

Ellis, W *Madagascar Revisited* John Murray, UK 1867. The Rev William Ellis of the LMS was one of the most observant and sympathetic of the missionary writers. His books are well worth the search for second-hand copies.

Eveleigh, M *Maverick in Madagascar*, Lonely Planet Journeys, 2001. A well written account of an exceptionally adventurous trip in the north of Madagascar.

Fox, L *Hainteny: the Traditional Poetry of Madagascar* Associated University Presses, UK and Canada 1990. Over 400 beautifully translated *hainteny* with an excellent introduction to the history and spiritual life of the Merina.

Kabana, J *Torina's World: the villages of Madagascar* 1997. A beautiful book of black-and-white photos aimed at giving American children a wider understanding of their counterparts in Madagascar. Available for $15.95 (including postage) from the author, Joni Kabana, 4855 Summit St, West Linn, OR 97068, USA.

Lanting, F *Madagascar, a World out of Time* Robert Hale, UK 1991. A book of stunning, and somewhat surreal, photos of the landscape, people and wildlife.

Murphy, D *Muddling through in Madagascar* John Murray, UK 1985. An entertaining account of a journey (by foot and truck) through the highlands and south.

Parker Pearson M & Godden, K *In Search of the Red Slave: Shipwreck and Captivity in Madagascar* Sutton, UK 2002. A new telling, with on-the-spot research, of the Robert Drury story.

Powe, Edward L *Ikotofetsy and Imahaka* Dan Aiki Publications, c/o E Powe, 530 W Johnson St, Apt 202, Madison, WI 53703, USA; tel: (608) 283 6357. Tales of two tricksters, part of oral tradition in Madagascar, originally collected in 1836 to teach Malagasy children about deception.

Sibree, J *Madagascar Before the Conquest: the Island, the Country, and the People* T Fisher Unwin, UK 1896. With William Ellis, Sibree was the main documenter of Madagascar during the days of the London Missionary Society. He wrote many books on the island, all of which are perceptive, informative, and a pleasure to read.

Ethnology

Bloch, M *From Blessing to Violence* Cambridge University Press, UK 1986. History and ideology of the circumcision ritual of the Merina people.

Mack, J *Madagascar: Island of the Ancestors* British Museum, London 1986. A scholarly and informative account of the ethnography of Madagascar.

Mack, J *Malagasy Textiles* Shire Publications, UK 1989.

Powe, E L *Lore of Madagascar* Dan Aiki Publications (530 W Johnson St, Apt 210, Madison, WI 53703) USA 1994. An immense work – over 700 pages and 260 colour photos – with a price to match: $300. This is the only book to describe in detail, and in a readable form, all 39 ethnic groups in Madagascar.

Rund, J *Taboo: a study of Malagasy customs and beliefs* Oslo University Press/George Allan & Unwin, UK 1960. Written by a Norwegian Lutheran missionary who worked for 20 years in Madagascar. A detailed study of *fady*, *vintana* and other Malagasy beliefs.

Sharp, L A *The Possessed and the Dispossessed: spirits, identity and power in a Madagascar migrant town* University of California Press, USA 1993. Describes the daily life and the phenomenon of possession (*tromba*) in the town of Ambanja.

Wilson, P J *Freedom by a Hair's Breadth* University of Michigan, USA 1993. An anthropological study of the Tsimihety people, written in a clear style and accessible to the general reader.

Natural history
Literature

Attenborough, D *Zoo Quest to Madagascar* Lutterworth, UK 1961. Still one of the best travel books ever written about Madagascar, with, of course, plenty of original wildlife observations. Out of print, but copies can be found.

Durrell, G *The Aye-aye and I* Harper Collins, UK 1992. The focal point is the collecting of aye-aye for Jersey Zoo, written in the inimitable Durrell style with plenty of humour and travellers' tales.

Jolly, A *A World Like Our Own: Man and Nature in Madagascar* Yale University Press, 1980. The first and still the best look at the relationship between the natural history and people of the island. Highly readable. A sequel about the ring-tailed lemurs of Berenty will be published in 2002/3.

Preston-Mafham, K *Madagascar: A Natural History* Facts on File, UK and US 1991. The most enjoyable and useful book on the subject. Illustrated with superb colour photos (coffee-table format), it is as good at identifying strange invertebrates and unusual plants as in describing animal behaviour.

Quammen, D *The Song of the Dodo* Hutchinson, UK 1996. An interesting account of island biogeography and its implications for nature reserves.

Tyson, P *The Eighth Continent: Life, Death and Discovery in the Lost World of Madagascar*. Perennial (HarperCollins), 2001. An American journalist's description of accompanying four scientific expeditions in Madagascar, with American, British and Malagasy scientists. This is interspersed with extensive information on Madagascar's history, archaeology and natural history.

Wilson, J *Lemurs of the Lost World: Exploring the Forests and Crocodile Caves of Madagascar* Revised 1995 and available from the author (see page 208). An interesting and informative account of the Ankarana expedition and subsequent travels in Madagascar.

Specialist literature and guides

Bradt, H; Schuurman, D; Garbutt, N *Madagascar Wildlife: a visitor's guide* Bradt Travel Guides (UK); Globe Pequot Press (USA) 2001 (2nd edition). A photographic guide to the island's most interesting and appealing wildlife, and where best to see it.

Dransfield, J & Beentje, H *The Palms of Madagascar* Royal Botanic Gardens, Kew, UK 1996. A beautiful and much-needed book describing the many palm species of Madagascar.

Dorr, Laurence J; *Plant collectors in Madagascar and the Comoro Islands* Royal Botanic Gardens, Kew, UK 1997. Biographical and bibliographical information on over 1,000 individuals and groups.

Du Puy, D; Cribb P; Bosser J; Hermans J & C *The Orchids of Madagascar* Royal Botanic Gardens, Kew, UK 1999. A checklist of all known Malagasy orchid species, along with a complete bibliography, superbly illustrated with colour photos. Pricey (£49.50) but orchid enthusiasts will not care.

Garbutt, N *Mammals of Madagascar* Pica Press (UK) 1999. The book we've been waiting for. Comprehensive, with wonderful photos and black-and-white illustrations, as well as authoritative text. My only complaint is it's too heavy to be used as a field guide.

Glaw, F; Vences, M *A Field Guide to the Amphibians and Reptiles of Madagascar* 1994. A thorough guide to the herpetofauna of Madagascar. In Britain this is available through the NHBS.

Hillerman, F E; Holst, A W *An Introduction to the Cultivated Angraecoid Orchids of Madagascar* Timber Press, USA. Includes a good section on climate and other plant life.

Inventaire Ecologique Forestier National Published in 1996 by the Direction des Eaux et Forêts. A brave and welcome attempt to make the island's botany more accessible.

Jenkins, M D, editor *Madagascar: An Environmental Profile* IUCN, Gland, Switzerland and Cambridge, UK 1987. Descriptions of the nature reserves, with checklists of flora and fauna.

Jolly, A; Oberle, P; Albignac, R, editors *Madagascar* Pergamon Press, UK and Canada 1994. This book in the 'Key Environments' series is mainly a translation of the French *Madagascar: Un Sanctuaire de la Nature*. Now a little dated, but nevertheless one of the best overviews of the natural history.

Martin, J *Chameleons* Facts on File, USA; Blandford, UK 1992. Beautifully illustrated with photos by Art Wolfe; everything a chameleon aficionado could hope for.

Mittermeier, M et al *Lemurs of Madagascar* Conservation International 1994. A detailed field guide to all Madagascar's lemurs.

Morris, P; Hawkins, F *Birds of Madagascar: a photographic guide* Pica Press, UK 1999. One of two new bird guides; not suitable for use in the field (too heavy, no distribution maps) but the authoritative text and photos provide serious birders with the details they need for reliable identification.

Nicholl, M E & Langrand, O *Madagascar: Revue de la Conservation et des Aires Protégées* WWF, Switzerland 1989. Currently available only in French, but an English edition is in preparation. A detailed survey of the reserves studied by the WWF, lists of species and excellent maps.

Rauh, W *Succulent and Xerophytic Plants of Madagascar* Strawberry Press, Mill Valley, CA, USA 1995 & 1998. Two of the five intended volumes on the subject. Detailed and comprehensive; lavishly illustrated with photos.

Richard-Vindard, G & Battistini, R (editors) *Biogeography and Ecology of Madagascar* W Junk, Netherlands 1972. Largely in English including chapters on geology, climate, flora, erosion, rodents and lemurs. Each chapter includes an extensive bibliography.

Sinclair, I; Langrand, O *Birds of the Indian Ocean Islands* Struik, South Africa 1999. The most user-friendly of the two new field guides to Madagascar's birds. Clear layout with good illustrations and distribution maps allow for quick reference on the trail.

Tattersall, I *The Primates of Madagascar* Columbia UP, USA 1981. A comprehensive description of the biology of Madagascar's lemurs.

Tyson, P & Mittermeier, R *The Eighth Continent: Life, Death and Discovery in the Lost World of Madagascar.*

Where to buy books on Madagascar

Discover Madagascar (Seraphine Tierney) 7 Hazledene Rd, Chiswick, London W4 3JB; tel: 020 8995 3529; fax: 020 8742 0212. Seraphine puts out a catalogue of books on Madagascar which are in print but may be hard to find in conventional outlets. She also sells Malagasy music cassettes and CDs.

Mad Books (Rupert Parker) 151 Wilberforce Rd, London N4 2SX; tel: 020 7226 4490; email: Rupert@madbooks.co.uk; web: http://www.madbooks.co.uk. Rupert specialises in old and rare (out-of-print) books on Madagascar, and will send out his catalogue on request. He will also search for books.

Eastern Books of London 81 Replingham Rd, London SW18 5LU; tel/fax: 020 8871 0880; email: info@easternbooks.com; web: www.easternbooks.com. An antiquarian bookseller (shop, catalogue and website) specialising in rare and out-of-print books on Madagascar and the Indian Ocean.

Editions Karthala (France) 22–24 Bd Arago, 75013 Paris. This French publisher specialises in Madagascar, both for new titles and reprints.

Natural History Book Service (NHBS) 2 Wills Rd, Totnes, Devon TQ9 5XN; tel: 01803 865913; fax: 01803 865280; web: www.nhbs.com.

Useful addresses
Conservation bodies
Association Nationale de Gestion des Aires Protégées (ANGAP)
BP 1424, Antananarivo; tel: 22 415 54/22 415 38; email: angap@dts.mg.
Contact: Mme Chantal Andrianarivo.

Marine conservation
Central
Office National de l'Environnement (Marine and Coastal Unit)
BP 822, Antananarivo; tel: 22 556 24/22 552 76; email: one@pnae.mg.
Contact: Mme. Haja Razafindrainibe.

Centre National de Recherche Environnementale (CNRE) (Coastal Management Unit)
BP 1739, Antananarivo; tel: 22 630 27; email: cnre@dts.mg
Contacts: Dr Jean Maharavo; Prof. Germain Refeno.

WWF Madagascar (Marine Programme)
BP 738, Antananarivo; tel: 22 348 85; email: wwfrep@dts.mg
Contact: Dr. Rémi Ratsimbazafy.

Wildlife Conservation Society (Marine Programme)
BP 8500, Antananarivo; tel: 22 528 79; email: wcsmad@dts.mg
Contact: Mr. Herilala Randriamahazo.

Regional
Institut Halieutique et des Sciences Marines (IH.SM)
BP 141, Toliara; tel: 94 435 52; email: ihsm@syfed.refer.mg
Contact: Dr Man Wai Rabevenana.

Centre National de Recherche Océanographique (CNRO)
Hell-Ville, Nosy Be. Contact: The Director.

Useful websites
General
www.madagascar-contacts.com – information on hotels, tour operators, etc.
www.air-mad.com – information from Air Madagascar.
www.madonline.com – chat and general information.
www.fco.gov.uk – British Foreign Office advice on safety.
www.unusualdestination.com – tour specialists based in South Africa.

Natural history
www.wwf.panda.org (international) – World Wide Fund for Nature.
www.wwf.org (USA).
www.wemc.org.uk – World Conservation Monitoring Centre.
www.duke.edu/web/primate – Duke University Primate Center.
www.conservation.org – Conservation International.

Madagascar on the net
Derek Schuurman
Increasingly, travellers view the web as a one-stop shop for information and on-line reservations. With very little effort, you can locate websites flaunting a huge variety of Madagascar-related topics. A big plus in examining these sites, is that many feature stunning (and often very rare) images, allowing one to get a visual idea of whatever it is about Madagascar that interests you.

At time of writing (October 2001) I can highly recommend the following sites to any potential 'Madophiles':

General country information
For general country information (Malagasy culture especially) my favourite website is 'Mada Gasi Kara' (http://archive.dstc.edu/au/AU/staff/andry/culture.html), painstakingly compiled by Andry and Malalanirina Rakotonirainy and Gino Ranaoivoarisoa, who say they will keep adding to the site 'until they get bored'. The marvellous **historical** section includes some rare, old black-and-white portraits of Merina monarchs. In the extensive cultural section is a fascinating MA dissertation by Philip Lismore on *Aloalo and Tombs*. In the **ethnology** section is information about the Malagasy ethnic groups and images of ceremonies include Sambatra and Fitampoha.

A useful online information service website has been put together by the Malagasy Embassy, Washington. See: http://embassy.org/Madagascar/ for up-to-date commentary and information on **politics**, **economy**, **sports**, **health**, **currency**, **foreign organisations** represented in Madagascar and more. The site includes the *Midi Madagasikara* in French and Malagasy, for daily news. Email: Malagasy@embassy.org.

There is also www.madagascarconsulate.org.za, a site primarily – but not exclusively for – Southern Africans wishing to visit and do business with Madagascar. This contains useful general travel information on **shopping** excursions, hotels and activities of interest for **business travellers**. English and French.

I also found some interesting updated **statistics** on the Peace Corps site at www.peacecorps.gov/countries/Madagascar/. It's the only source where I could find, for instance, an up to date population estimate (14,592,000).

The general-interest umbrella site 'Like You Madagascar' at www.lk-oi.com/en/voyage.htm, includes a number of sites with very useful information, for instance www.lk-oi.com/golf/en/index.htm, which has the most comprehensive information I have yet seen on **golfing holidays** in Madagascar. The island's 3 golf courses are reviewed with photos.

Also on 'Like You Madagascar' is the Za Tour site, worth seeing especially for its extraordinary series of scenery photographs taken by Nivo Ravelojaona of **Andringitra National Park**. See www.lk-oi.com/zatours3d/en/page2.htm for a rare virtual tour of this park.

Want to try your hand at **cooking** a Malagasy dinner? Then take a look at the African-Madagascar cookbook site, www.sas.upenn.edu/African_studies/cookbook/Madagascar.html. Not only does this site provide a comprehensive shopping list for ingredients plus the easy-to-follow recipes, but it also includes a menu, suggests appropriate table type and décor to create an intimate Malagasy ambience and advises on how a Malagasy dinner should be served.

Music

Check out www.froots.demon.co.uk/madagcd.html which lists all the known CDs put out by Malagasy muzo's. One of the links on this site is August Schmidhofer's extensive 'Reference of Malagasy Music' site at http://mailbox.univie.ac.at~schmida4/biblio/. Another interesting link here is to the 'Valiha High' project site by Hanitrarivo Rasoanaivo, leader of the Malagasy group Tarika. See www.froots.demon.co.uk/valihahigh.html.

National Parks

Treat yourself to a visual feast on some of Madagascar's most impressive wilderness places: the phenomenal site www.mobot.org/MOBOT/photoessay contains a stunning array of images of the following: Ranomafana, Périnet, Andohahela, Ampijoroa, Ankarana, Montagne d'Ambre and a particularly mind-blowing range of Masoala pics. Compiled by the Missouri Botanical Gardens, an organisation long active in Madagascar, this site (my absolute favourite Madagascar general natural history site) also has an extensive range of wildlife photos, notably invertebrates which are given marvellous coverage.

For **Ranomafana** National Park there is – among others – a fantastic site at www.sunysb.edu/doit/icte/ compiled by George Williams. It is, in my opinion, one of the best national park sites on the web. You will find maps, climate and geology information and comprehensive species lists for mammals, birds, reptiles, frogs and arthropods, plus flora including trees, orchids, bamboos, ferns and fungi. I was blown away by some of the photos on the site's species lists sections – check out the (extremely rare) photos of a Fanalouc in the wild, plus a grey-crowned greenbul on its nest. There are also remarkable video clips, such as those accompanying a set of photos of breeding male and female velvet asitys. (One extraordinary video clip is of the somersaulting display of the male asity).

Berenty Reserve is given brilliant coverage in the extensive website at www.duke.edu/gww/Berenty/index.htm. Here you can learn about rules for visitors, take a visual tour (good selection of photos) and print off species checklists and maps.

One of many sites on which **Périnet** features, is the Care Virtual Field Trip website at www.care.org/virtual_trip/Madagascar.care_Madagascar.html. The diary of their press officer Cynthia Glocker makes for an enjoyable armchair tour of Périnet, Antananarivo and the Masoala Peninsula.

A good site for **Masoala** National Park is at www.Stanford.edu/group/CCB/trop/maso.html. Great photos, maps and an overview of the conservation programme (and future plans) for the park.

Flora

With a flora as diverse as Madagascar's, there are just too many sites to list, but here are some memorable examples: check out 'Zoe's Baobabs' at www.buzau.com/baobab/taxon.html for a synopsis of all eight species of **baobab** (six are Malagasy endemics). Photos of most are included. The site has links to other, very worthwhile websites like 'Morondava Gorgeous' (www.morondava.com/curiosites.htm#baobab), a French site all about the Morondava/

Menabe region up to and including **Bemaraha**. It includes (very useful for this region!) daily weather forecasts and photos of remote places like Belo Sur Mer, Bosy, Tsingy de Bemaraha and Manambolo River and Kirindy.

For a **general botanical review**, the site www.mobot.org/MOBOT/Madagascar/ vegmad1.html is one of the best. The site, put up by the Missouri Botanical Gardens, includes a comprehensive overview (beautifully illustrated) of all the original habitat types with information plus photos of Malagasy plants. There are some alarming images of the environmental destruction. The site is filled with interesting facts – I learned that those tiny strips of forest along the high plateau streams are called '*thalwegs*'.

Wildlife

There are numerous sites pertaining to Malagasy wildlife. I will review some of the better ones for mammals and birds. Because most of the reptile and frog-related sites belong to people somehow involved with the wild animal trade/exotic pet trade, I refuse to list them here. (Just key in a search for a distinctive Malagasy reptile like 'Uroplatus' and see what I mean!).

Mammals

Jonah Ratsimbazafy has put together a great site on **lemurs** – see www.thewildones.org/ Animals/lemur.html. And surfers with questions about the lemurs of Madagascar are invited to email Jonah. Aside from good photographs there are also audio clips. Links include the highly praised Earthwatch lemur study projects.

There is also a delightful and informative essay on the Northamptonshire Wildlife Site by Mark Piper called 'Forest of the Sifaka', in this case the Coquerel's sifaka of Ampijoroa. See http://atschool.eduweb.co.uk/jblincow/triples/tripmedia.htm.

The NOVA/PBS Online Adventure by Pete Tyson (www.pbs.org/wgbh/nova/ Madagascar/expedition/), follows an online expedition to places such as Marojejy National Park (led by Dr Patricia Wright) and Ankarana National Park. In Marojejy (illustrated with unbelievably alluring visuals) the expedition was to study the rare silky sifaka.

Another report on the Luke Dollar **fosa** studies, written by Vicki Coke, points out that there may be as few as 2000 fosas left – a depressing statistic. See www.findarticles.com/m1511/4_21/ 60270450/p1/article.jhtml. You can also see www.earthwatch.org/expeditions/dollar.html for further information on the studies Dollar has been conducting in Ampijoroa (not just on fosas but also on some rather fascinating feral cats).

Madagascar's rather poorly understood **bat** fauna, is brilliantly covered in yet another remarkable website: www.abdn.ac.uk/~nhi770/madbats.html. The site is illustrated with excellent high quality photographs and echolocation calls – so you can see, hear and read about species like the remarkable endemic (and rare) sucker-footed bat, for instance. Bats of Madagascar is compiled by Daniel Bennett, Keith Ross et al.

I couldn't leave out the famed humpback **whales**, which attract so many visitors to eastern Malagasy waters every year from July–early October.

Whale enthusiasts must surf www.cnie.org/countries/Madagascar/biodiversity.html, which contains a detailed report by Maryalice Yakutchit on whale-watching expeditions by a scientific team to the Bay of Antongil in August/September, the optimum time in which to see the humpbacks. Apparently this 20 x 50 mile bay is as rewarding as nearby Ile Sainte Marie, the traditional whale-watching venue. There are excellent photographs throughout the report and all sorts of information, including maps on the astounding humpback migration routes.

Birds

Best on the general birding front is Dr Ronald Orenstein's 'Video Birding in Madagascar'. Author/Birder/Conservationist Dr Orenstein visited three sites in the standard birding route (Périnet, Ampijoroa, Ifaty) and captured many endemics on video, hence the marvellous virtual birding tour you can take when surfing his site, http://members.home.net/ornstn/Madagascar.html.

The best known endemic Malagasy family, the **vangas**, are covered in the site www.montereybay.com/creagus/vangas.html – worth looking at for an overview of the diversity amongst this family.

On the African Bird Club website, you can enjoy well illustrated, informative articles about various Malagasy birds, like blue pigeons, the gorgeous ground-rollers and those bizarre little sunbird-asitys, which Frank Hawkins covers in www.africanbirdclub.org/feature/asities.htm.

Strangely enough, the Malagasy birds which probably have the most extensive coverage on the web, are three of the very rarest endemics, the Madagascar **serpent eagle**, Madagascar **fish eagle** and the Madagascar **red owl**. All three are part of the Peregrine Fund's Africa & Madagascar Division's Madagascar based projects, so check out www.peregrinefund.org/notes_Madagascar.html for informative reports of the work being done to save these three rarities.

Herps (Reptiles and frogs)

As I mentioned, a large number of sites on the web belong to people who are involved with the exotic pet trade/wild animal trade. Aside from the previously mentioned Missouri Botanical Gardens' photo essay which includes lots of 'herps' – as do some of the reserve sites I have listed above – I did not find very many other sites in this category. One worth seeing is the chameleons feature by Chris Raxworthy, at www.pbs.org/edens/Madagascar/index.htm – it's part of the Living Edens documentary series website and Raxworthy provides an informative, reader-friendly article. The Living Edens trip in Madagascar took in Tsingy de Bemaraha, Kirindy, Ranomafana and Lake Alaotra.

'The breast-leaper... It is a small animal which attaches itself to the bark of trees and being of a greenish hue is not easily perceived; there it remains with its throat open to receive the flies, spiders and other insects that approach it, which it devours. This animal is described as having attached to the back, tail, legs, neck, and the extremity of the chin, little paws or hooks like those at the end of a bat's wing with which it adheres to whatever it attaches itself in such a manner as if it were really glued. If a native happens to approach the tree where it hangs, it instantly leaps upon his naked breast, and sticks so firmly that in order to remove it, they are obliged, with a razor, to cut away the skin also.'

Samuel Copland, *History of the Island of Madagascar*, 1822

Index